This major new publication is a history of the semantic tradition in philosophy from the early nineteenth century through its incarnation in the work of the Vienna circle, the group of logical positivists that emerged in the years 1925–35 in Vienna and was characterized by a strong commitment to empiricism, a high regard for science, and a conviction that modern logic is the primary tool of analytic philosophy.

In the first part of the book, Alberto Coffa shows how the semantic tradition originated in opposition to Kant's theory that a priori knowledge is based on pure intuition and the constitutive powers of the mind, and was developed in the course of various foundational studies in mathematics, geometry, and logic.

In the second part, Coffa chronicles the development of this tradition by members and associates of the Vienna circle. He examines the attempts by Schlick and Reichenbach to interpret Einstein's theory of relativity, the search by Carnap and Tarski for a definition of truth, the new semantic theory of the a priori offered by Wittgenstein and Carnap, the logical positivists' transcendental approach to epistemology, and their failure to deal adequately with realism and the empirical foundations of knowledge. Much of Coffa's analysis draws on the unpublished notes and correspondence of these philosophers.

However, Coffa's book is not merely a history of the semantic tradition from Kant "to the Vienna Station." The author critically reassesses the role of semantic notions in understanding the ground of a priori knowledge and its relation to empirical knowledge; he also questions the turn the tradition has taken since Vienna.

"This is an extraordinary and long-awaited book. Its history is meticulous, but it treats its subjects as philosophers to be responded to and even fought with, rather than as museum pieces. It is worth the wait."
Richard Creath, Arizona State University

"Alberto Coffa is an intellectual pioneer. His book is the first comprehensive treatment of the development of logical positivism that is rigorous and sophisticated from both a historical and a technical point of view. It will constitute an indispensable basis for all future research in the area."
Michael Friedman, The University of Illinois at Chicago

The semantic tradition from
Kant to Carnap

The semantic tradition from Kant to Carnap

To the Vienna Station

J. ALBERTO COFFA

Edited by Linda Wessels
Indiana University

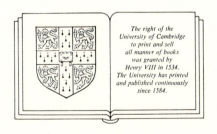

CAMBRIDGE UNIVERSITY PRESS

Cambridge
New York   Port Chester   Melbourne   Sydney

Published by the Press Syndicate of the University of Cambridge
The Pitt Building, Trumpington Street, Cambridge CB2 1RP
40 West 20th Street, New York, NY 10011, USA
10 Stamford Road, Oakleigh, Melbourne 3166, Australia

First published 1991

Printed in the United States of America

Library of Congress Cataloging-in-Publication Data

Coffa, J. Alberto.

The semantic tradition from Kant to Carnap : to the Vienna Station
/ J. Alberto Coffa ; edited by Linda Wessels.

p.   cm.

ISBN 0-521-37429-4

1. Semantics – History.   2. Kant, Immanuel, 1724–1804 –
Contributions in semantics.   3. Bolzano, Bernard, 1781–1848 –
Contributions in semantics.   4. Frege, Gottlob, 1848–1925 –
Contributions in semantics.   5. Vienna circle.   I. Wessels, Linda.
II. Title.
B840.C58   1991
149′.94 – dc20   90-40588
                                                          CIP

British Library Cataloguing in Publication Data

Coffa, J. Alberto

The semantic tradition from Kant to Carnap : to the Vienna
Station.

1. Meaning. Philosophical perspective, history
I. Title   II. Wessels, Linda
121.6809

ISBN 0-521-37429-4 Hardback

For
Theresa and Justa
and
Diana and Julia

Contents

Editor's preface

On Christmas Eve, 1984, Alberto declared that a "good penultimate draft" of his book would be finished by the end of the year. The day after Christmas he became ill, and in the early morning hours of December 30, he died. The typescript Alberto left behind was, indeed, almost completed: The research had been finished and the arguments and theses were already in place; all but the introduction and the last chapter had been written in full, and extensive notes for those had been drafted. Some portions of the typescript had already been carefully crafted, and the intended shape of much of the rest was clear. In many places Alberto's dry wit showed through — you could almost see behind the prose the tilt of his head, the lopsided smile, the brief twinkle in his eye. With the help of a number of people, that typescript has been readied for publication. Using the notes Alberto left, I have completed the introduction and final chapter. Repetitions, digressions, and minor errors have been removed, theses and arguments delineated more clearly, grammar corrected, prose smoothed — all, I hope, without disturbing the twinkle. The result is not what Alberto would have produced, but perhaps it is something he would have found acceptable. He had intended to write a conclusion, discussing some of the implications of his study for contemporary philosophy. I have not attempted to write that conclusion.

Alberto began writing this book in the spring and summer of 1981 while a fellow of the Center for Philosophy of Science at the University of Pittsburgh. He was extremely grateful to the center for the time that allowed him to begin this project, and to his colleagues in the Department of History and Philosophy of Science, Indiana University, for both the time and the supportive and congenial environment that allowed him to continue his work. During the writing of this book, Alberto had fruitful discussions with many people; many also supplied him with information about useful sources and materials, and provided both intellectual and spiritual support. I cannot begin to compile a complete list of people he would have thanked, but certainly on that list would have been those with whom he had long and regular conversations on the philosophical matters that are central to this book: Thomas M. Simpson, Eduardo Garcia

Belsunce, Hector Casteñeda, Simon Blackburn, and Alberto's students Frank Pecchioni and Tom Oberdan. There is no doubt that he would also have gratefully acknowledged the invaluable and constant support and encouragement of Adolf Grünbaum, his teacher and friend. To the many others whose assistance and influence should be acknowledged, I apologize for not including your names and thank you for the help you gave Alberto.

My own thanks go first to Gordon Steinhoff, who took on the heroic task of tracking down the sources of the quotations in the typescript, checking the quotations and translations for accuracy, completing the citations and references, and compiling the bibliography. I also gratefully acknowledge the assistance of Michael Friedman, who read the typescript at two different stages of my work on it and gave me numerous valuable suggestions for correcting and editing it. In addition, I thank Nicholas Griffin and an anonymous referee for their editorial suggestions, and Eduardo Garcia Belsunce, Edward Grant, and Tom Oberdan for lending their expertise where needed. Finally, I thank John Winnie for his suggestions and help on the typescript, and for the encouragement and support that sustained me through the long process of bringing it to publication.

Acknowledgments

Quotations from unpublished material are drawn from four sources: the Archives of Scientific Philosophy in the Twentieth Century, University of Pittsburgh Libraries; the Bertrand Russell Archives, MacMaster University; the Vienna Circle Archive, University of Amsterdam; the Wittgenstein Papers, microfilm distributed by Cornell University Library. My special thanks to Gerald Heverly, curator, and Stephen Wagner, research assistant, of the Archives of Scientific Philosophy, University of Pittsburgh Libraries, and to A. J. Fox, executive secretary of the Vienna Circle Foundation, University of Amsterdam, for their help in locating items in the Archives of Scientific Philosophy and the Vienna Circle Archive, respectively, and in checking the accuracy of quotations from material in their archives; thanks also to Nicholas Griffin for tracking down items in the Bertrand Russell Archives for me.

Passages from items in the Archives of Scientific Philosophy in the Twentieth Century that were authored by Rudolf Carnap, Frank P. Ramsey, and Hans Reichenbach are quoted by permission of the University of Pittsburgh; all rights reserved. The quotation from a letter by Kurt Gödel is included by permission of the Institute for Advanced Study, Princeton, N.J. Quotations from letters by Moritz Schlick are included by permission of the Vienna Circle Foundation.

Quotations from items in the Bertrand Russell Archives are included by permission of the Bertrand Russell Archives Copyright Permissions Committee.

Passages from items in the Vienna Circle Archive that were authored by Moritz Schlick are quoted by permission of the Vienna Circle Foundation. The unpublished letter by Rudolf Carnap from which a quotation is drawn has been copyrighted by Hanna Carnap Thost; all rights reserved. The quotation from that letter is included with the kind permission of Mrs. Thost. The quotation from a letter by Albert Einstein is included by permission of The Hebrew University of Jerusalem, Israel. Passages from a letter by Hans Reichenbach are quoted by permission of Maria Reichenbach.

Quotations from unpublished and posthumously published works by Wittgenstein are included with the kind permission of G. E. M. Anscombe and G. H. von Wright.

Introduction

The primary topic of this book is a decade in the philosophical life of what might loosely be called Vienna. Between 1925 and 1935 in the neighborhood of Vienna, the usually sluggish step of the Spirit suddenly quickened as some of his most enlightened voices started talking to one another. Wittgenstein, Tarski, Carnap, Schlick, Popper, and Reichenbach were, perhaps, no wiser than some of their contemporaries, but circumstances led them to interact during that decade, and the result of that dialogue deserves our attention.

When I started writing this book, I intended to explain in the preface that this was the history of epistemology since Kant, the way Carnap would have written it had he been Hegel. Since then I have come to think that while the Spirit may not be malicious, he is certainly forgetful. In Vienna he took a decisive step forward on the subject of the a priori; but he also moved sideways and backward on other crucial matters. Most of his erratic behavior could have been avoided had he been aware of some of his achievements in the preceding century. He may, perhaps, be excused since his best insights were due to the least noticeable of his voices.

Within the field of epistemology one may discern three major currents of thought in the nineteenth century: positivism, Kantianism, and what I propose to call the semantic tradition. What distinguished their proponents primarily was their attitude toward the a priori. Positivists denied it, and Kantians explained it through the Copernican revolution. The semantic tradition consisted of those who believed in the a priori but not in the constitutive powers of mind. They also suspected that the root of all idealist confusion lay in misunderstandings concerning matters of meaning. Semanticists are easily detected: They devote an uncommon amount of attention to concepts, propositions, senses — to the content and structure of what we say, as opposed to the psychic acts in which we say it. The others cannot see the point of wasting so much time on semantic trivia.

It would be hard to find a more crucial epistemological problem than that of the character of a priori knowledge. One of the basic intuitions

1

behind almost every epistemology since Plato's is that there are two radically different types of claims: the a priori and the rest. In pre-Kantian philosophy, many had tacitly assumed that the notion of analyticity provided the key to that of apriority. Kant saw that a different account was needed since not every a priori judgment is analytic, and offered a new theory based on one of the most remarkable philosophical ideas ever produced: his Copernican turn. In addition to this, Kant placed the idea of pure intuition at the center of his account of the scientific a priori. Positivists could not accept the consequences of this vision and saw no way out of the dilemma other than to deny the existence of the a priori, even in the case of logic.

Faced with the Scylla of asserting that $2 + 2 = 4$ is empirical and the Charybdis of explaining it through the operations of pure intuition, semanticists chose to turn the boat around and try to find a better route. That there is a priori knowledge – even of the synthetic type – was indubitable to all of them; but most semanticists regarded the appeal to pure intuition as a hindrance to the development of science. Part I describes the stages through which it came to be recognized that pure intuition must be excluded from the a priori sciences and that consequently the Kantian picture of mathematics and geometry must be replaced by some other.

Our story begins with Kant's views on analysis and some of his reasons for concluding that one must appeal to pure intuition in connection with the a priori (Chapter 1). We then turn to the leading episodes that undermined that conviction. Bolzano's reductionist project (Chapter 2), complemented by Frege's and Russell's logicist projects (Chapters 4 and 6), challenged Kant's convictions in the field of arithmetic. Helmholtz (Chapter 3), Poincaré, and Hilbert (Chapter 8) provided the decisive contribution to analogous developments in the field of geometry. By the end of the nineteenth century, it had become clear that a priori knowledge could not possibly be what Kant thought it was. Early in the twentieth century, the special and general theories of relativity appeared to pose yet another challenge to the Kantian view, now from the domain of physics (Chapter 10).

Semanticists were primarily interested not in showing that Kant had not solved the problem, but in solving it themselves. The basic assumption common to all members of that movement was that epistemology was in a state of disarray due primarily to semantic neglect. Semantics, not metaphysics, was their *prima philosophia*. In particular, they thought, the key to the a priori lay in an appreciation of the nature and role of concepts, propositions, and senses. Though no defensible doctrine of the a priori emerged from their writings (Chapter 7), the ground was laid by a patient sharpening of semantic insights in the writings of

Bolzano, Frege, Husserl, Russell, and the early Wittgenstein (Chapters 2, 4, 5, 6, and 8). Against this background, Wittgenstein and Carnap offered in the early 1930s the first genuine alternative to Kant's conception of the a priori (Chapters 13, 14, 15, and 17). Their view that meaning is responsible for the a priori was that period's most decisive contribution to philosophy.

Logical positivism started as a branch of neo-Kantianism that differed from other branches in taking science as an epistemological model (Chapters 9, 10, and 11). During the 1920s, the early members and associates of the group slowly broke away from their Kantian beginnings, Schlick and Reichenbach as they struggled to interpret the lessons of the new theory of relativity (Chapter 10), Carnap as he tried to develop his epistemological ideas as a theory of constitution (Chapters 11 and 12). Out of their high regard for science emerged a second major contribution of the Vienna group — a transcendental approach to epistemology, a new "philosophy of science" (Chapters 10, 17, and 18).

The Copernican turn that had inspired Kant's analysis of the a priori had also led to a theory of experience and an understanding of the link between knowledge and reality that naturally led to idealism. In the nineteenth century, many wanted to avoid idealism, but few knew how to do it short of refusing to think through the consequences of their convictions. Semanticists suspected that if Kant's tacit semantic premises were granted, then certain Kantian insights on the role of constitution in knowledge could only be interpreted as leading to idealism. Once again, they thought, the key to a reasonable attitude was a clear-headed semantics.

Empiricists have traditionally flirted with meaning but, in the end, have remained hostile to it. When meaning becomes anything more than a topic for oblique allusion, when it becomes an explicit subject of research, it appears as an alternative to empirical considerations. It begins to look like a factual domain that is impervious to scientific research. Those associated with the Viennese movement were above all empiricists and shared the traditional empiricists' horror of meaning. Unequipped with meaning, they found it difficult to avoid idealism (Chapters 9 and 10). Carnap came closer than the others to making sense of realism, but his distaste for all things metaphysical also prevented him from completing the incorporation of meaning into empiricism (Chapters 12 and 17). In the end logical positivism remained without meaning. The natural consequence was the debate in the early 1930s over "foundations of knowledge," which was not really about foundations at all, but about the link between what we know and the world (Chapter 19).

Our picture of the Viennese developments of Part II will not be balanced unless we bear in mind the truths and falsehoods the participants learned from the three great nineteenth-century traditions that together shaped their standpoints. In all fairness, this book should have included, in addition to Part I, two other introductory sections devoted to Kantianism and positivism. The finitude of my life, my mind, and my reader's patience were factors to consider. There was also the fact that nineteenth-century Kantianism and positivism are far better known than their less celebrated rival. Finally – why not admit it? – the proportion of insight to confusion is far, far greater among semanticists than among their more prestigious and respected colleagues.

PART I

The semantic tradition

1

Kant, analysis, and pure intuition

It was disastrous that Kant . . . held the domain of the purely logical in the narrowest sense to be adequately taken care of by the remark that it falls under the principle of contradiction. Not only did he never see how little the laws of logic are all analytic propositions in the sense laid down by his own definition, but he failed to see how little his dragging in of an evident principle for analytic propositions really helped to clear up the achievements of analytic thinking.

Husserl, *Logische Untersuchungen,* vol. 2, pt. 2

For better and worse, almost every philosophical development of significance since 1800 has been a response to Kant. This is especially true on the subject of a priori knowledge. The central problem of the *Critique* had been the a priori, and Kant had dealt with it from the complementary perspectives of judgment and experience. His "Copernican revolution" gave him a theory of experience and a non-Platonist account of the a priori. But when the *Critique* was well on its way, Kant discovered the notion of a synthetic a priori judgment, and he saw in this a particularly appealing way of formulating his project as that of explaining how such judgments are possible.

The constitutive dimension of Kant's theories of experience and the a priori will figure prominently in later developments. As we shall see, one of the turning points in our story will involve a Copernican turn, though the issue it concerns will be different from Kant's. Moreover, the early stages of logical positivism may be viewed as a development to the point of exhaustion of this aspect of Kant's original idea. In this chapter, however, we shall focus exclusively on the more superficial aspect of Kant's treatment of the a priori, involving synthetic a priori judgments; for it was the shallowness of Kant's treatment of this matter that led to doctrines which, in turn, elicited the semantic tradition.

One of the central points of agreement among the members of the semantic tradition is the idea that the major source of error behind Kant's theory of knowledge – especially of the a priori – is his confused doctrine of meaning and that the key to a correct doctrine of the a priori is the understanding of semantics. Our purpose in this first chapter is to examine the relevant features of Kant's epistemology and its semantic background. Our first problem will be to uncover Kant's semantic views.

In a sense, of course, he hadn't any; for part of the story we aim to tell is that of how semantics was born. In another sense he did, of course, for he was bound to have opinions, however tacit and unacknowledged, on what it is to convey information, on when we may succeed in doing so, and when we are bound to fail. Philosophers have often thought these topics unworthy of much attention. The analytic tradition that extends from Bolzano to Carnap places meaning at the heart of philosophy – or, rather, it finds that it has been there, unrecognized, all along and that the failure to think seriously about it is the root of the reductio ad absurdum of rationalism displayed in Kant's philosophy and its idealist offspring. The question is, Where does one look for the tacit semantics of those who did not address that topic explicitly?

In one of the many aphorisms Quine aimed at the semantic tradition, he noted that "meanings are what essences became . . . when wedded to the word." If this were right, those who would like to know what Kant thought about meanings would have to consult what he wrote about essences; since he wrote next to nothing on that subject, this would be the end of the search. Actually, meanings had a more honorable ancestor within the field of traditional logic, in the category of concepts or, more generally, representations. To find out what a post-Cartesian philosopher thought about meanings, we must look at the logic books he wrote or quoted from, for it is there that the notions of concept and judgment are treated. Meanings are what concepts became when wedded to the word.

Conceptual analysis

Kant was very proud of his distinction between analytic and synthetic judgments. He recognized that philosophers before him had understood the significance of the division between a priori and a posteriori judgments. But when Eberhard challenged his originality on the matter of analyticity, Kant replied, in an effort at irony, that everything new in science is eventually "discovered to have been known for ages" (Allison, *The Kant–Eberhard Controversy,* p. 154). Had he read Borges, he would have paraphrased him: "Great ideas create their ancestry" (see Borges, "Nathaniel Hawthorne," *Obras completas,* p. 678).

In fact, Kant had little reason to be proud. His treatment of the analytic–synthetic distinction is original in certain ways, as we shall see; but in the end, it is one of the least distinguished parts of his philosophy. In it, some long-standing confusions converge and others emerge, original with Kant; the latter were destined to have a long and damaging influence throughout the nineteenth century.

The picture of meaning dominant since the emergence of rationalism and empiricism took meanings to be inextricably associated with experience. It is plausible to think that in order to know the meaning of pain, love, rivalry, heroism, and so on, one must undergo certain experiences and that the more carefully one analyzes these experiences, the better one understands pain, love, and so on. It is but a small step to conclude that the meanings of 'pain', 'love', and so on consist precisely of those psychic phenomena that are the targets of our analysis. The same may be thought to hold for all expressions; they will mean something only insofar as, and to the extent that, they relate to human mental processes. Number expressions, for example, may be thought to derive their meaning from the mental processes in which they are involved – the natural numbers through processes of counting, geometric objects through acts of measurement, and so on.

On this way of looking at things, the basic semantic notion is that of "representations" (*Vorstellungen*) construed as "modifications of the mind" that "belong to inner sense" (Kant, *Critique*, A98–9), as mental states designed to represent something. A long tradition, canonized in the *Logique de Port Royal*, had declared ideas or representations the most important subject of logic, since "we can have knowledge of what is outside us only through the mediation of ideas in us" (Arnauld and Nicole, *La logique ou l'art de penser*, p. 63). In Leibniz's words, human souls "perceive what passes without them by what passes within them" (Clarke, *The Leibniz–Clarke Correspondence*, p. 83); indeed, "the nature of the monad" is "to represent" (Leibniz, "The Monadology" [1714], *Philosophical Papers and Letters*, pp. 648–9).

The word '*Vorstellung*' first became a technical term in Wolff's philosophy; it corresponded approximately to the earlier 'idea' and was intended to cover both intellectual and psychic processes. For Meier, author of the logic text that Kant followed in many of his courses on that subject, representations were "pictures or images (*Gemälde oder Bilder*) of those things that we represent to ourselves (*wir uns vorstellen*)" (Meier, *Auszug aus der Vernunftlehre*, sec. 24). In its pre-Kantian use, in Wolff, Lambert, and Meier, for example, 'representation' and 'concept' (*Begriff*) functioned as synonyms, and the pre-critical Kant largely followed this usage.[1]

One of the many ways philosophers have tried to understand meaning might be called the "chemical theory of representation," using an analogy occasionally found in the writings of Locke, Lambert, and even Kant. According to this theory, representations, like chemical compounds, are usually complexes of elements or "constituents," which may themselves be complex. Generally, when a representation is given to us, we are not consciously aware of this. Analysis is the process through which we identify the constituents of a complex representation. It is a process that must come to an end, after (perhaps) finitely many stages, in the identification of simple constituents. Moreover, the best way to know what a representation is, is to identity its constituents – preferably its ultimate simple constituents – and the form in which they are put together or linked to constitute the given representation. To know a concept fully, for example, is to define it; and definition (*Erklaerung*) is no more and no less than exhaustive and complete analysis.

Descartes's doctrine of ideas had promoted the notions of clarity and distinctness to the status of philosophical celebrities. Under the influence of the new rationalism, these two heterological notions soon came to be regarded as the highest virtue in the ethics of concepts and to figure prominently in the chapters of most logic textbooks. They took a more definite shape in the German philosophical tradition.

Even though representations are basically intended to represent other things, we can upon occasion turn the arrow of reference on them (Kant, *Critique,* A108). When we do so, when we become conscious of a representation, then, Kant said, it is "clear" (*klar;* e.g., *Logik,* p. 33). The much more crucial virtue of "distinctness" (*Deutlichkeit*) depends entirely on our mental relation to what Kant called the "manifold" given in representation. Consider intuitive representations first. If we intuitively represent (e.g., see) a house in the distance, we may not be consciously aware of the windows, doors, and other parts of it. But, claimed Kant, we surely see them, in some sense; for we know "that the intuited object is a house"; hence, "we must necessarily have a representation of the different parts of this house. . . . For if we did not see the parts, we would not see the house either. But we are not conscious of this presentation of the manifold of its parts" (*Logik,* p. 34; also *Logik Pölitz,* pp. 510–11; *Reflexionen zur Logik,* refl. 1676, p. 78; *Wiener Logik,* p. 841; Borges, "Argumentum Ornithologicum," *Obras completas,* p. 787). The venerable Wolff had praised "the great use of magnifying glasses towards gaining distinct notions" (*Logic,* pp. 27–8). Following his lead, Kant noted that when we look at the Milky Way with bare eyes, we have a clear but indistinct representation of it, since we do not see a discontinuous cluster of stars but, rather, a continuous streak of light. When we look at it through the telescope, however, our representation is (more) distinct (*Logik,* p. 35; also *Logik Pölitz,* p. 511). Echoing one of Leibniz's examples in his *Nouveaux essais* (bk. 2, chap. 2, sec. 1 and bk. 4, chap. 6, sec. 7), Kant illustrated the nature of a clear but indistinct representation: "Blue and yellow make green, but we are not always aware of the presence of these parts in green" (*Wiener Logik,* p. 841).[2]

Mutatis mutandis, the same is supposed to be true of conceptual representations. We may, for example, have a clear concept of virtue, and we may recognize some of its constituent marks without being entirely clear on what all or even most of them are. The process through which we achieve distinctness on this matter is precisely what Kant called analysis: "To analyze a concept [is] to become self-conscious of the manifold that I always think in it" (*Kritik,* B11/A7).

It is an essential element of Kant's doctrine of analysis that our understanding of the analyzed concept changes (for the better) during that process, whereas the concept does not:

When we resolve the concept of virtue into its constituents, we make it distinct through analysis. In so making it distinct, however, we add nothing to the concept, we merely clarify it. (*Logik,* p. 35)

When I make a concept distinct, then my cognition does not in the least increase in its content by this mere analysis . . . [through analysis] I learn to distinguish better or with greater clarity of consciousness what already was lying in the given concept. Just as by the mere illumination of a map nothing is added to it, so by the mere elucidation of a given concept by means of analysis of its marks no augmentation is made to this concept itself in the least. (*Logik,* p. 64)

As to definition, he had said in the *Wiener Logik* that it is "the most important chapter of logic" (p. 912) and went on to elaborate:

All our concepts, insofar as they are given, whether *a priori* or *a posteriori,* can be defined only by means of analysis through dissection (*Zergliederung*). For, when it is given, I can make the concept distinct only by making the marks (*Merkmale*) it contains clear. That is what analysis does. If this analysis is complete . . . [and] in addition there are not so many marks, then it is precise and so constitutes a definition. (p. 914; see also *Logik Philippi,* p. 455)[3]

On pain of indistinctness, analysis must terminate after finitely many steps; one must therefore find simple, indefinable, unanalyzable concepts at the end of this process.[4] About these obviously crucial indefinables, Kant had suspiciously little to say, though he did explicitly note that besides being indefinable and unanalyzable, these marks are also indistinct (*Logik,* pp. 34–5; *Logik Philippi,* p. 342). Total distinctness is therefore achieved when a complex concept is reduced to its indistinct constituents. This peculiarity may arise from a mere terminological oddity. It is harder to understand Kant's insistence that clarity, the only logical virtue of simple concepts, is not a topic for logicians, or indeed philosophers, but concerns only the psychologist (see, e.g., *Kritik,* B414 note; *Anthropologie,* p. 137; *Untersuchung über natürlichen Theologie,* pp. 284, 286, 290).[5] This would not be the last time a philosopher would consign to psychology those portions of epistemology that threatened to run his philosophy aground.

The preceding quotations provide ample evidence of Kant's commitment to the chemical doctrine of the concept. But they also display another important feature of his understanding of analysis, a feature that his idealistic successors would obliterate but that would be emphasized by a different tradition in nineteenth-century philosophy. Unless we are prepared to regard Kant's explanations of conceptual analysis as thoroughly blundering attempts to convey his meaning, there is no way to avoid the conclusion that he was tacitly endorsing a distinction between the mental acts in which concepts are involved and those concepts themselves. If our understanding of the concept *virtue* can be bad at one time and good at another, these two different acts or states of understanding must somehow concern or involve the very same concept. Hence, in some sense of being, there must *be* a concept of virtue that is both the target of mental episodes and distinct from them. This concept need not be extrasubjective; but it must at least be intersubjective, since the very same conceptual representation is involved in different representings, or psychic acts of representation, in the same or different persons. To be sure, like his teachers and his followers, Kant did not observe that distinction consistently; but without it, it would be very hard to make sense of the things he said about analysis of concepts and about analytic knowledge. About the former, for example, he typically claimed, "By means of analytic distinctness we recognize in something no more than we had originally thought in it; instead we recognize better, i.e., more disтinctly and clearly and with greater awareness, what we already knew" (*Logik Blomberg,* p. 131; see also *Critique,* A5–6/B9). Nor would it be possible to make sense of the countless references to the uncovering of tacit knowledge through analysis. Indeed, one of the few persistent themes throughout Kant's philosophy, from the early *Untersuchung über natürlichen Theologie* (1764) to his critical writings, was that philosophy is distinguished from other sciences in that its proper method is analysis of concepts, bringing forth or to the surface hidden knowledge, rather than constructing new knowledge. As in the Socratic model, the philosopher's task is to help people become aware of what they have known all along: "If we only knew what we know . . . we would be astonished by the treasures contained in our knowledge" (*Wiener Logik,* p. 843).

On one occasion, Kant went so far as to raise explicitly what we now call the "problem of analysis," the issue of the identity of *analysandum* and *analysans,* and his revealing answer provides evidence of his insecure grasp of the situation:

Is the concept in the definition totally identical to that defined [through the process of analysis]? . . . we must bear in mind: *materialiter,* i.e., *quoad objectum,* these concepts are always completely identical; only concerning the form they are not, indeed, they should be not entirely identical; concerning the matter, I always think the same object, only not in the same way, but in a different way;

what before the definition I represented confusedly, I now represent clearly. (*Logik Blomberg,* p. 265)

The distinction between matter and form — that root of so much philosophical confusion — is "explained" in the *Logik Philippi* as follows: "When I look at a worm under the microscope, the form of the worm changes but the object remains the same. . . . All philosophy concerns only form, since we consider an object piecemeal and become more clearly aware of the matter contained in it" (p. 341). This would appear to imply that in analysis the concepts with which we are concerned both before and after the analysis are the same but that our mode of knowledge of them is different (although these and similar passages may also be taken to display a confusion between a concept and its objects).

Even though Kant's views on the nature of hidden meaning and tacit knowledge called for a distinction between act and content in representations, it is also true that he often appeared to disregard that distinction and that whenever specificity was demanded, he chose to fall on the purely subjective side of the dichotomy. Had Kant been more sensitive to the distinction and to its overwhelming importance, he would have noticed that the link between concepts and analysis was much weaker than he thought. We shall see that as Kant went on to extend the ideas of analysis and synthesis from concepts to judgments, his emphasis on the subjective element in representation, to the neglect of its objective counterpart, combined with the chemical picture of concepts to produce a peculiarly Kantian confusion.

Analytic judgments

For Kant, the link between the analyticity of judgments and conceptual analysis was immediate. To begin with, "in a judgment, two concepts are in a relation" (*Philosophische Enzyklopädie,* p. 19), and in categorical judgments, the link is the subject–predicate relation. Categoric judgments are "the matter of all others" (*Reflexionen zur Logik,* refl. 3046, p. 631). Thus, all judgments have as their "matter" either concepts or other judgments (refl. 3046). A categorical judgment is analytic, Kant claimed, when the predicate concept is thought implicitly in, or is contained in, the subject concept; all other categorical judgments are synthetic (e.g., *Logic,* p. 117; *Prolegomena to Any Future Metaphysics,* p. 14).[6] Thus, an analytic judgment is the expression of the outcome of conceptual analysis.

Given its sources in the idea of conceptual analysis, it is hardly surprising that Kant's definition applies to judgments in the subject–predicate form. (Here 'subject' is construed in the traditional pre-Fregean manner, so that the subject of 'All As are Bs' is 'All As' or 'A'.) The familiar problems posed by the narrow scope of this definition do not concern us here, since they fail to reveal any serious flaws in Kant's picture of things. What does concern us is the much more crucial matter of the link between conceptual analysis and analytic judgments. These judgments are derived, according to Kant, "by dissection of the [subject] concept" (*Prolegomena to Any Future Metaphysics,* p. 17); they "merely break up the [subject concept] into those constituent concepts that have all along been thought in it" (*Kritik,* B11). A paradigm example of an analytic judgment is "Every *x* that conforms to the concept ($a + b$) of body also conforms to (b) extension" (*Logik,* p. 111). "In the analytic judgment we keep to the given concept, and seek to extract something from it" (*Critique,* A154/B193).

Superficially, it might seem that Kant was saying little more than the many others before him who had also been concerned with the issue of conceptual analysis. Eberhard, for example, thought the notion of an analytic judgment was clearly present in Leibniz's writings. This evaluation entirely misses the element of novelty that Kant had incorporated into the chemical doctrine of the concept. The difference between Kant's position on this issue and those of his predecessors becomes clear when we examine their answers to the question, How do we determine the constituency of a concept; what criteria determine whether a concept B is "in" the concept A?

When Kant started to think about this question, there were two standard answers, one emerging from a long and venerable tradition, the other first put forth by Leibniz. The Leibniz–Arnauld correspondence clearly displays the conflict between these two standpoints. With his characteristic blend of genius and insanity, Leibniz had conceived a project in which the simple constituents of concepts would be represented by prime numbers and their composition by multiplication. From the Chinese number theorem (and certain assumptions about the nature of truth) he inferred that – given this "perfect language" – all matters of truth could be resolved by appeal to the algorithm of division. "For example," he explained,

if the symbolic number of man is assumed to be 6 and that of ape to be 10, it is evident that neither does the concept of ape contain the concept of man, nor does the converse hold. . . . If, therefore, it is asked whether the concept of the wise man is contained in the concept of the just man . . . we have only to examine whether the symbolic number of the just man can be exactly divided by the symbolic number of the wise man. (*Logical Papers,* p. 22)

This procedure allows us to solve all questions concerning the truth value of universal affirmative propositions if we assume, with Leibniz, that in the true instances "the concept of the subject, taken absolutely and indefinitely, and in general regarded in itself, always contains the concept of the predicate" (*Logical Papers,* p. 22).

In response to Leibniz's astonishing claim that in every true proposition, whether necessary or contingent, the predicate is contained in the subject, Arnauld defended the historical view of the matter: In order for the predicate B to be in A, what is required is not just the truth but the necessity of 'All As are Bs'.

Sometime in the 1770s, Kant came to the conclusion that analyticity is neither truth (as for Leibniz) nor necessity (as for Arnauld) but something stronger than both: What is contained in a concept is less than what is true of it and even than what is necessarily true of its objects; to put it differently, analyticity is one thing and apriority another. It was then that he saw that there are a priori truths not grounded on conceptual analysis, that there are, as he chose to call them, synthetic a priori judgments. With this insight, his conception of philosophy changed radically. Earlier he had thought that the method of philosophy was analysis and that analysis could only ground analytic claims. Now he decided that philosophy was also, perhaps even predominantly, aimed at examining the foundations of very different sorts of judgments, those that are a priori but not analytic.

It would be hard to exaggerate the significance Kant attached to this discovery. The introduction of the *Critique* calls for a new science (sec. 3) designed to answer this previously unnoticed question: How can we have a priori knowledge of propositions in which the predicate concept is not part of the subject concept? "A certain mystery lies here concealed; if it had occurred to any of the ancients even to raise this question, this by itself would . . . have been a powerful influence against all systems of pure reason" (*Critique,* A10). But the existence of such remarkable judgments had been entirely overlooked, Kant thought. The fact that mathematical judgments were not analytic, for example, "has hitherto escaped the notice of those who are engaged in the analysis of human reason, and is, indeed, directly opposed to all their conjectures" (*Critique,* B14).

Whereas much of the *Critique* must have been written, or at least conceived, by the time he came to this new vision of conceptual analysis, Kant chose to place the consequences of this vision at the very beginning of the *Critique* and the *Prolegomena.* When Eberhard challenged Kant's originality on the subject of analysis and synthesis, Kant was furious, exhibiting his feelings in a celebrated polemical blast. And when in 1791 he drafted a response to a question posed by the Academy on what progress had been made in German philosophy since Leibniz and Wolff, Kant observed that "the first step" of the new critical philosophy had been to draw the analytic–synthetic distinction. He added, "Had this been clearly known in the time of Leibniz or Wolff, we would have found it not only reported but also emphasized as important by the treatises of logic and metaphysics" (*Preisschrift über die Fortschritte der Metaphysik* [1804]; see also *Critique,* B19).

Even so, an important question remains. Why didn't Kant think that his distinction was an utterly trivial consequence of the notion of conceptual analysis? The answer I would propose is this: When that distinction was conjoined with Kant's casual understanding of semantic matters, it appeared to entail nothing less than the Copernican turn. Once we realize that we know a priori some claims that cannot be grounded on a mere understanding of their content, it becomes clear that the things about which we have such knowledge cannot be as mind-independent as they were thought to be.

The heart of the problem is Kant's seemingly harmless assumption that the analytic–synthetic distinction is a correct explication of another one, between clarificatory judgments (*Erlaeuterungsurteile*) and ampliative judgments (*Erweiterungsurteile*). In all likelihood, Kant never realized that he was dealing with two different distinctions. Thus, some of his "definitions" of analytic and synthetic judgments tell us that the latter "extends my knowledge beyond what is contained in the [subject] concept" (Allison, *The Kant–Eberhard Controversy,* p. 141; see also *Logik,* p. 111; *Critique,* A8; *Prolegomena to Any Future Metaphysics,* sec. 2a). But it is essential to realize that we are dealing here with a second partition of the class of all (true, subject–predicate) judgments into those that we may ground, or identify as true, merely on the basis of the fact that we are clear about the concepts involved in the judgment, and those (other judgments) that call for an appeal to extraconceptual sources of knowledge. Roughly speaking, whereas Kant's first, *nominal* definition characterizes 'analytic' as true in virtue of definitions (analysis) and logic, the second one defines it as true in virtue of meaning.

The idea that his nominal definition coincides with the second version of 'analytic' is based on an assumption that apparently seemed so obvious to Kant that it did not deserve the slightest argument: *Concepts can provide a basis for knowledge only through a process of analysis.* Thus, he claimed that in a synthetic judgment,

I must advance beyond the given [subject] concept, viewing as related to it something entirely different from what was thought in it. This relation [between the subject and the predicate concepts] is consequently never a relation of identity or contradiction: and *from the judgment taken in and by itself,* the truth or falsity of the relation can never be discovered. (*Kritik,* A154–5/B193–4; my italics)

Elsewhere he put it more concisely: "It is evident that from mere concepts only analytic knowledge . . . is to be obtained" (*Critique,* A47/B64–5).[7] We shall return to examine the immense damage caused by the preceding confusion. But for now we shall proceed with the course of Kant's reasoning. Once the true synthetic judgments of Kant's nominal definition are confused with judgments not grounded on purely conceptual knowledge, the obvious question to ask is, What *are* they grounded on?

Kant had explained that all analytic judgments are grounded on a single principle, what he sometimes called the "principle of analytic judgments" (e.g., *Critique,* A149–50/B189), the principle of identity or contradiction. What he had in mind, presumably, was a principle allowing one to predicate of a given concept those other concepts that we "think" in it as constituents. However this may work, the interesting point is that Kant assumed that his analytic–synthetic distinction characterized, as it were, epistemic natural kinds, so he felt justified in concluding that there had to be another principle involved in the grounding of all synthetic judgments. He called it, of course, the "highest principle of all synthetic judgments" (see, e.g., *Critique,* A154/B193; A158/B197).

In synthetic subject–predicate judgments, we put together two concepts that are not related as part and whole. Having casually and unknowingly consigned all semantic grounds of knowledge to the category of conceptual analysis and thus to nominal analyticity, Kant did not even consider the possibility that synthetic judgments, nominally construed, might also have a semantic ground. "In synthetic judgments," Kant thought, "I must have besides the concept of the subject [and that of the predicate] something else (*X*), upon which the understanding may rely, if it is to know that a predicate, not contained in this concept, nevertheless belongs to it" (*Critique,* A8). Thus, he concluded that the synthesis of disjoint concepts could never be due to a link provided by the conceptual constituents of the judgment, but should always be mediated by a third element, an *X,* as he sometimes called it (e.g., *Critique,* A9/B13), not directly present in the judgment. This *X* could not possibly be a concept, Kant thought, since we would then have in addition to the subject and the predicate concepts, a third concept, and "from mere concepts only analytic knowledge . . . is to be obtained." Since Kant recognized no semantic building blocks other than concepts and intuitions, it followed that the ground of all synthetic knowledge, the glue that links the concepts in a synthetic judgment, must always involve intuition. This is the content of the principle of synthetic judgments: Synthetic judgments "are only possible under the condition that an intuition underlies the concept of their subject" (Allison, *The Kant–Eberhard Controversy,* p. 152; also see the letter to Reinhold, ibid., p. 164). For exam-

ple, after arguing that $7 + 5 = 12$ is not analytic, Kant added that in order to ground this judgment, "we have to go outside these concepts, and call in the aid of the intuition which corresponds to one of them, our five fingers, for instance" (*Critique,* B15). In all mathematical judgments, "while the predicate is indeed attached necessarily to the concept, it is so in virtue of an intuition which must be added to the concept" (*Critique,* B17).

Kant was not particularly modest about his discovery of this "highest principle of all synthetic judgments," designed to solve "the most important to all questions" of transcendental logic – indeed, perhaps "the only question with which it is concerned": How are synthetic a priori judgments possible? (*Critique,* A154/B193). As he wrote to Eberhard in bitter defiance:

It was therefore not merely a verbal quibble, but a step in the advance of knowledge, when the *Critique* first made known the distinction between judgments which rest entirely on the principle of identity or contradiction, from those which require another principle through the label 'analytic' in contradistinction to 'synthetic' judgments. For the notion of synthesis clearly indicates that something outside of the given concept must be added as a substrate which makes it possible to go beyond the concept with my predicate. Thus, the investigation is directed to the possibility of a synthesis of representations with regard to knowledge in general, which must soon lead to the recognition of intuition as an indispensable condition for knowledge, and pure intuition for a priori knowledge. (Allison, *The Kant–Eberhard Controversy,* p. 155)[8]

Kant's doctrine of pure intuition had multiple origins. We have identified two: the principle of synthetic judgments and the thesis of synthetic a priori knowledge.[9] The reasoning proceeds as follows: It is clear, to begin with, that in the nominal sense of 'analysis' there are a great many synthetic judgments that very few people would seriously regard as a posteriori. One could cite, with Kant, the examples of arithmetic and geometry, but there are more pedestrian examples, such as 'If this is red, then it is not blue', 'If this is one meter long, then it is not two meters long', and 'If a is taller than b and b than c, then a is taller than c'. In none of these judgments does the subject contain the predicate(s). Yet they are all surely necessary and hence, according to Kant, a priori. Moreover, by Kant's criterion, every judgment with a simple concept must be synthetic, and surely some such judgments are necessary.[10] Thus, using his nominal definition, Kant had no difficulty identifying synthetic a priori judgments. Indeed, the only considerations to be found in Kant's writings that resemble arguments for the existence of synthetic a priori judgments invariably appeal to the nominal version of Kant's distinction – arguing, quite plausibly, that this or that predicate concept is "obviously" not a constituent or not "thought in" this or that subject concept.

One can readily grant to Kant everything he wanted up to this point. But the next step in his reasoning is, in effect, to confuse synthetic in the nominal sense with ampliative, by assuming that synthetic judgments in the nominal sense cannot be given a purely conceptual ground. The reasons for this error will be examined later, but now we can see the critical roller coaster well on its way: *Something* must ground synthetic judgments, and it cannot be concepts; hence, it has to be intuitions, such as empirical intuitions of the sort Hume liked. But we have now discovered that some synthetic judgments are a priori, so they cannot be grounded by an empirical intuition. Hence, there must be a very special, nonempirical sort of intuition – let us simply call it 'pure intuition'.[11]

We have said that bad semantics was at the root of Kant's appeal to pure intutition. Having examined the motives that may have led him to confuse his two senses of analytic, it is possible to diagnose the problem somewhat more precisely, as emerging from a psychologistic conception of semantics. Consider, for example, the question of whether we have to understand the concept *bachelor* in order to ground the judgment that all bachelors are unmarried. One may imagine Kant's train of thought running along the following lines: Understanding the concept *bachelor* is surely necessary in order to engage in its analysis; but analytic judgments are no more and no less than the outcome of analysis. Therefore, an understanding of the concept – and not just of its structural features or its logical constituency – must be relevant to the grounding of analytic judgments. Or he may (also) have argued: To know or understand a concept is to know its definition; hence, conceptual knowledge is knowledge in virtue of definitions. Since analytic knowledge is exactly knowledge in virtue of (partial) definitions, all purely conceptual knowledge must be analytic.

These appealing but fallacious kinds of reasoning lose all of their attraction once one observes the act–content distinction.[12] Consider again

(*) All bachelors are unmarried.

According to the distinction drawn in the preceding section, two radically different acts of judgment correspond to this sentence; whether we associate with (*) one or the other will depend on how distinct our representation of *bachelor* is. If our representation is entirely distinct (and if *unmarried and male and adult* is the complete analysis of *bachelor*), then the subjective judgment we express by (*) may also be conveyed – even more explicitly – by means of

(**) All unmarried male adults are unmarried.

But if our representing of *bachelor* is indistinct, then the judgment we express by means of (*) will, in general, be quite different from the one

we express by means of (**).[13] We may therefore say that if our understanding of *bachelor* is indistinct, the mental episodes expressed by (*)
and (**) are quite different and that one purpose of analysis is to lead us
from the sorts of mental states associated with (*) to those associated
with (**). But it should be equally obvious that, psychology aside, the
contents of (*) and (**) are, by Kant's own standards, identical, since it
would otherwise be nonsense to insist – as Kant did – that only our
understanding of the concept has changed through the process of analysis, not what we were saying when we used it.

We are now ready to examine the extent to which our conceptual
knowledge of the constituents of the subject concept in (*) is involved in
the grounding of the judgment as analytic. When (*) is regarded as an
expression of our judgment as produced in a state of indistinct understanding of *bachelor,* it is indeed reasonable to say that our improved
understanding of that concept, our understanding of the meaning of
'bachelor', is essential to the grounding of (*), that is, for reaching the
conviction that (*) is true. But consider now (*) as expressing our judgment in a state of distinctness toward *bachelor* or, again, consider the
content of (*). To what extent does our understanding of the concepts
involved play any role in *its* grounding? Or, to put this question differently, could we ground the content of (*) – that is, of (**) – without an
understanding of all of the concepts involved? The answer is obvious
when we look at (**): of course! All we really have to understand in
order to provide a ground for (**) is the meaning of the concepts *conjunction* and *predication.* Thus, whereas the grounding of (*) *qua* indistinct subjective judgment through conceptual analysis calls for our understanding of all concepts involved, the grounding of what (*) says does
not.[14]

We can now see how Kant's neglect of the nonpsychological dimension of semantics may have led him to confuse the analytic and the purely
conceptual; for he would have been correct to think that an understanding of all concepts is essential for analysis (in the psychological sense)
and that analytic judgments are the outcome of analysis. The shift from
psychology to semantics is fatal to Kant's reasoning. The analysis of a
concept does, indeed, require an understanding of it; but the grounding
of an analytic judgment *qua* content calls only for an understanding of
what we have earlier called its structure.

Another way of stating Kant's problem is to say that he confused conceptual knowledge with definitional knowledge; that is, he confused
what can be grounded on concepts with the much smaller subclass of
what can be grounded on definitions. As Kant saw it, analytic knowledge
is possible only in the presence of conceptual complexity, but it should

have been clear that simple concepts, unaided by intuition, are as apt as their complex counterparts to act as grounds of a priori knowledge.

We have detected two tacit assumptions behind Kant's dealings with the analytic and the synthetic: According to the first, analytic coincides with true in virtue of concepts – or, as some would say much later, in virtue of meanings. On this assumption, considerations of a semantic sort are relevant to the establishment of only those judgments whose predicate is part of their subject. This implies that the ground of synthetic judgments does not lie in semantics. The second assumption tells us where it does lie. Given Kant's views on the nature of representation, it can only be assumed that the ground of synthetic knowledge is intuition – in the interesting cases, pure intuition.

Only through a complex and laborious process that took most of the nineteenth century did these Kantian confusions come to be recognized and neutralized. In the rest of Part I we shall look at the central stages of this process. It can be characterized most simply as the decline and fall of pure intuition. However much they may have disagreed on specific issues, the leading members of the anti-Kantian tradition we shall examine shared the conviction that Kant's system was built on a semantic swamp. They also agreed that the only way to avoid a similar fate was to place the theory of meanings, that is, the theory of concepts, judgments, and propositions, at the very top of their list of philosophical concerns. Semantics was born in the effort to avoid Kant's theory of the a priori. It was born in the writings of Bolzano.

2

Bolzano and the birth of semantics

All mathematical truths can and must be proven from mere concepts.

Bolzano, *Grossenlehre*

Kant was incorrect when he took logic to be complete.

Bolzano, *Gesamtausgabe,* ser. 2B, vol. 2, pt. 2

Modern Continental philosophy had always maintained close ties with scientific developments. In Kant the link became so close that the whole doctrine of the a priori had been motivated largely by a datum that had emerged from the sciences – an allegedly transparent feature of geometry, arithmetic, and the calculus that demanded philosophical explanation. Kant's successors in the nineteenth century were of two types: those who wanted to check whether what he said about the a priori sciences was true and those who didn't really care. The latter embraced his Copernican turn for "metaphysical" reasons. The former, by and large, devoted a great deal of time to an analysis of mathematical knowledge. As a result, their more gullible colleagues tended to look on them as low-level mathematicians trying to make a reputation in philosophy. "Mathematica sunt, non leguntur" is what Frege once guessed most philosophers would say about his writings. He was right. The same could have been said of the major writings of the semantic tradition.

The semantic tradition may be defined by its problem, its enemy, its goal, and its strategy. Its problem was the a priori; its enemy, Kant's pure intuition; its purpose, to develop a conception of the a priori in which pure intuition played no role; its strategy, to base that theory on a development of semantics.

If a theory is as sound as the problems it solves, it was reasonable to start a critical examination of the critical philosophy at the place where *it* had started, with an analysis of the character of the a priori knowledge from which Kant had derived his basic datum. The semantic tradition was not developed by people with a narrow-minded interest in the foundations of mathematics, but by those who suspected that Kant's understanding of arithmetic, the calculus, and geometry was based on irrepara-

22

ble misunderstandings and that these misunderstandings vitiated his general picture of the a priori. The following chapters sketch the story of the semantic tradition, a philosophical movement that, unlike positivism, took the a priori seriously and, unlike idealism, chose to look even more closely than Kant at his paradigm examples of the a priori.

While the idealists were removing every trace of objectivity from Kant's semantics, there was in a corner of the Austro-Hungarian empire, ignored by the leaders of German philosophy, a Czech priest by the name of Bernard Bolzano, who was engaged in the most far-reaching and successful effort to date to take semantics out of the swamp into which it had been sinking since the days of Descartes. Bolzano was the first to recognize that transcendental philosophy and its idealistic sequel were a reductio ad absurdum of the semantics of modern philosophy. He was also the first to see that the proper prolegomena to any future metaphysics was a study not of transcendental considerations but of what we say and its laws and that consequently the *prima philosophia* was not metaphysics or ontology but semantics. The development of these ideas in his monumental *Wissenschaftslehre* and in a variety of other writings established Bolzano as the founder of the semantic tradition.

Bolzano's philosophy was the kind that takes from and then gives life to science. His approach to semantics was developed in dialectical interplay with his decision to solve certain problems concerning the nature of mathematical knowledge. Kant had not even seen these problems; Bolzano solved them. And his solutions were made possible by, and were the source of, a new approach to the content and character of a priori knowledge. We shall illustrate the point by focusing on one of Bolzano's favorite mathematical topics, the calculus.

Intuition and the calculus

It would be grossly unfair to Kant to say that the main reasons he had for thinking that mathematics involves pure intuition were the semantic considerations examined in the preceding chapter. In fact, most mathematicians and philosophers at the time would have agreed that given the current state of mathematics, one could hardly draw any other conclusion. Geometry provided the most glaring example of the need to appeal to constructions in intuitions; but even the calculus, the most powerful branch of eighteenth-century mathematics, seemed to conform to that pattern.

In the British mathematical tradition, from which Kant appears to have learned most of what he knew about the calculus, Leibnizian infinitesimals were shunned; their role was played by rates of change. Motion – therefore, space and time – was placed at the very heart of the calculus. A variable was called a "flowing quantity" and its velocity a "fluxion." "I consider mathematical quantities," Newton wrote,

not as consisting of very small parts, but as described by a continual motion. Lines are described, and thereby generated, not by the apposition of parts, but by the continued motion of points . . . angles by the rotation of the sides; portions of time by continued flux. . . . Fluxions are, as near as we please, as the increments of fluents generated in times, equal and as small as possible, and to speak accurately [sic], they are in the prime ratio of nascent increments. (*Quadrature of curves* [1704], as quoted in Kline, *Mathematical Thought from Ancient to Modern Times,* p. 363)

Thus, the derivative, the limit of an infinite sequence of ratios, was conceived as the value of the ratio at that instant of time right before the increment vanished (whatever that might mean). Limits were also characterized as dependent on temporal notions. Newton explained in *Principia*:

Those ultimate ratios with which quantities vanish are not truly the ratios of ultimate quantities, but limits towards which the ratios of quantities decreasing without limit do always converge; and to which they approach nearer than by any given difference, but never go beyond, nor in effect attain to, till the quantities are diminished *in infinitum*. (p. 39)

The idea is to appeal to an infinite kinematic process with an end term, rather than to an infinite sequence with a limit.

Dubious theoretical considerations of this type were accompanied by no less dubious arguments in support of "claims" whose only merit was that they worked. For example, derivatives were calculated on the basis of indefensible sleights of hand, combining algebraic operations (such as division by an increment) with assumptions incompatible with algebra (division by 0). Even so, the calculus worked. It was not broken; why fix it? Those who thought of mathematics not as knowledge but as a scientifically useful technique, and those who did not think at all about such things, did not worry much about the "foundational" question. The first strident complaint came, in fact, from a philosopher.

Berkeley was the first to rise against the chaos at the foundation of the calculus. In 1734 he published a work designed to show that the boldest speculations of theologians compared favorably with the most sober statements of mathematicians on the foundations of the calculus. He noted with some glee that in England, following Newton, functions (fluents) were quantities that vary with time, and their derivatives (fluxions) "are said to be nearly as the increments of the flowing quantities, generated in the least equal particles of time; and to be accurately in the first proportion of the nascent, or in the last of the evanescent increments"

(*The Analyst,* p. 66). As to the "foreign mathematicians" (i.e., Leibniz and his followers):

Instead of flowing quantities and their fluxions, they consider the variable finite quantities as increasing or diminishing by the continual addition or subduction of infinitely small quantities. Instead of the velocities wherewith increments are generated, they consider the increments or decrements themselves . . . which are supposed to be infinitely small. (p. 67)

Leibniz's "ghosts of departed quantities" clearly made no more sense than Newton's "nascent increments." Berkeley drew his well-known conclusion:

Nothing is easier than to devise expressions or notations, for fluxions and infinitesimals. . . . These expressions indeed are clear and distinct, and the mind finds no difficulty in conceiving them to be continued beyond any assignable bounds. But if we remove the veil and look underneath, if, laying aside the expressions, we set ourselves attentively to consider the things themselves which are supposed to be expressed or marked thereby, we shall discover much emptiness, darkness, and confusion; nay, if I mistake not, direct impossibilities and contradictions. (*The Analyst,* p. 69)

At first few mathematicians took Berkeley's complaints very seriously, endorsing the pragmatist maxim attributed to d'Alembert: Allez en avant et la fois vous viendra! But by the end of the century – by the time Kant was arguing for the inevitability of the spatiotemporal character of the calculus – the very best mathematicians had begun to worry.

In 1784, three years after the publication of Kant's first *Critique,* the Berlin Academy proposed a question on the foundations of the calculus as its mathematical prize problem. The problem was, in effect, to explain the role of the infinitely small and the infinitely large in the calculus. The proposal explained:

It is well known that higher mathematics continually uses infinitely large and infinitely small quantities. Nevertheless, geometers, and even the ancient analysts, have carefully avoided everything which approaches the infinite; and some great modern analysts hold that the terms of the expression "infinite magnitude" contradict one another. The Academy hopes, therefore, that it can be explained how so many true theorems have been deduced from a contradictory supposition, and that a principle can be delineated which is sure, clear – in a word, truly mathematical – which can appropriately be substituted for "the infinite." (Grabiner, *The Origins of Cauchy's Rigorous Calculus,* pp. 41–2)

The first major contribution to this topic was Lagrange's *Théorie des fonctions analytiques* (1797). (The full title is almost a manifesto: "Theory of analytic functions, detached from any consideration of infinitely small or evanescent quantities, of limits or of fluxions, and reduced to the algebraic analysis of finite quantities.") There he explained that his two main purposes were to unify the calculus with algebra and, above all, to disengage the calculus from the "metaphysical" considerations involving infinitesimals and fluxions. The main problem with fluxions was their involvement with the "foreign" concept of motion and the obscurity of the associated notion of a limit.

Lagrange's main qualm about the notion of limit was that it was too vague and too geometric; as usually presented, it considered quantities "in the state in which they cease, so to speak, to be quantities"; and the ratio of two finite quantities "no longer offers a clear and precise idea to the mind, when the terms of the ratio become zero simultaneously" (see Grabiner, *The Origins of Cauchy's Rigorous Calculus*, p. 44). Lagrange's criticisms of standard foundations were decisive, and his project to eliminate infinity through a reduction to the theory of numbers (algebra) rather than through constructive processes remained a central feature of later nineteenth-century developments. But his own foundational work on the calculus aimed to avoid rather than to explicate the basic notions of limit, continuity, and the like. His proposed foundation was soon shown to be untenable.[1]

The next major step in this development was taken by Bolzano. Bolzano's mathematical work embraced an astonishing range of topics, including geometry, topology, the theory of functions, the theory of the infinite, and even the notion of the actual infinitesimal.[2] Here we shall illustrate only its philosophical thrust with a few references to Bolzano's role in initiating the research program that came to be known as the rigorization of the calculus.

It is worth pausing briefly to introduce a matter that will occupy us heavily in later chapters: the sense and purpose of foundationalist or reductionist projects such as the reduction of mathematics to arithmetic, or of arithmetic to logic. It is widely thought that the principle inspiring such reconstructive efforts was epistemological, that they were basically a search for certainty. This is a serious error. It is true, of course, that most of those engaging in these projects believed in the possibility of achieving something in the neighborhood of Cartesian certainty for those principles of logic or arithmetic on which a priori knowledge was to be based. But it would be a gross misunderstanding to see in this belief the basic aim of the enterprise. A no less important purpose was the clarification of what was being said.

The word 'rigor', normally used by mathematicians and historians to describe the purpose and the achievement of the major nineteenth-century foundational projects, is ambiguous; it is both a semantic and an epistemological notion. The search for rigor might be, and often was, a search for certainty, for an unshakable "*Grund.*" But it also was a search for a clear account of the basic notions of a discipline (an "ideological" reduction; see Chapter 11). Ignorant people may think it childish to worry about the difference between 'For every epsilon, there is a delta that works for all x' and 'For any epsilon and for all x, there is a delta . . .', since anyone can see it. Such people would be well advised to study the history of the calculus and consider the difficulties that emerged from a failure to distinguish between convergence and uniform convergence. Modern critics of foundationalist projects have been blind to their clarificatory dimension, sometimes confusing a search for meaning with a search for essences ("essentialism"). The epistemological perspective on foundationalist projects makes it especially easy to miss their basic achievements, since in few cases, if any, was an actual reduction achieved to what the reductionists regarded as a fully satisfactory basis of certainty. In most of the major cases, however, there was a clear advance in the direction of reducing the more obscure to the clearer. Bolzano's work is a good example of this.

It is now widely agreed that Bolzano's first decisive contribution to the rigorization of the calculus was his "Rein analytischer Beweis des Lehrsatzes" (1817). The problem examined in this paper is one the Kantians would have declared childish: How do we know that a continuous function taking values both above and below zero must take a zero value in between? What is essential is not, of course, the specific content of the theorem, but the particular perspective from which Bolzano approached it. The question was not, What argument are we to give in order to convince ourselves that this claim is true? It was, rather, What exactly does this claim *say?* As we shall see, Bolzano's lasting contribution to this problem was his insight into the structure of the required proof sequence; but this insight was, in turn, dependent on a clear and novel picture of the content of the intermediate-value theorem. In order to reach his specific conception of that content, Bolzano first had to explicate what was meant by the central notions in the theorem, especially the notion of continuity.

Bolzano began his paper by criticizing a variety of standard proofs of the theorem and, by implication, a variety of interpretations of its content. Some proofs, he explained, depend on a truth borrowed from geometry, to wit, that every continuous line with a positive and a negative coordinate must intersect the x-axis. But this geometric proposition is, first of all, a particular case of the theorem under consideration and, more importantly, is itself in need of proof – a proof that must no doubt derive from the more general theorem. Another equally objectionable form of proof introduces the notion of continuity in terms of the notions of time and motion. The latter, however, "are just as foreign to general mathematics as the concept of space." A correct proof must begin by giving a proper definition of the basic notions involved in the theorem and must prove the claim "analytically," that is, avoiding intuition and appealing only to basic assumptions concerning numbers and functions.

The first task, therefore, was to cleanse the notion of continuity of any spatiotemporal "dynamic" character and to turn it into an "analytic," arithmetical notion. Thus, we are told that

the expression *that a function fx varies according to the law of continuity for all values of x inside or outside certain limits* means only this: *if x is some such value, the difference f(x + w) − fx can be made smaller than any given quantity provided that w can be taken as small as we please.* (pp. 427–8)

This is, in effect, the first clear presentation of the epsilon–delta definition of continuity. Bolzano then stated the (so-called) Cauchy criterion for convergence, proving the necessity of that criterion and arguing for its sufficiency in a way marred by the unavailability of a definition of real number (which would emerge fifty years later). He then proved that a bounded set of real numbers has a least upper bound and from this finally derived the intermediate-value theorem.[3]

From the philosophical standpoint, leaving aside its specifically mathematical significance, the most interesting feature of Bolzano's proof is the careful elimination of anything that might have to do with geometry or spatiotemporal considerations. All "dynamic" notions of the calculus (continuity, limit, etc.) have been made static. The notion that a function "approaches" a value had become a misleading metaphor, which really said something about certain arithmetical inequalities that have no connection whatever with time. As a result of Bolzano's proof, the central notions of the calculus were on their way to being "arithmetized." The arithmetization − or "rigorization" − of the calculus would be completed in later years by Cauchy, Weierstrass, Cantor, and Dedekind.[4]

Bolzano saw a clear philosophical purpose behind this project. In a sketch of an autobiography, he once wrote (talking of himself in the third person):

From very early on he dared to contradict him [Kant] directly on the theory of time and space, for he did not comprehend or grant that our synthetic a priori judgments must be mediated by intuition and, in particular, he did not believe that the intuition of time lies at the ground of the synthetic judgments of arithmetic, or that in the theorems of geometry it is allowable to rest so much on the mere claim of the visual appearance, as in the Euclidean fashion. He was all the more reluctant to grant this, since very early on he found a way to derive from concepts many geometric truths that were known before only on the basis of mere visual appearance. ("Zur Lebensbeschreibung," *Gesamtausgabe*, ser. 2A, vol. 12, pt. 1, p. 68)

There is, indeed, no theme throughout Bolzano's mathematical and philosophical work more consistent than the commitment to take pure intuition out of a priori knowledge. In the field of mathematics, this took the form of persistently excluding spatiotemporal ideas from subjects other than geometry and continually questioning the value of any kind of intuition in mathematics.[5] Already in *Beyträge zu einer begründeteren Darstellung der Mathematik* (1810), Bolzano had raised the question of the nature of mathematics and its relation to philosophy. The critical philosophy, he explained, offers one answer:

It claims to have discovered a distinct and characteristic difference between the two fundamental types of human *a priori* knowledge, the philosophical and the mathematical, to wit, that *mathematical knowledge must be able* to represent – i.e., *construct* – adequately all of its concepts in a *pure intuition,* and thereby to *demonstrate* all of its theorems. *Philosophical knowledge,* on the other hand, lacking all intuition, must be satisfied with mere *discursive concepts.* The essence of mathematics would therefore be most properly expressed through this explanation: *It is a science of reason through the construction of concepts.* . . . As for me, I will frankly acknowledge that until now – as with in fact so many other doctrines of the critical philosophy – I have been unable to accept the correctness of Kantian assertions concerning *pure intuition* and the *construction of concepts through it.* I also still believe that surely there lies an internal contradiction in the *concept of a pure* (i.e., a priori) *intuition;* and even less can I convince myself that it is necessary to construct the concept of number in time, and that consequently the intuition of time is an essential part of arithmetic. (pp. 106–7)

Bolzano's "Rein analytischer Beweis des Lehrsatzes" was only one of a variety of contributions to this project of excluding intuition from mathematics. Since Kant had argued that all synthetic knowledge requires intuition, Bolzano's mathematical project involved an implicit challenge to the principle of synthetic judgments and, therefore, to the heart of Kantian semantics. Bolzano chose to make that challenge quite explicit.

The root of the problem

Bolzano agreed with Kant's teachers that all knowledge consists of representations; and he also agreed with Kant that representations are ultimately reducible to concepts or intuitions. But the chaos one finds in the literature both before and after Kant on the nature of these representations is characteristically replaced in Bolzano by a clear, careful statement of what they are.

To begin with, Kant's occasional ambiguities between subjective and intersubjective elements in representation are entirely eliminated. Bolzano started by distinguishing two senses of the word 'representation'. First, there are the representations that psychologists (and idealists) consider to the exclusion of all others, the mental states or determinations of the soul, as Kant had called them – such as my state of mind as I perceive a physical object. These are called "subjective representations" or "representations in us" (Bolzano, *Gesamtausgabe,* ser. 2B, vol. 18, pt. 2, p. 64). Second, there is the much more important intersubjective content of the psychological representation or, as Bolzano called it, the "representation in itself" or "objective representations."

The key to what objective representations are emerges from the fact that each meaningful grammatical unit is associated with a host of subjective representations but with only *one* objective representation, which has being even when the object of the representation does not. For example, "the subjective representations that occur in the minds of my readers when they see the word 'nothing' should be almost equal to one another, but they are nevertheless many. On the other hand, there is only one objective representation designated by this word" (Bolzano, *Theory of Science,* p. 62).

Whereas subjective representations are real, that is, "they have real existence at the time when they are present in a subject" (p. 61), objective representations are not. They are

not to be found in the realm of the real. An objective representation does not require a subject but subsists, not indeed as something *existing,* but as a certain *something* even though no thinking being may have it; also, it is not multiplied when it is thought by one, two, three, or more beings. . . . For this reason, any word, unless it is ambiguous, designates only one objective representation. (p. 62)

Objective representations are the substance (*Stoff*) or content of subjective representations. Their being in no way depends on the existence of subjective acts, just as the meaningfulness of expressions in no way depends on anybody's bearing the appropriate meanings in mind; and like meanings, there is only one for each linguistic unit unless the given expression is ambiguous. Clearly, Bolzano's objective representations are the "meanings" or "senses" of his successors in the semantic tradition.[6] The distinction between objective and subjective representations amounts to a separation of meaning from psychological processes.

Bolzano further distinguished between an objective representation and the object of that representation. For example, the objective representation associated with the word 'table' (i.e., the meaning of 'table') should not be confused with tables, the objects of that representation. Even though both are objective, only one of them is real and only one of them is the topic of discourse when the word 'table' is involved. One must consequently distinguish three semantically relevant elements associated with a grammatical unit: (a) the objective representation or meaning, (b) the object of the representation (e.g., the entity referred to by a proper name, *if any*), and (c) the psychological process that takes place when we perceive or think about the object of the representation (*Theory of Science,* p. 62). These distinctions had been acknowledged in one way or another by most major philosophers before Bolzano. What makes his contribution to this matter so remarkable is that he was the first one to recognize fully the enormous destructive implications of even a merely halfhearted recognition of these distinctions. As he once put it, the "proton pseudon" of the new idealistic philosophy is that "the *concept in itself* is not clearly understood, and is confused sometimes with the *thought* and sometimes with the *thing* that is its object" ("Uber der Begriff des Schönen" [1843], p. 6).

One of the most important consequences Bolzano drew from these distinctions was a radical reformulation of an implicit semantic assumption that had enjoyed widespread acceptance since the days of Leibniz, the doctrine that an appropriate analysis of a subjective representation should identify in it as many parts as there are in the object represented. Leibniz had argued, for example, that the representation (*idée*) of green is indistinct because even though it appears to us to be simple, it is, in fact, complex; for physics establishes that "green emerges from the combination of blue and yellow. Thus one is justified in thinking that the idea of green is composed of those two other ideas . . . hence there are perceptions of which we are not aware" (*Nouveaux essais,* p. 100). Kant was so impressed with Leibniz's point that he used this very example in his logic lectures to explain how representations could be clear but indistinct and how distinctness could be achieved through the identification of constituents (*Wiener Logik,* p. 841). And in one of his reflections, Kant noted that a representation must be isomorphic to what it represents: "[Representation] is that determination of the spirit (*Bestimmung der Seele*) that refers to other things. What I call referring (*Beziehen*) is when its features conform to those of the external things" ("Die Vernunftlehre," Reflexionen 1676, *Kants gesammelte Schriften,* vol. 16, pp. 76–7). But, he added, a representation does not stand to what it represents as the painting to its subject. The representation

is composed out of its component concepts in the same way in which the entire represented thing is composed out of its parts. Just as, for example, one can say that the notes of a musical piece are a representation of the harmonic connection of the tones, not because each note is similar to each tone but because the notes are connected to each other just as the tones themselves. (p. 78)

Bolzano thought that there was an important kernel of truth in all this, but that the intended point was blunted by the idealist "proton pseudon," the confusion between the objective representation and its object. Kant was assuming that "the parts of a representation are the same as the representations of the parts of its object" (Bolzano, *WL,* sec. 63). This is clearly false since, for example, the representation of a simple object may be complex (as in *the center of mass of the solar system*).[7] There is a tacit isomorphism in representation, Bolzano thought, but it is between the mental representation and its objective counterpart. And it is because this isomorphism is, for the most part, tacit or unconscious that semantic analysis is essential:

We think a certain representation in itself, i.e. we have a corresponding mental representation, only if we think all the parts of which it consists, i.e. if we also have mental representations of these parts. But it is not necessarily the case that we are always clearly conscious of, and able to disclose, what we think. Thus it may occur that we think a complex representation in itself, and are conscious that we think it, without being conscious of the thinking of its individual parts or being able to indicate them. (*Theory of Science,* p. 69)

Semantic analysis can remedy this difficulty by bringing subjective and objective representations to isomorphic match. Bolzano's doctrine re- directs conceptual analysis onto the path that will eventually lead to Frege's *Begriffsschrift.*

Finally, although the most obvious purpose of objective representa- tions is to represent their objects, Bolzano thought that their most impor- tant task was to join together into propositions the objective content of subjective judgments. Once again, one must observe here the distinction between the subjective and the objective realms. Subjective propositions – the judgments of standard logic treatises – are mental states con- stituted by mental representations. Their content, the propositions in themselves (as Bolzano called them), have objective representations as their constituents. "It seems indisputable to me," he wrote, "that every, even the simplest, proposition is composed of certain parts, and it seems equally clear that these parts do not merely occur in the verbal expres- sion as subject and predicate . . . but that they are already contained in the proposition in itself" (*Theory of Science,* p. 65). The constituents of the objective proposition expressed by the sentence *S* are, in fact, the objective representations associated with the grammatical units of *S.* Moreover, a proposition is not about its constituents but about the ob- jects of its constituent representations (see *WL,* secs. 48–52).

The preceding sketch provides an illustration of the sense in which Bolzano is responsible for the kind of picture-theoretic semantics that would develop decades later in the writings of Frege, Russell, and Witt- genstein. Philosophical semantics was not invented for its own sake, however, but for the sake of epistemology. It was invented so that the character of knowledge, in particular a priori knowledge, could be better understood. Let us now see how Bolzano put it to that use.

Modality, analyticity, and the a priori

Few issues divide philosophers more revealingly than their attitude toward the gap between what is and what must be, toward fact and modality. The basic issue might be illustrated as follows: Even though both

(1) This man is a featherless biped

and

(2) If all men are mortal and all Greeks are men, then all Greeks are mortal

are true, they appear to differ in an elusive modal trait. As some would put it, (1) merely *is* true, whereas (2) *must* be true. Alternatively, (1) is known only through observation, whereas (2) is known a priori. Before undergoing philosophical treatment, most people would agree that a modal feeling is associated with (2) but not with (1) and that this seems to be related to the difference between the modes of access to the truth of these statements. One of the perennial philosophical issues is whether the modal feeling associated with (2) is a reliable indicator of some important trait of the associated claim or whether it is no more than the product of confusion, worthy only of being purged from our thought. Most philosophers have taken the first position; the ludicrous character of the theories of modality and the a priori that they proceeded to offer may have been the powerful fuel that moved many sane philosophers to consider the second. Bolzano was one of the most prominent nineteenth-century proponents of the "positivist" standpoint that the modal feeling is deceptive and should be explained away. And yet no one in the nineteenth century came closer than he did to an appreciation of the facts that would lead, around 1930, to a new doctrine of necessity and the a priori. In order to see this, we must first examine Bolzano's contribution to the problem of analyticity.

There are two basic ways of construing logical necessity and related modal attributes of propositions. According to the first, what we might call the Leibnizian way, to determine whether a proposition P is logically true, we fix P and change the world, watching what happens to the truth value of P. To see whether (1) is logically true, for example, we examine different possible worlds to see whether this man is featherless in all of them. Finding that he is not, we conclude that (1) is not logically true.

According to the second procedure, when we want to determine whether P is a logical truth, we do not change the world; we change P instead and look at whether the truth values of the resulting propositions – evaluated in this fixed world of ours – change as well. Instead of envisaging new circumstances, we envisage, in effect, new claims about the given circumstances. This idea, loosely related to Aristotle's introduction of the variable into logical considerations, was first developed in Bolzano's writings.[8]

Russell once said that it makes no sense to say of a true proposition that *it* could have been false (*Principles,* p. 12). Perhaps unable to make sense of talk concerning different worlds, he was also unable to make sense of different truth values for *this* proposition. He would have concurred with Bolzano's judgment that "every given proposition is either true or false and never changes; either it is true forever, or false forever, unless we change some *part* of it, and hence consider no longer the same but some other proposition" (*Theory of Science,* p. 194).

According to Bolzano, this tacit change of the proposition is, in fact, what is involved in most modal claims:

We often take certain representations in a given proposition to be variable and, without being clearly aware of it, replace these variable parts by certain other representations and observe the truth values which these propositions take on. . . . Given a proposition, we could merely inquire whether it is true or false. But some very remarkable properties of propositions can be discovered if, in addition, we consider the truth values of all those propositions which can be generated from it, if we take some of its constituent representations as variable and replace them by any other representations whatever. (p. 194)

Whereas the treatment of modality in relation to possible worlds seems to leave no room for human choice, the Bolzano approach is clearly relative to a specification of the constituents that are to be regarded as variable. Which propositions will be associated with the one under consideration (as its "Bolzano companions") depends entirely on which of its constituents are considered variable. Thus, Bolzano introduced the notion of *general validity* (*Allgemeingültigkeit*): A proposition P is generally valid relative to the set $x_1, \ldots, x_n$ of constituents when all of its Bolzano companions (all propositions obtained by replacing $x_1, \ldots, x_n$ by arbitrary but grammatically admissible representations)[9] are true.

Bolzano briefly considered the possibility of leaving only logical concepts fixed, but observed that "the whole domain of concepts belonging to logic is not circumscribed to the extent that controversies could not arise at times" (pp. 198–9), and he therefore let the matter drop. To the extent that the distinction can be drawn, he proposed to call *logically analytic* all those propositions that are universally valid relative to all their nonlogical concepts. He reserved the term 'analytic' for the much less promising notion of a proposition that is universally valid relative to some constituent or other (pp. 197–8).

Whereas Bolzano's notion of analyticity does not appear to capture an interesting concept, the same could hardly be said about his general validity.[10] Much more important than singling out those of his notions destined to have a brilliant future, however, is recognizing the basic insight underlying Bolzano's approach to the subject of analyticity. This insight emerges most clearly when, after putting forth his own proposals, Bolzano (as usual) turns to examine the major alternatives available in the philosophical literature. After a detailed examination of the flaws in the Kantian notion of analyticity he concludes:

Generally, it seems to me that none of these explications sufficiently emphasizes what makes these [analytic] propositions important. I believe that this importance lies in the fact that their truth or falsity does not depend upon the individual representations of which they are composed. . . . This is the reason why I gave the above definition. (p. 201)

It would be hard to exaggerate the significance of this insight or the extent to which it undermines the basis of Kant's philosophy; for Bolzano is saying, in effect, that Kant's contention that truths based only on conceptual knowledge must be analytic is very nearly the opposite of the truth, since the basic feature of analytic knowledge, in Kant's nominal sense, is that it *ignores* most concepts or representations. Bolzano's point is precisely the one spelled out at the end of Chapter 1. That he was the first to make it (and the only one to see it clearly for quite a number of decades) was a consequence of the fact that he was the first to distinguish meticulously between the content of a conceptual representation and its psychological trappings.

Bolzano's insight led to an improved understanding of the notion of analyticity; but more significantly, it led also to the following question: If the conceptual resources that must be mobilized in order to justify analytic judgments are only a modest fragment of those available to us, what job do the remaining concepts do? Surely they must do some work! It seems absurd to suppose that the modest stock of concepts that pertain to logic justify some claims (the analytic ones), but that all remaining concepts have no comparable talents. If conjunction and implication suffice to establish the truth of 'If this is A and B, then it is A', then color concepts, for example, should be capable of contributing to the justification of some other claims. Which ones? Whatever the answer, we can see that Bolzano's careful semantic investigations show Kant's position on this matter to be an utterly untenable middle ground; for Kant insisted on the capacity of concepts to establish the validity of certain claims, but at the same time ignored the remaining vast continent of conceptual resources. Kant's semantic confusions led him to ignore the grounding force of descriptive concepts. That in turn led him to postulate pure intuition. When the confusions were exposed, it opened once again the question of whether arithmetical and geometric knowledge require something beyond the realm of concepts for their justification.

Considerations such as these likely played a role in Bolzano's later views on the nature of synthetic a priori judgments. As we have seen, he readily granted the existence of such judgments (in the nominal sense of synthetic):

Not everything that can be predicated of an object, even with necessity, lies already in the concept of that object. For example, one can predicate of every rectilinear triangle that the sum of its three angles = 180 . . . nevertheless, no one will believe that these properties of the triangle are contained as constituents of this concept. ("Logische Vorbegriffe," *Gesamtausgabe,* ser. 2A, vol. 5, p. 178)[11]

Kant's solution, involving the principle of synthetic judgments, was flatly rejected:

Kant poses the question, "What justifies our understanding in assigning to a subject a predicate that is by no means contained in the concept (or explanation) of the former?" – And he thought he had discovered that this justification could only be an intuition that we link with the concept of the subject and that also contains the predicate. Thus, for all concepts from which we can construct synthetic judgments, there must be corresponding intuitions. If these intuitions were always merely empirical, the judgments which they mediate should also always be empirical. Since, nonetheless, there are synthetic *a priori* judgments – (as such things are undeniably contained in mathematics and pure natural science); there must also be *a priori* intuitions – however odd this might sound. And once one has decided that there can be such, one will also convince oneself easily that for the purposes of mathematics and pure natural science, time and space are these intuitions. (*Beyträge zu einer begründeteren Darstellung der Mathematik,* pp. 234–5)[12]

What, then, is it that justifies the belief in these a priori judgments? Bolzano's most common explanations were of the empiricist type, thus inconsistent with the alleged a priori status of the relevant judgments. But in the *Wissenschaftslehre,* he finally came to recognize that his semantic insights could be put to good use at this very point:

What justifies the understanding to attribute to a subject *A* a predicate *B* which does not lie in the concept *A?* Nothing I say but that the understanding *has* and *knows* the two concepts *A* and *B*. I think that we must be in a position to judge about certain concepts merely because we have them. . . . Since this holds generally, it also holds in the case when these concepts are simple. But in this case, the judgments which we make about them are certainly synthetic [in Kant's nominal sense]. (*Theory of Science,* p. 347)

This says, in effect, that not only the *content* but also the justification of synthetic a priori judgments is purely conceptual.

This was no more than a flash of insight, however, and was not destined to play a major role in Bolzano's system. Bolzano's official account of how a priori knowledge is grounded was very different from the one we just saw in *Wissenschaftslehre.*

The basis of logical truth

Those willing to make sense of the modal difference between (1) and (2) will typically say that the truth of (1) both consists of a certain correspondence with facts and can be determined by an appeal to that correspondence, but will be willing to grant only that the truth of (2) may consist in that correspondence. It would be just plain muddle-headed to appeal to that correspondence in order to justify (2) – as muddleheaded as an attempt to determine empirically whether all bachelors are unmarried. The modalist will readily grant that the truth of

(3) All men are featherless bipeds

is entirely reducible to that of all of its instances, in the sense that there is nothing more to (3) than the conjunction of its instances such as (1), and these are merely factual. Hence, in cases like (3), the modalist will agree with Bolzano that an examination of a host of other propositions is essential to determine the truth value of (3), since (3) is, in the end, no more than the conjunction of those propositions. But for the modalist, the ground of (2) – and of necessary claims in general – does not emerge from below, from the facts, but from above. The modalist may grant that there is a fact that makes (2) true and that innumerable other facts make the Bolzano companions of (2) true as well. But these facts are, for the modalist, irrelevant to the justification of (2); something prior to and independent of these facts determines and explains the truth of (2) and, at the same time, its peculiar modal character. Traditionally, the "form" of the proposition was cited as the reason for its truth: (2) is true not in virtue of facts – which are, indeed, as (2) says they are – but in virtue of its form.

In his characteristic cool-headed manner, Bolzano noted the overwhelming weight of the tradition in favor of this approach and then examined the various attempts to explain the form–matter distinction. He concluded, quite rightly, that there is little but confusion behind the traditional ways of drawing the distinction. For those who would insist on using some notion of form, he offered an honest definition: The form of the proposition P relative to its constituents $x_1, \ldots, x_n$ is, in effect, the class of propositions that differ from P at most in the constituents in question (see *WL*, sec. 186). But Bolzano was clearly not very fond of those logicians and philosophers "blinded by the erudite twilight of the words 'form' and 'matter'" (*Theory of Science*, p. 164).

Bolzano concluded that the idea of form as traditionally construed was worthless, and he could see no other candidate for the role of a suprafactual ground of logical truth. Hence, he saw no reason to place (2) in a different category than (1); one might as well call them both analytic. In particular, the truth grounds of (2) are essentially of the same sort as those of (1):

The only reason why we are so certain that the rules *barbara, celarent,* etc. are valid, is because they have been confirmed in thousands of arguments in which we have applied them. This is also the true reason why we are so confident, in mathematics, that factors in different order give the same product, or that the sum of the angles in a triangle is equal to two right angles. (*Theory of Science,* p. 354)

The ground of (2), like that of (1), derives from below, from the facts.

The same attitude is clearly displayed in Bolzano's interpretation of Aristotle's celebrated definition of a syllogism as "a discourse in which, certain things being stated, something other than what is stated follows of necessity from their being so" (*Prior Analytics,* 24b19).

Here is Bolzano's comment:

The 'follows of necessity' [in Aristotle's characterization] can hardly be interpreted in any other way than this: that the conclusion becomes true *whenever* the premises are true. Now it is obvious that we cannot say of one and the same class of propositions that one of them becomes true *whenever* the others are true, unless we envisage some of their parts as variable. . . . The desired formulation was this: as soon as the exchange of certain representations makes the premises true, the conclusion must [*sic*] also become true. (*Theory of Science,* p. 220)[13]

In general, Bolzano's interpretation of statements of valid inference such as (2) is this: "Everybody feels that the sense of the assertion can only be to say that in each case where a substitution of representations makes the antecedents true, the consequent will also express a truth" (p. 253). For him the only way we can make sense of the idea of a necessary link between the premise and the conclusion of a valid inference is by assuming that some of the constituents of (2) are tacitly taken as variable and that we are required to examine the truth values of all of the appropriate instances. The basis of the necessity of (2) is the just plain truth of the appropriate instances. This leaves us with a strange category of analytic statements that includes not only (1) and (2), but also

(4) If this is red, then it is not-blue.

The modalist would want to regard (4) as necessary, but certainly not in virtue of its form. For him, the inference from 'This is red' to 'This is not-

blue' expresses a syllogism in the exact sense of Aristotle's characterization, and form surely plays no role in the necessity involved in this
inference. The idea that our acceptance of (4) should conform to the
inductive strategy of checking on the truth values of antecedents and
consequents for its instances is too ludicrous to even be taken seriously.
Bolzano might have appealed at this point to his doctrine of the conceptual ground of synthetic a priori knowledge. But if so, why not be equally
generous in the case of (logically) analytic knowledge? Having divided
his natural kinds in the wrong places, Bolzano was not properly disposed
to ask the right questions. It would take almost a century to reach once
again the level that Bolzano was approaching at this point, to rearrange
those categories, and to formulate the right questions.

Decades later others could see in Bolzano's work a nearly complete
version of a successful defense of a necessitarian standpoint. If concepts
can provide a justification for synthetic knowledge and if logical concepts are the only ones that are kept fixed in the case of logically analytic
knowledge, why not say that such knowledge is grounded on logical
concepts? Or, to put it in modern terms, why not say that logical truth is
truth in virtue of the meanings of the logical terms? Why not say that the
analyticity of (2) is based not on the fact that it and other sentences have
certain truth values, but rather on the fact that some of the constituent
words have certain meanings? By placing (1) and (2) in the same category of analytic judgments, Bolzano made it harder to see that in some
cases – such as (2) – the understanding of what is being said is not only
a necessary, but also a sufficient justification of logical knowledge.

Bolzano's indecisiveness on this epistemological matter is one of a
variety of indicators of the fact that, great as his contribution was, the
semantic tradition still had a long way to go. Bolzano excelled when his
subject was the content of a priori statements, where he argued with
unsurpassed technical and philosophical authority that claims widely
thought to involve intuition in their content, in fact, did not. But he was
far less successful when he turned to the justification of these avowedly a
priori claims. There his views were more conservative, and he tended to
infer from his justified rejection of standard aprioristic accounts that
nothing was left but a form of positivism. From *Beyträge zu einer begründeteren Darstellung der Mathematik* to the *Wissenschaftslehre,* he
kept repeating that the reason we are so confident of mathematical laws
such as that of the commutativity of multiplication is that "they have
been confirmed in thousands of arguments in which we have applied
them" (*Theory of Science,* p. 354).

Bolzano's sketch of a picture-theoretic semantics was also no more
than a sketch. The central ideal of logical analysis, the realization that
language is an extraordinarily misleading guide to content, was still in the

future.[14] For Bolzano language was a rather reliable picture of the form of objective propositions. He wrote as if, by and large, German sentences were isomorphic maps of the corresponding objective propositions. Thus, the objective proposition expressed by 'This triangle is large' consists of the representations *this, triangle, has,* and *largeness.* The isomorphism obtains even in the case of names: '35' and '53' were said to express representations whose constituents are identical (presumably, the representations *3* and *5,* whatever they may be) and to differ only in "the way in which these parts are connected" (*Theory of Science,* p. 69).[15] Finally, even the notion of content was not given its full role. Bolzano was still attached to the long-standing tradition that thinks of deductive relations as somehow analogous to causal connections and seeks to draw within the class of valid logical links a further distinction aimed at identifying the "proper ground" of certain claims. These and other matters would finally be settled a few decades later, in Frege's writings. Before we turn to them, however, we must consider what happened to Kant's views on geometry in the meantime.

3

◁=====================================▷

Geometry, pure intuition, and the a priori

In philosophy, an intuition can only be an example; in mathematics, on the other hand, an intuition is the essential thing.

Kant, *Logik Busolt*

For Helmholtz, however, there existed the option: either "necessity of thought" or "empirical origin." But it is appropriate to add to these: necessity of intuition, and this as pure.

Cohen, *Kants Theorie der Erfahrung*

So it is entirely implausible that outside the range of pure mathematics we will ever make use of these hypotheses of non-Euclidean spaces.

Riehl, *Phil. Krit.,* vol. 2

From the beginning of the nineteenth century, Kant's pure intuition had a rough time in analysis. The rigorization of the calculus banished intuition from the notions of function, continuity, limit, infinitesimal, and all else that had elicited Berkeley's justified complaint. The arithmetization of analysis cornered the pure intuition of time into arithmetic, where Frege would soon deal it a death blow (Chapter 4). Mathematics was not just the theory of abstract magnitudes, numbers, functions, and infinitesimals, however. It was also the science of space, geometry, and here Kantians could rest assured that intuition would never be dethroned. Or so it seemed for a while.

During the nineteenth century, geometry was the battleground of two major epistemological wars. The first, the subject of this chapter, concerned the role of pure intuition in knowledge; the second, surveyed in Chapter 7, took it for granted that that role was nil and questioned the nature of geometric concepts. It is interesting that in both cases the semantic tradition had nothing to contribute to these developments. As we shall see, a proper picture of geometry demanded a synthesis of Kantian and semantic insights that neither of these two conflicting traditions was in a position to undertake. For the time being, however, our topic is the nature and role of pure intuition in geometric knowledge.

The presence of pure intuition in geometry, Kant thought, is manifested by a peculiar type of necessity that attaches to geometric judgments. We begin by examining this idiosyncratic modality.

One of the central distinctions in Kant's theory of modality was between a kind of necessity derived from intuition (*Anschauungsnothwendigkeit*) and another derived from thought (*Denknothwendigkeit*). The former has its source in features of the human sensibility, the latter in features of the understanding.[1] Perhaps the best short explanation of this distinction occurs in a passage in Frege's *Grundlagen,* in which he is trying to explain why he thinks that arithmetic is a part of logic. "Empirical propositions," he writes,

hold good of what is physically or psychologically actual, the truths of geometry govern all that is spatially intuitable, whether actual or product of our fancy. The wildest visions of delirium, the boldest inventions of legend and poetry, where animals speak and stars stand still, where men are turned to stone and trees turn into men, where the drowning haul themselves up out of swamps by their own topknots – all these remain, so long as they remain intuitable, still subject to the axioms of geometry. Conceptual thought alone can after a fashion shake off this yoke, when it assumes, say, a space of four dimensions or positive curvature. To study such conceptions is not useless by any means; but it is to leave the ground of intuition entirely behind. . . . For purposes of conceptual thought we can always assume the contrary of some one or other of the geometrical axioms, without involving ourselves in any self-contradictions. . . . The fact that this is possible shows that the axioms of geometry are independent of one another and of the primitive laws of logic, and consequently are synthetic. Can the same be said of the fundamental propositions of the science of number? Here, we have only to try denying any one of them, and complete confusion ensues. Even to think at all seems no longer possible. (*The Foundations of Arithmetic,* pp. 20–1)

Frege is saying that the laws of geometry and arithmetic, unlike those of physics, are necessary. But whereas geometric propositions are necessities of intuition, the laws of arithmetic are necessary in a far deeper sense: Thought itself becomes impossible if we deny them. To the extent that logic is the pure theory of concepts, arithmetic must be a part of logic. The doctrine is, of course, not Kantian, but the ideological framework certainly is.

What does it mean to say that geometric laws are necessities of intuition? Kant's writings contain no more than a few confusing hints. Of course, he had no reason to be overly concerned about working out the details: Who would seriously doubt circa 1800 that geometry was necessary or that its necessity had something to do with geometric constructions?[2] But the situation changed shortly after Kant's death, when non-Euclidean geometry made its first public appearance. By the second half of the nineteenth century, people began to wonder first about the exclusive necessity of Euclidean geometry and then about the role of intuition in *any* geometry, Euclidean or otherwise. As neo-Kantians were forced to address this issue more extensively, it slowly emerged that the master's silence was not a sign of unspoken wisdom.

Revealingly, the cleverest among neo-Kantians silently pushed Kant's pure intuition to a corner of their doctrine of geometry; what they offered as the *truly* Kantian theory of geometry suspiciously resembled one of Helmholtz's central contributions to that field. By the end of the century, the neo-Kantians' writings on this topic had become an unwitting testimony to the fact that geometry called for a ground entirely different from the one Kant had envisaged. In conjunction with the rigorization of the calculus and with what Frege would soon be doing to arithmetic, these episodes converged to establish what Bolzano had claimed in 1810: that Kant's pure intuition plays no role whatever in mathematics.

Kant's mixed message

Kant thought that geometry was a good example of how little you could do in science with mere concepts. If you try to prove a geometric theorem from pure concepts, "All your labor is in vain; and you find that you are constrained to have recourse to intuition, as is always done in geometry. You therefore give yourself an object in intuition . . . [indeed] an object *a priori* in intuition, and ground upon this your synthetic proposition" (*Critique,* A47–8/B65). Well, exactly how do you give yourself an object a priori in intuition, and does the geometer really *need* to do that? There are three ways to read Kant's views on pure intuition, what we might call Platonist, constructivist, and structuralist. Let us consider them in sequence.

Every now and then one finds in Kant statements that suggest that pure intuition differs from empirical intuition in that the objects it represents are "pure" rather than empirical (see "Vorarbeiten zu Ausgleichung eines auf Missverstand beruhenden mathematischen Streits," *Kants gesammelte Schriften,* vol. 23, p. 201). In the *Critique* Kant gave a transcendental twist to the primary–secondary quality distinction when he argued that "qualities cannot be presented in any intuition that is not empirical," but quantities can: "The shape of a cone we can form for ourselves in intuition, unassisted by any experience, according to its concept alone, but the color of this cone must be previously given in some experience or other" (*Critique,* A715/B743). This seems to present the geometric cone as an object of a *different kind* than the objects given in empirical intuition, rather than as the form of objects given in empirical intuition. Here the difference between form and content (or matter) appears to correspond to the difference between innate and acquired, as if the colorless image of a cone could be formed by someone who had no previous experience, and this image would be a pure intuition. Whewell seems to have interpreted Kant along these lines when he thought of the Kantian intuition as an "imaginary looking" (*History of Scientific Ideas,* vol. I, p. 140; cited by Mill, *Logic,* bk. 2, chap. 5, sec. 5); and so did Riehl, albeit disapprovingly, when he saw in pure intuition an echo of Platonic forms (*Phil. Krit.,* vol. 2, p. 104). Consider also a typical reference to the "construction" of a geometric concept involved in the process of a proof: We construct it, Kant said, "by representing the object that corresponds to this concept either by imagination alone, in pure intuition, or in accordance therewith also on paper, in empirical intuition" (*Critique,* A713/B741). The explicitly drawn duality encourages us to think of pure intuition as given in a domain involving imagination and of empirical intuition as belonging to an entirely different domain.

Though these and other passages invite a Platonist construal, this interpretation is almost certainly at odds with Kant's intentions. There is a second interpretation that, like the first one, associates pure intuition with the givenness of objects (as one would expect of any sort of Kantian intuition) but takes these objects to be empirical. This interpretation focuses on Kant's remarks about the construction of mathematical concepts.

Few elements of the critical philosophy are better known than Kant's attempt to bring together what he had cast asunder in his distinction between sensibility and understanding. Detached as those two faculties may be, there can be no human knowledge unless they join forces: Concepts without intuition are empty, and intuition without concepts is blind:[3]

If our knowledge claims are to have objective reality, i.e., if they are to refer to an object and thereby have meaning and sense, it must be possible that the object be given in some manner. Otherwise the concepts are empty, and even though one indeed has thought with them, through this thinking nothing has really been known; one has merely played with representations. (*Kritik,* A155/B194–5)

Mathematical concepts are linked to intuition by the celebrated construction of the concept. Kant and his followers used this phrase repeatedly in allegedly explanatory contexts in which one can almost see them frowning down on their readers, daring them to exhibit their stupidity by asking what it means. The truth is that neither Kant nor his followers had any very definite idea of what that "construction" was. The plausibility of any Kantian thesis involving this notion is inversely proportional to the clarity with which it is explained. It is interesting that whenever Kant did make an effort to illustrate what he meant by "construction in intuition," an empirical intuition entered in. For example, Kant explained that the construction of a figure makes it "present to the senses" (*Critique,* A240/B299). When we prove a proposition about triangles we may construct the concept "on paper, in empirical intuition. . . . The single figure which we draw is empirical, and yet it serves to express the concept, without impairing its universality" (*Critique,* A713–14/B741–2). Moreover, "we cannot think a line without *drawing* it in thought, or a circle without *describing* it. We cannot represent the three dimensions of space save by *setting* three lines at right angles to one another from the same point"[4] (*Critique,* B154). The same is true of arithmetic: In order to produce the synthesis required for the proof that $7 + 5 = 12$, "we call in the aid of the intuition that corresponds to one of [those concepts], our five fingers, for instance, or, as Segner does in his Arithmetic, five points" (*Kritik,* B15;[5] Bolzano comments on these remarks in *WL,* sec. 305).

The structuralist interpretation differs from the first two in treating pure intuition as something quite unlike intuition, which is a singular representation. According to the structuralist Kant, what is pure and a priori is not a kind of object but a mode of knowledge of empirical objects. All objects of intuition are empirical, and pure intuition is the "mere form" of empirical intuition (*Critique,* A239/B298). It follows that pure intuition is not a sort of singular representation but a formal feature of such representations, a *lex menti insita,* as Kant once put it. When in this structuralist gear, Kant would explain that when we construct the concept of a triangle, for example, we do not really construct an instance of that concept or even give any particular object to intuition, but what we construct is only the form of an object. Indeed, given this construction the possibility of its object might still be doubtful (*Critique,* A223/B271; see also A239/B298).

However one interprets the nature of pure intuition, there are two related, but distinguishable problems faced by Kant's account of geometry: How does pure intuition support the necessity of Euclidean geometry, and why must a geometric argument be a chain of inference guided throughout by intuition (*Critique,* A717)?[6]

As we saw earlier, Kant explained that when we prove a proposition about triangles, we may construct that concept "on paper, in empirical intuition"; and he added that "the single figure that we draw is empirical, and yet it serves to express the concept without impairing its universality" (*Critique,* B741). One might have thought that what threatens the universality of the procedure is not the *empirical* character of the figure involved but the fact that it is a *singular,* specific object and that *it* is all that has been considered. Be that as it may, Kant added, "For in this empirical intuition we consider only the act whereby we construct the concept, and abstract from the many determinations (for instance, the magnitude of the sides and of the angles), which are quite indifferent, as not altering the concept 'triangle'" (*Critique,* A714/B742). Note that Kant wanted to abstract not only from those determinations that fix parameters that the concept leaves undetermined (such as those Kant enumerated in the preceding passage in parentheses) but also those in which the empirical object of our empirical intuition fails to qualify as an instance of the constructed concept (e.g., the three-dimensionality of the constructed triangle, the wiggly nature of its lines, etc.). Determinations of the first sort yield instances of the concept, while the second result in objects that are, at best (and in a sense badly in need of elucidation), mere approximations of instances of the given concepts. If, *per impossibile,* we were somehow given all instances of a concept in intuition, we could abstract from their idiosyncrasies by simply considering only what is true of all of them and thus achieve the intended result. But no object ever given to us in *any* kind of intuition is, for example, an instance of the concept of a triangle.

How do we decide which determinations are to be abstracted, which features of the constructed figure are relevant to a proof? Kant was, understandably, not terribly exercised by this question. His complete answer, such as it was, is encapsulated in that celebrated aphorism to the effect that the geometer "must not ascribe to the figure anything save what necessarily follows from what he has himself set into it in accordance with his concept [of it]" (*Critique,* Bxii). When pursued to its logical conclusion, however, this remark leads to an uncomfortable dilemma; for what necessarily follows from what the geometer has set in the figure either (a) follows from his concept of that figure, quite independently of *any* features of the figure ("formal" or otherwise), or (b) follows only when we examine in addition to the concept itself some *relevant* features of the figure. In the first case we have the position Russell came to endorse around 1900: The synthesis in mathematical and logical knowledge can be produced from concepts alone, without appeal to any kind of intuition.[7] This clearly conflicts with the principle of synthetic judgments and the associated link between mathematics and intuition. In the second case – probably Kant's own choice – we are left with the original question: Which of the various features exhibited by the empirically constructed figure (whether in the mind or on paper) are allowable grounds of inference? It would appear that by Kant's own standards, the only guides in this decision are the axioms and theorems of geometry. But *before* we can use the intuitional X to provide a ground for the synthesis expressed in the axioms, we must have those very axioms in order to determine what X is. Thus, Kant's prescription for identifying the features to be abstracted leads beyond Kantianism to the view that we cannot synthesize the axioms until we have them. In the Kantian idiolect, geometric axioms would have a regulative role and would therefore not pertain either to the domain of sensibility (intuition) or to the understanding (construed so as to exclude Reason). We shall soon see how some neo-Kantians chose to pursue this un-Kantian course in order to construe Kant as having anticipated Helmholtz's insights.

Helmholtz's challenge

The claim that Euclidean geometry is a necessity of intuition had been disputed by empiricists on the familiar grounds that what we cannot imagine may well exist. Mill, for example, had distinguished between the sense in which antipodes are inconceivable and the sense in which the enclosure of space by two straight lines is inconceivable. In the former case everyone can surely represent the circumstances under consideration even if they appear incredible. In the latter, however, "we cannot represent to ourselves" the alleged circumstances:

> We cannot represent to ourselves two and two as making five; nor two straight lines as enclosing space. We cannot represent to ourselves a round square; nor a body all black, and at the same time all white. These things are literally inconceivable to us, our minds and our experience being what they are. (*Hamilton's Philosophy,* pp. 69–70)

But even this strong sense of inconceivability is consistent with the possibility and even the truth of inconceivable claims; for even though we cannot represent round squares, things black and white all over, and so on, we can represent circumstances in which we could represent them.[8] The inconceivability arises only because our experience has taught us to associate or dissociate two representations:

> We should probably be as well able to conceive a round square as a hard square, or a heavy square, if it were not that, in our uniform experience, at the instant when a thing begins to be round it ceases to be square. . . . Thus our inability to form a conception always arises from our being compelled to form another contradictory to it. . . . We cannot conceive two and two as five, because an inseparable association compels us to conceive it as four; and it cannot be conceived as both, because four and five, like round and square, are so related in our experience, that each is associated with the cessation, or removal, of the other. . . . And we should probably have no difficulty in putting together the two ideas supposed to be incompatible, if our experience had not first inseparably associated one of them with the contradictory of the other. (*Hamilton's Philosophy,* pp. 70–1)

Mill illustrated our ability to represent the inconceivable with examples from several "a priori" disciplines. In arithmetic, for example, our commitment to the law that $2 + 2 = 4$ would vanish if whenever two pairs of things "are either placed in proximity or are contemplated together, a fifth thing is immediately created and brought within the contemplation of the mind engaged in putting two and two together" (p. 71). The production of this fifth thing must be "instantaneous in the very act of seeing, [so] that we never should see the four things by themselves as four: the fifth thing would be inseparably involved in the act of perception by which we should ascertain the sum of the two pairs" (p. 73). Clearly, Mill was thinking about adding up things like rabbits or cows, not things like solutions of third-degree equations or Roman consuls. As Frege would point out in *Grundlagen* (1884, secs. 7 and 8), the latter are not easily "placed in proximity" or involved in "acts of perception." A world in which when someone adds the first two Roman consuls to the next two a fifth one appears, presumably with his distinct proper name, his own political record, and so on, is not a world at all but the product of a confused mind; for in that world the decision to add would alter the past, and on pain of contradiction there could not be one person adding a group of objects and another not.

Mill's arguments against the a priori character of geometry were no better. For example, he quoted approvingly James Fitzjames Stephen's remark that a "world in which every object was round, with the single exception of a straight inaccessible railway, would be a world in which everyone would believe that two straight lines enclosed a space" and then observed: "In such a world, therefore, the impossibility of conceiving that two straight lines can enclose a space would not exist" (*Hamilton's Philosophy,* p. 72).[9] If Mill was the wisest positivist, as he probably was, the Kantians had little to fear from the positivist challenge to their doctrine.

The first decisive step in the overthrow of the notion of a necessity of intuition did not come from positivism. Widespread opinion notwithstanding, it did not come from the discovery of hyperbolic geometry either, or even from the recognition of its consistency. Ironically, it emerged from an attempt to show that the new geometries were not a challenge to Euclid.

In 1868 Beltrami published a paper entitled "An Attempt to Interpret Non-Euclidean Geometry," in which he introduced his celebrated pseudospherical model. Had the interpretation offered in that paper been successful, it would have established the consistency of hyperbolic geometry.[10] Despite appearances, the doctrines put forth could have brought nothing but comfort to Kantian souls. For Beltrami's ultimate goal was not so much to interpret as to *reduce* hyperbolic geometry to Euclidean geometry and to argue that there was no more geometric sense in the former than it could derive from the latter.

Beltrami's stated purpose was "to find a real substratum" for Lobatchewski's geometry, but only for its two-dimensional fragment (*Opere
matematiche,* p. 375). Beltrami concluded that the hyperbolic plane is,
in fact, the Euclidean pseudosphere in disguise, since the Euclidean metric of the Euclidean pseudosphere coincides (locally anyway) with that
of Lobatchewski's plane. He argued that no analogous interpretation
could be given for three-dimensional hyperbolic space, however, since
he thought that the part of space in which the interpretation is constructed must have a metric not reducible to the standard Euclidean form
$dx^2 + dy^2 + dz^2$:

Since until now the notion of a space different from [Euclid's] appears to be
lacking or transcends, at least, the domain of ordinary geometry, it is reasonable
to suppose that, even though the analytical considerations on which the preceding constructions rest can be extended from the field of two variables to that of
three, the results obtained in this latter case can not yet be constructed with
ordinary geometry. (p. 397)

And in his next study on the topic he would insist that his two-
dimensional model gives

a true and proper interpretation, since one can *construct* [the appropriate con-
cepts] on a *real* surface; on the other hand, those which embrace three dimensions can be represented only analytically, since the space in which such a
representation would materialize is different from the one that we generally call
by that name. ("Teoria fondamentale degli spazi di curvatura costante" [1868–9],
Opere matematiche, p. 427)

Far from posing any threats to Kant's philosophy, Beltrami's work was
consistent with and possibly even grounded upon it. Kant had never
doubted the logical consistency of non-Euclidean geometries. He would
surely have said of hyperbolic geometry that it is impossible but not
logically impossible (since its "negation," Euclidean geometry, is not
logically necessary but only intuitionally necessary). So the fact that
there is an interpretation of hyperbolic geometry is hardly surprising, nor
is it surprising that this interpretation has to be given in terms of Euclidean intuitable notions. Nor is it surprising that wherever that reduction
to Euclidean intuitions fails, we must abandon the project of giving an
interpretation to Lobatchewski's theory. One could hardly find a more
appealing package of good news for Kantians in a geometric monograph.
Yet less than three years later, Helmholtz would see in Beltrami's study a
refutation of the Kantian notion of the intuitional necessity of Euclidean
geometry. With characteristic boldness, Helmholtz recognized the potential of Beltrami's analytic representation. He was, in a sense, the first to
realize that what is now called the Beltrami–Klein model of hyperbolic

geometry is, indeed, a model of hyperbolic geometry. Let us first look briefly at this model.

To facilitate his metric analysis of the pseudosphere, Beltrami introduced an auxiliary surface, the interior of a Euclidean circle. An isomorphic mapping for the pseudosphere will induce a hyperbolic metric on this circle. The intrinsic metric of the pseudosphere is determined by associating with any two points P and Q on it the Euclidean length $d(P, Q)$ of the geodesic that links them along the pseudospherical surface. This metric function can be expressed as a function $f(X, Y)$ of the points X and Y that are the projections of P and Q, respectively, on the auxiliary circle. One may now choose to abandon Beltrami and look at $d(X, Y)$ not as a device for calculating the intrinsic Euclidean distance between P and Q (along the pseudosphere), but as giving the "distance" between X and Y. Thus construed, the function f defines a metric on the open surface inside the auxiliary circle that is hyperbolic, since it is the image of a hyperbolic metric under an isomorphism. By the new metric standard, the chords of the circle are infinitely long straight lines. Angles are correspondingly remetrized. Even though the open surface is a model of hyperbolic geometry, Beltrami did not think for a moment that this open surface could qualify as an "interpretation" (in his sense) of hyperbolic geometry. If it could, then by his own arguments three-dimensional hyperbolic geometry would also be interpretable. No doubt, the "arbitrary" (i.e., non-Euclidean) character of the metric defined by f was the decisive reason for ruling out the "auxiliary" space as a possible interpretation.

It was Helmholtz who observed that the "straight lines" in the above open surface are far closer relatives of standard straight lines than those found in Beltrami's preferred model. This was the basis of his well-known proof that we can intuitively represent non-Euclidean spaces, thus showing that Euclidean geometry is not a necessity of intuition.

The first step in Helmholtz's argument was to remove the ambiguity from Kant's notion of an intuitive representation:

By the much misused expression 'to represent' or 'to be able to think of how something happens', I understand that one could depict the series of sense-impressions one would have if such a thing happened in a particular case. I do not see how one could understand anything else by it without abandoning the whole sense of the expression. ("On the Origin and Significance of the Axioms of Geometry" [1870], *Epistemological Writings*, p. 5)

Helmholtz used this analysis of representation to show that non-Euclidean geometry is representable. He prefaced his argument with two "warm-up" stories designed to dislodge our faith in the truthfulness of intuition. The first was a Flatland case, in which two-dimensional beings living on a curved surface develop a non-Euclidean geometry on the basis of their perceptions. Since the idea that such beings might have anything like our perceptions is well-nigh incoherent, the philosophical point of this popular example is virtually nil. The second story overcame this difficulty by presenting a three-dimensional world, what we shall call a 'mirror universe'.

Imagine a spherical mirror on whose surface S all events in our Euclidean space are reflected. Now imagine a three-dimensional world delimited by S and a plane through the focal point of the spherical mirror. In this world, physical objects behave exactly the way they "appear" to behave in the mirror. Thus, for every object in our Euclidean space, there will be a corresponding object in the mirror universe. When an object O in our space moves away from S to infinity, the corresponding mirror object, O^*, will move away from S toward its focal point; O does not change shape as it moves, but O^* does, shrinking (by our metric standards) as it moves away from S.

How do we determine that the geometry of our space is Euclidean? We might, for example, draw a right triangle and measure its three sides; we observe that the measurements are 3, 4, and 5 units, respectively, thus confirming the Pythagorean theorem that separates Euclidean geometry from its constant-curvature rivals. But as I perform these measurements, a little man, looking and moving just like I do, but changing his shape as he moves, measures the sides of a triangle that looks very unrectangular (to us). Yet since his "meterstick" also changes its length as it moves, he also finds that it fits three, four, and five times, respectively, on the sides of the triangle. Unaware of the "fact" that his meterstick is changing size as he moves, the poor little man infers – at the same time *we* do – that his space must be Euclidean. In general, whenever a geometric statement concerning an object in our Euclidean universe is true (relative to our metric standards), the same statement will be true of the *corresponding* mirror object (relative to the metric standards in the mirror world). It follows that from the viewpoint of the mirror universe, the surface is also convex – rather than concave, as one might at first think, for all objects on S (and therefore S itself) are their own corresponding objects. In spite of the striking difference between the two universes, precisely the same geometry is valid in both; indeed, both are Euclidean. And the symmetry goes even further. From the standpoint of the mirror metric, we are the inhabitants of a mirror universe in which objects change shape as they move, shrinking as they move closer to their focal point. Whether things look "funny" or not is entirely a matter of perspective. Helmholtz did to intuition in geometry what Montesquieu had done a century and a half earlier to intuition in political philosophy.

Having softened our faith in intuition, Helmholtz delivered the decisive blow. Once again he set out to describe a three-dimensional universe that we can represent intuitively; but this time the geometry of the universe would be non-Euclidean. It is here that Helmholtz appealed to Beltrami's auxiliary sphere. Using Beltrami's results, Helmholtz set out to "deduce how the objects of a pseudospherical world would appear to an observer, whose visual estimation and spatial experiences had, exactly like ours, been developed in flat space" (p. 21). Beltrami's pseudospherical model, like Helmholtz's Flatland, was of no use because it was two-dimensional. Helmholtz concentrated instead on what was for Beltrami a merely analytic representation, the auxiliary circle – or, for the three-dimensional case, the auxiliary sphere. In a bold philosophical step, Helmholtz took the function f to be a metric in the space enclosed by the auxiliary sphere. According to this metric, the axioms and theorems of hyperbolic geometry are true. Moreover, the Euclidean straight secants are also straight lines. Helmholtz fashioned for the imagination a spherical universe endowed with the f-metric, or, in the more concrete terms preferred by Helmholtz, a universe in which the solid objects preserve f-length under transport to the same extent that the solid objects of our universe preserve their Euclidean length (for some Euclidean metric) under transport.

Can we intuitively represent this space? We have in fact just done so in general terms and could be as specific as required, appealing to the details of Beltrami's construction. But the representation given so far is, as it were, external. We can imagine this remarkable world in which "solid" objects change size in remarkable ways and even note the relativity of this description: We are no more entitled to judge the behavior of their metric standards by ours than they are to judge ours by theirs. But can we represent this world from the inside, not as an "impartial Euclidean" observer might, but as an inhabitant of that universe would? Helmholtz answered with an interspace traveler story. The Euclidean observer is sent to the center of the mirror universe, and we are told what that universe looks like to him. Since the straight lines in that universe are as straight as his old Euclidean lines, he

would continue to see the lines of light rays, or the lines of sight of his eyes, as straight lines like those existing in flat space, and like they actually are in [Beltrami's] spherical image of pseudospherical space. The visual image of the objects in pseudospherical space would therefore give him the same impression as if he were at the centre of Beltrami's spherical image. (p. 21)

In particular, since the "universe" is not infinite (by the Euclidean standards to which our space traveler is accustomed) but is bounded by the surface of a sphere of radius R, he would at first think (and "see") that all objects are roughly within a distance R. However, as soon as he started moving around (as he must, according to Helmholtz, if he were to be capable of geometry at all), he would encounter a number of surprises that would alter his way of thinking and therefore – according to Helmholtz – his way of seeing.

This challenge to the idea of *Anschauungsnotwendigkeit* is perhaps the most striking of Helmholtz's criticisms of Kant's philosophy of geometry. He also raised other questions about what Kantians called the "applicability" of Euclidean geometry. In particular, he wondered how Kantians could explain why the very same geometry that is allegedly grounded on pure intuition also happens to be so readily applicable to our empirical world. Helmholtz noted three difficulties. First, Kantians must assume that pure intuition gives them perfectly precise knowledge of the properties of, say, triangles or parallel lines if they are to be sure that Euclidean geometry is true – rather than some very small deviation from it. Second, even if we were endowed with such a supremely accurate mental eye, why should we think that the laws for the geometric triangles of pure intuition agree with the geometric laws governing the rather un-Platonic triangles we encounter in the world? Third, even if the laws of geometry in both the purely geometric and the empirical domains are the same, it does not follow that the metric behavior of ideal objects even remotely resembles that of their real counterparts (see, e.g., "Die Thatsachen in der Wahrnehmung" [1878], especially pp. 397–8). Helmholtz's mirror universe established that two geometric domains in which exactly the same geometric laws are fulfilled may disagree radically on congruence judgments.

It is unlikely that any neo-Kantian ever understood Helmholtz's third point.[11] In reply to the other two, they pointed out that Helmholtz's charges presupposed what we have called the Platonic interpretation of Kant's words and argued that this was quite wrong since for Kant there are no properly geometric objects. For support they could appeal to those passages in which Kant said that when constructing a concept, we construct not an object but "only the form of an object" (*Critique*, A223/B271; see also A239/B298). As we saw, even in light of that construction, "the possibility of its objects would still be doubtful" (*Critique*, A224/B271). The problem of the applicability of "pure geometry" to the world is solved as follows: The constructive synthesis through which the concept (of, say, a triangle) is constructed in imagination "is precisely the same as that which we exercise in the apprehension of an appearance, in making for ourselves an empirical concept of it" (*Critique*, A224/B271).

What distinguished the Helmholtzian neo-Kantians from their "philosophical" counterparts was their reaction to a passage like this: The former regarded it as a problem, the latter as a solution. The Helmholtzians noticed the obvious fact that such a passage perhaps suggests an interesting idea, but is nearly meaningless as it stands. They then did their best to asso-

ciate some clear and definite sense with such words, relating them to what
they or others had discovered in the fields of the psychology of perception
or geometry. The philosophical neo-Kantian response to such efforts was
invariably an echo of Cohen's professorial "The critics have not understood Kant" (*Die Gegner haben Kant nicht verstanden*).

Helmholtz's philosophies of geometry

Helmholtz's "On the Origin and Significance of the Axioms of Geometry"
is a paradigm of a seminal study. It is an explosion of new, deep, and often
conflicting ideas on the essence of geometry. In addition to refuting the
intuitional necessity of geometry (as recounted in the preceding section), the paper presents (a) Helmholtz's official empiricist philosophy of
geometry, which was destined to have a major influence in later decades;
(b) an implicit but quite clear refutation of a crucial part of (a); (c) an
aprioristic view of geometry, inconsistent with (a); and (d) the first
statement of geometric conventionalism – formulated as a possibility,
but not fully endorsed because of its obvious conflict with (a) and its
apparent conflict with (c). Helmholtz's official empiricism joined with
Mill's to inspire an increasingly influential but narrow geometric empiricism. His aprioristic doctrine was avidly grasped by neo-Kantians, who
liked it so much that they attributed it to Kant. Poincaré was the first to
see clearly beyond Helmholtz, recognizing not only the limitations of
geometric empiricism but, more significantly, the consistency and indeed the adequacy of Helmholtz's conventionalist and apriorist doctrines.

Helmholtz's official empiricist doctrine rested on his claim that empirical facts lie at the foundation of geometry. The most basic of these facts is
described by the axiom of free mobility, which says that geometric configurations can be moved up to each other without any change in their
form or dimensions (*Epistemological Writings*, p. 4). Helmholtz had
argued in "On the Facts Underlying Geometry" (1868, *Epistemological
Writings*) that from this axiom, plus the "fact" that space is infinite, one
could prove the central hypothesis of Riemannian geometry, that the
metric must have the form[12]

$$ds^2 = g_{ij}\, dx_i\, dy_j.$$

The assumption that space is infinite seemed justified by physical theory,
but what justifies the axiom of free mobility? Helmholtz took it to be an
"observational fact" ("On the Origins and Meaning of the Axioms of
Geometry," *Epistemological Writings*, p. 15), "something we have all
experienced from earliest youth onwards" (p. 4). But it is quite clear that
the inference from observation to free mobility is refuted by Helmholtz's

own mirror-universe example; for the inhabitants of both universes would "see" from their earliest youth onward that their metersticks and other solid objects satisfied the axiom of free mobility and would also "see" that the metersticks in the other universe did *not* satisfy the axiom. They could not both be right in their inference from experience to free mobility, yet by Helmholtz's reasoning, if one of them is right, so is the other. Hence, neither would be right, and Helmholtz's inference to the axiom is ungrounded.[13]

Side by side with this untenable geometric empiricism one finds in Helmholtz's writings a different and much more promising theory of geometry, for the roots of conventionalism are clearly under the surface of much that Helmholtz has to say about the essence of geometry. One might say that the purpose of geometric conventionalism, as developed by Poincaré and others in the late nineteenth century, was to perform a balancing act widely regarded as quite impossible: to grant to Kantians the a priori character of many scientific principles (geometry prominently included) and at the same time insist on their replaceability and on the existence of equally necessary alternatives to them. In *An Examination of Sir W. Hamilton's Philosophy,* Mill had expressed with characteristic clarity what was, no doubt, a widely shared view among both empiricists and their Kantian opponents. One of the latter had complained because Mill failed to distinguish between the necessity of thinking something and the thinking of that thing as necessary. Mill replied by acknowledging the distinction but noting that the ground for the latter is always an argument for the former. He added, "If I disprove the necessity of thinking the thing at all, I disprove that it must be thought as necessary" (p. 270). Much of the most interesting philosophy of science developed in the past few decades has been inspired by the opposite idea: Many fundamental scientific principles are by no means necessarily thought – indeed, it takes great effort to develop the systems of knowledge that embody them; but their denial also seems oddly impossible – they need not be thought, but if they are thought at all, they must be thought as necessary. This doctrine, whatever its intrinsic merits, is neither empiricist nor Kantian. It emerges directly from ideas that flourished, as we shall see, in Vienna around 1930. But its roots lie in the conventionalism of the late nineteenth century (see Chapter 7) and, even farther back, in the seminal writings of Helmholtz.

No one before Helmholtz was so acutely aware of *both* the need to allow for a variety of systems of geometry *and* the peculiar preempirical role that such systems play in the organization of our knowledge. The opening paragraph of Helmholtz's "On the Facts Underlying Geometry" (1868) states a remarkable fact concerning geometric axioms: To test the axioms we must first know which objects are rigid, which surfaces flat and which edges straight, but "we only decide whether a body is rigid, its side flat and its edges straight, by means of the very propositions whose factual correctness the examination is supposed to show" (*Epistemological Writings*, p. 39).[14] Statements exhibiting this extraordinary feature are not found only in geometry. Another example is Helmholtz's first axiom of the theory of measurement: "If two magnitudes are both alike with a third, they are alike amongst themselves" ("Numbering and Measuring from an Epistemological Viewpoint," *Epistemological Writings*, p. 94). According to Helmholtz, this axiom "is not a law having objective significance; it only determines which physical relations we are allowed to recognize as alikeness" (p. 94). The principle of causality also "has an exceptional status" because "it is the presupposition for the validity of all other [laws]; . . . it is the basis of all thought and conduct. Until we have it we cannot even test it: thus we can only believe it, conduct ourselves according to it" (Königsberger, *Hermann von Helmholtz*, vol. 1, p. 248).

How are we to interpret such statements? In his more lucid moments, Helmholtz suggested that to answer this question we must look closely at how to distinguish within our knowledge between what has "objectively valid sense" and what is merely "definition or the consequence of definitions, or depends on the form of description" ("On the Facts Underlying Geometry," *Epistemological Writings*, p. 39). Thus, at times he was inclined to think of geometric axioms as something like "definitions" and asserted that the "first axiom of arithmetic," the law that magnitudes equal to a third one must be equal to each other, "can be properly regarded as the definition of equality. The axiom must be satisfied in those cases in which two pairs of magnitudes must be recognized as mutually identical" (*Einleitung*, p. 27; see also "Numbering and Measuring . . .," *Epistemological Writings*, p. 78). Perhaps the most intriguing and striking statement of this position appears in "On the Origin and Significance of the Axioms of Geometry." After suggesting that geometric axioms deal with the mechanical behavior of rigid bodies under motion, he added:

Of course, one could also understand the concept of rigid geometric spatial configurations as a transcendental concept, formed independently of actual experiences and to which these need not necessarily correspond, as in fact our natural bodies do not correspond in an entirely pure and undistorted manner to the concepts that we have abstracted from them inductively. If we adopted this concept of rigidity understood as an ideal, a strict Kantian surely could then regard geometric axioms as *a priori* propositions given through transcendental intuition, and these propositions could not be confirmed or refuted by any experience because one should first have to decide in agreement with them whether given natural bodies should be considered rigid. But we should then add that under this interpretation, geometric axioms would certainly not be synthetic statements in Kant's sense; for they would then only assert an analytic consequence of the concept of rigid geometric configuration necessary for measurement, since one could accept as rigid only those configurations which satisfied the axioms. (*Schriften zur Erkenntnistheorie,* pp. 23–4)

The interpretation Helmholtz offered here as a possible retreat for a Kantian is exactly the one he had espoused in the remark quoted earlier from "On the Facts Underlying Geometry" (p. 39) concerning how we can decide whether bodies are rigid. We shall examine its implications shortly, when we look at the neo-Kantians' reading of this pregnant remark.

Plugging the leaks

When the Germans began to recover from idealism, the first thing that occurred to them was to go back to Kant and start over again, trying to get it right this time. 'Neo-Kantianism' is the blanket name for a variety of movements that had little more in common than a distrust of the post-Kantians who preceded them and the belief that what Kant meant (but didn't quite manage to say) was profound and true. In this general sense of the term, Helmholtz initiated one of the earliest neo-Kantian movements. In "Uber das Sehen des Menschen" (1855), he called for a re-evaluation and reinterpretation of transcendental philosophy in light of the new research in psychology of perception (pp. 76–7). The great historian of Greek philosophy Eduard Zeller would eventually join Helmholtz in his attempt to offer an image of Kantianism consistent with current science and philosophy. As we shall see, this movement would continue into the twentieth century, manifested in the work of Planck, Schlick, and many others inclined to add a scientific realist twist to transcendental philosophy.

What is generally known as neo-Kantianism, however, is a fragment of this larger movement that had a much weaker interest in science that did Helmholtz or, indeed, Kant. The most important exponent of this "philosophical" neo-Kantianism was Hermann Cohen, founder of the celebrated Marburg school; from this school would eventually emerge Natorp, Heimsoeth, Ortega, and Cassirer. Rickert and Windelband led a different branch of the movement that was more concerned with an extension of Kant's thought to the cultural sciences. Outside the Marburg school, Alois Riehl attempted to show that Kant's picture of knowledge was consistent with the rather unruly behavior since 1800 of the non-cultural sciences. One point on which the "strict" neo-Kantians agreed was that Helmholtz's criticisms of Kant had missed the mark. Wherever there was a genuine discrepancy, Helmholtz was wrong, and wherever

Helmholtz had made an interesting point, the point could be found in Kant, if you knew how to read him. In defending their hero, the neo-Kantians were greatly aided by the protean, dialectical nature of Kant's remarks on pure intuition (see the first section of this chapter, "Kant's mixed messages").

Helmholtz's position can be further clarified if we consider briefly the responses of neo-Kantians to Helmholtz's challenge. There were those who thought Helmholtz was simply not a very good philosopher and those who thought his philosophy was excellent but his Kantian scholarship bad. We shall examine one example from each group.

Cohen quite properly challenged Helmholtz's characterization of rigidity as a physical property that we can recognize in objects as a matter of empirical fact. But he observed, also correctly, that Helmholtz's writings contain a different account of the matter:

He thought that one could conceive the notion of a rigid geometric spatial configuration as a transcendental concept, and thereby consider the geometric axioms as sentences given through transcendental intuition. But in that case the geometric axioms would turn into analytic sentences. "For they would then assert merely what followed analytically from the concept of the rigid geometric configuration required for measurement." Here Helmholtz is relying on the usual nominal definition of analytic and synthetic, which we have long left behind. The concept of a geometric configuration in general, not to speak of one appropriate for measurement, has no connection with the concept of analytic truth but is, from its origin and character, a synthetic notion; for it presupposes intuition. (*Kants Theorie der Erfahrung,* p. 232)

To his credit, Cohen appears to have been the first to recognize clearly that Kant's use of 'analytic' is ambiguous. Cohen argued that there are two senses of 'analytic' and of 'synthetic' in Kant, in effect, the first and third senses identified in Chapter 1 (see *Kants Theorie der Erfahrung,* chap. 11). Kant sometimes meant by synthetic "predicate not thought in the subject," and at other times he meant "having intuition as the ground of the synthesis." Instead of regarding this as the outcome and source of several confusions, however, Cohen took the ambiguity to be another proof of Kant's subtlety. According to Cohen, the first definition is nominal, whereas the second is real. The distinction between these two sorts of definitions can be illustrated by an example due to the venerable Wolff, who had explained in his *Logic* that a nominal definition of a clock would be "a machine that shows the hours," whereas "if I point out its structure, I give a real definition" (pp. 41–2). Apparently, a real definition gives an account of the causes or sources of the features ascribed in the nominal. The conclusion is that Kant's second definition of 'analytic' is not equivalent to the first, but goes far deeper; it identifies the essence of analyticity.

Clearly, Cohen only succeeded in baptizing the difficulty, for he did not even notice that the extensions of the two definitions differ. Nor did he realize the difference between his "nominal" sense of 'analytic' and our crucial *second* sense – true in virtue of concepts. Like all other Kantians, he uncritically assumed that "knowledge claims that must be derived from given concepts . . . are analytic" in the nominal sense (*Kants Theorie der Erfahrung,* p. 115).[15]

Having missed this crucial distinction, it is only natural that Cohen would confuse the sense of analyticity suggested by Helmholtz's remark above with Kant's nominal sense, and that he should take its inadequacy to Helmholtz's intentions as sufficient reason for concluding that intuition is required for the purposes at hand. But this is clearly an indefensible construal of Helmholtz's words. According to Kant's "nominal" sense, we identify the analytic consequences of a concept C by looking at the constituents of $C.$ Nothing of the sort is involved in the relation invoked by Helmholtz, however, as Cohen observed. According to Helmholtz, the geometric axioms involving a particular geometric concept C follow analytically from $C,$ even though these axioms are not grounded on an analysis of $C.$ Rather, we do not have access to the concept C except through the endorsement of those axioms. As Sellars once put it, certain concepts presuppose laws and are inconceivable without them; a geometric axiom may not tell us anything about points, lines, and so on, but instead tell us something about the concepts of point, line, and so on. On this view, our knowledge of geometric axioms would be very much like what Kant regarded as transcendental knowledge, for it would deal not with objects of any sort, but with our knowledge of objects and, in particular, with that part of our knowledge that seems a priori.

Thus, however obscurely and confusedly, Helmholtz seemed to be appealing to a notion of analyticity that did not involve going into the concept to look for its constituents, but going outside it, to look for "analytic" links with other concepts. We might call this view "holistic," since it recognizes an intimate relation between a concept and a larger context, a propositional context, and takes this context to be in some sense prior to the concept. The propositional context is prior in the sense that the context defines the concept, or better, acceptance of the propositions that form the context is part of what is involved in recognizing the concept for what it is. The analytic consequences of the concept are the Fregean consequences of those claims that, as others would put it (Chapter 14), constitute the concept.

Unlike Cohen, Riehl tried to read Helmholtz's insights into Kant's writings. In *Der philosophische Kriticismus,* Riehl presented a version of Kant's conception of geometry that displayed the rather severe beating Kant's opinions had taken as a result of certain facts about geometry that had emerged over the previous few decades. Riehl recognized that some of the central elements in Kant's theory of mathematics were untenable and endeavored to adjust the doctrine to accommodate these recent, embarrassingly un-Kantian developments.

For example, Riehl frankly acknowledged that he could not make sense of the Kantian notion of a pure intuition in geometry (pt. 1, chap. 2, sec. 2). He saw no way to interpret that notion except as a revival of the idea that forms can subsist independently of the empirical entities in which they are embodied. As a true Kantian, Riehl regarded such objects as metaphysical fantasies of pre-Kantian philosophy. Consequently, there is no a priori representation, either conceptual or intuitional, that can be construed as an entity; instead, there are a priori functions of consciousness that are imposed as conditions of experience (p. 86). Form is no more than an abstract endpoint for an order of sensations (p. 104).

Nonetheless, Riehl thought that Kant was right about everything that mattered and his current critics wrong. If geometric axioms cannot be grounded on analysis or intuition, it does not follow that they must be grounded on fact. There is another possible ground of knowledge that Kant had in fact acknowledged but failed to explore with sufficient depth:

It is a prejudice to believe that what cannot be derived from pure mathematics must for that very reason be derived from pure experience. Above mathematics and experience there are the dominating principles of logic – and when one proves that certain knowledge claims are neither mathematical nor empirical, one has thereby proved that they have a logical origin. (p. 175)

This is, in fact, the case with Euclid's axioms: "Concerning the fundamental properties of space, what can never be decided either by intuition or by analysis is already decided logically" (p. 178). Geometric concepts are not derived from experience, according to Riehl, nor "proved by means of facts"; they are a priori concepts because they are created through the faculty of thought. Rather than having the facts verifying geometric concepts, we have that "conversely, the facts are to be verified through them" (p. 177). According to Riehl, this doctrine of geometric concepts as "logical" can be found (albeit tacitly and obliquely) in Kant's writings and, quite explicitly, in Helmholtz's:

No one has expressed more clearly than Helmholtz this independence of the ideal configurations of geometry from their corporeal representations in reality, and the dependence of our knowledge and judgment concerning the latter upon the former, as he does when he says that whether a body is rigid, its surface flat, and its edges straight is to be decided by means of the very (geometric) propositions whose factual (empirical) correctness was to be exhibited by the test. (p. 177)[16]

From his Helmholtzian premises, Riehl tried to derive the Kantian conclusion concerning subjectivity of geometric knowledge: "The subject is certainly not, as Kant taught, the sole carrier of the spatiotemporal relations of appearances; he is indeed the author of their determined thought form" (p. 116). And as in Kant, even though these forms are, in some sense, up to us, we do not really have a choice on what these forms will be: "This form of knowledge is necessarily valid for the conscious grasping of the relations of intuition" (p. 116). In other words, Euclidean space is really necessary after all − not a necessity of intuition, but a "logical" necessity, that is, a necessity grounded on concepts alone. But notice how far this is from Kant's ideas. Now conceptual necessity is not grounded on anything like an analysis of concepts; there is, indeed, no talk about analysis in the nominal sense. Rather, conceptual necessity emerges by some unspecified route, involving somehow the endorsement of certain axioms; these are accepted or recognized as true (in some sense of that expression, perhaps only misleadingly associated with its constituent phrases), somehow in virtue of the concepts involved − or, as some would put it later, in virtue of the meanings involved. When carried to its natural conclusion, this line of thought would lead to the view that even though each set of geometric axioms is, in the appropriate sense, "logically" true, it is also the case that each set of axioms is as good as any other. Helmholtz's "transcendental" version of geometry led inevitably to the principle of tolerance in geometry.

4

Frege's semantics and the
a priori in arithmetic

Wouldn't Locke's sensualism, Berkeley's idealism, and so much more that is tied up with these philosophies have been impossible if they had distinguished adequately between thinking in the narrow [objective] sense and representing; between the constituents (concepts, objects, relations) and the representations? Even if human thinking does not take place without representations, the content of a judgment is something objective, the same for all. . . . What we are saying for the whole content is true also of its constituents that we can distinguish within it.

> Frege, Draft of a reply to Kerry, *Nachlass*

The erroneous belief that a thought (a judgment, as it is usually called) is something psychological like a representation . . . leads necessarily to epistemological idealism.

> Frege, "Logik," *Nachlass*

Through the present example . . . we see how pure thought, irrespective of the content given by the senses or even by an a priori intuition, can bring forth judgments deriving solely from the content that springs from its own constitution, which at first sight appear to be possible only on the basis of some intuition. One can compare this with condensation, through which it is possible to transform the air that to a child's consciousness appears as nothing into an invisible fluid in the shape of drops.

> Frege, *Begriffschrift*

Before Frege, the best logic texts might have started with a paragraph such as this:

Every categorical proposition has a subject, a predicate, a copula, a quality, and a quantity. Subject and predicate are called 'terms'. For example, in 'the pious man is happy', 'the pious man' and 'happy' are terms of which 'the pious man' is the subject, 'happy' is the predicate and 'is' is the copula. The 'quality' of the proposition is affirmation or negation . . . the 'quantity' of a proposition is its universality or particularity. (Leibniz, *Opuscules et fragments inédits de Leibniz,* pp. 77–8)

Frege radically altered the character of logic. He rejected the traditional doctrine of all five of these categories and offered a new account that guided the development of logic for the following century. Frege re-

placed the partition between subject and predicate with one between object and function. He argued that the copula is not a separate element linking subject and predicate but merely a part or function of the concept displayed in its unsaturatedness; that the category of quality derives from a confusion between unasserted propositional content and its assertion; and that the proper interpretation of quantity requires a theory of quantification that recognizes the functional character of the quantified concept and the existence of higher-level concepts.

It is widely agreed that these discoveries signaled the birth of modern logic. They are, however, no more than the by-products of the much more fundamental enterprise that inspired Frege from his earliest writings: an investigation of the character of what we say when we convey information by means of judgments – not just of what we do say, but of what we could say or judge. From his earliest writings Frege's main concern was with meaning or content, with what he called "the logical" – that is, with semantics.

Begriffsschrift

According to Kant's early conception of mathematical knowledge, the distinguishing virtue of mathematical symbolism is that it represents isomorphically the features of its topic. In arithmetic, for example, Kant had argued that symbols, with their capacity to grow and diminish and their mutual relations, offer a model of the corresponding features of numbers. He thought the case of geometry was even more striking, because there the symbols actually resemble the symbolized. "Mathematical symbols," he argued,

are sensible vehicles of knowledge, so that one can be as confident with them that no concept has been neglected and that each single comparison has taken place through simple rules, etc., as one is of what one sees with one's eyes. The task is greatly facilitated by the fact that one must not think things in their general representation, but only about the signs known individually and with sensible knowledge. In the case of philosophy, on the contrary, words, the symbols of philosophical knowledge, serve only to remind us of the general concept being designated. One must always keep their meaning before one's eyes and the pure understanding maintained in constant effort; and how imperceptibly does a characteristic of an abstracted concept escape us, for there is nothing sensible to reveal to us its omission. (Kant, *Untersuchung über natürlichen Theologie,* pp. 291–2; see also *Critique,* A715–18/B743–6)

And elsewhere he added:

The signs employed in philosophical considerations are nothing more than words that fail to represent through their own composition the partial concepts that constitute the whole idea signified by the word; nor can their connection designate the relations of philosophical thoughts. That is why in each act of thinking for this mode of knowledge one must have the thing itself before one's eyes, and it becomes necessary to represent the general in abstracto, without being able to avail oneself of that important and helpful device of handling only single signs rather than general concepts of the thing itself. (Kant, *Untersuchung über natürlichen Theologie*, pp. 278–9)[1]

Thus, in Kant's youthful opinion, the symbolism of mathematics was what he might have called an *Anschauungsschrift*, a symbolic system designed to display in sensible intuition a reliable model of the domain of mathematical discourse. Because of the constructive nature of its topic, mathematics lends itself perfectly to isomorphic representation. Philosophy, in contrast, deals with given, nonconstructed concepts and therefore is not capable of this sort of treatment. In other words, there is an *Anschauungsschrift*, but there is no *Begriffsschrift*; and even if there were one, it would interest the mathematician and not the philosopher.

Frege's first book, his *Begriffsschrift* of 1879, put forth a program that directly opposed Kant. Its aim was to design a symbolism that would do for philosophy what Kant thought could be done only for mathematics – a symbolism that portrays not the things it is about but what we may say about them, that gives a picture not of things thought but of thought itself, objectively considered. "Right from the start," he explained in a retrospective account, "I had in mind the *expression of a content.* . . . But the content must be given more precisely than in a natural language" ("Booles rechende Logik," p. 13).

Unlike Bolzano, Frege recognized from the very beginning that for most sentences of natural languages "the connection of words corresponds only partially to the structure of the concepts" ("Booles rechende Logik," p. 13). But instead of drawing Kant's defeatist conclusion, Frege attempted to identify what others would call a "perfect language," a fragment of German that expressed perspicuously the content of what we say. "The business of the logician," he explained, "is to conduct an ongoing struggle . . . in part against language and grammar insofar as they fail to give clear expression to the logical" ("Logik" [1879–91], *Nachlass*, p. 7).

"The logical" – it would be a serious error to misunderstand what Frege meant by this recurring expression in his early writings. What Frege and Russell called "logical," what Husserl called a "logical" investigation, what Meinong called *"Gegenstandstheorie,"*[2] and what Wittgenstein termed a "logico-philosophical" observation are close relatives; they should not be confused with what is now called logic, after formalism and set theory have come to dominate the field. Their "logic" was our semantics, a doctrine of content, its nature and structure, and not merely of its "formal" fragment.

For example, Frege explained that an understanding of several languages reveals the fact that natural languages contain a large number of nonrepresentational features, elements that do not stand for anything "logical." He concluded that a familiarity with several languages is quite useful, because "differences between languages can reduce the difficulty in grasping the logical" ("Logik" [1879–91], *Nachlass,* p. 6; also in a later draft, "Logik" [1897], *Nachlass,* p. 154). When Frege defined as his goal "to isolate what is logical" ("Logik" [1879–91], *Nachlass,* p. 6) and "to separate sharply the psychological from the logical, the subjective from the objective" (*The Foundations of Arithmetic,* p. xxii), he was clearly implying that his target, the logical or objective element in thought, is not what remains in judgment when content is excluded but what remains when we discard the specifically *psychological* element.[3]

Frege devoted considerable effort to separating his own conceptions of "logic" from that of the mere computational logicians such as Jevons, Boole, and Schroeder. Whereas these people, he explained, were engaged in the Leibnizian project of developing a calculus ratiocinator, his own goal was the much more ambitious one of designing a *lingua characteristica.* Traditional logicians were concerned basically with the problem of identifying mathematical algorithms aimed at solving traditional logical problems – what follows from what, what is valid, and so on. Frege's goal went far beyond what we now call formal logic and into semantics, meanings, and contents, where he found the ultimate foundation of inference, validity, and much more.

Frege's criticisms of Boole are particularly revealing. In Boole's work, he complained, "content has been entirely ignored" ("Booles rechende Logik," p. 13). Boole's aim was to produce algorithms for solving logical problems, but his strategy could not satisfy "anyone interested in keeping the closest link in the relations between signs and the relations between the things themselves" (p. 13). Unlike Boole, "I did not want to represent an abstract logic in formulas, but to express a content through written signs in a more precise and surveyable (*übersichtlicherer*) fashion" ("Ueber den Zweck der Begriffsschrifts" [1882–3], *Begriffsschrift,* p. 97). "Boole's formula-language symbolic logic represents only the formal part of language, and that only incompletely" ("Booles rechende Logik," p. 14). "Boole's formula language presents only a part of our thought; the whole of it cannot be taken care of by a machine or replaced by a purely mechanical activity" (p. 39). It is the whole of our thought that concerns the *lingua characteristica.* "We can derive a real usefulness from [a formula language] only when the content is not merely indicated but constructed out of its constituents by means of the same logical signs that are used in the computation" (p. 39).

Frege's project involved identifying a fragment of the German language that fulfills two conditions: (a) Every German sentence has a translation into this fragment, and (b) the grammatical form of every sentence in this fragment mirrors isomorphically the constituents of the content it expresses, as well as their arrangement in that content. The fact that *Begriffsschrift* introduced symbols not available in pre-Fregean German, essential as it was for the practical feasibility of the project, was a semantically insignificant factor; for such symbols could be entirely eliminated in principle, in favor of standard German language expressions – precisely those in terms of which the meanings of Frege's symbols were expressed. Given this "perfect language," derivability relations and conditions for validity would follow without any need to appeal to algebraic tricks extrinsic to the propositions under consideration, but simply by an analysis of the constituents of the claims involved and their structural relations, as manifested perspicuously (i.e., syntactically) in their reformulation in the perfect language. In effect, the idea was to produce a language in which, even though inference was based on meaning, one need no longer think about meanings (just as Kant had said that the nature of mathematical symbolism makes it unnecessary to think about *its* meaning), since one could now restrict oneself to the signs "present to the senses" and their symbolic correlations. Little wonder that fifty years later a heretic disciple was tempted to cut the remaining link with meanings and take the perspicuous language as the whole concern of logic and scientific philosophy.

How is one to identify the details of this perfect language? Frege's strategy, and the epoch-making results that emerged from it, seem to have been inspired by a semantic conception that, oddly enough, he never made quite explicit. Indeed, the central elements of that semantics were *essentially* tacit; for as soon as he recognized their presence in his system (apparently in the late 1880s), he hastened to eliminate them.

The basic semantic categories

The similarity between Frege's early semantics and Bolzano's is quite striking. As we saw, Frege emphasized in the beginning of his *Grundlagen* the importance of separating "sharply the psychological from the logical, the subjective from the objective"[4] (p. xxii). One must be especially careful, he urged, to distinguish between objective and subjective representations; the former are "the same for all," but the latter are not. A word is often accompanied by a subjective representation that nevertheless "is not its meaning"; "the word . . . means an objective representation" (p. 37). Extending an undeserved olive branch to the past, Frege added, "It is because Kant associated both meanings with the word ['representation'] that his doctrine assumed such a subjective, idealist complexion, and his true view [!] was made so difficult to discover" (*The Foundations of Arithmetic,* p. 37).

There can be no doubt, however, that Frege's treatment of these matters is even farther removed from Kant's than Bolzano's. Unlike Kant, and in agreement with his general goal of desubjectivizing semantics, Bolzano had distinguished three elements associated with every representation: (a) the subjective representation, (b) its objective counterpart, and (c) its object. But having agreed with Kant that representations are either concepts or intuitions, he had a hard time producing an objective counterpart between the subjective intuition (e.g., the seeing of a rose) and its object (the rose). Bolzano was still far too dependent on that tradition in which all we see are "ideas" and "phenomena." "What I see when someone holds a rose before me," he explained, "is a representation" (*WL,* vol. 1, p. 217) – hence, presumably, not a rose, for roses, unlike objective representations, are in space and time and, unlike subjective representations, persist when the human mind vanishes.[5] The object of intuition appears to be subjective and the objective counterpart remains a mystery. We are in one of the darkest corners of Bolzano's philosophy.

From the very beginning Frege cast these Kantian hesitations aside: "Objective representations," he explained in the *Grundlagen,* "can be divided into concepts and objects," not into concepts and intuitions[6] (p. 37). Objective representations matter not for their own sake but for what we can do with them by linking them together, for when the link is appropriate, the outcome is something akin to a Kantian judgment minus its subjective, psychological component; it is the content of a judgment minus its subjective dimension. This is what Frege called a *content of possible judgment* (*beurteilbarer Inhalt,* henceforth, cpj). A cpj is the target of what Russell later would call propositional attitudes: understanding, assuming, asserting, wondering, and so on. Most importantly for Frege, these things are what we claim to know. Thus, an understanding of human knowledge depends on a proper understanding of cpj's: A theory of knowledge presupposes a semantics, and until we understand the latter, we ought not try to deal with the former.

The whole of Frege's early semantics centered around these three basic notions: concept, object, and cpj. The distance between Frege and Kant is underscored by the paucity of remarks on that most disturbing of Kantian problems, the character of the objects of knowledge and their constitution through the categories. Objects are no problem for Frege – they are the tables and chairs of everyday experience, the numbers and classes of mathematical knowledge, the truth values of his logic, and so on. His semantic interest is aimed almost exclusively at the other two topics, concepts and cpj's. Moreover, what he has to say about them has an oddly complementary nature, since his account of each depends on an account of the other, so that one is bound to understand them jointly or not at all. Whether dialectical or circular, Frege's reasoning on this topic does not lend itself graciously to didactic exposition. We begin by looking at the way he came to think about concepts, contrasting his views with the more standard picture of the matter.

The concept: roots of holism and unsaturation

According to the abstractionist theory of the concept that was still quite popular in Frege's time, the best way to understand what concepts *are* is to look at their genesis. It is important to emphasize that the young Frege agreed with this point, even if he disagreed with the abstractionist account of how human beings define or construct concepts. Abstractionists claimed that concepts emerge through a process that takes us from certain data to a concept via a process of elimination. The given at the starting point of this process appears to consist of intuitions. A succinct statement of the abstractionist theory is found in Husserl's early writings. Husserl began his *Habilitationsschrift* devoted to the concept of number, by explaining that he would assume

> that concepts originate through a comparison of the specific representations that fall under them. Disregarding the characteristics (*Merkmale*) that differ, one holds firmly to the ones that are common; and these latter are the ones which then constitute the general concept. (*Begriff der Zahl,* p. 299)

The standard designations of concepts as "general representations" and "common nouns" are motivated by the widely held belief that the essential characteristic of a concept is its capacity to refer to more than one thing. It was therefore widely held that a theory of the concept should explain, above all, that power of multiple reference. The abstractionist theory appears inspired by the curious idea that one can explain the generality of *reference* in a concept by involving a multitude of things in the story of how the concept came to emerge. But as Frege pointed out, the theory has no way to distinguish between a case in which one decides to neglect features of an object because they differ from those of others and one in which a person is simply forgetful and lets the details of a single instance drop out of his memory. Frege's biting and accurate critique of this procedure (as displayed in Husserl's *Philosophie der Arithmetik*) is worth recalling:

> [Detaching our attention] is particularly effective. We attend less to a property, and it disappears. By making one characteristic after another disappear, we get more and more abstract concepts. . . . Inattention is a most efficacious logical faculty; presumably this accounts for the absentmindedness of professors. Suppose there are a black and a white cat sitting side by side before us. We stop

attending to their color, and they become colorless, but are still sitting side by side. We stop attending to their posture, and they are no longer sitting (though they have not assumed another posture), but each one is still in its place. We stop attending to position; they cease to have place, but still remain different. In this way, perhaps, we obtain from each one of them a general concept of Cat. By continued application of this procedure, we obtain from each object a more and more bloodless phantom. (From Frege's review of Husserl's *Philosophie der Arithmetik* [1894], *Translations*, pp. 84–5)

If concepts cannot derive from abstraction, how *do* they emerge? In Frege's view, the process of concept formation is dependent on that of judgment. Frege noted that logicians, from Aristotle to Boole, had seen logic as a theory of inference in which the construction of concepts "is presupposed as something that has already been completed." He contrasted this with his own approach: "I start from judgments and their content, not from concepts. . . . I allow the formation of concepts to proceed only from judgments" ("Booles rechende Logik," p. 17); the representations of properties and relations "come simultaneously with the first judgment in which they are ascribed to things" (p. 19).[7]

Frege's strategy for dealing with the concept was to assume that we are given the cpj's and their constituent objects; we then generate concepts by carving them out of cpj's, as we exclude this or that object from the given cpj.[8]

In its basic outline, Frege's doctrine of concept formation corresponds rather closely to holistic remarks found in Bolzano and other previous writers. But nothing in the work of Bolzano, or of anyone else, compares with the richness of detail and results that emerged when Frege adopted this strategy. For one thing, most pre-Fregean philosophers, including Bolzano, relied rather blindly on surface grammar and on the subject–copula–predicate form. For another, the holistic doctrine became a fruitful semantic tool only when conjoined with another idea entirely original with Frege: that the step from judgment to concept is analogous to a similar step taken in mathematics, linking a function and its values.

The instrument of generality in mathematics is the variable, and its most frequent context is the function name. Consider, for example, the function

$$2 \cdot x^3 + x;$$

the values it assigns to 1, 2, and so on are

$$2 \cdot 1^3 + 1,$$
$$2 \cdot 2^3 + 2, \qquad \text{and so on.}$$

It occurred to Frege that if we look at this process backward, we obtain a very enlightening picture of the nature of a function. Instead of moving from the function to its values, move from the values (or, rather, from those *particular* names of the values) to the function (or, rather, to the name of the function):

From this we may discern that the essence of the function lies in what is common to these expressions; i.e., in what is present in

$$`2\cdot(x)^3 + x`$$

over and above the letter 'x'. We could write this as follows:

$$`2\cdot(\ \ )^3 + (\ \ )`.$$

("Funktion und Begriff" [1891], *Kleine Schriften,* p. 128)

The (name of the) function is therefore seen as deriving from (certain names of) its values by removing from the latter (the names of) one or more objects. Frege drew an important conclusion: The function not only correlates arguments and values but is also "unsaturated," "in need of completion," and like concepts, "predicative."[9]

Frege saw that the backward process from argument (name) to function (name) may be applied not only to expressions that designate numbers but to all meaningful expressions, including sentences, and recognized in this the key to the nature of general representation. For example, starting with

(*) John is tall,

we can take John (or 'John') out and are left with

   x is tall,

a function of a more general type than the mathematical variety, since it does not take numbers as values. According to Frege, this is the concept *tall* or, as he preferred to write it, *x is tall*. The holistic and the functional idea are now linked through the fact that the concept *tall* is the function we obtain when we carve out of a cpj such as (*) an object such as John.

In 1882 Frege explained to a correspondent (possibly Marty), "I do not believe that concept formation can precede judgment . . . but I think of a concept as having arisen by decomposition from a cpj" (Letter to Marty [?] [1882], *Wiss. Briefwechsel,* p. 164). He went on to explain how the construction takes place. Consider the cpj

(*) 3 > 2.

Depending on what we choose to regard as the "subject" of (*), the claim will be regarded as the attribution of different concepts to different objects. If we regard 3 as its subject, for example, then (*) says that 3 falls under the concept *being greater than 2*. A similar concept results if 2 is chosen as the subject. Finally, we can also regard '3 and 2' as a complex subject. As a predicate we then have the concept of the relation of the greater to the smaller. In general, I represent the falling of an individual under a concept by $F(x)$, where x is the subject (argument) and $F(\ )$ the predicate (function), and where the empty place in the parentheses after F represents nonsaturation. (p. 164)

Two years later he would explain in *Grundlagen:*

When from a cpj that deals with the objects a and b we subtract a and b, we obtain a remainder, a relation concept that is, accordingly, in need of completion in two ways. If from the sentence

"the earth is more massive than the moon"

we substract "the earth," we obtain the concept "more massive than the moon." If alternatively, we substract the object "the moon," we get the concept "more massive than the earth." But if we subtract them both at once, then we are left with a relation concept. (p. 82)

Frege's holist theory of the concept was revolutionary. Before Frege, singular and general representations had been considered two species of the same semantic natural kind. He was not simply rejecting the old idea of the concept as a "common name," as a name of more than one thing (although he was certainly doing that as well). Behind the term 'general representations' lay the idea that both sorts of representations emerge from basically the same process, such as that proposed by abstraction theories. According to these theories, there is a primordial sort of singular representation (the given), which is the most powerful, desirable, and complete form of representation; we obtain a less specific form of representation by weakening the features of the primordial ones. This character is mysteriously transmitted even to a priori concepts. On Frege's view, so-called general representations are so different from their singular counterparts that one might better regard them as falling into two radically distinct semantic categories. The difference is revealed by the difference in the procedures that lead to their emergence. Singular representations are proper names, and these are supposed to be given quite independently of judgment; general representations emerge only *after* judgment. Traditional logic texts treated concept, judgment, and reasoning in that order; Frege was proposing that the order of the first two be reversed. His new perspective not only showed how wrong it is to think of concepts as general names, ignoring their predicative (unsaturated) dimension; it also showed how wrong it is to think of concepts as *general* representations; for

x is identical with Sir Walter Scott

is a concept that, by its very essence, lacks the capacity to designate anything more than one object.

Quantification and arithmetic

Most of Frege's colleagues were suspicious of so much semantic subtlety. Why should one care about the nature of concepts? Here we can only scratch the surface of an answer by briefly recalling Frege's two major achievements of this early period: his theory of quantification and his analysis of arithmetic. As we shall see, they are entirely dependent on his semantic conception of things, and the picture they offer of mathematical knowledge is both an enormous improvement on earlier efforts and a further major step away from the Kantian position on the role of concepts and intuition in a priori knowledge.

Quantification

Traditionally, quantified sentences such as 'All As are Bs' and 'Some As are Bs' had been thought to make subject–predicate claims, their subjects being 'all As' and 'some As', respectively. As we shall see, Russell's *Principles,* written more than two decades after Frege's *Begriffsschrift,* was still inspired by this pre-Fregean view of quantification.[10] One could hardly provide more striking evidence of the revolutionary character of Frege's views.

Frege analyzed the content of

(1) All men are mortal

as follows: He first considered the apparently unrelated matter of how complex propositional contents emerge from simpler ones by means of logical operations such as negation and material implication. Consider, for example, how

(2) If John is a man, then John is mortal

is formed out of

(3) John is a man

and

(4) John is mortal.

According to Frege, the cpj expressed by (2) is uniquely characterized when we give what we would now call its truth conditions, that is, when we say that it is true in all and only those circumstances that make (4) true or (3) false.[11] A similar construction introduces all other connectives (negation suffices to define all the rest). At this point Frege had characterized the language of propositional logic. Next consider what

happens when we remove the object John (the word 'John'?) from (2);
Frege represented the result as

(5) If x is a man, then x is mortal

where the variable 'x' is no more than a convenient device to identify the
blank left by the departed name. As we know, (5) stands for a Fregean
concept, one that will be true of an object a precisely when a is not a
man or else it is mortal. Now (1) can be interpreted as saying *about that
concept* that every single object in the universe is an instance of it. A
quantified sentence such as (1) is therefore to be interpreted as involving a concept of "higher order," a concept that applies not, like (5), to
objects, but to (first-level) concepts, to (5) itself. The universal quantifier is no more and no less than a second-level concept that applies to
the first-level concept (5) precisely when (5) is true of every single
object — in other words, precisely when (1) is true. Appearances and
tradition notwithstanding, (1) does not say anything about all men, or
about *all men,* or about any particular man. Nor is quantification to be
construed in the medieval–Russellian manner, as an operation that trans-
forms the so-called subject concept (e.g., *man*) into a denoting expression (e.g., *all men*). It is a second-level concept whose topic is what we
now call the scope of the quantifier. The Fregean picture of quantification readily lends itself to iteration. Once existential quantification is
defined from its universal counterpart and negation in the standard manner, we can easily disclose ambiguities hidden in ordinary language —
such as that between simple and uniform convergence.

Frege's *Begriffsschrift* was not really a new language but a fragment of
German; everything that can be said in Frege's concept script can be said
equally unambiguously in German. Yet the German language does not
contain expressions that are manageable and unambiguous and that serve
the same purpose as Frege's new symbolism. That is why his notational
system became (pragmatically) essential. Given time and unlimited patience, one could explain in a natural language the ambiguities easily
sorted out in Frege's notation; but nothing in unreconstructed natural
languages can do nearly as well.

By combining his semantic insights with the new notational system,
Frege displayed explicitly in *Begriffsschrift* the first clear formulation of a
formal language with propositional connectives and quantification over
both individuals and first-level functions. Beyond this, the monograph
identified a set of "logical laws" and rules of inference for inferring other
laws from them, even though no effort was made to determine what
distinguishing feature of these formulas determines their membership in
that class. The system was developed with a subtlety and rigor far ex-

ceeding the standards displayed in later decades by Peano, Russell, and even Hilbert in his early logical writings. The role of inference rules, clearly recognized in *Begriffsschrift,* would remain a mystery to Frege's most distinguished colleagues until well into the twentieth century.

Remarkable as these achievements were, they were only the beginning. Five years later Frege would publish another short monograph aimed at showing that when we get our semantic facts straight, it becomes clear that Kant's philosophy of arithmetic – indeed, of the whole science of number – is incorrect.

Arithmetic

In *Grundlagen* Frege was concerned, once again, with the proper semantic interpretation of certain notions. Here, however, his emphasis was not on concepts traditionally assigned to the domain of logic such as quantification, copulation, and sentential connection, but on notions widely regarded as extralogical. His topic was number.

Three years after *Grundlagen* was published, Husserl explained in his *Habilitationsschrift*:

Today it is generally agreed that a rigorous and thorough development of higher analysis (the totality of *arithmetica universalis* in Newton's sense), excluding all auxiliary concepts borrowed from geometry, would have to emanate from elementary arithmetic alone, in which analysis is grounded. But this elementary arithmetic has, as a matter of fact, its sole foundation in the concept of number. (*Begriff der Zahl,* p. 294)

This was so because after half a century of work by Cauchy, Dedekind, Cantor, and Husserl's teacher, Weierstrass, a large portion of Bolzano's project to conceptualize analysis had been fulfilled. This achievement is sometimes known as the "arithmetization" of the calculus, because it reduced all of the mathematics of numbers to the science of natural numbers plus a vaguely logical discipline of classes. This project showed that whatever foundation there is to analysis is to be found in the theory of the natural numbers. One could conclude that any intuition present in analysis is to be found in arithmetic – hence the philosophical significance of the nature of arithmetic.

When Frege turned to examine this issue in *Grundlagen* (1884), he characteristically posed it at a pre-epistemological, semantic level. The questions he asked did not have the familiar Kantian ring: How does arithmetic acquire objective validity? How can it be applied? How do we come to know its objects and its justification? His basic questions were, What do number statements say and what do they say it about? The question of ground was not even raised.

Frege began by singling out for special attention what he called "number statements," statements that say there are n things of a given sort T; for example,

(*) Jupiter has four moons.

He reviewed the two basic doctrines on what these statements are about. According to the first one, (*) is about a certain object, perhaps the moons of Jupiter, or the class of those moons, or the "heap" or conglomerate that they somehow constitute. According to the second, (*) is not about any objective element but about some subjective counterpart such as our representation of moons, or certain mental processes of "addition," conjunction, or whatever. Frege described and criticized various versions of these two possible interpretations, refuting decisively every single one of them. This portion of the monograph, leading to Frege's own proposed solution, is one of the most dazzling examples of sound philosophical writing ever produced.

The key, according to Frege, is to recognize that the question "How many?" makes no sense if we identify an object as its target, but acquires sense if its target is a concept. If we point to the cards on the table and ask about them, "How many?" the right answer may be eighty (cards), two (packs of cards), or almost any other number we may choose. To allow for a definite, unique answer, we must make reference, explicit or implicit, to a concept (x is a card, x is a pack of cards, etc.). Since the number attribute is fixed only when the concept is determined, it is natural to regard the concept itself as the topic of the number statement. Thus, syntactic appearances notwithstanding, number statements, *like quantified statements,* are about concepts. In fact, Frege explained, they *are* quantified statements, even though ordinary language hides that fact.

For example, the number statement 'The earth has one moon' is about the concept *is a moon of the earth,* and it says that exactly one object (at least one and at most one) falls under it. To say that an object falls under a given concept is, according to *Begriffsschrift,* simply to apply an existential quantifier to it; and to say that at most one object falls under it is easy to do in terms of universal quantification, identity, and the propositional connectives. In a similar fashion one can render an interpretation of (*) and of all statements of the form 'There are n Fs', where 'n' is a *standard* numeral.

This brilliant solution, later described by Frege as the "most fundamental of my results" in *Grundlagen* (*Grundgesetze,* p. ix), showed that a wide range of statements previously regarded as extralogical and involving an appeal to either empirical intuition (Mill) or to pure intuition (Kant) involved only reference to concepts. Bolzano's hope of conceptualizing mathematics had been taken a giant step forward.

We shall return in Chapter 7 to Frege's conception of logic and arithmetic, and to some of the problems it left unsolved. But whatever the problems, there can be no doubt that Frege's work shed a great deal of light on the character of arithmetical knowledge. It is worth emphasizing once again that the clearer mathematics became in his hands, the further it moved away from Kantian doctrine. It wasn't so much that Frege had argued that arithmetic is analytic. Since he had defined 'analytic' as derivable from logic and definitions, one might consider his conception of logic so different from Kant's as to make a conflict on this issue virtually impossible. Rather, the basic conflict was, as we might expect, on the subject of intuition. On one thing Kant and Frege agreed: Logic is grounded at the level of the understanding where sensibility and its forms play no role (recall the quotation from Frege at the beginning of this chapter). The reduction of arithmetic to logic conflicted with the Kantian postulation of an appeal to sensibility in the realm of arithmetic. As we shall have reason to observe at a later stage, there is no explicit theory of the ground of analytic knowledge in Frege's writings; but these brief considerations indicate that he intended to place both the content and the ground of arithmetical knowledge at the level of Kant's analytic doctrine, to the exclusion of his aesthetic doctrine.

Quite apart from their relevance to Kantianism, Frege's early treatments of quantification and number statements provided the model for a reconstructive conception of language that would inspire a variety of schools within the analytic tradition. No one before Frege had taken so seriously the task of casting a language in which ordinary things could be said in an extraordinarily clear manner. No one before him had applied his translation techniques so effectively to the solution or dissolution of philosophical problems. We shall soon see that this aspect of Frege's approach appeared independently in the works of Russell, and then of Wittgenstein and Carnap. But we must now turn to yet another major discovery of Frege's, one that his successors were far slower to appreciate.

The discovery of sense

Few things have proved more difficult to achieve in the development of semantics than recognition of the fact that between our subjective representations and the world of things we talk about, there is a third element: what we say. Perhaps Chapter 5, which deals mostly with developments that took place more than a decade after Frege came to grips with the situation, should be read before this account of Frege's discovery; for that chapter describes the difficulties that many of the best philosophical minds encountered near the turn of the century largely because they were unable to understand that what we say, sense, cannot be constituted either from psychological content or from the real-world correlates of our representations. Psychologistic logicians had pursued the first approach; most of Frege's successors pursued the second. They all attempted to understand sense by forcing it into a world to which it does not belong.

As we have seen, many of the things Frege said during his first decade of research suggest that he also had started on the assumption that cpj's should have as constituents both the objects they deal with and the concepts attributed to them. The ominous hesitations on use and mention implicit in some of the references in the section on roots of holism and unsaturation are not Homer's nods, but symptoms of the fact that Frege had not thought through the implications of what he was saying. Moreover, from the very beginning, Frege had acknowledged a major exception to the general account of content, an exception that would become the rule in the picture of propositional content that emerged in the 1890s. Although we do not know much about the course of Frege's thought as he moved toward the recognition of sense, the opening remarks of "On Sense and Reference" (1892) give us an appreciation of the role played by one of the most influential factors: the nature of identity. Identity had posed a difficulty to Frege's cpj semantics from the very beginning. Consider, for example, the following identity statements:

(*) The author of *Waverley* = the author of *Waverley*

and

(**) The author of *Waverley* = Scott.

What does cpj semantics say about the content conveyed by these sentences? If we interpret identity as relational, its content will be a cpj containing the identity relation with both "holes" saturated by the objects named by the relevant terms. Then, since the author of *Waverley* is Scott, the content of (*) is identical to the content of (**). Consequently, if knowing that a sentence is true is knowing that its cpj is true, anyone who knows that (*) is true must also know that (**) is true. As Frege put it in "On Sense and Reference," "Now if we were to regard equality as a relation between that which the names 'a' and 'b' designate, it would seem that $a = b$ could not differ from $a = a$ (i.e. provided $a = b$ is true)" (*Translations*, p. 56). Frege seemed to have thought at first that this difficulty did not point to a problem within his semantics but revealed instead the very idiosyncratic character of the identity relation. Thus, he came to think that whereas all other relations relate their objects, identity says something about a very different domain. Let us look closely at what that domain was.

Superficially, section 8 of *Begriffsschrift* (in which the topic is discussed) appears to say that identity must be construed as a relation
between purely syntactic expressions, as if (*) and (**) were really about
'Scott' and 'the author of *Waverley*'. But a more careful reading shows
that this is not so. Frege's point is that different names of the same object
will, in general, be associated with different ways of determining which
object they name. For example, we might give to ourselves a geometric
point "directly in intuition" and baptize it with the proper name '*A*', and
then we might give it as the point fulfilling certain geometric conditions:

> To each way of determining the point there corresponds a particular name.
> Hence the need for a sign for identity of content (*Inhalt*) rests upon the follow-
> ing consideration: the same content can be completely determined in different
> ways; but the content of a *judgment* is that in a particular case *two ways of
> determining it* (*Bestimmungsweisen*) really yield the *same result*. Before this
> judgment can be made, two distinct names, corresponding to the two ways of
> determining the content, must be assigned to what these ways determine. (van
> Heijenoort, *From Frege to Gödel*, p. 21; Frege's italics)[12]

Clearly the cpj's (*) and (**) do not talk about names, nor do they, of
course, have names among their constituents. According to Frege, what
(*) and (**) *say* is that two methods of determining a referent yield the
same referent. If what they say is the cpj, then cpj's have as constituents
not the referents but the methods for determining them, that is, what
Frege will eventually call the "sense" of the corresponding singular
terms.

Thus, circa 1880, whereas the contents of most relational judgments
looked like the future Russellian propositions, the content of identity
statements looked like the future Fregean *Gedanke,* for they involved the
senses rather than the referents of the appropriate names. The main
difference with the views of his later self was that the young Frege
confused content and topic, thus concluding that the sense of the names
in question was the topic of the identity claim.

What happened circa 1890 is that Frege detected and removed this
major confusion from his system. First, he decided that identity does not
call for a special treatment after all, but that '$a = b$' *is* a relation between
what the names a and b signify. It does not follow, however, that the
content of this sentence is the same as that of '$a = a$'. In the spirit of
Begriffsschrift, he reiterated in "Uber Sinn und Bedeutung" (1892) that
when 'a' and 'b' refer to the same object, 'a' may differ from 'b' merely in
physical shape (as in 'England' and 'Inglaterra') – in which case '$a = a$'
and '$a = b$' *do* say exactly the same thing (have the same content); or 'a'
may differ from 'b' also in the *way* it designates or refers (*in der Weise,
wie es etwas bezeichnet;* p. 41). In the latter case the contents are obviously different even if the objects related are not. What was wrong with

the old solution to the puzzle of identity was that it misidentified the source of the trouble, for the trouble arose only when we failed to distinguish between what we say and what we say it about (or, as Bolzano would put it, between objective representation and its object). On the new solution, a sentence of the form '$a = b$' would concern not the topic (*die Sache selbst*) but the mode of designation (*die Bezeich-nungsweise,* p. 41) or, as Frege now called it, the sense (*Sinn*). It was clear that both topic and sense are essential, but they play radically different semantic roles.

Semantic dualism

Two styles of semantic analysis played a prominent role in the semantic tradition, what we will call semantic monism and semantic dualism. Monists and dualists agree on the broadly picture-theoretic assumption that for the purposes of semantic analysis we must partition a language into its basic grammatical units and associate with them appropriate semantic correlates. The conflict lies in the number and character of the semantic entities required: The monist thinks we need associate no more than one semantic entity with each grammatical unit, and all of these entities come basically from the same place, the world. The dualist thinks that we must associate two different elements with each piece of grammar: roughly its contribution to what the sentence says and its contribution to what it is about. The latter is in the world; but where the former is, and even whether this question makes any sense at all, are matters on which the dualist would normally hesitate.

We have seen that the semantic system underlying Frege's thought during the first and most creative decade of his intellectual life was a form of semantic monism. Then, around 1890, he recognized its presence and replaced it by a dualist system. According to Frege's official semantic doctrine after 1890, there are two radically different semantic categories associated with each independently meaningful expression: its sense and its significance. The words '*Sinn*' and '*Bedeutung*' had occurred in other semantic systems both before and after Frege. What distinguished Frege's usage was that he regarded these notions as semantic categories, rather than as names of specific semantic objects or relations. Wittgenstein would acknowledge in the *Tractatus* both a *Sinn* and a *Bedeutung*, for example; yet his system is a version of semantic monism, for on his view only names have a *Bedeutung* and only pictures have a *Sinn*. For Frege every meaningful grammatical unit does *two* semantically relevant things: It expresses its sense and it signifies its significance. By doing each of these things, the meaningful expression has the potential to contribute to two parallel processes whose ultimate goal is symbolically represented in the syntactic structure of the fully analyzed sentence.

Though Frege emphasized the distinction between what we understand and what we are talking about, he thought there must be a very intimate link between those two. Take a sentence such as

(1) The author of *Waverley* is tall.

The universe includes many objects and many properties, but only one of each affects in any way the truth value of (1). The only relevant object is the one who wrote *Waverley,* Scott; the only relevant property is *height.* Whether (1) is true or false depends entirely on whether a single object in the universe has a single property. And the interesting fact is that this information is entirely contained in sentence (1). Since that information consists of two different items, it is natural to think of (1) as being divided into two grammatical units corresponding to each of those items. We may therefore think of it as being partitioned into 'the author of *Waverley*' and '*x* is tall'. We then go on to recognize a very basic semantic feature of (1), that these grammatical units are associated with the truth-relevant parts of the world, that is, with those elements of the world that are the only ones relevant to the determination of whether what (1) says is true. Quite generally, Frege thought, the grammatical units of a claim are associated with the elements that constitute its topic and determine its truth value. For the case of direct discourse, the mode of language of science, it is natural to baptize the class of all such elements "the real world," for it includes all we talk about when we don't talk about talking. In direct discourse each grammatical unit is associated with a corresponding element in the real world, and Frege said of such elements that they are meant by the expression in question, or that they are its "significance" or "meaning" (*Bedeutung*).[13]

Grammatical units partition the world into what matters and what does not as far as truth is concerned; they give us what we have called the truth-relevant elements. Responsible use of language does not require that we have a definite idea of what that partition is, however (and herein lies a verificationist tale). All that is required for the purposes of communication or responsible discourse in general is that what we say be intelligible, and this usually has little to do with being able to tell whether what we say is true, or even with the possession of effective methods to identify either its referents or truth values.

That sense is nonetheless intimately related to the truth-value-relevant elements in the world is strongly suggested by a seldom-noticed fact: Frege took it as self-evident that the grammatical analysis appropriate to the study of sense coincides with the grammatical analysis appropriate to the study of significance. The understanding of the sense of a sentence is not, for Frege, a holistic phenomenon but comes about through the understanding of the sense of its parts. This is the natural explanation of the fact that we can understand sentences we have never seen before (Letter to Jourdain [1914], *Wiss. Briefwechsel,* p. 127) and is also the reason we need to talk about the sense of parts of the sentence, as well as that of the whole they constitute. But notice that there is, in principle, no reason the grammatical units that provide the building blocks of propositional sense should be the same that provide the truth-relevant features of the world, *unless* sense (and therefore understanding) are essentially a matter of doing something concerning those worldly units. Thus, even if the sense of those expressions that select truth-relevant elements need not be an *effective* method of getting at those elements, it must be some sort of device establishing a correlation, however ineffective, with them.

The realm of sense, ignored by most philosophers before Frege and challenged by many after him, was Frege's response to what has remained to this day one of the central topics of semantics, the character of propositional understanding. This involved at least two major problems: What is it that we understand, and under what circumstances does understanding take place (or how do we distinguish apparent propositional understanding from *the real thing*)?

The solution to these problems that would prevail among members of the semantic tradition after Frege was that the targets of propositional attitudes are certain real entities (for Russell, particulars or universals; for Husserl, essences, etc.) and that the basic attitude of understanding is, in effect, intuition (acquaintance, *Wesensschau,* self-evidence). In drawing a sharp distinction between sense and the real world, Frege was denying that the things we understand – that is, what we say and its constituents – are elements of the real world, whether individuals or properties, universals, concepts, or essences. He also denied that understanding is a glorified form of "seeing" aimed at these entities. Frege's subtle point is that while understanding does involve "giving" the object in question, it need not necessarily be "given" in the mode of acquaintance. Understanding and acquaintance should not be equated; indeed, the former is usually concerned with what might well be called "knowledge by description." What we understand when we understand a definite description, for example, is its sense; and this, in turn, is a way of giving the referent, but a way that need not be effective or even lead to an end result (a referent).

Thus, in Fregean doctrine the sentence is the real center of semantic activity. To understand the character of a constituent of a sentence is to know the job it is supposed to perform in connection with its partners in the sentence, in order to associate that sentence with each of its two semantic dimensions. The basic task of the sentence is to say something. What the sentence says is its sense, and the sense of each part is simply its contribution to this message. On the matter of sense, the parts of the sentence are mere instruments, totally subservient to the overriding goal, which is to constitute the sense of the sentence. The sense of a part of a sentence is interesting only because it helps us understand the sense of the sentence. The second semantic task concerns significance. Since the significance of a sentence is its truth value, the reason we are interested in the significance of its grammatical units cannot be related to the "construction" of the significance of the whole to which they belong. Indeed, the truth value of the sentence is determined not by its sense alone but by its sense plus the way things stand with certain elements in the real world. The second job of the parts of the sentence is, then, to determine what those truth-relevant elements are. Both the sense and the significance of the whole sentence "emerge" from that of the parts.

Frege's earlier semantic framework had provided the structure for some of the deepest foundational work of the century – including his theory of quantification and his analysis of arithmetic. Frege's philosophy after 1890 is the record of his remarkable but only partial success at grounding those foundational achievements on this newfound dualism. To explore the difficulties he encountered in this effort would require a more detailed analysis than is appropriate here. "It isn't all gold, but there is gold in it," Frege had written to his son concerning his unpublished papers. His published writings may not be all gold either, but on semantic matters Frege had seen far deeper than any of his contemporaries and had reshaped the course of the semantic tradition.

5

Meaning and ontology

O doubtful names which are like the true names, what errors and anguish have you provoked among men!

From Book of Crates, in Bertholet, *La chimie au Moyen Age,* vol. 3

In the last two decades of the nineteenth century, the semantic tradition took a turn toward ontology that would alienate those empiricists who, of course, wanted to avoid idealism, but not at the price of Platonism. A variety of issues were involved, all having to do with whether knowledge is independent of what is known: Are the objects of knowledge mind-independent? Is what we say about them mind-independent? Are their properties and relations mind-independent? These are very different questions, but the growing bias toward semantic monism tended to con-flate them.

These questions elicited two separate developments widely regarded as the landmarks of a certain type of realism. The first centered around the notions of intentionality and denoting; the second around the rights and wrongs of holism. The links between these doctrines and what came to be known as "logical atomism" is the topic of the following two chapters.

The purpose of most people involved in these developments was to oppose the growing tide of German idealism and neo-Kantianism. Wor-thy as the project was, it was marred by an excessive reliance on psychol-ogistic semantic categories and by a damaging confusion concerning the subject–predicate form. The former affected the semanticists' theory of empirical representation, leading to untold confusion via the so-called problem of our knowledge of the external world. The latter, our main interest at this point, led to the conflation of semantics with Platonism.

The subject–predicate form has been blamed for inspiring a number of philosophical confusions. Perhaps the best known is the doctrine that there are no ultimately relational propositions (that all relations are "in-ternal," as Russell put it). Russell identified the fallacy and its alleged links with idealism, and he talked more eloquently and permanently than anyone else about its dangers, which he certainly avoided. But there was a less celebrated confusion created by the tendency to think of subjects and predicates, one that Bolzano and Frege had quietly avoided but that inspired most of those who followed in Brentano's footsteps, Russell prominently included. It might be described as follows.

The notion of the "subject" of a proposition is ambiguous between the subject concept and the object(s) falling under it. The subject of *Adam is friendly,* for example, could be either the concept *Adam* or Adam himself, and Leibniz's famous predicate-in-the-subject doctrine trades on this ambiguity: Adam (but not *Adam*) must have the property of friendliness if the proposition in question is true. Taking 'subject' in its objectual sense, someone might think that all propositions must have a subject–predicate form, that there must be some thing that they are about and something they say about it. According to this picture, every basic statement can be analyzed as involving two properties, the subject concept and the predicate concept, respectively. It is essential to recognize that these concepts play very different semantic roles: The former is a mere instrument for identifying the topic or "subject" of the proposition; the latter is what is said about it. One can think of the subject concept as looking around until it finds something that exemplifies it; the latter is what the proposition talks about, its "logical subject" as Russell would call it. Once it has been found, the proposition is ready to convey its information by asserting of that object the predicate concept. In this picture of things, the penalty for vacuity of a concept depends on its location in the proposition. If the predicate concept has no instances, we have said something false; but if the subject concept has no instances, the price is far greater: We have said nothing. To put it differently, the presence of the subject concept in the proposition does not suffice to guarantee its meaningfulness; it must also have instances.

People tempted to think this way can be identified by a tendency to say things like the following: It is self-evident that every proposition must be about something; the claim that chimeras do not exist must be understood as saying about chimeras that they do not exist (and *not* about the concept of a chimera that it has no instances); quite generally, every representation and every belief must have an object other than itself; 'I am the subject of a proposition; therefore I am' is no less evident than Descartes's *Cogito.*[1] A primary character of thought, according to such persons, is its relation to objects, its aboutness. Their approach stands or falls with their understanding of the notions of *objects* and *aboutness.* In fact, it falls.

Neither Bolzano nor Frege felt the slightest temptation to reason along these lines. Frege, in particular, saw that there is no ambiguity in the notion of instantiation and analyzed existence as the having of instances. He went so far as to deny that 'All As are Bs' is about As *even* when there are As (which makes one wonder why we should examine their properties in order to see whether the claim is true). So very far was Frege from the temptation to believe in golden mountains. Others were not as lucky.

Misplaced objectivity

Five years before Frege's *Begriffsschrift* appeared, Brentano published a book destined to have a far greater influence in the nineteenth century, his *Psychology from an Empirical Standpoint.* Husserl, Stumpf, Meinong, and Twardowski drew lessons from his work that Brentano would later describe as absurd but that decisively influenced the course of twentieth-century Continental philosophy.

There are several intimate links between Brentano's work and the protoanalytic tradition that we have examined in earlier chapters. The most obvious are his hostility toward the Kantian-idealist movement and his interest in careful, patient, piecemeal intellectual work. There is also his emphasis on the metaphysical pre-Kantian, indeed, pre-Cartesian, classics, particularly evident in his attempt to link his idea of intentional in-existence with medieval themes and his attitude toward Aristotle. Finally, there is the fact that many of the main problems that concerned him were semantic.

There was a major difference, however: Brentano never quite came to grips with the fact that the problems in question were not psychological but semantic in nature, and therefore called for semantic solutions. The title of the book in which Brentano launched his new project is an accurate indication of the halfhearted, indecisive character of its break with Kant and his semantic ancestry. In fact, Brentano thought that logic itself derived its justification from psychology,[2] and he was greatly upset when his most distinguished disciple, Husserl, took Bolzano as his model.[3]

Brentano's most influential idea was stated in a celebrated and obscure paragraph of his *Psychology:*

> Every psychic phenomenon is characterized by what the Scholastics in the Middle Ages called the intentional (and sometimes the mental) in-existence of an object, and what we should like to call, although not quite unambiguously, reference (*Beziehung*) to a content (*Inhalt*), directedness (*Richtung*) toward an object (which in this context is not to be understood as something real), or immanent objectivity (*immanente Gegen-ständlichkeit*). Every psychical phenomenon contains something as its object, though not each in the same manner. In representation something is represented, in judgment something is acknowledged or rejected . . . in desiring it is desired, etc. (*Psychologie,* p. 115)

This intentional in-existence was for Brentano the characteristic trait of mental or psychic phenomena (perhaps roughly comparable to Kant's world of inner sense) that distinguished them from physical phenomena (those present to outer sense).

Brentano's principle of classification soon became so popular that two decades later Twardowski could start one of his books with "It is one of the best known positions of psychology, hardly contested by anyone, that every mental phenomenon intends an immanent object" (*On the Content and Object of Presentations*, p. 1). And Meinong, at about the same time, could assume, "The reader will concede without reservations that it is essential to everything psychic to have an object. . . . For no one doubts that we cannot have a representation without having something to represent, and likewise that we cannot judge without having something to judge" ("Uber Gegenstände höhere Ordnung und deren Verhältnis zur inneren Wahrnehmung" [1899], *Gesamtausgabe,* vol. 2, p. 381).

But the widespread and ever-growing agreement on what Brentano had said was not matched by a corresponding agreement on what he meant. The best philosophers among his followers saw no way of accepting Brentano's premise without also accepting the view that the object that is the target of the intentional act is not a mere component of the act, but must enjoy a mind-independent form of being.[4]

The first step in the process leading to this remarkable conclusion was the elimination of Brentano's confusion between the content and the object of a representation. In a logic treatise written under Meinong's editorship, Höfler had noted that whereas the content of a representation is part of the subjective act of representation, the object, in general, is not (*Logik,* par. 6). Twardowski devoted a whole monograph to the topic, his influential *On the Content and Object of Presentations.*

A good way to introduce the content—object distinction, according to Twardowski, is to notice an ambiguity in the notion of the "represented" (*Vorgestellter*). Following Brentano, he distinguished between determining and modifying uses of adjectives. 'Old friend' is an example of the former and 'false friend' of the latter: An old friend is a kind of friend; a false one is not. Twardowski's preferred example concerns a painting of a landscape. When we talk of the painted landscape, we might mean two different things, depending on whether 'painted' is intended in an attributive or in a modifying sense. In the former case, what is meant is the actual landscape that inspired the painter's artistic product; in the latter, what is meant is the painting itself. The same ambiguity obtains in the case of representations, for when we speak of "the represented" we might mean our subjective "painting," the content, or its target, the object. A person represents to himself an object, for example,

a horse. In doing so, however, he represents to himself a mental content. The content is the copy of the horse in a sense similar to that in which the picture is the copy of the landscape. In representing to himself an object, a person represents to himself at the same time a content that is related to this object. (*On the Content and Object of Presentations,* p. 16)

Once content is distinguished from object and the former placed in the psychic act, the obvious next question is, What and where are the objects to which psychic acts refer?

Twardowski and Meinong, the best known of the first generation of Brentano's disciples, saw in his writings a revolutionary answer to that question. As they read him, Brentano had refuted Bolzano's contention that there can be representations without objects. Since all (and only) psychic phenomena have reference to an object, and since all representations are psychic phenomena, it follows that all representations must refer to objects. What these objects are depends on whether the representation is empirical. *This rose* (thought in the process of looking at a rose) is an example of an empirical representation; representations for which there is no empirical object in sight to attach to them, such as *the golden mountain* or *the round square,* are nonempirical. It is the latter kind that concerns us at this stage, but first it is worth saying a word about the former.

The limited character of the rebellion against psychologism in the Austrian realist movement is illustrated by its version of the object of perceptual representation. Instead of saying that the object of a judgment of perception such as *This is a rose* (said while looking at a rose) is the rose in question, these semanticists accepted the idealist's notion that judgments involve phenomenal elements such as colors and sounds, and then reified those categories. Semanticists and idealists agree that the judgment concerns not roses in any ordinary sense but phenomenal colors, tactile sensations, and the like. But idealists, reasonably enough, can make no sense of phenomenal qualities in a mind-independent world; semanticists say they can. For all their virtues of rigor and insight, Brentano's writings must be apportioned much of the blame for the sense-datum approach to epistemology.

If in the field of empirical representation Austrian realism reified psychologism, in the field of representations without empirical objects it ontologized semantics. Where Brentano's sense of proportion had tempered his bold premises with a degree of hesitation and ambiguity, his disciples relentlessly pursued and embraced the consequences of those bold premises. They did what disciples tend to do: They reduced his system to absurdity. Twardowski's writings are perhaps the first to display with full clarity the problems that arise from a wholehearted endorsement of Brentano's hesitant views on representation.

Twardowski argued that, appearances notwithstanding, no representation, not even the inconsistent ones, can be without a corresponding object. Consider the worst possible candidate, *the round square.* Superficially one might think there is no such thing. Yet the fact that sentences such as 'The round square does not exist' are meaningful entails that, in some sense, there must be a round square; we must be talking about something when we deny the existence of the object in question. One could hardly ask for a clearer example of the subject–predicate fallacy described early in this chapter and subsequently reproduced by Meinong, Moore, and Russell.[5]

At this point emerged a familiar jungle: The objects of representation, according to Twardowski, may exist or not exist and be real or unreal. A (phenomenal) tree, a grief, an act of representation are real; an absence, a possibility, and the content of a representation are not. But what is unreal may exist: We may say truly (if somewhat Germanically) that there exists a lack of money; hence, an unreal thing must exist (*On the Content and Object of Presentations,* pp. 33–4).

Austrian realism, the doctrine that objectuality is a necessary condition for realism, soon found an echo in England. It is hard to judge the extent to which Moore's and Russell's shift from idealism to Austrian realism was influenced by the Brentano school. There is no question, however, that both Moore and Russell were familiar with and admired the achievements of that movement.[6]

Moore's and Russell's rebellion against idealism in 1898 started with what Russell described as the "distinction between act and object in our apprehending of things" (*The Problems of Philosophy,* p. 42).[7] Moore's "The Refutation of Idealism" of 1903 was based largely on the idea that for all the lip service idealists pay to the content–object distinction, they treat the object as immanent to the representation. And he drew with more sharpness and emphasis than Brentano the conclusion that phenomenal qualities (sense data) have a mind-independent life. Thanks to Moore it became commonplace in Anglo-Saxon philosophy to think that physical objects are invisible and that they are best construed as highly theoretical and bold inferences out of "the given."

Russell's early writings were less concerned with matters of empirical knowledge and displayed instead the consequences of the Austrian-realist doctrine on so-called objectless representations. In fact, one of the best-known statements of the Austrian-realist position on that issue occurs in Russell's *Principles,* in which he wrote:

Being is that which belongs to every conceivable term, to every possible object of thought – in short to everything that can possibly occur in any proposition, true or false, and to all such propositions themselves. . . . "A is not" must always be either false or meaningless. For if A were nothing, it could not be said not to be; "A is not" implies that there is a term A whose being is denied, and hence that A is. Thus unless "A is not" be an empty sound, it must be false – whatever A may be, it certainly is. Numbers, the Homeric gods, relations, chimeras and four-dimensional spaces all have being, for if they were not entities of a kind, we could make no propositions about them. (p. 449)

Oddly enough, this passage and many others like it appeared in a book that also contained the refutation of the view that every representation must have an object (Russell's first theory of denoting). Before we examine (in Chapter 6) this peculiar episode and its sequel, we must begin by introducing Russell's basic semantic ideas and their link with realism.

The propositional complex

In "Meinong's Theory of Complexes and Assumptions" (1904), Russell stated a thesis that he had "been led to accept . . . by Mr. G. E. Moore" and that was, in fact, one of Meinong's main contentions: "that every presentation and every belief must have an object other than itself and . . . extra-mental" (*Essays in Analysis,* p. 21). We have just met the extra-mental objects of representation; let us turn to the objects of belief.

Like Bolzano, Russell had come to realize the importance of distinguishing between propositional attitudes that pertain to psychology and their targets, which do not. But unlike his illustrious predecessors, Russell never came to grips with the fact that meaning cannot be constituted out of fragments of the real world. The psychologistic alternative to semantic monism led him (around 1910) to a self-destructive semantic standpoint that had no room for the notion of what a statement says.

Russell's semantic picture circa 1900 was, roughly speaking, what remains of Frege's when the domain of sense is dismissed and that of meaning is extended in a natural manner. Whereas Frege's semantic dualism associated with each grammatical unit two different semantic elements, a sense and a meaning, Russell always (except for a rather brief interlude between 1902 and 1905) associated a unique semantic object with each grammatical unit; when such objects joined with others to constitute a proposition, he naturally called them the "meanings" of the corresponding expressions in the sentence.

Originally, the main function of Russell's meanings was that of Frege's senses, to act as the building blocks out of which the propositional complex was constituted. Thus, Frege and Russell were in verbal agreement when they said that the proposition expressed by 'John loves Mary' has as constituents the semantic correlates (meanings, senses) of 'John', 'x loves y', and 'Mary'. But Russell's meanings were not at all like Frege's senses; in fact, they were hard to distinguish from Frege's meanings (*Bedeutungen*). If 'John' and 'Mary' are proper names, their Russellian meanings are John and Mary, and the Russellian meaning of 'loves' (or 'x loves y') is the concept *love* or x *loves* y, which is for Russell something as much a part of the external world as John and Mary. Like Frege, Russell thought of properties and relations as unsaturated.[8]

The central difference between Frege's "realm of meanings" and Russell's is that Frege's concepts remain forever incomplete and unsaturated, whereas in Russell's more permissive semantics the concept's need for completion is rather frequently fulfilled. Russellian concepts are saturated with objects – eventually, with objects of the appropriate types. The outcome of this process is not an evaluation (Russell's concepts are not functions in Frege's sense), but another object – a whole that displays a peculiar sort of unity in which the concept and all of the saturating objects appear as constituents. This is the Russellian proposition or propositional *complex*.

From the very beginning, in what the idealists regarded as a decisive inconsistency, Russell insisted on the element of unity that semantic complexes generally exhibit. He was particularly impressed by Meinong's "careful attempt" to deal with the very delicate problem of the unity of the complex. Russell agreed that

a melody of four notes is not a fifth note, and generally a complex is not formed by adding an object to the constituents . . . for red, green and difference do not make 'red differs from green'. . . . It is this special and apparently indefinable kind of unity which I should propose to employ in characterizing the notion of a complex. The kind of unity in question belongs, as is evident, to all propositions. ("Meinong's Theory of Complexes and Assumptions," *Essays in Analysis,* p. 28)

Thus, what we believe, assume, or deny when we believe, assume, or deny that red differs from green is a single thing: a complex, mind-independent entity that has as constituents the meanings of the words that make up the sentence in which we express the belief, assumption, or denial. For example, in his *Theory of Knowledge* Russell examined the difference between such phrases as 'Beggars are riders' and 'Beggars would be riders':

We may now add the question and the imperative, "are beggars riders?" and "beggars shall be riders." In all these, the relation between beggars and riders is the same; but in the first it is asserted, in the second suggested as a consequence of a hypothesis, in the third the object of a doubt, and in the fourth the object of a volition. We should not say that these four phrases "have the same meaning," yet they all have something very important in common. The word "proposition" is a natural one to use for expressing what they all have in common: we may say that they express different attitudes towards the same "proposition." (p. 107)

Compare this view with one that was part of Frege's early semantics. In *Begriffsschrift* Frege had explained that his assertion sign included symbols for two quite different operations:

The horizontal stroke that is part of the sign ⊢ *combines the signs that follow it into a totality, and the affirmation expressed by the vertical stroke at the left end of the horizontal one refers to this totality.* Let us call the horizontal stroke the *content stroke* and the vertical stroke the *judgment stroke*. (van Heijenoort, *From Frege to Gödel*, p. 12)

By way of example Frege considered the judgment "Opposite magnetic poles attract each other," which we may represent as

$$\vdash A.$$

The expression

$$-A$$

will not express this judgment; it is to produce in the reader merely the idea of the mutual attraction of opposite magnetic poles, say in order to derive consequences from it and to test by means of these whether the thought is correct. When the vertical stroke is omitted, we express ourselves *paraphrastically*, using the words 'the circumstance that' or 'the proposition that'. (van Heijenoort, *From Frege to Gödel*, p. 11)

Thus, if 'a' means an object and 'f' a concept,

$$\vdash f(a)$$

symbolizes the judgment that a is f, whereas

$$-f(a)$$

symbolizes the semantic content of that judgment. To make this distinction clearer, Frege considered a language in which a proposition like 'Opposite magnetic poles attract each other' is expressed as 'That opposite magnetic poles attract each other is a fact'.

To be sure, one can distinguish between subject and predicate here too, if one wishes to do so, but the subject contains the whole content, and the predicate serves only to turn the content into a judgment. *Such a language would have only a single predicate for all judgments, namely, 'is a fact'. . . . Our ideography is a language of this sort, and in it the sign ⊢ is the common predicate for all judgments.* (van Heijenoort, *From Frege to Gödel*, pp. 12–13)

According to this, a proper translation of $\vdash f(a)$ would be

It is a fact that a is f,

or

$\vdash$ that a is f.

Frege's purpose was the same as Russell's: to detach a propositional attitude (in this, assertion) from its target. But in Frege's case the target is a complex of elements, none of which could be regarded as part of the real world. In Russell's case, matters were otherwise.

Consider, for example, the proposition that Mont Blanc is more than four thousand meters high. We may not be surprised to find the concept *height* in it. But when Russell explained to Frege his theory of the proposition in 1904, Frege was shocked to find Mont Blanc among its constituents. In his response, Frege explained in a friendly way that

Mont Blanc itself, with all its snowfields, is not a constituent of the thought (*Gedanke*) that Mont Blanc is more than 4000 meters high. . . . The sense of the word 'moon' is a constituent of the thought that the moon is smaller than the earth. The moon itself (i.e., the meaning of the word 'moon') is not part of the sense of the word 'moon', for then it would also be a constituent of that thought. (*Wiss. Briefwechsel*, p. 245)

To this Russell replied: "I believe that Mont Blanc itself, in spite of all of its snowfields, is a constituent of what is strictly speaking asserted through the sentence 'Mont Blanc is more than 4000 meters high'" (Frege, *Wiss. Briefwechsel*, p. 250). What is Mont Blanc, snowfields and all, doing there?

In Russell's day (as in ours) there were many people who could make no sense of a question about the existence or reality of *X*s unless this was meant as a question concerning much larger contexts involving *X*. Russell was certainly not among them. He had a criterion of existence that was entirely independent of linguistic, propositional, or any other contexts: acquaintance. Russell was (often) convinced that there are many things we are not acquainted with; our knowledge of them is inferential and speculative. But he clearly thought that acquaintance was the touchstone of reality, so that the failure of acquaintance for *every* element of a category (e.g., classes or propositions) should count as strong evidence against the ontological legitimacy of the category. Under the circumstances, a natural approach to the question of propositions was to ask what it is that we are sometimes acquainted with, that we may believe and disbelieve, accept or reject, assume or question.

Moore had an answer. Propositions, he explained, are just plain facts. The proposition *Brutus killed Caesar* is simply the fact that Brutus killed Caesar, a circumstance with which at least Brutus and Caesar were acquainted. And if we think of this fact as a complex, it is natural to think also that Brutus and Caesar are themselves constituents of it. Since the fact in some obvious sense also involves the relation of *killing,* we may also say that *it* is yet another constituent of the fact. Now we have all the elements that Russell thought we should encounter in the proposition *Brutus killed Caesar.*

From this standpoint, what we say (when true) is no different from what happens. Therefore, in his article "Truth and Falsity" for Baldwin's *Dictionary of Philosophy and Psychology,* Moore argued against the "common supposition" that the truth of a proposition consists in some relation of correspondence that it bears to reality:

It is essential to the [correspondence] theory that a truth should differ in some specific way from the reality, in relation to which its truth is to consist. . . . It is the impossibility of finding any such difference between a truth and the reality to which it is supposed to correspond which refutes the theory. (p. 717)

Moore wondered, what could this difference be? Clearly displaying the blind spot for the domain of senses that was also characteristic of the Austrian-realist movement, Moore saw no more than two possible answers: (a) Propositions are, unlike facts, linguistic objects, that is, sentences, and (b) propositions are, unlike facts, mental copies of reality. He rightly objected that neither of these solutions would do, for the sentence merely derives its truth ground from something else, what it signifies, while the second alternative is based on a confusion between the content of a belief and its object. Thus, he concluded, "It seems plain that a truth differs in no respect from the reality to which it was supposed merely to correspond" (p. 717).

Russell thought this was very convincing, except for one small point that kept growing as time went by: If a true proposition is just the fact thought to make it true, what then is a false proposition? If truths are facts, what are falsehoods? What is it that we believe when we believe that Caesar killed Brutus? As we shall see (Chapter 8), this question would lead, by 1910, to the conclusion that there are no propositions – hence to the self-destruction of Russellian semantics.

The particular version of semantic monism endorsed by Moore and Russell was motivated primarily by a desire to avoid psychologism at all costs and by an inability to see that in semantic matters there could be anything between our subjective representations and the world.Their preference for realism required that propositions and their constituents be things we represent rather than representations; their blindness to the domain of Fregean sense forced the propositional constituents to be part of the ultimate furniture of the world. As it turned out, this drawback would be fatal to their realistic intentions. Like any other reasonable philosopher, Russell eventually felt the force of Kant's notion of constitution as applied to meanings; but his inability to detach meaning from the world turned that insight into another version of the old idealist project to construct the "external" world. Before looking at some of the elements in the long sequence of Russell's concessions to idealism, we should first examine briefly the nature of his original challenge to it.

Realism and holism

Few topics have elicited more heat and less light among philosophers during the past two centuries than the subject of realism. The developments we are in the process of reviewing are widely regarded as relevant to that issue. Russell and Moore are usually taken to be among the most extreme supporters of the realist position by those who challenge it. Yet Russell himself once said, "I do not regard the issue between realists and their opponents as a fundamental one" ("Logical Atomism" [1924]; *Russell's Logical Atomism,* p. 143). He may have come to think that to the extent that realism is defined as a doctrine about what is "real" or what "corresponds" to thought in the "external world," the hopeless obscurity of those phrases makes it impossible to formulate a doctrine on which it is worth taking a stand.

This difficulty is highlighted by the fact that realists and idealists can agree on virtually every verbal response they give to specific questions of reality: Russell once noted that Berkeley would surely agree that tables are real (*The Problems of Philosophy,* p. 15); Kant granted the independence of physical objects from mind and endorsed the correspondence theory of truth;[9] James endorsed the correspondence of thought and fact as the obvious essence of truth; and (as we shall see in Chapter 12) during his most intimate flirtation with phenomenalism, Carnap granted the existence and reality of every theoretical entity postulated by science. If these philosophers may legitimately talk like realists about reality and existence, what is it that divides them from the others?

Russell thought that "the fundamental doctrine of the realistic position, as I understand it, is the doctrine that relations are 'external' " ("The Basis of Realism," p. 158). And he added that "all arguments based on the contention that knowing makes a difference to what is known, or implies a community or interaction between knower and known, rest upon the internal view of relations" (p. 160). Elsewhere he explained:

The question of relations is one of the most important that arise in philosophy, as most other issues turn on it: monism and pluralism; the question whether anything is wholly true except the whole of truth, or wholly real except the whole of reality; idealism and realism, in some of their forms; perhaps the very existence of philosophy as a subject distinct from science and possessing a method of its own. ("Logical Atomism," *Russell's Logical Atomism,* p. 154)

The heart of the logical atomism that Moore and Russell started to develop in 1898 was, in fact, a rejection of the doctrine of internal relations. What exactly were they denying, and what was its link with realism?

Russell's official version of the doctrine of internal relations described it as the unexciting view that relations are not independent, since they can be reduced to properties. Bradley had argued that every relation "essentially penetrates the being of its terms, and, in this sense, is intrinsical" (*Appearance and Reality,* p. 347), and Russell naturally took him to mean that all relations are like *love* in that they alter the terms they relate and consist, in the end, in features of those terms. The doctrine has obvious links with Leibniz's monadology, and these were amply explored in Russell's *Critical Exposition of the Philosophy of Leibniz,* in which he explained that faulty logic and an excessive reliance on the subject–predicate form are the basis of idealism. During the first decade of this century, much of Russell's philosophical activity seems to have been guided by this interpretation of the issue; in this period he devoted a great deal of time to exposing as absurd the idea that all terms have constituents that somehow correspond to the relations in which they stand.

If this were all there were to the doctrine of internal relations, both it and the realism that opposed it would deserve to be placed in the museum of thankfully forgotten ideas. But there is a second interpretation of the idealist rejection of independence that makes Russell look far less silly. It is not that relational statements are to be analyzed as of the subject–predicate form, but that both relational and subject–predicate statements are misunderstood when seen as composites built up from detachable, independent semantic parts and that the only sense these parts can make is as unsuccessful efforts to detach portions of some broader wholes.

The presence of this holistic (or, as Russell called it, "monistic") element in idealism is repeatedly acknowledged by Moore and Russell in their specific objections to British habits. For example, in a discussion of Joachim's *The Nature of Truth,* after noting with evident glee that monists call pluralists like him "crude," Russell added:

The uninitiated might imagine that a whole is made up of parts, each of which is a genuine constituent of the whole, and is something on its own account. But this view is crude. The parts of a whole are not self-subsistent, and have no being except as parts. We can never enumerate parts $a, b, c, \ldots$ of a whole $\ldots$ the part a is not quite real. Thus W is a whole of parts all of which are not quite real. It follows that W is not quite really a whole of parts. ("On the Nature of Truth," p. 31)

In an exchange with Bradley in *Mind,* Russell formulated the main difference between them as follows: "I do not admit that [complexes] are not composed of their constituents; and what is more to the purpose, I do not admit that their constituents cannot be considered truly unless we remember that they are their constituents" ("Some Explanations in Reply to Mr. Bradley," p. 373). Bradley replied that "a relation apart from terms is to me unmeaning or self-destructive, and is an idea produced by an indefensible abstraction" ("Reply to Mr. Russell's Explanations," p. 76). A few years earlier Joachim had posed a key question: How does one have access to the constituents of the atomist's propositions?

Greenness is, for the theory [i.e., Russell's and Moore's theory] an ultimate entity in the nature of things, which has its being absolutely in itself. How, under these circumstances, greenness can yet sometimes so far depart from its sacred aloofness as to be apprehended (sensated or conceived); and how, when this takes place, the sensating or conceiving subject is assured that its immaculate *perseitas* is still preserved – these are questions to which apparently the only answer is the dogmatic reiteration of the supposed fact. ("The Nature of Truth," p. 42)

As we shall see in Chapter 7, the same question had recently been asked more artfully and powerfully by Poincaré, concerning geometric primitives. Russell's witty rejoinder to Joachim is worth recording:

Mr. Joachim alleges that the plain man is on his side. I have been tempted to ask some plain man what he thought greenness was, but have been restrained by the fear of being thought insane. Mr. Joachim, however, seems to have been bolder. Considering the difficulty of finding a really plain man nowadays, I presume he asked his scout, who apparently replied: "Well, sir, greenness is to me the name of a complex fact, the factors of which essentially and reciprocally determine one another. And if you, sir, choose to select one factor out of the complex, and to call it greenness, I will not dispute about the term, for I know my place, sir; but as thus isolated, your greenness is an abstraction, which emphatically, in itself and as such, is not *there* or *anywhere*." ("The Nature of Truth," p. 529)

Finally, we may note that in his "On the Nature of Truth," Russell noted the interconnectedness of two issues: the mind dependence of truth and the plurality of truths. And then he added that the latter question seemed to him "the more fundamental." The idealist version of monism entails "that nothing is wholly true except the whole truth, and that what seem to be isolated truths, such as 2 + 2 = 4, are really only true in the sense that they form part of the system which is the whole truth" (p. 29). When statements are "artificially isolated they are bereft of aspects and relations which make them part of the whole truth, and are thus altered from what they are in the system" (p. 29). If we substitute references to meaning for references to truth in these remarks, we obtain a reasonably good formulation of semantic holism. The idealists themselves occasionally performed that substitution. Joachim, for example, explained that the whole truth is an organic unity or significant whole "such that all its constituent elements . . . reciprocally determine one another's being as contributory features in a single concrete meaning" ("The Nature of Truth," p. 66).

It would therefore appear that the difference between realists and idealists is that one group insists on the *independence* of certain entities and the other rejects them as "indefensible" or "false" abstractions. The preceding remarks allow us to make a more definite statement concerning the type of independence involved. Consider a relational statement such as

(*) *a* is heavier than *b*.

Russell and Moore would say this asserts that

(**) The relation *is heavier than* holds between *a* and *b*.

Idealists (and, as we shall see, positivists in the 1920s) felt uncomfortable with this type of claim and usually refused to endorse it. But there is really no reason why they should not have. As the instances of Kant, James, and Carnap indicate, many of those who grant the idealists' basic points may accept these realistic-sounding utterances under an interpretation acceptable to them – and in later decades many would avail themselves of this possibility to endorse an idealistic philosophy and a realist rhetoric. How does the rhetoric differ from the reality?

The idealist who was the official target of Russell's atomism was, as we know, someone who explained both (**) and (*) as the attribution of certain properties to *a* and *b* – and on this debate Russell and Moore were clearly on the right side of the issue. The idealism we have seen reflected in our recent quotations does not disagree with atomism on how to analyze or reduce (*) however, but only on how to understand (**). For this second kind of idealist, (**) makes sense only insofar as it is taken to mean what (*) says. But for the atomist it is through (**) that we acquire a proper understanding of (*), at least in the sense that (**) gives us a better picture of what the claim is. Thus, both holists and atomists will agree in describing a particular situation as one in which the relation *being greater than* holds between two objects. But holists will explain this as no more than a restatement of the claim that one of those objects is greater than the other, whereas atomists will think they have uncovered an element, no less real than the objects under consideration, that is present "out there" and somehow gathers them into a particular type of factual or propositional unit. Notice that even this "atomistic" language could be endorsed by holists, provided that it were properly explained. The difference cannot be stated in any particular claim about what is or is not real, but emerges only when we consider what we might call the order of semantic explanation. (This point will be explained in greater detail in Chapter 12.)

Perhaps the best way to distinguish holists from atomists is to follow them in their divergent explanatory paths: Holists will explain the attribution of relations and properties to objects in terms of the truth of the sentences stating those facts, and then they will offer an account of the truth of those sentences that does not appeal to semantic features of their constituents. They will, for example, agree that *heavier than* may relate only physical objects. But they will read this as a peculiar statement of the point that 'is heavier than' makes sense only when flanked by names of physical objects; they will not be tempted to conjure images of an unsaturated entity anxious to grab two physical things in order to find semantic fulfillment. Atomists, in contrast, will take the explanatory path in the opposite direction. They will explain (*) through (**) and will then have to offer some noncircular account of how they have access to the semantic correlates of the parts of (**), its "indefinables." That is why, when asking about the meaning of indefinables, idealists may appeal to the sentence but atomists may not. Atomists will have to discover a prepropositional link with the constituents of propositions. This is the problem of the semantic pineal gland, raised by Joachim and Poincaré: How do we come to grasp the semantic units that lie at the basis of the atomists' construal of the propositional complex? It was on this very question that the atomist picture of knowledge came to grief in an episode that deserves separate treatment (Chapter 8).

Russell's semantic pineal gland was acquaintance. We understand sentences because we understand their constituent phrases, and we understand *them* because we stand in a very remarkable direct relation to the meaning of those terms: Those meanings are as present to us as an object was for Kant, when given in sensible intuition. Acquaintance is the unmoved mover of Russell's semantics, its ultimate explanatory factor, the crucial difference between his semantics and that of idealists, and, in the end, the cause of its failure. Acquaintance remained at the heart of Russell's philosophy for decades; yet in the years between his conversion to realism and his encounter with Wittgenstein, he slowly but constantly withdrew in the direction of an idealist semantics. Considerations relating to the paradox would soon lead Russell to argue that at least some, perhaps all, properties are "false abstractions" and that they may be properly treated only in broader propositional contexts.[10] Similar concessions will be examined in the next chapter. Most of them were guided by a discovery that Russell made while studying an aspect of the problem of intentionality, to which we now turn.

6

On denoting

Can we put the problem of philosophy thus? Let us write out all we think; then part of this will contain meaningless terms only there to connect (unify) the rest. I.e., some is there on its own account, the rest for the sake of the first. Which is that first, and how far does it extend?

Ramsey, Undated manuscript (ASP)

It is natural to think that the meaning of 'blue' or of 'the taste of a pine-apple' is an entity in the world with which we are sometimes acquainted, a color or a taste. For such cases it seems explanatory to say that to know a meaning is to be acquainted with what is meant. The same seems to apply also to proper names such as 'Scott'; to know what is meant by them, in the "strictest" sense, is to be acquainted with those objects.

But this simple "museum" semantics does not readily extend to most other cases. A friendship and a promise are things that, in some sense, we can be witness to; but it no longer seems explanatory to say that to understand those expressions is to be acquainted with anything in partic-ular. And what is it that we are acquainted with when after reading Jaeger's *Paideia* we have grasped the sense of that Greek notion? Indeed, the terms whose semantics are not plausibly explained through acquain-tance are of both general and singular types. Prominent cases among the latter are Bolzano's the 'golden mountain' and Meinong's the 'round square'. We surely understand them; but, once again, what worldly ele-ment are we acquainted with as we grasp their meaning?

One might take these difficult cases as evidence that the museum theory of meaning is simply an error, that it is not valid even in those simple cases where it seems appealing. Or one might insist on the basic idea and look for ways to reinterpret the recalcitrant areas of semantics to make them fit into the semantic monist pattern. The episodes that we are about to review constitute the first crisis within the semantic monist movement, arising when Russell recognized that Twardowski's and Meinong's solutions were more than an honest person could take. Russell's solution was not a challenge to the monist framework, however, but simply an effort to rescue it from the immense implausibility into which it had been cast by its Austrian proponents. The device he invented in order to rescue that semantic picture from its well-deserved demise is what we shall call the "incomplete symbol strategy." Russell's problems would have vanished had he chosen to distinguish meaning from world, as Frege had. But nothing would move him from his conviction that the ultimate furniture of the world was also the ultimate furniture of semantics.

The discovery of denoting: knowledge by description

Kant's opinion that there can be no knowledge without a blend of concept and intuition was a variation on a long-standing theme that would occur, once again, in the theories of propositional knowledge developed in the semantic tradition. In semantic terms, the question Kant had addressed concerned the role played by intuition (or acquaintance) in those propositions or judgments that express our knowledge.

The overwhelming weight of tradition had been in favor of a very tight link between those two elements. Aristotle had said that in sensual knowledge the sense contains the sensual object without its matter, so that, as Brentano put it, "the object which is thought is in the thinking intellect" (*Psychology,* p. 88). Aquinas claimed that the object thought is intentionally in the thinking subject, and Brentano derived from this and related ideas his own doctrine of the intentional in-existence of the objects of knowledge in its acts. Leibniz had explained that to have an idea of an object it is not necessary to be actually thinking about it but only to have the ability or "faculty" to do so. Since we can be affected by objects of which we have no idea, this faculty must be something more than mere receptivity, and, Leibniz thought, it must involve our possession of a method to generate the represented object in a way *"which not merely leads me to the thing but also expresses it"* ("What Is an Idea?" [1678], *Philosophical Papers and Letters,* p. 207). Finally, he explained, *A* expresses *B* when "there are relations (*habitudines*) which correspond to the relations of the thing expressed"; for example, "the projective delineation on a plane expresses a solid, speech expresses thoughts and truths" (p. 207).[1] Hume, in turn, believed that "it is impossible for us to *think* of any thing, which we have not antecedently *felt*" (*Enquiry,* sec. 7, pt. 1, p. 41). In Chapter 1 we saw Kant claiming that in order to represent, a representation had to be (in effect) isomorphic with its object.

Marty and Twardowski examined at length Brentano's idea of "improper representation" in order to establish that in the end Bolzano had been wrong in denying that "there corresponds to every part of the content of a representation a certain part of the object which is represented through it" (Twardowski, *On the Content and Object of Presentations,* p. 88).[2] In addition to the principle of the intentionality of con-

sciousness, phenomenologists introduced the "principle of phenomenological accessibility" (Becker, *Mathematische Existenz,* p. 502), according to which no state of affairs is thinkable that would be in principle
unknowable, in the sense of not being presentable in intuition. Finally, as
we shall soon see, Wittgenstein argued that the form of an object must be
contained in a proposition about it. One is not surprised to see him turn
against Russell's doctrine of knowledge by description (*Philosophical
Grammar,* pp. 163–71); this will be discussed in Chapter 13. In all of these
cases it is being assumed that a singular representation can represent its
object only if it satisfies a condition that makes knowledge by description
virtually impossible; for it is required that the source and the target of the
referential relation be in some respect identical – if not in content at least
in structure or formally. Barring semantic miracles it would appear that
this correspondence is possible only through the mediation of something
like intuition or acquaintance.

This common assumption seemed reasonable so long as one did not
try to spell out in detail how to make sense of standard knowledge claims
upon its basis. But when, in the second half of the nineteenth century,
semanticists turned to the task of explaining the character of mathematical knowledge, they found the assumption hard to live with.

One of the main problems examined in Husserl's *Philosophie der
Arithmetik* was that even though mathematical knowledge is our clearest
instance of sound knowledge, we can have accurate, reliable, (isomorphic) representation of its topic, numbers, only for the case of very
small numbers. We can represent accurately, for example, a class of three
objects by looking at or imagining three cats; but who can represent a
chiliagon with similar accuracy? In view of this failure of representation,
Husserl thought, one may well wonder how rigorous arithmetical knowledge is possible.

In order to solve this problem, Husserl used a distinction he had
learned in Brentano's lectures, between "proper and improper or symbolic representations. I am indebted to [Brentano] for a deeper understanding of the eminent importance of improper representations for all of
our psychical life, a point which no one before him had fully grasped to
the best of my knowledge" (*Philosophie der Arithmetik,* p. 193). In
agreement with this distinction, content can be given to us in two ways,
directly or indirectly. When we see a house, for example, a content is
given directly to us, and we then say that we have a proper representation of the house. But when the content is given through a description
like 'the house that is on such-and-such corner', what we have is a symbolic representation.[3]

A few years later, in his "Psychologische Studien zur elementaren Logik" (1894), Husserl elaborated this distinction:

There is a distinction between those representations that are intuitions and those that are not. Certain psychic experiences, known in general as "representations," have the peculiarity that they do not include their "objects" as immanent content (hence, not in actual consciousness) but *merely intend* the object in a sense that is still to be characterized more precisely. For the time being the following definition, which is obviously suitable but deliberately too complicated, will suffice. "Mere intending" means: to aim at a content not given in consciousness by means of one that is so given. (*Aufsätze und Rezensionen (1890–1910)*, p. 107)

One can see Brentano's hand in the hesitation between content and object that lends a characteristic air of ambiguity to Husserl's posture on the issue between realism and idealism. The point here, however, is that Husserl was distinguishing between intuitions that "actually embrace within themselves" the objects (or perhaps the contents) that they intend and a second strange category of improper, symbolic representations that do not embrace their contents or objects but point to them, as it were, from afar or, to coin a word, "denote" them.

Husserl's solution to the problem of arithmetical knowledge was to say that it often relies on symbolic representation. A large and remarkably obscure part of *Philosophie der Arithmetik* is devoted to an explanation of what these representations are and how they work; but the whole explanation collapses as soon as one distinguishes between psychology and logic, as Husserl would endeavor to do a few years later. In a retrospective essay written around 1913, Husserl referred with scorn to "the customary appeal in the Brentano school to [improper] representation (*uneigentliches Vorstellen*)," which, he now said, "could not help. That was only a phrase in the place of a solution" (*Introduction to the Logical Investigations*, p. 35). Frege had told that much to Husserl in 1894, in his review of the *Philosophie der Arithmetik* (*Collected Papers*, pp. 195–209). And by 1902 Russell had come to the same conclusion.

The analogy between Russell and Husserl's problems circa 1900 is quite striking. To begin with, mathematics provided in both cases the original stock of problems that led them to what both called "logical" investigations. Next, within mathematics itself, the foundational problems that initially seemed to trouble them most involved the representation of numbers and, in particular, the difficulty of representing the very large ones. As we are about to see, one of the central problems in Russell's early philosophy of mathematics was to account for our ability to have knowledge concerning infinite numbers, especially that knowledge recently uncovered by Cantor in his theory of the transfinite. Finally, in both cases the solutions offered appealed to a form of representation that was very unlike what it represented.

The differences between Russell and Husserl are, of course, equally marked. The most prominent among them is, perhaps, that Russell's strategy for dealing with his foundational problems was, from the beginning, to focus on the target of all epistemic attitudes, the proposition.

It is Russell's picture of the proposition at this time (circa 1900) that helps explain why *he* thought there was a major problem concerning our knowledge about infinity; for he had tacitly assumed that in order for a proposition to be about a particular entity, the entity itself had to be a constituent of the proposition. This doctrine of *confined aboutness,* as we shall call it, is only an extreme form of the intimate link between intuition and propositional knowledge that was described earlier in this section. It isn't hard to see how knowledge of infinity might become a problem on the assumption of confined aboutness. Consider, for example, the proposition that every natural number is either odd or even. How can we know this, Russell wondered, given that it is a proposition about an infinitely complex object and given also that our finite minds can understand only objects of finite complexity?

We know that Russell (like Brentano and Husserl) had carefully read Bolzano's *Paradoxes of the Infinite* and that he was struck by Bolzano's account of classes. According to Bolzano, classes are to be understood in terms of the concept of conjunction. To say that John and Mary are two, for example, is to assign a certain property to the class *John and Mary.* This class is a rather peculiar entity, a conjunction not of propositions but of objects. But Russell soon discovered that this account posed a problem for the case of infinite classes;[4] for if an infinite class is an infinite conjunction, it would appear that a proposition about infinite classes must be infinitely complex and hence beyond human comprehension. That is why the "theory of *and* applies practically [i.e., to human beings, though not to gods and angels] only to finite numbers" (*Principles,* p. 134).

At this point Russell turned to language for a clue. How do we, in fact, talk about infinite classes? Certainly not by means of infinitely long conjunctions. In fact, we frequently do so by means of quantification, as in 'All numbers are even or odd'. Perhaps, he thought, the solution to the problem of propositions about infinity lay in a correct theory of quantification. Thus, in 1900 Russell wrote to Moore:

Have you ever considered the meaning of *any?* I find it to be the fundamental problem for mathematical philosophy. E.g., 'Any number is less by one than another number'. Here *any number* cannot be a new concept, distinct from the particular numbers, for only these fulfill the above proposition. But can *any number* be an infinite disjunction? And, if so, what is the ground of the proposition? The problem is the general one as to what is meant by any member of any defined class. I have tried many theories without success. (Letter to Moore of 16 August 1900, Russell Archives)

Standard logic, Russell thought, was not much help. In his opinion, logicians from Bradley to Frege had given far too much importance to the role of concepts in quantification and had failed to determine what quantified propositions are *about*. Russell thought it self-evident that they are about the objects over which one quantifies and not about the correlated concepts (*Principles*, p. 90), since otherwise they would convey no knowledge about the objects in question.

Russell looked at the problem of quantification in the typical pre-Fregean fashion. For him, quantifier words such as 'all' and 'some' were to be interpreted not in isolation but in connection with the attached predicate. Whereas for Frege 'all' and 'some' were names of two specific second-order concepts, for Russell they had no meaning in isolation and were to be treated as fragments of larger grammatical units such as 'all men' and 'some men'. *These* were the grammatical units whose semantic analysis was "the fundamental problem of mathematical philosophy" in 1900. Russell's solution to that problem was his first theory of quantification, better known as his first theory of denoting. It disclosed, he thought, "the inmost secret of our power to deal with infinity" (*Principles*, p. 73).

As developed in the early drafts of *The Principles of Mathematics* (written about 1901), the doctrine of denoting is the theory of five words: 'all', 'every', 'any', 'some', and 'a', all of them quantifier words.[5] Definite descriptions were included almost as an afterthought, in the final stages of the manuscript, and there is reason to think that this thought was rather brief and uncommitted, as we shall see. What Russell had come to see in 1901–2 was that perhaps he had been wrong when he told Moore that *any number* cannot be a concept. Perhaps the reason we can deal with infinity in propositions of finite complexity is that quantifier expressions signify the presence of a very peculiar sort of concept, one that, unlike "normal" concepts, does not just sit there in the proposition, either linking its partners into a unified complex or allowing itself to be the focus of referential attention. Instead, these "denoting concepts," as Russell called them, play an altruistic semantic role in that they somehow manage to refer to (or, as he sometimes puts it, "indicate") other objects, thus allowing the proposition to be about things other than its constituents. Here is Russell's introduction of his new and revolutionary idea:

The notion of denoting, like most of the notions of logic, has been obscured hitherto by an undue admixture of psychology. There is a sense in which *we* denote, when we point or describe, or employ words as symbols for concepts. . . . But the fact that description is possible – that we are able, by the employment of concepts, to designate a thing which is not a concept – is due to a logical relation between some concepts and some terms, in virtue of which such concepts inherently and logically *denote* such terms. It is this sense of denoting which is here in question. . . . A concept *denotes* when, if it occurs in a proposition, the proposition is not *about* the concept, but about a term connected in a certain peculiar way with the concept. If I say "I met a man," the proposition is not about *a man*: this is a concept which does not walk the streets, but lives in the shadowy limbo of the logic-books. What I met was a thing, not a concept, an actual man with a tailor and a bank-account or a public-house and a drunken wife. (*Principles,* p. 53)

At this point the stage was set for one of Russell's most celebrated and important distinctions, that between knowledge by acquaintance and knowledge by description. Even though, as Russell still thought, we can understand a proposition only when we are acquainted with all of its constituents, we can not only understand but also know propositions that are *about* things with which we are not acquainted. If I can have knowledge of other minds, of unobservable particles and abstract entities beyond acquaintance, it must be because something I am acquainted with can make some propositions refer to such things. "An object," Russell explains,

may be *described* by means of terms which lie within our experience, and the proposition that there is an object answering to this description is then one composed wholly of experienced constituents. It is therefore [*sic*] possible to know the truth of this proposition without passing outside experience. If it appears upon examination that no *experienced* object answers to this description, the conclusion follows that there are objects not experienced. ("On the Nature of Acquaintance" [1914], p. 161)

It is easy to underestimate the extent to which this Russellian doctrine conflicts with traditional semantic dogma. Russell himself was, as usual, on both sides of the issue. But most of those who had preceded him (and not a few of those who followed him) were consistently on the wrong side of it. It is clear, of course, that Russell's theory of denoting conflicts with the thesis of confined aboutness as well as with the less specific claims concerning the link between knowledge and intuition to which we earlier alluded. A denoting concept, Russell explained, need in no way resemble what it denotes. An object of infinite complexity (such as an infinite class-as-many) may be denoted by a concept of complexity modest enough to be easily grasped by a human being:

With regard to infinite classes, say the class of numbers, it is to be observed that the concept *all numbers,* though not itself infinitely complex, yet denotes an infinitely complex object [the class of as many numbers]. . . . infinite collections, owing to the notion of denoting, can be manipulated without introducing any concepts of infinite complexity. (*Principles,* p. 73)

It is worth emphasizing that in the theory of denotation developed in *Principles,* denoting concepts have no obligation to denote: "The denoting concepts associated with [the concept] *a* will not denote anything when and only when '*x* is an *a*' is false for all values of *x.* This is a complete definition of a denoting concept which does not denote anything" (p. 74). Thus, Russell placed himself once again with Bolzano, rather than the Austrian realists, on the issue of whether there can be representations without objects. We are therefore not surprised that he explained to Meinong in 1904 that "in such a case as that of the golden mountain or the round square one must distinguish between *sense* and *reference* (to use Frege's terms): the sense is an object, and has being; the reference, however, is not an object" (Letter to Meinong, p. 16). Nor are we surprised to read in an article written a few months before the doctrine of "On Denoting" was conceived that *the present king of France* is a "complex concept denoting nothing. The phrase intends to point out an individual, but fails to do so: it does not point out an unreal individual, but no individual at all" ("Existential Import of Propositions" [1905], *Essays in Analysis,* p. 100; see also Review of A. Meinong [1905], *Essays in Analysis,* p. 81). Thus, the new theory of denoting did a great deal more than provide a solution to the problem of our knowledge of infinity; it completely undermined the Austrian-realist approach to semantics by eliminating the implicit confusion between what must have being in order for a claim to make sense and what that claim is about. Finally, the recognition of denoting concepts was inconsistent with monism and with the principle of confined aboutness. Now, some expressions, denoting symbols, have *two* semantic dimensions equally worthy of the logician's attention: a "meaning," that is, the object they contribute to the proposition, and a denotation. In 'All numbers are finite', for example, 'all numbers' has as its meaning the denoting concept *all numbers,* while it (or its concept) denotes the class of numbers, which the proposition is about. Similarly, both *Scott is tall* and *The author of Waverley is tall* are about the author of *Waverley,* that is, Scott; but only the first has him as a constituent (on the assumption that 'Scott' is a proper name).

But then, what are we to make of the persistence of confined aboutness throughout Russell's later work and of the Austrian-realist pronouncements so prominent in Russell's *Principles?* Whitehead is said to have commented that Russell was an entire Platonic dialogue in himself. The point was not that Russell's opinions changed through the years in dialectical fashion; this would not have been worth mentioning. Like every great philosopher, Russell felt the force of conflicting intuitions. Unlike most philosophers, however, he succumbed to those temptations without much regard for consistency. It has often been noticed that Russell gallantly and frequently refuted his earlier theories; and this is admirable. But it has not been noticed often enough that he didn't always discard the theories he had refuted. His views on aboutness are a case in point; those on denoting are another.[6]

Consider, for example, this question: What would the author of chapter 5 of *Principles* ("Denoting") have to say concerning the statement printed only pages away (p. 449), quoted at the end of section 1 of the preceding chapter? It suffices to examine a proposition of the form 'A is not', where A is a denoting expression – for example, 'The golden mountain is not'. Russell's argument with this particular case would go like this: 'The golden mountain is not' must always be either false or meaningless. If the golden mountain were nothing, it could not be said not to be; 'The golden mountain is not' implies that there is a term 'the golden mountain' whose being is denied and hence that the golden mountain is. Thus, unless 'The golden mountain is not' is an empty sound, it must be false – whatever the golden mountain may be, it certainly is. The golden mountain, the Homeric gods, and so on must have being, for if they were not entities of a kind, we could make no propositions about them.

These are precisely the sorts of things one would have expected Brentano's disciples to say; and one would have expected the author of chapter 5 of *Principles* to complain that this was a muddleheaded piece of reasoning. It could readily be granted that 'The golden mountain is not' would be an empty sign if 'the golden mountain' did not contribute a meaning to the corresponding proposition. But, of course, it does, regardless of whether it has a denotation or not. In general, the presence or absence of a denotation, that is, of "the logical subject," has nothing whatever to do with whether the statement in question is a mere noise or expresses a meaningful proposition.[7]

The conclusion to be drawn from this remarkable situation is that Russell's understanding of denoting at the time of *Principles* was unstable. It was *so* unstable that after putting forth a theory of the matter far better than those of his Austrian counterparts, Russell then paid scant attention to its implications.

Russell's second theory of denoting

Let us start by reviewing briefly the main elements of Russell's famous second theory of denoting symbols. Russell claimed that there are no denoting concepts, thus moving back to semantic monism. There is no particular entity, conceptual or otherwise, no "meaning," that denoting expressions contribute to a proposition. For example, definite descriptions have no meaning even though they do have (as in the old theory) "only sometimes a *denotation*" ("On Denoting" [1905], *Essays in Analysis*, p. 108). To understand the semantic character of a definite description is not to identify a certain thing, its meaning, but to give for each sentence in which it occurs a translation into another sentence in which it does not occur. In a language Russell would not have used, we could say that to "define" a denoting symbol is to give the truth conditions of all sentences in which it occurs. For the case of definite descriptions, the rule offered by Russell in "On Denoting" was this: 'F(the ϕ)' is to be interpreted as 'Exactly one thing is ϕ and that thing is also F'. Thus, 'F(the ϕ)' is not of the form '$F(x)$' but of the much more complex form indicated by the translation. The phrase 'the ϕ' does not contribute any simple or complex constituent to $F($ the $\phi)$, or, to put it differently, it has no meaning. It may, however, have a denotation; indeed, it will have one precisely when there is just one ϕ (pp. 114, 108).

Russell's theory can be seen as one more step along the path initiated by Frege's theories of quantification and of number statements. The heart of Russell's theory is the observation that sentences involving 'the F' are very close relatives of number statements; for what 'The F is G' says is that the number of Fs is one (a number statement) and that all of them are G. All one need add to derive Russell's theory is Frege's analyses of number statements and of quantification. The result is that 'The F is G' is not about the F (or even about *the F*) but about the concept Fa (and the concept G as well), and what we *really* say is that there is an F and no other (the number statement) and that F & G has instances. In the Fregean spirit, what appeared to be a statement in subject–predicate form is displayed as actually being about concepts and whether or not they are instantiated. Also in the Fregean spirit, the analysis dissolves any temptation to associate either the meaningfulness or the objectivity of the analyzed claim with the ontological features of what it might refer to.[8]

But why do we need a new theory of denoting? Russell said that the evidence for his new theory "is derived from the difficulties which seem unavoidable if we regard denoting phrases as standing for genuine constituents of the propositions in whose verbal expressions they occur" ("On Denoting," *Essays in Analysis,* p. 107).

The theories Russell aimed to refute are those that (like his earlier one) view denoting phrases "as standing for genuine constituents." He discussed two such theories: Meinong's and Frege's. Meinong assumed that an object of some sort is associated with every definite description in a way that, as Russell argued, entails the denial of the principle of contradiction. The Frege-type theory (closest to Russell's first theory of denotation) was subject to the following objection.

Consider "the cases in which the denotation appears to be absent." The "problem" is this: "If we say 'the King of England is bald', that is, it would seem, not a statement about the complex *meaning* 'the King of England', but about the actual man denoted by the meaning" (p. 108). But the same should be true of 'The King of France is bald', which "ought to be about the denotation of the phrase 'the King of France'" (p. 108). Since there is no such denotation, however, this seems to turn the proposition into nonsense (a clear echo of the Brentanophile statements of *Principles*). "Now," Russell argued,

it is plain that such propositions do *not* become nonsense merely because [their denoting symbols do not denote]. . . . Thus we must either provide a denotation in cases in which it is at first sight absent, or we must abandon the view that the denotation is what is concerned in propositions which contain denoting phrases. (p. 109)

The former course had been advocated by Meinong and, in a different way, by Frege. Russell added, "The latter is the course that I advocate" (p. 109).

It is clear that this is no objection at all, for it simply assumes, without argument, what a Frege-type theory explicitly denies: namely, semantic monism and the doctrine of confined aboutness.[9]

Nevertheless, although Russell had no real argument for his new theory of denoting, there can be no doubt that its outcome was one of the most interesting and influential philosophical ideas of this century: the strategy of incomplete symbols. This strategy is what justifies Ramsey's claim that "On Denoting" is, after all, a paradigm of philosophy.

The incomplete-symbol strategy

A major feature of "On Denoting" is its sharp recognition of the intransparency of language and its presentation of a definite program for the elimination of this defect. One way to put this is to say, with Wittgenstein, that Russell had discovered that "the apparent logical form of the proposition need not be its real logical form" (*Tractatus*, 4.0031). That observation had been articulated much earlier and better by Frege, concerning the domain of sense, but his views had been largely ignored. What was new with Russell was the discovery of a strategy for neutralizing the semantic temptation to produce what Russell now called (echoing the idealists) "false abstractions." The application of this strategy to the case of definite descriptions in "On Denoting" was far less significant than the strategy. It would soon be applied by Russell to other domains (classes and propositions) and would, quite generally, preside over an orderly retreat in the direction of holistic idealism.

Russell's earlier writings displayed a strong inclination to assume that language is, as he once put it, "transparent," that is, that to each grammatical unit in the sentence there corresponds a (possibly complex) element, its meaning, which occurs as a constituent in the proposition it expresses. In spite of conscious efforts in *Principles* not to be misled by grammar, Russell's early atomism resembled Bolzano's in the unrecognized assumption that grammar is mostly a sound guide to semantics and ontology.

It is essential not to confuse the transparency of language that "On Denoting" was meant to deny for the case of definite descriptions with what we may call the *perfect-language thesis,* the doctrine that there is a subclass of sentences in (say) English, or a conveniently extended version of English,[10] that is powerful enough to convey all possible information and is perfectly transparent. Russell's response to the intransparency of language in "On Denoting" does not deny but, in fact, presupposes that there is a fragment of English that is both transparent and complete. The project launched in that paper was to neutralize the effect of the misleading fragments of language by identifying a (preferably effective) method to associate with *every* sentence in the given language another one in the transparent fragment of that language that expressed the very same proposition. This would be impossible, of course, if there weren't a transparent rendering of *every* proposition.

The main *technical* achievement of "On Denoting" was, as we saw, the particular translation rule intended to eliminate definite descriptions from all sentential contexts. We have already presented the basic idea in the preceding section. In a terminology closer to Russell's, we might put it as follows: Consider an arbitrary sentence S that contains one occurrence of a definite description 'the ϕ'. If we remove 'the ϕ' from S, we have a concept name 'C'. We can therefore interpret S as having 'the ϕ' as its grammatical subject and 'C' as its predicate. Then, Russell claimed, the transparent (or more transparent) version of what S says is 'There is exactly one ϕ and it is C'. Russell soon noted that this translation technique was not quite unambiguous and resolved the ambiguity only for contexts involving propositional attitudes. The purpose, however, was to present a translation method that applied to *all* sentences containing definite descriptions.[11]

Russell's conception of the link between a perfect-language sentence and its meaning can be depicted as follows: Each nonlogical word contributes an object, its meaning, to the proposition in question; and the proposition is the combination of all such meanings in a way or "form" that is itself the meaning of the framework of logical expressions involved. With this image in mind, we define a symbol as *incomplete* when it contributes no simple or complex constituent to the proposition it helps convey. Thus, if 'a' is incomplete, there is in the proposition fa no single entity, simple or complex, that counts as the contribution of 'a' to that proposition. Since the meaning of 'a' is its contribution to such propositions, if 'a' is incomplete, Russell says that it has no meaning.

Let us call a sentence transparent, or *perspicuous,* when its grammatical structure accurately reflects the structure of the proposition it expresses, so that to each grammatical unit in the sentence there corresponds an entity (its "meaning") in the proposition. Then it is clear that if a symbol is incomplete, the sentence in which it occurs is unperspicuous and therefore semantically misleading. If what we are after is a language that reflects perspicuously what we mean, a perfect language, we must detect and eliminate all incomplete expressions.

It is worth emphasizing the distinction among these three different, indeed, independent, tasks: (a) showing that an expression is incomplete, (b) providing a rule to translate all sentences containing the expression into (more) transparent versions, and (c) showing that incomplete expressions lack a denotation.

It is a widespread and dangerous error to confuse (a) and (b), that is, to think that the elimination procedure to which (b) alludes counts for Russell as a reason, perhaps even the decisive reason, for thinking that a symbol is incomplete. To show that a symbol is incomplete is to give some sort of argument to show that the symbol in question contributes no constituent to the appropriate propositions. Of course, it would be pointless to engage in (b) if one did not already have some reason to think that the symbol under consideration *was* incomplete. But it would be an error to saddle Russell with the blunder of confusing success in (b) with success in (a).[12] Russell recognized most of the time that the fact that a translation rule can be given to eliminate an expression from all contexts in no way entails that the corresponding proposition lacks a constituent contributed by the given expression: The translation might, after all, be less perspicuous than the original statement. It was in view of this fact that in "On Denoting," as well as in several other places, Russell put forth an argument designed to establish that there are no denoting concepts and, in particular, no meanings of definite descriptions. And when he applied the incomplete-symbol strategy first to classes (in 1906) and then to propositions (before 1910), he was in both cases led to do so by his discovery of reasons for thinking that the symbols for these alleged entities were, in fact, incomplete.

The argument that Russell offered to establish that definite descriptions are incomplete symbols is worth examining, since, inter alia, it offers a vivid illustration of the grip semantic monism had on Russell's thought, even at a time when he said he did not think there were propositions. Here is one of the many appearances of the famous argument:

The central point of the theory of descriptions was that a phrase may contribute to the meaning of a sentence without having any meaning at all in isolation. Of this, in the case of descriptions, there is precise proof: If 'the author of *Waverley*' meant anything other than 'Scott', 'Scott is the author of *Waverley*' would be false, which it is not. If 'the author of *Waverley*' meant 'Scott', 'Scott is the author of *Waverley*' would be a tautology, which it is not. Therefore, 'the author of *Waver-*

ley' means neither 'Scott' nor anything else – i.e. 'the author of *Waverley'* means nothing, Q.E.D." (*My Philosophical Development,* p. 85)[13]

In other words, if the meaning of 'the author of *Waverley'* is Scott, then the proposition *The author of Waverley is Scott* is the very same proposition as *Scott is Scott,* since the very same constituents are located at the very same places. Since the latter is a tautology, so is the former. If, however, 'the author of *Waverley'* means some other thing, say, the number 2, then the proposition *The author of Waverley is Scott* has as constituents the number 2, Scott, and identity, correlated in such a way as to say something surely false (that Scott is the number 2). Notice the tacit appeal to confined aboutness; for if the "other thing" meant by 'the author of *Waverley'* were the denoting concept *the author of Waverley,* the proposition would be false only if we thought that it was about that very concept, rather than about what it denotes. Russell's argument is, of course, untenable unless one believes in semantic monism and confined aboutness; but it is the argument to which he kept appealing as the proof that definite descriptions are incomplete symbols. His later applications of the incomplete-symbol strategy were based on what he took to be weaker arguments of an inductive nature. Yet in all cases, he first came to think that a category of expressions could not be interpreted the way he had hoped in the heyday of atomism, and then proceeded to cope with the difficulty by applying the strategy.

Quite generally, what this strategy offered Russell was a way to save face as the new facts his research uncovered seemed to lead him in the direction first urged by Bradley and his followers. Definite descriptions and denoting symbols in general, then (at least) some properties and relations, then all classes, and finally propositions themselves were things that Russell's atomism had recognized as independently subsistent entities in 1900, but that by 1910 were what Bradley would call "illegitimate abstractions." The reasons that led Russell down this path were ones that Bradley's colleagues would probably not even have been able to follow, let alone discover. Yet the fact remains that Russell's project, when pursued relentlessly, seemed to lead to its own destruction. The incomplete-symbol strategy allowed Russell to preserve an image of conservative reform within his early atomist framework. The ultimate furniture of the world was still his real goal, though as years went by, one could but wonder what, besides sense data, would remain in the wake of the ontological massacre Russell was perpetrating.

7

Logic in transition

I have long struggled against the admission of ranges of values thereby of classes; but I have found no other possibility to provide a logical foundation for arithmetic. This question is: how are we to conceive of logical objects? And I have found no answer other than this: we conceive of them as extensions of concepts or, more generally, as ranges of values of functions . . . what other way is there?

Frege to Russell, 28 July 1902

The first task in discussing the foundations of (pure) mathematics is to make precise the distinction between it and other sciences, a task which in Principia Mathematica is surprisingly neglected.

Ramsey, Undated manuscript (ASP)

Logicism and the foundational crisis

In 1900 Russell underwent the one event in his intellectual life that he was willing to characterize as a "revolution": He met Peano and was struck by the capacity of Peano's work to shed light on the philosophical nature of mathematics. It was at this time that Russell conceived one of his most fruitful ideas, the logicist project.

Peano had identified a notational system, or a cluster of concepts, that seemed to have enormous expressive power. The hope was that it could be used to express all of mathematics, and Peano's school had been working for years at rewriting different fragments of mathematics in their peculiar notation. Russell suggested that its basic concepts might be reduced to purely "logical" notions, in an as yet undisclosed sense of that word, and that perhaps all the assumptions one needed were those of logic, whatever they might be.

Logicism is often defined as the thesis that mathematics is reducible to logic. This is correct as long as one understands that at this early stage, mathematics was a reality and logic a project. In Russell's practice, at any rate, the logicist motto was less a doctrine than a regulative maxim, intended as much to provide a guide to characterizing logic as to clarifying mathematics. This link between logic and mathematics was destined to have momentous implications. Among those pertaining to philosophy, none was greater than the effect it had on the role played by classes in logic.

Classes had been a part of logic since the days of Aristotle. Logic had traditionally been concerned with what we say and its internal relations; classes had been useful devices for translating talk of content into more manageable extensional terms. Thus, it was widely taken for granted that to every notion or concept there corresponded an extension, a class of things, the actual (or perhaps possible) instances of the concept in question, and that every class was the extension of some notion.

Until the nineteenth century classes remained, for the most part, the private concern of logicians, and logicians' problems were the sort that led them to question seriously the preceding assumptions. In the nineteenth century, however, classes began to take on a life of their own. It all started when Cantor and Frege brought classes to bear upon arithmetic, in their characterizations of the concept of number. This led to results that undermined the philosophical picture from which they had emerged. The first blow to the philosophers' conception of classes came from Russell's paradox (first communicated to Frege in 1902, see note 3, this chapter), which was thought to establish that the presence of a concept or intension does not guarantee the presence of the corresponding class. The second, heavier blow came in 1904 when Zermelo focused attention on the role of the axiom of choice, an assumption that implicitly questioned the necessity of intensions to guarantee the presence of classes. By the end of the first decade of our century, set theory had become a discipline that had no recognizable link with its traditional logical neighbors: concepts, intensions, and meanings. It had also become a hypothetico-deductive discipline whose main purpose was not to find a priori or even merely true assumptions but to save the mathematical phenomena.

Those who chose to preserve their commitment to the idea that this was still logic had to undergo a rather drastic change of mind as to what logic is. Frege concluded that the logicist program was dead and offered nothing in its stead. Wittgenstein eventually denounced the new turn of events as the product of unqualified confusion. Russell steered a middle course of indecision – or conflicting decisions; he joined the intensionalists on the subject of classes but, in the end, gave in to the new conjecturalist conception of logic that the mathematical community seemed, no doubt unwittingly, determined to promote.

Class struggle

By 1900 Russell had already rebelled against idealism. For him classes were no longer the outcome of classification processes but self-subsistent things, thriving mind-independently and waiting for someone to get acquainted with them. On that ground Cantor had built a famous paradise, a doctrine that was for Russell one of the greatest achievements of the human mind. Within that paradise everything seemed perfect, but for one troubling exception: Cantor's theorem that for every class there is another of higher cardinality.

Cantor's proof was extremely simple: Assume that there is a one-to-one correspondence f between a set S and its power set PS. Consider now the subset C of S whose elements are precisely those x's that are not members of their f-values (i.e., the x's such that $x \in f(x)$). Of course, C must be an element of PS and must therefore be the f-value of something in S — call that thing c. In other words, $f(c) = C$. At this point Cantor asked a question: Does c belong to $f(c)$ (i.e., to C) or not? If it does, then (since c belongs to its f-value, by the definition of C) it doesn't. And if it doesn't, then (since c is one of those x's that satisfy the defining condition of C [i.e., $x \notin f(x)$]) it does. So it does iff it does not — a contradiction. Cantor concluded that there could not be an f such as the one he had assumed; and with very little extra machinery, readily granted by Russell, he inferred his theorem that the power set of any set S has a cardinality greater than that of S.[1]

Russell was appalled. At first he thought that Cantor's theorem couldn't possibly be true. In an essay published in 1901 and devoted largely to an explanation of how Cantor's brilliant discoveries have solved centuries-old metaphysical problems, Russell pointed out that even the master is capable of making mistakes, since Cantor's theorem is false. Clearly, he thought, not *every* cardinal number has a greater one:

There is a greatest of all infinite numbers, which is the number of all things altogether, of every sort and kind. It is obvious that there cannot be a greater number than this, because if everything has been taken, there is nothing left to add. Cantor has a proof that there is no greatest number. . . . But in this one point, the master has been guilty of a very subtle fallacy, which I hope to explain in some future work. (*Mysticism and Logic,* p. 69)

In Russell's opinion, the essence of Cantor's proof was independent of the bijective nature of his function f and of the fact that its range was the whole power set of its domain. The main point, as he explained to Frege in 1902, was that given any class A, *any* subset B of the power set of A, and *any* function f from A onto B, the class of all things in A that are not members of their f-values, cannot be a value of f. It was late in 1900 that Russell first seriously addressed the question, What is wrong with Cantor's proof? He had recently established to his satisfaction that the class of all things and the class of all classes (which he may have regarded as its power set) had the same cardinality.[2] Russell tried to follow step by step Cantor's argument as applied to this case. He first defined a many–one function f between the universe and its power set, defined as follows: $f(x) = x$ if x is a class; $f(x) = \{x\}$ otherwise (*Principles,* sec. 349, p. 367). At this point, Cantor's reasoning focused attention on the class of all things in the universe that are not members of their f-values. This class, call it R, is the class of all classes that are not members of themselves. Cantor's result – as generalized by Russell – says that R couldn't possibly be a value of f; that is, for no object t is $f(t) = R$. But this is obviously false, since by our definition of f, $f(R) = R!$ There *must* be a mistake in Cantor's argument that there is no such t. Let us follow the remaining steps of the reasoning carefully.

Cantor assumed there is such a t (we know it is R) and examined the question of whether it belongs to $f(t)$ (in our case, by our definition of f, this is R again). Cantor said that we can now derive a contradiction: From the assumption that t belongs to $f(t)$ (i.e., that R belongs to R), derive the opposite. Russell saw that he was right. Let us try the other way. From the assumption that t does not belong to $f(t)$ (i.e., that R does not belong to R), Cantor said we can derive the opposite. What Russell now had in his hands was the Russell paradox.[3]

At first Russell saw in this no more than a difficulty for Cantor. But it eventually dawned on him that the contradiction he had derived depended only on assumptions he himself had been willing to grant. The shocking fact that all one needed to assume in order to derive the contradiction were premises that had been tacitly acknowledged by most mathematicians, and explicitly acknowledged by the single logician who had attempted to put the mathematical house in order, Frege. If one assumed, as Frege had in his *Grundgesetze,* that the concept *x is a class of classes not belonging to themselves* must have a class as its extension, the contradiction was inevitable

On the face of it, Russell's class R appeared no more dubious or remote than any other. But Russell's argument had made clear that its existence or subsistence was unacceptable. As this first domino fell, others started tottering. Russell noticed that it was a routine matter to generate further classes and relations in extension that led to very similar paradoxes and, therefore, could not exist.[4]

The conclusion was shocking but inescapable; it was not clear what classes were. As already noted, in December 1902, in the preface to *Principles,* Russell wrote that the discussion of indefinables "is the endeavour to see clearly, and to make others see clearly, the entities concerned, in order that the mind may have that kind of acquaintance with them which it has with redness or the taste of a pineapple" (p. xv). His struggle with the contradiction may have gone through his mind as he added: "In the case of classes, I must confess, I have failed to perceive any concept fulfilling the conditions requisite for the notion of *class*. And the contradiction discussed in Chapter x [i.e., Russell's paradox] proves that something is amiss, but what this is I have hitherto failed to discover" (pp. xv–xvi).

In appendix A to *Principles,* written after the book was completed, Russell noted that "it is very hard to see any entity such as Frege's range [*Wertverlauf*]" (p. 514), that is, Frege's "sets," but since "without a single object to represent an extension, Mathematics crumbles" (p. 515), Russell reluctantly concluded that "it would seem necessary . . . to accept ranges by an act of faith, without waiting to see whether there are such things" (p. 515).[5] Class theory was not the healthy organism that Cantoreans had taken it to be. The question was, How far does the cancer spread?

Surely not to the entire organism – or so Russell thought at first, for not only Cantor's paradise but the bulk of classical mathematics seemed to depend on classes. What was needed, he hoped, was limited preventive surgery, to be implemented by uncovering some hitherto neglected distinction that would help us understand the limit between reality and fantasy in the domain of classes.

Zermelo's axiom

The emergence of Zermelo's axiom is one of the most interesting episodes in the early history of mathematical logic. As soon as he made its use explicit, the axiom became the focus of philosophical dissent.

Borel, Poincaré, and Peano, and later Brouwer, Weyl, and Wittgenstein, either rejected the axiom or expressed serious misgivings about it. In all cases their concern was related to the broken link between extension and intension. The only alternative to their intensionalist standpoint seemed to be a picture of logic (and mathematics) as a physics of abstract objects. Indeed, their opponents seemed to think that reference to classes can somehow be taken for granted and that claims about them are like conjectures about atoms or tables. They seemed to think, that is, that for claims of logic (and mathematics), proper reference is presumed without question; truth value is therefore determined even though unknown; and believability is determined through inductive considerations entirely analogous to those that lead us to accept the existence of physical objects. From this standpoint, the way to respond to Russell's question about reality and illusion in the domain of classes is to do what Zermelo did in 1908 – to state an axiom system, a "theory" about classes, and to test it by checking whether it entails all of the desired and none of the undesired consequences.

Zermelo's reply to his critics in "A New Proof of the Possibility of a Well-Ordering" (1908, van Heijenoort, *From Frege to Gödel*) raised the epistemological issue in its clearest terms. Peano had noted that Zermelo's axiom was not derivable from the principles in his *Formulaire* and had displayed a certain skepticism concerning its truth. Zermelo's reasonable response was to ask, "How does Peano arrive at his own fundamental principles and how does he justify their inclusion in the *Formulaire?*" (van Heijenoort, *From Frege to Gödel*, p. 187). This was, no doubt, the hardest question one could ask in the field of logic at the time. As we shall see in the next section, no one had much of an answer. Zermelo's own guess was that the way to identify those fundamental principles was through the analysis of "the modes of inference that in the course of history have come to be recognized as valid and by pointing out that the principles are intuitively evident and necessary for science" (p. 187).

Peano had consigned questions of "intuitive evidence" to the domain of psychology: "Should we now state our opinion whether the proposition is true or false? Our opinion does not matter" (*Opere scelte*, vol. 1, p. 349). Zermelo thought this was a frivolous attitude, but he did not have an independent argument for the obviousness of his principle that couldn't also be used to support the obviousness of, say, Euclid's parallel postulate. He could, however, make a case for the "necessity for science" of the axiom of choice. In "A New Proof of the Possibility of a Well-Ordering," Zermelo listed a number of widely accepted results in set theory and argued that their traditional derivations tacitly relied on the axiom of choice. The principle had been an unnoticed part of mathematics. As we try to bring clarity to that discipline, our role is not to criticize but to make explicit what has been implicit: "Principles must be judged from the point of view of science, and not science from the point of view of principles fixed once and for all" (van Heijenoort, *From Frege to Gödel*, p. 189). In other words, there are (in mathematics) no standards above and beyond those implicitly recognized in scientific practice. If a principle is widely (even if tacitly) used, if it leads to widely acknowledged results that cannot be derived without it, and if it does not lead to contradictions, then all "philosophical" objections are misplaced, since they must rely on standards that do not matter to mathematics. The reasons for accepting mathematical axioms are, in a sense, inductive, in that they derive from the character of mathematical practice and not from any extramathematical form of intellectual activity.

In his reaction to Zermelo's axiom, Russell sided with the intensionalists. The axiom asserts (in the version independently discovered by Whitehead, known as the "multiplicative" axiom): Given an infinite family of nonempty classes, there is always another class that has exactly one element from each of the classes in the family. A class is said to exist even though no effort is made to establish the existence of an intension that would determine it. With what right could we make this assumption?

Both in the case of Zermelo's axiom and in that of the multiplicative axiom, what we are primarily in doubt about is the existence of a norm or property such as will pick out one term from each of our aggregates; the doubt as to the existence of a *class* which will make this selection is derivative from the doubt as to the existence of a norm. ("On Some Difficulties in the Theory of Transfinite Numbers and Order Types" [1906], *Essays in Analysis,* pp. 162–3)

The celebrated example of an infinite class of boots was designed to illustrate this difficulty, in view of the presence and absence, respectively, of a rule to divide the class into two halves. In the latter case, he explained, "we cannot discover any property" belonging to exactly half the boots (p. 157). "If the number of pairs were finite, we could simply choose one of each pair; but we cannot choose one out of each of an infinite number of pairs unless we have a *rule* of choice" (pp. 157–8). Quite generally, he was inclined to think that "a *norm* [i.e., "property" or "propositional function"] is a necessary but not sufficient condition for the existence of an aggregate" (p. 136).[6] The idea that there might be "lawless" classes of integers appeared to him "open to doubt." "It would seem," he added, that "an infinite aggregate requires a norm, and that such haphazard collections as seem conceivable are really non-entities" (p. 163).[7]

Yet the axiom of choice appeared to be necessary for the derivation of mathematics from "logic." The philosophical half of Russell's heart was with the intensionalists, the mathematical half with Cantor's set theory. With great relief, in late 1905, Russell realized that his incomplete-symbol strategy allowed him to postpone a decision. Russell thought he might be able to do away with class commitments entirely by methods analogous to those he had used to do away with the commitment to the "meanings" of definite descriptions. Initially this was no more than a hope. It soon became a theory. Late in 1905 he wrote to Jourdain: "I believe I can now deal satisfactorily with all the various contradictions; I do so by wholly denying that there are such things as classes and relations, which I treat in the same way as I treated denoting phrases in the current *Mind*" (Grattan-Guinness, *Dear Russell – Dear Jourdain,* p. 56). The no-classes theory to which Russell referred in this passage was explained in "On the Substitutional Theory of Classes and Relations" (1906, *Essays in Analysis*) and was based on the assumption that propositions are real – a view Russell would soon abandon for reasons to be examined in Chapter 8. By 1908 he had developed the no-classes theory that would be incorporated in *Principia*.

Roughly speaking, Russell's no-classes theories treat class symbols the way "On Denoting" treated definite descriptions, by identifying a general technique for characterizing the truth conditions of all sentential contexts in which they occur. In brief, all sentences containing a class symbol are to be replaced by sentences making a corresponding assertion about an associated propositional function or property. Talk about classes is thereby translated into talk about properties (propositional functions) that have as their extension the class in question. All class paradoxes are thereby solved, since as far as Russell's logic could tell, there are no classes. The corresponding intensional paradoxes did remain, of course; they would be handled through type theory. Also the new intensionalized interpretation of mathematics required axioms that were hardly distinguishable in syntactic structure from those that had generated so much dissent when conceived as referring to classes. Russell might have prided himself on noting that the axioms were now intelligible, however, and that they did not presuppose a dubious ontology. (After all, we are acquainted with intensions but not with classes.) But the difficult question remained, What reason is there to think that these axioms are logically true? Indeed, what reason is there to believe that they are true at all?

Conjectural logic

As the logicist project evolved, Russell's "logic" took shape, but the shape it took was rather unexpected. A year after the publication of *Principles,* Russell was still explaining, "The view advocated by those who, like myself, believe all pure mathematics to be a mere prolongation of symbolic logic, is, that there are no new axioms at all in the later parts of mathematics, including among these both ordinary arithmetic and the arithmetic of infinite numbers" ("The Axiom of Infinity" [1904], *Essays in Analysis,* p. 256). Yet as he joined Whitehead in the effort to fulfill the reductionist promises of *Principles,* he was forced to change his mind.

The first major surprise was the one we have just talked about. In 1904, while revising one of Whitehead's proofs of a certain statement that was required to develop (inter alia) the theory of cardinal multiplication, Russell discovered that the proof was circular. He tried other ways to prove the formula in question and found none. Eventually, he came to think that this "multiplicative axiom," as they started calling it, was, indeed, an axiom, an assumption without which mathematics could not be reduced to "logic."[8]

The next surprise was the axiom of infinity. In *Principles* Russell had followed Bolzano and Dedekind in taking this "evident" truth to be capable of proof from standard logical assumptions (sec. 339, p. 357). In response to a challenge by Kayser to the effect that an extra assumption was involved, Russell insisted in "The Axiom of Infinity" that there is no need to state an axiom of infinity. Yet shortly thereafter he changed his mind and, in fact, concluded (probably due to type-theoretic considerations) that the axiom asserts the existence of infinitely many individuals and is therefore a purely empirical assumption.[9]

These new axioms were, perhaps, required to deduce classical mathematics; but were they part of "logic"? What, exactly, was this "logic" to which Frege and Russell had decided to reduce mathematics? Even those who do not care about such questions might still wonder whether these axioms, logical or otherwise, are true; or whether there is any other reason to accept them.

Russell once said that he felt about the contradiction the way an honest Catholic would feel about a wicked pope. His attitude toward these "logical" axioms could not have been much warmer, especially when he noticed that he could avoid the contradiction but not the axioms. After a few efforts to dissolve the contradiction, Frege must have seen what was happening to logicism; he acknowledged the fact that it had been refuted. Russell saw the same events as an opportunity to redefine the project. He had sided with philosophers on the matter of classes, but when he saw no way to provide a "foundation" for mathematics without assuming these peculiar axioms, he decided it was time to revise those philosophical standards in the light of which logicism appeared to have failed. The idea was to search for a conception of logic that would render the new developments a confirmation of logicism. And Russell quickly found it:

In fact self-evidence is never more than a part of the reason for accepting an axiom, and is never indispensable. The reason for accepting an axiom, as for accepting any other proposition, is always largely inductive, namely that many propositions which are nearly indubitable can be deduced from it, and that no equally plausible way is known by which these propositions could be true if the axiom were false, and nothing which is probably false can be deduced from it. (*Principia*, p. 59)

A few years earlier, in response to one of Poincaré's attacks against "logistic," Russell noted that the claim for absolute certainty in the choice of a logical basis was no part of his logicist project. This is a common misconception concerning the nature of the evidence on which logistic relies, he explained, and added in a footnote, "Indeed, I shared it myself until I came upon the contradictions" ("On 'Insolubilia' and Their Solution by Symbolic Logic" [1906], *Essays in Analysis*, p. 193). "The method of logistic," he went on,

is fundamentally the same as that of every other science. There is the same fallibility, the same uncertainty, the same mixture of induction and deduction, and the same necessity of appealing, in confirmation of principles, to the diffused agreement of calculated results with observation. The object is not to banish "intuition," but to test and systematise its employment. . . . In all this, logistic is exactly on a level with (say) astronomy, except that, in astronomy, verification is effected not by intuition but by the senses. (p. 194)[10]

This is the new perspective on logical matters that Russell framed in response to the challenge to logicism. In his hands, logic began to resemble not only mathematics but even physics. There was, however, still an effort to preserve a link with the old ideals of apriority and certainty. Some propositions, Russell insisted, have a character of "inherent" or "intrinsic obviousness." This domain of "instinctive beliefs," as he also called them, "gives necessarily the basis of all other knowledge. . . . In the natural sciences, the obviousness is that of the senses, while in pure mathematics it is an a priori obviousness" ("The Regressive Method of Discovering the Premises of Mathematics" [1907], *Essays in Analysis,* p. 279). Intrinsic obviousness is the "basis of every science" (p. 279). Yet apart from telling us that intrinsic obviousness is not infallible, Russell had virtually nothing to say by way of elucidation or justification of this "basis of every science." The foundationalist hopes were still there; but the project they inspired had yet to produce anything that might be taken as confirmation of those hopes.

What is logic?

The semantic tradition offered an image of logical and other a priori knowledge that was far superior to all earlier accounts. But it had not completed that image with an explanation of what it is that makes a priori knowledge a priori known, nor had it fared successfully in its modest (if sometimes lengthy) attempts to explain the distinction between a priori and a posteriori. It was at the threshold of this very problem that the semantic tradition encountered its limits.

Kantians and semanticists differed from positivists in the enormous significance they assigned to the a priori. In earlier chapters we examined semanticists' undoing of the Kantian theory and their own constructive contributions. In one way or another, they faced three different issues, which it is now time to distinguish. We shall call them the questions of the *extent, intent,* and *ground* of a priori knowledge. In the case of logic, for example, to ask for the extent of logical truth is to ask for the class of statements that qualify as such. To ask for its intent is to ask what it is that makes them logical truths, or why the distinction was worth drawing in the first place. Finally, to ask for the ground of logic is to ask what reason we have to believe that a logical truth is true.

In the preceding section we described the struggle of Russell and others with the problem of how to make sense of the logic that was taking shape in their own hands. Overwhelmed by the complexity of the problems generated by the logicist project, Russell concluded that our access to a priori truths is no different in kind from our access to the rest. He also argued that there is nothing in the meaning of a priori claims that might allow us to distinguish them from their a posteriori counterparts. What, then, justifies their distinction? What is the intent of logical truth, and what is its ground?

Almost every major nineteenth-century philosopher felt the need to take a stand on the topic of synthetic a priori knowledge, but few thought there was much point in discussing its *analytic* counterpart. One might have hoped that the inadequacy of this attitude would have become clear as logic moved well beyond the principles of identity and contradiction. But even though the members of the semantic tradition were uniquely responsible for the creation of mathematical logic, they had little or nothing of significance to say on the questions of its nature and ground. There can be no doubt that logic, as we now know it, was born in the writings of Frege and Russell. In *Begriffsschrift, Grundgesetze,* and *Principia Mathematica,* they told us far better than anyone before which statements and patterns of inference are sanctioned by logic. But why does logic sanction them, and on what ground?

Frege's work was aimed at providing a logical foundation for arithmetic. There is no indication that he ever seriously worried about the foundations of logic itself, however. It isn't simply that it is hard to find an explicit statement in his writings about the intent and ground of logic. Rather, Frege did not even intend to explain why we are justified in believing logic. As we shall see in Chapter 8, Wittgenstein criticized Frege's appeal to rules of inference; he complained, for example, that the rule modus ponens does not provide a justification for the inference from '$A \Rightarrow B$' and 'A' to 'B'. The point is correct, but Wittgenstein was wrong in assuming that Frege intended the rule to play a justificatory role. The idea of a rule of inference was Frege's contribution to what he called the "ideal of a strictly scientific method." This ideal, he said,

which I have here attempted to realize, and which might indeed be named after Euclid, I should like to describe as follows. It cannot be demanded that everything be proved, because that is impossible; but we can require that all propositions used without proof be expressly declared as such, so that we can see distinctly what the whole structure rests upon. . . . Furthermore, I demand – and in this I go beyond Euclid – that all methods of inference employed be specified in advance; otherwise we cannot be certain of satisfying the first requirement. (*The Basic Laws of Arithmetic,* p. 2)

Thus, the purpose is systematic rather than foundational: to localize and minimize the required assumptions. And this purposeful avoidance of foundational questions extends to the case in which the axiomatized theory is logic itself. Frege's logical project is to display explicitly the logical axioms and logical rules, *not* to explain why one should accept them: "The question why and with what right we acknowledge a law of logic to be true, logic can answer only by reducing it to another law of logic. Where that is not possible, logic can give no answer" (p. 15). Evidently, Frege did not believe that "logic must take care of itself." What should? Frege did not know:

If we step away from logic, we may say: we are compelled to make judgments by our own nature and by external circumstances; and if we do so, we cannot reject this law — of Identity, for example; we must acknowledge it unless we wish to reduce our thought to confusion and finally renounce all judgment whatever. I shall neither dispute nor support this view; I shall merely remark that what we have here is not a logical consequence. What is given is not a reason for something's being true, but for our taking it to be true. (p. 15)

This is all Frege had to say on the topic. A few months before his death, he wrote a piece on the sources of knowledge; there are, he said, three sorts: sense perception, the "logical source of knowledge," and the geometric and temporal sources. There is little doubt about what the first and third items are, but Frege offered no explanation of the second. He did say that "a source of knowledge is what justifies the recognition of truth." But besides telling us that the logical source "is wholly within us," all of his remarks on that topic concerned the extent to which ordinary language may be responsible for errors in logic. The conclusion seems inevitable: The father of modern logic had no opinions on the ground of logical truth.

What about Russell? *Principia Mathematica* was, unquestionably, the most complete codification of logical truths to date. Yet in his review of Ramsey's *Foundations of Mathematics*, Russell acknowledged that "at that time I had no definition of mathematical [i.e., logical] propositions" ("Review of *Foundations of Mathematics* by F. P. Ramsey," p. 477).[11] To put it bluntly, he had no clear idea of what it was that he had codified.[12] Unlike Frege, however, he chose to display in public his private hesitations.

As we have already seen, Russell explained that the reasons we have for accepting a formula as a truth of logic are "inductive." In other words, our reasons for accepting axioms of logic are of the same type as those that lead us to accept axioms of geography: Either the axioms are intrinsically obvious, or we can deduce from them (and from no reasonable alternative) some intrinsically obvious claims. One problem is that for some (e.g., Frege) the intrinsically obvious included propositions of Euclidean geometry, while for others (e.g., Russell) it included propositions about tables and chairs — or about corresponding sense data.

Even more problematic was Russell's view that a priori propositions are not necessary. Since merely empirical claims and purely a priori propositions are entirely alike insofar as their relation to facts is concerned, "it seems impossible to distinguish, among true propositions, some which are necessary from others which are mere facts" ("Meinong's Theory of Complexes and Assumptions," *Essays in Analysis,* p. 26).[13] For example, "the law of contradiction is . . . a fact concerning the things in the world" (*The Problems of Philosophy,* p. 89). This denies that the law is about thought, but it also asserts that its topic is a mere fact, entirely lacking in modal force. The principle of contradiction is, inter alia, about trees, and it states "that if the tree *is* a beech, it cannot at the same time *be* not a beech" (p. 89).[14] As far as Russell's semantics could tell, the principle of contradiction and the statements of geography have the same basic semantic structure: They assert a certain fact that happens to be the case. Nothing in their "meaning" allows for that elusive distinction that we are after: "The difference between an *a priori* general proposition and an empirical generalization does not come in the *meaning* of the proposition" (*The Problems of Philosophy,* p. 106). From whence *does* it come?

Plato provided one standard way to account for the distinction between the a priori and the a posteriori: One thinks of them as claims referring to radically different domains. The a priori concerns certain rigid, immutable objects; the a posteriori deals with the changeable world of experience. Since the days of Aristotle, however, this view has been deemed by some to be too extravagant for belief. From then on, most epistemology has consisted of footnotes to Plato and Aristotle.

One of these footnotes was written by Wittgenstein in 1915. "My method," he wrote, "is not to separate the hard from the soft, but to see the hardness of the soft" (*Notebooks,* p. 44). It is tempting to think that he had Russell in mind, for three years earlier Russell had offered the following solution to the problem of the a priori: "The fact seems to be that all our *a priori* knowledge is concerned with entities which do not, properly speaking, *exist,* either in the mental or in the physical world" (*The Problems of Philosophy,* pp. 89–90). These entities are the meanings of certain very general expressions in our language; they are what Russell called "universals" and "forms":

The world of universals, therefore, may also be described as the world of being. The world of being is unchangeable, rigid, exact, delightful to the mathematician, the logician, the builder of metaphysical systems, and all who love perfection more than life. The world of existence is fleeting, vague, without sharp boundaries, without any clear plan or arrangement. (*The Problems of Philosophy,* p. 100)

The recognition of this world "solves the problem of *a priori* knowledge" (p. 100). Or so Russell hoped.

The trouble with Platonism had always been its inability to define a priori knowledge in a way that made it possible for human beings to have it. Identifying the *topic* of a priori knowledge, saying that *"all* a priori *knowledge deals exclusively with the relations of universals"* (*The Problems of Philosophy,* p. 103), is not enough to explain how we *know* it. One must add an explanation of how we have access to such universals and their relations: What is the semantic pineal gland that links the world of universals and forms with merely human epistemology? That is why any Platonism that is more than just a colorful rephrasing of common-sense beliefs must postulate *both* an incredible world and an incredible faculty of access to it.

Proponents of the chemical picture of representation had never been good at explaining how we come to possess the ultimate simples from which representational complexity emerges. The little they had to say on this matter had already been said by Hume: "Complex ideas," he had written,

may, perhaps, be well known by definition, which is nothing but an enumeration of those parts or simple ideas, that compose them. But when we have pushed up definitions to the most simple ideas, and find still some ambiguity and obscurity; what resource are we then possessed of? By what invention can we throw light upon these ideas . . . ? Produce the impressions or original sentiments, from which the ideas are copied. (*Enquiry,* sec. 7, pt. 1, p. 41)

Except for Hume's restriction to the domain of sense impressions, Russell would not have objected. Russell's solution to the problem of indefinables, his "semantic pineal gland," was intuition. He rarely used the term, since its Kantian resonances clearly displeased him, but that is the right word for what he called "acquaintance" and for its propositional correlate, self-evidence. In philosophy, Russell explained in 1900, "the emphasis should be laid on the indefinable and indemonstrable, and here no method is available save intuition" (*A Critical Exposition of the Philosophy of Leibniz,* p. 171). As we have already seen, he explained in *Principles* that

the discussion of indefinables – which forms the chief part of philosophical logic – is the endeavour to see clearly, and to make others see clearly, the entities concerned, in order that the mind may have that kind of acquaintance with them which it has with redness or the taste of a pineapple. (p. xv)

Ten years later he was still explaining that all knowledge starts with undefined terms and unproved propositions, and that "the undefined terms are understood by means of acquaintance. The unproved propositions must be known by means of self-evidence" (*Theory of Knowledge,* p. 158). Acquaintance and a Platonistic ontology were Russell's twin answers to the problem of the a priori. His philosophy of logic was the immediate consequence of this. It is worth looking briefly at his last attempt to articulate his conception of the matter, just before Wittgenstein explained that his whole approach was ill-conceived.

Russell explained in *Theory of Knowledge* that the ultimate furniture of the world contains three different categories of things: particulars, universals, and forms. The first two are the constituents of propositions (if there are such things); a proposition is a form, "the way in which the constituents are combined in the complex. It is such pure 'forms' that occur in logic" (p. 98).

Russell had always thought of logic as (inter alia) the most general of all sciences. If a proposition mentions anything specific, whether particular or universal, it cannot be logical. A "touchstone by which logical propositions may be distinguished from all others" is that they result "from a process of generalization which has been carried to its utmost limit" (*Theory of Knowledge,* p. 97). We may therefore think of reaching the logical through a process of elimination, by removing every single constituent from propositions. What remains is, of course, not a constituent of the proposition, nor does *it* have any constituents;[15] but it is nonetheless something and, indeed, something with which we are, in fact, acquainted as soon as we understand a proposition *of that form.*

Russell thought that we are certainly acquainted with forms, since otherwise he could not explain the fact that we can understand propositions we have never seen before. They are rearrangements of familiar objects in familiar forms. Since acquaintance with x entails the reality of x, it follows that forms are objects and not symbolic fictions like classes or propositions (p. 129). What objects could they be? The question echoes a similar one Russell had asked a decade earlier of propositions, and once again, he decided the answer should be: some sort of fact. Consider, for example, the complex *Socrates precedes Plato.* Its form must be an object with which we are acquainted, and it must be related to what we obtain by removing all constituents from that complex. Russell's choice was: *something has some relation to something.* Such facts are the subject of logic; and what distinguishes them from the others is that, apparently, it is enough to understand the claims that express them in order to know that they are true. It is enough because for statements of this type there is no distinction, as far as Russell can see, between understanding and acquaintance (p. 130) — hence no distinction between understanding and recognition of truth — since acquaintance is with the very fact that makes the "claim" true.[16] His argument for this: "I am unable introspectively to discover any difference" between acquaintance and understanding in the cases under consideration (pp. 130–1).

If this was Russell's view on the nature of logic, there is serious doubt that *Principia Mathematica* had much to do with that discipline. The

claimed link between understanding and truth for logical propositions
posed grave problems for the new axioms that were required. Within a
few years Carnap would remind Wittgenstein's allies that if they seriously
thought understanding in mathematics entailed recognition of truth, they
would have to conclude that they did not understand even the statement
of Fermat's last theorem.

Logical propositions had acquired a mysterious status. Russell noted
how strange it was that these "facts" had no constituents whatsoever. He
was pleased to note that they had "all the essential characteristics required of pure forms" (*Theory of Knowledge,* p. 129), but he also wondered, "Why, if pure forms are simple, is it so obviously inappropriate to
give them simple proper names, such as John or Peter?" (p. 130). Doesn't
this betoken a sort of complexity? What, exactly, is going on?

What is going on is that an approach to logic had finally reduced itself
to absurdity. The point did not escape the attention of the one student to
whom Russell showed the manuscript from which we have been quoting.
Wittgenstein's criticisms (see Chapter 8) led Russell to drop plans to
publish the book and, for a while, to abandon philosophical speculation
on fundamental, "logical" problems.[17]

We are witnessing here the death of Cartesian dreams:

It must be taken as a fact, discovered by reflecting upon our knowledge, that we
have the power of sometimes perceiving such relations between universals, and
therefore of sometimes knowing general *a priori* propositions such as those of
arithmetic and logic. (*The Problems of Philosophy,* p. 105)

"It must be taken as a fact . . ." and yet the path that logic had taken
under Russell's leadership had made it harder than ever to see this "fact"
as anything more than a refusal to face the fundamental problems, an
appeal to ancient hopes that the discoveries of the semantic tradition had
now made obsolete.

This type of Cartesianism had seemed attractive when compared with
what Kantians had done to philosophy. But finally it came time to recognize that the semanticists' project was in need of major revision. The first
clear indication of what the new approach might be emerged from unexpected territory: from a meditation on the foundations of geometry.
Ironically, the most outspoken opponents of the development that would
eventually lead to an understanding of the nature of logic were Frege and
Russell.

What is geometry?

Their desire to avoid the psychologism they saw in the Kantian answers
and their commitment to semantic monism left most semanticists with

no choice but the very Platonism that Kant had justifiably dismissed as dogmatic metaphysics. And when they asked for the ground of the a priori, the only answer they had was, in effect, intuition. It is ironic that after all those complaints against Kant's pure intuition, at the culmination of this revolutionary process we find an appeal to a form of intuition that Kant himself would have regarded as extravagant. As the semanticist position revealed its inability to cope with this problem, a new standpoint emerged that would combine the insights of the semanticists with a concession to Kantianism. The transition to this new perspective was initiated near the turn of the century, and its conflict with the semantic tradition was first displayed in a debate concerning the foundations of geometry.

Russell and Poincaré had been allies in the struggle to remove Kantian intuition from the field of geometry and transform it into a purely conceptual discipline; but once that war was won, they turned against each other. Their quarrel concerned a seemingly trivial topic: How do we have access to the basic, indefinable, geometric concepts? At about the same time, Frege and Hilbert were also examining that question. They did not realize that the issue they were debating held the key to the question of the nature of a priori knowledge, even in the field of logic.

Since the 1880s Poincaré had been advocating a remarkable doctrine concerning the nature of geometry, according to which no properly geometric axiom expresses either "an experiential fact or a logical necessity or a synthetic a priori judgment" (Pioncaré, "Analyse de ses travaux scientifiques," p. 127). What else could an axiom be? Poincaré's often repeated answer was that they are "definitions in disguise." In 1899 Hilbert published a monograph on the foundations of geometry in which he adopted a closely related standpoint, also describing geometric axioms as definitions (*Erklärungen*). When Russell found out about Poincaré's views and Frege about Hilbert's, their responses were, revealingly, the same: Geometers are thoroughly confused on the nature of definitions, and they need to be enlightened.

In fact, Frege and Russell had totally misunderstood the geometers' point; for they had even missed the problem their remarks were aimed to solve. Let us see how and why.

Russell and Poincaré

In 1897 Russell had published his fellowship dissertation under the title *An Essay on the Foundations of Geometry*. The *Revue de Métaphysique et de Morale* soon published a very enthusiastic review of it by Couturat in which he remarked that the work revealed a mind endowed with "a vast mathematical erudition" and an equally vast "understanding of philosophical problems." Amidst a flood of extravagant praise, Couturat added "That such a mind could not be found in France may be cause for regret but not for surprise" ("Essai sur les fondements de la Géométrie par Bertrand Russell," p. 354). The next volume of the *Revue* included a long, careful, devastating discussion of Russell's book by Poincaré ("Des fondements de la géométrie").

Of the many problems raised by Poincaré, the one that concerns us here is the one Russell called the "most important and difficult issue," that of the "definition" of geometric primitives. As part of his defense of conventionalism, Poincaré challenged Russell to explain what, in his view, were the meanings of a number of primitive notions. Russell replied:

M. Poincaré requests "a definition of distance and of the straight line, independent of (Euclid's) postulate and free from ambiguity or vicious circle" (Sec. 20). Perhaps he will be shocked if I tell him that one is not entitled to make such a request since everything that is fundamental is necessarily indefinable. And yet I am convinced that this is the only philosophically correct answer. Since mathematicians almost invariably ignore the role of definitions, and since M. Poincaré appears to share their disdain, I will allow myself a few remarks on this topic. ("Sur les axiomes de la géométrie," pp. 699–700)

There are, Russell explained, two kinds of definitions: mathematical and philosophical. Mathematical definitions (soon to become "knowledge by description") merely identify an object as the one and only that stands in a certain relation to already known concepts or objects (p. 700). For example, if we define the letter *A* as the one that precedes *B,* or the number 1 as that which precedes 2, what we have given is a mathematical definition of those objects:

But these definitions are not definitions in the proper and philosophical sense of the word. Philosophically, a term is defined when its *meaning* is known, and its *meaning* cannot consist of relations to other terms. It will be readily granted that a term cannot be usefully employed if it does not mean something. Its meaning can be complex or simple. In other words, either it is composed of other meanings or it is one of those ultimate elements that are constituents of other meanings. In the first instance one defines the term philosophically by enumerating its simple elements. But when it is itself simple, no philosophical definition is possible. . . . Definition is an operation analogous to spelling. One can spell words but not letters. M. Poincaré's request places me in the uncomfortable situation of a student who has been asked to spell the letter A without allowing him to use that letter in his reply. . . . All these truths are so evident that I would be ashamed to recall them, were it not that mathematicians insist in ignoring them. (pp. 700–1)

Applying these remarks to geometry, Russell concluded:

These observations apply manifestly to distance and the straight line. Both belong, one might say, to the geometric alphabet; they can be used to define other terms, but they themselves are indefinable. It follows that any proposition, whatever it may be, in which these notions occur, is either an axiom or a theorem and not a definition of a word. When I say that the straight line is determined by two points, I assume that *straight line* and *point* are terms already known and understood, and I make a judgment concerning their relations, which will be true or false, but in no case arbitrary. (pp. 701–2)

Russell's remarks would have been devastating if Poincaré had meant by giving a 'definition' what Russell thought he *should* have meant, that is, analysis. But Poincaré merely meant what the dictionary instructed him to mean, that is, a process through which meaning is assigned to an expression. As Mill had put it, a definition is a "proposition declaratory of the meaning of a word" (*Logic,* bk. 1, chap. 8, sec. 1, p. 133). On Russell's view, to define a word is to construct (synthesize) new meanings from old, the latter being regarded as constituents of the former. The dictionary sense of 'definition', in contrast, allows processes which do not assume that meanings are available prior to the definition (as in 'ostensive definition', 'coordinative definition', and the like). Thus, when Poincaré asked Russell to define geometric primitives, he was not asking for the analysis of the unanalyzable; he was requesting a sufficiently definite and geometrically acceptable characterization of what those primitive terms mean.

Russell could not see the point of the question. In addition, quite independently, he thought it obvious that one could establish a priori that the geometric axioms could not be employed in the process of assigning meanings to terms involved in their formulation. His reasoning involved an appeal to a principle that may be called the *thesis of semantic atomism.*

This principle says that if a sentence *S* is to convey information (or, as Russell or Frege would put it, to express a proposition), then its grammatical units must have a meaning *before* they join their partners in *S.* Recognition of the meaning of the constituent phrases must be independent of and prior to the acceptance of the statement in question. The harmless appearance of this principle will vanish as we begin to see the dominant role it came to play in these geometric debates. The basic fact to bear in mind is that *all* participants in the debates endorsed this principle. The philosophers used it to infer (by modus ponens) a conception of geometry that the geometers could not accept, while the geometers used it to infer (by modus tollens) a picture of geometric knowledge that the philosophers would not take seriously. Whether one was inclined to move up or down the argument chain depended entirely on one's attitude toward the character of indefinables.

At the end of our quotation from Russell's "Sur les axiomes de la géométrie" (pp. 701–2), we caught a glimpse of the train of thought that led him to regard as absurd the idea that axioms can be used to give definitions. His argument was, in effect, this: Since *obviously* the axioms of geometry express propositions (convey information), by the thesis of semantic atomism the geometric primitives must *somehow* acquire a meaning before they can contribute to the expression of the appropriate propositions. Poincaré was not satisfied with "somehow"; he wanted to know *how*. How, he asked, are we supposed to decide whether this or that entity is a point, a straight line, a plane? How are we to tell what distance is?

In a reaction typical of the worst tendencies in the semantic tradition, Russell promptly concluded that Poincaré was confusing epistemology with semantics. How we find out whether something is the case, he thought, can have no bearing on what that "something" is:

If there are such quantities as distance and angle, their measure can only be arbitrary so far as concerns the choice of a unit, and any different measure must be simply false; while if there are no such quantities, then they can have no measure at all. . . . How we discover two actual spaces to be equal is no concern of the geometer; all that concerns him is the existence of equal spaces. . . . The whole confusion appears to be due to not distinguishing between the process of measurement, which is of purely practical interest, and the meaning of equality, which is essential to all metrical Geometry. ("Geometry, Non-Euclidean," p. 671)

But clearly neither Poincaré nor his logical positivist followers meant to challenge (as others eventually would) the idea that before we can raise the question of testing, we must have solved the question of meaning. On the contrary, Poincaré agreed with Russell that the latter had to be solved before the former. It was Russell's answer to the question of meaning that Poincaré found entirely untenable, and because of this turned to his new interpretation of geometric axioms.

Though in his debate with Poincaré Russell refused to state and defend his own answer to this question of meaning, we know what it was: Geometric indefinables are first given to us in acquaintance.[18] Poincaré also knew what Russell had in mind. In "Des fondements de la géométrie" he suggested that Russell's answer would be as follows:

There is no need to define [the indefinables] because these things are directly known through intuition. I find it difficult to talk to those who claim to have a direct intuition of equality of two distances or of two time lapses; we speak very different languages. I can only admire them, since I am thoroughly deprived of this intuition. (p. 274; see also "Sur les principes de la géométrie," p. 75)

The emptiness of Russell's appeal to acquaintance becomes clear when regarded in the context of the relevant geometric facts.[19] By the end of the nineteenth century, the only reason anyone could possibly have for saying that the ultimate distinction between Euclidean and hyperbolic *distance* is given by acquaintance was the weight of a dead philosophy. One might insist that once we understand these notions, we have become acquainted with the concepts in question. But this could be viewed only as a linguistic ploy, designed to obscure the fact that acquaintance could not be asked to play in geometry the role that atomism had assigned to it. Circa 1900 it was no longer possible to suppose that acquaintance plays the specific semantic *explanatory* role in geometry that it was supposed to play in the atomist picture of knowledge, that is, that the construction of geometric theory would start with acquaintance, then proceed to a construction of claims, and perhaps conclude with the testing of these claims.

Poincaré's conventionalism was based on the idea that in order to understand geometry, one must stand Russell's argument on its head: Since geometric primitives do not acquire their meaning prior to their incorporation into the axiomatic claims, such axioms do *not* express propositions in Frege's or Russell's sense. A passage in his reply to Russell clearly displays the semantic dimension of Poincaré's views. Struggling to explain why he thought it is a mistake to conceive of the axioms of geometry as bona fide propositions, Poincaré said:

If an object has two properties A and B, and if it is the only one that has the property A, this property can be used as a definition; and since it will suffice as a definition, the property B [i.e., the attribution of B] will not be a definition: it will be an axiom or a theorem. If, on the contrary, the object is not the only one that has the property A, but it is the only one that has both properties A and B, A no longer suffices to define it, and the property B will be a complement of the definition, not an axiom or a theorem. In a word, in order for a property to be an axiom or a theorem it is necessary that the object that has this property has been completely defined *independently of this property.* Therefore, in order to have the right to say that the so-called distance axioms are not a disguised definition of distance, one should be able to define distance in a way that does not involve an appeal to those axioms. But where is that definition? ("Des fondements de la géométrie," p. 274)

Poincaré made the same point in a discussion of free mobility. Russell had argued that the axiom of free mobility is a priori, and he had formulated it as follows: *"Spatial magnitudes can be moved from place to place without distortion. . . . Shapes do not in any way depend upon absolute position in space"* (*An Essay on the Foundations of Geometry*, p. 150). Poincaré asked:

What is the meaning of "without distortion"? What is the meaning of "shape"? Is shape something that we know in advance, or is it, by definition, what does not alter under the envisaged class of motions? Does your axiom mean: In order for measurement to be possible figures must be susceptible of certain motions and there must be a certain thing that will remain invariant through these motions and that we shall call shape? Or else, does it mean: You know full well what shape is; well, in order for measurement to be possible it is necessary that figures can undergo certain movements that do not alter their form. I do not know what is it that Mr. Russell has meant to say; but in my opinion only the first sense is correct. ("Des fondements de la géométrie," p. 259)

With minimal sharpening, the argument is this: The axioms of geometry are widely regarded as statements that convey information about certain elusive geometric entities. If they do, then by the principle of semantic atomism it should be possible to "define," that is, to identify in some intersubjective manner, the meanings of their geometric primitives before they are incorporated into the axiomatic sentences. Up to this point the geometer and the philosopher agree; but now Poincaré brought in a new premise, the lesson that geometers had learned from the evolution of non-Euclidean geometry: There is really nothing we can say about the meaning of geometric primitives beyond what the axioms themselves say. There is, of course, nothing to prevent us from *deciding* to circumscribe those meanings further so that the terms in question would refer only to certain physical objects (light rays, etc.); but there is no particular meaning of that sort or of any more ethereal Platonic sort that geometry attaches to its primitives prior to its construction. Geometry does not depend on geometric *objects*, whether they be Platonic straight lines or Millian light rays; all it needs in order to have a life of its own is geometric concepts or meanings. And such meanings are constituted roughly in the way in which Kantians used to think that we constitute experience or its objects, through the employment of rules or maxims whose adoption is prior to and the source of the meanings in question.

Therefore, according to Poincaré, all we can say about the meanings of geometric primitives is what geometric axioms say. Under the circumstances, the thesis of semantic atomism prevents those axioms from conveying any sort of factual (nonsemantic) information. No wonder that they are neither analytic (in Kant's first sense) nor synthetic, since they are not propositions. No wonder either that they had always been regarded as extraordinary claims, endowed with a particularly strong sort of truth. The error was to think that they convey a privileged sort of information or information about some extraordinary domain. Their distinguishing feature is that they determine, to the extent needed in geometry, the meanings of geometric primitives. The conviction that they are necessary emerges from the fact that we would be talking about something else or, better yet, meaning something different from what is intended, if we denied them. Geometric axioms are definitions disguised as claims, and what they define are the indefinables.

Frege and Hilbert

At the same time that Poincaré was crossing papers with Russell, Hilbert was releasing a monograph that would soon become one of the land-marks of nineteenth-century geometry, his *Grundlagen der Geometrie.* O. Blumenthal reports that as early as 1891, commenting on a lecture by H. Wiener, Hilbert had said that "it must always be possible to replace [in geometric statements] the words, 'points', 'lines', 'planes', by 'tables', 'chairs', 'mugs'" (Hilbert, *Gesammelte Abhandlungen,* vol. 3, p. 403). Several years later he decided to put the idea to work. In the winter term of 1898–9 he offered a course on the foundations of Euclidean geometry, on which *Grundlagen* was based.

Frege had had a deep interest in geometry from very early on. For reasons he never explained and may never have seriously scrutinized, he thought that geometry was a clear instance of a priori knowledge based on pure intuition. He read Hilbert's monograph as soon as it was pub-lished, and his immediate reaction was disappointment. He wrote to a friend that the book was "a failure" (Letter to Liebmann [1900], *Wiss. Briefwechsel,* p. 148) and started corresponding with Hilbert in order to set him straight on the relevant logical issues.

It is hard to avoid a sense of déjà vu when one sees that Frege's main complaint was that Hilbert did not seem to understand the nature of definition. As is well known, Hilbert had started the *Grundlagen* stating what he called a definition, which turned out to be the axioms of his formulation of Euclidean geometry. Frege was appalled. "I think it is high time," he wrote, "that we came to an understanding about what a defini-tion is and what it is supposed to accomplish. . . . It seems to me that at the present time complete anarchy and subjective inclination reign su-preme" (Letter to Hilbert [1899], in *Wiss. Briefwechsel,* p. 62). What followed was a masterful and patronizing explanation of the classical picture of knowledge. The totality of the sentences of a theory, Frege explained, is to be divided into two groups, those in which something is asserted and those in which something is stipulated. The former are the axioms and theorems of the theory, the latter are the definitions:

It is absolutely essential for the rigor of mathematical investigations that the difference between definitions and all other sentences be maintained throughout in all its sharpness. The other sentences (axioms, principles, theorems) must contain no word (sign) whose sense and meaning (*Sinn und Bedeutung*) or (in the case of form words, letters in formulas) whose contribution to the expression of the thought is not *already* completely settled, so that there is no doubt about the sense of the sentence – about the proposition expressed in it. Therefore it can only be a question of whether this proposition is true, and on what its truth rests. Therefore, it can never be the purpose of axioms and theorems to establish the meaning of a sign or word occurring in them; rather, this must *already* be established. (pp. 62–3; my italics)

Clearly, a central role is played by the thesis of semantic atomism; and equally clear is Frege's conviction that *every* sentence of a theory that is not a definition must express a proposition and thereby convey (true or false) information. Given these two assumptions, Hilbert's axioms in sections 1 and 3 of the *Grundlagen* should be such that "the meanings of the words 'point', 'straight line', and 'between' are not given but are presupposed as known" (p. 61).

It is in this conclusion that Hilbert located "the crux of the misunderstanding":

I do not want to presuppose anything as known. I see in my explanation in section 1 the definition of the concepts point, straight line, and plane, if one adds to these all the axioms of group i–v as characteristics. If one is looking for other definitions of point, perhaps by means of paraphrase in terms of extensionless, etc., then, of course, I would most decidedly have to oppose such an enterprise. One is then looking for something that can never be found, for there is nothing there, and everything gets lost, becomes confused and vague, and degenerates into a game of hide-and-seek. (Letter to Frege [1899], Frege, *Wiss. Briefwechsel,* p. 66)

Compare Hilbert's statement about preaxiomatic procedures for capturing the indefinables of geometry with Poincaré's remarks about those who claim to be acquainted with (to intuit) them. For both of them, and eventually for all geometers, the preaxiomatic search for the indefinables is "a game of hide-and-seek" in which "everything gets lost, becomes confused and vague" because, in the end, "there is nothing there."

Besides semantic atomism, Frege and Russell shared a further doctrine, which we shall call "propositionalism." The propositionalist notes that all branches of knowledge, including logic and geometry, formulate their claims in statements that, syntactically speaking, do not seem to differ significantly from regular factual claims. The statement that no claim can be both true and false and the statement that two points determine a unique straight line seem to differ only in topic and degree of certainty from the statement that this table is brown. For the propositionalist this syntactic uniformity is as it should be, for all these statements are seen as playing essentially the same syntactic role: They tell us how things stand. According to the propositionalist, logic, geometry, physics, and ordinary talk all call for the same type of semantic analysis; in all cases we are dealing with "propositions" in the minimal sense that takes them to be vehicles of information. And only propositions can be regarded as the targets of what Russell called the "propositional attitudes" (assertion, assumption, belief, etc.) and as the subject matter of logical operations such as inference and proof.[20] For Frege and Russell, as for their predecessors, propositionalism was not so much a conscious assumption adopted after exploring the alternatives; they simply would not have known how to begin making sense of the claim that the most basic principles of knowledge, such as the laws of geometry or logic, are really not the sorts of things that say anything and therefore are not the sorts of things that could be true or false. In their view one might conceivably argue that geometric propositions make weaker claims than previously thought or even, at the limits of sanity, that they make purely logical claims. Frege thought this suggestion was ludicrous, but at least it had the virtue of being intelligible.

In his second letter to Hilbert, Frege made his first attempt to interpret what Hilbert was doing. "It seems to me," he wrote,

that you want to detach geometry completely from the intuition of space and to make it a purely logical discipline, like arithmetic. If I understand you correctly, the axioms that are no doubt usually considered the basis of the whole structure, on the assumption that they are guaranteed by the intuition of space, are to be carried as conditions in every theorem; not, to be sure, expressed in their full wording but as contained in the words 'point', 'straight line', etc. (Letter to Hilbert [1900], *Wiss. Briefwechsel,* p. 70)[21]

Frege said no more on this matter until 1906, when he raised the issue once again in the second part of "Uber die Grundlagen der Geometry." Hilbert's axioms and theorems, he explained, are not propositions but "improper sentences," that is, sentences from which one or more meaningful terms have been removed and replaced by variables. Hilbert did not really mean to assert either his axioms or his theorems, but only certain implications whose antecedents are conjunctions of his "axioms" and whose consequents are each of his "theorems." In fact, we reach the domain of sense – that is, of propositional knowledge – only when we quantify universally the free variables in each of these implications. Thus, "what Mr. Hilbert calls a definition will in most cases be an antecedent improper sentence, a dependent part of a general theorem" ("Uber die Grundlagen der Geometry" [1906], *Kleine Schriften,* p. 303). Part 2 of Frege's "Uber die Grundlagen der Geometry" was devoted entirely to an elaboration of if–thenism that was, as might be expected, much more thorough than any Russell ever gave.[22] Frege examined, for example, an "alleged" proof of a Hilbertian theorem, showing in painful detail how to reconstruct it as a proof of an implication of the appropriate sort. It should be emphasized, however, that while Russell put forth if–thenism as his own view of the matter, Frege never endorsed this doctrine but stated it only as the best sense he could make of Hilbert's words. And he thought it was obvious that this much sense was not sense enough.[23]

The discovery of syntax

In the spirit of tolerance, most who have examined these debates have argued that the outcome was a draw. It is said that the participants neglected to make the distinction (later made by Russell) between pure and applied geometry; had they done so, they would have noticed that they were talking past each other. Hilbert and Poincaré were surely talking about uninterpreted geometries, so were, of course, right in denying that there were any propositions in them. But Frege and (initially) Russell were talking about interpreted geometry. They were therefore right in viewing them as sets of true or false propositions.

The problem with this "resolution" of the conflict is that it creates the impression of a compromise or of a higher synthesis while, in fact, granting everything to one side and nothing to the other; for to endorse the interpreted–uninterpreted distinction as a *sufficient* account of the character of geometric claims is to grant Poincaré's and Hilbert's whole case. If all there is to geometry besides its uninterpreted form is the populous democracy of geometric models, then the noble class of propositions that constitutes *real* geometry according to Frege and the young Russell is lost among the uncountable multitude of swindlers that pass for interpretations. The idea that propositions about his watch could be part of "geometry" was, for Frege, unspeakably silly. Any account of geometry that did not include a way to distinguish between propositions about points – *real* points, that is – and propositions about watches was, in his view, hopelessly inadequate.

The real issue was whether geometric axioms have to be understood as expressing propositions. Poincaré and Hilbert saw more clearly than anyone else at the time that the propositionalist reading was inadequate. Moreover, their efforts to convince the propositionalists of the peculiar role of geometric axioms were the first serious attempts to acknowledge a distinction that was destined to have a long and illustrious history in the twentieth century. Wittgenstein's domain of showing, his later grammar, Carnap's syntax, Sellars's categorial frameworks, and Kuhn's paradigms are some well-known members of the continuing series of attempts to find the right way of looking at that peculiar kind of knowledge that seems necessary and not vacuous, yet at the same time does not quite state any factual claims. Poincaré may have officially started the search when he observed that geometric axioms present themselves "in disguise," pretending to be claims but really being something else; and he also fixed the broad category in which they belong, since by calling them definitions, he clearly intended to assign to them a role in the determination of meaning.

Poincaré's conventionalism adumbrated, however indecisively, the first promising alternative to Kant's guess concerning the nature of apriority and necessity. Convention is sometimes thought to conflict with necessity. Yet convention, semantically interpreted, is merely the opposite side of necessity. In the range of meanings, what appears conventional from the outside is what appears necessary from the inside. The "linguistic" (better, semantic) theory of the a priori that would emerge decades later in the writings of Wittgenstein and Carnap would simply say that all necessity is semantic necessity, that all a priori truth is truth *ex vi terminorum,* that when a statement is necessary, it is because its rejection would be no more than a misleading way of rejecting the language (the system of meanings) to which it belongs. Thus, in the case of a priori claims, one and the same linguistic form may be seen as playing two radically different linguistic roles: When regarded from outside a linguistic framework, it must be seen as part of the definition of one such framework, a definition in disguise; when regarded from within the defined framework, that very sentence now expresses a claim, one true in virtue of the constituted meanings and therefore necessary.

Hilbert's formalism was inspired largely by the same motives as Poincaré's conventionalism. This convergence is hard to see because of long-standing prejudices about the character of formalism, which have also helped distort our understanding of the syntacticist stage in logical positivism. We will have to face those prejudices at the appropriate place, but we might as well say a word about them right now.

Hilbert's project was the culmination of developments starting with Pasch's celebrated *Vorlesungen über Neuere Geometrie* of 1882. Pasch still thought that in order to understand the meaning of geometric primitives, there was no other way but to exhibit the corresponding empirical correlates, and that the meanings of axioms similarly depend on their correlation with certain figures. But what distinguished him from most predecessors was his insistence that "the process of inference must be independent in all its parts from the *meaning* of the geometrical concepts, just as it must be independent from the diagrams" (p. 98). Thus, he endeavored to produce axiomatic formulations that provided a sufficient basis for geometry even when judged by standards as exacting as Frege's. Yet Pasch completely misunderstood what Poincaré clearly saw: the role played by meaning in his own considerations. By failing to think through his ideas on the role of ostensive definition, he did not recognize the untenability of geometric empiricism. But, more importantly, by tacitly granting to Kantians and positivists an intimate link between intuition and meaning, he misdescribed his own project as that of the elimination of meaning from geometry, thereby promoting the confusion between the purely formal and the meaningless. That Pasch's actual achievement could have been interpreted as the elimination of meaning from geometry is an indication of the extent to which Kantian presuppositions had become common ground in the intervening century. If Kant was right, concepts without intuitions are empty, and no geometric derivation is possible that does not appeal to intuition. But by the end of the nineteenth century, Bolzano, Helmholtz, Frege, Dedekind, and many others had helped determine that Kant was not right, that concepts without intuition are not empty at all. The formalist project in geometry was therefore designed not to expel meaning from science but to realize Bolzano's old dream: the formulation of nonempirical scientific knowledge on a purely conceptual basis. Once the Kantian prejudice was removed, one could see the hidden message of formalism concerning the meaning of geometric primitives: It is not that meaning is given at the beginning, in order to be immediately taken away so that geometers can do their work properly; rather, as Poincaré and Hilbert argued, meaning is first given by the very axioms that constitute the discipline.

To be sure, in these geometric writings one finds no more than glimpses, oblique adumbrations of things to come. The fog would not start to lift until three decades later; and even then, the myth that geometric formalism conceives of geometry as marks on paper would become the myth that syntax relates not to meaning but only to marks on paper. It would take a long time to realize that besides the suspect sense of meaning offered by the Platonist tradition, there is the sense that 'meaning' has in the English language, and that in this sense, formalism and syntax have a great deal to do with meaning. The next major step toward a clarification of these matters was taken in one of the strangest books ever written.

8

◁══▷

A logico-philosophical treatise

Whenever I have met unbelievers before, or read their books, it always seemed to me that they were speaking and writing in their books about something quite different, although it seemed to be about that on the surface. . . . Listen, Parfyon. You asked me a question just now; here is my answer. The essence of religious feeling does not come under any sort of reasoning or atheism, and has nothing to do with any crimes or misdemeanors. There is something else here, and there will always be something else – something that the atheists will forever slur over; they will always be talking of something else. – Prince Myshkin.

Dostoevsky, *The Idiot*

The logic of mysticism shows, as is natural, the defects which are inherent in anything malicious. While the mystic mood is dominant, the need of logic is not felt; as the mood fades, the impulse to logic reasserts itself, but with a desire to retain the vanishing insight, or at least to prove that it *was* insight, and that what seems to contradict it is illusion.

Russell, *Our Knowledge of the External World*

It isn't easy to decide whether Wittgenstein should be included among the members of the semantic tradition or among its most ferocious enemies. On the surface, at any rate, Wittgenstein's problems and techniques were those of the semanticists; beneath the surface, however, things are less clear. The difficulty is not so much that Wittgenstein's purposes were quite different from those of Frege, Russell, and their fellows, but that their philosophical hopes seemed to be Wittgenstein's fears; their projects, Wittgenstein's targets; their enemies, Wittgenstein's friends. Nor is it that Wittgenstein had a radically different view of the nature of logic, mathematics, and science than everyone else in that group; there had always been a large degree of pluralism within the tradition. But for all semanticists, scientific knowledge had been a model, a source of inspiration and of spiritual comfort. For Wittgenstein, however, it was of only secondary interest, to be dealt with much as Kant had dealt with pure theoretical reason: Set limits on it in order to leave room for something more substantial. Even Kant was too much a rationalist for Wittgenstein's taste, since in spite of their limitations, Kant remained enthusiastic about science and about rationality in general. If Wittgenstein was a fifth column among semanticists, it is because from the very beginning his heart was with one of the most romantic, unrational versions of idealism. If it ever looked otherwise, it is in part because he joined the enemy camp in order to display its failure from within and in part, also, because he was more successful at scoring points against his favorite team than against his opponents.

Wittgenstein's philosophy went through a number of stages. Two of them influenced logical positivists decisively. The first stage, characterized by the doctrines of the *Tractatus Logico-Philosophicus,* is the topic of this chapter; the second will be discussed in Chapters 16 and 17.

The *Tractatus* may well be the most difficult philosophical book written in this century. Two facts conspired to produce this result: The thoughts in it are very hard to explain – we are told; and Wittgenstein was singularly uninterested in or incapable of explaining his views to others. Almost everything he wrote was in the nature of a diary, a record of his thoughts, a conversation with himself or with God – hence, he did not feel the need to meet a potential interlocutor even halfway.

Ortega once wrote a piece entitled "In Defence of the Theologian and against the Mystic" (a project Wittgenstein would have detested), in which he noted a somewhat disturbing feature of mystics' dealings with religious subjects. The writings of mystics, he noted, are often classics in their own languages. With unsurpassed eloquence mystics take us stage by stage up the circuitous path leading to their mystical experiences. But when the hour of truth comes, when the real substance of their stories is about to emerge, all of their eloquence vanishes. They let go of our hands and say, "Words elude me at this point. . . . I must proceed now to my silent mystical experience; I wish you luck in getting your own." Something not entirely unlike this happens in the *Tractatus.* Its final aphorism tells us that "whereof one cannot speak, thereof one must be silent," and as Wittgenstein explained to von Ficker in 1919, it is what comes (or should have come) after this statement that really mattered to him: "My work consists of two parts: the one presented here plus all that I have *not* written. And it is precisely this second part that is the important one" (*Prototractatus,* p. 15).

Perhaps it will not be inappropriate to approach the *Tractatus* with a strategy fit for mystical writings, by attempting to ascend through stages to the ultimate vision awaiting the lucky ones right after proposition 7.

The first circle: links with the past

The semantics described in Wittgenstein's *Tractatus* is somewhere between Frege's and Russell's both in problems and in solutions, but on both scores, it is closer to Russell's. Even though the *Tractatus* talks extensively of *Sinn* and *Bedeutung,* these expressions do not designate, as in Frege, two semantic categories that apply to every linguistic unit. They refer, instead, to specific semantic elements: Not everything has a *Bedeutung,* only names do; and not everything has a *Sinn,* only pictures do. Wittgenstein did not think about semantics in Frege's way. From the very beginning he thought that the ultimate constituents of what we say are also the ultimate furniture of the world – the objects.[1] It is therefore worth considering more closely the links with Russell.

The Russellian conception of analysis and the associated doctrine of a perfect language are clearly part of Wittgenstein's view. "In statements (*Sätze*)," Wittgenstein asserted,

thoughts can be so expressed that to the objects of the thoughts correspond the elements of the sentence (*Satzzeichen*). These elements I call 'simple signs', and the statement 'completely analyzed'. The simple signs employed in statements are called 'names'. The name means (*bedeutet*) the object. The object is its meaning (*Bedeutung*). . . . The name represents the object in the statement. (*Tractatus* 3.2–3.22)

In 1915 he wrote in his notebook:

It is clear that the constituents of our statements can and should be analyzed by means of definitions, if we want to approximate the real structure of the statement. *In any case, then, there is a process of analysis.* . . . Analysis makes the statement more complicated than it was; but it cannot and ought not to make it more complicated than its meaning (*Bedeutung*) was to begin with. When the statement is as complex as its meaning, then it is *completely* analyzed. But the meaning of our statements is not infinitely complicated. The statement is the picture of the fact (*Tatsache*). (*Notebooks,* p. 46)

Frege would have gladly endorsed this picture-theoretic conception had it been associated with the domain of senses. But Russell had shifted the picture theory to the range of *Bedeutungen,* and Wittgenstein followed.

The link between Russell and Wittgenstein should not be exaggerated, however. Russell had been swept from one philosophical standpoint to another, with little consistency of purpose through the changes. In fact, when Wittgenstein first met him, Russell was in the process of unwittingly dismantling the core structure of the semantic project that he had eagerly promoted ten years earlier. The problem concerned Russell's theory of the proposition.

Since 1898 Russell had been trying to give shape to a theory of the proposition, with little fortune. Russell's early enthusiasm for relations had led him to conclude at first that if we believe (assume, etc.) a proposition, there must be an ego, a relation of belief (assumption, etc.), and a thing, the proposition in question. As we know, he had begun by acknowledging Moore's identification of propositions with facts; but as he tried to determine what a false proposition might be, he slowly came to think that there could be no such thing. If there were false propositions, there would have to be not only things such as *that Napoleon was a General* but also things like *that Napoleon was defeated at Marengo.* The former objects are surely there, but where are the latter?

For a while Russell entertained the possibility that the ultimate furniture of the world included not only facts but also "objective non-facts" or "fictions" (see "On the Nature of Truth," p. 46). In his 1904 review of Meinong's *Uber Annahmen* Russell explained that there are two basic approaches to knowledge: One says that "knowledge is the affirmation of a true complex, error that of a false one" ("Meinong's Theory of Complexes and Assumptions," *Essays in Analysis,* p. 63); the other contends that there are no false complexes, and therefore "judgment has no object except when the object is a *true* proposition" (p. 63). Russell thought it obvious that there were true propositional complexes (Moore's facts). He also thought that the analysis of a propositional attitude should not depend on the truth value of its target. If, for example, belief is a two-place relation between an ego and a proposition when the proposition is true, it must also be a dyadic relation when the proposition is false. Otherwise there would be intrinsic features of belief that would allow us to detect all falsehoods a priori. So he was at first inclined to go along with the first approach.

But what Russell was pleased to describe as his "vivid sense of reality" (*Russell's Logical Atomism,* p. 79) prevented him from holding such a view for long. A few years later he explained:

[Meinong's] view is, that there is an entity, namely the 'proposition' (*Objektiv*), to which we may have the dual relation of assumption or the dual relation of belief. Such a view is not, I think, strictly refutable, and until I had discovered the theory of 'incomplete symbols' I was myself willing to accept it, since it seemed unavoidable. Now, however, it appears to me to result from a certain logical naivete, which compels us, from poverty of available hypotheses, to do violence to instincts which deserve respect. (*Theory of Knowledge,* p. 108)

The instinct that deserved respect is that there is no such thing as, for example, *that Napoleon was defeated at Marengo.* So there are no false propositions. Therefore, propositional attitudes may not be analyzed as relations to propositions; therefore (*sic*), there are no propositions.

In order to mitigate the effects of this "final solution" in the field of semantics, Russell recalled that the incomplete-symbol strategy helps make sense of situations in which the category of symbol plays a semantic role even though (in Russell's sense) it "means" nothing. By 1910 he had concluded that propositions are incomplete symbols and that "some context is necessary before the phrase expressing a proposition acquires a complete meaning" (*Theory of Knowledge,* p. 109). What he meant by this is hard to explain without confusing use and mention or something else; but, roughly speaking, the idea was as follows.

Russell thought that the question "What is a proposition?" suffers from the same problem as "What is a class?" or "What is the round square?" It cannot be answered. The closest we can get to finding an answer involves looking at a broader context. The idealists were, once again, right in thinking that Russell's and Moore's propositional complexes were "false abstractions." In *Principia* Russell explained that

> a "proposition," in the sense in which a proposition is supposed to be *the* object of a judgment, is a false abstraction. . . . That is to say, the phrase which expresses a proposition is what we call an "incomplete" symbol; it does not have meaning in itself, but requires some supplementation in order to acquire a complete meaning. This fact is somewhat concealed by the circumstance that judgment in itself supplies a sufficient supplement, and that judgment in itself makes no *verbal* addition to the proposition. Thus, "the proposition 'Socrates is human'" uses "Socrates is human" in a way which requires a supplement of some kind before it acquires a complete meaning; but when I judge "Socrates is human," the meaning is completed by the act of judging, and we no longer have an incomplete symbol. (p. 44)[2]

Thus, the proper context from which they cannot be detached is judgment or belief. That is why the closest thing there is to a theory of the proposition is a theory of judgment.

The new theory was given its first full presentation in 1910. Its basic ideas are two: There is no more to propositions than there is to judgment, and judgment is not a relation between the judging mind and the proposition but a many-termed relation between the mind and the diverse constituents of what was thought to be the proposition. Russell still believed, with Brentano, that "in all cognitive acts . . . the mind has *objects* other than itself to which it stands in some one of these various relations" ("On the Nature of Truth and Falsehood" [1910], *Philosophical Essays,* p. 150; my italics). Since judgment or belief is listed as one of those cognitive relations, the principle applies to it as well. When I understand, entertain, believe, judge, or assert that John is tall, I do not stand in a relation of any sort to Bolzano's *Satz an Sich,* or to the Fregean sense of 'John is tall', or to Meinong's *Objektiv,* or to Russell's and Moore's old proposition *that John is tall.* I stand in relation only to what used to be regarded as the constituents of that proposition (and are still regarded as the constituents of the fact, if the judgment is true). What obtains, then, is a relation not between me and *that John is tall* but between me, and John, and tallness.

This approach is at odds with the purposes that had inspired Russell's philosophy in the first place, for it immediately entails the surrender to psychologistic semantics. Russell's original project was to oppose psychologism and subjectivism in logical or semantic matters. The strategy had been to develop the basic intuition that what we believe and know has a certain type of independence from the human mind; that what two people believe (even when false) might be the same; that logical relations of inference, consequence, and the like may – indeed, should – be analyzed without reference to the judging mind. The central tenet of the project had been that the nature of and the relations among the things that we may say are quite independent of whether anyone has said or will ever say them or hold any propositional attitude toward them.

If Russell's new theory of the proposition was correct, then these were vain dreams. Logic could not be regarded as a theory concerning the inferential relations of arbitrary propositions but, at best, of those that have and will be judged. No sense could be made of the idea that some propositions are a priori and others not; whatever sense there might be in this must be derived from properties of judgment – an idea that idealists had been advocating all along. Truth and falsehood could not exist in a world without minds. Russell did not miss this consequence. In 1912 he noted that it was "fairly evident that if there were no beliefs there could be no falsehood, and no truth either" (*The Problems of Philosophy*, p. 120). If so, no sense could be made of the truth value of an unasserted antecedent of an implication. Even if one extends Russell's doctrine beyond judgment to other propositional attitudes, it still follows that logic makes sense only when there are minds to judge or to engage in propositional attitudes. If truth and falsehood are mind-dependent, the type of semantics that Gödel and Tarski would develop in later years (Chapter 16) would have to be based on philosophical psychology and involve a theory of propositional attitudes. By 1910 Russell had driven himself full circle back to the psychologistic stage from which Brentano had initiated the march of the Austrian-realist tradition.

Russell seems to have sensed that something was amiss. In the manuscript of his *Theory of Knowledge* that he showed Wittgenstein in 1913, he let his old instincts loose for a moment when he recalled that "it is fairly obvious that the truth or falsehood which is attributed to a judgment or statement is derivative from the truth or falsehood of the associated proposition" (*Theory of Knowledge*, p. 108). But in the next two paragraphs he explained that "in my opinion" neither true nor false propositions are entities, and both must be regarded "as alike unreal, i.e. as incomplete symbols" (p. 109). A few pages later Russell's opinion was bracketed in an attempt to make these two doctrines consistent.

Russell's attempt to breathe some life into his defunct propositions began with the psychologistic assumption that the proposition must emerge from propositional attitudes – not necessarily from judgment but, preferably, from the one propositional attitude presupposed in all others: understanding. Russell analyzed our understanding that xRy as

$$U(S, x, R, y, \phi),$$

where U is the relation of understanding, S is the subject, x, R, and y are the constituents of the (quasi-resuscitated) proposition that xRy, and ϕ is the form of that complex. From this mind-dependent notion Russell defined the proposition that xRy as

There is a U and an S such that $U(S, x, R, y, \phi)$.

This, he concluded, "is the same for all subjects and for all propositional relations which we should regard as concerned with the same proposition. Thus there is no formal obstacle to defining this as the proposition" that xRy (p. 115).

Even though there is no "formal" obstacle (whatever that might mean), the definition fails to serve the purposes propositions were intended to serve in the semantic tradition – as Russell proceeded to point out. The main problem, he explained, "is that we cannot be sure that there are propositions in all cases in which logic would seem to need them" (p. 115). We would like logic to tell us about the inferential relations of propositions, quite independently of whether anyone has thought of them or has been acquainted with their specific constituents – a condition Russell imposed on understanding. Russell concluded that "we cannot know of the existence of propositions other than those that have been actually thought of" (p. 116). With that he let the matter drop.[3]

This is the point at which Wittgenstein entered. When Russell gave his young student the manuscript of his *Theory of Knowledge,* the topic on which Wittgenstein focused his criticism was the theory of judgment. We know little about the specific nature of his objections (see the subsection on types and forms, this chapter); but we do know that shortly after raising them, Wittgenstein wrote to Russell, "I am very sorry to hear that my objection to your theory of judgment paralyses you. I think it can only be removed by a correct theory of propositions" (Wittgenstein, *Letters,* p. 24). And when, a few months later, Russell insisted on his theory of propositions as incomplete symbols, Wittgenstein impatiently replied that "the proposition . . . is *of course* not an incomplete symbol" (*Letters,* p. 35).

By 1913 Russell had left semantic monism in ruins. On Wittgenstein's view, the first thing that had to be done in order to reconstruct semantics was to find the right answer to the question, What is a proposition? The key to that question, he thought, was a notion that neither Russell nor Frege had taken seriously enough: form.

The second circle: objects, facts, and their forms

Like Frege and (the early) Russell, Wittgenstein thought that as we analyze statements, we usually find that other statements occur as their
constituents (as in 'John believes p' or 'p and q'). The analysis is not
concluded until we reach the ultimate simples, which are, of course, not
statements but something else. Therefore, before we reach the endpoints
of propositional analysis, there must come a stage at which we encounter
the simplest complexes that convey information. This frontier between
the range of statements and that of its constituents, between what we can
say and mere names, is what Wittgenstein called the elementary statements (*Elementarsätze*). The radical character of Wittgenstein's reductionism is displayed in his doctrine that *all* information that could possibly be conveyed is already present at that level. Anything that can be said,
can be said by means of elementary statements. From this it follows that
semantics need not worry about anything beyond the domain of elementary statements and their semantic correlates.

According to Wittgenstein's reductionism, the only symbols that contribute constituents to propositions (that are not incomplete, as Russell
would put it) are the constituents of elementary statements,[4] the
"names," as Wittgenstein called them, whose semantic correlates are the
ultimate constituents of the world, the "objects." In order to understand
what an elementary statement is, we must understand what its form is.
This, in turn, depends on understanding the form of its constituent names
and their links with the forms of the objects they name.

As we know, Frege and Russell were struck by the power of a distinction between those constituents of what we say that can stand on their
own two feet and those that cannot. Russell thought that the constituents
of propositions are either concepts or objects; Frege, that they are either
saturated (objects) or unsaturated (senses of concept words or relation
words). Wittgenstein's decision to use a single word, '*Gegenstand*', for
all ultimate constituents reflects his conviction that there is something
wrong in the bipartition that both Frege and Russell had accepted. One of
the favorite questions among Wittgenstein scholars used to be whether
the *Tractatus* was nominalistic or realistic, which was sometimes translated into the question of whether Wittgenstein admitted only Fregean
objects as constituents of facts or whether he allowed concepts as well.
There can be little doubt that had the question been put to Wittgenstein,
his answer would have been that *neither* concepts *nor* objects in Frege's
sense are constituents of anything in his semantics.

Objects

Frege's distinction between concept (function) and object was, as we
know, introduced as an *alternative* to the traditional subject–predicate

analysis; so was Russell's. Few people have been more vocal than those two philosophers in their denunciation of the dangers and confusions implicit in the subject–predicate picture of semantics. It is therefore puzzling to find Wittgenstein saying that the concept–object distinction must be rejected because it is identical to the old subject–predicate distinction (*Philosophical Remarks,* pp. 119, 136;*Philosophical Grammar,* pp. 202, 205). Fregean concepts, he thought, were the properties of substrata (*Philosophical Remarks,* p. 120; *Philosophical Grammar,* p. 202), though, of course, he did not say why he thought so. He found this unacceptable.

A hint of what may have been in Wittgenstein's mind emerged during one of his conversations with his Viennese audience in 1929 (Waismann, *Vienna Circle,* pp. 41–2). Basically, what he told them is this: As long as we think only of the misleading picture of things implicit in ordinary language, we will take the subject–predicate form as dominant, and we will naturally be tempted to conclude that the world consists only of two sorts of things, those that are designated by subject expressions and those that are designated by predicate or relation expressions. *That* is the basic intuition behind the Frege–Russell distinction between concept and object.[5] As soon as we look beyond ordinary language to other forms of representation, Wittgenstein explained, the appeal of this dichotomy vanishes. For example, ordinary language would describe this room by alluding to tables, chairs, and so on, as well as to relations among them. But consider the following alternative description: The *phenomenal* room is now to be described by means of a two-dimensional surface given by an analytic equation and by assigning phenomenal colors (aġ la Carnap) to each of the points on the surface. This method of representation, according to Wittgenstein, is no less faithful to the basic facts than the first one, since it is surely closer to the level of "primary language" (as discussed later). When this form of representation is chosen, the temptation to talk about objects and concepts vanishes. Which are the objects and which the concepts? There must, of course, be ultimate elements of analysis, but it is not correct to partition them into the two Fregean categories.

These ultimate elements of analysis, these *indefinables,* are precisely Wittgenstein's objects.[6] The fact that he chose to assign all of them to a single category reflects his disagreement with Frege's and Russell's dichotomy. But it might also be taken to imply that the ultimate constituents of propositions are not of two radically different sorts but only of one, [7] that is, that Frege and Russell erred in finding too many varieties of indefinables. The truth is rather the opposite. Wittgenstein's main complaint against the Frege–Russell bipartition was that it sins even in trying to establish a priori the variety of categories of forms that there may be. This point emerges quite clearly when we turn to the central philosophical feature of Wittgensteinian objects, their form.

The form of objects

Wittgenstein said virtually nothing directly about the character of objects. There is no example of an object in the *Tractatus* and not even a hint of what these things might be.[8] But there is a great deal of talk about something *of* objects, their form. Understanding this may be the closest we can hope to come to understanding what objects are.

Perhaps the best way to approach Wittgenstein's doctrine of the form of objects is to compare it with Frege's doctrine of the unsaturatedness of first-level concepts. Even though Wittgenstein's objects were quite unlike Frege's, they were like Frege's concepts in that they were also unsaturated and in need of completion. Unlike Frege's concepts, however, they possessed a much more discriminating nature, a greater unsaturatedness, as it were. Let us examine each of these two features in turn.

It used to be said that the Tractarian picture of a proposition as a sequence of names was indefensible since 'John, Peter, Mary', for example, does not say anything. If we put a number of Fregean objects together, what we get is not a claim but a bunch of objects. But Wittgensteinian objects have "holes," like Frege's concepts, so that when we put them together, there may emerge a unit of a new, nonobjectual sort. Wittgenstein preferred a different analogy for expressing the same point: He compared objects to the links of a chain (*Tractatus*, 2.03), and he explained to Ogden that the point of the metaphor "is *that there isn't anything third* that connects the links but that the links *themselves* make connexion with one another" (*Letters to C. K. Ogden*, p. 23). In a similar vein, in 1929 he examined the question of how to analyze a proposition of the type *color c is located at place p* and observed:

It is clear that there is no relation of 'being at' obtaining between a color and a place, at which the color "is located." There is no in-between term between color and space. Color and space saturate (*sättigen*) each other. And the way in which they penetrate each other makes the visual field. (Typescript of vols. 1–4, p. 5, Wittgenstein Papers, 208)[9]

There is a crucial difference between Frege's concepts and Wittgenstein's objects, however. The holes in Frege's first-level concepts have a unique form, while those in Wittgenstein's objects have a plethora of forms. This metaphor is the reflection of a point Wittgenstein first made in connection with the doctrine of types. We must pause here to remind ourselves of how Russell came upon that doctrine and what its point was.

Types and forms

Russell's paradox, as stated for classes, could be solved by means of the no-classes theory: If there are no classes, there are no class paradoxes.[10]

The contradiction was derived from the assumption that there is a certain class, and the conclusion was therefore that there is no such class. But for the parallel case of the intensional contradiction, the relevant assumption is not one of existence but of meaningfulness; all that is assumed is that $F(F)$ makes sense, that it is either true or false. What we seem to have here is the first conclusive proof that some sentences that appear to make sense are, in fact, senseless.

In Wittgenstein's view, Russell's intensional paradox was not so much a dreadful problem to be solved for the sake of consistency, but rather an extraordinarily fortunate accident that brought to the surface a previously undetected confusion in traditional conceptions of language. If $F(F)$ is not, in fact, significant, there must be a host of other similarly misleading expressions, equally lacking in meaning. What we need, Wittgenstein thought, is *not* a trick to avoid the paradox, like Russell's theory of types, but a precise diagnosis of the disease upon which Russell had accidentally stumbled.

As Wittgenstein read it, Russell's theory of types attempted to solve the difficulty by identifying a system of rules that prevented the construction of expressions of the delinquent (meaningless) sort. It was, he thought, as if someone had decided to suspend the use of modus ponens in a region of argument in order to prevent the derivation of a contradiction; the theory attempted to prescribe, where what we had to do was more in the nature of describing. We did not need to impose rules of types. God had already done that. All we had to do was recognize His works in an appropriate symbolism, one that would make the type rules superfluous. Wittgenstein's first statement of this attitude appeared in a letter to Russell of January 1913; its point must be seen in the context of the views Russell was holding at the time.

In his *Theory of Knowledge* Russell had explained that if we understand aRb, then must we be acquainted not only with a, b, and R, but also with a fourth elusive element (not a thing, not a constituent of the proposition, but something nonetheless), the form of dyadic relational complexes, represented by 'xZy' (where 'x', 'Z', and 'y' are variables of the appropriate types). Here is Russell's account of why we understand propositions we have never seen before:

Let us suppose that we are acquainted with Socrates and with Plato and with the relation "precedes," but not with the complex "Socrates precedes Plato." Suppose now that someone tells us that Socrates precedes Plato. How do we know what he means? It is plain that his statement does not give us *acquaintance* with the complex "Socrates precedes Plato." What we understand is that Socrates and Plato and "precedes" are united in a complex of the form "xRy", where Socrates has the x-place and Plato has the y-place. It is difficult to see how we could possibly understand how Socrates and Plato and "precedes" are to be combined unless we had acquaintance with the form of the complex. (*Theory of Knowledge,* p. 99)

As usual whenever a question about "understanding" arose, Russell answered in terms of acquaintance. To understand a word is to know its meaning, and to know a meaning is to be acquainted with something, that meaning (e.g., *The Problems of Philosophy*, p. 104). This might be understood in a harmless manner, as a colorful rephrasing of the claim that we understand something. Russell did not mean it that way. For him, references to acquaintance were intended to be *explanatory:* To understand a meaning is to relate to it the way I relate to a sense datum when it is present in consciousness. And this was true not only of particulars and universals, the constituents of propositions and facts, but also of forms.

It was a natural concomitant of this view that even though forms are not constituents of propositions, they are quite independent of the entities that could be correlated "in those forms." Thus, "we might understand all the separate words of a sentence without understanding the sentence. . . . In such a case we have knowledge of the constituents, but not of the form. We may also have knowledge of the form without having knowledge of the constituents" (*Our Knowledge of the External World*, pp. 52–3). One may gather from scattered information that before 1913 Wittgenstein held a similar view (*Notebooks*, p. 117; *Letters*, pp. 13, 19). He thought that objects (particulars) and relations (in the old sense of these terms) were constituents of propositions, and independently of these things, and somehow "above" them, there was something else that Russell called the "form of the complex" and Wittgenstein the "copula."

In his letter to Russell of January 1913, Wittgenstein reported a change of mind on atomic complexes (roughly, in the direction of Frege's analysis) and then added:[11]

Every theory of types must be rendered superfluous by a proper theory of the symbolism: For instance if I analyze the prop Socrates is mortal into Socrates, Mortality and $(Ex, y) \epsilon_1(x, y)$ I want a theory of types to tell me that "Mortality is Socrates" is nonsensical, because if I treat "Mortality" as a proper name (as I did) there is nothing to prevent me to make the substitution the wrong way round. *But* if I analyze [it] (as I do now) into Socrates and $(Ex)x$ is mortal or generally into x and $(Ex)\phi(x)$ it becomes impossible to substitute the wrong way round, because the two symbols are now of a different *kind* themselves. (*Letters*, p. 19)[12]

Wittgenstein was telling Russell that he no longer agreed with the arguments in *Principles* that concepts can occur both in subject and in predicate position; revealingly, his point concerned substitution, which was, as we shall soon see, the most apparent feature of the form of objects. He was offering what would later become his definitive objection to Russell's theory of judgment (or, better yet, of the proposition): If there were no features intrinsic to the constituents of a complex that prevented them from being interchangeable, then in a complex such as

(*) that this book is on top of this table,

it should be possible to put a penholder where the relation *is on top of* stands. The result is the complex

(**) that this book penholders this table.

Equivalently, the sentence displayed in (**) and expressing the complex in question should be meaningful; it clearly is not (*Notebooks*, p. 96).

As Wittgenstein saw it, we do not need type rules to cope with things such as (**); rather we need to recognize that there simply are no such things as the complex allegedly described in (**). There are no such things because the constituents of that alleged complex have forms; that is, they are so constituted as to allow for certain sorts of links but not others, and *consequently,* syntactical appearances notwithstanding, there is no statement that represents it (*Notebooks,* 2.9.14, p. 2). If a linguistic system is like English in that it allows for configurations of symbols that appear to express the alleged complex (**), then what we need is not to add to that system a theory of types, but to throw that system away and replace it by one that does not allow such misleading symbolic configurations.

The idea was illustrated at a meeting with Vienna circle representatives, when Wittgenstein agreed that the following was a good explanation of the intended point: In a normal language such as German or English, not only can we formulate the statements 'A is north of B' and 'B is north of A' but we can also formulate their conjunction, and someone could be misled into thinking that there is a conceivable circumstance that this new configuration represents. The Russellian strategy for avoiding this difficulty would be to add a rule forbidding the introduction of conjunctions of that sort. The Wittgensteinian strategy was to adopt a different system of representation, in this case a map, in which one could still say the meaningful, that A is north of B, or that B is north of A, but could no longer display a configuration of symbols corresponding to the old 'A is north of B and vice versa' (Waismann, *Wiener Kreis,* pp. 79–80).[13]

The preceding considerations indicate how, from Russell's contradiction together with his attempted solution of its intensional version, Wittgenstein was led to think that objects, the ultimate constituents of propositional analysis and the ultimate furniture of the world, must have forms. These forms might be regarded as certain propensities to attach to or reject other objects, and in this respect, Wittgenstein's objects were very much like Fregean concepts. But we have also said that in a sense, they are unlike them. It is now time to see why.

It is ironic that several authors have seen in Frege's modest hierarchy of concepts an anticipation of the theory of types. There is, in fact, no

philosopher whose thought has been more hostile to type-theoretic thinking than Frege. In the famous hierarchy of concept levels, he paid attention
only to the first two stages and expressed a clear reluctance to go beyond
it. Much more to the point, Frege's first-level concepts, the ones that apply
to objects, are strikingly undiscriminating – absolutely any object in the
universe can fit into a concept and saturate it. From the first inaccessible
cardinal to the president of France, from a particular shade of color to truth
values and sneezes, every object in the universe is a proper argument for
the concept *is greater than 3.* If, as Anscombe once put it, Frege's concepts
have holes, the first thing to say about these holes is that they all have the
same "form" and, correspondingly, all objects must also have the same
"form." Indeed, in Wittgenstein's technical sense of form, it turns out that
this can be proved; for even though Wittgenstein said next to nothing
about what form *is,* he did explain himself on what it is to have the same
form: Two objects have the same form when, upon replacement of one of
them by the other in an arbitrary state of affairs, the result is still a state of
affairs. Thus, explaining to Waismann and Schlick that there cannot be one
subject–predicate form, he noted that "if there were only one, all substan-
tives should be intersubstitutable [*salva significatione*] and so should all
adjectives, for all intersubstitutable words belong in a single class" (Waismann, *Wiener Kreis,* p. 46).[14]

Similarly, in his *Theory of Knowledge* (which Wittgenstein read and,
by some accounts, "demolished"), Russell wrote, "two complexes have
the same form if the one becomes the other when the constituents of the
other are successively substituted for the constituents of the one" (p.
113). Two decades later this notion of form would make a notorious
appearance in a different branch of the semantic tradition. In his monograph on truth Tarski explained:

[The] concept [of semantical category], which we owe to E. Husserl, was introduced into investigations on the foundations of the deductive sciences by
Lesniewski. From the formal point of view this concept plays a part in the construction of a science which is analogous to that played by the notion of type in
the system *Principia Mathematica* of Whitehead and Russell. But, so far as its
origin and content are concerned, it corresponds (approximately) rather to the
well-known concept of part of speech from the grammar of colloquial language.
Whilst the theory of types was thought of chiefly as a kind of prophylactic to
guard the deductive sciences against possible antinomies, the theory of semantical categories penetrates so deeply into our fundamental intuitions regarding the
meaningfulness of expressions, that it is scarcely possible to imagine a scientific
language in which the sentences have a clear intuitive meaning but the structure
of which cannot be brought into harmony with the above theory. ("The Concept
of Truth in Formalized Languages," p. 215)

He then offered the following explication for the notion of 'same semantical category':

Two expressions *belong to the same semantical category* if (1) there is a sentential function which contains one of these expressions, and if (2) no sentential function which contains one of these expressions ceases to be a sentential function if this expression is replaced in it by the other. . . . By applying the principle of abstraction, all the expressions of the language which are parts of sentential functions can be divided into mutually exclusive classes. (p. 216)

If Tarski's sentential functions are replaced by Wittgenstein's elementary statements, we have the linguistic correlate of the notion of form: To each semantic category there corresponds a form and (in the ideal case) vice versa.[15]

The form of statements

When objects saturate each other in the fashion appropriate to their forms, a certain whole emerges. This whole is the closest thing in Wittgenstein's semantics to Russell's propositional complex.[16] It is what Wittgenstein called a *Sachverhalt* (henceforth Sv), a (possible) elementary circumstance,[17] "what corresponds to an Elementarsatz if it is true" (Letter to Russell of 19 August 1919, *Letters,* p. 72).

Like his predecessors, Wittgenstein had distinguished between language and what it represents, and he sought through analysis the constituents of linguistic and ontic complexes. The minimal molecule at the level of language is the elementary statement, and at the level of semantic it is the Sv. The constituent atoms of these molecules are names and objects, respectively. A particular statement and a particular Sv are configurations or "structures" (as Wittgenstein called them) of their constituent atoms. None of this seriously challenged tradition. But pre-Wittgensteinian monistic semantics was based on the idea that each linguistic configuration should map isomorphically the semantic configuration it aims to express and that the essence of linguistic representation lies in preservation of structure. This, Wittgenstein thought, is a superficial view of the matter, for it ignores form. At both the linguistic and the "worldly" level, the forms of the constituents induce a form on the new holistic units they constitute. "The logical form of the statement must already be given in the forms of its constituents" (*Notebooks,* 1 November 1914 (6), p. 23) and "If I know an object I also know all the possibilities of its occurrence in elementary circumstances" (*Tractatus,* 2.0123).

In 1929 Wittgenstein explained to Waismann, "A statement may be varied in as many dimensions as there are constants in it. And that is the

number of dimensions of the space in which the statement lies" (Waismann, *Wiener Kreis,* p. 91). For example, if the statement under consideration is the concatenation of the names *a* and *b,* then the logical
(or semantic) space in which it can be represented is two-dimensional,
and the coordinate axis associated with each of the objects (or names)
associates with each of its points an object of the same form. If John and
is tall were objects and they were the only objects in *John is tall,* then
this would be represented by a point in a two-dimensional semantic
space; another point would represent, for example, *Mary is short,* assuming that Mary has the same form as John and that *is tall* has the same form
as *is short.* If, following Wittgenstein, we call "the connection of the
elements of a picture . . . its structure" (*Tractatus,* 2.15), then the form
of a statement is the class of all structures that may be generated from it
by appropriate substitutions, or if we want to insist on an aphorist style,
we might say of the connection of the elements of a picture that "its
possibility is its form of representation" (2.15) or, better yet, "form is the
possibility of structure" (2.151).

Thus, a particular Sv displays a particular structure; the nature of its
constituent objects determines a class of other structures obtained by
substituting equiform objects. This class of all the *possible* structures
associated with the original structure displays the form of the Sv, which
underlies its visible structure. It is this form, rather than the surface
structure, that a correct linguistic representation must match. Not only
must a propositional picture be capable of offering an isomorphic map of
the specific arrangement of the objects in the Sv depicted; it must also be
modifiable, in conformity with its form, so as to represent isomorphically
all other structures of the same form. To the possible connections of
objects there must correspond isomorphic possible connections of their
names. What Wittgenstein called "multiplicity" was, apparently, this formal element. The requirement that a symbolic system and a corresponding reality have the same multiplicity demands that the symbolic system
and its objective correlate have exactly the same numbers of elements
and that these are capable of exactly the same structural arrangements.

The motivation for the requirement that an appropriate symbolism
have the same multiplicity as what it symbolizes is that the other two
alternatives have evident drawbacks. If the multiplicity of the symbolic
system is smaller than that of what it represents, there will be possible
circumstances we will not be able to describe. If the multiplicity is
greater, the problem is more familiar − it is called 'philosophy'. All of
philosophy (up to, and perhaps including, Wittgenstein) had consisted of
attempts to say things that cannot be said. Good philosophy attempts to
say what can be shown, the *sinnlos;* bad philosophy attempts to say what
cannot even be shown, the *unsinnig,* the utter nonsense. Most philoso-

phy had been bad philosophy, based on confusions concerning language. These confusions were roughly of the sort displayed by Russell's paradox: The language we use has a greater multiplicity than what it talks about. We can therefore form expressions whose syntactic appearance is like that of perfectly meaningful claims, but from them we are led to some form of chaos. *All* bad philosophy is the use of expressions like Russell's '*F(F)*'. A "correct *Begriffsschrift*" would make bad philosophy impossible; it would also display the way to show and only show what good philosophy tries to say.

Form is the key to meaning. Indeed, it may be said that Wittgenstein held a correspondence theory of meaning: Statements need not correspond to reality the way true sentences do, but there must nonetheless be some element in the symbol that is identical with some element in the circumstances symbolized, in order for the former to symbolize the latter; this element is form. A name, a symbol for an object, can represent that object only if it has the same form as the object: "The forms of the entities are contained in the form of the proposition which is about these entities . . . the proposition contains the form of an entity which it is about" (*Remarks on the Foundations of Mathematics*, p. 36). And a thought can represent a reality only if they have the same form: "What the picture and reality must have in common in order to be able to represent it after its manner – either truly or falsely – is its form of representation" (*Tractatus*, 2.17; see also *Notebooks*, 20 November 1914, p. 15).

Let us pause to survey this territory from the vantage point we have now achieved. There are basically three things that concern the Wittgensteinian logician in the treatment of statements and what they represent: their constituents, their form, and the associated facts. At the level of language, the reductionist analysis took us first from arbitrary statements down to elementary statements, and beyond them to their simple constituents, the names. Then we moved to their worldly correlates – the objects – examined their form, and started moving upward toward Sv's. Yet the world is neither objects nor forms but everything that is the case, the facts. Thus, we have to move upward beyond elementary circumstances.

One of the seven Tractarian pillars (*Tractatus*, 2), says, "What is the case, the fact, is the obtaining of Sv's"; not Sv's, but their obtaining. Names and statement forms are essential in that they provide the scaffolding required for the purposes of communication, but those purposes are ultimately fulfilled by something else, by statement facts in which those names are constituents and those forms are displayed. The reason for this is that what we want to communicate is what we regard as *fact*, and Wittgenstein thought that this could be depicted only by means of other facts. Thus, objects are represented by names (which may have been endowed with a form of sorts through grammatical rules), forms by forms, and facts by facts. If, *per impossibile,* John and Tall were objects, they would be represented by names like 'John' and 'is tall', their forms by the forms induced on 'John' and 'is tall' through linguistic rules (although the ideal symbolism, as in the map analogy, would not require such rules), and finally, the fact that John is tall would be represented by some fact concerning the symbols 'John' and 'is tall'. A correct symbolism would allow for substitutions of all names of the same form for 'John' in 'John is tall', but not for 'tall'. The symbol 'John is tall' would have the same form as the fact that John is tall, *because* the symbols 'John' and 'is tall' would have the same form as their corresponding objects. In this language there would be no symbol for forms. There would be no symbol for the form of the fact that John is tall, for example. But that form would nonetheless be displayed by the language. The proposition that says John is tall would, at the same time, show what the form of that fact is, since its form is precisely the form of that fact: Its possibilities of meaningful rearrangement are a perfect replica of the possibilities of rearrangement of the corresponding objects.

We have been talking about the representation of facts by means of linguistic facts, but what we want to be able to represent includes things such as

that Hitler was wise and benevolent.

The word 'fact' may not be appropriate here. That is why in the *Tractatus* Wittgenstein did not talk of linguistic facts representing nonlinguistic facts, but said instead that only facts can represent *senses* (*Sinne*), since senses are the possibilities of the holding or not holding of an Sv. The remaining question is, What is sense? The answer depends on the notion of a *Sachlage* (henceforth Sl).

The third circle: Wittgenstein's *Sinn*

In the beginning were the objects and their forms. Having decided on which objects to create, God still had more work to do, since the world is the totality not of objects but of facts.

Sv's are of two sorts: those that obtain (*Bestehende* Sv) and those that do not (*Nichtbestehende* Sv). A fact (*Tatsache*) is the obtaining of a circumstance (*Tractatus,* 2) – not a circumstance, or even one that obtains, but the obtaining of one. An Sl is the holding or not holding of circumstances – not necessarily a fragment of the *actual* holding or not holding of circumstances chosen by God in the act of creation, but any possible one (2.11). Thus, an Sl can be seen as a fragment of a world that

God could have created or, equivalently, as a class of possible worlds (all the worlds agreeing on that particular fragment).

This notion provides the key to Wittgenstein's theory of the meaning or sense of a sentence. He explained that a picture presents (*darstellt*) a possible Sl in logical space (*Tractatus,* 2.202), and what the picture presents is its sense (2.221). Since he also thought that every statement is a picture of reality (4.01), we seem justified in concluding that the sense of a statement is always a possible Sl.[18]

Further clues to the nature of sense are given in *Tractatus,* 4.2, which offers an indirect way of identifying the sense: "The sense of the statement is its agreement and disagreement with the possibilities of the obtaining and non-obtaining of Sv's." Unscrambled the claim appears to be that if we were given all the possibilities of obtaining and nonobtaining of Sv's, all "maximal Sl's" we might call them, or all possible worlds, then to know the sense of a statement is just to know with which of those possible worlds it agrees and with which it does not – or, equivalently (by 2.222), in which of those possible worlds the statement is true. This is just another way of identifying the appropriate Sl, since the Sl in question is simply the element common to all the maximal collections of Sl's with which the statement agrees. To put the matter in more pedestrian terms, we might represent an Sl as a fragment of what Carnap called a state description, and what I have called a maximal Sl as a state description. The sense of a statement would then become the Sl in question or, alternatively, the class of all possible worlds that have it as a part. This alternative would be the one described in *Tractatus,* 4.2. Once again, one may notice the link between these ideas and semantic monism since, like Russell, Wittgenstein concludes that the object *a* occurs in the sense of *'fa'*.

To understand a statement, we said, involves knowing its form and therefore the form of what it represents. But to understand a statement *is* to know (*kennen*) its sense (4.021). When I understand a statement, I know the Sl it presents (*darstellt*). This ties up with the famous doctrine that to understand a statement is to know (*wissen*) what is the case when it is true, for the Sl that is its sense is precisely that – what is the case if the statement is true. It also explains why the sentence shows how things stand if it is true (4.022), since what the sentence shows is its sense (4.022).[19]

Closely connected with these points is one of Wittgenstein's earliest ideas, what he called at first the "bipolarity business," the root of his later verificationism. Already in a text from 1913 Wittgenstein had made the observation that "what we know when we understand a proposition is this: we know what is the case if it is true and what is the case if it is false"

(*Notebooks,* pp. 93–4). He noticed shortly thereafter that far from it being a mere accidental correlation, "the being true or false actually constitutes" the having of sense (p. 112). If an alleged statement is to be a genuine vehicle of information, if it is to be a real statement, it must have two poles, the truth pole and the false pole; that is, there must be *both* circumstances that make the statement true *and* circumstances that make it false. The absence of *either* of those poles guarantees the absence of both, because it guarantees the failure of sense. (Since sense is the possible facts common to the possible worlds in which the statement is true and since no possible fact is present in all possible worlds, both tautologies and contradictions have nothing at all as sense.)

Now we know what sense is, we know the "general form of the proposition," we know what it is to *say* something, what conditions are to be fulfilled in order for an apparent vehicle of information actually to be such. By implication, we have also determined what lies outside the sphere of sense.

The fourth circle: showing and saying

What, one may well ask, is the purpose of this baroque semantic edifice? In the semantic tradition feats of this sort had always been performed for the greater glory of science, to cleanse it from blemishes and give it as solid a foundation as possible. Why engage in this extraordinary search for the essence of the proposition? Where was the fire that fueled this amazing enterprise?

Most philosophers will agree that Wittgenstein was, after all, human, and hence was likely to be inspired by reasons that reason might not always comprehend. It is therefore worth observing that, like Prince Myshkin, Wittgenstein came to believe very early on that the truly important things in life are not among those whereof one may speak. When Parfyon Roghozin asked Myshkin whether he believed in God, the gentle prince would not give a direct answer. Some commentators (e.g., Guardini) have explained that the answer was too obvious; but it seems more plausible to think that in Myshkin's mind *any* answer to that question would have been wrong. The atheist professor who answers one way is no more confused than the Catholic theologian who contradicts him. The sort of reasoned discourse in which both engage, the domain of saying, is fit only for the lower purposes of science and other pragmatic matters. Everything that really counts, that gives meaning to life and thereby to the world, is entirely unsayable.

The *Tractatus* tells us that "all propositions are of equal value," that "in the world . . . there is no value . . . there can be no ethical propositions," that "propositions cannot express anything sublime," that "even if all *possible* scientific questions be answered, the problems of life still have not been touched at all," and that "the sense of the world must lie outside the world" (6.4–6.421, 6.52). Besides what we can say, "there is indeed the inexpressible. This *shows* itself; it is the mystical" (6.522). Even though these doctrines appear at the end of the *Tractatus,* there can be little doubt that they stood at the very beginning of the train of thought that inspired it. Wittgenstein *wanted* to establish with classical rigor that there is a special, superior place for something like that moment of insight and peace at the very beginning of Myshkin's epileptic fit, when he was overcome by "a feeling, unknown and undivined till then, of wholeness, of proportion, of reconciliation, and of ecstatic devotional merging in the highest synthesis of life." In the end, Wittgenstein did come up with a distinction between what language says and a different domain of things that we may aim to say but always unsuccessfully.

In 1919, in response to some questions Russell had raised about the *Tractatus,* Wittgenstein wrote that Russell had missed the "main contention" of the book: "The main point is the theory of what can be expressed (*gesagt*) by prop[ositions] . . . and what can not be expressed by prop[ositions], but only shown (*gezeigt*); which, I believe, is the cardinal problem of philosophy" (Letter of 19 August 1919, *Letters,* p. 71). Whether one agrees with Wittgenstein or not, there is, as we shall see, a recognizable and insightful train of thought leading from the analysis of form presented earlier to the conclusion that we cannot say what modus ponens "says," or what is "said" by anything involving formal concepts as a topic. Whether there is any link at all between the view we are about to explain and God, or the meaning of life, or any of the mystic images that Wittgenstein was hoping to rescue from the claws of Reason, is a matter I must leave for better minds to determine. The purpose here merely is to make some sense of what Wittgenstein showed about showing in the field of logic.

Two decades before the *Tractatus,* Lewis Carroll had presented a striking paradox stemming from the traditional way of thinking about logic. In his celebrated dialogue between Achilles and the Tortoise, he had the latter arguing that a valid inference can be drawn only after we have completed infinitely many tasks, for we must acknowledge infinitely many premises before we are entitled to endorse the conclusion. His point was basically this: We all agree that from 'If A then B' and A, B follows logically. But Carroll notes that if we *fail* to grant *either*

(1) $A \ \& \ A \Rightarrow B$

or

(2) $(A \& A \Rightarrow B) \Rightarrow B,$

we will not be entitled to infer

(3) $B.$

"Hence," he wrote, "*before* granting (3), I must grant [not only (1) but] (1) and (2)." But, in fact, if I do not grant *also* that (1) and (2) entail (3), I am still not entitled to infer (3). "Surely, my granting (3) must *wait* until I have been made to see the validity of this sequence" (Carroll, *Symbolic Logic,* p. 472). And so on ad infinitum.

The paradox is entirely spurious because of the role time plays in it. Carroll's reasoning is, in fact, a revealing illustration of the way psychology and logic were fused before objective content was detached from the mental acts related to it. Whether an inference is justified does not, of course, depend on whether we have noticed anything at all. But when the reference to time and psychology is excluded, there still remains a problem for the semantic construal of logic. If the justification of the inference from (1) to (3) requires an appeal to the logical law (2), why don't we need to appeal to further logical laws in order to justify the inference from (1) and (2) to (3); and so on ad infinitum? Doesn't the justification of logical inference involve an infinite regress?

Since Aristotle, several philosophers had recognized something like this regress, and it had been acknowledged that the regress must somehow be broken. A favorite way to break it, recently revived by Russell, was by an appeal to self-evidence or intuition. The inference from one claim to another must be backed up by a logical law; but the regress stops at the law, because we now say that it is known immediately in intuition.

In *The Problems of Philosophy,* while explaining his views on logic, Russell invited his readers to imagine a discussion between two men trying to determine what day it is:

One of them says, 'At least you will admit that *if* yesterday was the 15th to-day must be the 16th'. 'Yes', says the other, 'I admit that'. 'And you know', the first continues, 'that yesterday was the 15th, because you dined with Jones, and your diary will tell you that was on the 15th'. 'Yes', says the second; 'therefore to-day *is* the 16th'. (p. 71)

Everyone will recognize this as an instance of the soundest sort of reasoning there is, logical reasoning. But *why* is it so solid? What are the root and the justification of its infallible accuracy? Russell explained that the argument is acceptable *only because* it can be subsumed under a very special sort of law: Its conclusion

depends for its truth upon an instance of a general logical principle. The logical principle is as follows: 'Suppose it known that *if* this is true, then that is true.

Suppose it also known that this *is* true, then it follows that that is true'. . . . This principle is really involved . . . in all demonstrations. . . . If anyone asks: 'Why should I accept the results of valid arguments based on true premises?' we can only answer by appealing to our principle. In fact, the truth of the principle is impossible to doubt, and its obviousness is so great that at first sight it seems almost trivial. (*The Problems of Philosophy,* pp. 71–2)

In the model of logical representation developed by Frege and Russell and now widely regarded as standard, one thinks of a proper axiomatization of a discipline as involving, besides the specific assumptions or axioms of that discipline, a set of logical axioms and logical rules of inference. Both the logical and the nonlogical axioms are thought to occur as part of the same language and to differ only in the scope of their validity and perhaps also in the abstractness of the domain with which they are concerned. Thus, a correct and complete account of the inference from $A \lor B$ and $-A$ to B will involve logical laws (perhaps $((A \lor B) \& -A) \Rightarrow B$) and logical rules (perhaps modus ponens). All of this machinery must be mobilized for the purpose of inferring B, and without any of it, the inference would not be justified. This is the point that Russell was trying to exemplify in the preceding quotation (taking account of the fact that, unlike Frege, Russell seldom paid attention to the distinction between logical rules and logical laws). In Russell's case, at any rate, it is clear that the appeal to laws is intended to play an explanatory and justificatory role: "If anyone asks: 'Why should I accept the results of valid arguments based on true premises?' we can *only* answer by appealing to our principle" (i.e., modus ponens; *The Problems of Philosophy,* p. 72; my italics).

The problem that emerges from this perspective is, What justifies the logical laws and rules? The standard answer was intuition. But we have recently examined the most detailed account of what this would involve in the field of logic, and we have seen the view collapse into virtual incoherence. In Wittgenstein's view, an accurate diagnosis of the situation has been prevented by the propositionalist prejudice, by the insistence on looking at logic and other a priori disciplines as being expressed in statements that convey facts, just like any a posteriori statement – except that the facts in question are somehow otherworldly. If logical laws were essentially like all other statements, they would require some sort of justification, as every statement does. The best among Wittgenstein's predecessors had tried to provide that justification, but with no success. Wittgenstein's solution was to say that logic, and the a priori in general, has no justification, since it cannot even be conveyed by means of claims. There isn't a "hard" domain of a priori truths and a "soft" domain of empirical truths; all the truths there are, are empirical. That does not eliminate the a priori but rather locates it as a "hardness in the soft," as what one might perhaps call a formal aspect of all meaningful, factual discourse.

In Wittgenstein's view, the depsychologized version of Carroll's paradox suffices to establish the bankruptcy of all attempts to provide a foundation for inference on the basis of more general statements: If B will not follow from $(A \lor B)$ & $-A$ unless we explicitly add the assumption that $((A \lor B)$ & $-A) \Rightarrow B$, then by the same token B will not follow from *these three assumptions* unless we add the further assumption that all of these premises, properly generalized, entail B; and so on ad infinitum (see *Lectures, 1930–32,* p. 56). To the pseudo-Fregean alternative that deductive inference is justified by rules, Wittgenstein's response would be to ask for a non-question-begging justification of those rules. In later years it would become apparent that any such "justification" would presuppose the very claim it was supposed to establish and therefore also lead to an infinite regress or a circle.

Wittgenstein had focused on this problem from early on. In 1912 he had written to Russell: "Logic must turn out to be of a TOTALLY different kind than any other science" (*Letters,* p. 10). Two years later he found a way to articulate his point. He had come to think that logic must differ from other theories already at the level of how it conveys its message, of how it says what it says. He concluded that he had to draw a distinction between regular "saying," the sort of thing for which it matters how things stand, and something that superficially seems like saying but is entirely different from it. To see what he meant we must examine his way of thinking about logic.

Wittgenstein's new solution started by going back to the first stage of the problem: Do we need to "know" something besides $A \lor B$ and $-A$ in order to conclude that B? *If* Carroll and Russell were right in thinking that the inference to B requires an appeal to the corresponding logical law, and also right in thinking that the law is independent of those premises even to the point that it could be rejected while the premises are accepted, then it seems that there is no way to stop the infinite regress. Russell's appeal to self-evidence put forth as a model for the explanation of logic the idea of a special kind of relationship to a special kind of claim. Wittgenstein, however, put forth the idea that logic is fully explained by an appeal to a familiar kind of relationship to the most familiar kinds of claims. The so-called logical law that is said to justify the inference to B is not a law, and it does not justify anything at all. It is, in a sense, a necessary statement, but it is quite unlike all other statements in that what it "says" bears no relationship to how things might stand and relates only to the nature of language. For example, the logical law that was thought to justify the inference to B is something we see when we understand the premises A and $A \Rightarrow B$. In this picture of things, logic emerges not from the intuition of extraordinary claims but from our understanding of the ordinary ones. Logic "shows itself" because it is something we recognize as soon as we understand the language we are talking, something that in no sense depends on how anything stands in the world or in the mind, but only in the understanding of language:

If p follows from q, I can conclude from q to p; infer p from q. The mode of inference is to be understood from the two propositions alone. Only they themselves could justify the inference. "Laws of inference" which — as in Frege and Russell — are supposed to justify the inference, are senseless and would be superfluous. (*Tractatus*, 5.132)[20]

That the truth of one proposition follows from that of another is something "we see from the structure of the propositions" (*Tractatus*, 5.13). If so, it would be an error to think that the conclusion of Russell's date example "depends for its truth upon an instance of a general logical principle." The *truth* of the conclusion (as Russell knew) depends only on the facts of the matter; and our inferential knowledge of it depends only on the recognition of the particular claims that have been accepted as premises, as well as an understanding of what it is to accept something as true. Similarly, to say that Russell's version of modus ponens is "really involved . . . in all demonstrations" is as plausible as saying that the restatement in the course of an argument of a previously endorsed claim "strictly speaking" involves an appeal to an instance of the law of identity (that p implies p).[21]

What, then, about logic and its laws? "My fundamental thought," Wittgenstein explained in the *Tractatus*, "is that the 'logical constants' do not represent (*vertreten*). That the *logic* of facts cannot be represented" (4.0312). This means that we cannot think of logic as the most general laws of a *Begriffsschrift*. The "old logic," Wittgenstein had explained in 1914, "gives so-called primitive propositions; so-called rules of deduction; and then says that what you get by applying the rules to the propositions is a *logical* proposition that you have *proved*" (*Notebooks*, p. 108). The tacit presupposition is that, as in the model case of Euclidean geometry, we can also identify in logic some primitive truths from which one can deduce all others. This is the root of the misunderstanding.

Logic is radically different from every other type of knowledge because its "justification" lies not in how things stand but in the understanding of language. As I understand the language in which $A \lor B$ and $-A$ are formulated, I ipso facto recognize that whatever A and B might be, if those two statements were true, B would also be true. One might perhaps say that I "see" the law that $((A \lor B \,\&\, -A) \Rightarrow B)$, for all As and Bs; but this way of putting things is the one that makes us think of logical laws as very general truths and thereby to appeal to intuition or self-evidence: "The self-evidence of which Russell talks so much can only be discarded in logic by language itself preventing every logical mistake. That logic is a priori consists in the fact that we *cannot* think illogically" (*Tractatus,* 5.4731).

The basic point is that in this new picture of things, the focus is not on the "seeing" of a certain very general and a priori truth but on the recognition of certain meanings, on *understanding.*[22] In general, it would appear that *everything* that "shows itself" emerges entirely from our understanding of language.

What shows itself is not restricted to the field of logic. When we go beyond the molecular structure of the proposition and examine its internal constitution, we find the source of further "claims" that appear to be a priori but that also belong to the range of what shows itself once the essence of a language is recognized. These "laws" emerge from the character of formal concepts. Here bipolarity is no longer of any use in helping us detect the idiosyncratic character of these claims, since in the case of most statements about formal concepts, we seem to be able both to assert and to deny the apparent claim. We seem to be able to assert *and* to deny that numbers are objects or that there are more than two things in the universe. The reason for the unsayability of these claims emerges from the fact that 'object', 'number', and the other basic notions they involve are not really concepts but formal concepts; thus, they do not designate properties an object might or might not have, but features of the very essence of the entities involved.

Ontologically speaking (which was Wittgenstein's way of speaking at this stage), it is very hard to make any sense of all this. But if the "internal," the "formal," is interpreted as that which is determined entirely by our understanding of language, then we may perhaps interpret these as remarks concerning what we need to know in order to understand what we are talking about, as opposed to what we need to know in order to be aware of those properties it has and it might not have had.

Now we see that the decision to identify the bounds of sense, to chart the limits of language from within, was inspired not by an interest in the charted territory but in what lies beyond it. Beyond the range of meaningful discourse lies, first of all, the vast and arid land of utter nonsense, inhabited philosophy, and much else. The discovery of this domain caused great excitement among positivists in Vienna. Wittgenstein, who did not share their antimetaphysical zeal, did not much care about that outcome of his endeavor. What he did care about was the remaining domain, not the *sinnvoll* or the *unsinnig,* but the *sinnlos,* what shows itself. All good metaphysics, all of the truly important things in philosophy, had finally been given their proper place – right outside language. Language is the key to all metaphysical knowledge; it is the vehicle through which we recognize it, but not in any previously imagined manner. These "truths" emerge not from the acknowledgment of facts — these could always be otherwise — but through the recognition of meaning. From logic to solipsism, everything that is a priori is what we must see when we know how to communicate. Language and meaning had become the very heart of metaphysics.

PART II

Vienna, 1925–1935

9

Schlick before Vienna

In the second half of the nineteenth century Kant was regarded with enormous respect by the most reasonable part of the German philosophical community. This attitude was inspired partly by the intrinsic value of Kant's work, but partly also by the dramatic contrast between his sober, reasonable approach and the romantic flights of those who followed him on the German scene.

Early in the twentieth century, that periodic German revolt against reasonableness started once again; and once again Kant compared favorably with the Schelers and the Heideggers that began to capture the imagination of the philosophical masses. Little wonder that those more inclined to take things calmly organized a *zurück zu Kant* movement of their own, emphasizing the scientific aspect of Kant's work, much in the fashion of Helmholtz, Zeller, Riehl, and also the Marburg school. All of the leaders of Viennese positivism began their philosophical path as neo-Kantians of this kind. Schlick was the first among them.

With Schlick, we are back in the world of Kantian questions and semi-Kantian answers, so different from that of the semantic tradition. The little he knew of that tradition before Vienna was primarily its hypostatic version in the writings of Brentano's students and, to a lesser extent, in Russell's. Like so many others before and after him, Schlick concluded that a nonpsychologistic theory of meaning was incompatible with empiricism.

Though Schlick knew and cared little about the semantic tradition, like all neo-Kantians he cared very much about mind. As we shall see, for almost every issue he raised, one does not have to dig very deep in order to uncover the human mind. The mental character of the inner world is obvious; but even the perceivable parts of the "outer" world turn out to be constituted by qualities such as shapes and colors that, on closer examination, reveal themselves as children of the mind. Unlike most of Kant's followers, however, Schlick also cared seriously about contemporary science. The particular brand of neo-Kantianism he endorsed had been inaugurated in the writings of Helmholtz and developed by other great scientists, including Schlick's mentor, Max Planck. Schlick was the first to attempt a systematic formulation of the picture of knowledge implicit in Helmholtz's writings. Its centerpiece was a doctrine of scientific realism destined to become quite popular among postpositivistic philosophers of science. But as Schlick developed the details of this conception, it became apparent that his concessions to Kantianism had made the defense of realism an extraordinarily burdensome task.

From the commonsense standpoint of both Kantians and positivists, the semantic developments reviewed in Part I appeared as retrogressions to an intolerable dogmatic-Platonic metaphysics. Indeed, the wisest semanticists had wanted to reject Platonism but had nothing of substance to say about how this could be done in a way that was consistent with their project. Carnap's sterilization of semantic realism was still far in the future. Psychologistic "naturalized" semantics seemed to most the natural ally of all sensible empiricists. Yet one century earlier psychologistic semantics had also presided over the developments leading to idealism. Bolzano, Frege, and their followers had claimed that this was no accident and that however hostile to empiricist sensitivities, their type of semantics was required in order to develop a sensible realistic account of empirical knowledge. Schlick's effort to work out a defense of empirical realism on standard pre-Fregean semantic assumptions offers impressive evidence that they were right.

Our purpose here is to present, first, the largely tacit semantic ground on which Schlick's case for realism was built and then to display his elaboration of Helmoltz's picture of the link between knowledge and reality.

Schlick's semantics

In one of the most penetrating statements of his *Logic,* Mill had noted:

An inquiry into the nature of propositions must have one of two objects: to analyse the state of mind called Belief, or to analyse what is believed. All language recognizes a difference between a doctrine or opinion, and the fact of entertaining the opinion; between assent, and what is assented to. . . . Philosophers, however, from Descartes downwards, and especially from the era of Leibnitz and Locke, have by no means observed this distinction; and would have treated with great disrespect any attempt to analyse the import of Propositions, unless founded on an analysis of the act of Judgment. A proposition, they would have said, is but the expression in words of a Judgment. The thing expressed, not the mere verbal expression, is the important matter. When the mind assents to a proposition, it judges. Let us find out what the mind does when it judges, and we shall know what propositions mean, and not otherwise. (bk. 1, chap. 5, sec. 1)

Schlick's early work fits rather well to Mill's model of a psychologistic logician. According to the early Schlick, representations are mental images (*GTK,* sec. 4) and may be explained as follows:

When I utter such words as: 'the sea' or 'Rostock' or 'cat', the phenomena, the mental products, which appear in your consciousness on hearing these words, are just what we call representations. But these representations are in your mind, not only when you think of the objects named, but also when you actually see them before you. . . . Representations, like all mental objects, cannot be defined, but only experienced. ("What Is Knowing?" [1911–12], pp. 125–6)

Similarly, it makes no sense to talk of propositions except as abstractions embodied in acts of judgment ("The Nature of Truth in Modern Logic" [1910], p. 54). Meaning "has its habitation only *in* the mental experience . . . we cannot, that is, regard the logical propositions as structures devoid of any mental character" (p. 54). For example, it is absurd to think, as Husserl and Hilbert did, that one can establish the existence of solutions to certain systems of equations unless one actually produces such solutions explicitly in thought. In his *Logical Investigations* Husserl had argued that the solution to the *n*-body problem may transcend all human cognitive powers, "but the problem has a solution" (p. 191). Schlick responded that this can only mean that *n* gravitating bodies actually move in a certain way. A "solution" would be a mathematical judgment, and if the passing of such a judgment is beyond human capabilities, then there is no solution ("The Nature of Truth in Modern Logic," p. 52).

One could hardly illustrate more clearly the view that there is nothing whatever between psychology and the real world. On this score, of course, Schlick and Russell agreed against Frege: Nothing at all deserves philosophical recognition except for the inner and the outer world. Schlick acknowledged the mental acts of judgment and representation, as well as the physical matters they sometimes aim to represent, but there is nothing else between them. For example, "when I remove everything generated by the mind from the representation of 2, we have nothing left; the residue can at most consist of two real objects or mental processes" ("Das Wesen der Wahrheit nach der modernen Logik," p. 407). What Russell and Schlick did disagree on was where to place the realm of semantics. For Russell, what we say can be objective only if we regard it as constituted out of the elements in the real world. For Schlick, as for Mill's psychologistic logician, the realm of meaning pertains to the mental world.

Science consists of judgments whose ultimate constituents are representations. But since the essence of science is generality and precision, and since intuitions are both singular and imprecise, there must be another form of representation that lies at the heart of the scientific enterprise. There must be something like what used to be called a general representation. What is it? Or to put it differently:

What sort of visual image arises in my mind, for example, when I hear the word 'dog', and thus think of dogs quite generally? Now, that is rather hard to say. Mostly it will happen that a vague image forms in my consciousness of a dog belonging to some particular breed, such as a St. Bernard, to be at once followed by the afterthought that not just this one, but all other kinds of dogs as well, should be taken into account; and this afterthought may again figure in consciousness in that at once, in faint outline, the visual representations of other dogs, dachshunds, bulldogs and so on, make a blurred, momentary appearance. This much, at least, is clear: it is quite impossible for me to frame a clear representation of a dog that is neither a St. Bernard, nor a bulldog, nor a dachshund, nor any other particular sort of dog. . . . You can thus easily see that real general representations as such are impossible. ("What Is Knowing?" p. 128)

Even though we represent generally, we do so not with general representations but with the only representations Schlick acknowledged – singular representations; in representing generally, the singular representation is accompanied by a conscious recognition that it is to count only as a representative (p. 129).

The logical structure of judgments emerged from Schlick's refusal to detach semantics not only from psychology but, in true Kantian fashion, also from epistemology. "In the opinion of everyone," he explained, "including ourselves, every judgment must be based on something given, about which it is enunciated. . . . A judgement is made possible only by some fact, some datum of consciousness, which it designates" ("The Nature of Truth in Modern Logic," p. 49).[1] Mill had warned against the error of looking for the essence of the proposition in the act of judgment; Schlick would look for it in the act of *true* judgment or knowledge. When we add to this strategy the view that the essence of knowledge is most clearly revealed in its simplest prescientific forms, we can see why Schlick concluded that a good way to find out what propositions are is to look at what a child does when recognizing a dog as his or her dog and thinking, 'This dog is my dog'.

In this act, according to Schlick, we can distinguish two constituent representations: first, the perception designated by 'this dog', the very vivid image (not the dog) now present to the child while looking at the dog (or at its image?). Next, we have the reproduced, less vivid representation (a memory) designated by 'my dog'. What the act of judgment does, prima facie, is declare them to be alike ("What Is Knowing?" p. 126), or perhaps it declares the space-time points somehow associated with those representations to be identical (*GTK*, secs. 9, 31). Without much further ado, Schlick concluded that every basic judgment is like the child's in that it has the subject–predicate form ("What Is Knowing?" pp. 137–8) and it expresses the discovery that the predicate concept is in the subject. We now have two theories for the price of one: a subject–predicate theory of the proposition and a theory of knowledge as recognition – the source of Schlick's so frequently reiterated aphorism: All cognition is recognition.

From premises like this together with a doctrine of experience that, as we shall see, Schlick also endorsed, German philosophers of the previous century had gently slid into idealism. In order to avoid a similar fate, there were two problems Schlick had to solve. First, he had to explain the objective character of scientific knowledge in a way that was consistent with his subjectivistic picture of judgments; second, he had to show how we can come to know that our representations represent extramental objects not constituted by the mind.

Schlick's efforts to cope with the first problem centered around his notion of a "concept." He was fully aware of the fact that as science progresses the subjective element is eliminated in favor of increasing objectivity. Yet objectivity cannot be achieved by means of judgments whose constituents are Schlick's representations, since they are essentially tied to subjective elements. Concepts are the tools intended to turn the subjective into the objective.

Schlick's concepts "are merely signs, which first acquire a meaning when they are coordinated with objects . . . a concept has no content of its own and hence is nothing at all until it designates something" (*AE,* p. 329).[2] Concepts must fulfill two purposes: Like representations, they must somehow mediate between us and determined portions of the real world; unlike representations, they must be "sharply defined, firmly circumscribed" ("What Is Knowing?" pp. 129–30; see also *GTK,* p. 20), thereby achieving intersubjective validity.

Schlick acknowledged only one way to obtain conceptual sharpness: via definition, either explicit or implicit.[3] Consider the former first. On the face of it, through explicit definition "knowledge becomes possible in a form practically free from doubt" (*GTK,* p. 27). If someone hands me a piece of metal and asks me whether it is silver, for example, as long as I am restricted to the perceptions of touching and seeing and to a comparison of these perceptions with my memories of earlier similar perceptions with genuine silver, my conclusion will be highly unreliable. But once science defines the concept of silver in terms of atomic weight and so on, "I need only see whether the substance possesses [the defining] properties" (*AE,* p. 26).[4]

Whatever the virtues of this sort of definition, it hardly takes us beyond the domain of subjective, private experience; for, as Schlick hastened to add, "the characteristics into which a definition resolves the concept of a real object must, in the end, be intuitive in nature. The presence of these features in a given object can be ascertained only by intuition" (*GTK,* p. 28). In explicit definition, "very soon we come upon features that simply do not admit of being further defined. The meaning of words that designate these ultimate characteristics can be demonstrated only through intuition, or immediate experience" (p. 29). An indefinable characteristic is explained by stating "what must be done in order to become acquainted with its content." The meaning of 'green', for example, can be defined only "by pointing to the foliage of a tree" or some similar operation (*Problems of Ethics,* p. 8; see also *GTK,* p. 37). The vagueness intrinsic to all empirical intuition thereby infects all explicitly defined concepts.

If we really want to get rid of the subjective element, Schlick claimed, we must appeal to a different sort of concept formation: implicit definition (*GTK,* secs. 6, 7). This sort of definition was first clearly illustrated in Hilbert's treatment of geometry. Geometric concepts are regarded as entities "whose whole being is to be bearers of the relations laid down by the system [of axioms]. This presents no special difficulty since concepts are not real things at all" (*AE,* p. 32). Implicitly defined concepts are rigorous because they are entirely detached from the given in intuition. For that very reason, they are also entirely detached from the real world. Such concepts "have no association or connection with reality at all. . . . None of the concepts . . . designate anything real; rather, they designate one another. . . . Accordingly, the construction of a strict deductive science has only the significance of a game with symbols" (*GTK,* p. 37).

Schlick's quandary is obvious: Explicit definition from given primitives gives representations that are linked to reality, but it can guarantee no more intersubjectivity than is available in its starting point. Since its starting point always consists of the subjective targets of ostension (singular representation), it preserves the link with reality at the price of failing to give a solution to the problem under consideration. In contrast, implicit definition (allegedly) achieves sharpness, but the price is a complete lack of relation to the world. At the end of Schlick's prolonged consideration of concepts, we are no wiser than at the beginning.

Schlick's second problem, we said, was to explain how representation relates to the real world. The key to this link is the notion of coordination (*Zuordnung*). It would be hard to exaggerate the role assigned to coordination in Schlick's picture of things. Mental representations refer to things outside our mind because we have somehow established a coordination between the former and the latter. Judgments state extramental facts because we have somehow managed to coordinate the former with the latter. In fact, coordination ends up being the *only* function of thinking:

Thought does not dissolve [as in Kant] into various categorial functions; on the contrary, in our view "thinking" signifies only one function, that of *coordinating*. The coordinating of two objects with one another . . . is in fact a fundamental act of consciousness not reducible to anything else. It is a simple ultimate that can only be stated, a limit and a basis, toward which every epistemologist must finally strive. . . . In thinking, there is basically no relation other than that of coordination. (*GTK,* p. 383)

Schlick's extramental world was as remote from everyday experience as the Kantian thing-in-itself. Under the circumstances, it is natural to ask that familiar question always put by idealists to realists: How does one establish this coordination between our representations and this external reality?

More orthodox Kantians, like Reichenbach (Chapter 10), had a definite answer to the question in their theory of constitution. Schlick realized that this path led to idealism. By calling coordination a "simple ultimate," he was obliquely acknowledging his inability to offer a better answer. But, though he could not explain how the job would be done, he did have a great deal to say about what the job was. This is worth examining in order to appreciate the magnitude of the problem that Schlick's approach left unsolved.

Consider first what coordination is supposed to do in the field of concepts. To the extent that representation has anything to do with reality, Schlick thought that its link is always primarily to the given by means of acts of ostension. He asserted, for example, that a typical general term such as 'wax' designates a complex of phenomenal qualities (*GTK,* p. 376). But he also wanted to say that we have knowledge of noumenal objects such as the wax-in-itself and of things in themselves generally. Therefore, we must be able to talk about such things; hence, our representations designate not only phenomena, but also things-in-themselves. This is made possible by what looks like a minor semantic miracle: The phenomenal qualities directly designated by an expression such as 'wax' designate the things-in-themselves that have elicited such phenomena, and (here is the miracle) the relation of designation is transitive (p. 89).

One is tempted to conclude that Schlick was confusing coordination with reference. Coordination is, presumably, transitive; one might argue that just as names are coordinated with mental states and the latter with their phenomenal counterparts, so those phenomenal qualities are also coordinated, perhaps via causality, with things-in-themselves. But virtually every process is coordinated with an unlimited number of counterparts – for example, each event in a causal chain with all of its successors. Hence, coordination must be a many-valued relation, and therefore ambiguous, whereas designation, by Schlick's own standards, cannot be. As a tool for the analysis of reference, coordination is worthless.

Coordination was also supposed to give the semantics of judgment and the essence of truth. Since saying is a kind of naming, judgments are names. But of what? Obviously, of facts or states of affairs; and when a judgment names a fact, we say that it is true. The question about the essence of truth must be a special case of the question, When is a name a correct name? A correct name, Schlick thought, is one that is employed without ambiguity and in conformity with a previously agreed upon designative use. The "only" requirement we make of a sign is that "it should be *univocal*" ("The Nature of Truth in Modern Logic," p. 94). To say of an inventory number, for example, that it is "the *correct* number, means that it was the number the maker [of the goods] has assigned, once and for all. . . . So it is with all designations. The aim is to achieve a univocal coordination" ("What Is Knowing?" p. 136).

Now we can see the essence of truth. If an astronomer names an asteroid '@36' and another observes an asteroid and issues the judgment 'that is asteroid @36', the truth-relevant fact is the following: If the asteroid is indeed @36, then the second astronomer has given it the correct name; if not, he has given the name '@36' to a new object and (here is the crucial point) thereby created an ambiguity. Presumably, Schlick thought that in the latter case, '@36' becomes ambiguous because it has been used to "mean" different objects. This assumes, however, that the second astronomer was not making a false claim about the asteroid he was observing, but only baptizing it as '@36'. Thus, all saying is naming and, indeed, baptizing. It is true saying if the baptism agrees with the original naming and false otherwise.[5]

The extent to which Schlick identified true judgment with naming is worth examining more explicitly. Schlick noticed in passing that there are people who hold a picture theory of truth. After a few offhand remarks, he claimed to have "completely demolished" the theory. He urges that we

dismiss from our minds altogether the notion that a judgment can be *more* than a sign in relationship to a set of facts, that the connection between the two can be anything more intimate than mere correspondence, that a judgment is in a position somehow to describe, express or portray adequately a set of facts. . . . A judgment pictures the nature of what is judged as little as a musical note pictures a tone, or the name of a man pictures his personality. (*GTK,* p. 61)

Since truth is no more than the coordination of signs with facts, it would in principle be child's play to design a procedure that generates all truths: Simply baptize one fact after another. If knowledge were identical with truth, "the sciences would have a very easy task indeed," for all we would have to do is "to designate all the things in the world [including, of course, the facts] simply by inventing individual signs for each of them, and then committing to memory the meaning of each sign" (*GTK,* p. 66).

Schlick's position is worth comparing with the circumstances surrounding the life of the Uruguayan positivist Ireneo Funes (known as "the Memorious"). Funes was an extreme case of a certain sort of empiricist: so memorious that he was able to baptize and remember everything he had ever seen or imagined; so dull that he could not understand even the principle underlying the construction of the standard numerals. Fortunately, the former virtue compensated for the latter vice. He had names for all numbers: "In place of seven thousand thirteen he would say, for example, Maximo Perez; in place of seven thousand fourteen, the railroad; other numbers were Luis Melian Lafinur, Olimer, sulfur, the reins, the whale, the caldron, Napoleon, Agustin de Vedia. In place of five hundred he would say 'nine'." (For an intriguing report of Funes's untimely death under the pressure of overwhelming memories, see J. L. Borges, "Funes, el Memorioso," *Obras completas,* pp. 485–90.)

Funes's un-Davidsonian powers allowed him to baptize facts as well as regular objects, but always in a similarly unstructured fashion, with no name bearing any systematic relation whatever to any other name. Funes could not understand a sentence that he had not seen before. According to Schlick (but not, of course, according to Frege or Wittgenstein) Funes could well have spoken a language that did not differ essentially from our own. Funes's problem, as diagnosed by Schlick, was not with language but with knowledge. He could have talked as we do and even identified as many truths as we can; but he could not have had knowledge of them:

Truth requires nothing but uniqueness of coordination; as far as truth is concerned, it does not matter what sign is used for that purpose. Knowledge, on the other hand, means unique coordination with the help of certain definite symbols, namely, those that have already found application elsewhere. . . . Thus our use of judgments to designate sets of facts must, so far as judgments contain knowledge, be of a different sort. We do not need to learn separately which fact is designated by a particular judgment; we can tell this from the judgment itself. A cognitive judgment is a *new* combination made up exclusively of *old* concepts. (*GTK,* pp. 66–7)

One could hardly have been much farther from the semantic message that Wittgenstein was in the process of setting down in the pages of the *Tractatus.*

The hamstringing of realism

According to a familiar debate in the field of Kant scholarship, there are two ways of interpreting the thing-in-itself, depending on whether the morified 'in-itself' is understood adjectivally or adverbially.[6] On the first interpretation, things-in-themselves are a proper subclass of the class of things, a world populated by intelligible, transcendent objects of which human minds can know nothing, and disjoint from the proper domain of knowledge, the world of sensible objects. On the second reading, there is only one domain of things but two ways to consider them: (a) in relation to a knowing, preferably human, subject and (b) independently of such relations. Consequently, when a thing enters into an epistemic relation with a human subject, *it* (and not an appearance of it) appears to the subject with features that partly depend on the subject. (It was the aim of the first *Critique* to determine the extent of that dependence.) Since these two interpretations differ above all in the ranges of objects they postulate, we shall label them the "two-world" and the "one-world" views, respectively.

If things-in-themselves are interpreted in the two-world sense, it is natural to suppose that there are objects different from what we see, touch, and otherwise encounter in experience. If they are *also* viewed in the one-world sense, *and* it is assumed furthermore that all knowledge of an object must involve its givenness – that the only way we can engage in epistemic relations with an object is if it is actually or possibly *given* (i.e., that there is no knowledge by description) – then it is natural to conclude that we couldn't possibly know anything about things-in-themselves. Under that curious set of assumptions, to say that the thing-in-itself is unknowable is simply to say that we cannot engage in epistemic relations with something unless we can engage in epistemic relations with it.

The two-world interpretation of Kant's doctrine is, perhaps, the most widespread.[7] It is certainly fostered by a great number of his remarks and by the entirely defensible view that the thing-in-itself is the last link in a chain of ideas that originated with the distinction between primary and secondary qualities. The aim of that dichotomy had been to distinguish between those qualities that, as we might put it, hide the nature of things-in-themselves and those that reveal it. The imperialist expansion of the domain of secondary qualities in modern philosophy is the root of what Bennett has called the doctrine of the "veil of perception" ("Substance, Reality, and Primary Qualities"). In Kant, according to the two-world interpretation, all qualities are secondary, including the spatiotemporal ones, for they are all misleading guides to the character of the mind-independent world.

The two-world philosopher thinks no one has ever seen a table, a real table, that is. We have all seen colors, shapes, and other phenomenal objects that have carelessly been identified with tables. But tables themselves are invisible – not because we can see through them, but because we cannot see up to them.[8] Our vision always collides with the veil of perception; it collides, for example, with Eddington's table number one.

Eddington once explained that whenever he sat to write a philosophical lecture, the first thing he encountered was (were?) his "two tables," the two tables on which he happened to be leaning as he picked up his two pens to write on his two sheets of paper (*The Nature of the Physical World,* pp. xi–xii). The first table is a colorful, solid object with which we are acquainted in everyday perception. The second table is the one physics tells us about. Apparently, it is an entirely different object. Whereas the first table has no holes, this second one consists mostly of holes, that is, of interelectronic empty space. Whereas the former has colors in the standard phenomenal sense, the latter has nothing of the sort, even though it is involved in certain wavelike or photonlike phenomena that somehow relate to color perception. And so on. On the two-world view, the first table belongs to the phenomenal world, and the second is as invisible as the Kantian thing-in-itself. In fact, Helmholtzian neo-Kantians *identified* the second table with the "table-in-itself."

Quite generally, in the two-world view the real world is a remote land of which human eyes can never catch a glimpse. It is unobservable by mere humans, though perhaps beings with extraordinary powers might be capable of getting acquainted with it.

To most of Kant's followers, the assumption of humanly unknowable things-in-themselves appeared absurd. Idealists, positivists, and most neo-Kantians chose to give up the idea that there are any such things. But a few neo-Kantians decided to deny their unknowability instead. By the end of the nineteenth century, the best neo-Kantian philosophers (Marburg school, Riehl) had severely circumscribed the role of intuition in knowledge. A small movement, constituted mainly by philosopher-scientists (Helmholtz, Planck; but also Zeller, Schlick, and others), reexamined the Kantian conception of knowledge, especially in regard to the role played by sensibility (intuition) in *empirical* knowledge. They concluded that if we remove the inappropriate restrictions Kant had imposed on legitimate knowledge, if we realize that concepts without intuition can yield empirical knowledge, the way is opened for knowledge of things-in-themselves; such knowledge derives not from sensibility but from the understanding, acting under the guidance of science (see e.g., Schlick, *GTK,* p. 223).

Within this version of neo-Kantianism, there were two different pictures of the way science discloses the secrets of the things-in-themselves. The first is illustrated in Helmhotlz's writings. When in 1855 Helmholtz called for a return to Kant (in his celebrated "Über das Sehen des Menschen"), he tacitly assumed the two-world interpretation and suggested that science may provide a way of finding out about the arcane domain of things-in-themselves. Helmholtz's idea was that although all qualities are secondary, there is in addition a formal element in experience, and this could be a reliable guide to the structural features of the outside world. He argued that the phenomenal world as a whole may be regarded as a code language that, when properly decoded, could give us information about these structural features. Essential to this idea is a distinction between form and content, which would eventually play a large role in Schlick's philosophy. Helmholtz, Hertz, Wittgenstein, Russell, and many of their contemporaries had high hopes for this distinction; after decades of illustrious and strenuous efforts to make clear sense of it, however, no one had yet given an account that was intelligible and served the intended purposes.

If, however, one thinks in terms of just one world and of experience giving us access to it, there is also a problem that might be described as the search for the thing- (considered-) in-itself. If knowing a thing-in-itself is knowing something about it while knowing nothing about it, then (as recently noted) this is not likely to happen. But if knowledge is humanly possible without adding intuition to concept, if even when the idiosyncrasies of the human sensibility are excluded, we can still have knowledge, then the project of finding out what things are like when "considered-in-themselves" is at least coherent. But now this will not mean the search for a special world of unperceivable objects, let alone the search for knowledge of an object of which we know nothing. It will be the search for a picture of things that excludes not knowledge but the human sensibility. This is the task that Planck defined as the essence of good science: eliminating the anthropomorphic element from our picture of the universe.

Planck's picture of science was, of course, the mirror image of that of Mach and other positivists. For Mach, truth in science was entirely a matter of sense and sensibility, and the farther science went in the direction of insensible inhuman postulation, the farther it departed from truth and reality. For Planck, on the other hand, the more closely attached we remained to human experience, the more likely it was that the picture offered by science was a distorted guide to the unexperienced portion of reality.[9]

There is a crucial difference between the scientific neo-Kantianism of Helmholtz and of Planck. Under Helmholtz's program, the aim is to remove content from the given in order to derive a purely structural picture of things-in-themselves. Under Planck's, the aim is to remove the human sensibility. Recall the old puzzle about whether there is sound in the woods when the tree falls and no one listens. A solution that refers to air vibrations and the like illustrates Planck's approach – it describes how things are when human senses are absent. But by no stretch of the imagination could this be construed as also giving the purely structural, formal elements of the situation. Only if one confuses, as so many did and still do, the psychological or the phenomenal sensible content of a representation with the semantic content of a statement of fact can one draw the absurd conclusion that a picture without subjective, phenomenal elements (such as Planck called for) must also be a purely formal, contentless, structural characterization.

Schlick's stand on these issues is perhaps the most essential element of his pre-Viennese philosophy. Its character emerges most clearly in connection with one of the problems that worried him most, the "psycho-physical antinomy." As stated in "Ideality of Space, Introjection and the Psycho-Physical Problem" (1916, *Philosophical Papers,* vol. 1) the problem is as follows: Phenomenal qualities must be located somewhere in space, yet all places seem occupied by something else. The interesting thing is not so much his solution to this problem, or even the problem itself, as the presuppositions that led Schlick to think that this was one of the very major issues of philosophy.

Consider a white piece of paper. The whiteness we see is a sensory quality that, Schlick explained, is a secondary quality; as such, it is not a property of the physical object in which it appears to inhere but is only a state of consciousness (p. 194). Sensory qualities are nonetheless localized in space. Qualities such as "the white of the paper, do in fact have a place; the only question is, which?" (p. 195). At first one might think that the answer is: wherever the paper is. But physics tells us that the white of the paper does not exist "at the place of the physical object 'paper'." The paper of physics, like Eddington's second table, does not have a phenomenal color. In response to this difficulty some philosophers have been tempted to place the quality in the brain, a doctrine Avenarius labeled "introjection." This is surely absurd. But if not in the brain, where? Every place seems to be occupied by a qualityless physical object – whence our antinomy: Phenomenal qualities are in space, but there is no place in space to place them.

Schlick thought that Kantians and positivists had made a decisive contribution to the understanding and solution of this problem and that there was a basic unity in their apparently divergent proposals. Both Kant and Avenarius recognized that

mental qualities are something immediately given. . . . The white of the paper in front of me has never been in my head. Any attempt to locate it anywhere but right out there at the place where I see it, invariably comes to grief. It just *is* there . . . this is a fact immediately experienced, and in facts of consciousness there is nothing that can be quibbled over. (p. 197)

Also, both had shown that

sensory qualities are . . . not produced in consciousness by the action of bodies, and only then re-projected outwards by the former upon the latter; they actually attach to the bodies from the first, exist at the very places where they are experienced, and thus belong to consciousness, for everything spatial belongs, as an appearance, to consciousness. (pp. 199–200)

To Avenarius's denial of introjection and reprojection corresponds Kant's doctrine of the ideality of space (and time). The goal in both cases is the same: to reject the "characteristic distinction between the perceived object outside the mind and the perceptual representation within it" (p. 198), that is, the distinction between a representation and its phenomenal object. We have learned from Kant and Avenarius "that consciousness is not somewhere in space, but space, on the contrary, in consciousness" (p. 201) – and together with space, time, and indeed with both of them, everything else that may lie in them (*GTK*, sec. 33).

Schlick thought that these considerations, though necessary, were not sufficient to solve the problem completely. Kant and Avenarius explained that the white of the paper is not in the place occupied by the paper; it is in phenomenal space, out there where we are pointing when we (think that we) are pointing at the paper. But the Kant–Avenarius "solution" poses another problem: Where is the paper? It is on this central question that Kantians and positivists let Schlick down.

Positivists and, more generally, "philosophers of immanence" tried to solve the difficulty by denying the existence of Schlick's paper; for them there were no things-in-themselves. Schlick would have none of this and, for reasons to be examined in a moment, he sided with Kant in asserting that there are things-in-themselves such as this piece of paper.

But there are two major problems with Kant's stand. First, the claim that the thing-in-itself is entirely unknowable leaves Kant's philosophy in a position of unstable equilibrium. Idealists simply let the system move into its most natural rest state when they denied the existence of such things. But there is a second plausible modification that is worth exploring: Deny the idea that things-in-themselves are unknowable. Kant's inability to detach knowledge from intuition prevented him from realizing that we can have knowledge about things-in-themselves; in particular, that we can locate them in space and time – not the forms of sensibility of phenomenal space and time but "transcendent" space and time (*GTK*, sec. 29). About transcendent space and time Schlick said very little beyond the fact that they are represented by ordering schemata.

The second problem, Schlick thought, is that whereas positivists had taken the given far too seriously, Kant had not taken it seriously enough. Kant's attitude toward the given is best revealed in the name he chose to describe it: "appearance" (*Erscheinung*); this implicitly contrasted it with real being (*Wesen*). Schlick was not complaining that Kant took a two-world view and thus reified appearances, but that he did not reify them enough ("Appearance and Essence" [1918], *Philosophical Papers*, vol. 1, p. 277; *GTK*, sec. 27). Kant erred less than the positivists, but he erred nonetheless, in not drawing a sharp enough distinction between the equally real worlds of phenomena and noumena:

We arrive at a satisfactory picture of the world only when we concede to *everything* real, the contents of consciousness no less than all being outside it, the same *type* and *degree* of reality, without any distinction. All are in the same sense self-subsistent. . . . This is to say that processes in my consciousness are not

merely conditioned by a transcendent world, of which they would be appearances; they stand, rather, alongside this world beyond consciousness with perfectly equal reality and legitimacy, and condition in their turn the processes
therein. ("Appearance and Essence," *Philosophical Papers,* vol. 1, pp. 284–5)

They are in no sense two domains of different kinds, but merely parts of a
single domain of reality; one part happens to belong to our consciousness, the other not.[10]

Once we give the given its proper place (as it were) in nature, we are
ready to solve the psychophysical antinomy. The solution lies in noting
that each of us lives in a private phenomenal space and speaks of it in
our private phenomenal language. "The intuiting individuals each have
their own appearance-spaces" ("Ideality of Space . . .," *Philosophical
Papers,* vol. 1, p. 201). In fact, they have a different space for each sense
modality (*GTK,* sec. 29); one space contains the white of the paper,
another its softness, and so on. And each of these private spaces is to be
carefully distinguished from transcendent space, where Schlick's paper
is located. It was at this point that Kant's *Ding-an-sich* chauvinism did
him wrong, according to Schlick; for Kant used the word 'appearance'
to refer not only to "the manifold of intuition (the 'elements' of the
positivists)" ("Ideality of Space . . .," *Philosophical Papers,* vol. 1, p.
200), but also to genuine physical objects. The latter, however, are "not
the content of some casual particular intuition, but the *object* of all
possible intuitions. This physical object . . . is divested of all 'secondary
qualities' and hence essentially unintuitable, no longer representable to
the senses" (p. 200).

The questions that remained unanswered were, What reason do we
have to think that these things-in-themselves exist, and what ground do
we have to think that science gives us information about these essentially
unintuitable objects of all possible intuition (*sic*)? In stating his answers
Schlick moved beyond Kant, not to Hegel but to Helmholtz. To decide
how sound this move was, we must examine his reasons for rejecting the
other, better-known resolution of the Kantian crisis, what Schlick called
the "philosophy of immanence."

The philosophy of immanence is the doctrine that all objects of knowledge are immanent, intentionally in-existent, present only in the act of
knowledge. Its supporters include not only classical idealists, but also
neo-Kantians of the Marburg school (such as Cohen and Natorp), positivists (such as Avenarius and Mach), and neutral monists (like Russell).[11]

The immanentist position appears to be supported by two closely
related and seemingly sensible ideas: that we should accept the existence
only of what is at least in principle observable, and our old friend, the
Kantian doctrine that knowledge is possible only when concept and
intuition join together to give us information about the world. The former
offers sensible inductive grounds for discarding things-in-themselves; the

latter tells us why, even if there were such things, we could know nothing about them. To the latter point, Schlick replied with vigor and insight, proposing to develop a picture of knowledge in which intuition played little or no role. Regrettably, his anti-intuitionist zeal took him all the way to the other end of the spectrum, where he ended up arguing that knowledge is strictly incompatible with intuition. His reason for this was basically the peculiar theory of knowledge as recognition and coordination that we examined in the section on Schlick's semantics, this chapter.[12]

But even if knowledge of the forever unobservable were logically possible, what reason would there be to believe that unobservable things exist? The immanentist grants that belief in mind-independent things is part and parcel of the prephilosophical or commonsense view of the world, but finds this view incorrect, that is, false. Schlick, in contrast, found it quite literally true, but its truth was purely accidental. It is worth seeing why.

The prephilosophical view of things has two prominent features: It assumes that there are things-in-themselves, real objects that are entirely independent of mind, and it also assumes that we can see, touch, and otherwise recognize quite directly the existence of these objects. Immanentists dismiss the latter claim as grounded on philosophical and scientific ignorance, and since they see no other reason for the belief in things-in-themselves, they drop *it* too.

As we saw, Schlick wholeheartedly granted the immanentists' first point. Idealists "did succeed in proving . . . the impossibility of the extra-mental existence of objects that are *representable*" (*AE*, pp. 247–8), since "distinguishing consciousness from its contents is meaningless" (*GTK*, p. 269).[13] The prephilosophical view of things, he explained, conflates what is given to consciousness with mind-independent objects. The prephilosophical observer errs in thinking that he does not infer from certain perceptions that there are, for example, tables: "On the contrary, he says 'I see a table'. Without drawing any inference at all, he takes the object to be the immediately given, and does not distinguish it from the representation or image of the object" (*GTK*, p. 177). Philosophy knows better: All we are ever given, all we can see, hear, point to, or otherwise refer to (barring semantic miracles) consists entirely of mental phenomena.

We don't *really* see tables or loaves of bread or anything extramental; we *infer* from mental data the existence of such things, and the reasons for that inference will soon be examined. But if, in order to satisfy the prephilosophical mind, we want to go along with its misleading mode of speech and say that we "observe" tables and loaves of bread, we should realize that in the same sense we observe "unobservable" electrons (e.g., in a Wilson cloud chamber):

There is not the slightest difference between the two cases. And the [Machian] claim, often heard, that the existence of molecules cannot be regarded as proved until such time as we can *see* them, is wholly unwarranted. Seeing an object proves to me that it exists only insofar as I can infer this from the given visual sensations; and to make the inference I need a series of premises about the constitution of the sense organs, about the nature of the processes through which these sensations are aroused, and much more. . . . To perceive an object is in the end to experience the effects that issue from it. Whether the effects are nearer or more distant cannot be the ground for any fundamental difference. (*GTK,* p. 218)[14]

Schlick's "realism" had managed to make electrons as observable as chairs not by bringing electrons closer to us but by turning everyday chairs into remote objects boldly postulated by theoretical speculation.

We can interpret Schlick as having introduced two different senses of "observation": There is, on the one hand, what we *really* see, touch, and so on, the given; and there is, on the other, what we observe indirectly or inferentially, as it were, including tables and electrons. What we observe indirectly, according to Schlick, are the things lying somewhere along the causal chain culminating in the "direct" observation. On this causal construal of observation, however, we observe (albeit indirectly) a great deal more than we ever thought we did or could. A professor lecturing in front of an audience is observing either a private mental world or a truly astonishing display of human endeavor reaching back to the embarrassingly intimate details of the emotional proceedings that, years ago, started the causal chains leading to each of the students' births. According to Schlick, there is no "fundamental difference" between this "peeping Tom" sense of observing, in which our observant professor sees all of these things, and the sense in which he or she sees just the students.

Given Schlick's complete surrender to the immanentist's argument against the commonsense view of what we observe, how did he intend to avoid the immanentist conclusion? Like Kant, Schlick seemed to think that things-in-themselves are *obviously* there; in particular, he seemed to assume that once the argument for the impossibility of things-in-themselves is refuted (a task Schlick completes quite successfully), philosophy can relax its critical stance and allow our natural common sense to take over (*GTK,* p. 229). But Schlick's problems at this point were no smaller than Kant's.

The only reasons common sense has for believing there are things-in-themselves concern the things we see, touch, and otherwise observe "directly." But Schlick had argued at great length that all such reasons are worthless since, according to him, every single commonsense belief of the form 'that is a thing-in-itself' or 'that is mind-independent' is quite false. Schlick's appeal to common sense to support his views on the thing-in-itself is therefore no more convincing than an appeal by Hitler to the Talmud in order to support his doctrine of the master race. Common sense has nothing (good) to say about Schlick's bold postulation of his world of things-in-themselves.

Did Schlick have other reasons for postulating things-in-themselves? It is hard to say. There are here and there opaque references to the impossibility of a causal account of nature such as he hoped to achieve, without assuming things-in-themselves (e.g., *GTK*, p. 231). There is also a reference to the fact that "coincidence events" in different phenomenal spaces (I see the spider walking on my arm while I feel it crawling) lead us to postulate an underlying transcendent space-time with corresponding events in it. The details of this story are left to others, but there is little reason to believe that they can be filled out unless the common-sense beliefs Schlick has dismissed are admitted as true.

In Schlick's hands, realism had been turned from the boring, trivial commonsense view that it was before Kant into an exciting, bold, and utterly unbelievable conjecture. Its basic doctrines were as follows: We each live in our own private world of given data – when we point at a table, for example, what we "really" point at is a phenomenal table, a different one for each of us; beyond these innumerable phenomenal tables, there is a table-in-itself that no one has or will ever see (except in the "peeping Tom" sense of seeing); the phenomenal tables are not the appearances of the table-in-itself but something else, things at least as real as the physical table with which they are coordinated (in ways it seems impossible to explain). The world of common sense has been torn to pieces: Its time is subjective and transcendentally ideal (*GTK*, sec. 28) and so is its space (sec. 29); all sensible qualities "are elements of consciousness. . . . They belong to the subject, not to objects" (p. 265). Like phenomenal objects, physical objects are made up of qualities, but these qualities are of a sort never available to human intuition. Schlick had argued convincingly that immanentists are committed to solipsism or to a monadology complete with preestablished harmony. Both positions were unacceptable, but it was hard not to be committed also to their disjunction given the premises Schlick granted. Schlick managed to avoid the disjunction only by introducing assumptions that were scarcely less miraculous than preestablished harmony. Though he saw more clearly than most of his colleagues that intuition had to be purged from the Kantian conception of knowledge, Schlick's concessions to the Kantian framework and his semantic blindness left him virtually unarmed to conduct his struggle on behalf of realism. Schlick's vestigial Kantianism was soon to be shaken, however, not by discoveries in semantics or epistemology, but by a new development in physics.

10

Philosophers on relativity

This morning I read your article about Cassirer with true enthusiasm. I
have not read anything so clever and true in a long time.[1]

Einstein to Schlick, 10 August 1921 (VCA)

In the early stages of their intellectual development, the founding fathers
of logical positivism were at least as close to Kant as they were to classical positivism. We have just seen that Schlick tried to argue for the
essential unity of the epistemological approaches of Kant and Avenarius,
and we have also seen the strong Kantian inspiration of his *Allgemeine
Erkenntnislehre*. Around 1920 Reichenbach judged Kantianism to be the
most appropriate standpoint for interpreting the theory of relativity. At
about the same time, Carnap was writing a Kantian-style meditation on
the nature of space, and he would devote most of the remainder of the
decade to that most Kantian of projects, the development of a theory of
constitution (Chapter 11). There can be little doubt that logical positivism started as a branch of neo-Kantianism differing from its rivals in that
movement only in its concern for clarity and its appreciation of science
as a model for epistemology. Yet these differences would, in the end,
make all the difference.

The 1920s were a soul-searching decade for the logical positivists.
During those years they struggled with the Kantian language in which
they had chosen to couch their views of science and knowledge. Very
slowly they came to realize how inadequate that language was to the
message they were trying to convey. In the next two chapters we shall
look at Carnap's efforts to give the theory of constitution an un-Kantian
twist. Our topic now is an even more significant departure from Kantian
orthodoxy, initiated by Schlick around 1920 and motivated by the theory
of relativity.

Kantians had displayed a remarkable ability to withstand all apparent
refutations of their doctrine generated by science. When non-Euclidean
geometries were invented, it was rightly noted that Kant had never denied their conceivability, only their "objective validity," the possibility of
intuiting in agreement with them. When Helmholtz explained that even
this was wrong, he was told (by H. Cohen) that he had misunderstood
Kant's conception of representation. Riehl had even found grist for the

Kantian mill in Helmholtz's doctrines, as would Cassirer. And they could all rejoice in Poincaré's demonstration that geometric empiricism is untenable.

In the field of arithmetic the logicist developments had threatened yet another Kantian stronghold. The entire extent of the Kantians' contribution to this topic was to hold their breath. Finally in 1902 their prayers were answered when Russell discovered his paradox. Frege recanted from logicism, and Russell embarked on a project that could not seriously be described as the reduction of mathematics to *logic*, but only to a (partly) contingent set of assumptions about properties or intensions and about the number of things there are. Others chose to reduce mathematics to certain existential conjectures about peculiar mathematical objects called "sets." The Kantians could watch these confusing developments with glee, and in the second and third decades of the century, they saw with even greater glee a revival of interest in intuition as a key to mathematical truth.

Early in the century, the special theory of relativity appeared to pose yet another obstacle through its relativization of space and time; and a decade later, the general theory of relativity came along with yet another challenge. Riehl had explained not very much earlier that "it is entirely implausible that outside the range of mathematics it will ever be possible to make any use of hypotheses of non-Euclidean spaces" (*Phil. Krit.,* vol. 2, pt. 1, p. 180), and at the time that seemed to be the reasonable thing to say from a Kantian standpoint. Now, however, not only did the best theory of the cosmos challenge Newton, but it was formulated in terms of a non-Euclidean geometry. It was time for Kantians to clear their throats once again and do a little explaining. The first explanation came from Hans Reichenbach in *The Theory of Relativity and a Priori Knowledge* (1920).

Dogmatic slumber

According to Reichenbach, there are several respects in which Kant's epistemology must be modified in view of Einstein's work, but it is still the case that the best standpoint from which to grasp the essence of relativity is Kantian. More specifically, Reichenbach argued, instead of joining the positivist masses in their claim that all knowledge is a posteriori, we must realize that the key to an understanding of relativity is an appreciation of the nature of the a priori. Our best guide for this task is still Kant, though we must follow his lead with great caution.

The main reason for caution is the fact that Kant used the expression 'a priori' in two very different senses: "First it means 'apodictically valid', 'valid for all times', and secondly, 'constituting the concept of object'"

(Reichenbach, *Relativitätstheorie und Erkenntnis Apriori*, p. 238). Kant thought (for reasons to be discussed later) that these two senses were inextricably linked; but he was wrong. Reichenbach's first task was to separate these two notions, to dismiss the former and to offer his own understanding of the latter as the key to all epistemology.

The theory of relativity had established once and for all that there are no judgments of the type Kant called a priori that are valid for all time. In order to prove this point it does not suffice to point out that Euclidean geometry had been abandoned by the new physics; one must proceed through a far more convoluted set of considerations. What had become apparent through Einstein's work, Reichenbach thought, was that systems of principles with equal rights to be regarded as a priori have empirical implications that may turn out to be false. Reichenbach observed that there are clusters of principles that have a character comparable to that of Kant's causality in that, when regarded in isolation from their partners in the cluster, it is difficult, perhaps impossible, to conceive of circumstances that would warrant their rejection. Yet none of these principles is valid for all time, Reichenbach claimed, because when we place them in the context of the remaining a priori principles in the group, it emerges that they entail empirical consequences.

For example, Reichenbach claimed that the equivalence of all (inertial) coordinate systems, the principle of action by contact, and the absolute character of time are as a priori as any Kantian principles. Yet together they entail an empirical claim whose denial is a basic part of the special theory; for, Reichenbach argued, if we assume the equivalence of coordinate systems and the principle of action by contact, then there can be an absolute time, the same for all reference frames, only if there is no upper limit for physically attainable velocities.[2] It follows that, in general, "it is quite possible to discover a contradiction between the constitutive principles and experience" (*RAK*, p. 67).

It would be an error to see in these considerations any intention to deny the distinction between the a priori and the empirical. By declaring those principles revisable and even capable of conflicting with experience, Reichenbach was not aiming to deprive them of their a priori character; for recall that we still have the second sense of a priori, as "constituting the concept of object": "It was Kant's great discovery that the object of knowledge is not simply given but constructed, and that it contains conceptual elements not contained in pure perception" (p. 49). Perception offers not the object of knowledge but "only the material of which it is constructed" (p. 48). Such constructions are achieved by acts of judgment, and in these acts certain principles play a peculiar role. If there is no a priori in the sense of "for all time" or even "independent of experience" (p. 105), there are nonetheless "a priori principles" that

embody a constitutive activity prior to knowledge. Reichenbach's understanding of these constitutive principles coincides with Kant's in the
decisive doctrine that "the conceptual schema, the category, creates the
object; the object of science is therefore not a 'thing in itself' but a
reference structure based on intuition and constituted by categories" (p.
49). Once the vacuity of Kant's first sense of a priori is noticed,

> the more important does its second meaning become: that the a priori principles
> constitute the world of experience. Indeed there cannot be a single physical
> judgment that goes beyond the state of immediate perception unless certain
> assumptions about the description of the object in terms of a space-time manifold
> and its functional connection with other objects are made. (p. 77)

Reichenbach's theory of the a priori was therefore his theory of constitution, which was presented as a development of Schlick's views on
coordination. Following Schlick, Reichenbach saw coordination as the
heart of knowledge, arguing that "the principles of coördination are
much more significant for the cognitive process than for any other coördination" (p. 53). There is, however, a common misconception about the
role of coordination in knowledge that has promoted certain dogmatic-
realist errors. In order to avoid them we must realize that there are two
radically different types of coordination: those in which all of the coordinated elements are defined *prior* to the coordination and those in which
only one side is so defined. For example:

> If two sets of points are given, we coordinate them by associating with every
> point of one set a point of the other set. For this purpose, the elements of each set
> must be *defined;* that is, for each element there must exist another definition in
> addition to that which determines the coordination to the other set. Precisely
> such definition is lacking on one side of the epistemic coordination. The equa-
> tions, that is, the conceptual side of the coordination, are of course sufficiently
> defined, but one cannot say the same thing about the "real." On the contrary, the
> "real" is first defined by coordination to the equations. (*Relativitätstheorie und
> Erkenntnis Apriori,* p. 227)

What is peculiar about the type of coordination employed in knowledge
is that only one side of the coordination, the conceptual one, is defined
before we proceed to establish the coordination; the coordinating principles themselves "define the individual elements of reality and in this
sense *constitute* the real object. In Kant's words: 'because only through
them can an object of experience be thought'" (*RAK,* p. 53). The underlying principles of coordination "are equivalent to Kant's synthetic a
priori judgments" (p. 47).

In Reichenbach's hands the a priori–a posteriori distinction became
the distinction between "axioms of coördination" and "axioms of connection" (p. 54). The latter connect certain state variables with one
another (as in Einstein's relativistic equations); the former "contain gen-

eral rules according to which connections take place" (p. 54). Reichenbach's examples give us a better idea of what he had in mind. The axioms of arithmetic, for example, are presupposed as rules of connection in physics and "are therefore coördinating principles" (p. 54). Similarly, if a mathematical vector is coordinated to a physical force, the mathematical properties of the vector must be ascribed to the force in order to enable us to think of the force as an object. Therefore, the axioms "referring to vector operations are constitutive principles, that is, categories of a physical concept" (pp. 54–5). And when we speak of the path of an electron, we must think of it as remaining identical with itself; that is,

we must make use of the principle of genidentity as a constitutive category. . . . This connection between the conceptual category and the experience of coördination remains as an ultimate, not as an analyzable, residue. But this connection clearly defines a class of principles that precede the most general laws of connection as presuppositions of knowledge. (p. 55)

The preceding illustrates the sense in which Einstein's theory of relativity confirms Kant's analysis of the concept of object (see Reichenbach, "The Present State of the Discussion on Relativity" [1921], p. 27). But there is a second, more specific confirmation of Kantian doctrine by relativity on the topic of the ideality of space and time. Reichenbach expressed "astonishment" that the principle of relativity "had not been asserted long before Einstein by Kantian-oriented philosophy. . . . Kant's philosophy is more compatible with Einstein's theory than with Newton's, and it is surprising that Kant himself did not realize that his views were inherently incompatible with those of Newton" ("The Present State of the Discussion on Relativity," p. 27). Basically, the idea was that Newton's doctrine of space is tied up with a realistic conception of space that conflicts with Kant's transcendental idealism. For Kant there can be nothing to space and time beyond relations to subjectivity, so the objectivity of those two notions must consist of a system of "transformations" linking the totality of subjective spatiotemporal perspectives. But in Reichenbach's opinion, this is the guiding philosophical principle behind Einstein's relativity. On this matter Reichenbach's thought and that of Cassirer were in perfect harmony. Since Cassirer's account in his *Einstein's Theory of Relativity* (*Einstein'schen Relativitätstheorie,* 1921)[3] was the clearer and more thorough, we can turn to him for an explanation of this element of Kantianism in relativity.

In order to grasp the philosophical kernel of relativity, Cassirer explained, one must first recognize the conflict between the realist or correspondence theory of truth (Cassirer called it the "dogmatic" theory) and the idealist alternative:

The latter does not measure the truth of fundamental cognitions by transcendental objects, but, conversely, it grounds the meaning of the concept of the object on the meaning of the concept of truth. Only thus will we overcome finally that conception that sees knowledge as *depicting* (*Abbilden*), whether absolute objects or immediately given "impressions." The "truth" of knowledge is transformed from a mere pictorial into a pure functional expression. (*Einstein'schen Relativitätstheorie*, p. 54)

Leibniz's monadology was offered as a clear example of this conception of truth. Monadologic truth comes about not in virtue of the fact that different pictures of the world are related to their topic as copies to an original, but in virtue of their "functional" correspondence with each other. According to Leibniz one fact expresses another when there is an isomorphic relation between what can be said of the one and what can be said of the other. Kant freed this notion of its underlying metaphysical assumptions (preestablished harmony) and based on it his picture of objects and objectivity. Knowledge is, indeed, relative to human perspectives, but this relativism avoids the skeptic's conclusion by basing the notion of objectivity on the intrinsic correlation between the different subjective standpoints.

Reichenbach made essentially the same point in terms of coordination. He explained that the essence of scientific truth lies in coordination, yet not in the sense in which a traditional realist might think. To say that truth is unique coordination would be to endorse the correspondence theory of truth only if one thought of the type of coordination that presupposes both correlated terms as independently defined. No doubt, for those types of coordination in which we may define both of the correlated series, it makes sense to understand the uniqueness of coordination that is the essence of truth as the correspondence with a single, given object. This makes sense because we have definitional access not only to the arguments but also to the values of this coordination, and a comparison is therefore possible. If this sense of "uniqueness of coördination" is to apply, "it must be possible to determine whether or not a given element is the same as a previously coördinated one. Such a determination is not possible for reality" (*RAK,* p. 45), because we have no way of comparing our opinions about reality with anything besides *other* opinions about reality:

The only fact that can be determined is whether two numerical values derived from two different measurements are the same. We cannot know whether a coördination with this result always refers to the same element in the real world. The question is therefore meaningless; but if the values obtained by the measurements are consistently the same, then the coördination possesses that property which we call truth or objective validity. Therefore, we define: *Uniqueness* of a cognitive coördination means that a physical variable of state is represented by the *same value* resulting from *different empirical data*. (*RAK,* p. 45)[4]

For example, if a set of computations starting from Einstein's theory leads to the result that there should be a deflection of light of 1.7 inches near the sun and a different set of computations starting from observational data leads to the conclusion that the deflection of light near the sun has a radically different value,[5] then we have an inconsistency of sorts – two chains of reasoning that coordinate different values with the same physical event:

We call true that theory which continuously leads to consistent coordinations. Schlick is therefore right when he *defines truth in terms of uniqueness of coordination*. We always call a theory true when all chains of reasoning lead to the same number for the same circumstance. This is our only criterion of truth. (*Relativitätstheorie und Erkenntnis Apriori*, p. 233)

Both Reichenbach and Cassirer found in relativity a consistent application of this epistemological picture. They agreed that (in Cassirer's words) the epistemological achievement of the theory of relativity is that

more clearly and more consciously than ever before, the advance is made from the picture theory of knowledge to the functional theory. As long as physics retained the postulate of absolute space, one could still make sense of the question as to which of the different paths of a moving body that result when we consider it from different systems of reference represents the proper and "true" motion. (*Einstein'schen Relativitätstheorie*, p. 55)

But now,

the assertion has lost all meaning for us that any space, whether Euclidean or non-Euclidean, is the "real" space. Precisely this was the result of the general principle of relativity, that by it "the last remainder of physical objectivity" was to be taken from space. Only the various relations of measurement within the physical manifold, within that inseparable correlation of space, time, and the physically real object, which the theory of relativity takes as ultimate, are pointed out. (*Einstein's Theory of Relativity*, p. 432)

Reichenbach's and Cassirer's views on this particular matter clearly depend on the original reading of relativity in terms of reference frames and their associated coordinate systems. Their basic intuition appears to be that the relativity of space and time to reference frameworks is merely a mathematical version of the Kantian subjectivity of those notions, and that the laws of transformation linking all frames, like the structural links between one Leibnizian monad and another, embody the entire content of their claim to objectivity. This would be a reasonable conclusion if coordinate frames pertained to the essence of relativity. Yet in 1909 Minkowski had offered a coordinate-free formulation of the special theory, according to which the coordinate dependence of space and time emerges as the mere appearance of an underlying, unrelativized space-time manifold that is no less absolute than Newton's space.

Cassirer's main reference to Minkowski was to emphasize how "projection into space and time" has become relatively arbitrary and also how "the transformation equation reestablishes objectivity and unity since it permits us to translate the results found in one system into those of the other" (*Einstein'schen Relativitätstheorie,* p. 93). As to Minkowski's claim that space-time now possesses the independence (*Selbstständigkeit*) previously attributed to space and time, Cassirer viewed it as a momentary retrogression to dogmatic thought patterns that were, once again, corrected by the general theory: "Even this union [of space and time] becomes a shadow and an abstraction according to the results of the general theory of relativity, and . . . only the unity of space, time and things has independent reality" (*Einstein'schen Relativitätstheorie,* p. 93). Neither space nor time nor space-time are a "reality"; only their combination with phenomenal objects is real – in that elusive sense in which phenomenal things are real for Kant.

Yet once again, at about the same time that philosophers were speculating in this fashion, mathematicians were undermining the basis of their argument. Thanks to Weyl's and Cartan's work, it would soon become apparent that the general theory could and should be given a coordinate-free, invariant formulation. It slowly emerged that coordinate systems, far from being the very heart of the relativistic picture of knowledge, are a computational artifact – perhaps essential for the purposes of prediction, but largely irrelevant and often misleading when it comes to the actual content of the theory. If the theory of relativity might be thought to support an idealist construal of space and time, it is no less absolutistic about space-time than Newton's theory was about space. This purely mathematical development undercut Reichenbach's and Cassirer's claims about the link between relativity and the ideality of time and space. But there still remained the question of the other alleged confirmation of Kantianism by relativity, concerning the constitutive role of certain postulations.

Awakening

Schlick was probably the first major philosopher to draw the philosophical lessons of relativity. Like most of his colleagues in that enterprise, his first reaction had been to view the theory from a Kantian perspective. In "The Philosophical Significance of the Principle of Relativity" (1915), for example, he still worried about whether the (special) theory conforms to "our *a priori* intuition" (*Philosophical Papers,* vol. 1, p. 162).

Until the emergence of the general theory of relativity, Schlick had

exhibited a somewhat eclectic attitude toward the conflict between sophisticated (German) positivism and Kantianism, arguing that the differences were more apparent than real. In effect, Schlick had focused on the
constitutive dimension of both philosophical currents and on their theories of experience, to the almost complete neglect of their conflicting
attitudes toward the a priori. Now the theory of relativity had forced his
attention to the question of whether there is an apodictic a priori. A
careful, prolonged analysis of the situation finally led him to conclude that
there is no such thing and, more importantly, that this would entail a
decisive break with the Kantian tradition. Schlick was the first one of the
scientifically oriented neo-Kantians to understand that the philosophical
lessons of relativity demanded not the correction but the elimination of
Kantianism. The central ideas behind this change of mind were first
expressed in response to Reichenbach's and Cassirer's accounts of relativity.

Schlick on Cassirer

For all his earnest commitment to the study of science, Cassirer's epistemological works reveal an even greater commitment to a revival of
Kant's ideas. In *Substance and Function* (1910), after a careful reading of
Poincaré, Cassirer had explained that the theory-ladenness of observation makes a decision concerning the "correct" geometry impossible.
Since the measuring instrument is involved in a system of presuppositions that includes geometric and physical assumptions, "we can expect
no clear decision from [measurements] with regard to the conflict of
geometric systems" (p. 107). This position borders on Kantian heresy,
for it seems to imply the possible objective validity of non-Euclidean
geometry. Even so, Cassirer argued that Kant was right in holding that
geometric systems of conditions have absolute validity; for, he said, it is
only the pure system of conditions erected by mathematics that is absolutely valid; the assertion that there are things corresponding to these
conditions in all respects possesses only relative and thus problematic
validity (p. 111).

If there was a distinctively Kantian doctrine of geometric knowledge, it
was that there is a privileged a priori system of geometry grounded on
intuition – in fact, pure intuition. By the time Cassirer was writing, it had
become monumentally implausible to say that there is a privileged a
priori system of geometry. So he would say instead that mathematics
erects "pure systems of conditions," and it is these systems that are
"absolutely valid." Behind the arresting language lies nothing but the very
modest and sensible claim that mathematicians are free to construct any
axiomatic systems they please; and to say that these systems are "absolutely valid" is to say absolutely nothing.

In *Einstein's Theory of Relativity,* responding now to the general theory of relativity, Cassirer started his analysis by making a variety of apparent concessions to the new physics. Yet once again, the changes they forced on Kantian philosophy are not essential. Cassirer argued, for example, that Kant's pure intuition and his doctrine of geometric knowledge are not to be abandoned but suitably modified to adjust to the new situation. Pure intuition is still really there as a "methodological presupposition," and its presence is detected as follows: "It lies in the concept of 'coincidence' to which [relativity] ultimately reduces the content and form of all natural laws" (*Einstein'schen Relativitätstheorie,* p. 84).[6] His second and final effort to identify "the *a priori* of space" in the new theory was the remark that it involves "no assertion concerning any definite particular structure of space in itself, but is concerned only with that function of 'spatiality' in general, that is expressed even in the general concept of the linear element" (*Einstein's Theory of Relativity,* p. 433), that is, in the Riemannian expression for the metric element:

$$ds^2 = g_{ik}\, dx_i\, dx_k.$$

Finally, the essential correctness of Kant's position on geometric knowledge emerged, as usual, from an adaptation of Helmholtz's "transcendental" considerations. Helmholtz was right in thinking that geometric axioms are presupposed in the determination of what is to count as a geometric object; but he was wrong in concluding that under this interpretation, the axioms of geometry would no longer be synthetic in Kant's sense:

What this objection overlooks, however, is that besides the form of analytic identity that Helmholtz has here in mind, and that he contrasts with the form of the empirical concept as if the form of analytic identity were unique, there are also fundamental *synthetic positions of unity* (*synthetische Einheitssetzungen*) and that the axioms of geometry are precisely of this sort. Positions (*Setzungen*) of this kind refer to the object insofar as in their *totality* they "constitute" the object and make its knowledge possible; but not one of them, taken in and of itself, may be regarded as an assertion about things or relations among things. (*Einstein'schen Relativitätstheorie,* p. 107)

This was Cassirer's effort to explain in what sense the synthetic a priori was still alive and well in the field of geometry: Between the notions of analytic identity (Kant's nominal analyticity) and the empirical, there is a tertium quid that is synthetic and constitutive, and the theory of relativity only confirms the presence of such principles. As we know, a hundred years earlier Bolzano had recognized that tertium quid for what it was. But the lessons of semantics did not travel fast in Kantian territory.

By 1920 the theory of relativity had become a topic of great concern among philosophers. The theory had elicited a good deal of philosophical silliness, even among otherwise respectable people (including some of

Brentano's prominent students); serious responses were slow to arrive. Schlick had acquired a well-deserved reputation as a balanced and informed judge on this matter, so when Cassirer and Reichenbach announced the publication of their books, *Kant Studien* asked him to review them. Schlick's review article, "Critical or Empiricist Interpretation of Modern Physics?" (1921, *Philosophical Papers,* vol. 1), is the work to which Einstein refers in the opening quotation of this chapter. It is the first clear statement of the inconsistency between Kantian philosophy and relativity. This remarkable article may well be regarded as the point of departure of a new direction for scientific philosophy.

Schlick began by setting out clearly the conditions Kantians must satisfy in order to make the case that their philosophical standpoint has been confirmed by, or is at least consistent with, the theory of relativity. Kant could hardly be blamed for not knowing non-Euclidean geometry or relativistic physics. The geometry and the physics of Kant's time were not as necessary as he thought, but "that is by no means our concern here." The critical viewpoint could still be vindicated, and one might even argue that relativity confirmed Kant's basic convictions: "All that would be needed is for the ultimate foundations of the theory [of relativity] to disclose themselves as synthetic propositions of absolutely necessary validity for all experience" (*Philosophical Papers,* vol. 1, p. 325). The question is, What are these propositions?

For this must assuredly be noted: anyone who upholds the critical claim, must, if we are to accord him credence, also really set forth the *a priori* principles which must form the solid basis of all exact science. For transcendental philosophy, as Cassirer rightly says, space and time are . . . 'sources of knowledge'. We therefore have to demand a statement of the cognitions of which space, for example, is the source. The critical idealist must designate them as definitely and clearly as Kant was able to point to the geometry and 'general theory of motion' which alone were known and recognized in his day. (p. 325)

Kant did not claim that pure intuition was the source of some unspecified type of synthetic a priori knowledge; he explicitly identified that knowledge as including Euclidean geometry and fragments of Newtonian physics. We now know that these examples were wrong, but this, of course, does not refute Kant's epistemology, since there might be other synthetic a priori principles. What is entirely unacceptable is to retreat to a level of vagueness and generality that Kant would have despised as philosophical chicanery. It will not do, for example, to say (as some Kantians say) that physics treats of "mere" empirical time and empirical space, so that its decision about such topics is of no great philosophical interest. Kant's pure intuition is not supposed to be a domain independent of the empirical world but, rather, "the cognitive source of those *a priori* principles that are needed for the construction of empirical time and empirical space" (p. 325). The question a Kantian must answer is, therefore, What are those new synthetic a priori judgments that the theory of relativity has uncovered?

It cannot be sufficiently emphasized that an adherent of the critical philosophy can vindicate himself only by producing such a system of judgements. Every attempt to reconcile Einstein with Kant must discover synthetic *a priori* principles in the theory of relativity; otherwise it must be regarded from the outset as a failure. (p. 325)

Schlick then proceeded to review and refute Cassirer's efforts to identify "the *a priori* of space" in *Einstein's Theory of Relativity.* Pure intuition cannot seriously be reduced to "coincidence events," since these would surely be placed by Kant in the domain of *empirical* intuition; as for the attempt to find the a priori of space in the formula for the linear element, Schlick requested a formulation of the set of axioms included in this claim and the reason for regarding them as a priori.[7] Finally, on Cassirer's effort to "Kantianize" Helmholtz, Schlick had already noted in "The Philosophical Significance of the Principle of Relativity" that "Kant attributed much to the pure form of intuition which in truth must be regarded as the contribution of understanding" (*Philosophical Papers,* vol. 1, p. 163). As we shall presently see in connection with Reichenbach, Schlick had seen better than most of his colleagues that the role of implicit definition in geometric and other knowledge can be taken not as confirmation of a Kantian epistemology, but rather as a further reason to depart from it.

In view of the inadequacy or indefiniteness of all of Cassirer's efforts to prove that Kant's notion of pure intuition is vindicated by the new physics, Schlick decided to write to Cassirer asking him to state precisely wherein lies the synthetic a priori element in modern science. Cassirer's reply, as quoted in Schlick's review article, is that the ultimate synthetic a priori principles of all science "really consist only of the idea of the 'unity of nature', that is, of the law-abiding character of experience in general, or, more briefly perhaps, of the 'univocal nature of coordination'" (Schlick, "Critical or Empiricist Interpretation of Modern Physics?" *Philosophical Papers,* vol. 1, p. 326). In response, Schlick accused Cassirer of turning Kantianism into an epistemological doctrine incapable of refutation and *therefore* unacceptable. Unitary obedience to natural law is, Schlick noted, a *conditio sine qua non* of science. No theory will even qualify as scientific unless it fulfills that condition. It follows that no development in the field of science could ever pose a threat to the critical philosophy and *therefore* that no scientific development could ever confirm it:

For it would now no longer be possible ever to claim of a physical theory that it confirmed the critical philosophy: the latter would have, rather, to be compatible with *every* theory, in the same way, and without possibility of selection, so long as such a theory satisfies the mere conditions of being scientific. (p. 326)

These remarks announce not only the disentanglement of scientific empiricism from its neo-Kantian origins but also the emergence of a new methodological attitude toward epistemology. We shall return to this subject in the last section of this chapter.

Schlick on Reichenbach

Cassirer's book had given Schlick the opportunity to explain why Kant-ianism should be abandoned rather than modified; Reichenbach's gave him the opportunity to display the inadequacy of Kantian terminology and ideology to the task of conveying relativistic insights. The central points were made not in the brief comments on Reichenbach included in his review for *Kant Studien,* but in private correspondence.

On 26 November 1920 Schlick wrote to Reichenbach commenting on his *The Theory of Relativity and a Priori Knowledge.* After praising him for the sharpness with which he drew the distinction between the two senses of a priori, he noted that in his view, the specifically Kantian position on the topic was the identification of those senses. Kant was not original in thinking that the mind plays a constitutive role and that there are necessary, apodictic claims. What was new was the link he drew between these two doctrines:

He explained them [i.e., apodictic claims] and justified their validity by disclosing the fact that the most general laws of nature are the principles of our *knowledge* of nature (as principles of the possibility of experience). In other words (since for him this was the same): he identified the self-evident general statements of natural science with the principles that constitute the objects of experience. It is here, i.e., in the identification of the two concepts of a priori that you have so properly distinguished, that I find so essential a doctrine of the critical philoso-phy that one cannot undermine it without placing oneself far from the Kantian philosophy. (HR 015-63-22, p. 1, ASP)[8]

Schlick conceded that the existence of constitutive principles is undenia-ble. The point, he thought, had been widely (if implicitly) recognized by a variety of philosophers, including Hume and Leibniz. The major excep-tion appears to be "extreme sensualism, the untenability of which is as clear to me as it is to you. The presupposition of object-constituting principles seems to be so obvious that I have upon occasion failed to emphasize it sufficiently in my AE" (p. 1).[9]

The real question, therefore, is whether the constitutive principles are what Kant thought them to be: synthetic a priori judgments:

Besides this possibility there of course remain two others: that these principles are hypotheses, or that they are conventions. In my opinion the latter is, in fact, the case – and it is the main point of this letter that I cannot see what is the real difference between your a priori statements and conventions. . . . The decisive places where you describe the character of your a priori correspondence principles seem to me to be nothing short of accomplished definitions of the concept of convention. (pp. 2–3)[10]

The point was once again emphasized in Schlick's review article. There he reiterated the idea that someone who perceives the necessity of constitutive principles for scientific experience should not thereby be called a Kantian, since it all depends on how these principles are understood. Cassirer had correctly argued that both empiricism and Kantianism grant to experience the decisive role in knowledge, and both recognize that measurement presupposes laws. But when he examined the nature and validity of these laws, the only alternative to Kantianism that he recognized was sensualism or strict positivism, the Machian doctrine according to which "one can read off" the nomic element in experience "by immediate perception" ("Critical or Empiricist Interpretation of Modern Physics?" *Philosophical Papers,* vol. 1, p. 324). This alternative is incorrect: "Between the two [standpoints] we still have the empiricist viewpoint, according to which these constitutive principles are either *hypotheses* or *conventions;* in the first case they are not *a priori* (since they lack apodicticity), and in the second they are not synthetic" (p. 324). And in a brief reference to Reichenbach's *Theory of Relativity and a Priori Knowledge,* Schlick added that he "should designate Reichenbach's *a priori* principles as conventions" (p. 333), in Poincaré's sense (bearing in mind Poincaré's geometric conventionalism).

Conventionalism had played no role in Reichenbach's philosophy up to that point. Reichenbach referred to Poincaré's geometric conventionalism in *Theory of Relativity and a Priori Knowledge* only to dismiss it as inspired by his neglect of geometries of variable curvature. Now we know that Poincaré was wrong, Reichenbach explained, because *"Euclidean geometry is not applicable to physics"* (p. 3).

In his letter of 26 November 1920 Schlick corrected Reichenbach's scholarship and his philosophy: Poincaré had taken spaces of variable curvature into account (though not in the text cited by Reichenbach), and more to the point, Poincaré was right in thinking that one can choose the physical laws so as to make them conform to any geometry. The only thing that prevents us from adopting Euclidean geometry in relativity theory is the demand for simplicity. Kantians are wrong in thinking that we *must* use Euclidean geometry, but they are certainly right in thinking that we *may* use it (HR 015-63-22, ASP).

In his reply of 29 November 1920 Reichenbach agreed that the theory of relativity could be expressed in a Euclidean framework, yet he was still reluctant to refer to geometry and the other coordinative principles as "conventions":

You ask me why I do not call my a priori principles *conventions*. I think we can very easily reach an agreement on this question. Even though several systems of principles are possible, it is always only a *group* of system principles that is possible; and in this limitation lies an epistemic content. Each possible system signifies through its possibility a *property* of reality. What I miss in Poincaré is an emphasis on the fact that the arbitrariness of principles is circumscribed as soon as one *combines* principles. That is why I cannot accept the name "convention." Moreover, we are not certain that two principles, that today we put together as constitutive principles and that are both, according to Poincaré, *conventions*, will not tomorrow be separated because of new experiences, so that the alternative between these two conventions will end up being synthetic knowledge. (VCA)[11]

This reflects clearly, if not the epistemology, at least the semantic stand-point of an intelligent Kantian. First of all, there is the unshakable convic-tion that in order to understand the nature of knowledge, we must draw a sharp distinction between two types of judgment, the a priori and the empirical. Moreover, as Reichenbach developed his own views on this dichotomy, no distinction is drawn between those acts whereby we state what we mean and those whereby we state our beliefs about the world. All judgments, constitutive or otherwise, are about the world – though for the constitutive ones, this fact emerges only when in holistic clusters. The implicit rejection of a distinction between fact and meaning, be-tween the constitution of what we say and of what we say it *about,* is inspired not by a careful examination of the difficulties involved, but by the characteristic Kantian neglect of all matters relating to semantics.

Reichenbach's main problem was that his account of the a priori had made it virtually indistinguishable from the empirical. The only recogniz-able difference was that the a priori element can conflict with experience only in conjunction with similar principles. Had he read Duhem more carefully he would have known that this is not much of a difference. When a few years later he came to see that his understanding of the a priori–a posteriori dichotomy would not do, he had two options: to follow the positivists or to drop that distinction and try Schlick's sugges-tion that it be explicated on the basis of the notion of convention. Reich-enbach chose the latter, and a decade later had become the most elo-quent proponent of relativistic conventionalism.

There was another matter on which Reichenbach would also have been well advised to follow Schlick's suggestion. Reichenbach shared Schlick's realist instincts, but he did not find the expression of these instincts within a Kantian framework any easier than Schlick had years earlier. Thus, in *Theory of Relativity and a Priori Knowledge,* Reichen-bach had remarked on "the strange fact" that in coordination "it is the defined side that determines the individual things of the undefined side [i.e., reality], and that, vice versa, it is the undefined side that prescribes the order of the defined side. *The existence of reality is expressed in this mutuality of coordination*" (p. 42). Through coordinative "definition" we constitute the objects of knowledge, and yet at the same time, and as an indication that the constituted object was out there even before we constituted it, that very thing that we "determined" is "determining" us. This, Schlick now thought, is not a deep and inscrutable paradox but an incoherent remark:

> I believe that only the undefined side determines – through the mediation of perception – the conceptual side, and not vice-versa. Your theory seems to me to emerge from the fact that it is so easy to confuse the concept of reality with reality itself . . . an illusion to which the Marburg neo-Kantians have fallen prey. The determination of the length of a rod (p. 38) does not seem to me, for example, to belong to the definition of the real rod – the real is always beyond all definition – rather it is the determination of a characteristic of our *concept* of a rod. (Letter to Reichenbach, 26 November 1920, HR 015-63-22, p. 4, ASP)[12]

The point Schlick was making relates to the issue that Cassirer had raised in connection with Helmholtz. Schlick was now saying that constitutive axioms, even though not analytic in Kant's nominal sense, are nonetheless conceptual. Instead of seeing them as constituting experience or its objects, we must interpret them as constituting concepts. To be sure, the doctrine is merely suggested at this point, and Schlick could never quite articulate its link with the notion of implicit definition. We may observe, however, that there was no doctrine more central than this to the development of logical positivism in the late 1920s and early 1930s, and it will recur in a variety of guises throughout the rest of this book.

The transcendental method

One of the many novelties that Kant's first *Critique* brought to the field of epistemology was a new attitude toward skepticism embodied in his transcendental method. Modern philosophy had developed under a skeptical obsession, with some philosophers nervously trying to establish that there really is knowledge and others despairing of the possibility of proving it. Kant's transcendental method turned the situation around. The basic question of the new epistemology was not *whether* there is knowledge. Its starting point was that there obviously is knowledge and experience and synthetic a priori cognition. The question was not whether but *how* all of this is possible. Thus, instead of trying to construct knowledge from an ultimate basis of givenness and simplicity, Kant took knowledge as a datum and tried to identify its "conditions of possibility." Leaving aside the details of Kant's application of his method, this general aspect was destined to have a lasting influence even outside the field of orthodox Kantianism.

Reichenbach was totally committed to this general aspect of Kant's project, but he did object to Kant's application of the method in his analysis of reason. In fact, he saw in this feature the root of Kant's erroneous identification of the two senses of a priori.

As Reichenbach saw it, the "given" in Kant's application of the transcendental method was not so much knowledge or science as *reason.* Kant thought that he could find behind the changeable aspect of science the operations of an unchangeable faculty, reason, and that the transcendental method should guide us in the search for its characteristics. *If* the constitutive principles were to be derived from this unchangeable reason, then one could well see why those principles should be apodictic and valid for all time. Yet, according to Reichenbach, reason is not a system of fixed propositions; it is merely a capacity "that becomes fruitful in application to concrete problems" (*RAK,* p. 72). In the end Kant had nothing firm with which to link his transcendental method beyond the criterion of self-evidence. Thus, his system of a priori principles ended up being "merely a canonization of 'common sense'" (p. 73), or of what had become common sense after Newton. Kant's error was, therefore, to apply the transcendental method to the wrong thing: "If he searched for the conditions of knowledge, he should have analyzed *knowledge;* but what he analyzed was *reason*" (p. 72). Knowledge, that is, science, is the proper target of the transcendental method and the touchstone of epistemology: "There is no other method for epistemology *than to discover the principles actually employed in knowledge.* Kant's attempt to detect these principles in reason must be regarded as a failure" (p. 75).

Schlick's analysis of the philosophical implications of relativity is a clear application of Reichenbach's new transcendental standpoint. As we have already seen, he argued that an epistemology is to be *dismissed* if it is formulated in such a way that it can no longer conflict with any conceivable scientific theory. The criterion of adequacy for an epistemology is its capacity to exclude some conceivable scientific developments and to conform to our best scientific theories.

It would be hard to exaggerate the importance of the shift toward this new transcendental standpoint. The members of the semantic tradition had always been the greatest admirers of science and had repeatedly demonstrated their willingness to take it as a model. Yet the way in which it was so taken was normally inspired by the foundationalist ideals of pre-Kantian philosophy.

Russell's "On Scientific Method in Philosophy" (1914) offers an excellent example of this traditional attitude. There he reiterated his well-known view that it is "from science, rather than from ethics and religion, that philosophy should draw its inspiration" (*Mysticism and Logic,* p. 75). Yet, he went on to add,

there are two different ways in which a philosophy may seek to base itself upon science. It may emphasize the most general *results* of science, and seek to give even greater generality and unity to these results. Or it may study the *methods* of science, and seek to apply these methods, with the necessary adaptations, to its own peculiar province. Much philosophy inspired by science has gone astray through preoccupation with the *results* momentarily supposed to have been achieved. (pp. 75–6)

Russell's prime examples of scientific philosophy gone astray were the energeticist doctrines fashionable in Germany at the time and the philosophy of evolution. The folly of such efforts to derive philosophy from the content of currently successful science becomes apparent as soon as that science changes its content, as it inevitably will. The scientific method is the only element of permanence in science, and it is consequently the only feature of science that philosophers must try to apply in their own investigations. "It is not results, but *methods,* that can be transferred with profit from the sphere of the special sciences to the sphere of philosophy" (p. 76).

If so, philosophers need not worry excessively about the character of current science. Or, at any rate, once they have shaped for themselves a good enough idea of the scientific method, they need no longer concern themselves with the details of science. In later years Russell himself would, of course, engage in careful studies of the theory of relativity and other scientific theories, and he would put such knowledge to philosophical use. Even so, his picture of philosophy remained one in which philosophers stand on a ground of their own, learning a great deal from science but preserving a set of epistemological standards that originate elsewhere. The idea that the main criterion of correctness for an epistemology is whether it adequately describes the best current science would have seemed to him absurd.

Schlick, Reichenbach, and – ten years later – Popper (Chapter 17) initiated a new challenge to this standpoint by giving a scientific twist to the transcendental method. In doing so, they created a new type of epistemology that is known in Anglo-Saxon countries as "philosophy of science." Russell remained the most eloquent proponent of the opposite, foundationalist perspective within the analytic tradition. It was so eloquent, in fact, that in 1921 he managed to convert to his cause the future leader of Viennese positivism.

11

◁══▷

Carnap before Vienna

... only I imagined that this science [i.e. physics] should be preceded by
still another one, in which it would first be demonstrated and explained
that we pass many experiential judgments, and under which circumstances
we are justified in doing so. For I already felt as a boy that most of the
judgments we call experiences are not known by us directly, but only
inferred from certain others, and frequently I became lost in reflections
about out of which premises we might actually derive the same consequences. You may now laugh about the uselessness of such an inquiry; yet I
confess that I still today believe that there should be such a science, only I
no longer think it must be pursued in advance by anyone who wants to
study physics.[1]

Bolzano, *Lebensbeschreibung*

The exact sciences frequently work with concepts (which are occasionally
even their principal concepts) of which they cannot say exactly what they
mean; and on the other hand: the traditional methods of philosophy can
help here a little.[2]

Carnap, Circular letter, 7 April 1920 (ASP)

When in his later years, recollecting his intellectual development, Carnap
listed the major influences on his thought, the names he gave were those
of Frege, Russell, and Wittgenstein. But in 1920 he sent a very different
list of names to Dingler. Kant, Riemann, Helmholtz, Mach, Avenarius,
Poincaré, Natorp, Ostwald, Einstein, and Weyl were, he said, the people
he was studying (Carnap's draft of a letter to Dingler, 20 September
1920, RC 028-12-11, ASP). Two months later he wrote again, enumerating the topics he would like to work on: meaning and justification of the
application of non-Euclidean geometry in physics; the methodological
significance of the rigid body in physics; the synthetic (i.e., nonempirical) method in physics; the a priori character of physical laws; the empirical and the nonempirical components of the law of conservation of energy; the relation between relativity theory and experience; and so on
(Carnap's draft of a letter to Dingler, 14 November 1920, RC 028-12-12,
ASP). Clearly Carnap was on the verge of becoming a philosopher of
science of the sort for which Popper and Reichenbach would eventually
provide the paradigms. Within the next few years, in fact, he published a
few excellent papers reporting the results of research already in progress

207

by 1920. But something happened in 1921 that decisively deflected the course of Carnap's thought from philosophy of science and toward more traditional philosophical issues. "My philosophical insights," Carnap once explained,

are usually gained not in moments of inspiration but rather through a slow process of growth and development. It is only on rare occasions when a book or a talk made a strong, lasting impression on me. This happened one day, in the winter of 1921 while I was in bed with influenza reading Russell's book which had just arrived. (Mia Reichenbach's typescript, 1962, RC 090-02-05, pp. 3–4, ASP)

The book was *Our Knowledge of the External World,* and Carnap recalled in his autobiographical remarks for the Schilpp volume (*The Philosophy of Rudolph Carnap*) how moved and inspired he was by Russell's eloquent defense of the role of logic in philosophy. "The study of logic," Russell had written, "becomes the central study in philosophy: it gives the method of research in philosophy" (*Our Knowledge of the External World,* p. 243). "All this supposed knowledge in the traditional systems must be swept away, and a new beginning must be made" (p. 244). He continued:

The one and only condition, I believe, which is necessary in order to secure for philosophy in the near future an achievement surpassing all that has hitherto been accomplished by philosophers, is the creation of a school of men with scientific training and philosophical interests, unhampered by the traditions of the past, and not misled by the literary methods of those who copy the ancients in all except their merits. (*Our Knowledge of the External World,* p. 246)

Carnap wrote: "I felt as if this appeal had been directed to me personally. To work in this spirit would be my task from now on!" ("Intellectual Autobiography," p. 13). Logic was, no doubt, the most promising road for those who wanted philosophy to follow the secure path of science. Appropriately enough, the first major project that Carnap chose to undertake was to place Kant's own philosophy on that secure path.

By 1924 Carnap had completed what may be regarded as a first sketch of the *Aufbau,* a manuscript revealingly entitled "Vom Chaos zur Wirklichkeit" ("From Chaos to Reality"; Letter to Schlick of 19 December 1924, RC 029-32-46, ASP). As the manuscript grew into a book, Carnap emphasized its Kantian lineage by first planning to call it *Konstitutionstheorie* (*Theory of Constitution*). But besides Kant and logic there was a further inspiring principle.

Russell's supreme maxim

When the *Aufbau* was published in 1928, its opening page displayed the motto of the foundationalist-constructionist tradition. It was Russell's

"Supreme Maxim of Scientific Philosophizing": Wherever possible, substitute logical constructions for inferred entities.

A wide variety of activities may be interpreted as applications of Russell's advice. The paradigm cases were the logicist reduction and Whitehead's method of extensive abstraction. But in 1924, in his "Logical Atomism," Russell went so far as to present his theories of descriptions, classes, and judgment as applications. If they are, then Russell's formulation of his maxim is extraordinarily misleading. One might be tempted to say that the theory of descriptions replaces inference to the golden mountain by a construction involving universals such as *being a mountain* and *being golden.* But then, by parity of reasoning (as Russell liked to say), we should also conclude that the theory replaces the inference to the author of *Waverley* (or, if you insist, to the sense datum of which I am currently aware) by a construction out of universals. Clearly this is nonsense; the theory of descriptions has nothing to do with anything that might seriously be described as a step from inference to construction from data. And the same is true of all other applications of the incomplete-symbol strategy. Russell's maxim was vitiated from the very beginning by ambiguities.

What the applications of Russell's maxim seem to have in common is this: We start with a system of expressions that serves some essential semantic or epistemic purpose but that, for some reason or other, is also regarded as problematic. Then we replace that system by another that no longer suffers from those particular problems and that, moreover, preserves a certain sort of link with the original one. Depending on the type of problem and the required link, we shall have radically different projects, most of them usually described as "reductionistic."

Reductionist strategies may be used to deal with the three main aspects of epistemology: meaning, ontology, and foundations. Given a body of knowledge we may wonder what its claims mean, what they are about, and what type of reason – if any – we have to believe them; reductionism may be offered as an answer to each of those questions.

We may, for example, want to know what imaginary numbers *really are* or whether the topic of thermodynamics is *really different* from that of statistical mechanics. Inspired by this type of ontological purpose, Frege was extremely upset because mathematicians did not really know what numbers *are,* and his brand of reductionism was partly designed to tell them (see Chapter 17).

Yet one may ignore or dismiss ontological issues and still find reductionism attractive because it clarifies the meanings of previously unclear expressions. One may, for example, think that there are no imaginary numbers or remain agnostic on the matter, while at the same time being interested in the meanings of such expressions as 'imaginary number' and 'square root of -1'.

What Quine has called the "ideological" element includes these two dimensions of reduction. They should, however, be clearly distinguished from each other. The quest for understanding is, of course, quite different from the quest for the ultimate furniture of the world. It was the former goal that had inspired the most celebrated examples of reductionism, from Bolzano's treatment of the calculus to Mach's historicocritical studies aimed at clarifying obscure notions in physics. Carnap's concern with what he called the "legitimacy" of concepts (*Physikalische Begriffsbildung*, p. 3) belongs squarely in this tradition. This type of reductionism was the instrument used by many of those who saw the search for clarity as a worthy goal.[3] As we shall see, Carnap regarded the first of the two ideological projects, the one concerned with meaning, as all-important; he thought that the second, concerned with ontology, was meaningless.

The third dimension of reductionism, the foundational, is embodied in what Quine has called the "doctrinal" aspect of reduction processes. Here we are no longer asking what p means or what it is about, but what reason we have for believing that it is true. The reason offered by reduction depends on the ideological stage in a way best displayed by a consideration of the character of reduction in science.

Within the field of science, the words we are concerned with, the ones we may be uneasy about and would like to legitimize through reduction, are always associated with a successful body of theory. Indeed, the reason we want to legitimize them, rather than ignore them altogether, is that we usually don't know how to do without them. We may feel uneasy about the meaning or the referent of the 'square root of -1' or about the reasons we have for believing what we say with it; but we are certainly aware of a number of fine things we can do with a theory involving that expression that we couldn't do without something equivalent to it. These fine things usually depend on the appeal to equations or, more generally, to sentences containing the questionable expressions. If we feel that mathematics is not just a set of calculational techniques with applications, but a set of truths, we will naturally be led to regard those sentences as parts of a theory that, to put it paradoxically, we have ample reason to believe is true without really having much of an idea about what it says and why it is true.

Let C be the questionable concept word and T the theory or set of sentences that involve it and that we "know" to be true. If T is, in the end, all that counts about C, we can couch the boundary condition that a concept C^* must satisfy in order to be a legitimation of C as follows: C^* must be legitimate (i.e., it must have been derived from legitimate concepts by methods that preserve legitimacy) and it must be such that when C is interpreted as meaning C^*, what T says turns out to be true. The *doctrinal* question examines the grounds for believing that T is true.

The ideological reduction has transformed T into a theory T^* that is, one hopes, clearer than T. If we can identify in the language of T^* formulas known to be true for specifiable and defensible reasons, and if T^* is deducible from or highly confirmed by these claims, then the doctrinal task has been achieved.

This reductionist technique was first displayed in the reduction of the calculus to arithmetic initiated by Bolzano and culminating in the work of Dedekind and Cantor on the continuum. That familiar process hardly needs more than a superficial review at this point.

Each of the diverse domains of complex, real, rational, integer, and natural numbers has an associated class of truths, that is, corresponding theories. The arithmetization of the calculus succeeded in reducing each of those theories to a simpler one in that sequence: The theory of complex numbers was reduced to that of the reals, the theory of reals to that of the rationals, and so on. The strategy was always the one we have just described: First define the primitives of the broader theory on the basis of those of the simpler one; then prove the axioms of the broader theory, as translated in agreement with the given definitions, on the basis of the axioms of the simpler one. For example, an imaginary number had been defined by Hamilton as an ordered pair of real numbers. When the operations among complex numbers were appropriately redefined, the laws of complex-number theory became (more) intelligible statements about (classes of) real numbers, and the reason these statements were true was displayed in their proofs from (presumably more plausible) axioms concerning real numbers. By the time Frege started to think about these matters, Dedekind and Cantor had solved the toughest problem in this sequence, the reduction of the continuum to the "atomistic" domain of the rationals.

When the mathematicians completed the reduction of the calculus to arithmetic, the philosophers took over. As we saw, Frege and Russell argued that arithmetic itself was reducible to logic, in an even more demanding sense of reduction than the one just explained. If they were right, most of mathematics would turn out to be logic in disguise: That was the logicist doctrine.

Whitehead and Russell were the first to see in this reductionist episode a model for epistemology. The idea was to do with all our knowledge claims about the empirical world what logicism had tried to do with mathematics, taking as the basis of reduction not just pure logic but also some given domain of data. The topic of reduction in this generalized project was not just the basic concepts of empirical science but almost all everyday concepts, however harmless they may seem. One might wonder about the purpose of this extended project.

Ontically speaking, one can see why the reductionist strategy is worth pursuing when the concept words under consideration appear to designate things that are strange and unfamiliar (like 'imaginary number' or 'electron') or even when they appear to represent familiar objects or processes, but in fact do not (as in the case of 'natural number' or 'simultaneity'). But it is harder to see why the project is worth pursuing in connection with familiar objects such as tables and chairs. The point of reducing or "constructing" the everyday world surely could not be that we don't have an honest idea of what is meant by words like 'table' and 'chair'. Nor could it be that we don't really know what tables and chairs are. Or could it? What, to repeat, is the point of this extension of reductionism?

Russell's answer was: in order to solve the problem of our knowledge of the external world. This problem is a direct consequence of Hume's skeptical philosophy and of the reification of idealism examined in Chapter 5. Hume's confusion on semantic matters had led him to think that all we can see and hear, all we can refer to, is in the mind. Brentano's disciples, and later Moore and Russell, had staged a mock rebellion against this view, arguing that even though everything empirical we can refer to is, indeed, of the nature of sounds and sights, these things have a mind-independent subsistence. The question that remained was, What about tables and chairs? These "realists" agreed with Hume that we never have and never will see a table. Under the circumstances it was natural to wonder what reasons we have for believing that there are such things. Reasonably enough, Hume and his followers had concluded: none whatever. "The problem of the external world" is the problem of finding a reason to conclude that there is, after all, an external world. This "problem" has nothing to do with empiricism, of course, but is merely the consequence of semantic confusions, which have been democratically distributed among empiricists and their opponents.

By 1914 Russell's semantics was in disarray. Its natural tendency had led Russell to make fatal concessions to psychologism. When he then turned to an idea of Whitehead's that seemed to offer a job for logic in the realm of philosophy, he paid the price of further concessions to psychologism. In a retrospective account, Russell recalled that Whitehead

said to me once: "You think the world is what it looks like in fine weather at noon day; I think it is what it seems like in the early morning when one first wakes from deep sleep." I thought his remark horrid, but could not see how to prove that my bias was any better than his. At last he showed me how to apply the technique of mathematical logic to his vague and higgledy-piggledy world, and dress it up in Sunday clothes that the mathematician could view without being shocked. This technique which I learnt from him delighted me, and I no longer demanded that the naked truth should be as good as the truth in its mathematical Sunday best. (*Portraits from Memory,* p. 39)

Following Whitehead's cue, Russell embraced Moore's old picture, according to which all we are given in empirical experience is sense data, and attacked the "problem" of the external world by giving up the project of discovering a reason for believing in the external world and instead constructing a replica of it in the domain of sense data.

Russell's first effort was presented in *Our Knowledge of the External World,* the book that Carnap had so admired. But the true sources of the project were displayed a few years later, in a further development of the basic ideas: "All empirical evidence consists, in the last analysis, of perceptions; thus [*sic!*] the world of physics must be, in some sense, continuous with the world of our perceptions, since it is the latter which supplies the evidence for the laws of physics" (*The Analysis of Matter,* p. 6). But the objects we can know noninferentially, the things we are acquainted with, are not physical objects:

In former days, my apparatus of non-inferential knowledge included tables and chairs and books and persons and the sun and moon and stars. I have come to regard these things as inferences . . . now, as the result of an argument, I have become unable to accept the knowledge of them as valid knowledge. . . . What seems like perception of an object is really perception of certain sensible qualities together with expectations of other sensible qualities. (*The Analysis of Matter,* pp. 181–2)

That tables are inferences means that they are not given in acquaintance. From the fact that they are not given in acquaintance, the inventor of knowledge by description concludes that "the knowledge of them is not valid knowledge," and therefore we must construct a surrogate of the "inferred" unperceived chair out of things we perceive. Thus, to the extent that we have reason to believe that there are tables and chairs, these objects must be "continuous" with the data of sense. Since experience is awareness of reified data – or perhaps the reified awareness-of-data, depending on the Russell vintage you are tasting – and since the presence of data can only be evidence for the presence of similar or "continuous" data, it follows that if we really have reason to believe anything at all about tables, then tables must be clusters of data, of things we are or could be acquainted with.

The role that evidence played in these considerations is reminiscent of the role it played in Russell's theory of the a priori. Here, as there, his train of thought leads inevitably to the conflation of ground and topic. From the obvious assumption that the data of experience are the ground of empirical knowledge, plus their reification and the tacit denial of knowledge by description, Russell inferred his supreme maxim and the idea that meanings, that is, the things our knowledge is about, should be constructed out of the material of acquaintance. This is a refined version of the Kantian idea that mind constitutes experience: In order to make sense of empirical knowledge we must construct the objects of experience from its data. If Russell had been a semantic dualist, he could have easily distinguished what we say from what we say about it, and he could therefore have granted that while human beings may constitute the former, only God can make, say, a tree. And even if he had remembered about knowledge by description, Russell could still have recognized that there is no need to pretend that we are constructing the world, but only our propositions about it. As it was, a plausible epistemology and an implausible semantics led Russell back to the Kantian womb. This is the Russell whom Carnap read and admired in 1921.

Russell had not merely revived the old idealist project; he (and Whitehead) had turned it into an exciting challenge for technically minded people and had also given it what seemed a fair chance of success by endowing it with the techniques of *Principia Mathematica*, which had worked so well in the case of logicism. But neither Russell nor Whitehead had offered more than sketches of exactly how to construct the world. Carnap would be the first to work out the details.

Constructing the world

There can be little doubt about the young Carnap's allegiance to Russell's program. But in Carnap's hands, the project took a very un-Russellian turn, indicative of the emergence of an unprecedented attitude in the field of semantics. Among a multitude of statements that Russell and earlier foundationalists could have signed as their own, one finds in Carnap's more thoughtful statements of his purpose a doctrine and an attitude that from Russell's standpoint must have appeared not just false or inconsistent with the project, but flatly incoherent. Later we will examine this remarkable twist that Carnap gave to the Russellian project. But we must first cast a quick glance at the nuts and bolts of his construction.

The object of the *Aufbau*, Carnap explained, was to apply the techniques of *Principia Mathematica* to the "problem of the analysis of reality," that is, to the "reduction of 'reality' to 'the given'" (sec. 3). As we shall see, he did not quite mean this – at least not the way anyone else would. But the standard, incorrect interpretation of these words will offer a thread of coherence to Carnap's strategy that was otherwise hard to recognize.

The reduction of reality was to be achieved by displaying a system for the constitution of concepts (*Konstitutionssystem*, henceforth C-system;

Konstitutionstheorie will be referred to as C-theory). The task of C-theory is divided into four different problems (sec. 26): the determination of the basis, the level forms, the object forms, and the system form.

The constitution of reality, if conceived as a construction, must start from something, the basis, and by means of certain procedures, the level forms, it must generate everything – every object and every concept. The problem of the system form is to select the sorts of things that will count as basis and level forms and to identify the general conditions to be satisfied by a constructed concept in order to qualify as the construction of one of the preconstructionally available ones. Carnap noted that it is in principle as legitimate to start with sensations and construct physical objects as it is to start with physical objects and construct sensations. In fact, it is conceivable that the whole world could be constructed starting from Hegel's Absolute or a close relative thereof (sec. 56).

In order to solve the problem of the system form, one must first decide what one's goals are. If we are concerned with matters of "epistemic primacy," with what is known before what, it will be advisable to choose as the basis the given. An object *A* is epistemically prior to another *E* when *E* is recognized through the mediation of *A* (sec. 54). Since the given is the only thing recognized in and of itself, that would be the appropriate starting point for such purposes. As to the level forms, logic provides a most valuable tool; the specific mode of application must be guided by the "information available in the special sciences" (sec. 53). The purpose of C-theory is not to sit in judgment of any serious science but to find out, with the help of science, exactly what science is saying. Finally, the concepts constructed need not agree with their pre-constructed counterparts in "sense" or psychological representation, but only in "logical value," that is, extension.

The basis problem is simply to determine the particular notions that constitute the ground level of the construction. Since the motive is epistemological, the basis must be a close relative of the chaos of sensations. Carnap's famous choice is the relation of recollection of similarity that holds between two experiences precisely when in one of them I remember the other and detect a similarity of some sort between them. (The given coincides with the field of this relation, assuming that our subject is a memorious one.) The choice of a single primitive as the basis is inspired by increased simplicity and, one suspects, by the magnitude of the technical challenge. The failure to construct the entire world from a single primitive could hardly be taken as a serious objection to the program.

The problem of level forms is to determine what specific logical, constructive devices can be used to proceed from each level of the construction to the next. It is presupposed that the construction moves by stages, from the base to even high stages of "quasi-object"[4] construction. The theory of types and the logical techniques available no doubt played a role in convincing Carnap that this was the way to proceed. But it is not easy to reconstruct an argument for this course of action that is both reasonable and consistent with the other doctrines of the book. Carnap's chosen level forms were the techniques of class and relation construction.

Finally, Carnap was rather imprecise in explaining the problem of object forms. Apparently, it is the question of what specific form the construction will take. Given the basis and the level forms, there might still be several ways to move up from the basis to the desired goals of the construction. The solution to this problem offered in the *Aufbau* was, by far, its best-known and most widely criticized feature. It is therefore convenient to remember that, according to Carnap, "the determination of the content of the stated constructions does not belong to the thesis of the present treatise" (sec. 122). It is, nonetheless, worth looking closely at the object forms chosen by Carnap, beginning with a survey of the several worlds that were supposed to emerge from them, the preanalytic range of objects and concepts that Carnap was committed to construct.

Carnap's classification of worlds was sketched in his "Dreidimensionalität des Raumes und Kausalität." There he said that even though sense experience is necessarily spatiotemporal and qualitatively structured, the connections of its elements into "things" with "properties" and their correlation through "causes" are, by no means, conditions of possibility of experience. Experience with no more than its necessary form is what Carnap called the "first level of experience," and its content was the "primary world." He criticized the neo-Kantian school for ignoring the primary world. In fact, its idea that the forms of experience of the second level are necessary and unique make it that much harder to recognize the distinction between primary and secondary worlds: "Their true achievement, namely, the proof of the object-creating function of thought, remains correct, however, and lies at the foundation of our conception of the secondary world" (p. 108).

In the *Aufbau* the primary world becomes the autopsychological world, a solipsist's dream world of given qualities spread out in two-dimensional space and time, the very universe that Schlick had treated as the only reality that is ever given to human beings. The secondary "common" world is called the physical world, with objects constituted as clusters of phenomenal qualities in three-dimensional space and not attached to any single individual mind. Among the things to be found in this world are the bodies of a number of people, including my own. All of those bodies that move and produce certain sorts of noises are regarded as endowed with a mental life. These "lives" are the heteropsychological worlds, the mental episodes of all empirical subjects, including me. Besides this there are the world of physics and the world of social institutions, and, who knows, there might be more. Carnap's goal was to construct all of them.

The basis, as indicated, is the relation *recollection of similarity,* which holds between temporal cross sections of the stream of experience (its terms are what Goodman calls "erlebs," elementary experiences). By an artful application of techniques found in *Principia Mathematica,* Carnap managed to mimic the process of analysis through what is, in reality, a process of synthesis. This "quasi-analysis," as Carnap called it, was one of the earliest ideas to emerge in the development of the project. The problem it solved is this: We start with erlebs and want to identify their constituents, that is, the localized qualities (e.g., 'this particular hue, saturation, and brightness at this particular location of this erleb'), but we seem to be unable to get to them through a process of constructions, because construction would take us from the simpler to the more complex, whereas we are trying to move in the opposite direction. In the process of quasi-analysis, explicit (constructive) definition is used to identify certain classes of erlebs, which are argued to share the "constructed" quality.

The constructed qualities can then be used to construct the physical world. Its ground is a four-dimensional array of real numbers, representing space-time, which is to be covered with qualities. The goal is, roughly speaking, to project the two-dimensional picture that each erleb gives me onto a three-dimensional domain. The two-dimensional doglike shape present in this particular frame of my visual field is to be blown up and out into a three-dimensional cluster of qualities: The obvious ones on this side of the dog's surface; others, less obvious and inferred, elsewhere around and inside the dog. The process of assigning qualities to places is no longer carried out by means of explicit definition. Carnap offered instead certain canons to which the world constructor must conform. For example, the canons instruct us to put the doglike qualities, interior and all, behind the constructed sofa, when the doglike shape appears to be absorbed by the sofa in successive frames of the erleb movie.

Once we are done constructing the three-dimensional inflation of our erlebs, we notice that we have constructed certain persons and things that provide the prime matter for further constructions. I have never met my grandfather, but an old postcard speaks of him and so does my recently constructed mother. Since she moves and makes noises in the appropriate ways, I will construct a heteropsychological world of erlebs for her (although "her" erlebs are, like everything else, clusters of mine).

Projecting those erlebs and others into the world (with corrections from
the postcard and other memorabilia), I will construct my grandfather and
then his father and so on *ad indefinitum*. In this way I will construct all
persons and things I have any reason to believe have ever existed; for
how else would I have reason to think so, if not through the testimony of
people and other sources?

Each of these empirical subjects that have been constructed is instructed to do with its erlebs exactly what the transcendental subject did
to construct *them*. They will first construct their autopsychological
world and then the physical world. Now there will be as many physical
worlds as there are empirical subjects. These worlds, Carnap thought,
will differ in their qualitative aspects (a plausible assumption if they were
not all made up of the same erlebs), but they will coincide in certain
structural features. The world of physics is generated by abstracting
these common features from the variety of physical worlds. (Carnap was
here endorsing, verbally anyway, another doctrine that Russell held for a
while, the idea that all physical knowledge is knowledge of structure.)
And this, in effect, completes the construction.

The preceding remarks offer a sketch of what is, no doubt, the best-
known part of the *Aufbau*. However admirable its technical achievement, the philosophy that is manifested in these pages is far from original
and, as we shall see in the next chapter, far from defensible. The most
original and defensible part of the *Aufbau* lies elsewhere, in the anticipation of conceptual holism.

Holism in the *Aufbau*

In the late 1960s Dummett began to publish a series of works that gave
new life to the study of the analytic tradition and, in particular, to Fregean studies. Before Dummett it was habitual among the later Wittgenstein's friends to regard Frege as an evil influence on modern philosophy,
as the man who had confused everything by bringing too sharp and
narrow a logical mind to deal with the broad, imprecise problems of
philosophy. Dummett has reversed this picture, turning Frege into the
source of some of the deepest insights concerning meaning.

One of the centerpieces of Dummett's new picture is his interpretation
of Frege's mysterious holistic aphorism: A word has significance only in
the context of a sentence. Through the years Dummett's interpretation
has changed, but roughly speaking, his account of it goes along the
following lines.

Consider two people arguing about whether there is such a thing as
intellectual responsibility. Since 'there is' occurs in the formulation of the
problem, one might think that the debate concerns a matter of ontology.

There are, to be sure, philosophers who will pose that very question, meaning to ask whether there is an entity that deserves the name 'intellectual responsibility', and they will wonder how our world relates to it, where it is located, and so on. These are misguided heirs of the tradition discussed in Chapter 6, and surely one need not go along with them in order to understand what the debate is about.

One might also interpret the disagreement as one concerning whether the notion of intellectual responsibility, in some of its standard uses, has a manageable meaning and serves a useful purpose, perhaps setting an ideal toward which we may strive. Those on one side may argue that anything we might normally be tempted to say "about" intellectual responsibility is bound to betray some philosophical confusion and that we would do far better if we ignored that notion altogether. The question is not one of Russellian existence but of the legitimacy of a concept.

Dummett argues that a large number of the claims that involve what seem to be existential quantifiers and therefore seem to be existence claims, or "reality" claims, as Carnap would put it, can be properly interpreted only in light of the holistic maxim. Here is a typical situation of this sort, involving the question of whether the 'number 28' stands for an object:

But what then *are* we asking? We are on the verge of introducing a philosophical sense of 'exists' which is distinct from the ordinary application of 'there is . . . '. Admittedly we do not ordinarily say that there is such a number as 28; but we do say that there is a perfect number between 10 and 30 and that that number is 28. But all the same, we want to add, the number 28 does not *exist* (in the philosophical sense). One of the consequences of [Frege's holistic maxim] is the repudiation of this philosophical existence. . . . If we can find a true statement of identity in which the identity sign stands between the name and a phrase of the form 'the x such that Fx', then we can determine whether the name has a reference by finding out, in the ordinary way, the truth-value of the corresponding sentence of the form 'There is one and only one x such that Fx'. There is no further philosophical question whether the name . . . *really* stands for something or not. (*Truth and Other Enigmas,* pp. 40–1)

Quite generally, the idea is that many questions of the form 'Are there *really* A's', as posed by philosophers, usually have no sense at all unless they are interpreted as questions concerning the meaningfulness or the legitimacy of the notion X. And in that case, Dummett adds, the answer to the question is given in accordance with Frege's aphorism, which he interprets as saying that to give the meaning (or perhaps the referent) of an expression is to give the truth conditions of the sentences in which it occurs.

One must grant that something like this doctrine was struggling to emerge in Frege's early writings. The doctrine may also have made an appearance in the *Tractatus.* The fact is that the holism Dummett sees in Frege's early writings does not clearly come to life until much later, for it is one of the important contributions to philosophy of Viennese positivism. Indeed, the first *explicit* statement of what Dummett takes to be Frege's intended point occurs not in Frege's or Wittgenstein's writings, but in Carnap's *Aufbau,* in which we are told that "to give the meaning (*Bedeutung*) of an expression of an object consists in giving the truth criteria (*Kriterien der Wahrheit*) of the sentences in which the sign of this object can occur" (sec. 161).

The point had already been made in *Physikalische Begriffsbildung,* in which Carnap dismissed the question of what concepts *are* and claimed that the only valid question in the neighborhood of that one is, When does a sign stand-for-a concept? (p. 3; the hyphens are intended to emphasize the nonrelational character of "standing for"). This early shift to the formal mode was inspired by the fact that "whenever we speak meaningfully of concepts, we are always dealing with concepts designated by means of signs or which could at least in principle be so designated; and so in the end we are always talking of these signs and their laws of application" (p. 4). The way to introduce a concept word, or to legitimize one already in use, is to "determine under what circumstances it can be used for the representation of states of affairs (*Sachverhalten*)" (p. 3). A word stands-for-a-concept, according to Carnap, when there is a rule that associates with each sentence in which the word occurs the circumstance in which the sentence is true; indeed, the concept *is* the rule in question. Thus, "*the construction of a concept is the selection of a law for the application of a sign* . . . in order to represent states of affairs" (p. 4). In natural languages, these rules are usually tacit. One purpose of philosophical analysis is to make them explicit. These explicit rules relate to their tacit counterparts much in the way that codified law relates to the unwritten law of custom (p. 4). The laws in question are somehow associated with the recognition of the appropriate states of affairs.[5]

In the *Aufbau* Carnap explained that concepts are legitimized through reduction to others, which are presumably already legitimate. A concept *a,* he explained, is reducible to others, *b, c,* and so on, when all assertions "about" *a* (i.e., all assertions involving *a*) can be transformed into assertions about *b, c,* and so on (secs. 2, 35).[6] Thus, the constitution of the concept of 2/7 from 2 and 7 consists in the "presentation of a rule through which all statements about 2/7 can be transformed into statements about 2 and 7" (sec. 35). Explicit definition guarantees eliminability, but it is by no means the only way to achieve that goal, as illustrated by Russell's incomplete-symbol strategy.

When this idea of constitution was introduced in section 2 of the *Aufbau,* there was no indication that the intended translation was to be achieved by means of explicit definition. In fact, the only example that Carnap gave at that point did not involve definitions at all. All fractions are reducible to natural numbers, Carnap explained, because all statements about fractions are reducible to statements about natural numbers. Thus, he explained, '3/7 > 2/5' can be translated as 'for any x and y that are natural numbers, if $7x = 5y$, then $3x > 2y$'. This statement formulates the truth condition of the former in terms that do not involve an explicit reference to fractions. It is assumed that the same can be done for all other statements containing fractions.[7]

The picture that emerges from these considerations is strikingly like the conception of holism attributed by Dummett to Frege. And yet there is no trace of holism in the constructive part of the *Aufbau,* that is, in the construction of the object forms. All we find there is an atomistic conception of constructivism, grounded on the exclusive use of explicit definition. The transition from holistic insights to explicit definition, reminiscent also of a similar transition in *Grundlagen,* was generated by Carnap's hopelessly confused treatment of contextual definition.

In sections 27, 38, and 39, the holistic treatment just reviewed appears to be reinforced when Carnap puts forth Russell's notion of contextual definition as the paradigm of a constitutional device that does not involve explicit definition. If we cannot define explicitly a word, Carnap says, we can legitimize it by doing with it what Russell did with incomplete symbols. What Russell did, as *we* know, was eliminate the phrase by introducing a rule that associates sentential contexts in which it occurs with other sentences (the "translation" or truth condition), which no longer employ the symbol in question. In section 38, Carnap observes that a constitution is always achieved through definition, either explicit or contextual. Of the former, all he says is that its nature is "well-known" (sec. 39), and for definitions in use he refers to *Principia Mathematica,* vol. 1, pp. 25, 69, which are exactly the references to give if one wants to point to Russell's theory of incomplete symbols.[8]

So far, everything appears to be in order. But when Carnap begins to display through applications his understanding of definitions in use, it becomes apparent that what he so-calls has no connection with what Russell and we so-call; for Carnap's "contextual definitions" are Russell's and our explicit definitions.

First of all, Carnap argued that the transformation rule involved in the constitution of a concept must apply to propositional functions, since it must "be applicable to all sentences of a certain sentence form" (sec. 39). If the expressions to which the rule applied did not have free variables, he thought, the rule would not apply to several sentences but only to this particular one. The translation rule must therefore identify another propositional function containing the very same free variables.[9]

This is a strange line of reasoning, particularly in view of the fact that *none* of Russell's examples of definition in use satisfy the condition that Carnap regarded as unavoidable. However indefensible, one can see how this train of thought led to the notion of explicit definition. Adding to this already considerable confusion, Carnap proceeded to offer two examples, one of explicit and the other of contextual definition. The former is '2 = Def 1 + 1 '; the latter is 'x is a prime number = Def x is a natural number and x is divisible only by 1 and by x'. Carnap noted that one might be tempted to think that 'prime number' could be defined explicitly, perhaps as 'the prime numbers = Def the numbers such that something or other'. But this, he explained, is mere appearance: "Expressions such as 'those such that . . .' . . . are (very useful) abbreviations for *definitions in use;* they correspond to the class-signs in logic" (sec. 39).

The mass of confusion accumulated in Carnap's treatment of definition entirely annihilates the holistic dimension of his thought in the sample of a C-system that has become the only memorable part of the *Aufbau.* But the holistic intention was there, inspiring a variety of doctrines that would remain at the center of Carnap's philosophy as the fog lifted. The most important of them was Carnap's remarkable attitude toward realism.

12

⟨══════════════════════════════════════⟩

Scientific idealism and
semantic idealism

Positivism and realism can to a considerable extent run a parallel course.
In particular, the realist can adopt the idea of the process of constitution,
i.e., the definition of constructs by means of coordinating propositions.
Yet this idea does not lead him to a theory of *objects,* but to a theory of
concepts.

> Reichenbach, "The Aims and Methods of Physical Knowledge,"
> *Selected Writings, 1909–1953,* vol. 2

Carnap's *Aufbau* and *Pseudoproblems* display the first explicit statement
of what seemed an unprecedented attitude concerning realism. Around
1930 Wittgenstein explained a related doctrine to audiences in Vienna
and Cambridge. Under the pressure of these two authorities, the view
became a characteristically Viennese product in that it was widely accepted in Vienna and widely regarded as absurd most everywhere else.
Kaila was expressing a not uncommon reaction among the non-Viennese
when he spoke of the "catastrophic results" of Carnap's philosophy on that
particular issue and observed that Carnap's ideas, if correct, "are apt to
deprive even empirical research of its *élan*" ("Logistic Neopositivism"
[1930], p. 4). Planck had raised similar charges against Machian positivism
in "The Unity of the Physical World-Picture," and in the early 1930s he
thought he was witnessing a revival of the attempt to deny the existence of
the external world ("Positivismus und reale Aussenwelt"). In 1927, after
reading Carnap's manuscript, Reichenbach had written to him:

It seems doubtful to me whether one can abstract the way you do from the
relation of the objects [i.e., Carnap's concepts] to something real. . . . You may
well call the axiom of reality metaphysical; but without this axiom your system of
constitution would be a mere game of chess, and also the whole of science. . . . I
think . . . that your neutrality [between idealism and realism] is a pretty dream.
(Letter of 20 February 1927, RC 102-64-02, p. 2, ASP)[1]

There was, as we shall see, much truth in these reactions. But there was
also much confusion, for behind their misleading formulations, Carnap
and Wittgenstein had something very important but very difficult to say

concerning existence and reality. Our purpose in this chapter is to examine the nature of Carnap's message.

When one considers what Carnap had to say about realism around 1928, most of the relevant texts arrange themselves into three different categories: those that appear to support an idealist position, those that endorse what we shall call a relationist position, and, finally, those that support a version of holism. A proper understanding of Carnap's attitude demands a separate treatment of each of these categories. Idealism was probably his position when he started writing the *Aufbau*, though not when he concluded it. The remaining two views were designed to explain how the philosopher can contribute to what Carnap called the problems of reality and essence, respectively.

Carnap had two major points to make about realism. The first was that discussions of that topic had been hampered by the conflation of two radically different types of problems and of two different interpretations of those problems. To begin with, Carnap explained, we must distinguish between questions of reality and questions of metaphysical essence or nature (*Wesensprobleme*). A question of reality is of the form 'Is *X* real?' or 'Does *X* exist?'; a question of essence has the form 'What is *X*?' (Each can be put in three Anglo-Saxon monosyllables: What is there? and What is it?). The answer to a question of reality is a simple yes or no; an answer to a question of essence is more complicated.[2]

Moreover, questions of reality and questions of essence have a good and a bad interpretation. (Carnap said "empirical" or "scientific" instead of *good*, and "metaphysical" or "philosophical" instead of *bad*.) The good interpretations receive a full and satisfactory answer from science. In the case of questions of reality, philosophy makes a modest contribution through construction theory and the notion of the real-typical (see the following section); the answers to good questions of essence are to be read straight out of the science textbook. For example, when we ask in the proper frame of mind for the reality and the nature of rabbits, we shall be fully satisfied by the answers 'Sure they are real!' and 'They are short-eared, long-tailed, burrowing mammals . . .', respectively.

The bad interpretations, in contrast, try to answer a prescientific or suprascientific question. The bad interpretation of questions of reality asks whether there *really* are rabbits, quite apart from what leporidology has to say about the matter.[3] The bad interpretation of questions of essence asks for the prescientific or extrascientific nature of something, as in 'Are rabbits really clusters of sensations?' Both of these questions, Carnap thought, were quite senseless. *But* whereas the former was hopelessly meaningless, there was something of philosophical interest somewhere in the neighborhood of the latter. There had better be, since otherwise the reduction in the *Aufbau* would be an answer to a nonsensical question.

Carnap's second point is much harder to identify, since it lies well below the surface of his writings of this period, though its effects are quite apparent. Its topic is a question that arises *after* one decides to give science the final word on all matters of reality: What is it that science has thereby decided?

Before Carnap, certain types of discourse were widely regarded as carrying ontological commitments. If we believe in unreconstructed mathematics, we must agree with Plato that there are numbers. If we go along with Bolzano and Frege, we must believe that there are even more things in this universe than Plato thought. And if Meinong was right, the mere fact that we understand a claim such as that the round square is blue guarantees that there *is* – in some remarkable sense of 'is' – an object that is both round and square.

Yet many philosophers had also sensed that there was something wrong with reading the existential claims of abstract disciplines as implying anything in the field of ontology. One standard attempt to avoid the implication had been to identify two senses of existence – a harmless and a harmful one, as it were – and to contend that only the harmless one is involved in the relevant existential claims.[4] No one before Carnap or since has made a more sustained effort to argue that only the harmless sense of existence makes any sense and to explain exactly what that sense is. This conception of reality is what lies behind the first appearance of that peculiarly Carnapian attitude toward philosophical matters that he chose to designate with that most misleading expression "tolerance." Carnap's tolerance was based on a sterilization of existence so effective as to allow him to talk both as a Platonist and as an anti-Platonist – without being either – and so undiscriminating as to deprive him of the power to draw any interesting distinctions between the reality of concepts and the reality of chairs.

Idealism and the problem of reality

In *Pseudoproblems* (sec. 10) Carnap told of a group of geographers considering the question of whether reports claiming the existence of a previously uncharted mountain are correct. They are at the purported location of the mountain, perform the appropriate observations, and reach a unanimous decision based on standards generally agreed upon by their scientific community. Their answer is affirmative. But as they start writing the joint report confirming the reality of the mountain, one of the geographers remembers that he is an idealist. He therefore adds a footnote pointing out that in his view the mountain does not *really* exist, that all they have witnessed are certain items of human experience. Upon hearing this, the Platonist geographer feels obligated to add his own qualification, indicating that, of course, the mountain in question, like any other earthly mountain, is not real and that there is only one real Mountain in some far beyond. The scientific realist encourages all of them to postulate boldly the existence of a mountain-in-itself beyond the realm of actual and possible observation, knowable only through structural features. The story was intended to illustrate the distinction between good and bad questions of reality. Carnap's verdict was that in their moment of sanity, all of these people used the good ("empirical") concept of reality, whereas in their moment of philosophy they used the other one.

It is characteristic of Carnap's writings in this transition period that the point of this clear example is quite muddled by the "serious" remarks that surround it and that probably played a role in alienating Carnap's realist critics; for those remarks identified the metaphysical notion of reality with the idea that there is a reality independent of the knowing subjects. This concept, Carnap said in the *Aufbau*, *"cannot be constructed"* (sec. 176), not only in his preferred C-system, "but in any experiential (*erkenntnismässig*) constructional system, even in a system which does not proceed from an autopsychological basis, but from the experiences of all subjects or from the physical." Carnap's less than half-hearted effort to establish this incredible claim depended on taking the definition of "independent of my consciousness" to be "not changeable by an act of my will." He argued that this was unacceptable because it would lead the realist to accept that butter is not real and the idealist to accept that Alpha Centauri is real.

Carnap's careless treatment of this crucial matter must be taken as an indication of a lingering bias toward idealism. Carnap was at least misleading and probably confused when he described the view he opposed as asserting a reality "independent of cognizing consciousness" (*Aufbau*, sec. 175) or asserting that physical things "are not only the content of my perception, but, in addition, they exist in themselves" (*Pseudoproblems,* sec. 9). Since he believed in the theory of evolution, he must have believed that there were some things before there was consciousness, or at least have been willing to endorse and reconstruct that sentence. Thus, the assertion

(*) There are objects even when there is no consciousness

should be of no more concern, or call for more special treatment, than

(**) There is a mountain at location *L.*

Carnap confusedly suggested that realists accept both claims, while the right way to look at things recognizes the factuality of the latter claim but not of the former. This is clearly inconsistent with the thrust of his argument, however. The difference between Carnap and his opponents cannot be reflected in any disagreement concerning (*), which does not carry over to (**) and to every other reality claim; the disagreement concerns the way they read *both* (*) and (**).

This mixture of sensible observation and thoughtless party-line idealism is characteristic of much of Carnap's work in the late 1920s. The best of his work in this period, however, represents an enormous and partially successful effort to identify the kernel of truth buried in the idealist's confusing doctrines.

As we saw in the preceding chapter, nothing is easier than to produce a long list of quotations from the *Aufbau* that, if literally taken, could be asserted only by someone committed to the doctrine that all there is, is reified experience. Here is a typical statement from a lecture entitled "Von Gott und Seele," delivered by Carnap in June 1929 but never published:

Quite generally, everything that we talk about must be reducible to what I have experienced. Everything that I can know refers either to my own feelings, representations, thoughts and so forth, or it is to be inferred from my perceptions. Each meaningful assertion, whether it concerns remote objects or complicated scientific concepts, must be *translatable* into a statement that speaks about contents of my own experience and, indeed, at most about my perceptions. (RC 089-63-02, p. 12, ASP)[5]

It is hard to imagine a more explicit commitment to the sort of ontological bias toward experience recently promoted by Mach and Russell.

Moreover, the distinction between objects and quasi-objects in the *Aufbau* seems intended to emphasize the same bias. Following Frege without much conviction or understanding, Carnap distinguished between the saturated and the unsaturated parts of a sentence (see sec. 27). Each constructed element in the *Aufbau* corresponds to an unsaturated expression, and all unsaturated expressions "designate nothing in and of themselves" (sec. 27).[6] Even so, Carnap thought that instead of saying that these expressions designate nothing at all (no object), it is preferable to make a concession to realistic (in this case, Meinongian) modes of speech and say that they designate "quasi-objects." Quasi-objects are, therefore, fictions. One can well understand why realists would have been suspicious of Carnap's neutrality when they heard him say that "the 'objects' of science are almost without exception quasi objects" (*LSW*, sec. 27) or that "each object which is not itself one of my experiences (erlebs), is a quasi object; I use its name as a convenient abbreviation in order to speak about my experiences" (*LSW*, sec. 160).[7] We seem to be facing one of those familiar developments leading from positivism to idealism in one very small step.

This implicit idealism was mitigated by the recognition of what Carnap misleadingly called a "concession to the realistic mode of speech" (*LSW*, sec. 162). What he meant by "realistic" in this context included not only the views of Meinong and the early Russell, but also those of Berkeley and Mach. Claims are in the "realistic" mode of speech when they seem to be talking about something, whether it be material (as in Planck), Platonic (as in Russell), extrasubsistent (as in Meinong), or experiential (as in Mach).[8] For example, Carnap explained that anybody who *asks* such questions as whether physical things exist when unobserved, whether other persons exist, and whether classes exist is a "realist"; questions of this sort "(*independently of how they are answered*) imply a realistic standpoint" (*Aufbau*, sec. 176, my italics). Thus, when Carnap said that the construction of the *Aufbau* shows that our knowledge is *about* experience, he was making one of those misleading and confusing concessions to "realism" – in this case, to ontological idealism, the doctrine that all there *is*, is experience. It is clear that he did not mean what he said. What he *did* mean is not as easy to figure out.

There can be little doubt that these linguistic concessions to "realism" (i.e., to ontological idealism) were originally intended quite literally and that the project of constructing the world was conceived at a time when Carnap was an idealist – wittingly or otherwise.[9] The most apparent traces of this early stage, and possibly the clearest suggestion of idealistic leanings, occur in the construction of the physical world examined in the preceding chapter. That construction clearly illustrates the sense in which Carnap said that the *Aufbau* places all objects in a system, the constructional system of scientific objects. On the basis of evidence we construct some tables but not others; some shadows but not others. We also construct mirror images, visual images, color solids, and a great deal more. We do not construct mermaids, unicorns, God, or Satan, not because we couldn't but because "science" (i.e., some consistent subclass of what reasonable people believe) does not suggest that we should. This is the context in which Carnap would allow us to pose and to answer the question 'What is real?' under its good interpretation.

Are unicorns real? Carnap's answer was: certainly not, for "science" has not instructed us to construct them. Are tables real? This time the answer is clearly: yes, for all those we have constructed. Are shadows, mirror images, and virtual images real? Here we hesitate, and in this hesitation Carnap saw a clue to the problem of reality: the hidden notion of the "real-typical" (see the *Aufbau*, secs. 172–4). Something is real-typical, or the type of that which is real, Carnap explained, if it is the sort of thing that is automatically regarded as real when we construct it in the process of constituting the world. Common usage is unequivocal in indicating that both tables and unicorns are real-typical; if we were equally clear on the real-typical character of shadows and mirror images, we would not hesitate to infer their reality from the fact that we have constructed them. And as with shadows, so with very many other things: events, wholes composed of real things, relations between real things or classes of these, and so on. At places, common usage is downright erratic, sometimes asserting and sometimes denying reality to entities with no logically recognizable difference. What better proof, Carnap wondered, of the "rather arbitrary and frequently vacillating boundary of the concept of the 'real-typical'" (*LSW,* sec. 173)?

The space-time order of the physical world is only one of the domains to whose members we may attribute reality. Once we have completed its construction, we construct many other "orders," and the question of reality is resolved in them essentially as it was in the case of physical objects. Nominalists will complain that Carnap's dog Luchs is real in a sense in which his brown color or his property of being a dog is not. Carnap replied that this is an unjustified distinction (sec. 158); it is true that the color *brown* and the species *dog* cannot be placed in the space-time order, but Luchs cannot be placed in the color solid (where *black* lies) or in the "zoological solid" (where *dog* lies). According to Carnap, there is a perfect symmetry between these situations; he saw no ground for promoting the space-time chauvinism that had led several philosophers, including Schlick, to regard as real only what belongs in the spatial or temporal framework.

We see here the root of the idea that "the reality of anything is nothing else than the possibility of its being placed in a certain system" and that "the question about the Reality of the physical world as a whole . . . has no sense" (*Philosophy and Logical Syntax,* p. 20).[10] When seen against the background of the preceding considerations, this position takes the notion *is real,* whatever its subject, to be not a property but a relation to a framework.

How do these doctrines relate to traditional realism? On the face of it, the links with scientific realism appear closer than one might expect. First, like scientific realists, Carnap refused to draw a line between those objects that are introduced into the system of science for purely instrumental purposes and those that are more closely tied to observational data. The claim that 'we see tables but not electrons' would not move the author of the *Aufbau* to draw any conclusions about the reality of the former or the unreality of the latter. Carnap would go so far as to argue for the reality of the Freudian unconscious (sec. 132). Anything located in the system of science is automatically real, provided that it is real-typical or we choose to make it real-typical. Quite generally, on scientific reality claims Carnap would agree with the scientific realist; more precisely, he would ascribe reality to every real-typical thing to which the realist ascribes reality; indeed, he would go along with any of the realist's attributions of reality, provided that the realist acknowledged the conventional element involved.

The scientific realist will find this agreement shallow and Carnap's concessions to realism empty. Even if the Carnapian attributes and denies reality to things in unison with the realist, the Carnapian's words sound hypocritical, as if the Carnapian were a homophonic fifth column whose true purpose is the demise of realism. Is the realist right?

Consider first the situation in mathematics. Imagine the realist (in this case, the Platonist) asking Carnap whether he thinks that there exist prime numbers. Carnap will perform the appropriate calculation and establish that 3, for example, is prime and so will answer in the affirmative. The Platonist will say that he has been misunderstood, that what he wanted to know is whether Carnap thinks that there *really* are prime numbers. At this point Carnap says that he thinks he already answered that question. The Platonist nervously insists that what he is asking is whether Carnap admits an ontic commitment to numbers. Carnap will reply that he is not sure he understands, but he thinks he just said yes. The Platonist is now furious and asks about the independent existence of numbers. At that point Carnap stands up and leaves.

Perhaps the empirical domain offers a better area for unmasking the Carnapian homophonist. One could argue, for example, that the electrons and the unconscious whose reality Carnap has granted have nothing whatever to do with the real thing. Carnap has said many times that the autopsychological objects are "in part my experiences themselves, in part classes of such experiences," that physical objects are "classes of my experiences," heteropsychological objects "consist of a new arrangement of the autopsychological objects in relation to certain physical objects," and that even the cultural objects are "orders of heteropsychological . . . objects" (*LSW,* sec. 160). So it is all really experience, Carnap's experience, in disguise. Carnap *says* that electrons are real, but he merely means that certain collections of sensations are real.

This reasonable and plausible confusion is, to be sure, caused mainly by Carnap's concessions to the "realistic" mode of speech. Carnap did talk like an ontological idealist with embarrassing consistency, but he was – or was slowly beginning to be – something else: a semantic idealist. In order to explain what this means we must look at the problems posed by questions of essence and their resolution by means of holism.

Idealism and the problem of essence

The realist's complaint against Carnap was not merely that he talked like an idealist, but, of course, that what he was doing seemed to be exactly what idealists had always wanted to do. After all, he was constructing the world! Wasn't reduction to experience the characteristic feature of the worst form of idealism?

Before Carnap and since Quine, reduction had been regarded as relevant primarily to matters of ontology. Ontological reductionists such as Mach, Whitehead, and (a certain) Russell engaged in processes of reduction in order to determine what there is *and* what it is. Mathematical reductionists often intended to tell us things such as that complex numbers are classes of classes of reals, that reals are classes of rationals, and so on; empirical reductionists traditionally tried to deal with ontological problems outside the scope of mathematics by means of the same technique. For them reductionism was an answer to what Carnap had called a question of essence.

The remarkable thing about the *Aufbau* is that, as everyone knows, it contains the most developed exercise within that reductionist tradition, but it also contains the sharpest condemnation to date of the ontological purpose that had inspired it. Carnap asserted that there is no better answer to the question of what something is than what the scientist tells us. What, then, is the point of doing what Carnap was doing? What is the purpose of constructing the world?

'Construction' is not quite the right word; for where we use the word 'construction', Carnap normally used another one: 'constitution'. As noted in the preceding chapter, the original title of the *Aufbau* was "Konstitutionstheorie" ("Theory of Constitution"); the actual title was a reluctant concession to Schlick (Correspondence with Schlick in March 1926, RC 029-32-23, RC 029-32-24, and RC 029-32-27, ASP).[11]

Constitution is one of a handful of landmark notions that dominated nineteenth-century developments in epistemology. Hosts of philosophers tried to develop the Kantian idea that experience and its objects are constituted through our categories. Most sensitive thinkers had felt the force of Kant's point, but they would have been hard-pressed to assign a manageable meaning to that elusive notion. Following the ontological bent of traditional idealism, they compared constitution to construction, thus suggesting that what our mind does with the objects of experience is comparable to what the engineer does with bridges and the carpenter with tables. Many philosophers recognized the absurdity of this claim but did not know how to avoid the inference from reduction to ontology.

Carnap may have been the first among admirers of the idea of constitution to come up with a reasonable theory about the nature of that activity that both grasps the kernel of truth in the Kantian doctrine and excludes the ontological-idealist implication. The centerpiece of Carnap's new doctrine of constitution was his conceptual holism, introduced in the preceding chapter. The role that doctrine played in the *Aufbau* was one of implementing a major revision of idealistic principles. From the very beginning, idealism had taken a clearly ontological approach in its denial of things-in-themselves and its endorsement of experience as the only topic of genuine knowledge. Throughout the nineteenth century, several neo-Kantians and positivists had obscurely sensed that their constructive insights concerned semantics rather than ontology, that the main point they wanted to make against "realism" did not have to do with what there is but how we mean; consequently, their enemy was not an opinion about what is real (hence nothing that could reasonably be called "realism") but an opinion about how we can make sense or speak with objective significance. Yet in the end they usually expressed their position as one about what there is and what there isn't. Among those who influenced logical positivists, those who exhibited the most noticeable confusions of this sort were, of course, Mach in his version of neutral monism and Russell in his more recently adopted variety of that doctrine.[12]

The transition of these idealist insights from the field of ontology to that of semantics did not really start to take place until the late 1920s. It is in Carnap's *Aufbau* and *Pseudoproblems* that one can finally recognize the gigantic decisive shift from ontic to semantic idealism beginning to develop, even though the confusion between ontic and semantic matters still plagued Carnap's efforts.

Let me begin by stating the idea far more sharply than Carnap did in the *Aufbau*. First, for Carnap reduction was a version of constitution, and the ambiguities of the latter are reflected in the former. The ambiguity of constitution is this: There are two things we might want to constitute: the world or what we say about it. The only apparent reason we may have for constituting the world is that we are trying to answer the *bad* interpretation of a question of essence: What is *X*, apart from what science says it is? The rejection of this type of question entails the rejection of constitution as construed by idealists. Since ontological reductionism is one form of ontological constitutionalism, that doctrine is also rejected.

There is, however, a crucial philosophical matter in the neighborhood of essence, a question of semantics. The later parts of the *Aufbau* deal with an aspect of this question,[13] and conceptual holism emerged in that book as an answer to it: "The *question* concerning the *essence of a type of object* is incorrect; what one means to ask in such cases finds adequate answer when one gives the *connection between concepts*. Connection between concepts means: *connection between the sentences* in which they occur" (Notes for lecture delivered 5 November 1932, RC 089-61-01, p. 2, ASP).[14] Carnap had already explained in the *Aufbau* that a legitimate form of the question of essence asks about the meaning, rather the *Bedeutung*,[15] of a term, and the proper answer was described in this passage: *"To say what an object is* or, in other words, to give the Bedeutung of an object sign, *is simply to give the truth-criteria for the sentences in which the sign can occur"* (sec. 161). The link between reductionism and holism emerged in Carnap's characterization of constitution in the *Aufbau.* After stating once again that familiar theme, that his system shows how all objects can be constituted starting from his experiences, he finally added: "In other words (for this is the meaning of the expression 'to constitute'): all (scientific) assertions can be transformed into assertions concerning my experiences so as to preserve their logical value" (sec. 160). To put it differently, to constitute X is not necessarily (as many have assumed) to define it explicitly, but to give the experiential truth conditions for each sentence in which X occurs – a condition fulfilled by explicit definition but also by a host of other procedures, as illustrated by Russell's incomplete-symbol technique.

Carnap's reductionism was therefore not an exercise in ontology but one of several available ways to implement a holistic doctrine of meaning. By embedding reductionism in a holistic framework, Carnap deflected the implications of the Kantian doctrine of constitution away from ontology and onto semantics. Carnap could not express his point clearly, largely because of the enormous empiricist prejudice against meaning that he was only beginning to overcome.

Realism and the bad concept of reality

The hardest question concerning reality remains untouched, for what we have said so far may leave us wondering what a scientific realist should find objectionable in Carnap's views. After all, the typical scientific realist is not concerned with essences, and may freely grant Carnap's reinterpretation of reductionism as well as his holistic doctrine. What, then, is the remaining conflict with realism, properly so-called?

Our examination of the "good" concept of reality in the preceding section, and, indeed, many of the things that Carnap said, might lead us to believe that in Carnap's view, as long as one takes science as the ultimate guide in attributions of reality, there is no way to go wrong. This is a mistake. It is one thing to endorse, with Carnap, the doctrine that "science is the measure of all things: of those that are, that they are, of those that are not, that they are not"; it is a completely different thing to determine what that attribution of existence amounts to. Science solves the problem of reality by telling us what there is; but science does not tell us *what* it tells us when it tells us what there is.[16] It is on this topic that Carnap disagreed with the scientific realist, for the realist interprets the attribution of reality within an ontological framework that Carnap found objectionable. It is this framework, more than anything else, that Carnap meant by the word 'realism'. Our purpose now is to try to understand that framework and Carnap's objections to it.

Before Carnap, it was widely assumed that there is a very intimate link between some of the things we say and ontology. To put it in its most convincing form, the idea was that whenever we endorse statements involving talk about numbers or propositions or electrons or chairs, we must, in all consistency, agree that among the things in the universe there are numbers or propositions or electrons or chairs. Those who do not believe that the things in question are something (rather than nothing) cannot responsibly use the relevant linguistic fragments, or hold the relevant beliefs, *unless* they manage to "reduce" or translate their statements into others that avoid the fearful ontic commitments. This was the common assumption of nominalists and realists, for example, the difference between them being that nominalists rejected the dubious entities (and hence the associated form of discourse) while realists accepted the form of discourse (and therefore the entities). Short of reduction, all parties agreed that it was irresponsible to talk a language with ontic commitments one could not accept and that it was *incoherent* to promote the acceptance and use of languages with conflicting ontic commitments.

As we know, there is a sense in which Carnap would want to agree with this common assumption; but the difference between *that* sense and the one intended by the conflicting parties becomes clear when we notice in Carnap's attitude what the realist will regard as an incomprehensible indifference to matters of ontology. We have just said that Carnap was a naturalist who had a job for philosophy. We should add, however, that in the true Wittgensteinian spirit, the job was suicidal (jumping off the ladder once you climbed it, as it were); for Carnap thought that there was no specifically *philosophical* reason to be happy or unhappy about the truth or falsehood of any statements of reality, whether they concern electrons, sets, propositions, or the Holy Ghost. As long as science places such objects in its system, there is no reasonable reaction but to acquiesce with indifference. Wittgenstein may have been wrong about surprises in logic, but there were certainly no surprises for Carnap in ontology.

In a few years Carnap's indifference to ontology would be compounded by an even stranger feature, soon to become a trademark of his philosophical style: Carnap's inclination to talk in the language of philosophers with whom he disagreed. Most careful readers of his later work have been struck by the elusive flavor of unreality associated with much of what Carnap said when he wrote about specifically philosophical matters. At different stages in his intellectual development, one finds him talking the way X would, while at the same time telling us that he regards

X's philosophical position as meaningless — whether *X* is a constructivist, classical logicist, idealist, Platonist, or realist. More often than with most other philosophers, one is left wondering whether Carnap really meant what he said and, if so, exactly how he meant it. But Carnap would argue that the feeling that his attitude was incoherent or frivolous, or that he couldn't possibly mean what he said, was itself a testimony to the widespread, if tacit and uncritical, endorsement of "realism"; for it is only when we look at things from that unjustified perspective that these alleged conflicts appear to be conflicts.

The roots of this attitude can already be clearly detected in the late 1920s, in Carnap's treatment of the conflict between realism, phenomenalism, and transcendental idealism (*Aufbau,* secs. 177–8). By the time of *Pseudoproblems,* his line was that in the sense in which the "conflicting" standpoints make sense, they do not conflict at all and, indeed, that they are all correct; hence, we may talk as a realist *and* as an idealist without thereby saying anything false in either language or anything inconsistent in their conjunction.

The story of the geographers in *Pseudoproblems* was intended to illustrate the good questions of reality and their dependence on science. But the story also offers a clue to Carnap's indifference to ontology; for as he would soon observe, the very same story could have been told with mathematicians wondering whether there are more than five prime numbers in a given interval or with logicians wondering whether a certain proposition follows from another.

A traditional empiricist would gladly grant all of this and then conclude that the metaphysics thus unmasked should be committed to the flames. The remarkable thing about Carnap's approach is that instead of doing this, he would actively search for and often find a way to reinterpret what all conflicting parties were saying so as to turn their metaphysical doctrines into something a reasonable person might want to say. Far from despising philosophers or philosophy (as many of his Neurathian emissions might lead one to believe), Carnap's attitude reflects an astonishing degree of optimism toward the instincts, if not the opinions, of most philosophers. In the *Aufbau* he quoted with approval the claim that "all philosophers are right, but they express themselves with varying degrees of ineptness; and it could not be otherwise since they use the *given* language and thereby speak a hundred sublanguages, instead of inventing a pasigraphy"; he added, "This neutral language is the goal of the theory of constitution" (sec. 178). If constitution would soon vanish from the forefront of Carnap's concerns, the neutral language would become an ever more dominant goal.

It would be a gross error to confuse this emerging "tolerant" attitude with a version of eclecticism. On the contrary, in the *Aufbau* Carnap explained that the philosophical standpoints of *both* Mach and his scientific realist opponents were quite wrong, because they were "realists" in Carnap's still unexplicated sense: They all interpreted what they said precisely in the way that Carnap considered indefensible or incoherent. Only when this indefensible element of "realism" was eliminated from what the conflicting parties said did their views become correct. Hence, Carnap's earliest form of "tolerance" tolerated, indeed encouraged, apparently conflicting philosophical doctrines – but not before insisting that in the realistic sense in which they had been put forth, they should all be committed to the flames.

The peculiar nature of the strategy Carnap would pursue in later years, constructing that "pasigraphy," or neutral language, was entirely dependent on the idiosyncratic way in which he interpreted reality assertions. We have already described the circumstances under which Carnap would agree to say that there is a mountain or that a certain mountain is real. Since he would also grant that mountains are physical objects, he was also willing to agree that there are physical objects, that there are things in the universe, that there *really* are physical objects, and so on. He would be reluctant to say these things in the presence of philosophers, however, since among them such utterances are highly correlated with a certain confusion. The hard question around which we have been circling for pages is, What is this confusion? What is this objectionable realistic intent?

Quine once noted that the person trying to argue that 'Pegasus does not exist' is not about Pegasus has a hard time even stating that position coherently. Carnap faced a similar difficulty: It is far easier to describe the conflict between him and the realist *from the realist's standpoint,* although Carnap found himself agreeing with everything the realist said he denied.

From the realist's standpoint (though not from Carnap's), it seems that what is at issue is a conception of the link between language on the one hand and the world on the other. (The Carnapian homophonist would, of course, agree.) Some words refer to some things, and they thereby allow us to make claims about these entities.[17] But as the realist sees it, Carnap was inviting us to apply a semantic epoch, saying what realists do without accepting in his heart the ontic commitments of what he was saying. For example, the homophonist will use set-theoretic language as shamelessly as his Platonistic colleagues, and in the appropriate circumstances he will say, 'There are sets such that . . .', or 'There are numbers such that . . .'. But (the realist thinks) he will not really mean it; he will not regard any of these claims as *truly* existential. If asked whether there is a prime number between 7 and 12, the homophonist will perform the standard calculations and give the standard answer. When asked whether there *really* is such a number, an already familiar dialogue will ensue.

The Carnapian homophonist cannot agree with the realist's reading of their conflict. Indeed, it may seem, even from his own viewpoint, that Carnap was not opposing a theory or doctrine but only an attitude. As we just saw, if there are statements outside the range of purely philosophical talk that the homophonist will not pronounce in unison with the realist, it is not because he disagreed with them but because he feared they were symptoms of an objectionable attitude. But there is, in fact, a philosophical doctrine that Carnap was rejecting in his denunciation of realism.

First of all, one could say that the homophonist's target is a doctrine concerning the difference between content and grounds for reality claims. The objectionable form of realism will agree that the homophonist's computations determining that 7 is prime provides an excellent, indeed decisive, reason for concluding that there are prime numbers, but this (and all reasons of this sort) is no more than one mode of access to a truth that has, as it were, a life of its own. It might even be the case that human beings happen to have no other form of access to such truths. The realist will distinguish between what we are saying and the particular grounds that we have for saying it, even in this particular case. The homophonist's attempts to divide 7 by 3, 4, . . . and their ensuing failure are no more than the route to a truth, not the content of that truth. The homophonist recognizes the very same grounds, however, as the realist; the homophonist does not recognize them *as* grounds but as something else. It is as if all there were to the assertion under consideration from the homophonist's standpoint were the grounds, and so the homophonist would be in the incoherent position of accepting that there are good reasons to believe *p* without being able to assign any meaning to *p*. For the realist there is something above and beyond all paths to such reality statements that gives them their content. This is something Carnap would not grant. The reality statement is determined entirely by those circumstances that the realist would regard as merely confirmational or as routes toward its truth.

There is another related element in the doctrine Carnap was denying. Carnap's "realism" is an opinion underlying the philosophies of the *Tractatus* and of Russell's atomism, a specific philosophical doctrine concerning explanation in matters of semantics − the thesis that the traditional "realist" picture of things, with words and meanings on the one side, language on the other, and finally semantic relations linking the two, has explanatory value. As we know, the homophonist does *not* reject the fact that there are classes and tables, nor that there are expressions for classes and for tables. But the homophonist does deny that this fact helps us understand anything at all in the field of semantics. The import of this rejection and its ground are the topic of Chapter 14.

In conclusion, we are now ready to assess the extent to which Carnap managed to extricate himself from ontological idealism and define a defensible position on matters of ontology. Earlier we raised the question, What is the purpose of constructing the world? Despite all we have said, there is no coherent answer to that question short of a commitment to ontological idealism. Recall once again that Carnap's example of construction beyond the autopsychological level aimed to construct not what we say about the world, but the world itself – not what we say about Napoleon, but Napoleon himself, an exciting four-dimensional life story, from trips to Marengo to trips to the boudoir. But Carnap should have known that we do not need to construct Napoleon: Someone or something else took care of that long before we could do anything about it. What we need to construct or constitute is what we say about him; the obscure recognition of this fact is what emerged in the later, less celebrated, less technical portion of the *Aufbau.*

We also noticed earlier the extent to which Carnap agreed with the scientific realist on what the realist takes to be real. Even so, the position displayed in the construction of the physical world (and beyond) is more properly described as an exercise in "scientific idealism." It has emerged in recent years, largely as a result of Putnam's work, that the key doctrine of scientific realism concerns not so much the truth of science as its possible falsehood. In order to be a scientific realist, it is not necessary, or even reasonable, to believe that science is true; but it is necessary to believe that it might be false, *always* false. This is a test that Carnap's construction of the world fails miserably, for it leaves us without the ability to distinguish between truth and well-grounded belief, or between what science says and what is the case. If Carnap were right, science could never be false. As science changes, Carnap would instruct us to reconstruct the world. Frege could have told him that all that changes under those circumstances is what we believe, the claims we are willing to endorse. Indeed, Bolzano and probably a good many medieval logicians could have explained the same point to Carnap. But the recognition of this fact required a benevolence toward meaning that, once again, Carnap was only beginning to acquire.

Carnap had succeeded in defining an anemic sense of existence wonderfully fit to defuse Platonism. It is as if he had taken abstract discourse as his target and then mechanically extended his results everywhere else. For those who think that electrons are somewhat more substantial than sets and that absolutely everything we say about the former may be wrong, Carnap had nothing to offer. He did have, however, a great deal to offer to those who thought that existence statements were inevitably entangled with "ontic commitments." Finally, Carnap's wisest words were to those who felt the force of idealistic premises but were reluctant to apply them to ontology.

Carnap's scorecard was and remained mixed. His solution to the problem of reality was scientific idealism; his solution to the problem of essence was semantic idealism. The former led to a kind of relationism that was hard to detach from its idealistic motivation; the latter was based on a reinterpretation of constitution and reduction through holism that left room for a reasonable realism. In both cases there was a link with traditional idealism, and also a difference. Scientific idealism differed from the standard version in little more than an overwhelming bias toward science. But semantic idealism was the kernel of a more radical and thoughtful challenge to tradition, for it involved a reinterpretation of idealism that preserved everything defensible in that doctrine while depriving it of implications concerning what there is.

13

◁══════════════════════════════════════▷

Return of Ludwig Wittgenstein

I am today in disagreement with *very, very* many of the formulations of the book [i.e., the "essay"] . . . everything that has to do with "elementary propositions" or "objects" (or at least most of it) has now turned out to be incorrect, and must be completely reworked.[1]

> Letter from Wittgenstein to Schlick, 20 November 1931 (VCA)

Mathematics is ridden through and through with the pernicious idiom of set theory. . . . Set theory is false because it apparently presupposes a symbolism that doesn't exist instead of the one that does exist (the only one possible).

> Wittgenstein, *Philosophische Bemerkungen*

Shortly after Schlick moved to Vienna in 1922, he must have heard about a strange little book written by an obscure Viennese philosopher. The book was impenetrable, but it came with a remarkably favorable introduction by Russell, the philosopher who commanded more respect than anyone else among scientifically minded people.[2] Hahn and Reidemeister were apparently the first to have been impressed by the logicomathematical doctrines of the *Tractatus,* and in 1926 it was decided that Schlick's circle should hold special sessions to discuss the book, sentence by sentence (see Menger, "Introduction," p. xii; and Carnap, "Intellectual Autobiography," p. 24).

It is easy to see why the *Tractatus* would have struck many scientifically minded Viennese as extraordinarily attractive. Leaving Russell's endorsement and its references to logic aside, the few intelligible doctrines it espoused were bound to please them: Philosophy should no longer be conceived as a discipline, involved in producing theories about peculiar objects, but rather as an activity, aimed at clarifying meaning; the domain of sense coincides with that of the natural sciences, so everything that can be said meaningfully lies within the province of science; logic and other a priori "claims" say nothing at all, so an empiricist need not worry about how to provide a foundation for them; and so on. In the long struggle between the village atheist and the village priest that constituted so much of German popular philosophizing, Wittgenstein appeared to positivists to be squarely on the side of the former. Little did they know that he was appalled by the godless materialism of the village atheist.

After a failed attempt at protracted self-destruction through school teaching, Wittgenstein returned to Vienna in 1926. Schlick had been trying to meet him since 1925, and his efforts were finally rewarded when he was invited to lunch with Wittgenstein at his sister's mansion on 19 February 1927. Mrs. Schlick recalls the "great joy and anticipation . . . expectations and hopes" of her husband: "I observed with interest the reverential attitude of the pilgrim. He returned in an ecstatic state, saying little, and I felt I should not ask questions" (Waismann, *Vienna Circle*, p. 14). Schlick invited Wittgenstein to meet with his Vienna circle colleagues in order to discuss the *Tractatus*. It was like inviting Christ to discuss the Gospels with Voltaire. Wittgenstein eventually agreed to meet in neutral territory with those positivists who could behave properly. In his "Intellectual Autobiography" Carnap described the preparations for his first encounter with Wittgenstein as follows:

Before the first meeting, Schlick admonished us [i.e., Carnap and Waismann] urgently not to start a discussion of the kind to which we were accustomed in the Circle, because Wittgenstein did not want such a thing under any circumstances. We should even be cautious in asking questions, because Wittgenstein was very sensitive and easily disturbed by a direct question. The best approach, Schlick said, would be to let Wittgenstein talk and then ask only very cautiously for the necessary elucidations. (p. 25)

The meetings started in 1927 and concluded in 1932.[3] The positivists derived their understanding of Wittgenstein's position from these meetings and from other direct or indirect contacts with Wittgenstein, rather than from his impenetrable book.[4]

It is difficult to ascertain the relation between the doctrines of the *Tractatus* and those that Wittgenstein was explaining to the friendly positivists in the late 1920s. The format of their sessions with him, as described by Carnap, was not the most appropriate for inquiring about the extent to which what Wittgenstein was then saying clarified or conflicted with his stance in the *Tractatus*. There can be no doubt, however, that his views on fundamental matters were changing rather quickly in this period.[5] In this chapter we will examine some of the doctrines that Wittgenstein explained to his positivist audience in the late 1920s and early 1930s. It goes without saying that the clearer our account of these views is, the farther it will be from Wittgenstein's actual words, and perhaps even from his intended meaning.

The critique of understanding

Even though Wittgenstein's plentiful writings of this period offer an impression of anarchy and free association, there is a unifying theme: Wittgenstein was trying to survey the main ways in which we (think we) manage to communicate. Unlike most others, Wittgenstein was enormously skeptical about the degree of uniformity displayed by what goes on in different cases and insisted that behind misleading syntactic analogies lies a wide variety of radically different semantic processes. The impression of chaos and randomness that emerges from the manuscripts and talks of this period is due partly to his decision to survey as broad a territory as possible and to describe faithfully the different semantic dimensions displayed in language.

Wittgenstein's main concern was still the same: language or, better yet, the nature and limits of the human ability to convey information by whatever means. But his attitude toward that topic had changed radically; the old "transcendental" reasoning about what *had* to be the case given the meaningfulness of language was waning, while a very different picture of language was slowly emerging. The most obvious indication of this shift was Wittgenstein's new set of terminological preferences.

It may be unfair to compare stylistically a supremely polished piece like the *Tractatus* with the drafts and private notes Wittgenstein had written since 1929. But the *Notebooks* provide a good reference point. Whereas the early doctrines could hardly be explained without invoking such terms as *'Sachverhalt', 'Sachlage',* and *'Komplex',* these words do not appear in Wittgenstein's later writings and talks, except in retrospective accounts of his earlier views. 'Object' (*Gegenstand*) is also banished to the ghetto of suspect notions, even though the talk about *Bedeutung* remains as fluent as ever. It isn't as if Wittgenstein now thought that what he had said in terms of those suspect notions was false – no doubt he would have been able to find a way to read them as steps in the right direction.[6] But the decision to stop talking that way signifies that he now thought those old claims were at the very least conducive to philosophical error – if not false. As we shall see, the *kind* of error they induce was partly suggested by the fact that all of the suspect notions were intended to apply to things out there in the world, rather than to language.

What remained from the *Tractatus* language in the late 1920s was talk about *Bedeutung,* about the multiplicity of the proposition, its pictorial character, and its form. *Bedeutung* was no longer a relation between a name and a *Gegenstand;* it was a more ethereal element, which one would hardly expect to find in the ultimate furniture of the world (or as an "element of being" [*ein Element des Seins*]; *Notebooks,* p. 62); for *Bedeutung* was now a place in grammar, something constituted by rules. Meaning had moved to grammar, and even things one would usually regard as partly involving the world, such as ostensive definitions, were now presented as purely intralinguistic. These stylistic changes appear to reflect a step away from what one might call a language-world picture of things (a "realist" picture, in one of the many senses of that confusing word). The puzzle is that the linguistic notions that remained seemed to make sense only in connection with those that had been dropped. What the proposition depicts was supposed to be the *Sachlage,* and its form was supposed to coincide with that of certain *Sachverhalten,* which in turn was determined by that of certain objects. How can one insist on the pictorial character of propositions while ignoring the target of that depiction? How can one insist on the predominance of form in philosophy while studiously avoiding all reference to a real-world correlate? How could one assign a dominant role to the preservation of multiplicity while acknowledging only one term of that relation? The answers to these questions emerged from a new emphasis on understanding and its links with constructive processes.

Wittgenstein's new philosophy might well be described as a "critique of understanding." Even though the matter was never put in quite such general terms, it is clear that Wittgenstein had decided to place at the center of his considerations understanding – in a sense that, appearances notwithstanding, may not be too remote from Kant's. As already noted, the concern was still with the semantic nature of each part of language. It was as if Wittgenstein now thought that the nature of a linguistic element (be it an indefinable, a proposition, or a propositional system) was best revealed by looking at what is involved in our understanding of it.

As we have seen, Wittgenstein examined in this period the semantic character of a wide variety of statements, aiming to uncover the drastic differences between different linguistic functions that are obscured by the uniformity of syntactic representation. Here are four paradigm instances of the sorts of statements with which he was concerned: 'Blue is a primary color'; 'There is no greatest prime number'; 'Space-time curvature is a function of matter–energy distribution'; 'I now see the color red'. Most philosophers before Wittgenstein had discussed at great length the grounds of each of these claims and felt inclined to draw a number of distinctions in that regard. But no one before him seriously examined the question of whether the most important differences might lie at the level of what these "claims" say. Indeed, Wittgenstein would explain around 1930 that each of the above-mentioned statements calls for a semantic analysis that is *toto caelo* different from that of each of the others; and one may trace his conviction concerning these semantic differences back to his recognition of the different ways in which they relate to our understanding.

The first statement is one that others would call "true in virtue of meanings." Wittgenstein would argue that it is, in fact, constitutive of the meanings that appear to be involved in it and that its acceptance is therefore a condition of possibility of our understanding of those meanings (Chapter 14). The second statement, a mathematical claim, cannot be understood until we are in possession of the sort of constructive technique that mathematicians call its "proof" (or disproof). The third statement (a hypothesis) appears to be essentially like the fourth, in that it concerns possible facts – though a rather large, indeed infinite, number of them. The *Tractatus* had explained that understanding statements of fact is knowing when they are true and when they are false. If infinity were a very large number, one could state the truth conditions for hypotheses (as infinite conjunctions of basic statements) and therefore regard them as limit cases of standard propositions. But a proper analysis of infinity would show the absurdity of its extensional interpretation (as in set theory) and would force the conclusion that hypotheses are yet another type of statement. Hypotheses, like rules of grammar and mathematical statements, are incapable of truth and falsehood and therefore cannot be regarded as genuine propositions.[7] Only when we reach the last example, a genuine proposition, do we come to the domain where truth and falsehood about the world are fully available.

Each of these four types of statements deserves careful examination. Chapter 17 is devoted to grammar and part of Chapter 18 to hypotheses. In the rest of this chapter we shall focus on the remaining two types of statements.

Verificationism as the truth in solipsism

For decades Wittgenstein's friends have responded with patronizing grins to the positivists' assumption that the "world" of which Wittgenstein had spoken was the phenomenal, given world. The *Tractatus* said nothing definite on the matter; but Wittgenstein's papers do, and what they say agrees with the positivists' interpretation of his words.

In fact, Wittgenstein was quite upset with those who, inspired or misled by the Kantian notion of "appearance," assigned a second-rate status to the given and thought that genuine reality, whether unknowable or knowable only through science, lay somewhere behind appearance:

What I wanted to say is that it's strange that those who ascribe reality only to things and not to our representations move about so unquestioningly in the world of representation and never long to escape from it. In other words, how much of a matter of course the given is. It would be the very devil if this were a tiny picture taken from an oblique, distorting angle. This which we take as a matter of course, *life,* is supposed to be something accidental, subordinate; while something that normally never comes into my head, reality! That is, what we neither can nor want to go beyond would not be the world. (*Philosophische Bemerkungen,* p. 80)

For a while (in the late 1920s), Wittgenstein called this given domain or "what we really know" (Waismann, *Wiener Kreis,* p. 45) the "primary world" (*Philosophical Remarks,* p. 98), and the language in which we speak about it the "primary language."[8] "Ordinary physical" language is the source of "all our forms of speech," and it "cannot be used in epistemology or phenomenology without casting a distorting light on their objects" (*Philosophical Remarks,* p. 88). "The worst philosophical errors always arise when we try to apply our ordinary – physical – language in the area of the immediately given" (*Philosophical Remarks,* p. 88); and the "immediately given" is, as usual with positivists, reified experience.[9] In his Cambridge lectures of 1931–2 Wittgenstein is reported to have said, "The world we live in is the world of sense-data; but the world we talk about is the world of physical objects" (*Lectures, 1930–32,* p. 82). And also:

There is no fact that the earth is round over and above the various facts such as the shape of the shadow on the moon at an eclipse, ships disappearing over the horizon etc; just as there is no fact that this is a physical object over and above the qualities and judgments of sense-data about it. (pp. 80–1)

Like most philosophers at that time, Wittgenstein thought that the conflict between realism and idealism had to be overcome rather than decided in favor of one of the alternatives. But his solution had an even more clearly idealist bias than Carnap's. He explained, for example, that idealists "were right in that we never transcend experience. Mind and matter is a division *in* experience. Realists were right in protesting that chairs do exist" (p. 80). Where they *both* go wrong is when they start trying to use seriously the word 'real'. When the solipsist says that only his toothaches are real and those of others are mere fictions, he provoked the realist's response

that surely his pain is real. And this would not really refute the solipsist, any more than the realist refutes the idealist. The realist who kicks the stone is correct in saying that it is real if he is using the word "real" as opposed to "not real." His rejoinder answers the question, "Is it real or hallucinatory?", but he does not refute the idealist. (p. 23)

This is because the idealist's claim involves a sense of reality without a counterpart, something like what Carnap had called the "metaphysical" concept of reality.

It was at this point that Wittgenstein and Carnap parted company. Having concluded that the dispute between realists and idealists was based on a confusion and did not allow a proper formulation, they agreed that there was nothing more to say on the matter. For Carnap this meant the matter was to be dropped; for Wittgenstein, however, this was where things finally became interesting. If there is nothing more to say, there is still a great deal to show: "What solipsism *intends* is quite correct, only it cannot be *said* but it shows itself" (*Tractatus,* 5.62).

As usual with what "shows itself," one has to make an extraordinary effort to see it. In this case, Wittgenstein would try to display what the solipsist meant through an appeal to phenomenology and to his new method of analysis. The matter was of great significance because this "fact" to which the solipsist was pointing (however incompetently) was the root of much of Wittgenstein's epistemology, including his verificationism.

The greatest obstacle to seeing the "truth" in solipsism, Wittgenstein thought, is the role played by 'I' and other personal pronouns in ordinary language. The normal use of 'I' is "one of the most misleading representational techniques in our language" (*Philosophical Remarks,* p. 88). In particular, solipsists have been misled into formulating their very perceptive philosophical observation as a fact concerning the ego (in claims such as '*My* pain is the only real one' or, more generally, 'Only what happens to *me* is real; the rest is *my* construction'). On the contrary, the best way to state the insight is to note that "what the solipsist wants is not a notation in which the ego has a monopoly, but one in which the ego vanishes" (*Lectures, 1932–35,* p. 22).

Consider, for example, the visual field. There is a temptation to think that there *must be* a person, a physical subject, behind this given datum. But this is a false impression:

Suppose all the parts of my body could be removed until only one eyeball was left; and this were to be firmly fixed in a certain position, retaining its power of sight. How would the world appear to me? I wouldn't be able to perceive any part of myself, and supposing my eyeball to be transparent for me, I wouldn't be able to see myself in the mirror either. (*Philosophical Remarks,* pp. 100–1)

What about when we close our eyes: we don't stop seeing. But what we see in this case surely can't have any relation to an eye. And it's the same with a dream image. . . . Even the word 'visual space' is unsuitable for our purpose, since it contains an allusion to a sense organ which is as inessential to the space as it is to a book that it belongs to a particular person; and it could be very misleading if our language were constructed in such a way that we couldn't use it to designate a book without relating it to an owner. It might lead to the idea that a book can only exist in relation to a person. (p. 103)

The theme of these variations is a familiar one in the idealist and neo-Kantian tradition. Dilthey had brought to prominence the view that the ultimate "given" for philosophical purposes is not merely the data of sense but life itself and that our very idea of reality has its roots in that of life.[10] Ortega, for example, had been repeating for years that "life is the root reality," all else (including my ego and its objects) being derived or constructed from it. Wittgenstein's incursion into science fiction in the preceding quotations was designed to display the subjectless character of what "we" see, hear, or, in general, sense; better yet, of life. Of course, around 1930 the life in question was for Wittgenstein still not much more than the life of an eye or of a group of sense organs, not the communal life of a human being in a social context.

The 'I' that is to be eliminated is the empirical ego, the 'I' of whom we say things like 'I am in this room', the 'I' localizable in space and time and therefore closely related to my body. This is the 'I' of ordinary language that "only has meaning with reference to a body" (*Lectures, 1932–35*, p. 62). In the *Notebooks* Wittgenstein had written, "The I is not an object" (p. 80). To put the point in terms that are, to be sure, quite meaningless, Wittgenstein was saying that all there is for each of us is the world given to us and that this given lacks a subject in the ordinary sense of the word, since what we call a subject is a construction no less than any other "object" of experience.

Another way to approach the solipsist's ineffable point relies on Wittgenstein's new conception of analysis.[11] The way to show that 'I' does not stand for anything linguistically essential is to show there is a language form that is identical to the usual one in semantic power but that does not tempt one to think of the given as endowed with a privileged empirical subject. This technique has the further advantage of displaying not only the solipsist's error, but also the solipsists's point – in a showing sort of way.

Wittgenstein considered a language, *L,* that differs from ordinary language in that when L. W. is in pain, everyone, including L. W., must say, 'There is pain'. In contrast, when someone else, say N. N., is, as we would put it, in pain, everyone, including N. N., should say, 'N. N. behaves as L. W. does when there is pain' (*Philosophical Remarks,* sec. 58, pp. 88–9).[12] Of course, there is another similar language in which N. N. plays the role of L. W. and, indeed, many other similar languages in which other persons take the place of L. W. These languages, Wittgenstein thought, would be equivalent in their capacity to convey factual information, and they would also express the same relevant facts as English or German. This shows that 'I', 'he', and so on can be eliminated from our language without loss of content. From my viewpoint, there is pain and color and sound; and then there is behavior of other things (people). From your viewpoint, there will be behavior when I say there is pain, but that is your problem. By depriving solipsists of the use of 'I', Wittgenstein prevented them from making their point in the usual way, but he allowed them to make it in the correct way:

Among all the languages with different people as their centres . . . the one with me as its centre has a privileged status. This language is particularly adequate. How am I to express that? That is, how can I rightly represent its special advantage in words? This can't be done. . . . The privileged status lies in the application. (*Philosophical Remarks,* p. 89)

What Solipsists *say* is that only the present moment has reality,[13] and the truth in this (properly sublimized to the domain of showing) is the conviction that "our propositions are only verified by the present" (p. 81). Here is the bridge between solipsists' confused insight and Wittgenstein's semantics.

Indeed, it would appear that Wittgenstein's doctrine of meaning in the period we are dealing with was less a consequence of speculations on the nature of meaning and language than of his metaphysical opinions concerning "the world." His opinions on the nature of propositions are best seen as deriving from his remarkable attitude toward solipsism.

Propositions are tools for conveying information about how things stand; they tell us something about "the world" in such a way that what they say agrees or fails to agree with the facts. With each proposition we must associate the fragment of reality whereof it speaks truly or falsely, and, we are told, that is really all there is to the proposition. Therefore, with each proposition we must have two different factors: a fragment of reality *and* the association or mode of correlation between the statement and the reality in question. Let us consider these two factors separately.

Since the time of the *Tractatus*, Wittgenstein had been explaining that propositions must be capable of both truth and falsehood, for to understand them is to know what is the case in each of those circumstances. As early as 1914 he had written that "to have meaning *means* to be true or false: the being true or false actually constitutes the relation of the proposition to reality, which we mean by saying that it has meaning (*Sinn*)" (*Notebooks,* p. 112). But we have just seen what that "reality" is and how seriously one must take the old Tractarian claim that "the world is my world." The *Tractatus* had also explained that the proposition (now, the propositional system) is like a yardstick in that its very essence is to fulfill a certain purpose involving the correlation of a certain given entity (the yardstick or the proposition) with something else (the measured objects or the world). But "you cannot compare a picture with reality, unless you can set it against it as a yardstick. You must be able to fit the proposition on to reality. The reality that is perceived takes the place of the picture" (*Philosophical Remarks,* pp. 77–8). Therefore, if the world is my world, the only things I can say (the only things capable of truth and falsehood) are those that can be "fit . . . on to reality," those that aim to describe or represent my world linguistically. Propositions can be verified only by my world, "so they must be so constructed that they can be verified by it" (*Philosophical Remarks,* p. 81). As we shall see in a moment, the proposition involves an expectation concerning an event: "Our expectation anticipates the event. In this sense, it makes a model of the event. But we can only make a model of a fact in *the* world we live in, i.e. the model must be essentially related to the world we live in" (*Philosophical Remarks,* p. 71) – the solipsist's world, that is.

Consider now the second element associated with the proposition, the method or procedure – what others might call the technique for verifying it. Let us begin with a proposition like 'There is a match in my matchbox'. How does one come to incorporate it (or exclude it) from a body of knowledge? Most people will agree that the best thing to do is to open the box and look. For members of the semantic tradition, and for those empiricists who were beginning to recognize their point in the early 1930s, this was only one of several methods for determining the truth value of the claim – a particularly distinguished and reliable method, to be sure, but only one among many. As we shall see in Chapter 19, a number of positivists pursued, in the early 1930s, a doctrine of syntactic ascent, describing the process in question as one in which we compare the sentence under scrutiny with other "basic" or "protocol" sentences. Wittgenstein's standpoint was quite different.

Like so many other defenders of intuition in knowledge, Wittgenstein thought that the allegedly privileged method of testing described earlier (open the box and look) was not just one method of confirmation among others but a supremely privileged one. What Wittgenstein added to this common attitude among early-twentieth-century German philosophers was a particular claim about the nature of this privilege: The procedure in question is nothing less than what the proposition says – its sense. Quite generally, what a proposition says is that if we do certain things, we must expect other things to happen to us. Consider, once again, the analogy with yardsticks. "The method of taking measurements," Wittgenstein now explained, "is related to a particular measurement *in precisely the same way* as the sense of a proposition is to its truth or falsity" (*Philosophical Remarks*, p. 78, my italics). It couldn't be too far from the mark to say that the sense of a proposition is the method for comparing it with "the world" to determine its truth value. Wittgenstein was also saying that if meanings are the sorts of things we can understand, these truth conditions must be subject to human access. "To 'understand'," he explained to his Cambridge students in 1930, "is to be led by linguistic convention to a right expectation; and of the expectation we can only say that it must have the same logical multiplicity as the event" (*Lectures, 1930–32*, p. 5). Moreover, "the linguistic convention is conveyed by linking the proposition with its verification" (p. 5).

The old Tractarian doctrine that a proposition says what is the case if it is true now takes on a constructivist dimension:

Every significant proposition must teach us through its sense how we are to convince ourselves whether it is true or false. "Every proposition says what is the case if it is true." . . . Whereas – and this is the point – you cannot have a logical plan of search for a *sense* you don't know. The sense would have to be, so to speak, revealed to us: revealed from without – since it cannot be obtained from the propositional sign alone – in contrast with truth, which the proposition itself tells us how to search for and compare with it. (*Philosophische Bemerkungen,* p. 170)

In one of his lectures Wittgenstein gave as an example the proposition 'The clock will strike in five minutes'. To understand this, Wittgenstein thought, is to be able to "find the way from where you are to where the issue is decided" (*Philosophical Remarks,* p. 77) and to know how to decide it. Thus, one must first master a procedure that in this case instructs you to perform a task in temporal space (wait for five minutes) and then another in auditory space (listen to the clock).[14] Thus, to understand the proposition 'The clock will strike in five minutes' is to recognize a procedure (wait for five minutes, listen) *and* to recognize the appropriate expectation concerning its outcome (see *Lectures, 1930–32,* A2). To *believe* that proposition is to have also the correlated expectation; to *verify* it, finally, is to fulfill that expectation. When the propositional task is performed, what we encounter at its endpoint is an event in our life, a modest fragment of reality; and that portion of life, when measured against our expectation, will give its conclusive verdict on the truth or falsehood of the proposition.[15] This process, the verification, "is not a mere token of the truth, but determines the sense of the proposition" (*Philosophical Grammar,* p. 459; also see *Philosophical Remarks,* p. 200).

Two important semantic consequences emerge from this picture of things. First, if a proposition must be associated with the type of procedure just described, there are far fewer propositions than most people think. Indeed, Wittgenstein believed that most of the things people would call "propositions" are not properly so called. Genuine propositions must be capable of truth or falsehood, which, for Wittgenstein, meant the same thing as conclusive verification or conclusive falsification in terms of the given.[16] A "proposition" is therefore, in effect, a prediction that some particular contingent event will take place in my life; it will be verified if the event takes place, falsified if it does not. Any "proposition" that can be "verified" by more than one occurrence is, ipso facto, not a proposition but something else, often a hypothesis. The overwhelming majority of the sentences we normally employ are not genuine propositions. Leaving aside the mathematical statements discussed in the following section and the grammatical propositions of Chapter 14, the statements most commonly confused with propositions are hypotheses: "A proposition is verified or falsified in experience. . . . 'Propositions' about physical objects and most of the things we talk about in ordinary life are always really hypotheses. For example – All men are mortal" (*Lectures, 1930–32,* p. 53). Another example is 'There is a book lying here' (*Philosophical Grammar,* p. 219). We shall examine in Chapter 18 the theory of hypotheses that regards all of these ordinary claims as hypothetical.

The second consequence relates to an extraordinary category of statement uncovered by this type of semantic analysis. If 'There is a book lying here' is not a proposition, what is? Just as the old philosophy could not give us any definite examples of objects or of constituents of thought, the new one cannot give us any definite example of a proposition. Wittgenstein did say that 'Here there is a sphere in front of me' is a proposition (*Philosophical Grammar*, p. 221); but this cannot be taken at all seriously if, as we just saw, 'There is a book lying here' and 'Here there is a chair' (*Philosophical Grammar*, p. 220) are hypotheses. Better candidates are 'It looks as if there is a sphere in front of me' (*Philosophical Grammar*, p. 221) or more inarticulate expressions of the 'red, here, now' type. The closest Wittgenstein came to giving us an idea of what he might have in mind was by giving analogies such as this one:

If someone tells me "Look into this telescope, and make me a sketch of what you see," the sketch I make is the expression of a proposition, not of a hypothesis. . . . The best comparison for every hypothesis . . . is a body in relation to a systematic series of views of it from different angles. (*Philosophical Grammar*, pp. 220–1)

It is clear that Wittgenstein's commitment to transcendental arguments remained stronger than his ability to learn from experience. It would be left to the positivists to draw the appropriate consequences of this inability to identify clear-cut examples of "propositions," and they would do it during the protocol-sentence debate of 1932 (Chapter 19).

In the meantime, Wittgenstein had concerned himself into the doctrine that there *must* be a very special type of semantic element relating to the crucial life event at the end of the verification procedure, the event that places us in connection with reality, or perhaps we should say (meaninglessly, to be sure) the event that *is* the reality with which we want to link. That single source of reality, the present moment, is sometimes the subject of linguistic description, as when we think 'red here now' (however subconsciously) in the process of awareness of that presence. These proposition events are what Schlick came to call *"Konstatierungen,"* the terminal station at the level of language, the point where there is nothing more to say, when we must simply let the world tell us if what we said is true.

One of the insights with which the solipsist is to be credited, according to Wittgenstein, is the recognition of the privileged character of this part of language; for it is the solipsist who has seen, behind misleading syntactic analogies, the privileged character of direct descriptions of the world. The solipsist is "right in treating 'I have toothache' as being on a different level from 'He has toothache'" (*Lectures, 1932–35*, p. 23). The former is not the sort of thing that calls for verification; it is the limit case, the endpoint, of the process of verification. Schlick would soon be explaining that these sentences are *so* true, when true, that one cannot even ask if they are true; and he would also say that as with analytic statements (*sic*), to understand them is to know their truth value. The extraordinary character of these "propositions" would become another of the central issues in the debate on protocol sentences. We turn now to Wittgenstein's treatment of mathematical and other "formal" notions.

Wittgenstein's conception of mathematical statements bears a striking resemblance to the verificationist picture we have just presented, to the point that one is tempted to see his interpretation of mathematics as an extension of verificationism. Wittgenstein himself often drew a link:

As the immediate datum is to a proposition which it verifies, so is the arithmetical relation we see in the structure to the equation which it verifies. It is the real thing, not an expression for something else for which another expression could also be substituted. That is, it is not a symptom of something else, but the thing itself. . . . How a proposition is verified is what it says. . . . The verification is not *one* token of the truth, it is *the* sense of the proposition. (*Philosophical Remarks*, p. 200)

But there is a crucial difference between empirical and mathematical claims; the former have a world to refer to, however subjective and phenomenal, whereas the latter do not. The difference between "genuine" propositions and their mathematical counterparts corresponds to the difference between concepts and forms;[17] the former are, in Wittgenstein's view, methods to *find out* whether something is true, whereas the latter are methods to *do* something.

Constructivism in mathematics

One of the best-known responses to the "crisis in mathematics" stemming from Russell's paradox and other similar ones was Brouwer's intuitionism. A small but determined group of distinguished mathematicians argued that the paradoxes were a mere symptom of a deep-rooted disease in the body of mathematics. According to them, during the nineteenth century and due largely to the nefarious influence of the "extensional standpoint" (of which set theory was merely the reductio ad absurdum), mathematics had lost contact with its true constructive spirit. Many thought then (and think now) that an interpretation of mathematical statements that makes them true or false independently of our knowledge of them is bound to be Platonistic, since it must postulate the "independent existence" of a realm of mathematical entities that *makes* those statements true, whether we know it or not.

Brouwer and his successors undertook a complete revision of mathematics based on the by now familiar idea that mathematical knowledge is grounded on intuition; and since we can have intuition only of the finite, our only access to genuine knowledge about infinity is through constructive processes repeatable without end. The point was conceded by Brouwer's alleged archenemy, Hilbert, who conceived metamathematics as aimed at establishing from "sound" mathematics (i.e., mathematics acceptable to intuitionists) the formal consistency of classical mathematics. Husserl's philosophy, possibly the most influential and widely respected in Germany at the time, had placed intuition once again at the heart of philosophy; and a number of Husserl's followers – including Weyl, Becker, and Kaufmann – had drawn support from that philosophy for an intuitionist philosophy of mathematics.

Wittgenstein's philosophy of mathematics was well in tune with this constructivist fashion of the 1920s in the Germanic countries; but it differed from the mathematicians' doctrines, as one might expect, in its emphasis on language and meaning. In this respect Wittgenstein's approach resembled Frege's and Russell's, though it would be hard to find any other significant agreement between them on the nature of mathematical knowledge. Indeed, in Wittgenstein's view the Frege–Russell formulation of mathematical discourse in their respective *Begriffsschriften* distorted the real nature of mathematics. We shall try to convey some idea of the extent of Wittgenstein's disagreement with them by considering several paradigmatic examples.

It is sometimes said that constructivism explicates truth as proof. This is at least misleading, since the notion of proof is no less subject to challenge than that of mathematical truth. The constructivist sees nothing in mathematical truth beyond a certain sort of construction. Such constructions may be called "proofs," but not everything that *others* would call proofs qualifies as such for the constructivist. The heart of the matter for Wittgenstein was not truth or proof but meaning, and a constructivist conception of it.

Once Wittgenstein said that "the proper mathematical proposition is a proof of a so-called mathematical proposition" (Manuscript of vol. 1, *Philosophische Bemerkungen,* begun 2 February 1929, p. 59, Wittgenstein Papers, 105),[18] and he often noted that we understand a mathematical proposition only after we have proved "it."[19] Thus, a proof is not a proof of some antecedently understood statement asserting something about mathematical entities, but the theorem acquires whatever meaning it has from the algorithmic process of derivation. From this perspective it follows that no one understands Fermat's theorem or any other mathematical "conjecture"; that there is no such thing as looking for a proof we do not already have tacitly in mind;[20] that we never understand a false mathematical proposition; that no generalization of experience can be a mathematical proposition (*Philosophical Grammar,* p. 360); and so on.

Like most constructivists, Wittgenstein thought that there was no proof procedure more essential to mathematics than induction. It is therefore interesting to see how his views of that form of reasoning differed from what he called the "extensional" interpretation advocated by Frege, Russell, and the promoters of a set-theoretic approach.

The nonconstructive way of looking at reasoning by induction sees it as involving the application of a "principle of induction" with two antecedents (a base and an induction step) and one consequent (a universal conclusion). Thus, when we prove by induction that all natural numbers have the property P, we first establish that 0 has P, then that if n had P, so would $n + 1$; then, appealing to the principle of induction, we conclude that *all* numbers have P. In Wittgenstein's view this is an utterly confused way of presenting things. To begin with, it is an error to think that there is any "inference" or "conclusion" in this sort of reasoning. We simply prove the base case, then offer the reasoning from n to $n + 1$, and that is all. One may, perhaps, say that these two steps show what the meaningless standard conclusion was intended to say. But there is *nothing* to the statement 'All numbers have P' beyond what the proof of the "premises" displays. Wittgenstein explained to Waismann in 1929:

Most people think that complete induction is only one way to reach a determinate proposition; that one adds to the method of induction a particular inference: *therefore* the proposition holds for all numbers. My question is: What is this "therefore"? There is no "therefore"! The complete induction is already the proposition we wanted to prove, it is everything and not just the proof procedure. The method is not a vehicle that takes us somewhere else. In mathematics we do not have first of all a proposition that has sense in and of itself, and then the method to determine the truth or falsehood of this proposition; there is only the method, and what we call "the proposition" is only an abbreviated name for the method. (Waismann, *Wiener Kreis,* p. 33)

Behind this way of looking at things lies a conception of mathematical knowledge that could hardly be more opposed to Frege's central ideas. The project initiated in *Begriffsschrift* and pursued by Russell and Whitehead was based on the assumption that the very same language that we use to express propositions of empirical science is appropriate for expressing logical and mathematical statements. In particular, the same sense of quantification and of the remaining connectives is involved in making assertions about numbers and assertions about tables. The system of *Begriffsschrift* or of *Principia Mathematica* was intended to present a language adequate for the expression of every scientific claim, where "science" includes logic and mathematics.

Brouwer had challenged in 1907 the idea that mathematical formulas ought to be seen as conveying information in roughly the same sense as "scientific" sentences. He had explained, for example, that

mathematical formulas ought not to be considered as "truths" existing independently, but only as an expedient to remind us as efficiently as possible by means of symbols of the way in which a certain structure was imbedded in another structure. For instance, the formula $13 = 6 + 7$ reminds us of the fact that a set originating by juxtaposition of two sets along which we could count up to 6, respectively up to 7, was imbedded in a set along which we could count up to 13. ("On the Foundations of Mathematics," p. 96)

Compare this way of looking at things with Frege's. For him, the expressions on both sides of the identity sign were names of objects, and the statement said that these objects were one and the same. Brouwer, in contrast, saw the left-hand term of the equation as a symbol for an operation to be performed on the outcome of certain mental processes, and the whole equation as saying that two processes (generating the number 13 in some "primeval" sense, and generating the numbers six and seven in that sense, and then "adding" them up) gave the same result. Even though Brouwer and Frege would, of course, assent to the very same elementary arithmetical statements, each one would regard what the other *claimed to assert* through that assent as either meaningless or trivially false.

Wittgenstein's position was far closer to Brouwer's than to Frege's, though he was even farther removed than Brouwer from the idea that mathematics has a topic, even a mental topic. Mathematics does not deal with numbers, nor does it deal with primeval intuitions of time. It doesn't deal with anything: "In mathematics *everything* is algorithm and *nothing* is meaning; even when it doesn't look like that because we seem to be using *words* to talk *about* mathematical things" (*Philosophical Grammar*, p. 468). Consider the statement

(*) There is a 5 in the fourth place in the decimal expansion of pi.

According to Wittgenstein, this does not say that a certain object occurs in a certain place (unless this is meant as a rephrasing of the original, problematic statement). Rather, what it means is that there is a certain law or algorithm for calculating the digits in the decimal expansion of pi and that when we get to a certain stage in that procedure, the outcome will be the same that we would obtain through the primeval technique for generating 5. The calculation procedure both determines the sense of the statement and guarantees that the matter is decidable.

Even though (*) is perfectly meaningful and, in some sense, true, its apparent consequence,

(**) There is a 5 in the decimal expansion of pi,

is just as meaningless as a random collection of syllables. The reason is that there is no "law" or algorithm associated with (**) that would allow us to determine its truth value, and this is simply another way of saying that it has no sense.

The reason we might suppose otherwise, Wittgenstein thought, is that we tend to argue as follows: As we calculate the decimal expansion of pi, either there will come a point when we find a 5 (as, indeed, we do) or we will never, ever find a 5. In the first case (**) is true; in the second case, false. Quite apart from any Platonistic assumptions, we have given truth conditions to (**) and have therefore guaranteed its meaningfulness.

This piece of reasoning is, according to Wittgenstein, utter nonsense – the sort of nonsense that emerges from the most confused part of mathematics: set theory and its attendant "extensional" mode of thought. The main problem with the preceding reasoning is best stated in connection with the second disjunct of its first step: It involves the idea that the decimal expansion of pi is something with a life of its own, quite independent of the method we use to generate it. The method for calculating the decimal expansion of pi is a recursively enumerable function that associates with each natural number (each location in the decimal expansion) a natural number between 0 and 9. Apparently no one questions that the decimal expansion of pi has infinitely many terms (in the sense that there is a procedure for generating that unending sequence), or that the method of calculation assigns a definite value to each "location," or that the value is "determinate," in the sense that the very same number will be obtained as a result by whoever chooses to follow the procedure whenever he or she chooses to do so. What is questioned is either the existence of these numbers before we create them or our ability to refer to them or represent them "at a distance" (as did Leibniz; see Chapter 6). And there is no doubt that from this viewpoint, set theory is the root of all mathematical evil:

Set-theory attempts to grasp the infinite at a more general level than a theory of rules. It says that you can't grasp the actual infinite by means of arithmetical symbolism at all and that therefore it can only be described and not presented (*dargestellt*). The description would encompass it in something like the way in which you carry a number of things that you can't hold in your hands by packing them in a box. They are then invisible but we still know we are carrying them (so to speak, indirectly). . . . With this there goes too the idea that we can use language to describe logical forms. In a description of this sort the structures . . . are presented in a package, and so it does indeed look as if one could talk about a structure without reproducing it in the proposition itself. (*Philosophical Remarks*, p. 206)[21]

What is wrong with the extensional conception? Apparently, there is nothing wrong with it in the finite case, but it is inadmissible beyond that. It is as if there were a limit to the sizes intelligible to us; as if it could make no sense to say that a class is infinite. Why?

Once Ramsey asked Wittgenstein what was wrong with saying that we can imagine a man living forever: "Isn't that extensional infinity?" he asked, and can't we imagine a wheel rotating for ever? Wittgenstein replied: "What a peculiar argument: 'I can imagine . . .'! Let's consider what experience we would regard as a confirmation or proof of the fact that the wheel will never stop spinning" (*Philosophical Remarks,* pp. 304–5). He then argued that whatever items of evidence we might adduce are fine, but that instead of regarding them as evidence for extensional infinity, we should view them as determinants of meaning, as telling us what was *really* meant by anyone who says the sort of thing Ramsey said.

To Wittgenstein's request, "Let's consider what would confirm them," Ramsey's reply might well have been, "Let's not." After all, as Bolzano, Frege, or Russell would have insisted, the question concerns the happening of something, not the reasons we might have for believing it happened. Wittgenstein thought that the only road to the meaning of Ramsey's statement was through what others would call its confirmatory circumstances; for him Ramsey's remark made only as much sense as could be stated in terms of those conditions involving the given in experience that would completely verify it.

Why did Wittgenstein take this position? The reason he would probably have cited is the statement he was already calling "my old principle" by 1930 (*Philosophical Remarks,* p. 289), the verifiability principle: "It isn't possible to believe something for which you cannot imagine some kind of verification" (p. 89). "How a proposition is verified is what it says. . . . The verification is not *one* token of the truth, it is *the* sense of the proposition" (p. 200). "According to my principle, two assumptions must be identical in sense if every possible experience that confirms the one confirms the other too" (p. 282).

One final look at the matter of existence will further clarify the disagreement between Wittgenstein and the intuitionists on mathematical ontology. His views on this matter bear a striking similarity to Carnap's.

The familiar ontological questions that had troubled the semantic tradition had sometimes been discussed and resolved in terms of the notion of independent existence. The question often asked and answered was whether numbers, propositions, concepts, and senses have an existence independent from us. To this, Wittgenstein answered, "Does chess exist independently of us, or not?" (*Philosophical Grammar,* p. 321). Even though the question was aimed at Frege, its targets were both Platonistic *and* intuitionistic assumptions. Wittgenstein's goal was not, of course, to deny the independent existence of chess or anything else; nor was it (in the intuitionist fashion) to assert their existence as mental constructions. His purpose was to call attention to the extraordinary pressure that the question puts on the word 'existence'. Do we really know what is being asked when someone asks whether chess exists independently of us? There is, of course, a human institution, a game that we call chess. But few would seriously argue that one is asking a definite, clearly understood question when one asks about its independent existence. The same is true when one asks about the independent existence of mathematical entities.[22] That does not mean, of course, that numbers and chess do not exist. "The reason why there are infinitely many cardinal numbers," Wittgenstein explained, "is that *we* construct this infinite system and call it the system of cardinal numbers" (*Philosophical Grammar*, p. 321). This might sound like an endorsement of the intuitionistic identification of existence with construction; but it is not. In mathematics,

existence is what is proved by the procedures we call "existence proofs." When the intuitionists and others talk about this they say: "This state of affairs, existence, can be proved only thus and not thus." And they don't see that by saying that they have simply defined what *they* call existence. (*Philosophical Grammar*, p. 374)

In his Cambridge lectures Wittgenstein explained to his students:

If there were such a thing as existence which is proved when an existence theorem is proved, then perhaps one could say every existential proof must do a certain thing. Weyl talks as though he has a clear idea of existence independent of proof, and has made what looks like a statement about the natural history of proofs in saying that only such-and-such prove existence. There is no concept of existential theorems except through the special existential theorems. Every existential proof is different, and "existential theorem" has different meanings according as what is said to exist is, or is not, constructed. (*Lectures, 1932–35*, p. 117)

Having reviewed Wittgenstein's views on genuine and mathematical propositions, we are now ready to turn to a different category, that of grammatical rules. It is here that after the varied excursions of the past four chapters into neo-, paleo-, and crypto-Kantian territory, we finally reencounter the central theme of the developments reviewed in Part I, the link between meaning and the a priori.

14

A priori knowledge and the constitution of meaning

The great problem round which everything that I write turns is: Is there an order in the world a priori, and if so what does it consist in?

Wittgenstein, *Notebooks*

To a necessity in the world there corresponds an arbitrary rule in language.

Wittgenstein, *Lectures, 1930–32*

Wittgenstein said that "there are no true a priori propositions" (*Lectures, 1930–32,* p. 13; *Tractatus,* 2.225), Carnap tirelessly denied the synthetic a priori, and Schlick went so far as to define empiricism as the rejection of synthetic a priori knowledge. In spite of all this there can be no doubt that the major contribution of Wittgenstein's and Carnap's epistemologies in the early 1930s was their interpretations of all a priori knowledge, both analytic and synthetic. Their theories of philosophical grammar and of logical syntax may well be regarded as the first genuine alternatives to Kant's conception of the a priori.

By the beginning of the twentieth century, no philosopher of consequence was satisfied with Kant's solution to the problem of the a priori. Many had come to understand far better than Kant what was involved in particular instances of a priori knowledge; but efforts to build general accounts of what that form of knowledge was and the way it was grounded were far less successful. In Part I we examined some of the alternatives to Kant's theory that had been put forth by Kantians or anti-Kantians. As we saw, none of them had achieved a doctrine comparable to Kant's in scope and plausibility. Around 1930, a number of the insights that had slowly been emerging in the course of the developments reviewed in Part I finally coalesced into a new interpretation of the a priori, an interpretation that was first presented in the writings of Wittgenstein and Carnap.

Those before them who had attempted to explain the character and ground of a priori knowledge had considered the fine structure of judgment as well as any distinctions between the semantic tasks performed by different kinds of statements, to be irrelevant. For example, for Kant a priori and a posteriori judgments were species of a semantically uniform

259

genus, *judgment;* therefore, everything that "Logic" told us about judgment would, ipso facto, be applicable to the a priori. According to this picture of things, in order to understand the difference between the a priori and everything else we would have to go beyond the study of judgment to a transcendental theory of mental activity; the strategy was to look at how we can *know* such claims rather than at what it is that they *say.*

The semanticists had rightly challenged Kant's failure to distinguish consistently between content and propositional attitude, but no one before Wittgenstein and Carnap had thought of challenging the underlying assumption of semantic uniformity, nor speculated that its denial might hold the key to the a priori. Wittgenstein and Carnap argued that the main difference between a priori statements and the rest lies at the level of what they say. A priori statements, they asserted, do not differ from others merely in the strength with which the mind or other things entitle us or force us to believe what they say. It lies rather in the extraordinary role these statements play in the process of making it possible for us to say anything at all.

Even though Carnap's and Wittgenstein's trains of thought were largely independent of each other and, as we shall see, there were radical differences between them, their doctrines also show a remarkable degree of agreement.[1] Nowhere is this clearer than in the matter of the a priori.

Indefinables and intuition

It would be hard to exaggerate the significance Wittgenstein attached to the a priori–a posteriori distinction around 1930 or the strength of his opposition to the traditional accounts of that dichotomy. These are displayed clearly, for example, in the notes taken by Moore and others of the lectures Wittgenstein delivered at Cambridge in the early 1930s.

Moore reports that Wittgenstein emphasized from the very beginning a distinction between two sorts of propositions. First of all, Wittgenstein explained, we have those that can be "compared with reality" and either "agree or disagree with it" ("Wittgenstein's Lectures," p. 257). These are the ones he sometimes called "experiential" or "scientific," that is, those that state facts. Then there is the second group, much harder to characterize than the first. Of this group

> he sometimes said that they are not propositions at all [but] were those which have been traditionally called "necessary," as opposed to "contingent." . . . They include not only the propositions of pure Mathematics, but also those of Deductive Logic, certain propositions which would usually be said to be propositions about colours, and an immense number of others. Of these propositions he undoubtedly held that, unlike "experiential" propositions, they cannot be "compared with reality." (p. 262)

Clearly, the "propositions" that Wittgenstein singled out for special treatment are our old friends the a priori truths. What is even more significant is that his treatment of them appears to differ from all preceding accounts, in that it is based on a semantic distinction. The notes of Wittgenstein's Cambridge lectures for 1931–2, edited by Lee, contain this remark: "*A priori* and empirical are not two kinds of proposition. What is there in common between them that we should call them 'propositions'? An *a priori* proposition would have to be one whose meaning guaranteed its truth. But meaning requires us to verify" (Wittgenstein, *Lectures, 1930–32,* p. 76).[2]

In order to appreciate Wittgenstein's position, we begin by recalling briefly the primary features of its main opponent: the propositionalist assumption of semantic uniformity in our knowledge claims.

Imagine that an Oriental despot instructs his subjects to write down *everything* they know. In due course they will inscribe such sentences as 'It rains or it does not rain', '2 + 2 = 4', 'Space-time is pseudo-Riemannian', 'All humans are mortal', 'This pen is brown', 'My hand hurts', and so on. Whatever the differences among the items of knowledge, all of these sentences seem to convey some sort of information and, correspondingly, all of them are the apparent targets of propositional attitudes such as assertion, belief, and assumption. The uniformity of syntactic representation (the fact that they all seem like statements), as well as the apparent uniformity in the range of epistemic attitudes we may adopt toward them, naturally suggests that all of the sentences that constitute a body of knowledge are alike in semantic function, their task being to say (truly or falsely) what is the case concerning either concrete or ethereal entities. Propositionalism, as we called this doctrine in Chapter 7, contends that the attitude of endorsing a sentence and incorporating it into a body of knowledge can be understood only as a rational act, if we see it as the end result of a process in which we first recognize what information the sentence conveys and then determine that what it says is the case. According to propositionalism, there is no other account of what is involved in rationally accepting a statement. Prior to assertion and judgment, prior to the incorporation of a sentence into a body of knowledge, it must be possible to understand it, to tell what it says; as semanticists would put it, it must be possible to recognize the concepts, senses, or meanings of the constituents of the sentence.

It is essential to focus on the role of understanding and its location relative to a priori claims in the propositionalist picture. Roughly speaking, we are dealing with a three-stage process. First, we understand the primitives or indefinables; second, as we combine these notions, we understand the claims we frame with them; finally, we may determine their truth values by checking whether the facts they state are the case. Since a priori claims do not differ semantically from the rest, we must run through the same process with them, except for the odd fact that as we complete the second stage, when we finally understand an a priori claim, we notice that there is no need to check the facts at all: Meaning suffices to determine its truth value. True a priori claims are "true in virtue of meanings." On this view "it looks as if one could *infer* from the meaning of negation that ' $- - p$' means p. As if the rules for the negation sign *follow from* the nature of negation. So that in a certain sense there is first of all negation, and then the rules of grammar" (*Philosophical Grammar,* p. 53). More generally, it is "as if understanding were an instantaneous grasping of something from which later we only draw consequences which already exist in an ideal sense before they are drawn" (p. 55).

In Part I we looked at the string of successes stemming from the propositionalist picture. But we also saw that this way of looking at semantics had a problem: that of indefinables. The propositionalist solution was, very roughly, that we "instantaneously grasp" the meaning of primitives (e.g., of 'distance' and the other geometric indefinables) and then derive the proper axioms and theorems. For a long time this view was thought to be, at the very worst, harmless. But when non-Euclidean geometries emerged, it became apparent that this standpoint was an obstacle to an appreciation of that field.

The traditional view that we should know what distance is (or what 'distance' means) before we can decide which distance axioms are true or which measurement procedures are appropriate for measuring distance was eventually challenged by Helmholtz, Poincaré, and Hilbert. They promoted developments leading to the idea that both the distance axioms and the method for measuring distance "define" or "constitute" what distance *is,* and according to this, the endorsement of geometric axioms and of systems of measurement is prior to the determination of what they are about. Yet none of its nineteenth-century proponents seems to have seen in this new picture of geometry the roots of a wider challenge to the role of intuition in knowledge. Indeed, Poincaré and later Hilbert postulated a form of intuition as a basis for arithmetic and thereby of most of mathematics. And phenomenologists had a large segment of scientific opinion on their side when they took to be of primary importance the project of explicating the link between knowledge and intuition.

There were others who had come to think that Russell's 'acquaintance' and Husserl's *'Wesensschau'* were the names of two monumental confusions and that all efforts to assign a role to nonempirical intuition in epistemology were bound to fail. They believed there was no way to escape the impasse short of reformulating the problem of indefinables. But they did not know quite how to do it.

Schlick had been groping with this difficulty for years. His celebrated attacks against phenomenology in *Allgemeine Erkenntnislehre* (1918) and elsewhere were inspired by a growing conviction that epistemology and intuition exclude one another; and his early enthusiasm for implicit definition was, no doubt, partly related to his obscure perception that the procedure in question had something to do with the problem of indefinables. He had taken a further step forward in this process by noticing that constitution primarily affects concepts. But he had not seen the connection between these two observations and the topic of the a priori. The decisive step in this development came when Wittgenstein linked the problem of indefinables with that of the a priori. Wittgenstein transposed Kant's Copernican turn to the field of semantics.

A new Copernican turn

Goethe once wrote, "The greatest art in theoretical and practical life consists in changing the *problem* into a *postulate*" (quoted in Cassirer, *Substance and Function and Einstein's Theory of Relativity*, p. 371). He may well have been thinking of Kant's Copernican turn, the idea that "objects must conform to our knowledge" (*Critique*, Bxvi) and not the other way around. This doctrine had been the heart of Kant's conception of the a priori, based on the idea that mind constitutes the objects of experience. Wittgenstein's and Carnap's insights on the a priori belong in the same family as Kant's. One could, in fact, mimic Kant's famous "Copernican" pronouncement to state their point: If our a priori knowledge must conform to the constitution of meanings, I do not see how we could know anything of them a priori; but if meanings must conform to the a priori, I have no difficulty in conceiving such a possibility.[3] What we witness circa 1930 is a Copernican turn that, like Kant's, bears the closest connection to the a priori; but its topic is meaning rather than experience.

Wittgenstein's position is best approached by way of examples from traditional a priori disciplines such as logic and geometry. Consider first a typical (if, at that time, recently challenged) logical law, the principle of double negation. Most sentences containing the negation sign readily lend themselves to the type of semantic analysis that Frege and Russell would have proposed. For example, the sentence 'John is not tall' says something because each constituent grammatical unit has an associated meaning and because these meanings are properly combined to generate that claim. It would be absurd to say that in order to understand 'John', 'not', or 'tall', one would first have to believe that sentence. In order to *believe* it one must first understand it, and one cannot understand it unless one recognizes those meanings. Likewise, we first recognize the meaning of negation and of the other propositional constituents, then we grasp the meaning of the full claim, and finally, we try to gather reasons that allow us to decide whether the asserted fact is a fact. This is precisely what propositionalists think we must *always* do, even when we come to the law of double negation. (This also leads them to intuitionism on the matter of indefinables.)

We may surely disagree on whether John is tall without thereby disagreeing on the meaning of negation. But may we agree on that meaning and disagree about the law of double negation? Wittgenstein thought not. If not, then it looks as if negation is somehow "there" regardless of what we do about 'John is tall', but also as if its being there is not independent of what we do with the law of double negation. Indeed, it looks as if a priori statements are involved with meanings even more intimately than the way in which true claims relate to what makes them true. The meaning of negation does not make the law of double negation true in the sense in which Cicero makes some claims about him true. Rather, that logical law determines the meaning (Wittgenstein, *Lectures, 1932–35*, p. 4). Better yet, the acceptance of the law of double negation is part of what is involved in the recognition and adoption of the classical notion of negation, so that the law could be said to contribute to the definition or constitution of a meaning of negation (*Lectures, 1932–35*, p. 4; *Philosophical Grammar*, pp. 52–3, chap. 10).

There cannot be a question whether these or other rules are the correct ones for the use of 'not' (that is, whether they accord with its meaning). For without these rules the word has as yet no meaning; and if we change the rules, it now has another meaning (or none), and in that case we may just as well change the word too. (*Philosophical Grammar*, p. 184)[4]

Wittgenstein had turned the problem of the a priori on its head, postulating it as a solution to the problem of indefinables.

A second example that recurs in Wittgenstein's writings and lectures of this period is his treatment of geometric axioms. In his Cambridge lectures, Wittgenstein told his students that Euclidean geometry is "a part of grammar" (Moore, "Wittgenstein's Lectures," p. 276), and he explained at some length to his Vienna circle audience in 1929 that one should resist the temptation to think that geometric axioms convey any information. In fact, he told them that "the axioms of geometry have the character of postulations concerning the language in which we wish to describe spatial objects. They are rules of syntax" (Waismann, *Weiner Kreis*, p. 62; also Wittgenstein, *Philosophical Grammar*, p. 320; *Philosophical Remarks*, pp. 216–17; *Lectures, 1932–35*, p. 51). "Geometry," he explained elsewhere,

isn't the science . . . of geometric planes, lines and points. . . . The relation between geometry and propositions of practical life, about . . . edges and corners, etc. isn't that the things geometry speaks of, though *ideal* edges and corners, resemble those spoken of in practical propositions and their grammar. (*Philosophical Grammar*, p. 319)

And in a sharper statement of these views (addressed to Schlick), Wittgenstein wrote:

Does geometry talk about cubes? Does it say that the cube-form has certain properties? . . . Geometry does not talk about cubes but, rather, it constitutes the meaning (*Bedeutung*) of the word 'cube', etc. Geometry now says, e.g., that the sides of a cube are of equal length, and *nothing is easier* than to confuse the grammar of this sentence with that of the sentence 'the sides of a wooden cube are of equal length'. And yet, one is an arbitrary grammatical rule whereas the other is an empirical sentence. ("Diktat für Schlick" [1931–33], p. 5, Wittgenstein Papers, 302)[5]

Beyond logic and geometry, the grammatical sentences disguised in the "form of empirical propositions" include a host of traditional instances of the a priori. Among others, Wittgenstein mentioned claims concerning the infinite divisibility and continuity of space (Waismann, *Vienna Circle*, p. 230), the order structure of time (*Lectures, 1932–35*, p. 14), the law of causality, and the thesis of determinism (*Lectures, 1932–35*, p. 16). The preceding examples may, however, suffice as an illustration of Wittgenstein's standpoint.

From this new perspective, the old feeling that among claims there is a distinguished class that expresses a particularly strong type of knowledge was entirely justified. The problem was that people blind to differences in types of judgment had not been able to understand what those alleged claims really are: They are our access to certain meanings, definitions in disguise, devices that allow us to implement an explicit or tacit decision to constitute certain concepts. Wittgenstein had said, Moore recalls, "that the meaning of any single word in a language is 'defined', 'constituted', 'determined' or 'fixed' . . . by the 'grammatical rules' with which it is used in that language" ("Wittgenstein's Lectures in 1930–33," p. 252). Thus, the ground of the necessity of a priori laws, of our inability to find a situation in which they would not apply, lies in the fact that rejecting them is a misleading way of refusing to apply the meanings they constitute. From this standpoint, necessary claims do not tell us anything that is the case both in our world and in many others, as Leibniz thought, or anything that is the case for *formal* reasons, whatever that might mean, or anything that one is forced to believe due to features of our mind. They do not tell us anything that is the case; so they had better not be called claims or propositions. Since their role is to constitute meanings and since (apparently) we are free to endorse them or not, it is better to abandon the old terminology (a priori "principles," "laws," etc.) that misleadingly suggested a propositional status and to refer to them as "rules." And since, like grammatical rules, their substance is semantic, the science that investigates the nature of the a priori will be a "philosophical grammar."

One should not be misled by Wittgenstein's (and Carnap's) antimeaning rhetoric of this period. Moore recalls that in his early Cambridge lectures Wittgenstein once made

the rather queer statement that "the idea of meaning is in a way obsolete, except in such phrases as 'this means the same as that' or 'this has no meaning,'" having previously said in [1932] that "the mere fact that we have the expression 'the meaning' of a word is bound to lead us wrong: we are led to think that the rules are responsible to something not a rule, whereas they are only responsible to rules." ("Wittgenstein's Lectures in 1930–33," p. 253)

It should be obvious by now that this attitude, no less than Carnap's fiery condemnations of meaning in the early 1930s, is a rejection *not* of meaning but of a particular conception of it, the picture-theoretic or "realist" conception. In a sense, Carnap and Wittgenstein wanted to insist that all a priori truth is truth in virtue of meaning. If they rejected this formulation, and more generally the appeal to meanings, it is because history and, in Wittgenstein's case, introspection associated that appeal with an explanatory picture that placed meanings first in the semantic order and then postulated mysterious relations that link us with them.

The point emerges rather strikingly in a remark that, according to one student, Wittgenstein made during one of his Cambridge courses in 1934–5. He had been discussing the old type-theoretic issue of meaningless combinations of signs and had taken as an extreme illustration of the problem an attempt to apply negation not to a proposition but to an object, for example, an apple. If someone said that we can negate apples by simply saying that 'apple' is not true, then, Wittgenstein explained, "the reply would be that 'negation' and 'apple' don't fit" (*Lectures, 1932–35*, p. 141). At the next meeting Wittgenstein returned to the problem and (reportedly) said:

You want to say that the use of the word "not" does not fit the use of the word "apple." The difficulty is that we are wavering between two different aspects: (1) that apple is one thing or idea which is comparable to a definite shape whether or not it is prefaced by negation, and that negation is like another shape, which may or may not fit it:

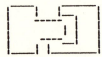

(2) that these words are characterized by their use, and that negation is not completed until its use with "apple" is completed. We cannot ask whether the uses of these two words fit, for their use is given only when the use of the whole

phrase "not apple" is given. For the use they have *they have together.* The two ideas between which we are wavering are two ideas about meaning, (1) that a meaning is somehow present while the words are uttered, (2) that a meaning is not present but is defined by the use of the sign. If the meanings of "not" and "apple" are what is present when the words are uttered, we can ask if the meanings of these two words fit; and that will be a matter of experience [i.e., of fact]. But if negation is to be defined by its use, it makes no sense to ask whether "not" fits "apple"; the idea of fitting must vanish. (p. 144)

The first of these two positions, drawing and all, is probably the one that inspired the *Tractatus*[6] and (certainly) some of its predecessors. The second is the new semantic picture, the outcome of the Copernican turn in semantics.

This new picture of things does not really deny that there are meanings to which our statements must somehow conform if they are to make sense, any more than Carnap should have denied in the *Aufbau* that reference is a relation between words and what they refer to. Nor does it deny that there are truths in virtue of meaning. What *is* being denied is that statements such as these play an explanatory role in philosophy or in science. The law of double negation *is* true in virtue of the meanings of the negation and implication; but we must not interpret this as saying that the *reason why* the law is true is that negation and implication are what they are. The semantic explanatory route does not go from Wittgensteinian "objects" or meanings to the laws concerning them and then to our reasonable linguistic behavior, but the other way around, from our linguistic behavior to meanings. The ultimate explanatory level in semantics is not given by references to unsaturation or to the form of objects or meanings, but by reference to the meaning-giving activity of human beings, an activity embodied in their endorsement of rules. Consequently, to the extent that a reference to these semantic entities has been introduced into philosophical discourse for merely explanatory purposes, as in the picture-theoretic model of things, it is only natural that this reversal of perspective would lead one to be as hesitant about reference as Carnap was in the *Aufbau* (see sec. 161) or as hesitant about meaning as Wittgenstein was in the early 1930s.

The new stand does not merely make the a priori intelligible; it also departs from tradition in assigning to it a surprising feature that is best described in contrast to one of Mill's doctrines. Recall Mill's defense against criticism of his arguments against necessity (Chapter 3): "Surely, if I disprove the necessity of thinking the thing at all, I disprove that it must be thought as necessary" (*Hamilton's Philosophy,* p. 270). On one natural reading of this statement, it is precisely what the new account of necessity denies. Is it necessary that the double negation of p is equivalent to p? No doubt about it, provided that we mean by negation and implication what we do mean. But is it necessary that we think it at all?

Of course not! We might not have the concepts in question; and under certain accounts, it might even be *preferable* not to have the concepts in question.

One can now see the intimate link between these new ideas and a form of conventionalism. In the end, to put the point ironically, Wittgenstein's conventionalism gives us a doctrine of necessity, for it tells us that what people call necessary is indeed necessary when one looks at it, as it were, from the inside; but in order to understand it fully, one must also look at it from the outside – and what one sees *then* is that it is conventional. Moreover, one also sees that these conventions were really definitions in disguise; syntactic appearances notwithstanding, these sentences have more to do with the identifications of meanings than with the making of claims. The statements that constitute what Carnap would soon call a language framework are, within that framework, necessary; that is, to the extent that we are using that system, we cannot deny them. But we can also detach ourselves and see them from afar. Then they are seen to be what Poincaré said geometric axioms are – conventions. Carnap's principle of tolerance says (inter alia) that a priori claims are not really claims but "definitions," constitutors of meaning, and that we are free to constitute them in a variety of ways, which need not be tied up with verificationist scruples. But how wide is our degree of freedom? Here lies the main conflict between Wittgenstein's and Carnap's approaches to the a priori.

Is grammar responsible to anything?

A central question is whether this process of constitution is in any way accountable to any reality. Are grammatical rules in some defensible sense "knowledge" claims after all, or is the analogy with Poincaré's conventionalism to be pursued to the end? Can the world of meanings be constituted in radically diverse ways, or are we circumscribed to a restricted range of alternatives?

Superficially it might appear that Wittgenstein's answer to these questions must be that rules are in no way accountable to any reality, that the analogy with geometric conventionalism must be pursued to its ultimate implications. Wittgenstein noted that one may endorse the view that time is infinitely divisible or the view that it is not, that the temporal structure is linear or that it is circular, that all events have a cause or that some do not, quite independently of facts. Determinism and indeterminism, for example, "are properties of a system which are fixed arbitrarily" (*Lectures, 1932–35,* p. 16). In all of these cases, it makes no sense to talk of correctness or incorrectness, for this would presuppose that rules are responsible to a preexisting meaning (*Lectures, 1932–35,* p. 4; *Philo-*

sophical Grammar, pp. 184, 246). But they are not, and therefore grammar is arbitrary (*Philosophical Grammar,* pp. 184–6). It follows also that there is no genuine conflict between apparently contradictory rules any more than there is a conflict between Euclidean geometry and hyperbolic geometry. A change of rules is a change of meaning (*Philosophical Grammar,* pp. 111, 184–5; *Lectures, 1930–32,* pp. 57, 58; Waismann, *Vienna Circle,* p. 71; *Philosophical Remarks,* p. 178 – with *'syntaktische'* instead of *'synthetische'*). Grammar is arbitrary because there are no facts that it could agree or conflict with.

The odd thing is that when Wittgenstein raised explicitly the issue of the ground of grammar and its arbitrariness, he very rarely said anything like what we have just inferred from his words. What he did offer as an explanation of a lack of ground in grammar is an extraordinarily convoluted argument that makes one wonder what exactly was going through his mind.

Its opening line is harmless enough: We cannot really point to anything that could be offered as a ground for a grammatical rule (Waismann, *Vienna Circle,* pp. 104–5; *Philosophical Grammar,* p. 185). But to judge from the rest of the argument, this impossibility is due not to the simple absence of a ground but to something more difficult to explain. Here is how the reasoning goes: A statement that justifies a grammatical rule such as 'There are four primary colors' must take the form 'Since there are (in fact) exactly four primary colors, the rule must be "There are four primary colors".' From bipolarity it now follows that 'There are not four primary colors' is perfectly meaningful, which is what we were trying to deny via the justification of the rule. Hence, if we could justify a rule, it could be violated (*Lectures, 1930–32,* p. 47; *Philosophical Remarks,* pp. 53, 55; Moore, "Wittgenstein's Lectures," pp. 272–3).

As with most of Wittgenstein's arguments, it is very hard to tell what it assumes and what (if anything) it establishes. The interesting thing about it, however, is its Tractarian aftertaste. Recall that the *Tractatus* had offered a correspondence theory of meaning, according to which something present in the fact we are trying to depict must also be present in the linguistic object through which we try to depict it. This is true not only locally but also globally; not merely atomic facts, but the world or reality has a form or an essence, and language as a whole, if it is to depict reality, must share that form.

This might seem to conflict with a grammatical tolerance that other portions of the *Tractatus* seem to suggest; for it was also claimed there that it is impossible to depict form (2.172, 2.173); thus, there is no condition that could be stated in any language that must be satisfied in order for it to qualify as a language, that is, as a system for communication. It follows that according to the *Tractatus,* nothing at all can be said that can distinguish between a pictorial system capable of representing reality and one that cannot do so. In particular, it would be impossible to justify the syntax of our language by constructing a claim to the effect that the syntax of the language has the same form as the reality it deals with and then showing that this sentence is true.

This inability to justify grammar does not lead to linguistic conventionalism or Carnapian tolerance, however. Indeed, it is consistent with the Tractarian conviction that there is only one sort of proper grammar, the one that agrees in the appropriate way with the form of reality. The misleading impression of grammatical tolerance entirely vanishes once we note that in the *Tractatus,* grammatical intolerance has simply moved from the domain of saying to that of showing. We cannot *say* that grammar should have the form of reality; *but it should.* And even though language cannot say that it has the form in question, it can show it, so it must be *shown* that the forms of language and reality are the same.

How far from this standpoint had Wittgenstein moved in the early 1930s? Many of the passages cited earlier appeared to be inspired by the spirit of geometric tolerance and so suggest one answer. But many other passages suggest the opposite. Thus, around 1930 Wittgenstein wrote that "language derives the way it means only from its meaning (*Bedeutung*), from the world" (*Philosophische Bemerkungen,* p. 80) and that "philosophy as custodian of grammar can in fact grasp the essence of the world, only not in the sentences of language, but in the rules for this language" (*Philosophical Remarks,* p. 85). In 1932 he told his Cambridge students that "grammar is a mirror of reality" (*Lectures, 1930–32,* p. 9) and that "it is not entirely a matter of arbitrary choice. It must enable us to express the multiplicity of facts, give us the same degree of freedom as do the facts" (p. 8). Echoes of showing and saying are also clearly detectable: That grammar allows us to state true and false propositions tells us something about the world, but what it tells us cannot be expressed in propositions (*Lectures, 1930–32,* pp. 9–10); and the reasons for the unsayability of the unsayable are still the same old ones (*Lectures, 1930–32,* pp. 9–10). Moreover, rules of syntax, like logic in the *Tractatus,* are prior to the *how* but not to the *what* (Waismann, *Vienna Circle,* p. 77) – whatever that may mean. Worst of all, there is the frenzy of grammatical intolerance displayed in the hundreds upon hundreds of pages that Wittgenstein devoted to the extermination of all forms of nonconstructive mathematics.

The conclusion to be drawn from all this is that there are at least three different attitudes toward grammar in the middle Wittgenstein. To begin with, as we have seen, he often talked of rules of grammar in a conventionalist tone of voice, as if to change them were no more difficult than to stop playing chess and start playing checkers or to replace a meterstick by a yardstick (see, e.g., *Philosophical Grammar,* p. 185). The impressions conveyed in these passages is that we are dealing merely with trivially different modes of representation of the very same facts and that, consequently, there can be no grounds for the choice of one system over another except for reasons of expediency, taste, and the like.

At other times Wittgenstein talked as if it were difficult to imagine circumstances under which one might be inclined to adopt a grammatical system different from the one we actually use (e.g., *Lectures, 1930–32,* p. 49; *Philosophical Grammar,* p. 110). The preference for a grammatical system, he appears to say on these occasions, is no less justified than the fear of fire or our belief in inductive reasoning. If so, to think of circumstances in which an alternative grammatical system will be acceptable is no easier than thinking of circumstances in which people will regularly jump in a fire every time they see one or assume that nothing will happen the way it always has. A change of grammar seems, in these cases, not like a mere change of representational system, but a paradigm change of cross-cultural proportions.

Finally, at other times Wittgenstein appeared to say that some grammatical rules are downright wrong and that those who want to endorse them should not do so. Whereas one might try to explain the difference between the first two attitudes toward grammar as corresponding to the difference between grammar regarded as a calculus and as an applied grammar (grammar seen from the outside and from the inside, respectively), this distinction could not account for the immense amount of energy Wittgenstein devoted to establishing the absurdity of nonconstructivist mathematics. One may readily grant Wittgenstein's insights concerning the factuality of meaning (as we shall, in Chapter 17) without thereby overlooking the contrast between Wittgenstein's serene tolerance toward the good savage that adds 2 and 2 and gets 5 and the religious zeal with which he denied Cantor his concept of number. There is a dubious intellectual path from a statement such as "The axioms of mathematics are . . . sentences of syntax. . . . The 'axioms' are postulations of the form of expression" (*Philosophische Bemerkungen,* p. 189) to the remark that "set theory is false" (*Philosophische Bemerkungen,* p. 211).

The analysis of the a priori was the topic of Wittgenstein's philosophical grammar. It was also the subject of Carnap's logical syntax. In order to appreciate the distinctive features of Carnap's position, we must begin by tracing the un-Wittgensteinian path by which he reached it.

15

The road to syntax

I see mainly three phases: 1. 1925–30, in the center: Wittgenstein's Tractatus, next: my Aufbau conception, which simplified everything very much;
danger of dogmatism. Refusal of metaphysics through a too strongly simplified scheme. All difficulties appear solved. The dragon was slain. Now
things need only to be clarified a little through explanations. 2. The new
phase comes out of two additions: 2a. (Mainly since 1929?) physicalism,
unity of science; bridges between the branches; the attention goes not only
to physics, but further to psychology and sociology. 2b. Syntax mainly
since 1931 (my first sketch: Jan. 1930 [*sic*]; stronger influence through
Tarski's lecture in Vienna, February 1930, disregarded by Schlick and Waismann). Gradually it became ever clearer: all of our problems are syntactic
problems. Serves to strengthen the thesis of the unity of science. Not:
everything is solved, but a set of new jobs to be tackled.[1]

Letter from Carnap to Neurath of 23 December 1933 (ASP)

The protocols of the Vienna circle sessions held in 1931 (RC 081-07,
ASP) offer an image of conflicting attitudes toward Wittgenstein's
thought, from Waismann's unswerving support to Neurath's thoughtless
rejection. Carnap took the middle ground of critical interest, convinced
that there were insights behind the confused message reaching him but
unwilling to let the matter stand where Wittgenstein had left it.

One source of constant puzzlement was Wittgenstein's view that *the
best* philosophy is meaningless and consists of certain strange things
called *"Erläuterungen"* (clarifications). A closely related puzzle was the
nature of what Wittgenstein had called "syntax" or "grammar," which,
apparently, was the only activity appropriate for philosophers. Could this
new form of philosophical activity be legitimate in spite of the alleged
meaninglessness of its products? Wittgenstein had thrown away the ladder after climbing it; but had he remembered to step off first?

Wittgenstein's emissaries – Schlick and Waismann – had been less
than successful in articulating his solution to that problem. At one of the
meetings, Gödel asked how one distinguishes between the meaningless
Erläuterungen that Wittgenstein instructs us to produce and the meaningless metaphysics that he instructs us to avoid. Apparently, no enlightening answer was available. Then, on 15 January 1931, Gödel gave a
paper on what appeared to be an entirely unrelated matter, for it con-

cerned his recent discovery of the incompleteness of arithmetic. Carnap listened and concluded that there might be a link after all.

In his "Intellectual Autobiography," Carnap recalled that

the whole theory of language structure and its possible applications in philosophy came to me like a vision during a sleepless night in January 1931, when I was ill. On the following day, still in bed with a fever, I wrote down my ideas on forty-four pages under the title "Attempt at a metalogic". These shorthand notes were the first version of my book *Logical Syntax of Language.* (p. 53)

It took him three years to sort out the new ideas and set them down in a satisfactory form. A few days after submitting the manuscript of *The Logical Syntax of Language* to the printer, Carnap paused to reminisce about its origins: "Historically," he wrote to Neurath, "my 'Syntax' has two roots: 1. Wittgenstein, 2. Metamathematics (Tarski, Gödel)" (Letter of 23 December 1933, RC 029-03-06, p. 1, ASP).[2] We already have an idea of what Carnap *might* have learned from Wittgenstein concerning grammar;[3] our task now is to survey the foundational developments as they appeared to Carnap when he began speculating on the character of logic and mathematics.

The monolinguistic project

There is almost nothing in the published record that would allow us to form a definite idea of Carnap's philosophy of logic before *The Logical Syntax of Language.* His major text on this subject is the *Abriss der Logistik* of 1929, which is concerned primarily with the application of *Principia* to problems in epistemology and philosophy of science. Little can be concluded from it concerning Carnap's conception of logic. Fortunately, Carnap's Nachlass contains logical writings and correspondence from this period that enable us to frame a rather precise picture. Perhaps the most illuminating document in this area is the ninety-three-page typescript entitled "Untersuchungen zur allgemeinen Axiomatik," which Carnap wrote about 1929 (RC 080-34-03, ASP; hereafter referred to as "Untersuchungen").[4]

The first part of this text was typed and circulated for comments; the second part remained in shorthand form. From our own perspective, which was Carnap's by the mid-1930s, the purpose of this book could be described as that of producing a formal explication of the basic proof-theoretic and model-theoretic notions of Hilbert's metamathematics within a type-theoretic language *but* eliminating the standard assumption that an object language is under consideration. Carnap's aim was, in effect, to stand up for the Russellian monolinguistic approach, in opposition to the growing trend in metamathematics toward a Hilbertian two-language approach to foundational matters.

Since the beginning of Hilbert's geometric and metamathematical studies, problems of consistency and completeness had become the foci of attention for foundational research. The Russellian approach did not seem to be particularly hospitable to such considerations, which seem to demand a sharp distinction between the language *for* which those notions are defined and the language *in* which they are defined. Wittgenstein's *Tractatus* appeared to be even more hostile than Russell to that distinction. Understandably, outside Poland the Russellian tradition had been largely neglected by those developing the new metamathematical ideas. (The Polish school followed a middle course, attentive to the need for distinguishing language levels while at the same time keeping as closely as possible to a Russellian–Husserlian–Twardowskian perspective.) Carnap's book was thus inspired by the somewhat epicyclic aim of showing that everything of value in metamathematics can (or should) be expressed within the monolinguistic framework of *Principia Mathematica*. His effort offers instead an unwilling testimonial to the hostility between the Russellian approach and metamathematical questions, a feature already revealed in the discussion of Chapter 7.

The immediate occasion for the writing of Carnap's "Untersuchungen" was a passage in Fraenkel's *Einleitung* in which he discussed the ambiguities in the idea of completeness, one of the most crucial notions of recent metamathematics. In section 18 of his treatise, Fraenkel had introduced three apparently different conceptions of completeness in relation to an axiom system (henceforth, AS). There is, to begin with,

the conception according to which the completeness of an AS requires that the system should encompass and deal with the totality of the theory it is intended to ground, so that each pertinent question which can be framed in terms of its basic concepts must be answerable either one way or the other by means of deductive inferences from its axioms. (p. 347)

A second, closely related sense is suggested by the history of the parallel postulate: There are statements that not only are underivable from a given AS, but are such that both they and their denial are compatible (*verträglich*) with the AS. For these ASs,

the issue whether certain relevant questions are to be answered one way or the other is left undecided, not merely in the sense of deducibility with the currently available or future means of mathematics, but rather in an absolute sense (*in einem absoluten Sinn*) (representable by means of independence proofs). Such an AS can be justifiably regarded as incomplete. . . . Let A be a relevant statement in the AS; independently of whether one can deduce the correctness or falsehood of A in the system, or whether one can secure such deducibility merely theoretically, only *either* the correctness *or* the falsehood of *A* – but not both of these possibilities – should be compatible with the system if it is to qualify as complete. Here we are not setting the exaggerated requirement that the decidability of *A* be assured. Rather, all one requires is what one might call an internal determination of the domain through the axioms. (pp. 348–9)

According to the third and final sense, an AS is complete

when the mathematical objects and basic relations which fall under [an AS] are determined *formally and unequivocally* in such a way that between two different realizations one can establish a connection by means of 1–1 isomorphic correspondence. (p. 349)

These are the metamathematical notions Carnap would attempt to explicate. Since they all pertain to ASs, his first task was to explain what an AS is.

Carnap began by explaining that ASs are put forth in order that one might draw consequences from them; but this can be done only when a logic is available. This logic must be "contentual" or material (*inhaltlich*),[5] since otherwise "we would not be in a position to operate with it; and to deduce is to operate, since it means to construct from given configurations of signs and in agreement with certain rules other configurations of signs" ("Untersuchungen," p. 4).[6] Under the influence of Russell, Carnap had been blinded to the Fregean distinction between logical rules and logical laws and therefore interpreted the former as a subclass of the latter. Consequently, he misconstrued the claim that an AS must be embodied in a context of rules of inference as the claim that ASs must be fragments of an all-encompassing logical language such as that of *Principia Mathematica.*

In a complete reversal of Wittgenstein's position, Carnap held that *only* logical propositions say anything at all, genuine axiom systems being only apparent conveyors of information. Unlike the basic concepts of logic, the primitive notions of an AS have no determinate meaning and are consequently to be interpreted as variables of some appropriate type. Correspondingly, the system of *basic propositions* (*Grundsätze*) of logic ought not to be confused with the *axioms* of an AS; for an axiom is a propositional function, and an AS is a conjunction of axioms. It follows that "the system of logical statements whose presupposition was required for every AS can not itself be an AS in the sense intended here" ("Untersuchungen," p. 4).[7]

What we usually call a "theorem" of an AS is, again, a propositional function. Since "properly speaking" one can prove only statements (*Aussagen*), one cannot really prove these "theorems." In agreement with Russell's if–thenism, mathematics should not be construed as asserting these contentless statements but only the implications from the ASs to the theorems. As Carnap put it, if we denote by $f(R)$ a formula of PM (the language of *Principia Mathematica*) that contains R as its only nonlogical sign (variable), then to say that another expression $g(R)$ is a theorem in the AS $f(R)$ is really to say that we can prove (presumably, in PM), for any relation R of the appropriate type, if $f(R)$ then $g(R)$.[8] In this case we say that $g(R)$ is a consequence (*Folgerung*) of $f(R)$.

A further preliminary matter relates to the conflict between what Carnap calls the "constructivist" and the "absolutistic" interpretation of logicomathematical expressions. To the extent that Carnap defined it explicitly, the conflict refers basically to the interpretation of existential statements. For the absolutist such statements are to be interpreted without restrictions, whereas for the constructivist the statement 'There is an F' must be associated with a method for identifying an instance of F; otherwise, the existence statement must be regarded as meaningless. Unlike intuitionism, which Carnap dismissed, constructivism accepts the principle of excluded middle. Even though Carnap thought that the constructivist interpretation of mathematical statements was the correct one,[9] his treatment was intended to be neutral with respect to this issue, and thus he introduced for each metamathematical notion both an a-version (absolute) and a c-version (constructive), leaving it up to the reader to decide which interpretation to use. (The c-versions always have a c prefixed to their names; a-versions may not.)

The first semantic concept to be explicated was that of a *model* of an AS. Let $f(R, S, T)$ be an AS (with 'R', 'S', 'T' its only primitives, or free variables); then we say that the relation system (R_1, S_1, T_1) is a *model* of $f(R, S, T)$ when R_1, S_1, T_1 are relations of the appropriate types definable within PM and $f(R_1, S_1, T_1)$ "is true" ("Untersuchungen," p. 44). (Whether Carnap properly distinguished between true and provable in PM – or in the correct logical system – is dubious.) Often nonmathematical relation systems with nonabstract objects as their terms will also make $f(R, S, T)$ true, but Carnap called these structures "realizations," restricting the term 'model' to mathematical relation systems.

An AS $f(R)$ is "*satisfied*' (*erfüllt*) if it has a model: $(E)f$; consequently, it is '*c-satisfied*' if one can present a model; '*empty*' if it has no model: $-(E)f$" (Carnap's notation '$(E)f$' is an abbreviation for '$(ER_1)\ldots(ER_n)$ $f(R_1\ldots R_n)$'); "Untersuchungen," p. 46).[10] An inconsistent propositional function is the conjunction of a propositional function and its negation. "If an AS has a contradictory consequence, it is called '*inconsistent*' . . .: $Eh(f \Rightarrow (h\ \&\ -h))$; consequently, it is '*c-inconsistent*' when one can present such a propositional function [my emphasis]. . . . If an AS has no inconsistent consequence we call it '*consistent*': $-(Eh)(f \Rightarrow (h\ \&\ -h))$" (pp. 46–7).[11]

Carnap then proved a number of theorems, among them (a) that an inconsistent axiom system is empty, (b) that an empty axiom system is inconsistent, (c) that a c-empty AS is c-inconsistent, and (d) its converse. Their revealing proofs will be examined in the next section.

Next came Carnap's analysis of isomorphism. For the simplest case of two relations P, Q of the same type, the relation isom(P, Q) is defined as in PM. There followed an elaborate attempt to extend this notion to a relation between arbitrary relation systems, regardless of their type distribution. Using this notion of isomorphism, Carnap introduced a distinction between two kinds of axioms (or ASs): formal and material. A formal axiom is one for which all structures isomorphic to a model are also models; a material axiom is one that is not formal. The intended point of Carnap's distinction can be explained as follows: Consider the AS T consisting of these three claims: There are three R-terms, each term stands to the other two in the relation R, and R is irreflexive. Intuitively we want to say that T is, in Fraenkel's sense, nonramifiable since it determines the "form" of R. But trivially we can "ramify" it with infinitely many axioms, for example, 'The number 20 is an R-term', such that both they and their negations can be consistently conjoined to T. The common element of all such ramifications, however, is – as *we* would put it – that they provide a (partial) interpretation of the nonlogical primitives or – as Carnap put it – they assert something about the character (*Bestand*) of R, about the nature of its terms. No ramification of T is possible when we restrict ourselves to assertions that concern only the "form" of R, and this was the intuition that Carnap's explication of form versus content was intended to grasp.

At this point Carnap was ready to explicate Fraenkel's notions of completeness, beginning with the second one, nonramifiability (*nicht-gabelbarkeit*). We first say that an AS $f(R)$ can be *ramified* with $g(R)$ when $g(R)$ and $-g(R)$ can be conjoined to $f(R)$, respectively, without contradiction (i.e., both $f(R)$ & $g(R)$ and $f(R)$ & $-g(R)$ are consistent). An AS is *nonramifiable* (*nicht-gabelbar*) when for every *formal* axiom $g(R)$, the AS cannot be ramified with $g(R)$.

Fraenkel's *third* completeness notion (Carnap's "monomorphic," Huntington's "sufficient," Veblen's "categoric," Fraenkel's and Weyl's "complete") was defined as follows: An AS system is *monomorphic* when all of its models are isomorphic.

Carnap then examined the link between these two notions of completeness. He defined f to be *compatible* (*verträglich*) with g when $(E)(f \& g)$ and incompatible (*unverträglich*) with g when the conjunction is inconsistent, that is, when $(Eh)((f \& g) \Rightarrow (h \& -h))$. He then proved that '$f$ and g are compatible' is equivalent to 'f & g is satisfied', to 'f & g is consistent', and to '$-g$ is not a consequence of f'. Also, if f and g are compatible, then f is satisfied. The incompatibility of f and g is equivalent to the inconsistency of f & g, to its emptiness, and to the claim that from f, $-g$ follows ("Untersuchungen," p. 80b).

To say that $f(R)$ is ramifiable with $g(R)$ is equivalent to saying that g is formal and both f & g and f & $-g$ are satisfiable; and also that g is formal and that neither g nor $-g$ is a consequence of f (pp. 80b–81a). Carnap concluded that 'polimorphic' and 'ramifiable' are equivalent notions.[12]

Carnap finally turned to an explication of Fraenkel's *first* notion of completeness, decidability. An AS $f(R)$ is (a-) *decidable* (*entscheidungs-definit*) if it is satisfied, and for each formal $g(R)$ either it or its denial is a consequence of $f(R)$. The corresponding c-concept states that for each $g(R)$ "one can exhibit a procedure through which, in each case, the consequence can be established" ("Untersuchungen," p. 95b).[13]

Given these explications, Carnap then argued that the notion of decidability is essentially superfluous, for a-decidability is equivalent to the two proceding notions of completeness, and c-decidability is and will most likely remain an empty notion. Carnap believed the last claim because he thought it could be shown that the c-decidability of any AS is equivalent to the c-decidability of the whole of mathematics as embodied in PM. With this, the purpose of explicating the notions of completeness had been achieved.

The limits of Russellianism

It is important to emphasize once more the Russellian character of Carnap's "Untersuchungen." No doubt, Russell would have explicated the relevant metamathematical notions much as Carnap did, even though he would have dealt with the matter of truth versus construction in a different light. Indeed, the most interesting lesson to emerge from Carnap's "Untersuchungen" concerned the relative location of the next stage in Carnap's logical development, his syntacticism vis-à-vis Russell's position.

It is sometimes thought that Carnap's philosophy of logic started from an insane pre-Russellian syntacticist perspective according to which logic can deal only with languages and that only later did Carnap achieve a level of Russellian sanity as the facts of semantics slowly made their presence felt. On the contrary, we now see that Carnap started as a Russellian in logic and that his shift to syntax was motivated by the slowly emerging recognition that the monolinguistic framework was inappropriate for the formulation of metamathematical notions. One might say that the "Untersuchungen" did to Russellianism what the technical part of the *Aufbau* had done to epistemological constructivism: By demanding that the project make good its promissory notes, Carnap helped display its bankruptcy. Let us briefly consider the problems made apparent by Carnap's effort to treat monolinguistically those notions that, in Hilbert's opinion, called for a two-language treatment.

Carnap's definitions of 'isomorphism', 'model', 'consistency', 'completeness', and the like were often quite close to the metalinguistic translations of the corresponding semantic notions, as provided by Tarski's definition of truth. For example, using Tarski's definition of truth, for each interpretation I we can translate an object-language axiom S into a metalinguistic statement $\phi(I)$ (equivalent to 'S is true in I'), and then the statement 'S is categoric' can be translated as (roughly) 'For all I_1 and I_2, if $\phi(I_1)$ and $\phi(I_2)$, then I_1 and I_2 are isomorphic', which is, nearly enough, Carnap's explication of categoricity.

The similarity is deceptive, however, for the refusal to treat axiom systems as parts of entirely independent language units makes all the difference in the world. Carnap's ASs are conceived not as parts of an object language but as scattered fragments of *the* language in which the investigation is being conducted. The metalanguage, one might say, has lost its object language and must find a replica of it within itself. As in Russell, the distinction between a proof and a true implication is not sharply drawn. In the process the crucial notion of rule of inference, so central to Hilbert's investigations, is entirely lost. As a result, Carnap's monolinguistic perspective is incapable of providing an adequate framework for *either* syntactic *or* semantic metamathematical notions.

Consider, for example, Carnap's arguments in support of the theorems stated earlier. Here is Carnap's proof of theorem (2) that an empty axiom system is inconsistent:

The AS $f(R)$ is empty:	$-(E)f$	(1)
($\sim$) L26 [i.e., from $-(E)f$ infer $f \Rightarrow -f$]	$f \Rightarrow -f$	(2)
Taut L19 [i.e., $f \Rightarrow f$]	$f \Rightarrow f$	(3)
From (2) and (3), following L21:	$f \Rightarrow (f \& -f)$	(4)
($\Rightarrow$)	$(Eb)(f \Rightarrow (b \& -b))$	(5)

("Untersuchungen," p. 48)[14]

Carnap's proof of theorem 3 (that a c-empty AS is c-inconsistent) proceeds as follows: "[Let the AS] fR be c-empty; that means [*sic*] that in the proof of theorem 2 we can prove (1) $[-(E)f]$. Therefore, as shown above, (4) can be proved" (p. 49).[15] Correspondingly, the proof of theorem 4 appeals to the fact that to say that fR is inconsistent "means" that $(Eb)(R)(fR \Rightarrow (bR \& -bR))$ can be proved. Apparently, the distinction between absolute and constructive has now become the distinction between truth and proof.

The blinding effect of Carnap's stand is revealed in the preceding proof of theorem 2. Verbally, there is no significant distinction between Carnap's theorem 2 and Gödel's completeness theorem: Both raise and answer questions concerning the link between consistency and satisfiability. But Carnap's explications of the pertinent notions leave him blind to the central problem Gödel posed. Take, for example, the first step of Carnap's proof. He asks us to assume that the axiom system $f(R)$ is empty, and then he writes, in effect,

(*) $-(ER)fR$.

What are we being asked to assume concerning (*): That it is true, or that it is a theorem of PM? That there is a model of the axiom system under consideration, or that one can prove a metalinguistic assumption that there is one? Carnap thought we could adopt a neutral attitude toward this question, for he appeared to believe that there are two ways to *interpret* (*): constructivistically, in which case we assume that (*) is provable, or absolutistically, in which case we assume that it is true. But notoriously, a proof of (*) might be associated with highly nonconstructive proof procedures and arguments, for its truth might be fully constructive. Gödel's completeness problem emerged from a perspective that classifies mathematical fact in a way that is incongruous with that of Carnap's Russellian perspective.

The same difficulty arises with each of Carnap's definitions. We saw that he characterized the consistency of f, for example, as $-(Eh)(f \Rightarrow (h \& -h))$. Are we being asked to assume that the formula is true or that it is logically demonstrable? The answer is, both and neither: A constructivist "attitude" will read the definition as requiring the provability of the defining formula, whereas an absolutist attitude will read it as demanding its truth. One could even be tempted to explain along these lines why constructivists prefer syntax and absolutists semantics; and one could then hope to rise above it all in soaring tolerance, leaving matters of interpretation undecided. This would not be the last time Carnap would attempt to be neutral on an issue where neutrality could only be grounded on misunderstanding.

Beyond this, there is the question of the status of logic vis-à-vis the explicated concepts. These notions, Carnap insisted, are defined only for ASs. But logic is not an AS. Hence, it would appear, metamathematical concepts make no sense when referred to logic ("Untersuchungen," p. 98). In particular, Carnap did not really say what he meant by the claim that logic is decidable, nor can we know for sure, therefore, what he meant when he concluded that the only decision problem is that of logic. The Hilbertian temptations to which Carnap was ready to succumb were bursting out of his Russellian framework.

Enter Tarski

The point of Hilbert's metamathematics, long recognized in Göttingen and Warsaw, was slow to travel to positivist Vienna. Some, like Wittgenstein, never saw it; others, like Carnap, came to recognize it only slowly and very reluctantly. In Carnap's case the recognition was effected largely through the mediation of Gödel's and Tarski's work, with Tarski's influence possibly being the decisive one.

"The first contact between the Vienna Circle and the Warsaw group," Carnap recalled in his "Intellectual Autobiography,"

was made when, at the invitation of the Mathematics Department, Alfred Tarski came to Vienna in February 1930. . . . Of special interest to me was his emphasis that certain concepts used in logical investigations, e.g., the consistency of axioms, the provability of a theorem in a deductive system, and the like, are to be expressed not in the language of the axioms . . . but in the metamathematical language. (p. 30)[16]

The effect of Tarski's talks on Carnap's attitude toward his "Untersuchungen" must have been decisive. He must suddenly have realized that there was a far better way to do it all – the Polish way. As the need to take language as a subject of logical research began to emerge, Carnap may have recognized for the first time the point of some of the lessons of his old teacher at Jena.

There is no doubt that Carnap could have avoided many of the confusions of "Untersuchungen" had he chosen to pay more attention to Frege's lessons, particularly on the distinction between rules of inference and axioms and on the need to be careful about use and mention.[17] It would be a major error, however, to think that the metamathematical viewpoint to which Carnap was quite blind at this time was implicitly contained in Frege's writings. On the contrary, Frege's thought was as hostile as Russell's to metamathematics and the associated two-language approach to logical matters. As Gödel once pointed out, the standpoint of *Principia Mathematica* is a considerable step backward from the level of rigor achieved by Frege's work. But even if the use–mention problems are removed, there remains a crucial difference in philosophical standpoint between Frege and Russell, on the one hand, and Hilbert, on the other. As we endeavored to show in Chapter 7, the Frege–Hilbert debate bears not only on matters of geometry but on logic as well. It is worth recalling that Frege could make sense of Hilbert's consistency and independence proofs only by reinterpreting them in terms essentially identical to those of Russell's if–thenism. One could hardly lay too much emphasis on the point: Frege's clear recognition of the role of rules is one thing; the two-language semantic picture and the associated notions of interpretations, truth-in-an-interpretation, and all the rest are an *entirely* different matter. Frege not only failed to introduce these ideas but was actively hostile to them.[18]

In order to evaluate the character of Tarski's influence on Carnap circa 1930, we should begin by recognizing that Tarski's metamathematical work before 1935 (with the possible exception of his monograph on truth, to be discussed in the next chapter) was essentially syntactic in spirit. This is so *even* when the problems under consideration were semantic.

Perhaps the clearest illustration of this occurs in Tarski's "Some Methodological Investigations on the Definability of Concepts" (1934, *LSM*), in which he set out to justify Padoa's method. As is well known, in "Logical Introduction to Any Deductive Theory" (1900), Padoa had claimed, without proof, that a term '*a*' is not definable in a theory *T* on the basis of the remaining primitives of *T* when "after an *interpretation* of the system of undefined symbols that verifies the system of unproved propositions has been determined, all these propositions are still verified if we suitably change the meaning of the undefined symbol *x only*" (van Heijenoort, *From Frege to Gödel*, p. 122). Thus, if $F(a; b_1, \ldots, b_n)$ is the closure of the conjunction of the (finite) class of axioms of *T*, and if $b_1, \ldots, b_n$ are all of the nonlogical primitives in those axioms, then, as we would now put it, '*a*' is not definable in terms of $b_1, \ldots, b_n$ in *T* precisely when there are two interpretations of the language of *T* that differ only in the meaning they assign to '*a*', and both make $F(a; b_1, \ldots, b_n)$ true. Tarski's explication developed along quite different lines.

A constant feature of Tarski's early treatment of semantic matters is that in agreement with Carnap's analysis of ASs in "Untersuchungen," the axioms of the theory *T* under consideration are conceived not as elements of an independent object language to be examined from a PM-style metalanguage, but as a scattered fragment of a PM-like type-theoretic system. Under these circumstances it becomes possible to reinterpret Padoa's notion of the explicit definability of '*a*' to mean the existence of some formula $\phi(x; b_1, \ldots, b_n)$ in PM such that one can deduce (in PM) from $F(a; b_1, \ldots, b_n)$ the formula (definition):

$$(x)((x = a) \Leftrightarrow \phi(x; b_1, \ldots, b_n)).$$

This allowed Tarski to offer as a foundation for Padoa's method a theorem (roughly) to the effect that '*a*' is not definable in *T* relative to the primitives $b_1, \ldots, b_n$ when the following formula is provable in "logic" (e.g., in PM; see *LSM*, p. 304 and the reference in fn. 1):

$$(Ex)(Ex')(Ey_1)(Ey_2) \ldots (F(x : y_1, y_2, \ldots) \, \& \, F(x'; y_1, y_2, \ldots) \, \& \, x \neq x').$$

The same attitude inspired Tarski's explication in "Methodological Investigations on the Definability of Concepts" of one of Fraenkel's versions of completeness, the concept of categoricity. Assuming that *T* and $F(a; b_1, \ldots, b_n)$ are as before, Tarski said that *T* is categorical when the following formula can be proved in PM (is "logically provable," *LSM*, p. 310):

$$(x_0)(x_0')\ldots(x_n)(x_n')(F(x_0,\ldots,x_n)\ \&\ F(x_0',\ldots,x_n') \Rightarrow$$
$$I(x_0, x_0',\ldots, x_n, x_n')),$$

where $I(x_0, x_0'\ldots, x_n, x_n')$ is a PM sentence asserting that there is a bijection R from the universe of individuals V onto itself, such that the images of x_0, x_1, and so on under it are x_0', x_1', and so on, respectively. (Thus, if x and x' are individuals, xRx'; if x and x' are classes of individuals, the class of individuals standing in the relation R to the elements in x is x', etc.) Large portions of Carnap's "Untersuchungen" had been devoted to the development of an equally general conception of isomorphism very similar to Tarski's.

Yet another example of the similarity of motives inspiring Tarski and Carnap is provided by Tarski's explication in "On the Limitations of the Means of Expression of Deductive Theories" (1935, *LSM*) of another "semantic" concept, Fraenkel's notion of ramifiability. An AS T is non-ramifiable, according to Tarski, when one can prove in PM

$$(x)(y)\ldots(F(x, y, \ldots)) \Rightarrow S(x, y, \ldots)) .\lor. (x)(y)\ldots(F(x, y, \ldots) \Rightarrow$$
$$-S(x, y, \ldots))$$

for each sentential function $S(x, y, \ldots)$ in T.[19]

The preceding considerations are not intended to equate Tarski's merits with Carnap's. None of Carnap's confusions are visible in Tarski's early work. Rather, they illustrate that by 1930 Carnap still had little to learn from Tarski's treatment of *semantic* issues. In his *syntactic* investigations of this early period, Tarski applied with great ingenuity the two-language approach, producing results quite outside the scope of Frege's and Russell's methods. As soon as he faced a semantic issue, however, the reference to an object language vanished, and Tarski offered a perfectly standard "intralinguistic" explication of the facts under consideration. Of course, like Frege, Russell, and Carnap, Tarski dealt with semantic issues from the very beginning; but his treatment of them was bound to be as insufficient as that of his predecessors until he recognized that the two-language approach had a role to play beyond syntax. Since the key to the extension of the two-language approach to the field of semantics is the definition of truth, it is hardly surprising that Tarski could not have helped Carnap on semantic matters during their early encounters. Indeed, even once Tarski discovered his celebrated definition, it took him several years to recognize the role it could play in the characterization of such concepts as consequence, categoricity, and ramifiability. As we shall see, even though Tarski had reached his conception of truth by 1931, Carnap was the first to pose the proper questions in *The Logical Syntax of Language* in connection with the notion of consequence.[20]

If, in 1930, Carnap could not learn anything from Tarski on semantics, he had a great deal to learn from him on syntax. It was in his early treatment of syntactic issues that Tarski displayed the power of the meta-mathematical approach to logic ("metalogic," as Carnap suggested he call it). Carnap learned from Tarski that metamathematical research deals with sentences "roughly in the same sense in which spatial entities form the field of research in geometry" (Tarski, *LSM,* p. 30). When Dürr wrote to Carnap early in 1931 requesting literature on "metalogic," Carnap's reply (23 March 1931, RC 028-14-01, ASP) referred only to papers by the Polish school, prominently chapters 3–5 of Tarski's *LSM.* All of these fell squarely within the domain of what Carnap would soon be calling "logical syntax," which includes, of course, Tarski's pre-1935 treatment of consequence and completeness.

16

Syntax and truth

It is my firm conviction that, if ever a history of the rational philosophy of the earlier half of this century should be written, this book [Carnap's *The Logical Syntax of Language*] ought to have a place in it second to none. . . . It was through this book that the philosophical world, to the west of Poland, was first introduced to the method of analysing languages in a "meta-language," and of constructing "object-languages" – a method whose significance for logic and the foundations of mathematics cannot be overrated; and it was in this book that the claim was first made, and, I believe, completely substantiated, that this method was of the greatest importance for the philosophy of science.

Popper, *Conjectures and Refutations*

We now know what Carnap knew early in 1931 when his thoughts on Wittgensteinian grammar and metamathematics finally converged. The product of that fusion was *The Logical Syntax of Language,* a book that displayed a new theory of mathematical knowledge and offered it as a model for epistemology.[1]

The single most decisive stimulus to the train of thought that culminated in that book was Gödel's 1931 paper on the incompleteness of formal theories of arithmetic, "Uber unentscheidbare Sätze," which contains a discovery whose intellectual significance was comparable to Einstein's relativity theory.

The relevance of Gödel's conclusions to Hilbert's program are widely acknowledged. But its relevance to what one might call "Wittgenstein's program" was no less decisive. Wittgenstein had explained in the *Tractatus* that "the characteristic mark of logical sentences is that one can recognize (*erkennen*) from the symbol alone that they are true; and this fact in itself contains the whole philosophy of logic"; he then designated as "one of the most important facts that the truth or falsehood of non-logical sentences can *not* be recognized from the sentence alone" (6.113).

Wittgenstein's point includes two distinguishable doctrines: (1) The truth value of logical propositions is determined by the character of language, and (2) this determination is embodied in constructive procedures that allow someone who understands the given language to "recognize" the truth values in question.

The division between the range of what is linguistically determinate and what is not would eventually become the heart of the positivist conception of the a priori. Following the constructivist fashion of the 1920s, the positivists had interpreted that linguistic determinacy in terms of constructive procedures such as derivability via effective rules of inference. But Gödel's "Uber unentscheidbare Sätze" had shown that no such set of rules would suffice to determine that mathematical sentences widely recognized as true *are* true. Thus, Gödel's work seemed to threaten the idea that a logicist understanding of mathematics could be placed in the framework of a Wittgensteinian conception of logic.

Constructivists had two choices: They could stick to their guns and say that constructive proof is still all there is to mathematical and logical truth, thus dismissing the idea of general validity as meaningless and denying the philosophical significance of Gödel's work; or they could declare themselves refuted and alter their views on mathematical truth and consequence. The first was Wittgenstein's way; the second Carnap's.

It is ironic that Carnap's syntactic philosophy is sometimes thought to be refuted by Gödel's discoveries, which, we are told, establish the need to go beyond syntax. In fact, Gödel's discoveries were decisive in determining both the problems that Carnap would face and his solutions to them. Far from having been written in ignorance of Gödel's results, Carnap's *LSL* was inspired by an appreciation of the significance of Gödel's work that only a handful of logicians could match at the time. Few people realized as clearly as Carnap the extent to which Gödel's "Uber unentscheidbare Sätze" had reactivated an old philosophical problem: What precise sense can we make of the notion of truth involved in Gödel's two major theorems? It is well known that Tarski not only saw the problem but also solved it. It is less widely know that, next to him, it was Carnap who came closer than anyone else to finding a solution.[2]

Carnap's definition of mathematical truth

The main problem behind the technical developments in *LSL* was to define two notions: mathematical truth and logical consequence. Carnap's *starting* point was the recognition that truth and theoremhood are different things and that consequence and proof are equally far apart. "One of the chief tasks of the logical foundation of mathematics," Carnap observed, "is to set up a formal criterion of validity, that is, to state the necessary and sufficient conditions which a sentence must fulfil in order to be valid (correct, true) in the sense understood in classical mathematics" (p. 98). Up to now, he added, it had been generally thought that the notion *valid* or *true on logical grounds* could be explicated in terms of processes of derivation (p. 41). 'Consequence', for example, had been explicated (prominently in Tarski's writings) as a purely syntactic notion. However, in view of Gödel's results, "for our particular task, that of constructing a *complete criterion* of validity for mathematics, this procedure, which has hitherto been the only one attempted, is useless; we must endeavour to discover another way" (p. 100).

Carnap was never tempted to say that some mathematical statements are neither true nor false. Even in his strictest constructivist period, he did not consider dropping the principle of excluded middle – which, like most others, he did not distinguish from bivalence (the law that every proposition is either true or false). Even though Carnap's extreme reluctance to endorse a concept of truth different from that of well-grounded belief was defeated only after he learned of Tarski's work, he seems never to have seriously doubted that in the range of mathematics, proof was one thing and truth an entirely different one. When Gödel convinced him that proof could not even grasp extensionally the concept of mathematical truth, Carnap's instinctive reaction was: something else must! The most interesting technical portions of *LSL* are devoted to the task of explicating the notion of mathematical truth.

If urged to present his explicandum in the dreaded material mode, Carnap would have said that the languages under consideration in *LSL* are interpreted as dealing with the natural numbers (or an isomorphic domain of "locations") and all classes that may be built up from them. Since the domain of discourse is well defined, each sentence in those languages should have a truth value. Any closed logical sentence in any of Carnap's languages is either true or false – whether we know it or not, whether we can prove it or not. Thus, the class of mathematical truths is well determined, and the problem is to "define" it, that is, to find a necessary sentence entailing sufficient conditions for it. The definition would have to "decide" every mathematical sentence one way or the other; that is, it would have to force *every* such sentence into either the "truth" box or the "false" box, and not into both. Moreover, all mathematical axioms must end up in the "truth" box, which must also be closed under the consequence relation. The name that Carnap chose to characterize this "truth" box was 'analytic', but one should not be misled by the use of that ambiguous word: "in relation to [logical languages], certainly, 'true' and 'false' coincide with 'analytic' and 'contradictory', respectively" (p. 216).

There is a certain lack of coherence in Carnap's treatment of analyticity and consequence in *LSL*, suggesting that there may have been two stages in the development of his ideas on the topic. Carnap's first and least interesting strategy for defining mathematical truth and consequence is the one applied to language I as well as to the general characterization of "consequence-concepts" (c-concepts) in section 48. The idea was apparently inspired by an incorrect diagnosis of the problem: the assumption that what is wrong with standard proof-theoretic characterizations of mathematical truth is that the rules they use are not strong enough. Given this diagnosis, the correct strategy would be to define truth and consequence as syntactic generalizations of *theorem* and *deduction,* respectively. Thus, for language I Carnap defined 'analytic' as the consequences of an empty class of statements, and the consequences of a class of formulas were conceived as the supertheorems that could be derived from that class using logical axioms, the standard rules of deductive inference, and some other rules whose actual application is normally beyond the scope of human capabilities. Carnap's preferred "indefinite" rule is infinite (transfinite) induction: From $F(n)$, for each natural number n, infer $(x)Fx$. Hilbert and Tarski had studied this rule, and Gödel's recent work had brought it to prominence by emphasizing the fact that even though the rule is intuitively sound, it is not a derived rule in standard systems of arithmetic.[3]

The second strategy for defining truth and consequence in *LSL* appears in section 34, when analyticity is defined for language II. The essentially semantic nature of this new approach becomes clear when we notice that the centerpiece of the new notion of truth was not a generalization of the notion of inference, but the radically new idea of *valuation.* Carnap never explained the reason for this change of strategy, but one may conjecture that at some point he realized that the first technique had worked for the case of language I only because of the weakness of its expressive power. By Gödel's theorem, any system of rules representable in the object language would inevitably fail to decide all mathematical statements.

In "Some Observations on the Concepts of w-Consistency and w-Completeness" (1933, *LSM*) Tarski had faced the same situation in connection with the idea of consequence. As we know, up to this point he had given a purely proof-theoretic analysis of what he called the "ordinary" notion of consequence (truth-preserving inference). But Gödel's work also led him to question the adequacy of that method. In "Some Observations on the Concepts of w-Consistency and w-Completeness," he discussed at length the rule of infinite induction and its role in improving proof-theoretic explications of consequence. But he recognized that this strategy would not work in general:

The profound analysis of Gödel's investigations shows that whenever we have undertaken a sharpening of the rules of inference, the facts, for the sake of which this sharpening was felt to be necessary, still persist, although in a more complicated form, and in connexion with sentences of a more complicated logical structure. The formalized concept of consequence will, in extension, never coincide with the ordinary one. (*LSM,* p. 295)

Whereas Tarski concluded from Gödel's results that the notion of consequence could not be formally explicated on the basis of the logical resources at hand or even of foreseeable extensions thereof, Carnap proceeded to identify a technique that allowed him to define those concepts for a wide class of language.[4] Leaving aside the approach in terms of strengthened inference rules, Carnap developed a new technique closely associated with Tarski's notion of satisfaction, and on this basis he introduced non-proof-theoretic characterizations of consequence and mathematical truth, both defined for a large class of languages.

Carnap did not seem to be aware of the magnitude of the shift that had taken place as he moved from his account of c-concepts for language I to the account in section 34. A combination of philosophical prejudices led him to present the semantic ideas contained in that section in such a contorted fashion that even Carnap could not recognize them for what they were. Yet when we look under the thick crust of nominalist and verificationist dogma, what we find bears an interesting relation to Tarski's work, as we shall now see.

Language II is, in effect, a simple theory of types and a "coordinate language," that is, a language whose terms of level zero are number expressions and, in particular, whose individual names are all numerals. The logical primitives of II are the propositional connectives $=$ and '(successor), quantifiers (both bounded and unbounded) for variables of all types, and the minimum operator K (both bounded and unbounded) – for example, $Kx(\ldots x \ldots)$ stands for 'The least x such that $\ldots x \ldots$'. The system of type indices T may be defined as follows: (1) $0 < T$. (2) If $t_1, \ldots, t_n < T$, then $(t_1, \ldots, t_n) \leq T$. (3) If $t, \ldots, t_n < T$, then $(t_1, \ldots, t_k : t_{k+1}, \ldots, t_n) \leq T$ (Carnap allowed functions to have a sequence of values). (4) That's all. Variables are introduced as follows: For every type index t we have denumerably many variables $x_t, y_t, \ldots$, which are called "variables of type t." The variables of type 0 are also called "numerical variables." Finally, there are denumerably many propositional variables $p, q, r, \ldots$. There is one primitive constant 'O'; this together with all expressions $0', 0'', 0''', \ldots$ (called St; also written '1', '2', '3', $\ldots$) are called the "constant numerals," and are all of type 0. There are no more constants of type 0, but there may be as many constants of type t ($t \neq 0$ and $t \leq T$) as one wishes. There are, consequently, infinitely many languages of type II depending on the choice of nonlogical primitives. The rules of formation are the usual ones. The type of a complex expression is defined so that a function taking arguments of types $t_1, \ldots, t_k$ and values of types $t_1, \ldots, t_n$ will be of type $(t_1, \ldots, t_k : t_{k+1}, \ldots, t_n)$, and a predicate taking arguments of types $t_1, \ldots, t_n$ will be of type $(t_1, \ldots, t_n)$. The axioms of language II include the standard propositional and functional axioms and rules of inference, the Peano axioms, a version of the axiom of choice, the law of extensionality for predicates and functors of all types, and the axioms for the minimum operator.

Carnap's strategy for defining 'analytic' was roughly this. First he identified an effective procedure that associates with each closed sentence of language II another sentence S^* provably (in II) equivalent to S. S^* is in prenex normal form; that is, it consists of a string of zero or more quantifiers followed by a quantifier-free matrix with a different free variable for each of its prenexed quantifiers. In the limiting case of zero quantifiers and zero free variables, if the formula has no descriptive signs it will be either '$0 = 0$' or '$0 \neq 0$' (th. 34b). The problem of defining 'analytic' for a language II without descriptive primitives is thereby reduced to that of defining it for these prenex sentences.

Take the simplest prenexed formula '$(x)Fx$', where 'x' is of type 0 (therefore, a number variable). Carnap said this formula is analytic when each element in the class of instances in II $\{ `F(0)', `F(1)', `F(2)', \ldots \}$ is analytic. This is unobjectionable under the assumption that the domain of discourse of II is (isomorphic to) the class of natural numbers — for we would then have exactly as many individual names in II as we need. But Carnap thought at first that he could apply the same (substitutional) interpretation of quantification to all types. For example, if 'F' is of type (0), '$(F)M(F)$' will be analytic when all appropriate substitutions of expressions of type (0) for F in '$M(F)$' turn out to give analytic sentences. In 1932 Carnap showed his definition to Gödel and received, in response, yet another gentle push in the direction of semantics.

In a letter written on 11 September 1932, Gödel explained to Carnap that the idea would not do as it stood:

Consider, for example, the formula $(F)(F(0) \lor -F(0))$; in order to determine whether it is analytic, one must determine whether all formulas of the form $P(0) \lor -P(0)$ are analytic. To this end each constant predicate P must be replaced by its definiens; but these may contain again bounded predicate variables and so forth, so that one comes to an infinite regress. This is made clearest by noting that under certain circumstances *the same* formula can always recur. If, for example, in the formula $(F)(F(0) \lor 0 = 0)$, one substitutes for F the constant predicate $(F)F(x)$ and derives the normal form, one gets back the original formula. In my opinion this error can be avoided only if we recognize as the range of variability of the function-variables not the predicates of a particular language but all classes and relations in general. This does not involve a Platonistic standpoint, for I assert that this definition for "analytic" can be carried through only within a particular language that already has the concepts "class" and "relation." (RC 102-43-05, ASP)[5]

Carnap acknowledged the point.[6]

One may reasonably conjecture that it was Gödel's objection that led Carnap to search for a radically new approach to the characterization of 'analytic' and to place the notion of *valuation* at the heart of the correct definition of mathematical truth.[7] As we shall now see, Carnap's new approach was based on the idea that in order to define 'analytic' we must begin by correlating expressions with what he calls their "values," presumably what they are agreed to stand for (dare one say it? — their "referents"). The quantifiers are no longer treated as incomplete symbols calling for syntactic analysis on a narrow syntactic basis.

The revised definition of valuation starts as before: Expressions of type 0 may take only numerals in II as valuations; beyond type 0, however, we valuate no longer with expressions of the corresponding type but, rather, with classes of the appropriate type, which are ultimately built from the numerals. By a possible valuation of an expression of type (0) "we shall here understand a class (that is to say, a syntactical property) of accented expressions" (*LSL*, p. 107), that is, of numerals; the possible valuations of type (0:0) will be the functions from numerals to numerals and so on. *All* classes of numerals, *all* functions from numerals to numerals, and so on, regardless of whether they are definable in the system, are to be included among the possible valuations for the expressions of the relevant type.

In effect (def. VR 1 of sec. 34c) we can see Carnap as introducing the concept of a *range of possible values Vt for an expression of type t* as follows: V_0 is the class of numerals; $V(t_1, \ldots, t_n)$ is the power set of the Cartesian product $Vt_1 \times \cdots \times Vt_n$; $V(t_1, \ldots, t_{j-1}:t_j, \ldots, t_n)$ is the set of all functions from the Cartesian product of $Vt_1 \times \cdots \times Vt_{j-1}$ into $Vt_j \times \cdots \times Vt_n$. A *valuation* for a quantifier-free matrix with variables and nonlogical primitives ("value-bearing signs") v_i of types t_i is an assignment to each v_i of an element of Vt_i. The valuations of the primitive signs are extended in the natural manner to all defined terms. Consider, for example, a valuation v such that $v('x') = {}$ '7' and $v('+')$ is the standard correlation between pairs of numerals and the numeral representing their sum (we are assuming that '+' is not defined). Then $v('x + 3')$ = '10'.

More generally, we have (def. VR 2 of 34c): (1) '0' is the valuation of '0'. (2) If *St* is the valuation of Z_1, *St'* is the valuation of Z_1'. (3) If $v_1, \ldots, v_n$ are the valuations of the terms $A_1, \ldots, A_n$, respectively, and if v_{n+1} is the valuation of (the appropriately typed) F_{ij}, then the valuation of $F_{ij}(A_1, \ldots, A_n)$ is the object correlated with the n-tuple $(v_1, \ldots, v_n)$ by v_{n+1}. Since the only well-formed expressions that have not been given a type are the sentences, they are the only ones awaiting an evaluation. This will be done employing, in effect, the sentences '0 = 0' and '0 ≠ 0' as the "honest" syntactic version of Frege's truth and falsehood. (The choice of logically determined sentences as representatives is a further confusing aspect of Carnap's strategy.)

At this point we are ready to explain what it is for a matrix to be mathematically true or analytic relative to a given valuation of all of its value-bearing signs. The idea is simply to find the truth value of the matrix relative to that valuation by evaluating it "from inside out" so to speak, starting from the propositional atoms in the matrix and moving outward. Since no quantifiers are involved at this stage, the process can be concluded in finitely many steps. Theorem 34c.1 states that for every quantifier-free reduced matrix M and for every evaluation of its value-bearing signs v, the described process of evaluation (in conjunction with the reduction process) leads in a finite number of steps from M and v to either '$0 = 0$' or '$0 \neq 0$' (i.e., the truth values of all matrices are determined, for each appropriate v).

Let us postpone for a moment the details of this process. Once we are given the notion of *analytic relative to a valuation* for quantifier-free matrices, only one small step remains; we must extend that idea to the prenex formulas in the obvious fashion (i.e., in the fashion that has become obvious since Tarski; see defs. DA2C and DA3). For example, if the formula is

(*) $(EG)(Ex)(y)Gxy,$

we say that (*) is analytic if there are two valuations v' and v'' of the types of 'G' and 'x', respectively, such that for every valuation w of the type of 'y', 'Gxy' is analytic relative to the valuations v', v'', and w. '$(x)(Ey)(x + 1 = y)$' turns out to be analytic, for example, because (we can prove in the syntactic metalanguage that) no matter how we valuate 'x' (e.g., $v('x') = $ '3'), given the definition of '$+$', there will always be a valuation of 'y' (in this case $v('y') = $ '4') such that the matrix will turn out to be analytic.[8] Finally, bearing in mind that an arbitrary formula F is equivalent to its reduct F^*, we define a closed formula in II as analytic if its reduct F^* is analytic.

The link between all this and the semantics that would emerge from Tarski's work is clear enough. But the similarities should not be exaggerated. The key difference is manifested at the heart of the enterprise, the characterization of 'analytic in a valuation' for quantifier-free matrices. A paragraph ago we skipped over its details. Let us now focus on them.

Suppose, for example, that S_1 is the matrix we are evaluating, and suppose that 'F' is a predicate symbol of type (0); then,

if V_1 is a particular valuation for 'F' of this kind [i.e., a class of numerals], and if at any place in St_1 'F' occurs with [a numeral] St_1 as its argument (for example, in the partial sentence '$F(2)$'), then this partial sentence is – as it were (*gewisser-massen*) – true on account of V_1 if St_1 is an element of V_1, and otherwise false. . . . The definition of 'analytic' will be so framed that S_1 will be called analytic if and only if every sentence is analytic which results from S_1 by means of evaluation on the basis of any valuation for 'F'. (*LSL*, p. 107)

Nowhere was Carnap closer to the semantic conception of truth than at this point. At about the same time Carnap was writing these words, Tarski was publishing a paper in which he explained, in effect, that Carnap's S_1 was under the envisaged conditions not just, "as it were, true," but true in V_1, period. How far Carnap was from that relaxed attitude toward truth becomes apparent in the passage left out of the preceding quotation: "Now, by the evaluation of S_1 on the basis of V_1, we understand a transformation of S_1 in which the partial sentence mentioned [i.e., '$F(2)$'] is replaced by '$0 = 0$' if St_1 is an element of V_1 and otherwise by '$0 \neq 0$'" (*LSL*, p. 107). To illustrate the point further, we present Carnap's treatment of the two basic types of atomic sentences:

Let a partial sentence S_2 have the form $Pr_2(Ar_1)$; and let the valuations for Ar_1 and Pr_2 be V_1 and V_2, respectively. If V_1 is an element of V_2, then S_2 is replaced by '$0 = 0$'; otherwise by '$0 \neq 0$'. Let a partial sentence S_2 have the form $A_1 = A_2$, but not '$0 = 0$'; and let the valuations for A_1 and A_2 be V_1 and V_2, respectively. If V_1 and V_2 are identical, S_2 is replaced by '$0 = 0$'; otherwise by '$0 \neq 0$'. (*LSL*, p. 110)

Carnap's rules of evaluation determine the truth value of a quantifier-free matrix for a given valuation of its value-bearing signs. But Carnap would not allow himself to use this "realistic mode of speech." He said instead that his rules tell us how to transform one sentence into another, so that in the end all mathematical sentences of II will be transformed into either '$0 = 0$' or '$0 \neq 0$'. The former are analytic sentences.

Carnap was clearly making an enormous effort not to say what one would naturally say under the circumstances: that he had identified a process that determined the truth values of all the arithmetical claims of II in the domain of the natural numbers. By embedding his ideas in a Procrustean nominalist mold, he had deprived himself of the possibility of grasping their true nature and their link with the nonmathematical notion of truth.

Meanwhile, back in Warsaw

According to Tarski's account in *LSM*, we can distinguish three stages in the evolution of the ideas incorporated into his "Concept of Truth in Formalized Languages." The earliest version, submitted to the Warsaw Scientific Society in March 1931, had as its centerpiece the thesis that a truth predicate can always be defined for languages of finite order. The version published in 1933 included a revision of the original text, partly inspired by Gödel's "Uber unentscheidbare Sätze" and leading to the conclusion that the truth predicate is not definable for languages of infinite order. Finally, the German version of the monograph, published in 1936, was an extension of the Polish text. In a new postscript Tarski withdrew his earlier conclusion about the indefinability of truth and argued that the truth predicate can *always* be defined for languages of arbitrary order in metalanguages of appropriate complexity. We shall first review the central ideas of Tarski's monograph; in the following section we shall examine their link with Carnap's theory of 'analytic'.

Tarski's problem was, Can we define truth? Carnap had posed a similar question, but Tarski had the good idea of first asking a prior question: What is a definition?

In Tarski's early work on definition, he aimed to explicate two different senses of definability (see *LSM,* chap. 13, p. 386, note 1). On the one hand, there was the purely syntactic problem of determining for a theory T already including a predicate P in its language whether P is definable in $T,$ relative to (some of) the remaining primitives $t_1, \ldots, t_m$. Under Tarski's explication, the question became that of whether an expression of the form

(S) $P(x_1, \ldots, x_n) = F(x_1, \ldots, x_n; t_1, \ldots, t_m)$

is provable in $T,$ where $F(x_1, \ldots, x_n; t_1, \ldots, t_m)$ is a formula containing the same free variables as P and no primitives other than $t_1, \ldots, t_m$. For extensional languages, the question of whether a term is definable in this purely syntactic sense is, in effect, the question of whether it is dispensable, whether it can be *eliminated* from the underlying theory without loss of content. To this category of problem belongs, for example, the question of whether mass is definable in classical mechanics; Padoa's method was designed to deal with situations of this sort (see, e.g., Tarski's treatment of Padoa's method in *LSM,* chap. 10). We shall refer to these as problems of proof-theoretic definability (P-definability).

An entirely different problem of definability (discussed, e.g., in *LSM,* chap. 6) is posed when we start with a well-defined semantic object (usually an individual or a class) and ask whether we can identify in a given language a propositional function whose extension is the object in question. If there is, we may say that the propositional function *defines* that object. We shall call this a problem of model-theoretic definability (M-definability). In the proof-theoretic case we are raising the problem of the eliminability of an expression from a theory, while in the model-theoretic case we are dealing with the possibility of introducing a new expression into the language (in our case, a truth predicate). The model-theoretic problem is concerned not with the introduction or elimination of expressions but rather with the question of whether the expressive power of a language suffices to capture a certain semantic object.

In order to pose properly a question of (P- or M-) definability, we must therefore begin by specifying the language (and, for P-definability, the theory) relative to which the question is to be understood. In the case of a predicate (like Tr) that is supposed to apply to sentences, there is a further complication, since we must specify both the language that will provide the instances of the predicate and the one that will constitute the framework in which the question is posed. These two languages might conceivably coincide, but at least the latter must be formally characterized if the problem of definability is to have a precise meaning.

Let ML be the (meta)language in which Tarski posed the problem of the definability of Tr, and OL the (object) language for which Tr is to be defined. Tarski's ML is, in effect, a syntactic metalanguage for OL extended to include a translation of OL *and nothing else.* In particular, Tarski wanted to exclude all semantic primitives (such as *truth* or *designation*) from his ML.[9] Besides logical and syntactic primitives, therefore, ML would include translations of all the nonlogical primitives of OL. Tarski also assumed that we have an axiomatic structure (AS) in ML, its axioms being a standard and sufficiently powerful logic, plus an axiomatic account of the syntax of OL and (if OL is also endowed with an AS) additional axioms that translate all the axioms of OL.

Now, even though Tarski's ML comes with an axiomatization, the problem that he was posing was not one of P- but of M-definability. Tarski was not assuming that the language ML already contains a truth predicate Tr whose eliminability is under consideration, nor was he asking whether an equivalence of the sort (S) can be proved in ML. He assumed instead a language without any semantic primitives, a purely (extended) syntactic language, and he also assumed that there is a well-defined class of true sentences of OL. The question that he raised was whether there is a propositional function ϕ in ML whose extension is the class in question. If there is one, we may trivially introduce the predicate 'Tr' in ML through the axiom ("definition") '$Tr(X) = \phi(X)$'.

The propositional function ϕ must qualify, to begin with, as a *formally correct* definiens. In the case of P-definability Tarski had explicated formal correctness, in effect, as follows: A propositional function ϕ (in the language of T) is a formally correct definition of a predicate P in the theory T, relative to the primitives $t_1, \ldots, t_n$, when (a) ϕ has the same free variables as P and all of its primitives are taken from the list $t_1, \ldots, t_n$, and (b) we can prove $\phi = P$ in T. The condition of formal correctness for M-definability, however, cannot possibly fulfill requirement (b) and is therefore circumscribed to condition (a). A formally correct M-definition, therefore, is any propositional function whose free variables pertain to the appropriate categories and whose nonlogical signs are the ones to which we intend to reduce the definiendum.

When a problem of P-definability is posed, the requirement of formal correctness fully determines both the problem and its solution, for either there is a theorem in T of the appropriate sort or there is none, whether we know it or not. But when a problem of M-definability is posed, the formal requirement vastly underdetermines the problem. This becomes obvious as soon as we notice that in the case of the class of true sentences, for example, any propositional function of ML whose extension is a class of OL sentences fulfills the requirement of formal correctness as intended by Tarski. One must therefore add further conditions restricting the class of acceptable solutions, and these conditions should obviously take account of the semantic aspects of the problem. This is what led Tarski to introduce his second requirement, material adequacy.

To say that a definition of the class of true sentences of OL must be materially adequate is simply to say that if $\phi(x)$ is the propositional function that M-defines the intended class, then for each sentence X of OL, one should be able to prove in ML the formula of the form $\phi(X) = p$, where 'p' is to be replaced by a metalinguistic sentence "having the same meaning" (p. 187) as X. This is the heart of Tarski's celebrated convention (T); for if we introduce the sentential predicate 'Tr' in ML by adding the axiom '$Tr(X) = \phi(X)$', we have the famous condition '$Tr(X) = p$' ('Snow is white' is true iff snow is white).[10]

The point of convention (T) is that its satisfaction will guarantee that the truth predicate 'Tr' will have the class of true sentences as its extension and thus qualify (in the semantic sense) as a definition of it; for if OL is fully interpreted (as it is in the languages considered by Tarski), then all sentences of OL as well as their metalinguistic translations will be endowed with a truth value, whether or not it is known to us. If a predicate 'Tr^*' that applies only to sentences of OL also satisfies convention (T), then for each sentence X of OL we will be able to prove in ML that $Tr^*(X) = p$; hence, $Tr^* = Tr$. On the assumption (obvious to Tarski) that metalinguistic theorems are true, we thus have that an OL sentence X will be an instance of 'Tr' precisely when its translation p (and therefore X itself) is true. For interpreted languages, then, the problem of finding a formally correct and materially adequate $\phi(X)$ is a *precise* version of the problem of whether we can find a predicate whose extension is the class of true sentences in OL.

We can now restate the goal of Tarski's paper: It is, in effect, to determine the extent to which one can hope to find for arbitrary OLs a materially adequate and formally correct definition of truth.

Tarski's first target was ordinary language (sec. 1), and here his results were entirely negative. In virtue of Lesniewski's version of the liar paradox (which, as we shall see, Carnap had also discussed in *LSL*), Tarski concluded that *Tr* cannot be defined *within* ordinary language. The question of whether it can be defined *for* it from some other language was not examined owing to the imprecise nature of ordinary language.

Tarski next turned to the examination of formalized languages (sec. 2), raising the question of whether truth can be defined (not within but) for them, from appropriate metalanguages. The languages with which Tarski was concerned were formalized but by no means "formal" in Hilbert's sense. Indeed, he was unequivocal in his conviction that for "formal" languages the problem of defining truth "is not even meaningful" (p. 166), as it surely is not if one needs to assume a given class of true sentences as a starting point:[11] "We shall always ascribe quite concrete and, for us, intelligible meanings to the signs which occur in the languages we shall consider" (p. 167). These languages are, moreover, the vehicles of deductive systems of intuitively true claims. Thus, they are normally assumed to be endowed with an axiomatic structure that captures, however partially, a domain of truth. "The sentences which are distinguished as axioms," Tarski explained, "seem to us to be materially true" (p. 167). The intuitive conditions imposed on the languages under investigation therefore include "a strictly determinate and understandable meaning of the constants, the certainty of the axioms, [and] the reliability of the rules of inference" (p. 211). Moreover, the reason for including a translation of the OL axioms in the metalanguage is that "as soon as we regard certain expressions as intelligible, or believe in the truth of certain sentences, no obstacle exists to using them as the need arises" (p. 211). The object of Tarski's investigations were, therefore, not languages but interpreted axiomatic systems of a mathematical nature (since certainty would hardly be claimed for any other systems) that embody fully interpreted, true – indeed, certainly true – mathematical claims.[12]

The general type of language with which Tarski was concerned has a type-theoretic structure, even though he preferred the philosophical foundation provided by Husserl's theory of categories to the one displayed in *Principia Mathematica* (p. 215). Every meaningful expression in these languages has an *order* that is characterized (p. 218) in essentially the same way as Carnap's *levels*: The order of individual names and variables is 1; the order of a predicate or functor is greater by 1 than the highest level of its arguments. Roughly speaking, the order of a predicate expression *F* measures how many times we have to collect elements already available into new classes in order to have objects of the type appropriate for interpreting the symbols in *F*.

In *LSL* Carnap had used the hierarchy of levels to observe that II contains infinitely many "concentric language-regions II_1, II_2, . . . , which form an infinite series" (p. 88):

Not counting [predicate and function symbols], all the symbols already occur in II_1, and thus in every region. . . . In II_1, [predicates and functions of level 1] occur both as constants and as free variables, but not as bound variables. Further, in a region II_n ($n = 2, 3, . . .$) [predicate and function expressions] occur as constants and as free variables up to the level n, but as bound variables only up to the level $n - 1$. (The line of demarcation between II_1 and the further regions corresponds approximately to that between Hilbert's elementary and higher calculus of functions.) (p. 88)

Tarski defined 'languages of infinite order' as "languages which contain variables of arbitrarily high order" (*LSM*, p. 220); thus, all of Carnap's II_i's are of finite order, but their union, II itself, is of infinite order.

In sections 3 and 4 Tarski concentrated on languages of finite order. The *pièce de resistance* of the 1931 version occurs in these sections, in which Tarski shows – against Carnap's expectations – that there is a very general strategy for defining a materially adequate truth predicate in the extended syntax of such languages.

As is well known, the definition is based on the notion of satisfaction, which differs from Carnap's concept of valuation in nothing of philosophical significance, except for the fact that its range is not restricted to linguistic entities even at the first stage of the process. The main difference with Carnap arises in connection with the other major technical insight: the idea of defining truth recursively in a fashion that parallels the recursive definition of a well-formed sentence. For example, when Carnap asked whether '$P \lor Q$' is analytic in a given valuation, his answer involved an often complex reduction process that transformed the sentence into another one and, in the end, into '$0 = 0$' or '$0 \neq 0$'; when Tarski asked essentially the same question his answer was "if P is analytic in that valuation or Q is analytic in that valuation."[13]

Using this definition of Tr and the metalinguistic translation of the OL axioms, one can establish that the OL axioms are true and (presumably) that the OL rules preserve truth. Thus, in general one can prove in ML that all OL theorems are true (for a qualification, see *LSM*, note on p. 237). Since one can also show that some OL sentences are not true (the denials of the true ones), we have a metalinguistic proof of the consistency of the OL theory. As Tarski indicated, "The proof carried out by means of this method does not, of course, add much to our knowledge, since it is based upon premises that are at least as strong as the assumptions of the science under investigation" (p. 237). Indeed, this method amounts to asking the axioms under investigation to determine whether they are consistent. We already know that if they are inconsistent, they will lie, allowing us to prove (among other things) their own consistency. We also know, by Gödel's results, that in standard OLs the axioms will entail their consistency *only if* they are inconsistent. What Tarski added is that in their metalinguistic rendering, axioms do not necessarily lie, for consistent axioms, no less than inconsistent ones, will entail the consistency of their OL translations.

Section 5 contains the analysis of languages of infinite order. As we know, Carnap had defined in *LSL* a predicate ('analytic') whose extension is the class of sentences of II true under the standard arithmetical interpretation. Yet in this section Tarski argued that such a truth predicate cannot be defined either *in* or *for* infinitary languages. Languages of infinite order include variables of arbitrarily high finite order that, Tarski feared, require for their semantic treatment the use of expressions of "infinite order" in the metalanguage. "Yet," Tarski added, "neither the metalanguage which forms the basis of the present investigations, nor any other of the existing languages, contains such expressions. It is in fact not at all clear what intuitive meaning could be given to such expressions" (p. 244). Such a language would conflict with Husserl's and Lesniewski's theory of semantic categories;[14] but "it is scarcely possible to imagine a scientific language in which the sentences have a clear intuitive meaning but the structure of which cannot be brought into harmony with [the doctrine of semantic categories]" (p. 215). This is because "language, which is a product of human activity, necessarily possesses a 'finitistic' character, and cannot serve as an adequate tool for the investigation of facts, or for the construction of concepts, of an eminently 'infinitistic' character" (p. 253).

According to Tarski, the 1931 version of his monograph included only "certain suppositions" to the effect that truth was indefinable for languages of order w (p. 247); but after submitting the paper to the Polish Academy, Tarski read Gödel's "Uber unentscheidbare Sätze" and saw a way to develop a rigorous version of the intended point. The basic new result is theorem 1 of section 5, stating for infinitary languages that "in whatever way the symbol '*Tr*', denoting a class of expressions, is defined in the metatheory, it will be possible to derive from it the negation of one of the sentences which were described in . . . the convention *T*" (p. 247), that is, a sentence entailing '$Tr(X) = -p$', where 'p' is replaced by a translation of X. An immediate consequence is that "assuming that the class of all provable sentences of the metatheory is consistent, it is impossible to construct an adequate definition of truth in the sense of convention *T* on the basis of the metatheory" (p. 247). This result should not, of course, be confused with what is now known as "Tarski's theorem," the claim that the truth predicate for OL is not definable *within* OL. That claim is, to be sure, contained in the proof of theorem 1, but the main point of this theorem was that one *cannot* define truth for an OL *even in its ML* when OL is of infinite order. (This is the point he chose to emphasize, for example, in the abstract of "The Concept of Truth in Formalized Languages," which he read to the Viennese Academy in 1932.) This is because the theory of semantic categories determines that no meaningful language is more powerful than the language of order w. To ask for the definition of truth for an infinitary language is therefore to ask for the definition of truth in a language within itself, and by Tarski's theorem, no consistent language can do that.[15]

Such were the basic philosophical ideas contained in the first published version of Tarski's monograph. The German translation included a new postscript (translated in *LSM*) that registered a radical change of perspective. There Tarski withdrew the main negative conclusion of section 5; he no longer believed in the theory of semantic categories. By appealing to Cantor's theory of transfinite ordinals, he showed that the same procedure used to define truth for languages of finite order can be extended to apply to the infinite case.[16] Truth is, after all, definable for languages of arbitrary order. The earlier negative result of section 5 remained in the form of a theorem about the impossibility of defining truth within the OL under investigation; but if the ML is essentially stronger than its OL, the definition is always possible in that ML.

Tarski's truth and Carnap's truth

The analogies between many of the technical ideas in *LSL* and Tarski's monograph are striking. We have seen how Carnap's distinction of levels paralleled Tarski's "orders" and how, like Tarski (for the case of 'truth'), Carnap explained that 'analytic' for a language of finite level can be defined in a language of higher level (e.g., sec. 34d, p. 113). Carnap also argued that we can do no better, that is, that we cannot expect to define 'analytic' for a language of level n *within* that language, on pain of contradiction (th. 60c.1; a version of Tarski's theorem), and we have seen how he proved this by means of an argument that, like Tarski's, combined Lesniewski's and Gödel's insights. Moreover, like Tarski, Carnap realized that one could use the metalinguistic definition of 'analytic' to prove the consistency of the object language: He proved the 'analyticity' of the axioms of II and the fact that its rules of inference preserve analyticity, and concluded from the existence of nonanalytic statements in II that the language was consistent. Yet, like Tarski, he reflected on the modest epistemological significance of this consistency proof (Tarski, *LSM,* pp. 236–7; Carnap, *LSL,* p. 129). Last, but not least, there was the role played by Carnap's *valuations* and their close link with Tarski's satisfaction functions. Little wonder that in "The Concept of Truth in Formalized Languages," Tarski referred to section 34 of *LSL* as containing ideas "quite similar" (p. 277) to the ones developed in his monograph.

In two respects Carnap even went beyond Tarski: (a) As we saw, his "tolerance" allowed him to overcome the restrictions of semantic categories and to acknowledge a predicate that defined the class of arithmetical truths in II; (b) these same freedoms allowed him to recognize that the formal explication of consequence is not, as Tarski thought at first, impossible.

I would not dream of comparing Tarski's and Carnap's logical skills. But on the subject of semantics around 1933, technically speaking, Carnap and Tarski were not that far apart from one another. It is therefore interesting to ask why Tarski, rather than Carnap, got there first.

We have already detected one of the reasons: Carnap's nominalism, his decision to replace talk about objects by talk about their names. Gödel's letter of 1932 had dealt a death blow to this approach; but Carnap hoped at first that he could abandon his reductionist nominalism for all levels but the lowest. Thus, even though no effort was made to reduce quantification at all levels to anything remotely related to discourse about language (Carnap had, in effect, become a homophonist for higher-level mathematical discourse), Carnap incongruously insisted on interpreting individual expressions as designating numerals. But this waning nominalism was far from being the only source of confusion.

Verificationism had played a major role in the early stages of Carnap's work on syntax. In the first draft of *LSL,* he had displayed an "intolerant" preference for what later became language I, and we are familiar with his early reluctance to endorse concepts that are not effective or, as he called them, "definite." But, as we have also seen, this penchant for definiteness was not strong enough to lead him to dismiss the call of the indefinite concepts emerging from Gödel's results. The evolution of Carnap's logical thought in the early 1930s was one of increasing acceptance of indefinite concepts and thereby of specific semantic patterns, slowly allowing for their introduction within the boundaries of meaningful discourse. This admission was, however, gradual, and at the time of publication of *LSL* it had not been completed. *LSL* still displays a lingering verificationist bias, and together with the syntactic nominalism, this may have been the main reason for Carnap's failure to develop his ideas into a semantic framework.

At several places in *LSL,* Carnap bordered on the semantic conception of truth. A typical passage is the following one, in which he turns to consider a sentence with descriptive primitives:

Let [the predicate expression] pr_1 be descriptive; here a valuation of the same kind as for [the predicate variable] p is possible. Here also, [the sentence] S_1, in which pr_1 occurs, will be called analytic if the evaluation on the basis of any valuation for pr_1 leads to an analytic sentence. In contradistinction to the case of a p, however, S_1 will here only be called contradictory if the evaluation on the basis of any valuation for pr_1 leads to a contradictory sentence. For, in the case of a p, S_1 means: "So and so is true for every property," and this is false if it does not hold for even one instance. Here, in the case of the pr_1, however, S_1 means: "So and so is true for the particular property expressed by pr_1" where we have a [descriptive predicate expression] pr_d and therefore an empirically and not a logically determinable property; and this sentence is only contradictory – that is to say, false on logical grounds – if there exists no property for which S_1 is true. (pp. 107–8)

Carnap was looking at a nonlogical sentence and asking when it is analytic and when contradictory. He was *not* asking when it is true. But an answer to that question was implicit in his reasoning. Since the sentence with a descriptive predicate says that it is true (*sic*) for a particular interpretation of that predicate, in order to show that this claim is contradictory it does not suffice to show that under a different interpretation the sentence comes out mathematically false. In the middle of this reasoning Carnap found himself arguing, quite against his "better" judgment, about a phrase 'true for the particular property expressed by pr_1'. What, exactly, could he have thought he meant by that phrase? Had he sat down to work this out, he would have encountered the "triviality" that to say that S_1 is true (under those circumstances) is to say that the coordinates under consideration are elements of the class associated with pr_1 by the interpretation.

But it was not to be. In section 60b Carnap raised explicitly the question of whether truth could be defined within the confines of his syntactic techniques, and he argued that it could not. The argument – one of the worst Carnap ever advanced – began with a Lesniewski-type analysis intended to show that the assumption that a truth predicate can be defined in the object language leads to a contradiction. Carnap assumed that the syntax of OL is formulated within OL and that it contains the predicates 'Tr', 'Fa', and 'K' (for "true sentence," "false sentence," and "not a sentence," respectively). In their customary usage, he said, truth and falsehood are supposed to satisfy the following assumptions: (a) Let N be the name (in OL) of an expression S in OL; then $Tr(N)$ iff S; (b) for every expression E, '$Tr(E)$', '$Fa(E)$', and '$K(E)$' are sentences; (c) every expression that is a sentence is either true or false but not both. But these assumptions, Carnap explained, lead to a contradiction. The sentence S: '$Fa(S)$' suffices to show this; but in order to avoid the confusing effect of direct self-reference, Carnap derived the contradiction from the assumptions that

(A_1) $Tr(A_2)$

and

(A_2) $Fa(A_1)$.

From (b) we have that either $Tr('Fa(A_1)')$ or $Fa('Fa(A_1)')$. From the first disjunct and (a), we derive $Fa(A_1)$, and thereby $Fa('Tr(A_2)')$. From (c) and (a) this leads to not-$Tr(A_2)$ and thus to not-$Tr('Fa(A_1)')$. Analogous reasoning leads us from the second disjunct to *its* denial.[17]

"This contradiction," Carnap explained,

only arises when the predicates 'true' and 'false' referring to sentences in a language S are used in S itself. On the other hand, it is possible to proceed without incurring any contradiction by employing the predicates 'true (in S_1)' and 'false (in S_1)' in a syntax of S_1 which is not formulated in S_1 itself but in another language S_2. (p. 216)

Up to this point Carnap had paralleled Tarski's reasoning prior to his introduction of the concept of truth. He was now posing the question of definability for the metalanguage. Like Tarski, Carnap had no objection to including in the metalanguage a full translation of the object language.[18] But he was so convinced that this extra portion could have no philosophical significance that he didn't even think it worth further consideration. (Tarski would soon make him change his mind on this.) It is here that Carnap made the single most damaging error in his treatment of semantic matters, as he offered an utterly confused argument for the impossibility of defining 'truth' in a syntactic metalanguage. The reason the definition of truth is beyond the scope of syntactic techniques is, he explained, that

truth and falsehood are not proper syntactical properties; whether a sentence is true or false cannot, in general, be gathered from its design, that is to say, by the kinds and serial order of its symbols. (This fact has usually been overlooked by logicians, because, for the most part, they have been dealing not with descriptive but only with logical languages, and in relation to these, certainly, 'true' and 'false' coincide with 'analytic' and 'contradictory', respectively, and are thus syntactical terms.) (p. 216)

With the "wisdom" of hindsight, many readers will readily grant Carnap's point: Truth is not a syntactic predicate, and that is why semantics was such a major discovery and its acknowledgment a revolution in Carnap's philosophy. This is wrong on two counts: Carnap's argument is indefensible, and his conclusion is false. Truth *can* be defined in what he called the syntax of a language. This is obvious as soon as we realize that Carnap allowed his syntax languages to include translations of their object languages (see, e.g., p. 228). As noted earlier, Carnap thought that this portion of the language was simply excess baggage, a repetition of what one already had at a different level. But because they included this excess baggage, Carnap's syntax languages were indistinguishable from Tarski's semantic metalanguages, and truth is consequently definable in them.

It follows that Carnap's argument against the possibility of defining truth in them is wrong, and its flaw is revealing. Carnap said, to repeat, that "whether a sentence is true or false cannot, in general, be gathered from its design." In general, whether a sentence is true or false cannot "be gathered" through the techniques available in syntax. Notice that whether a sentence is analytic (in Carnap's sense) cannot be gathered from the .techniques available in Carnap's syntax; and more to the point, whether a sentence is true or false cannot be gathered by means of the techniques available in semantics either. What could have led Carnap to think that whether a concept *C* is definable on the basis of certain techniques depends on whether those techniques allow us to identify the instances of *C?* The obvious answer is: a verificationist prejudice.

Carnap had radically departed from verificationist dogmas both in his endorsement of tolerance and in his rejection of the idea that understanding a sentence is essentially linked to the possibility of determining its truth value (see *LSL,* pp. 101–2, quoted in the first section of Chapter 19, this volume). But conversion is a complicated process. It is one thing to decide to abandon a church; to take your heart from it is another. The decisive role played by indefinite concepts in *LSL* is testimony to the strength of Carnap's decision; but his failure to see the weakness in his argument against the syntactic characterization of truth shows that the process of conversion was far from complete.

Carnap used to tell his students a story about the first time Tarski explained to him his ideas on truth. They were at a coffeehouse, and Carnap challenged Tarski to explain how truth was defined for an empirical sentence such as 'This table is black'. Tarski answered that 'This table is black' is true iff this table is black; and then, Carnap explained, "the scales fell from my eyes."

A superficial observer will no doubt regard this as an extraordinarily silly response to an extraordinarily trivial observation. Placed in the context of our preceding analysis, one may well see what Carnap meant. He had been *so* close to Tarski's idea: His metalanguages were of exactly the right kind, he had introduced the crucial idea of valuation, and he had implicitly (and, upon occasion, explicitly) appealed to the idea of valuation to talk of nonformal truth. He had been the first to define truth for a particularly difficult case that Tarski regarded as intractable. But the main issue, the very *problem* of defining truth in general, had remained totally beyond his grasp. Carnap's *mathematical truth* did not appear in his work as the species of a genus of *truth* that applies to languages independently of subject matter, and his *consequence* was similarly vitiated by a shortsighted dependence on the idiosyncrasies of the languages for which it is defined (see Tarski's "On the Concept of Logical Consequence" [1936], *LSM,* esp. pp. 413–14). The price Carnap paid for his philosophical prejudices was that in order to reach his goal, he had to apply extraordinarily convoluted and artificial methods, which made it impossible to understand exactly what was going on. One can well imagine the embarrassment with which Carnap came to see that it could all have been done far better, and far more naturally and generally, if verificationism and his horror of reference had not burdened so heavily his train of thought. Little wonder that unlike the other truth-fearing positivists (Neurath, Reichenbach, et al.), Carnap immediately and enthusiastically embraced Tarski's ideas when they came his way.

17

◁══════════════════════════════════════▷

Semantic conventionalism and the factuality of meaning

> Some writers, for example Carnap in his "Logical Syntax of Language," treat the whole problem [of defining logic] as being more a matter of linguistic choice than I can believe it to be. In the above-mentioned work, Carnap has two logical languages, one of which admits the multiplicative axiom and the axiom of infinity, while the other does not. I cannot myself regard such a matter as one to be decided by our arbitrary choice. It seems to me that these axioms either do, or do not, have the characteristic of formal truth which characterizes logic, and that in the former event every logic must include them, while in the latter every logic must exclude them. I confess, however, that I am unable to give any clear account of what is meant by saying that a proposition is "true in virtue of its form."
>
> Russell, *Principles*

Quite apart from its contributions to logic and in uneasy alliance with them, Carnap's *LSL* contains a radically new approach to the philosophy of mathematics that he and others would soon take as a model for epistemology as a whole. Carnap's attitude toward philosophical considerations was roughly that of the scalded cat toward boiling water.[1] He was second to none in his ability to state clearly and argue cogently formal-level philosophical issues; but the deeper and less obviously formal those issues become, the harder it is to find either a clear statement or an argument for Carnap's position. That is why even though the philosophical heart of *LSL* is a certain attitude toward semantic matters, one is largely on one's own in the effort to figure out what that attitude is.

Syntax and meaning

The philosophy of mathematics had traditionally dealt with three different types of problem: foundations, ontology, and meaning.[2] Foundational questions concern the justification of mathematical knowledge: What kind of reason can support the claim that $2 + 2 = 4$ or that the axiom of choice (Russell's "multiplicative axiom") is true? Ontological questions are about the sorts of entities that such knowledge involves: Are there really numbers, classes, and so on; are they objects or something else? Meaning questions, finally, attempt to determine what makes sense and what does not. Foundational and ontological questions had been part of the philosophy of mathematics possibly since its origin in Greece; the matter of semantics was not easy to detach from the other two. The rediscovery of semantics in the nineteenth century had made that task easier, though semantic monists helped perpetuate the confusion of meaning and ontology, and at the same time that idealists and positivists promoted the parallel conflation of meaning and justification.

There is no topic to which Carnap devoted more time and thought in the late 1920s and early 1930s than the foundations of mathematics. There is, however, very little to be found in his writings that could qualify as a straightforward statement of his position vis-à-vis the standard attitudes held at the time. Of the three most popular standpoints – logicism, intuitionism, and formalism – it is often thought that Carnap favored the former. Even so, there can be no doubt that for all his tolerance, Carnap regarded all three positions as utterly meaningless. He was, as usual, quite willing to reinterpret and endorse the words and actions of the proponents of these doctrines in ways they all would regard as absurd. But in the intended sense, Carnap thought that those three standpoints were quite indefensible. The main reason is that they were primarily efforts to answer questions of justification and ontology, while for Carnap the diverse forms of mathematics and the diverse logics to which they were reducible had no foundations and no ontic commitments at all.

Perhaps the best way to approach Carnap's position is to consider his alleged ally, the logicist. If Carnap looks like a logicist, it is because of the privileged role the language of *Principia Mathematica* played in his thought and because – like Frege and Russell – he believed that mathematics can be reduced to logic. This reductionist theme is more likely to confuse, however, than to explicate Carnap's attitude. After Frege's defeat and Russell's reinterpretation, the project of reducing mathematics to logic had radically altered its philosophical purpose, even if on the technical surface it offered an appearance of continuity. In Carnap the sense of the project was altered once again, to the point that its links with Russell's intentions, not to mention Frege's, were modest indeed. As in the case of the *Aufbau* reductionism, Carnap's adherence to a traditional slogan was predicated on the assumption that it should be given a radically new meaning.

In fact, Carnap's version of logicism posed a far greater challenge to Frege's and Russell's views than either Brouwer's or Hilbert's philosophies. Before Carnap, the debate about "foundations" (notice the word) had assumed that the main purpose was to uncover the right way of doing mathematics and its ultimate base of support. Some found this base in logic construed as a maximally general theory, others found it in intuition; but it was unthinkable to the parties in this debate that mathematics should have no foundation. For all of them the axiom of choice was, as a matter of fact, either true or false. For Carnap, however, there was no fact of the matter that could make it true or false; as we shall see, there wasn't even a fact of the matter that could make it meaningless.

Frege's and Russell's logicism had started as the attempt to establish that mathematics is as solid as can be by showing that it is as solid as logic. If Frege and Russell did not know what the justification of logic was, they (initially) did not doubt that it had one and that there could be no firmer basis for knowledge. So when they looked for a foundation for mathematics, they took it for granted that none could be better than reduction to logic. Not surprisingly, the first internal crisis in the logicist program developed when Frege and Russell realized what Poincaré had suspected all along, that the "logic" required to provide a foundation for the whole of mathematics was a far more dubious discipline than most of the mathematics it was supposed to support. At that point Frege gave up the project, while Russell and Whitehead turned it into a search for definitions that would translate every mathematical sentence into a "logical" language, and a search for formulas in that language sufficient to establish the sentences so translated. By the time of *Principia,* it had become rather clear that as a foundational enterprise, logicism was dead. In Russell's and Whitehead's hands, logic had lost all pretensions of becoming the ground of mathematics and had turned into its humble servant. Neither Whitehead nor Russell seem to have fully realized at the time what they had unwittingly done to the foundationalist dimension of logicism. Carnap did, and his response to this development was neither Frege's abhorrence nor Russell's resigned acceptance, but the decision to base in these surprising developments a new picture of logic.

Carnap's rejection of the ontological motivation in logicism is equally apparent. Frege and Russell had asked what sorts of things were the topic of arithmetic, and they had decided that numbers must be objects (Frege) or reducible to universals (Russell). As we know, the role played by acquaintance in guiding the course of Russell's philosophy of mathematics was due largely to the fact that acquaintance was, for him, the criterion of existence. These concerns were part of an intellectual universe to which Carnap did not belong and which he probably didn't even try to understand. As we saw in Chapter 12, even during the Russellian period of his "Untersuchungen," Carnap was accusing Russell of "realism" because he *asked* the question whether there are classes (even though he then proceeded to give a negative answer).

On the matter of foundations, Carnap's attitude by the time of *LSL* was that to the extent that the foundation of a discipline excludes alternatives to it, mathematics has no foundation. In his opinion, the search for the basis of *Principia Mathematica* or some other mathematical system, whether type-theoretic, set-theoretic, constructivist, or classical, or the search for a justification or a refutation of, say, the "multiplicative axiom," is exactly as ill inspired as the search for a foundation for Euclidean geometry or the parallel axiom. From Carnap's viewpoint, the early-twentieth-century debate on foundations is a perfect replica of the nineteenth-century debate on the nature of geometry, and the solution comes in both cases through the replacement of foundationalist hopes via a policy of syntactic ascent, in the spirit of the development reviewed in Chapter 7.

The debate that Frege, Russell, Poincaré, and Hilbert pursued was, in a way, on the question of whether for foundational purposes we should focus on what the axioms of geometry *say* or on pragmatic and syntactic features of the axiomatic sentences. The first option was the obvious one, but geometric developments in the nineteenth century had slowly forced a shift of attention away from content to a syntactic dimension. The question of what the true geometric propositions are made sense while people thought that the *words* with which those propositions were expressed had a definite sense available independently of the sentences in which they occurred and of our attitudes toward them. But when this belief vanished and when Helmholtz's point concerning the constitutive role of axiomatic sentences was recognized, the question about geometric propositions began to vanish as well. One could still think about geometric statements as expressing propositions and still ask about the class of all geometric truths; but this would include all theorems from all geometries, so that there would hardly be any motive to think in those terms any more. After Poincaré's and Hilbert's revolution, the geometric sentence had become the focus of attention,[3] and its prominent feature was its constitutive role. This syntactic ascent, this focus on the (structural features of) the sentence as the most sensible account of meaning for a certain domain – often the a priori domain – was the technique that Carnap now extended to the entire field of foundations and, as we shall see, to epistemology as a whole. The slogan was still there; mathematics *was* reducible to (or indistinguishable from) "logic." But the logic in question was not *the* right logic in which Frege, Russell, and Wittgenstein believed; Carnap thought there was no such thing. Clearly there was reason for Russell to wonder, What did Carnap think logic was?

The analogy with geometry extends, according to Carnap, beyond foundations to the matter of ontology. Frege – like most other philosophers – had taken it as self-evident that there is a well-defined topic for geometry, however difficult it might be to identify precisely. Anyone who endorses Euclid's axioms (in, e.g., Hilbert's version) must agree that there are three noncollinear points, and there also are the lines determined by them, and so on. For Poincaré and Hilbert, this made no sense except as a statement that the axioms in question are consistent and that we intend to interpret the words 'point', 'straight line', and so on in ways that make the axioms true. In the same spirit, Carnap would endeavor to deny that there are any ontic commitments in logic and mathematics.[4]

If he rejected the foundational and ontological aspects of mathematical philosophy, Carnap's syntactic philosophy was a response of sorts to its third, semantic component. One must, however, penetrate through a thick crust of prejudice and confusion before the point is recognized.

First of all, one must clear away a common misconception about the link between formalist approaches and meaning matters. It is sometimes said of syntax, as of formalism, that it concerns only ink marks, chalk lumps, and other material objects that may function as signs. If so, then syntacticists, whatever their interests, could not possibly be concerned with any traditional philosophical question, since no such question could be resolved by focusing on words. But in fact, syntacticists' problems are not *that* different from those that concerned most members of the semantic tradition – problems leading to the clarification and, to the extent that is possible, the foundation of mathematical knowledge.

When formalists look at what mathematicians have to say about, for example, complex numbers, their attitude is the same as that of traditional semanticists: They do not quite understand what is going on and they want to make sense of it. Traditional semanticists will try to solve this problem by figuring out, for example, exactly what 'the square root of −1' designates or what the square root of −1 *is* (a problem of essence, a question of ontological reductionism). Syntacticists, however, think that such an appeal to "meanings" – to use the word in Russell's sense – is entirely lacking in explanatory value and that however useful they may be for the odd purposes of mathematical ontology, these meanings serve no purpose for the intended goal of *clarification* and *understanding.* Carnap's alternative proposal was that a satisfactory explanation will remain at the level of the symbols we use and our behavior toward them.

The opposition will claim that syntacticists are trying to debase scientific knowledge to the level of a mere game with signs or to that of discourse about the distribution of ink in the universe. No doubt, several nineteenth-century formalists (Hilbert not included) had formulated their opposition to the traditional semanticist approach in terms that justified this interpretation. But not all formalism was thus misinspired.

Frege and Hilbert had both been struck by the fact that, by and large, mathematicians agree on which sentences about a "mathematical domain" (e.g., numbers or geometric objects) are true, and yet there is nothing resembling agreement among them concerning what the entities in that domain are. Frege's reaction was to conclude that, literally speaking, mathematicians did not know what they were talking about (a point Russell would soon embody in a famous aphorism) *and* that it was essential that somebody tell them. In an effort to demonstrate the ludicrous character of the situation, Frege once observed that Weierstrass, Heine, and Cantor define number in different ways, one as a sequence of things of the same type, another as a written configuration, and the third as something that cannot be grasped by the senses:

Clearly each of them associates a different sense with the word 'Number'. The arithmetics of these three mathematicians must therefore be entirely different from each other. A sentence for one of them must express a proposition entirely different from the proposition expressed by an identical sentence of the other. It is as if the botanists disagreed on what to mean by 'plant', so that one of them would say that it is a self-developing organic structure, another one, an artificial human product and a third one, a thing not at all perceivable through the senses. . . . Now it is astonishing that the sentences of these radically different sciences, which are all called Arithmetic, entirely agree in their wording; and it is even more astonishing that researchers in these sciences do not realize that their disciplines are radically different. They all think that they are doing arithmetic, indeed, the same arithmetic. ("Logik in der Mathematik" [1914], *Nachlass,* p. 233)

Could it be, he asked rhetorically, that arithmetic is a "science that proves sentences without knowing what it proves?" (p. 234). Surely it is not the *sentence* that is proved, since mathematical proofs can be translated into different languages and we do not say that what one proves in Euclidean geometry depends on whether the proof is in German or in French. "There must be something there, however, that is not lost in the translation. What could that be if not the sense?" (p. 234).

That it *couldn't* be the sense was established by Frege's own research. There is, to begin with, the extraordinary implausibility of the idea that virtually no mathematician understands arithmetic and that Frege is the first one to tell them what they are talking about. Moreover, Frege's account of the meaning of arithmetical words unintentionally entails its mathematical irrelevance.

According to Frege a number is, roughly speaking, the class of concepts that have that number of instances. The number 1, for example, is the class (call it C) that has as its elements the concept *is a natural satellite of the earth* and all concepts equinumerous with it. Therefore, when we say that $1 + 1 = 2$, Frege can explain exactly what we are talking about: We are saying about C that it stands in a certain complex relationship to a different class of concepts (the one that contains *x is an author of Principia Mathematica* and all concepts equinumerous with it). But given Frege's definitions, it follows that in a universe that differed from ours only in that the earth has two moons, the claim that $1 + 1 = 2$ would be about entirely different objects. In general, one could easily imagine a world differing from ours in arithmetically irrelevant features, in which every (Fregean) number is different from what it is in our world. All arithmetical truths would still be represented by the same sentences; our reasons for believing in them and our convictions about what they say would remain unchanged. And yet according to Frege, the topic of that otherworldly arithmetic would differ from ours just as much as the topic of Weierstrass differs from that of his colleagues. To the extent that a variety of topics justifies Frege in attributing a variety of arithmetical senses to Weierstrass and his colleagues, the irrelevant variety of topics in these imaginary universes would be associated with similarly irrelevant variations of sense. Thus, even from the standpoint of Frege's own characterization of number, it could not seriously be argued that what matters for an understanding of arithmetic is the recognition of the particular entities designated by '1', '2', and so on. What matters must be features common to the infinite variety of things designated by those numerals in every conceivable universe.

Wittgenstein and Carnap were among those "formalists" who knew that mathematics is not about words but who believed that there was much more to formalism and much less to the traditional semantic approach than Frege thought. Talking to his Vienna circle audience on Frege's opposition to formalism, Wittgenstein explained:

Frege rightly opposed the view that the numbers of arithmetic are signs. The sign '0', after all, does not have the property that when added to the sign '1' it gives the sign '1' as a result. In this critique Frege was right. But he did not see what is justified in formalism, that the symbols of mathematics are not signs, and yet they have no 'meaning' (*Bedeutung*). For Frege the choice was as follows: either we are dealing with ink marks on paper or else these ink marks are signs *of something,* and what they represent is their meaning. That these alternatives are wrongly conceived is shown by the game of chess: here we are not dealing with the wooden pieces, and yet these pieces do not represent anything – in Frege's sense, they have no meaning. There is still a third possibility; the signs can be used as in a game. (Waismann, *Weiner Kreis,* p. 105)

In Wittgenstein this point remained in the programatic-aphoristic stage. Carnap took up the challenge of working out the idea and its technical implications.

Carnap's syntax was no more concerned with specific symbols than Wittgenstein's. From a syntactic point of view, he explained, it is irrelevant which of two symbols one uses "so long as the rules of formation and transformation are analogous" (*LSL,* p. 6). Quite generally:

Assume that two languages, S_1 and S_2, use different symbols, but in such a way that a one–one correspondence may be established between the symbols of S_1

and those of S_2 so that any syntactical rule about S_1 becomes a syntactical rule about S_2 . . . and conversely. Then, although the two languages are not alike, they have the same *formal structure* . . . and syntax is concerned solely with the structure of languages in this sense. (pp. 5–6)

The focus was on language as structure, and the goal was to challenge the Fregean idea that Weierstrass and his colleagues did not really understand arithmetic. The semantic "life" of mathematics must be something that Weierstrass did understand, and Carnap's candidate for that role was the structural character of that discipline. To be sure, Carnap's rhetoric recommended rejection of meaning, but his true purpose in this regard is best described as the correction of a bad picture of meaning.

Indeed, by the early 1930s Carnap had more than one bad picture of meaning to reject: Wittgenstein's semantic constructivism was the second major target of Carnap's analysis. The link between Carnapian syntax and semantics came briefly to the surface during his discussion of the Tractarian idea that analyticity is recognized from the symbol alone. Carnap pointed out that this is based on a narrow idea of analyticity and on a confusion between what is linguistically determinate and what can be effectively decided:

The same error seems to occur in Schlick [*Fundament,* p. 96] when he says that as soon as a sentence is understood, one also knows whether or not the sentence is analytic. "In the case of an analytic judgment, to understand its meaning and to see its *a priori* validity are one and the same process." He tries to justify this opinion by quite rightly pointing out that the analytic character of a sentence depends only upon the rules of application (*Verwendungsregeln*) of the words concerned, and that a sentence is understood only when the rules of application are clear. But the decisive point is that it is possible to be clear about the rules of application without at the same time being able to envisage all their consequences and connections. The rules of application of the symbols which occur in Fermat's theorem can easily be made clear to any beginner, and accordingly he understands the theorem; but nevertheless no one knows to this day whether it is analytic or contradictory. (*LSL,* pp. 101–2)

So to understand a sentence is to be clear concerning the "rules of application." Carnap did not say what these rules are, but given the context in which the remark occurs, there can be little doubt that they are the syntactic rules that he had given for the case under consideration (Fermat's theorem). To the extent that what we understand is *meaning,* syntax must be taken to embody Carnap's approach to at least a fragment of the theory of meaning. By implication, he was saying that the mastery of a system of syntactic rules is all there is to an understanding of the relevant meanings, at least in the fields of mathematics and logic.[5] And he was also dismissing the Wittgensteinian construal of syntactic meaning that identifies the bounds of sense with those of decidability.

If syntax was Carnap's theory of meaning, the question that remains is, How broad a territory of semantics does it cover? At one point in *LSL* Carnap observed that people have opposed "formal" logic to a logic of "content" or "meaning":

> If all that is meant by this is merely that, if the meanings of two sentences are given, the question of whether one is a consequence of the other or not is also determined, I will not dispute it (although I prefer to regard the connection from the opposite direction, namely, the relations of meaning between the sentences are given by means of the rules of consequence). (p. 258)

Then he asked:

> Now, is it the business of logic to be concerned with the sense of sentences at all . . . ? In a way, yes; namely, to the extent that sense and relations of sense can be grasped formally. Thus, in syntax, we have grasped the formal side of the sense of a sentence through the notion of *content.* (p. 259)

The content of a sentence S is, on Carnap's account, the class of its nonanalytic consequences.

To be sure, Carnap talked as if his (formal) consequence relation sufficed to explicate all there is to objective meaning: "Our discussion of general syntax has already shown that the formal method, if carried far enough, embraces all logical problems, even the so-called problems of content or sense (in so far as these are genuinely logical and not psychological in character)" (p. 282). It follows that, officially anyway, Carnap's approach left no room for anything semantic between the purely logical and the psychological. Apparently, Carnap was assuming the familiar dogma that all matters of meaning that make any sense are questions either of psychology or of strict formal logic. Carnap at times appeared very close to this narrow view of things in *LSL* (see esp. sec. 62), but his principle of tolerance seems to embody the obscure recognition of the fact that there may be more than formal logic and empirical research after all.

In accord with Carnap's strained indifference toward what is properly speaking "philosophical," this properly speaking philosophical principle is never stated with any care, and no effort was made to offer a direct argument for its truth. Carnap's official response to a request for an argument would probably have been to say that the principle is not true but is only a proposal. But Carnap's official philosophy of meaning is, fortunately, not the whole story.

There is a widespread image associated with Carnap's attitude toward "ultimate" philosophical questions (such as that of the foundations of mathematics) that depicts it as a version of utopian socialism in the field of epistemology. We think of Carnap as contemplating the messy mathematicians and philosophers as they build what seems to him a Tower of

Babel; he stares at them in astonishment, shrugs his shoulders, and shaking his head walks away from the noise to a remote and quiet place where he builds a variety of linguistic phalansteries intended to conform to the variety of Babelonian tastes. When he invites everyone to move into the structure of their choice, no one comes. Carnap shakes his head once more and hopes for a more reasonable future, although he promptly says to himself that what "reasonable" means is a matter of conventions and proposals and one shouldn't quarrel about *that* either. If asked whether any of the Babelonians are saying something false or something meaningless, Carnap will smile tolerantly and say, "Who am I to judge? I certainly don't understand what they are talking about, but I am no longer a dogmatist like Wittgenstein. Let each do as he chooses and let us all live in peace."

There is much in Carnap's writings after his conversion away from Wittgensteinianism in 1932 that suggests this dreadful image of brotherly love; yet we have had abundant occasion to remark on the overwhelming fratricidal dimension in Carnap's tolerance. Its presence after 1932, as we shall further document, is as unquestionable as its presence before his rejection of Wittgensteinian dogmatism. The simultaneous occurrence of these conflicting attitudes reflects Carnap's inability to take a firm stand on the hardest semantic question that faced the positivists about 1930, that of the factuality of meaning. We must examine this matter before we try to appreciate the sense of Carnap's new principle of tolerance.

The factuality of meaning

Perhaps the single most decisive effect of Wittgenstein on the Viennese positivist scene was to turn their attention to the problem of the factuality of meaning. It was only after the positivists met him that they started thinking explicitly about the question of whether *in fact* this or that sentence means anything. And this question was posed at two different levels.

We have seen that Frege and Wittgenstein were greatly impressed by the fact that we can understand sentences that have not been explained to us; unlike names, meaningful sentences that we have never seen before are *recognized* as meaningful without the need for an additional convention that gives them a meaning. The other side of this coin is the fact that we also *recognize,* without the need for additional conventions, that some *other* sentences convey no meaning at all. Given a language, it is a fact determined (at a distance, as it were) that some as yet unexamined claims are meaningful and others not. In this sense one may say that meaninglessness is a language-relative matter of fact.

But there is another sense in which meaninglessness is a matter of fact *prior* to the specification of a language. For centuries, philosophers of an empiricist persuasion had been dismissing certain philosophical and scientific claims on grounds roughly to the effect that they could make no sense of them. This type of criticism was hardly intended as autobiographical; nor was it language-relative in assuming, say, that the challenged point was unintelligible in German but might make sense in French. The *tacit* assumption was that there are certain general conditions that must be fulfilled in order to convey information. Kant's Transcendental Dialectic shows that this conviction was not circumscribed to the empiricist camp.

Wittgenstein's *Tractatus* finally brought this long tradition to the surface. A basic assumption of his project was that meaningfulness and meaninglessness are not merely relative to specific language systems; there are, in fact, general conditions that a system of signs must satisfy in order to qualify as a language and therefore also general conditions that determine the failure of meaningfulness. Once meaning is available, we can redistribute it at will, "by convention"; but we cannot originate sense by convention, since no act of semantic convention is possible in the absence of resources to express sense. The point is, in effect, that there is an objective factual difference between a representational system and a mere jumble of symbols, that there are conditions to be discovered – rather than agreed upon – such that fulfilling them is necessary and sufficient for being an information-conveying device. The emergence of sense is not the result of an act of the will but the outcome of acting in conformity with predetermined conditions of meaningfulness.[6] The aura of mystic obscurity with which Wittgenstein surrounded the problem and the way he linked it with idealism were decisive factors in blinding the Viennese positivists and other reasonable people to the enormous significance of this matter. Yet there can be no doubt that Wittgenstein's basic point was correct, regardless of whether the conditions of meaningfulness were as narrow as he thought, or even of whether they were immune to scientific investigation.

When the positivists first read the *Tractatus,* they looked only at the brighter side of Wittgenstein's doctrine. From the late 1920s to the early 1930s, "criteria of meaning" were designed in order to identify factual conditions that fixed the bounds of meaningfulness, and positivists gleefully applied them in order to argue that almost every philosopher in sight was saying nothing at all. Then, in the early 1930s, some of them began to wonder in what sense these theories of meaning were true. As they pursued this question, it dawned on them that their approach to the problem of meaning presupposed that mortal sin in positivist religion, a domain of fact specific to philosophy and apparently outside the range of the natural sciences. The *Tractatus* had brought to the surface an internal contradiction within the positivist tradition. At that point positivists divided into two major groups: those who, like Schlick and Waismann, chose to preserve the semantic dimension of positivism and those who, like Neurath, Reichenbach, and Popper, allowed the old positivist instincts to take over once again, flatly denying the factuality of meaning. Carnap remained in a class of his own, unable to make up his mind about the right way to go and opting, in the end, for a strategy intended to ignore the problem.

The arguments of what Neurath called the "right wing" of the circle (Schlick, Waismann, and their followers) were Wittgenstein's; we need not review them once again. But we haven't yet met the opposing "left wing." Before we examine Carnap's systematic hesitations on this matter, it will be worth looking briefly at the position adopted by the most committed proponents of the traditional positivist line on meaning matters.[7]

The most powerful proponent of a radical semantic conventionalism within the Vienna circle was Neurath. There is, however, no way to tell what, if any, were his reasons for adopting this standpoint. We may simply record Carnap's grateful acknowledgment in *LSL* of Neurath's "emphasis on the fact that all rules of the physical language depend upon conventional decisions and that none of its sentences – not even the protocol sentences – can ever be definitive" (*LSL*, p. 321). Neurath's general philosophical stance will be discussed in Chapter 19. For an elucidation of the left-wing position and for relevant arguments, we must turn to the works of Reichenbach and Popper.

In *Experience and Prediction* Reichenbach noted that the claim that a statement is meaningful when it *can* be verified is ambiguous since there are several senses of possibility, including logical and physical possibility. Then he added:

If we are now to make a choice between these two definitions . . . we must clearly keep in our mind that this is a question for a volitional decision and not a question of truth-character. It would be entirely erroneous to ask: What is the true conception of meaning? or which conception *must* I choose? Such questions would be meaningless [*sic!*] because meaning can only be determined by a definition. What we could do would be to propose the acceptance of this decision. (p. 41)

In particular, the actual procedure of science (since Einstein, anyhow) offered several examples of the application of the concept of physical – as opposed to logical – meaning:

Einstein's rejection of absolute simultaneity is of this kind; it is based on the impossibility of signals moving faster than light, and this, of course, is only physical impossibility. Applying instead the concept of logical meaning we can say that absolute simultaneity is meaningful. . . . [From the standpoint of the logical theo-

ry of meaning we could say that] for our world absolute simultaneity has no
meaning, but for another world it might have a meaning. (p. 43)

If consistently pursued, these conventionalist remarks have a destructive
effect upon Reichenbach's best work and, in the end, upon themselves.
For example, Reichenbach's classic analysis of the conventionality of
simultaneity would depend entirely on the adoption of a semantic convention that, on Reichenbach's own view, there is no *factual* reason to
adopt. If this were right, simultaneity would not be in fact a matter of
convention, but rather, certain conventions would lead to the consequence that we should regard simultaneity as a convention. From this
perspective Reichenbach's analyses in his *Philosophy of Space and Time*
do not concern surprising features of the world but surprising consequences of certain semantic conventions that one might well choose not
to adopt. And since these consequences are not invariant under changes
of convention, their interest becomes extremely dubious. More generally, the claim that "it is meaningless" to ask for a factual account of
meaning, that is, the thesis that what is meaningful and what is not is a
matter of convention, must be put forth either as a convention or as a
statement of fact. In the former case, Reichenbach's wrath seems unjustified; in the latter, more likely alternative, the question is, Which facts
of the matter has Reichenbach uncovered to establish the conventionality of meaning?

   This forgettable semantic doctrine was frequently forgotten by Reichenbach when he got down to the business of actual philosophizing, in
which he was usually inspired by a rather extreme form of semantic
intolerance. One often finds him arguing about the precise meaning of
this or that claim with far greater ego involvement than the mere proposal of a convention could possibly inspire. His analysis of "superempiri-
cal" statements in section 8 of *E & P* is one case in point; a more important one, to be examined in the next chapter, is his controversy with
Popper on the content of laws of nature. Popper's position was that such
laws are universal conditionals and that they are falsified by a single
negative instance,[8] whereas Reichenbach thought this was *false* − and
not just a convention he did not like. For him no law of nature is *in fact* a
universal conditional since "each law of nature, formulated as a statement
about real things, represents a probabilistic implication" ("Bemerkung,"
p. 428).

   Reichenbach's extreme semantic intolerance was more frequently displayed in connection with determinism. He repeatedly explained that
"we can never speak of strictly determined events, and it is therefore
meaningless to use the language of determinism when speaking about the
limit itself; such assertions necessarily remain empty" ("Causality and

Probability" [1930], *Selected Writings, 1909–1953*, vol. 2, p. 337). And elsewhere, as he analyzed a strict causal claim of the form 'State A is always followed by state B', he explained that in "the assertion of that implication nothing, absolutely nothing is said (*ist . . . nichts, aber auch gar nichts ausgesagt*) about reality" ("Der physikalische Wahrheitsbegriff," p. 164). The frown and the bang on the table that are clearly implied stand in uneasy alliance with the idea that this is offered as no more than a friendly proposal.

Popper offered an even clearer and more consistent example of the same phenomenon. In "Replies to My Critics" he noted that among the very many important things he explained to Carnap and Feigl in talks they had in 1932, one of the central issues concerned the topic of semantic essentialism: "In our daily conversations in the Tyrol, one of the main points was my contention that the idea of (absolute) 'meaningfulness' or 'meaninglessness' was dogmatic and untenable" (Schilpp, *The Philosophy of Karl Popper*, p. 968). As we shall see, the main features of Popper's semantic conventionalism were already present in his *Logic of Scientific Discovery*, but its clearest presentation occurred years later in a retrospective account of his relationship with Carnap. There Popper explained that the naturalistic or essentialist theory of meaninglessness (as he called it), which he had refuted in the Tyrol, is the standpoint of Russell and Wittgenstein, among many others. It may be characterized as

the doctrine that every lingustic expression purporting to be an assertion is either meaningful or meaningless; not by convention, or as a result of rules which have been laid down by convention, but as a matter of actual fact, or due to its nature, just as a plant is, or is not, green in fact, or by nature, and not by conventional rules. (*Conjectures and Refutations*, p. 259)

This doctrine, and the related type-theoretic and semantic ideas, have

long since turned out to be mistaken. Admittedly, it is true that we can, with Russell, construct a language (embodying a theory of types) in which the expression in question ['a is an element of the class a'] is not a well-formed formula. But we can also, with Zermelo, and his successors . . . construct languages in which the expression in question is well-formed and thus meaningful; and in some of them it is even a true statement. . . . These are, of course, well-known facts. But they completely destroy the idea of an 'inherently' or 'naturally' or 'essentially' meaningless expression. For the expression 'a is an element of the class a' turns out to be meaningless in one language but meaningful in another; and this establishes that a proof that an expression is meaningless in some languages must not be mistaken for a proof of intrinsic meaninglessness. In order to prove intrinsic meaninglessness we should have to prove a great deal. We should have to prove not merely that an alleged statement, asserted or submitted by some writer or speaker, is meaningless in *all* (consistent) languages, but also that there cannot exist a meaningful sentence (in any consistent language) which would be recognized by the writer or speaker in question as an alternative formulation of what he intended to say. And nobody has ever suggested how such a proof could possibly be given. (pp. 263–4)

That a person of Popper's stature could offer this parody as a serious account and refutation of Russell's and Wittgenstein's views on the factuality of meaning is an impressive testimony to the blindness on semantic matters affecting all those raised in the Kantian and positivist traditions. None of the philosophers to whom Popper attributes this theory of meaning ever held the view that a linguistic expression is either meaningful or meaningless "due to its nature," or any other opinion in the neighborhood of what Popper was criticizing. One does not need Zermelo set theory to determine the childish triviality that absolutely every expression (including $'x \neq x'$) can be used to mean a true claim. The question was never whether an expression is meaningless intrinsically or in every language; the question was, rather, a close relative of Kant's problem in the Transcendental Dialectic: Are those who try to say certain things implicitly violating objective rules that doom their efforts to failure? It is conceivable that such a question is based on a confusion, but Popper's "refutation" is based on the most thorough misunderstanding of the question under consideration.

Like most of those frightened by meaning, Popper turned to conventionalism as the only alternative. The methodology developed in *The Logic of Scientific Discovery* included a number of conventionalist theses explicitly designed to replace doctrines appealing to meaning. The devastating effect of these theses on Popper's methodology will be examined in the proper context, in Chapter 19.

Whereas most of his colleagues had made a firm commitment one way or another, Carnap could not make up his mind. His inability to sort out the issues pertaining to the factuality of meaning is most clearly displayed in the peculiar blend of insight and confusion embodied in his principle of tolerance.

The principle of tolerance

The worst side of the principle embodies the semantic conventionalism that we have just encountered in Reichenbach and Popper, the idea that in matters of meaning there is nothing interesting to discover and everything to decide upon. This attitude is apparent, for example, in the arguments Carnap offered against the Tractarian thesis that "the truth or falsehood of non-logical sentences cannot be recognized from the sentence alone" (*Tractatus*, 6.113). This, Carnap said, is "absolutism." According to Carnap, it all depends on how we decide to construct our languages. It is entirely a matter of convention whether we use a language whose rules of inference are purely logical or whether we also include "physical" rules – rules that lead us, for example, from the empty class to the axioms of quantum or (one might add) of the phlogiston theory. If such rules are given, "the truth or falsity of certain synthetic sentences . . . can also be recognized from their form alone. It is a matter of convention whether we formulate only L-rules [logical rules], or include P-rules [physical rules] as well" (*LSL,* p. 186).

This passage displays, among other things, what an extraordinary view of truth Carnap held at the time and how hesitant was his grasp on the link between syntactic rules and meaning. There is, of course, a sense in which physical rules might be incorporated into the characterization of a language; but the link between a synthetic sentence and its truth value is not up to us – not unless *all* synthetic sentences may be made a priori. There is no truth by convention; there is only meaning by convention and then truth in virtue of meaning. The idea that a sentence conveying some sort of information could be made true by convention is simply incoherent. If a language includes the rule to infer the sentence 'There are mermaids' from the empty set, then it will follow that the sentence is linguistically determined, but it will not follow that the sentence, in its standard sense, is true (unless, as Russell once put it, truth can be determined by the police). Alternatively, one could think of the sentence in question as meaningless prior to its association with the rule and as receiving whatever meaning it may acquire from the rules in which it occurs. In that case it would be extraordinarily misleading to call the rules in question "physical rules," as Carnap did. Under the envisaged circumstances, 'There are mermaids' would not say that there are mermaids. It would in fact say nothing, since the claim would be analytic; consequently, it would still be false to say, as Carnap did, that the truth or falsehood of certain *synthetic* sentences can be recognized from their form alone.

Fortunately, we said, semantic conventionalism is only part of the story. For example, when Carnap was not distracted by his novel hostility to Wittgensteinian ideas, he granted the very point he had denied in reference to Wittgenstein. As we saw in Chapter 16, a few pages after his challenge to Wittgenstein's semantic "dogmatism," Carnap noted that whether a sentence is true or false cannot in general be determined through syntactic considerations (see quotation from *LSL,* p. 216 in the last section of Chapter 16, this volume). If this were thought to be a matter of convention, one could hardly infer from this claim the undefinability of truth, as Carnap did.

Moreover, it is impossible to take seriously the view that the thesis of metalogic, the doctrine that all philosophy is about language, is *no more* than a proposal, an invitation to look at things from a certain perspective; or to believe that Carnap's painstaking constructions of languages for constructivists and classicists were not really inspired at least by the suspicion that other philosophers had in fact misunderstood the situation. When he explained that the problem of foundations and other philosophical questions were "at bottom (*im Grund*) syntactical, although the ordinary formulation of the problems often disguises their character" (*LSL,* p. 331), Carnap was inadvertently expressing the non-conventional character of his convictions. He would never admit it openly, because that admission would place him in an arena in which he did not want to perform. But there is no coherent reading of *LSL* that takes seriously the semantic conventionalism in that book.

If Carnap's application of his linguistic techniques in *LSL* is to have any relevance to the foundational problems that others were debating, it must be because behind the first-level semantic conventionalism there is a second-level semantic factualism that poses a genuine challenge to all other philosophies of mathematics. Under this interpretation – which makes sense of Carnap's actions but which he never explicitly endorsed – Carnap was proposing first of all an object-language conventionalism, arguing that if you accept and I reject, say, the multiplicative axiom, we are not disagreeing on a matter of fact, however ethereal the fact, but we are following different paths in the characterization of the language we intend to use. My acceptance of that axiom is not a manifestation of the fact that I have identified a true statement, but part of the process through which I identify the language I will use. The multiplicative axiom is not a factual claim, but a convention. But *this* statement is not a proposal for a convention. It is a factual claim about the nature of mathematical axioms. This is the second-level factualism, the presupposition that there is a fact of the matter concerning the difference between the stage at which we produce the semantic machinery involved in communication and the stage at which we are finally communicating – or, if you will, the analytic–synthetic distinction. The role of sentences in the former stage is, as we know, the key to the new theory of the a priori.[9]

This second-level semantic factualism is, once again, not an explicit doctrine of *LSL,* but rather a part of the vague philosophical atmosphere that surrounds the book. In order to sharpen its image, it is convenient to place the doctrines of *LSL* in the framework of the Tractarian ideas from which they stem.

As traditionally understood, the *content* (as opposed to the justification) of a philosophical statement differs from that of other disciplines only in the more abstract and ethereal character of its objects. In the *Tractatus* Wittgenstein had denied this, arguing that all meaningful discourse pertains to science and that all philosophy is meaningless. In fact, he had partitioned the class of things people may say into two categories: the meaningful (science) and the meaningless. But within this domain of what lacks *Sinn,* he had drawn a more important distinction between the *sinnlos* (senseless) and the *unsinnig* (nonsense). Nonsense is to be thrown away, and it includes the worst kind of philosophy. But the level of the senseless (closely related to that of showing) is where the best philosophy lies. Efforts to formulate by means of sentences these things that show themselves – such as what the solipsist means, or that there are more than two things in the universe, or that a logical statement is true – inevitably lead to nonsense. Moreover, what shows itself seems to show itself only in one place, in the actual application of the techniques we use to communicate with one another, that is, of language. That is why philosophy is a critique of *language* rather than of pure reason or of something else. And the main purpose of that critique is not to avoid misleading language forms but to recognize the kernel of truth in traditional philosophical doctrines as a point pertaining to what language shows.

One of the key distinctions between the separation of the factual from the philosophical was determined by the notions of formal and genuine concepts. According to Wittgenstein, the "old" logicians (Frege and Russell) had failed to notice that *x is an object* and *x is a book* are concepts in radically different senses of that word: "One cannot, *e.g.* say 'There are objects' as one says 'There are books'. . . . The same holds of the words 'Complex', 'Fact', 'Function', 'Number', etc." (*Tractatus,* 4.1272). All of these are "formal" concepts: "That something is an object falling under a formal concept," Wittgenstein had explained, "cannot be expressed by a proposition. But it is shown in the symbol for the object itself" (4.126). And he had argued that formal concepts are expressed by different types of variables: In the *Tractatus* variables were as "constant" as proper names, the main difference being that they do not designate a particular object but express a particular form.

In accord with this general way of looking at things, Carnap's first step was to take the distinction between the *sinnvoll* and the *sinnlos* and transform it into a distinction between two kinds of language: (a) object languages, those with which we talk about the world, and (b) meta-languages, those with which we philosophize. Thus, in *LSL* Carnap said that the class of all real or apparent knowledge claims can be divided into two large categories: those that (in fact) succeed in conveying true or false information about the world and those that do not. Sentences in the first group he called "object-sentences" or "real object-sentences," for they really refer to objects; those in the second group that are not the product of grammatical confusion (those that are not nonsense) he called "pseudo-object-sentences" and also "quasi-syntactical sentences of the material mode of speech" (*LSL*, pp. 284–5; *Philosophy and Logical Syntax*, p. 60). Philosophers have little or nothing to say about the former; but they have a great deal to say about the latter. Indeed, if Carnap is right, philosophers have traditionally regarded it as their professional duty to examine, accept, and reject sentences of just this sort – except that since the beginning of philosophy, they have (in fact) grossly misunderstood the character of what they have been doing. As Wittgenstein would put it, philosophers have been uttering nonsense; they have been unaware of the nature of the activity in which they were professionally engaged. Carnap's intention was not so much to let them know what it was they had been doing as to give them a choice. He would describe the only meaningful activity anywhere in the neighborhood of what they had been doing – the syntactic reconstruction of philosophical statements as quasi-syntactic sentences. If they accepted this as an interpretation of their activity, their claims would become part of Carnap's transmuted version of Wittgenstein's *sinnlos;* they would not be about any (extra-linguistic) entities, but they would be meaningful nonetheless. If they did not, their claims would be consigned to the Wittgensteinian flames of the *unsinnig.*

Here are some prominent examples of Carnap's pseudo-object-sentences: Time is one-dimensional; space is three-dimensional; the mathematical continuum is composed of atomic elements; (or) it is not; the only primitive data are relations between experiences; the sense qualities belong to the primitive data; a thing is a complex of sense data; (or) it is a complex of atoms; the system of colors is known a priori to be three-dimensional when ordered according to similarity; its three-dimensionality is an internal property of the arrangement; every color is at a place and every sound has a pitch; time is continuous; every process is univocally determined by its causes; the metric structure of space is Euclidean; (or) it is non-Euclidean (*LSL*, sec. 79; *Philosophy and Logical Syntax*, pp. 84–8). These are precisely the sorts of things philosophers – or scientists in a philosophical mood – are likely to talk about. It is essential to note that most of them are also the sorts of claims traditionally regarded as prime candidates for a priori knowledge. Empiricists old and new would regularly attempt to show that in some unexpected sense they are really empirical, like everything else that makes any sense and is not logic. Carnap was recognizing that they are not empirical and that they are not "logical" either, in the sense in which everyone else was using that word at the time. So we need an explanation of what they are.

When stated as in the preceding paragraph, these claims are in what Carnap called the "material mode." This mode is misleading, because it has led people to believe that these statements are about things such as numbers, space, time, and so on. Their proper interpretation is evident when we formulate them in the "formal" mode, which makes it clear that they are not about the world but about the structure of an object language in which, in turn, we talk about the world. This is the "thesis of metalogic," first stated in "Die physikalische Sprache als Universalsprache der Wissenschaft"[10] in the following terms: "The meaningful philosophical propositions are metalogical propositions, i.e., they deal with forms of language" (p. 435). Few points are made more persistently and consistently than this one about the "misleading" character of the material mode. If the mode is misleading, it must be because it suggests something *false;* and if the formal mode is better, it must be because it avoids that suggestion and tells the unvarnished *truth.* It must therefore be true, and not just a proposal, that all philosophical claims are about language. Once again, the best philosophy of *LSL* makes no sense except on the assumption of second-level factualism.

Another crucial element of Carnap's syntactic picture relates to Wittgenstein's formal concepts, which here occur under the guise of "universal words" (*Allwörter*).[11] Like Wittgenstein, Carnap will agree that one must draw a distinction between genuine and formal concepts; and he also agrees that if *F* is a universal word, *'Fa'* is a pseudostatement. Yet what Wittgenstein tried to achieve through the notion of showing Carnap accomplished through syntactic ascent: That *a* is an object is not "shown," but it may be *said* at the metalevel in the proper translation of that claim into the formal mode ('In language *L* '*a*' is an object-name'). Moreover, once the claim is recognized as one relative to language, once it is seen as part of a description of a language framework, its conventional character becomes apparent and so does the possibility of alternatives.

If Wittgenstein's arguments for the distinction between formal and genuine concepts (the doctrine of showing) are unintelligible, Carnap's are nonexistent or worse.[12] Even so, one must bear in mind that in philosophy, as in any other discipline, changes are more often motivated and justified by the clear failure of the available attempts at solution than by the quality of the reasons offered to support the new views. Carnap's solution had as its best "reason" the fact that it was aimed at articulating a feeling *cum fundamento in re* that we have seen struggling to emerge, perhaps since Helmholtz, and that was clearly displayed in the work of Poincaré and Wittgenstein. To Carnap's credit, never before had we been told so clearly that there is a large, essential element in all knowledge that is easily mistaken for the ordinary type of factual claim but that is actually a tool for the constitution of the representational apparatus; that these apparently factual claims are "definitions in disguise"; and that what they define is a linguistic framework. And we had never been told that this framework may be chosen with a degree of freedom comparable to the one we enjoy in the case of geometry and that consequently no questions of ontology or of justification arise.

For all their analogies with Wittgensteinian doctrine, Carnap's views go far beyond Wittgenstein's in one essential respect: Even though logic and the whole range of what cannot be said were, for Wittgenstein, incapable of truth and falsehood, there was nonetheless a sense in which that odd type of information was responsible to an independent reality, however otherworldly it might be. The unsayable is not true, but there is something it is right about: "The essence of language is a picture of the essence of the world; and philosophy as custodian of grammar can in fact grasp the essence of the world, only not in the propositions of language" (*Philosophical Remarks,* p. 85). Carnap's principle of tolerance completely obliterated this dimension of Wittgenstein's thought, and to the extent that it succeeded, it displays an understanding of linguistic frameworks as *entirely* constitutive of meanings rather than as obliquely reflecting an independently given "essence of the world." Carnap's principle of tolerance severed the last link between Wittgenstein's constitutive doctrine and extrasemantic elements. Constitutive principles are not responsible to anything at all except to the general conditions of meaningfulness.

The conditions of meaningfulness remained unspecified, however. In *LSL* Carnap's attitude was that of a revolutionary urging us to let a thousand flowers bloom without having much of an idea about what was likely to grow from the seeds he was planting. He knew that the limits of proper semantic behavior were far wider than Wittgenstein thought, and he had made his point by analyzing at length a case of what Wittgenstein regarded as nonsensical. It was now up to Wittgensteinians to explain what was wrong with Carnap's language II, a challenge they never took up. But Carnap also knew that "anything goes" could not be the right alternative to Wittgensteinian semantic dogmas; yet he gave no indication of what the new ruling dogma should be. His tolerance was therefore a welcome correction to verificationist excesses. But it was also the name Carnap gave to his own inability to determine the right attitude toward matters of meaning.

18

<==>

The problem of induction:
theories

Contrary to Kant's belief, synthetic judgments *a priori* do not exist. . . . But one problem remains still unsolved which since then has caused greatest difficulties to philosophy; and moreover no consistent empiricism can be developed as long as it remains unsolved: that is the problem of induction. Since Hume's splendid critique, this problem dominates all epistemology and, now that the solution suggested by Kant has been proved untenable, one had to find another.

> Reichenbach, "Autobiographical Sketch," *Selected Writings, 1909–1953,* vol. 1

In earlier chapters we saw how the domains of mathematics and logic had been taken care of (albeit differently) by Wittgenstein and Carnap. Most positivists were willing to go along with one or the other of them on those topics; but they were far more interested in empirical knowledge. Once again, as in the case of mathematics, the leading questions were semantic and foundational: What does science say, and what kinds of reasons do we have for believing what it says? These two questions were the kernel of what was misleadingly called at the time the "problem of induction."[1] A variety of ways of looking at it had been taking shape for decades. Their proponents finally confronted one another in Vienna in the early 1930s. The showdown was, as usual, inconclusive, but it greatly sharpened the conflicting positions and helped reveal their respective virtues and vices. Moreover, beneath the wide variety of responses, one may detect further evidence of the methodological shift toward the transcendental approach adumbrated in Chapter 10.

One of the major developments in empiricist thought in the 1920s and 1930s was the gradual replacement of the constructive-foundational method of the positivist and semantic traditions by the transcendental method. Roughly speaking, the foundational approach interprets epistemology as the search for the simple, the indefinable, and the given and the construction and foundation of everything else on that basis. In contrast, the transcendental approach starts from basic facts of undeniable complexity and looks for the conditions that make them possible. For the foundationalist, epistemology is the construction of the complex out of the simple, of the definable out of the indefinable, of the inferred out of the given in acquaintance, of the uncertain out of the certain. For the transcendentalist, it is the search for circumstances that help make sense of a domain whose ultimate validity is never seriously in question; it is primarily the search for an explanation of how certain basic facts of knowledge could be possible rather than a justification and confirmation of their undeniable actuality.

In its first appearance in Kant, the transcendental method was applied to the "fact" of synthetic a priori knowledge and to the possibility of experience; in the *Tractatus* the basic fact was the phenomenon of linguistic communication. As we are now about to see, a new breed of neo-Kantians changed the face of empiricism when they looked at science once again and decided that the foundational approach was not acceptable. Their choice was to apply the transcendental method to a new set of "basic facts." For Popper in the early 1930s the datum was the rationality of science in its historical development; for Reichenbach it was the rationality of "inductive behavior," that is, of the practices involved in distinguishing between what it is reasonable to believe and what is not. We begin our review of these developments by looking at an early expression of the conflict between transcendental and foundational methodologies as applied to the problem of induction.

The transcendental method

The *Aufbau* is cautiously noncommittal or ambiguous on most of the crucial foundational questions one might ask about scientific knowledge. Many positivists who had been as moved as Carnap by the project of reducing absolutely everything to reified experience had also thought that part of the reason for undertaking that reductionist project was that empirical claims can talk only about past experience, since otherwise we could not fully justify them. For them, 'All men are mortal' is not a statement about all men but about those we know have died, and 'The sun will rise tomorrow' is an oblique description of things I have seen rather than a statement about what the sun will do tomorrow. Everything Carnap said in the *Aufbau* is consistent with the rejection of these absurd views – and we know that he was struggling to place that reductionist project in a radically different setting. Yet there can be little doubt that when he let his instincts loose, Carnap would speak on behalf of that most primitive form of positivism. Reichenbach, who had been able to dig beneath the surface of Carnap's writings through correspondence and conversations, asserted in his review of the *Aufbau* that Carnap's reduction of scientific assertions "conflicts with the undeniable and fundamental fact that scientific statements are not only reports of past experiences but also predictions of future experience" ("Rudolf Carnap, *Der logische Aufbau der Welt*," p. 200). In July 1929, in a letter to Schlick, Feigl talked about Carnap's efforts to convince Kaila that 'The sun will rise tomorrow' is, strictly speaking, meaningless and that only 'The sun will probably rise tomorrow' is truly meaningful – its meaning being a record of past observations (Letter of 21 July 1929, VCA).

The basic accuracy of these reports is confirmed by a discussion that Carnap had with Reichenbach in 1929, reported in *Erkenntnis*. The discussion concerned a paper by Waismann on the subject of probability, in which he had defended a roughly Wittgensteinian view. Reichenbach had criticized Waismann from an empiricist standpoint and Carnap rose to his defense. In his analysis of Waismann's contribution, Carnap wrote:

[Reichenbach] said . . . that if one accepts Waismann's interpretation, a probability statement about the future will not contain anything beyond a report of what has been experienced in the past, and consequently, it will say no more than we already know. I would like once more to leave aside the specific application to the concept of probability and raise the fundamental question: Should a scientific statement say more than what we already know? Presumably Reichenbach will answer "No" and he will introduce a distinction between what we know immediately from experience and what is only inferred immediately from it. Then I would reformulate my question as follows: Could we, with the help of some inference process, infer from what we know something "new," something not already contained in what we know? Such an inference process would clearly be magic. I think we must reject it. ("Diskussion über Wahrscheinlichkeit," p. 269)

Reichenbach replied:

. . . as epistemologists, our task is not to sit in judgment of probabilistic assertions. This seems to me to be the error in [Carnap's] question. In my view, we are obligated to accept knowledge as it is, and we must see what sorts of operations are displayed in knowledge. . . . From the standpoint of classical logic I of course should not infer from anything something that goes beyond what I already know. But we are not satisfied with a process of this type either in science or in daily life. Carnap's question whether the scientist should assert something that he does not know makes it sound as if the theory of probability required us to do something nearly immoral. . . . My answer to Carnap is therefore "Yes, but there are certain principles to which the inference beyond the state of knowledge must conform if it is to be allowed." ("Diskussion über Wahrscheinlichkeit," p. 270)

This exchange reflects the emergent distinction among positivists between "philosophers" and "philosophers of science." The former search for a reconstruction of science and sit in judgment, not on scientists' statements, but on what they mean. The latter take scientists' interpretation of science – as displayed in their behavior rather than in their words – as the touchstone and the ultimate judge of philosophical theories. For the former, the theory of knowledge is a discipline inspired by logic and other prescientific sources that stands above all sciences, with standards of its own. For the latter, "the theory of knowledge [is] the methodology of the empirical sciences" (Popper, *Grundprobleme,* p. 6).

To be sure, Carnap's claims for the rights of philosophy upon science were not based exclusively on a narrow-minded epistemology; there was also the remarkable success that the method had had in nineteenth-century foundational studies and the partial success of its extension to physics in recent years. Moreover, those who claimed to take science itself as their guide had to begin by decoding its message, and it was not clear how in doing so they could avoid the interference of those dreaded philosophical ideas. Even so, there was a clear difference between those who, like Reichenbach and Popper, worried seriously about tailoring their doctrines to the best scientific practice and those who, like Carnap, let logic take them where it chose.[2]

Reichenbach's approach to philosophical questions was inspired by what he would later call the "postulate of utilizability" (see *E & P,* pp. 69–71), a version of the transcendental approach to epistemology. According to this postulate, when a philosopher is concerned with a particular notion, the task is not to analyze it or clarify it or, even less, to determine what it is that people have in mind when they appeal to that notion. The proper goal is to give an account of what would make the actual use of that notion seem rational and justified (see, e.g., "On Probability and Induction," p. 33; *E & P,* sec. 15). For example, Reichenbach once defended his doctrine of single-case probabilities against the charge that his frequentist account does not conform to anybody's intentions by noting:

The explicans given by me has the property of making a man's behavior justifiable whenever he is in a situation which, in correspondence with established usage, he describes by means of the term "probable." . . . This is a sufficient reason to accept my explication. ("The Verifiability Theory of Meaning," p. 52; see also *E & P,* p. 309 and sec. 38., and *The Theory of Probability,* p. viii)

The postulate of utilizability is not easily applied to the analysis of irrational behavior, but it was Reichenbach's guiding principle in his analysis of what he took to be the paradigm of rational behavior, science. Thus, whereas Carnap examined the "scientific" inference that the sun will rise tomorrow from the perspective of someone who has found out elsewhere what one can and cannot reasonably infer from given evidence, Reichenbach took as his *datum* the fact that the inference is reasonable (since it is sanctioned by scientists) and sought an explication that displays its rational character. It is therefore not surprising that whereas Carnap concluded that scientists cannot possibly mean what they say, Reichenbach argued that because scientists mean what they say we must acknowledge a principle of induction as a condition of possibility for those inferences:

> Our conviction as to the justifiability of probability predictions is such a fundamental fact that it is impossible to disabuse ourselves of it. Philosophy cannot consist in criticizing fundamental convictions on the basis of preconceived opinions as to the possibility of inferring certain propositions. Rather, we must simply accept such convictions, leaving to philosophy only the job of fitting them into a system. The justification of our belief in strict logic is, after all, in no better a position. ("The Problem of Causality in Physics" [1931], *Selected Writings, 1909–1953,* vol. 1, p. 341)

As we saw in Chapter 10, Schlick and Reinchenbach were the first among empiricists to promote this type of transcendentalism and to display it in a number of enlightening studies on the philosophies of relativity and quantum physics. But it was Popper who became the better known and more eloquent exponent of that position.[3] Reichenbach did not publish an epistemological treatise until 1938, when *Experience and Prediction* came to light; and then he devoted that book almost entirely to his version of the problem of induction, the problem of how we can go from what we know ("experience") to what we do not know ("prediction"). Moreover, the emerging epistemology was not, like Popper's, the statement of a bold, inspiring program with definite social and political implications, but a relatively pale echo of the insightful analyses of theories that Reichenbach had offered in earlier years.

Popper combined Reichenbach's interest in the specific details of contemporary science with Carnap's respect for logic. But he had a far broader picture of knowledge to offer than Reichenbach's. He recognized much faster than Reichenbach the role of truth, and his respect for logic did not blind him to the idea that there was more to philosophy than the combinatorics of languages. Contrasted with Schlick's Wittgensteinian hesitations, with the reductionist Sturm und Drang of the *Aufbau,* and with the surrealistic atmosphere of *LSL,* Popper's early work shines as a refreshing blend of insight and common sense, combining a host of new ideas with a warm respect for tradition. The *Furor Teutonicus* with which Neurath and Carnap were vibrating at the time in their denunciations of traditional philosophy contrasts sharply with the far more reasonable attitude that Popper displayed toward the past, especially toward Kant.

By 1932 Popper had finished a draft of the first part of his *Two Problems of Epistemology (Die beiden Grundprobleme der Erkenntnistheorie,* henceforth *Two Problems*). Regrettably, the manuscript had to be drastically shortened and revised in order to comply with the publisher's demands, so that when the book was eventually published late in

1934, as *The Logic of Scientific Discovery,* it was a far less detailed and forceful presentation of his ideas.[4] The early manuscript is a better guide to the epistemological situation in Vienna in the early 1930s.

Popper's "problem of induction"

Popper clearly enjoyed the game of *épater le positiviste.* The purpose of his book, he explained, was to develop a theory that borrows from Kant his "problem, his method and essential parts of his solutions" (*Grundprobleme,* p. 18). He did say that *"there are, no doubt, synthetic a priori judgments"* (p. 32), that his purpose, like Kant's, was to develop a "theory of experience," and that the proper method of epistemology was Kant's transcendental method (p. 7). But when these opinions were explained – as Popper did, and quite clearly – it turned out that the ideology underlying this terminology was much farther from Kant's than Carnap's: *"There are, no doubt, synthetic a priori judgments, but they are often a posteriori false"* (p. 32); the "theory of experience, and indeed, of scientific experience" tells us that scientific experience is a method, a method of conjecture and refutation; finally, the "transcendental method" that would turn out to be Popper's leading epistemological maxim involved testing the claims of epistemology by looking at science to see whether successful scientific theories conform to those claims.[5]

According to Popper, the "two major problems of the theory of knowledge" are the problems of induction and demarcation. Roughly speaking, the former concerns the justification of scientific knowledge and the latter its distinction from pseudoscience. Kant's first *Critique,* as Popper read it, is devoted largely to these two great problems; the Transcendental Analytic deals with the problem of induction and the Transcendental Dialectic with the problem of demarcation (*Grundprobleme,* p. 17). Before Popper, no one had been as close as Kant to a solution of these problems. Yet Kant's solutions are not perfect: the Analytic grants too much to rationalism by allowing far too many synthetic a priori judgments, and the Dialectic grants too much to empiricism by demanding too close a link between concepts and experience (pp. 17–18). Popper's purpose was to develop a Kantian standpoint that avoided both excesses. Part 1 of *Two Problems* deals with the problem of induction.[6] It is one of the most interesting and revealing documents of this pre-Tarskian stage of Viennese positivism.

As already noted, Popper's "problem of induction" was the problem of the content and justification of the most general scientific claims: "With what right can such statements be laid down? What exactly does one mean by them?" (*Grundprobleme,* p. 3). We recently saw Carnap and Reichenbach at odds on a version of that problem: We can observe only finitely many events, but science asserts general laws, statements that seem to claim validity for the unobserved and even for an infinite domain of events. Their question was, in effect, "With what right can such statements be laid down? What exactly does one mean by them?" Their specific approach to the problem was "inductive" in the now-standard sense of that word. But Kant's Analytic is not concerned with induction in that sense. "The problem of induction" contained for Popper the ambiguity it already had in the writings of Schlick and Reichenbach. The ambiguity is reflected, for example, in two successive formulations of the problem in Popper's *Logic of Scientific Discovery*, first as "the question whether inductive inferences are justified" (p. 1) and then as "the question concerning the validity (*Geltung*) of general statements of experience" (*Logik der Forschung*, p. 2).[7] The latter formulation is the one to bear in mind.

Traditional solutions to this problem, Popper explained, may be classified according to the way they interpret the content of laws. From this standpoint there are three types of solution: The first and most important one takes laws to be what Popper revealingly called "normal" statements, statements that are decidable; the other two positions construe laws to be probabilistic statements and as rules, respectively. These were, indeed, the basic views on the character of scientific knowledge at the time Popper was writing. Let us consider them in sequence before we turn to Popper's own solution to his problem of induction and to Carnap's reformulation of the whole issue from his new tolerant standpoint.

Wittgenstein's solution: laws as instructions

Physics is not like history. It predicts. If one were to think of physics as a mere report concerning facts already observed, it would lack its most essential element, its relation to the future. It would become the telling of a dream. (Waismann, *Wiener Kreis*, p. 101)

With these words, recorded by Waismann early in 1930, Wittgenstein had taken the same side as Reichenbach in his opposition to Carnap's vision of science, and he had thereby displayed the need to offer a nonreductionist interpretation of laws and hypotheses. According to him, an essential feature of hypotheses (perhaps *the* essential feature)[8] is their link to observational statements whose truth is not yet known. In a similar vein, Schlick had argued in "Causality in Contemporary Physics" (1931) that in order to find out what laws are, one should ask how they are tested: "For the physicist . . . the absolutely decisive and essential thing, is that the equations derived from any data now also hold good of *new* data" (*Philosophical Papers*, vol. 2, p. 185). The "essential characteristic" of a law of nature "is the *fulfillment of predictions*" (p. 185). In order to understand the nature of laws we must examine their link with predictions.

Traditionally it had been thought that hypotheses and laws relate to their associated predictions as the general does to the particular. According to this view 'All swans are white' is not essentially different from a finite conjunction of statements of the form 'If *a* is a swan, then it is white', and its assertion amounts to the assertion of all those instances. But this, Wittgenstein claimed, makes no sense:

It had always been thought that an hypothesis is a proposition (*Satz*) whose truth is less firmly established. People thought: in the case of an hypothesis we have not tested all of the cases, that is why we are less certain of its truth – as though the distinguishing criterion were, so to speak, *historical.* In my conception an hypothesis is *ab initio* a completely different grammatical structure. (Waismann, *Vienna Circle,* pp. 210–11)[9]

The crucial difference between hypotheses and "ordinary" propositions lies in the fact that hypotheses involve universal quantification. Some statements come with quantifier words explicitly displayed somewhere in the sentence, but most of them do not. Yet, as we saw in Chapter 13, Wittgenstein thought that a large number of apparently unquantified statements such as 'My brother is playing the piano in the next room' are really universally quantified and therefore hypothetical (and therefore neither true nor false). How does one tell? How does one decide whether something includes a hidden reference to an indefinite multiplicity, the way hypotheses do? According to Wittgenstein, the decisive clue is that the statement in question appears to be capable of confirmation through a variety of sources. This has *got* to be mere appearance, he thought, since there are no grounds for believing any statement other than the most conclusive, irrefutable, irreversible reasons. We might think, for example, that there are several ways to confirm short of certainty the claim concerning my brother's piano playing. I might open the door and look at him; or I might remember that I saw him alone in the room a moment ago and that no one has gone into the room since then; and so on. The truth of the matter, Wittgenstein thought, is that none of these "observations" in any way helps support the truth of the statement about my brother. Whenever we think that a proposition can be verified in more than one way, what we have is an unverifiable hypothesis and several independently verifiable genuine propositions. All that we verify in such cases is statements such as that I can see a brotherlike entity in the next room, that I can bring forth a certain memory, and so on. As Waismann once put it, "What I have verified are different facts which count as symptoms of something else" ("Hypotheses" [composed before 1936?], p. 44).[10]

When we quantify over a finite domain, Wittgenstein thought, the correct interpretation is the old one: When we quantify on a finite form ('All primary colors are pretty'), the content of this claim is a finite conjunction of "instances" ('Red is pretty & . . . & green is pretty'), and when we quantify over a concept ('All men in this room wear trousers'), the content is the conjunction of instances together with an extremal clause ('Schlick wears trousers & . . . & Wittgenstein wears trousers & those are all the men in this room') (Waismann, *Vienna Circle,* pp. 44–5). But when what others would call the domain of quantification turns out not to be finite, this model should not be extended – as classical logicians attempted to do – but replaced by something radically different. Wittgenstein still believed that a proposition asserts all that follows from it, so that a universal proposition about four things is more complex than one saying the same about only three of them. "But a generality with an infinity of special cases is of an entirely different logical kind. . . . It does not assert an infinite number of propositions" (Wittgenstein, *Lectures, 1930–32,* p. 17). On the notion of infinity itself, Wittgenstein explained:

Infinite is not an answer to the question "How many," the infinite is not a number. It is an infinite possibility in language of constructing propositions. The word "all" [in the finite case] refers to an extension; but it is impossible to refer to an infinite extension. Infinity is the property of a law, not of an extension. (p. 13)

This way of thinking about infinity was by no means idiosyncratic, since the 1920s witnessed a return to the Kantian idea that concepts alone do not suffice for foundational purposes.[11] For example, the alleged arch-enemy of intuitionism, Hilbert, had argued in "On the Infinite" (1925) that existential claims are harder to understand than one might think, since in the interesting cases, they involve the difficulties associated with the notion of infinity. In the finite case, he explained, 'There exists' is "an abbreviation for" the conjunction of finitely many instances; but in the general case this is not so. In order to illustrate the point Hilbert wrote down the largest prime number known at the time (call it p) and noted that by a Euclidean theorem there must be another prime between p and $p! + 1$:

A statement such as 'there exists' an object with a certain property in a finite totality conforms perfectly to our finitary approach. But a statement like 'either $p + 1$ or $p + 2$ or . . . (ad infinitum) . . . has a certain property' is itself an infinite logical product. Such an extension into the infinite is, unless further explanation and precautions are forthcoming, no more permissible than the extension from finite to infinite products in calculus. Such extensions, accordingly, usually lapse into meaninglessness. (p. 144)[12]

It is worth noticing that these difficulties with quantification stem from an analysis of this notion that is radically different from Frege's. For Wittgenstein and Hilbert the basic sense of quantification is spelled out in terms of conjunctions or disjunctions of elementary formulas; for Frege it is explained in terms of instances of concepts. For Wittgenstein, "the understanding of general propositions *palpably* depends on the understanding of elementary propositions" (*Tractatus,* 4.411); for Frege it did not.

In Wittgenstein's conception, quantifiers do not belong in a proper logical language, any more than definite descriptions do in Russell's picture of things. A proper language should have only conjunctions and disjunctions playing the role of quantification; the presence of dubious cases of quantification would be manifested by the inability to formulate infinitely long conjunctions or disjunctions. Frege recognized, of course, that quantification is equivalent to such infinite constructs when they are meaningful; but its sense in no way depends on the meaningfulness of such constructs. The basic explanatory idea is that of exemplification or instantiation; all we need to know in order to understand quantification is what it means to be an instance of a concept. To quantify existentially is merely to say of a concept that it has an instance, and under this interpretation it is transparent that what I *say* does not *depend* on my prior understanding of the elementary statements that instantiated the existential claim; nor does what I say change with the size of the domain about which I am saying it. If I say that there is a table, what I say does not depend on whether the number of tables in the universe is even or odd, large or small, or even infinitely large. Either way, I am saying of a certain concept only that it has instances. Therefore, if we think of objects, tables, for example, as independent of what we might say about them, then it appears that given a concept such as *x is a table,* the truth of the claim that it has instances has nothing whatever to do with infinity.

Wittgenstein could not accept Frege's opinion because of the verificationist character of his semantics. For him nothing can be true (indeed, nothing can be said) if in the natural course of things we cannot come to know for certain that it is true or that it is false. As mentioned in Chapter 13, Wittgenstein asked Ramsey how one would verify an infinitely long conjunction.[13] Because one cannot, universally quantified statements must be interpreted as something radically different from genuine claims.

Schlick followed Wittgenstein in applying the restricted notion of quantification to laws. Since in the case of laws a definitive verification is impossible, Schlick concluded that laws do not have the "logical character of an *assertion*" (*Philosophical Papers,* vol. 2, p. 187), that is, "of statements that are true or false" (p. 195). What, then, is a law? We know already that it is not an assertion about reality and that its essential characteristic is its link with predictions. These two points are really all that is involved in the doctrine that hypotheses are instructions for the construction of propositions not already verified, instructions linking those statements that describe the given and the giveable in experience.

One favorite Wittgensteinian picture represents hypotheses as three-dimensional bodies (Waismann, *Vienna Circle,* p. 100). A hypothesis "is a law for forming expectations. A proposition is, so to speak, a particular cross-section of an hypothesis" (*Philosophical Remarks,* pp. 285–6). Echoing Wittgenstein, Waismann explained:

The phenomena we observe are then, as it were, the individual cross-sections we make in different places through the body. In other words, the individual experiences are inserted in the hypothesis like cross-sections in a three-dimensional body. *Strictly speaking,* what we can verify is always only *one* such cross-section. In cases where it looks as if we had verified the same proposition in different ways, we have really verified different cross-sections of the same hypothesis. ("Hypotheses," p. 44)

Hypotheses are

the connecting link we insert between the actual experiences of the past and the actual experiences of the future. Indeed, to an astronomer it never really matters whether the law of gravity 'is valid for all eternity' – this would be a question which we could never come any closer to answering . . . – but whether it *stands the test,* whether he *succeeds* with this assumption. (pp. 39–40)[14]

Schlick thought that this new conception of laws automatically solved the problem of induction. That problem, he explained, "consists, of course, in asking for the logical justification of general propositions about reality. . . . We acknowledge, with Hume, that there is no logical justification for them; there cannot be any, because they are simply not genuine propositions" ("Causality in Contemporary Physics" [1931], *Philosophical Papers,* vol. 2, p. 197).

But, of course, to claim that laws cannot be justified because they say nothing is not to solve the problem of induction but to invite a reformulation of it.[15] There surely is *some* epistemologically significant difference between the hypothesis that my brother is in the next room and its denial, between the hypothesis that the sun will rise tomorrow and its denial, between the laws of Einstein's theory and those of Newton. If hypotheses say nothing at all, we may not talk about what justifies our belief that they are true; but there remains the question of how one can reasonably choose which ones to believe or, at any rate, act upon. Schlick's solution was therefore quite empty. A proper solution from a Wittgensteinian standpoint would have had to rely entirely on the fine structure of the predictive character of laws in order to rank them by epistemic merit. An account of this type was first presented by Popper in *Two Problems.*

Reichenbach's solution: laws as probabilistic
statements

Reichenbach's solution is interesting both for its virtues and for its vices. It was inspired by pregnant insights, such as the idea that any account of hypothetical knowledge must make sense of its capacity to generate justified predictions about unobserved facts and the idea that a proper epistemology must be based on a principle weaker than certainty. But it is also interesting to see how these insights were deflected from their proper purpose by Reichenbach's blindness toward semantic matters.

We have recently seen Reichenbach's justified astonishment at Carnap's refusal to think that science can assert anything we do not already know (through observational means). Scientific knowledge involves as its essential element the possibility of predicting what is not known with certainty. We can predict that the sun will rise tomorrow, and this is not a misleading reformulation of previous observations of the sun but a statement about an event in the future. Wittgenstein said in the *Tractatus,* "That the sun will rise tomorrow, is an hypothesis; and that means that we do not *know* whether it will rise" (6.36311). Reichenbach took this to mean that when we contrast that prediction with a randomly chosen one, such as that I will grow another leg tomorrow morning, "we know exactly the same amount in the two cases – namely, nothing" ("The Problem of Causality in Physics," *Selected Writings, 1909–1953,* vol. 1, p. 340).

This is one point where Reichenbach chose to apply his transcendental method. Our actual behavior belies the skeptical conclusion concerning those predictions: We make plans on the assumption that the sun will rise tomorrow, but we do not spend the night adding a third leg to our trousers. Between Wittgensteinian knowledge and ignorance there must be a continuum of degrees of rational belief associated with factual statements. In order to solve the problem of the nature and justification of scientific knowledge, one must begin by recognizing and accepting the fact that we endorse knowledge claims about the unknown (contra Carnap) and that we are justified in doing so in conformity with rules (contra Popper).

Apart from the skeptical and positivist errors, Reichenbach thought there was a further error to be avoided in order to solve the problem of induction. Even if positivism was wrong, one should avoid the most traditional confusions concerning truth, wisely avoided by positivists and Kantians. The worst offender was what Reichenbach called the "standard" solution, the appeal to that "auxiliary construction," the classical concept of truth. This standard solution contends that the prediction statement in itself (*an sich*) is true or false; only our knowledge is incomplete. We can indeed approach this ideal of truth in our knowledge, but one can never attain it. This is the common understanding of the problem: the undecidability is transferred to human imperfection, and the ideal of strict truth for statements in themselves is preserved. ("Der physikalische Wahrheitsbegriff," p. 161)

However popular, this view is untenable and its conception of truth is empty because "it fails to offer a procedure by which we approach this ideal truth" (p. 161). Truth is an ideal limit in a process of approximation. This ideal

possesses the significance only of a limit, and just as the limit is not something that exists in itself, but simply takes on the meaning possessed by the process of approximation, the scientific concept of truth can acquire meaning only through the formulation of the method of approximation actually used in science. (p. 161)

This is why he thought probability must come before truth in epistemology and why all attempts like Wittgenstein's, Waismann's, and eventually Carnap's to base probability on truth are doomed to failure.

Perhaps the main source of confusion in Reichenbach's rejection of truth was not so much verificationism as his characteristically Kantian-positivist inability to draw Bolzano's and Frege's distinction between content and assertion. The blend of concept and intuition required for what Kant called "cognition" (*Erkenntnis*) was easily turned into a blend of content and evidential justification; and in the process it seemed dogmatic and metaphysical to talk of judgments outside contexts where they are justified. In agreement with that style of thinking, the Bolzanian content of a sentence is, for Reichenbach, an impossibly unrealistic construct that applies only to fictional circumstances that could never be realized in actual, empirical fact (which he cannot consistently distinguish from known fact). This refusal to detach content from ground is the source of Reichenbach's views concerning the "fundamentally probabilistic character of science" ("Causality and Probability," *Selected Writings, 1909–1953*, vol. 2, p. 339) and his attendant rejection of determinism. In his view all nonlogical statements are probabilistic: "Every physical statement, whether about a single physical system or about the validity of a physical law in general, is a probabilistic statement" ("Der physikalische Wahrheitsbegriff," p. 166). For example, "The statement that a street is between 1 and 100 yards long must therefore be regarded as a probability statement" ("Causality and Probability," *Selected Writings, 1909–1953*, vol. 2, p. 336).

What Reichenbach meant, of course, is that even the statement that this street is between 1 and 100 yards long is not knowable with Cartesian certainty. Yet he could not distinguish between this reasonable observation and the utterly unreasonable one that every empirical claim attributes a probability to something. "In the domain of predictive statements only probability statements have sense, not strict truth statements" ("Der physikalische Wahrheitsbegriff," p. 169). Thus, he was quite unmoved by Popper's devastating criticism that Reichenbach's approach gives the nonsensical result that the probability of a hypothesis will be $\frac{1}{2}$ (rather than 0) when every second member of the propositional sequence contradicts it (*The Logic of Scientific Discovery*, sec. 80). Reichenbach replied, "I can see nothing nonsensical about it" ("Induction and Probability," *Selected Writings, 1909–1953*, vol. 2, p. 378).

This train of thought led Reichenbach to conclude that classical logic is inadequate for the interpretation of empirical knowledge. In his view Carnap's problems with epistemology were due to his commitment to Frege's and Russell's logic, where there are only two truth values: truth and falsehood. We may, perhaps, assign truth or falsehood to fully verified statements (such as those describing "facts of zero level"). If we circumscribe our attention to reports such as those inscribed in the scientist's protocol (report book) there is no problem: "The truth of these statements is easily decided for they assert nothing more than the occurrence of perceptual experiences" ("The Physical Concept of Truth," *Selected Writings, 1909–1953*, vol. 1, p. 345). But science is never satisfied with what Kant called the perceptual level. It must proceed to the level of judgments of experience, and here, Reichenbach thought, we are in the realm of prediction:

How is the truth of predictions to be decided? The protocol of the experimental physicist may be true while the prediction based upon it is false. *The truth of a prediction is therefore of a different kind from the truth of a report statement, this is the great epistemological problem of scientific truth.* ("Der physikalische Wahrheitsbegriff," p. 159)

This problem has often been obscured by the fact that – in accord with the "classical" picture of truth – one assumes a fictitious observer determining at a time still in the future what the observational truth is about the predicted situation. But this is unacceptable, "for what we need is a truth decision *before* that confirmation; we need to know how to evaluate predictions as predictions; transforming them into report statements at a later time is not the answer" ("Der physikalische Wahrheitsbegriff," p. 159).

Clearly, for all his alleged semantic tolerance, Reichenbach's rejection of the "classical" view was based on a conception even narrower than Wittgenstein's, since the small class of claims Wittgenstein called propositions did include sentences of unknown truth value, sentences that were as true or false for Wittgenstein as they were for Bolzano, quite independently of whether they referred to the future. In contrast, for Reichenbach, the only "truth values" one can assign are the ones we can attribute to propositions right *now,* so that even when the proposition is fully verifiable in the future, its "truth value" is neither 0 (falsehood) nor 1 (truth), but a number measuring the reliability of the claim in question at the present time.

Thus misinspired, Reichenbach proceeded to construct his new logic as follows: Probabilistic logic consists of a technique for assigning "truth values" (numbers from 0 to 1) to the sentences of a scientific language, where these numbers reflect the degree to which it is rational to believe the given statements. Roughly speaking, the idea is that the weight of an atomic expression 'Fa' ($W(Fa)$) will be the proportion of true (*sic*) sentences (the frequentist probability) in the "best," presumably finite, sequence $\langle Ft_1, Ft_2, \ldots \rangle$ of which we have direct knowledge. The weight of molecular (nonquantified) expressions is generated from those of the atomic constituents by means of probabilistic laws.[16] In analogy with the traditional method of truth tables, we have (a) a technique for assigning certain valuations to atomic elements and (b) a technique for extending those valuations from the elementary to the molecular cases. But this is as far as the analogy goes.

It is clear that Reichenbach's construction has only the remotest connection with logic. Reichenbach told how to find the correct evaluation for the formulas in L (by finding the appropriate frequentist probability and then extending it to molecular formulas in a nonextensional fashion), but he did not say which truth values are to be treated as distinguished, nor did he identify the formulas with a distinguished truth value for arbitrary evaluations. This is the exact opposite of what logic is supposed to do. Logicians are not interested in the "correct" assignment of truth values — that is *precisely* not their job; the task is to define distinguished truth values and then identify those formulas that have distinguished truth values under *all* valuations. Logicians never care about the assignment of truth values at any given knowledge state; but that is all that Reichenbach's "logic" cares about. Thus, Reichenbach's presentation of his logic as an alternative to classical logic was based entirely on a misunderstanding.

As a contribution to the problem of induction, Reichenbach's logic did not fare much better. He made an effort to associate numbers with claims in ways that involve frequencies. But Popper's criticism of Reichenbach's assignment of weights to laws establishes conclusively that those numbers cannot seriously be construed as measures of the degree to which the claims in question may rationally be held as true.

By 1935 Reichenbach had come across another effort to justify a frequentist assignment of probabilities to judgments, his famous vindication
of induction. That effort was also unsuccessful, but its history pertains to
a later stage in the development of positivism.

Laws as normal statements and Popper's solution

The guiding idea behind *Two Problems* was the transcendental principle
according to which

epistemological assertions and concepts can and must be critically tested in
relation to the actual justification procedures of the empirical sciences – and
only in relation to them. . . . The theory of knowledge is the science of science: It
relates to the specific empirical sciences as these relate to empirical reality.
(*Grundprobleme*, p. 7)

This technique would guide Popper not only in his search for worthy
epistemological conjectures, but also in the process of criticizing and
refuting alternatives.

A "normal" statement, Popper explained in *Two Problems*, is one that
is "conclusively decidable" (p. 40) or "decidably true or false" (p. 42).
Pre-Humean positivists (and those who had misunderstood Hume's lessons, such as Reichenbach) thought that experience could provide the
source of knowledge needed to decide universal statements or statements about the unknown. But since Hume, we have known that *if* laws
are decidable and *if* they are based on experience, then they can only be
reports of past experience. This implication (let us call it "Hume's thesis") was the basic fact behind Popper's critical analysis of the problem of
induction. "Strict positivism" was Popper's name for the view (apparently
Carnap's in 1929) that laws can only be reports of past experience. Kant
saw "that the consequences of Hume's argument leave open only two
alternatives [within the normal-statement interpretation]: the position
here designated *strict positivism* (roughly, Hume's standpoint) and the
position of apriorism" (*Grundprobleme*, p. 59).

Both the Kantian and the strict positivist accept Hume's thesis, and
both assume that laws are normal statements. Hence, they conclude that
to the extent that laws are grounded on experience they cannot refer to
the unknown. They diverge only on whether at this point one should
apply modus ponens or modus tollens. The strict positivist assumes that
scientific laws can be supported only by experience and concludes that
we can never be justified in accepting a universal law or a prediction,
literally interpreted. For the strict positivist, universal laws should be
read as misleading reports of the already observed (*Grundprobleme*, pp.
47–8) or, better yet, à la Mach, as economic forms of expression that

carry the tacit proviso "so far as we have already observed" (p. 48; see also p. 42). The Kantian, in contrast, assumes that some of our nomic knowledge concerns the future or the unknown and concludes that laws are not always grounded on experience. Popper thought that both the Kantian and the strict positivist solutions were incorrect. Why?

Hume and Kant assumed that experience *can* be the ground of validity (*Geltungsgrund*) of some claims but not of others, "that experience is in a position to establish with certainty (*sicherzustellen*) the validity of our knowledge, through only the validity of *particular* reality statements" (*Grundprobleme,* p. 62). Popper would eventually challenge this standpoint, but in *Two Problems* he agreed:

This presupposition that we are justified in grounding on experience [*auf Erfahrung zu gründen*] . . . some assertions about reality, this presupposition that experience is admissible as a ground of validity in general, should not be doubted in and of itself; in any case, every experimental science, indeed, all knowledge about reality in general rests on it. . . . Hume was surely right in not regarding this ultimate datum with scepticism. (p. 62)[17]

This assumption is what Kant called the "possibility of experience"; in Popper's opinion it was not only true but a priori true, though he would remain undecided on whether it was analytic (pp. 62–3).

It would be a mistake to look for hidden subtleties in this straightforward statement. Like almost everyone else in his neighborhood, Popper was still taking for granted that "normal" statements, such as observational reports, can be conclusively established or disproved on the basis of observational data. Elsewhere in *Two Problems* he explained that for "predictions" or individual sentences such as 'Napoleon carried a sword', one may identify truth and confirmation without contradiction because

when it is verified by experience, it is *conclusively* verified. It is *true*. . . . But with strictly general assertions of reality things are different: A hypothesis can be confirmed throughout a long period of time and even today; but perhaps tomorrow it will no longer be confirmed. (p. 155; see also p. 256)

We shall soon encounter further evidence of the same attitude.

If there is a "decidable" empirical basis, what is wrong with strict positivism? Kant had rejected it, claiming that Hume's criticism was self-destructive, since the empirical basis (the only one that Hume acknowledged) presupposed the same sorts of general principles involved in the justification of general laws. The deduction of the categories and of the corresponding *Grundsätze* was Kant's argument to establish that all forms of scientific experience and all forms of objectivity, however modest and untheoretical they may seem, presuppose regularities. "Kant's solution to Hume's problem" can be stated as follows: "General reality statements can be true or false [*sic*] no less than particular reality state-

ments, for the former presuppose no more and no less than the latter"
(*Grundprobleme,* p. 68). Popper expressed great sympathy with Kant's
line of reasoning, but not with his conclusion. He would soon be explaining at great length how wrong it is to assume that laws of nature "can be
true or false." So the refutation of strict positivism must be elsewhere.

Popper's refutation of strict positivism involved the transcendental
method, for it emerged from a comparison of strict positivism "with the
actual procedure of the empirical sciences" (p. 48). Strict positivism
turns science into an irrational activity, Popper explained, because if laws
were summaries of reports of past observations, there would be no way
to make sense of the fact that scientists make predictions *and* test their
theories by determining whether those predictions are true (p. 49).
When Eddington predicted that the light ray from a certain star would
reach a certain spot on earth, he did not rest content in the knowledge
that this remark safely summarized his past experience; he traveled to
Principe to see if the prediction was true. Since the philosopher's job is
not to show that scientists behave incoherently but to reveal the structure of their coherent behavior, strict positivism must be abandoned.

According to Popper, Kant recognized that laws apply beyond the field
of past experience. But like Hume, he did not challenge the assumption
that they "can be true or false" and was thereby led to infer their a priori
character. Kant succeeded in establishing that all knowledge is a search
for laws (p. 78) and that objectivity is the intersubjective testability of
laws (p. 67). *If* there is knowledge, there must be laws; that much is true.
But Kant was wrong in assuming that there *must* be knowledge. "If we
desire knowledge we must seek after natural laws. . . . But we must by no
means presuppose that there are strictly general regularities; it suffices to
know that our knowledge consists in the search for strictly general regularities – as if there were such" (p. 79). The "as if" is all we are entitled
to assert – not, as in Kant, the unconditional necessity of regularities.
This disposes of the second version of the "normal-statement" picture of
hypotheses.

Given Hume's thesis, Kantianism and strict positivism are the only
alternatives if one assumes that laws are normal statements. Since Popper
thought that both of these doctrines were refuted, he concluded that the
interpretation of laws as normal statements must be false. Modern
positivism had recognized this fact but failed to offer a positive and
defensible theory of laws. Popper sought to establish this by criticizing
the theories of Wittgenstein and Reichenbach. In his criticism of the
doctrine of laws as instructions, Popper noted that many statements
other than laws can be read as "instructions for the construction of
statements." For example, the laws of Newtonian mechanics may be seen
as providing, in an appropriate context, instructions to construct the

statement 'This projectile will have a parabolic trajectory'; but this prediction may in turn be seen as involving the instruction to construct the sentence 'This projectile will fall at this particular place', and so on (pp. 161–2). The characterization of laws as instructions is therefore not specific enough, and the key difference between laws and "genuine" propositions must lie elsewhere.

Popper's guess was that the real motivation lies in a confusion concerning the behavior of laws toward truth and falsehood. Strict inductivists and Kantians were guilty of having assumed "that natural laws can be true or false" (p. 256).[18] We know this is wrong, because "general reality assertions can never be true (for science) – this was established by our critique of the normal-statement standpoint" (p. 159).[19] The new inductivists (Wittgenstein, Schlick, Waismann) had recognized the fact that hypotheses cannot be true, but they had wrongly concluded that they could not be false either, and this is what led them to look for a representation of laws as something other than statements. Reichenbach's probabilistic project shows that he is guilty of essentially the same mistake. What they all failed to see – what everyone before Popper failed to notice – is the crucial asymmetry of laws vis-à-vis their behavior toward truth values. In fact, natural laws "can never be [demonstrably] true":

Whereas particular reality statements are in principle completely *verifiable or falsifiable,* things are different for general reality statements: They can indeed be conclusively *falsified,* they can acquire a conclusive *negative truth value* (*Geltungswert*), but not a positive one:[20] the positive value is of an essentially *different kind* than the negative; it is, if you wish, a pragmatic value that can be designated a "corroboration value." (p. 256)

Most positivists had, indeed, come to think that laws cannot be "true" (i.e., conclusively verified); and they had learned from Duhem that no particular law can be "false" (conclusively refuted) either. Popper's alternative proposal was based on the idea that Duhem's claim is untenable. In his opinion, there can be no doubt that some general statements are conclusively refuted. For example, the statement that all books are bound in red leather in conjunction with the premise 'This is a book' leads to the prediction that this book is bound in red leather:

I can falsify this prediction. Therefore, one of the assumptions must be false. The second assumption was a specific reality statement that can be conclusively verified. Therefore, the other assumption is *conclusively falsified.* Can one raise any objection against these trivial considerations? I don't think so. Such an objection should deny the *conclusive verifiability of specific reality assertions.* (Such objections go beyond the problem of induction and . . . should not be taken seriously.) (pp. 260–1)

Blinded by Duhem's argument and by the idea that conclusive refutation is impossible, positivists failed to see that the relation of laws to truth is quite different from their relation to falsehood, and this asymmetry is the key to *both* of the fundamental problems of epistemology. Popper's solution to the problem of induction would be to say that the reasons we have for the acceptance of a law are always negative: We have tried hard to refute the law and we have not yet succeeded. The problem of demarcation was solved by the criterion that characterizes as scientific what could in principle be refuted.

The preceding summary of Popper's views in *Two Problems* makes it clear that Popper's solutions to his "two fundamental problems" were based on that great positivistic and neo-Kantian favorite, the confusion between truth and conclusive verification or certainty. Once that confusion is granted, it follows that those who worry about the "truth" of laws are wasting their time. Those people are inductivists and probabilists. They fail to see that

natural laws are *fictions;* for they do not represent any real state of affairs. The assertion that there are general states of affairs is rationalistic. . . . It is remarkable that the logical positivist Carnap talks without further ado about *general states of affairs,* in opposition to the individual ones. (p. 279)

If one further grants the conclusive decidability of observational statements, it follows that laws can be "false"; and if one will settle for nothing less than conclusive evidence, the reasonable thing to do is to concern oneself only with this "truth value."

Reichenbach was no less involved than Popper in the confusion between truth and certainty, and like Popper, he recognized that, at least in the case of laws, certainty is an unattainable ideal. Yet he quite plausibly thought that genuine knowledge might be characterized by something less than certainty but more than sheer epistemic indifference. Like most other positivists, indeed, like most other human beings, Reichenbach thought that there are less than perfect reasons to believe what we believe. Thus, he was unimpressed by Popper's dilemma between absolute verification and total epistemic ignorance concerning the truth value of true laws. Moreover, by 1932 Neurath had been urging his colleagues in the Vienna circle for quite some time to acknowledge that nothing at all, not even one of Popper's basic sentences, is ever conclusively verified. Under his influence, the positivists finally turned to the question of the empirical basis of empirical knowledge. Those who tried to take a stand found themselves, as we shall soon see, in very strange corners.

Popper's remarkable response to Reichenbach's and Neurath's challenge was presented in *The Logic of Scientific Discovery* and was the philosophical equivalent of a *salto mortale:* First, he admitted that there is no certainty in science or anywhere else, in effect withdrawing the arguments offered in *Two Problems* against Duhem. He then added that nothing at all is known *even* with probability and that there is no such thing as "reasons to believe" that science or anything else is true. He argued brilliantly that science is not knowledge in the philosophical sense of *episteme,* involving absolute certainty. Reichenbach and Neurath had recognized the point and the other positivists quickly accepted it. But then Popper went on to say that science is not knowledge even in the ordinary sense of the word and that there is no reason whatever to believe that what scientific assertions say is true. He was, in effect, reviving that extreme form of Pyrrhonian skepticism that Hume had described as the doctrine that "all is uncertain, and . . . our judgment is not in *any* thing possest of *any* measures of truth and falsehood" (*A Treatise of Human Nature,* p. 183).[21]

These doctrines annihilate the case that Popper had built in *Two Problems* for his deductivist solution to the problem of induction, and no new case was offered in its place. Yet the same solution – the same *sentences,* anyway – were offered in *The Logic of Scientific Discovery.* He still said that a statement is scientific when it is refutable and that the problem of induction is solved by the observation that clever efforts to refute a theory are all one can offer in its "support." Yet refutation was no longer the logical conflict between a theory *T* and certain factual statements that we know or have good reason to believe are true, but between *T* and statements that we have *decided* to regard as true, by convention. Moreover, the contradiction between *T* and the "refuting" statements was itself the result of another convention. Thus, the solution to the problem of how laws are justified was that they are not; and Popper's surrealistic description of scientific testing was that it is a process whereby we accept certain statements by convention and then determine whether in conformity with some other conventions these statements conflict with the theory being tested. The inspiring rhetoric of *The Logic of Scientific Discovery* suggested a *great* deal more than this, all of it in the spirit of the now-abandoned ideas of *Two Problems,* and most of it in stark conflict with Popper's revised standpoint. But the philosophy behind the persistent rhetoric no longer had anything to offer in support of the notion that science bears any interesting epistemological relation to reality.

Conventionalism had started as an insightful doctrine about a previously uncharted domain of knowledge. By the early 1930s in Vienna, it had become a security blanket that positivists embraced whenever they did not know what to do with a problem. The worst aspects of this development will emerge in the next chapter, when we examine the debates on the character of the empirical basis. But the influence of this attitude is already clear at the level of hypotheses. Further evidence of the very mixed value of the conventionalist message is found in Carnap's radically revised theory of hypotheses of the early 1930s.

The new Carnap

By 1933 Carnap had abandoned his earlier strict positivist stance in the sense that he now thought of it as one possibility among many. In his new tolerant mood he decided that it was wrong to put forth a view of hypotheses intended to exclude any other, as if there were a truth or falsity of the matter. There isn't. Different theories of hypotheses ought to be regarded as alternative proposals, some more useful than others, perhaps, but none of them ever true. Carnap explained, for example, that if one thinks (as he used to, in his dogmatist years) that a sentence is meaningful only if it is completely verifiable, then laws are excluded from the language of science and must be reinterpreted either as misleading reports of past observations (as he had thought they were) or as instructions for the construction of predictions (à la Wittgenstein) and therefore as "syntactical rules" (*LSL,* p. 321). Either of these alternatives is fine, so long as neither is put forth as the "correct" way of looking at things. The claim that a sentence is meaningful only if completely verifiable is now no longer a true statement about meaning but an admissible and arbitrary statement of what we intend to mean by the word 'meaningful' – much as if we were to say that a sentence is meaningful if believed true, if believed by Carnap, or if believed by all deranged aviators. One may choose any notion of meaning one wishes; under a "nonverificationist" doctrine of meaning, laws may be included in the language of science as normal quantified statements. Carnap now thought that this was "better adapted to the ordinary use of language in the actual sciences" (*LSL,* p. 321), although he did not explain why adaptedness to the ordinary use of language was a decisive consideration. It certainly wasn't when he started to construct the world.

Carnap was therefore willing to tolerate the positions of Wittgenstein and of his former self.[22] His tolerance did not extend to either Reichenbach's or Popper's views, however. Of Reichenbach, all he would say in *LSL* was that "there can be no rules of induction," because the content of a law always exceeds that of any finite class of protocols (p. 317). (If the definition of 'content' were really a mere convention, it would be hard to understand this as an objection to anybody's views.) And in response, no doubt, to Popper's *Two Problems,* Carnap pointed out:

There is in the strict sense no refutation (falsification) of an hypothesis; for even when it proves to be L-incompatible with certain protocol-sentences, there always exists the possibility of maintaining the hypothesis and renouncing the acknowledgement of the protocol-sentences. Still less is there in the strict sense a complete confirmation (verification) of an hypothesis. . . . Further, it is, in general, impossible to test even an isolated hypothetical sentence . . . the remaining hypotheses must also be used. Thus *the test applies, at bottom, not to an isolated hypothesis but to the whole system of physics as a system of hypotheses* (Duhem, Poincaré). (*LSL,* p. 318)

If we ignore for a moment the semantic conventionalist dimension of his views, Carnap's position on hypotheses in *LSL* can be characterized as a form of object-language holism. The adequacy of hypotheses is to be judged on the basis of their relation to observation or protocol sentences; and the adequacy of the latter is a matter for scientists to decide (although the philosopher may be allowed to observe, presumably as a matter of contingent empirical fact, that all protocols are revisable). The link between hypotheses and protocols was described in agreement with the standard hypotheticodeductivist position (including a sketch of the D–N model of explanation [pp. 319–20]). But neither confirmation nor refutation can, in fact, be targeted to single sentences; only an act of convention may lead us to "blame," and thereby to drop, this or that element of a theory when a clash with fact (rather, a conflict between sentences) arises. The idea that empirical content may be apportioned "sentence by sentence" had been dropped.

Nothing within the scope of epistemology has an immutable nature – or a mutable one, for that matter. There are simply no facts of epistemology. Once the psychologist, the sociologist, the biologist, and all the other honest scientists have spoken their piece about the character of knowledge, there is still a modest little corner left for the philosopher. But what is specific to the philosopher does not consist in the performance of acts of knowledge but of (friendly) acts of the will, in which stipulations and conventions are proposed. Everything is revisable, *and* nothing in particular *need* be revised. Thus, the revisability of protocols already mentioned is only one aspect of a more radical revisability of everything in sight:

If a sentence which is an L-consequence of certain P-primitive sentences [i.e., physical laws] contradicts a sentence which has been stated as a protocol-sentence, then some change must be made in the system. For instance, the P-rules [i.e., the physical transformation rules] can be altered in such a way that those particular primitive sentences are no longer valid; or the protocol-sentence can be taken as being non-valid; or again the L-rules which have been used in the deduction can also be changed. (*LSL,* p. 317)

Yes, even logic is subject to revision on the basis of what might loosely be described as empirical grounds:

No rule of the physical language is definitive; all rules are laid down with the reservation that they may be altered as soon as it seems expedient to do so. This applies not only to the P-rules but also to the L-rules, including those of mathematics. In this respect, there are only differences in degree; certain rules are more difficult to renounce than others. (p. 318)

This holistic position sounds exactly like a doctrine later advanced by Quine *against* Carnap. One may, however, wonder whether Carnap's holistic remarks were carefully worded statements of his views or hasty concessions to Neurath's persistent, overbearing pressure.

We can clarify the matter by considering briefly Schlick's reaction to Carnap's claims that on the matter of giving up logic or physics "there are only differences in degree" and that there is really no fact of the matter to the question of whether the truth value of a synthetic statement is determined by linguistic facts. This doctrine was considered in Chapter 17, when we were examining Carnap's rejection of Wittgenstein's linguistic "dogmatism" and its implications for the nature of logic. Schlick focused on its implications concerning the nature of physics, and he stated his views in a paper entitled "Are Natural Laws Conventions?" ([1935] *Philosophical Papers,* vol. 2).

Schlick began that paper by stressing the insights implicit in the conventionalist developments stretching from Helmholtz to Poincaré and Wittgenstein. Thanks to them, he explained, we now have a better grasp of the grammatical character of geometry. But how far ought this conventionalism to extend? The language in which we speak of physical relations must have its own grammar, "and there is no doubt that this is determined by convention. Are natural laws these conventions perhaps? Do the natural laws perhaps represent nothing else but the grammar of the natural sciences . . .?" (p. 438). Some philosophers and scientists have given an affirmative answer to this question; but this answer "rests on a grave logical error which . . . can be cleared up in a few words" (p. 438). It is no trivial mistake, however, for it displays the most thorough and, indeed, "dangerous" misunderstanding of the nature of scientific knowledge.

The question whether something is conventional or factual, Schlick explained, is itself not to be decided by a convention. There is a sharp, objective distinction between these two notions. A convention may be maintained under all circumstances. "Experience might well suggest but can never compel its abandonment" (p. 438). Standing by a convention may be inadvisable and even wrongheaded, but it may never be "false." Yet statements of fact are always true or false; their acceptability is determined by circumstances quite outside our will.[23] For example, we might stubbornly insist on using Euclidean geometry in the formulation of relativistic physics. We would be doing something quite unnatural, but we would not be saying anything false.

Would the same be true of, for example, the law of energy conservation? If we think of that law as entirely embodied in the equation $E = W + Q$ and we notice that E can be determined only through measurements of W and Q, we may easily be tempted to conclude that the law is a definition. The essence of the energy equation is not apparent in those symbols, however, but in something that "cannot be read out of the equation itself but must be added as a special comment" (p. 439), that the value of E is independent of the path by which the transformation takes place. One can, of course, *turn* this law into a convention by postulating inaccessible and unobservable energies whenever experience seems to conflict with it. But then one will simply have changed the meaning of the law; one will have chosen not to mean by the words in that natural law what the physicist now means. The principle will have become a convention at the price of completely modifying its meaning.

In general, Carnap thought, nomic conventionalism stems from a failure to observe consistently the distinction between the vehicle of information, that is, the sentence, and the information conveyed.[24] Mathematically minded people are used to dealing with a discipline in which meaning lies entirely within the domain of the symbolism and the associated calculations. After a physical theory has been developed, "the mathematician amuses himself by investigating the mutual connections, derivabilities, and transformabilities of the single statements" (p. 441). In this type of work, one loses track of what is definitional and what is factual simply because one has given up the essential semantic factors.[25]

When Schlick's paper was read (by Feigl) at the 1935 Paris conference – presumably without the specific reference to Carnap quoted later – Carnap could not imagine who its target was. This is a revealing indication of the extent to which he had failed to think through the implications of his Neurathian remarks. Carnap wondered if the target might be the archconventionalist Dingler. He wrote to Schlick about this and was shocked to hear that the target was Carnap (Letter from Schlick to Carnap, 14 November 1935, RC 102-70-10, and from Carnap to Schlick, 4 December 1935, RC 102-70-11, ASP). In the published version of Schlick's paper, a concluding footnote spelled out the connection for Carnap to see:

When Carnap explains . . . that one can construct a language with "extra-logical" transformation rules by, for instance, including natural laws among the principles (i.e., they are considered as grammatical rules), then this way of putting things seems to me misleading in the same sense as is the thesis of conventionalism. It is true that a sentence (a sign sequence) which, under the presuppositions of customary grammar, expresses a natural law can be made into a principle of language simply by stipulating it as a syntactical rule. But precisely by this device one changes the grammar and, consequently, interprets the sentence in an entirely new sense, or, rather, one deprives the sentence of its original sense. It is then not a natural law any more at all; it is not even a proposition, but merely a rule for the manipulation of signs. This whole reinterpretation appears therefore trivial and useless. Any interpretation which blurs such fundamental distinctions is extremely dangerous. ("Are Natural Laws Conventions?" *Philosophical Papers,* vol. 2, p. 445)

Whether motivated by Schlick's criticism or for reasons of his own, the fact is that Carnap soon came to terms with the fact that the extreme conventionalism (or pragmatism) that Neurath had inspired was inconsistent with the basic doctrines of his *LSL.* The Carnap who had seen no clear-cut difference between what pertains to logic and what pertains to physics or facts cannot be seriously regarded as the author of *The Logical Syntax of Language.* He was not the one who conceived those sharp distinctions that lie at the very heart of the syntacticist project; he was not the one who devoted so much time to the characterization of 'analytic' or to the doctrine that truth is definable in logic and mathematics but nowhere else; above all, he was not the one who inspired a whole conception of philosophy as based on the sharp and quite ungradual distinction between what goes on in the metalanguage (proper philosophy, syntax, the formal mode) and what goes on in the object language (factual research). The pragmatist Carnap did make a brief appearance in various corners of *LSL;* but he could make no sense of the main philosophical thesis of that book, that philosophical research (in the metalanguage) and factual research (in the object language) are essentially distinct types of activities.[26]

One may therefore look (as Carnap eventually did) for a different, nonpragmatic interpretation of Carnap's holistic pronouncements, one that makes them consistent with the main thrust of *LSL.* One may argue, for example, that when Carnap talked about the revisability of logic, what he had in mind was in fact the revisability of *language,* that is, the possibility of giving up one language form for another when pragmatic circumstances make that advisable. The principle of tolerance had, after all, been proclaiming that possibility from the very beginning. When Carnap said, in effect, that logic (language) is revisable for empirical reasons, he was not saying that logic is empirical – indeed, he would soon be quite literally shocked to discover that some very clever people at Harvard thought just that.[27] Pragmatism obliterates the distinction between the abandonment of a factual claim and the abandonment of a language framework. Both may be grounded on empirical reasons; but they will be very different reasons. A factual claim may be false; it may assert empirical facts that are not the case. We may have empirical reasons to believe that it asserts a falsehood and thereby to reject the claim. A language framework, however, cannot possibly be false; it cannot possibly clash with anything at all, empirical or otherwise. Consequently, it makes no sense whatever to say that experience might offer grounds to conclude that it is false. Nonetheless, the principle of tolerance offered alternatives of which some use must be made. A linguistic framework may be replaced by another one, and there may be good pragmatic or, if you will, empirical reasons to do so – for example, one framework may allow us to do things we want to do but could not do without it. In this way there may be empirical grounds for replacing a logical system by another, without questioning the view that both logical systems are a priori, in the sense of Chapter 14.

From as far back as we have evidence about his opinions, to the very end of his philosophical speculations, Carnap held firm to the a priori–a posteriori distinction, that mortal enemy of all pragmatism, claiming that there is a domain of a priori knowledge and another of empirical fact. The thesis of tolerance asserted that both were revisable on empirical grounds, but that only one made claims that could conflict with facts. Under the pressure of Neurath, the lure of syntax, and the fear of Wittgensteinian dogmatism, Carnap temporarily lost his philosophical balance and treated the a priori–a posteriori distinction as relatively insignificant. As others produced a more consistent development of pragmatism, Carnap would quickly understand how wrong he had been in this appraisal. The "pure" Carnap, the one most frequently displayed in the pages of *LSL,* is the one who once wrote, in reply to Quine's challenge, the following words:

I should make a distinction between two kinds of readjustment in the case of a conflict with experience, namely, between a change in the language, and a mere change in or addition of, a truth-value ascribed to an indeterminate statement (i.e., a statement whose truth value is not fixed by the rules of language, say by the postulates of logic, mathematics and physics). A change of the first kind constitutes a radical alteration, sometimes a revolution, and it occurs only at certain historically decisive points in the development of science. On the other hand, changes of the second kind occur every minute. A change of the first kind constitutes, strictly speaking, a transition from a language Ln to a new language $Ln + 1$. ("Replies and Systematic Expositions," Schilpp, *The Philosophy of Rudolf Carnap,* p. 921)

If the difference between giving up protocols, laws of physics, and laws of logic is, in some sense, gradual, that sense is less significant epistemologically than the sense in which it isn't.

19

◁══════════════════════════════════════▷

The problem of experience: protocols

The question concerning "protocol sentences," their function and structure, is the new form in which philosophy . . . presents the problem of the ultimate foundation of knowledge.

> Schlick, "Uber das Fundament der Erkenntnis"

. . . the *problem of protocol statements* . . . is the crucial problem of the logic of science (epistemology); in it lie also the problems usually treated under the catchword "empirical justification," "test" or "verification."

> Carnap, "Uber Protokollsätze"

Our most sublime scientific knowledge, in the final analysis, has no other foundation than the facts admitted by common sense; if one puts in doubt the certainties of common sense, the entire edifice of scientific truth totters upon its foundations and tumbles down.

> Duhem, *The Evolution of Mechanics*

Traditionally, the notion of experience played two essential but distinguishable roles in the theory of knowledge: Experience functioned as the rock bottom of all empirical justification and as the key to the link between our beliefs and reality. Experience was the ultimate foundation of all empirical knowledge, and it was also our only guarantee that what we think we know has what Kant called "objective validity." In this way our views of experience affected our views both on foundationalism and on realism.

Around 1930, a number of positivists began to question the adequacy of the foundationalist standpoint that had inspired much of traditional philosophy, and they detected a source of error in a certain doctrine of experience. The new attitude that these "fallibilists" developed toward experience succeeded in presenting a more reasonable picture of the role of certainty in knowledge; but, unexpectedly, it also succeeded in severing all links between knowledge and reality, offering an epistemology that differed from idealism only in rhetoric. The difficulty was already present in Russell's epistemology.

Russell had articulated a conception of knowledge that was not original with him, but that expressed forcefully and eloquently a paradigmatic challenge to the Kantian conception of knowledge. Its essential elements were the rejection of any type of constitution and the admission that virtually everything we believe could be wrong, including our logical beliefs and our beliefs in a mind-independent reality. There is a set of "instinctive beliefs" that we find "ready in ourselves as soon as we begin to reflect" (*The Problems of Philosophy,* p. 24).

Philosophy should show us the hierarchy of our instinctive beliefs, beginning with those we hold most strongly. . . . There can never be any reason for reject- ing one instinctive belief except that it clashes with others; thus, if they are found to harmonize, the whole system becomes worthy of acceptance. (p. 25)

"All or any of our beliefs may be mistaken," but "we cannot have *reason* to reject a belief except on the ground of some other belief" (p. 25). By organizing our instinctive beliefs, by adjusting some for the benefit of greater coherence, we can arrive at a systematic organization of knowl- edge. Even though "the *possibility* of error remains, its likelihood is diminished by the interrelation of the parts and by the critical scrutiny which has preceded acquiescence" (p. 26). If anybody had asked Russell about his reason for this claim, he would have shrugged his shoulders and pointed out that there is always room for a skeptical challenge. Russell always granted that skepticism is irrefutable, but somehow managed to conclude that it doesn't matter. In fact, it isn't merely that it is irrefutable, but that from Russell's standpoint one cannot make even a mildly plaus- ible case against it without entirely begging the question. From Russell's epistemological premises one can reach his foundationalist standpoint only through a blind leap of faith. He was happy to take it; but in the early 1930s the Viennese began to wonder whether *they* should take it too.

Foundations and experience

The standard attitude toward hypotheses and their justification before the stormy developments we are about to review was clearly displayed in Schlick's early statements concerning verification. Recall that in *Allge- meine Erkenntnislehre* Schlick argued that we must distinguish between the definition of truth (what truth is) and its criterion (the way we come to recognize it). Truth, he explained, "reveals itself to us only in specific experiences of verification" (*AE,* p. 186), and these experiences are al- ways the "*recognition of the identity of two judgements,* one of which is a judgement of *perception,* and hence a judgement whereby an actual experience is immediately expressed" ("The Nature of Truth in Modern Logic," p. 75; see also *GTK,* p. 165). Suppose we want to decide whether a hypothetical judgment *J* is true. First we deduce a specific, observable consequence *J'* from *J* and then place ourselves in a position to face the circumstances to which *J'* refers. As we encounter those circumstances, we express a second judgment J'' that describes them. If J' and J'' are identical, we have *verified J*. This does not mean, of course, that we have established the truth of J; we have confirmed it, if no contrary evidence is available.

Characteristically, the whole procedure assumes as a matter of course that judgments of experience such as J'' are true and known to be true; characteristically also, Schlick offered no explicit reason for granting this assumption. His definition of truth in "The Nature of Truth in Modern Logic" was "one-to-one coordination of judgements with facts" (p. 99), but his criterion of truth entirely ignored the fact in question, for its ultimate source was the feeling of inner evidence that "is simply nothing else but the *feeling of identity* intimated in consciousness by the likeness of the two judgements" (p. 78). Unless J'' is true, this "feeling of identity" is worthless as an indication of the truth of J', let alone of J. But why believe that J'' is true? Verification was the *only* criterion of truth that Schlick gave; yet it is obvious that we cannot apply it to decide whether judgments of experience are true.

It would be hard to exaggerate the significance of this difficulty. As we saw in the preceding chapter, by the early 1930s the leading positivists were agreed that the question of the factual adequacy of a theory T was reducible to the study of the type of relation that must hold between T and certain observational statements O. A great deal of attention and debate focused on the question of whether the link between T and O must be deductive, inductive, or some other type; almost everyone agreed, however, that the relation in question was not empirical but in some sense a priori. If the factual adequacy of an empirical theory has a non-a priori dimension, that feature must emerge in an account of the empirical basis. In other words, the link between knowledge and reality depends entirely on the link between basic statements and reality, and, as Schlick's example illustrates, it was widely assumed that the key to this link was experience. Empiricism was, after all, the view that knowledge is somehow based on experience, since experience is, by and large, the most reliable guide to the way the world is. Scientific experience was thought to be linguistically embodied in observational statements whose reliability and certainty was rarely explicitly considered but which most empiricists implicitly granted.

This traditional picture of things was shattered through a process that started with the seemingly harmless decision to reformulate it in Carnap's formal mode.

Protocol sentences

Protocol sentences made their appearance in 1931, shortly after Carnap's discovery of the thesis of metalogic (Carnap, "Intellectual Autobiography," pp. 53–4), the claim that all philosophical discourse concerns language rather than extralinguistic matters. Carnap saw that talk about experience, facts, reality had been a source of unending confusion. Schlick's experience, for example, seemed to be a private psychological process of no concern to intersubjective science. Whatever is of substance in this misleading talk in the material mode of speech will be preserved, without the misleading implications, when we move up to the formal mode. There, instead of facts and experience, we talk of protocol sentences.

One imprecise but vivid characterization of the protocol language is that of a language in which the "original Protocol" is written. The scientist's Protocol is the book in which he registers the theoretically unpolluted results of his daily observations in the laboratory. "Protocol sentences" are the statements in that book (or, better yet, all sentences in the minimal language in which that book is written):

> We think of [the Protocol] as containing the sentences of the original protocol, perhaps of a physicist or a psychologist. We thereby idealize the procedure as if all of our experiences, perceptions, and feelings, thoughts, etc., both in science and in our everyday life, were first set down in writing, in a protocol, so that the further elaboration would always have as its starting point a protocol. What is meant by the "original" protocol is what would be preserved if we drew a sharp distinction between the setting down of the protocol and its elaboration in a scientific process, so that the protocol would not include any sentences derived indirectly. (Carnap, "Die physikalische Sprache," p. 437)

Since protocol sentences are the "proper" linguistic counterpart of experience, verificationism becomes the doctrine that "a word sequence has sense only when its derivability relations to protocol sentences are determined" (Carnap, "Uberwindung der Metaphysik," pp. 222–3). The empirical test of a theory is no longer its mysterious confrontation with experience; properly speaking, a "person S *tests* (verifies) a system-sentence by deducing from it sentences of his own protocol language, and comparing these sentences with those of his actual protocol" (Carnap, "Psychology," p. 166). Even truth is decided on the basis of protocols: "The decision concerning truth and falsehood lies with the protocol sentences" ("Uberwindung der Metaphysik," p. 236).

The old language–world bipartition, the simplest, most trivial element at the basis of every sane account of the nature of knowledge, was transmuted into the division between the language of the system of science, or system language, and the protocol language ("Die physikalische Sprache," pp. 438–9). The distinction between protocol language and system language was, at first, clear-cut. Carnap argued that the system language and the protocol language should be clearly distinguished even when the former concerns the psychological domain. There is a difference, for example, between the protocol sentence 'I am excited now' and the psychological-system sentence 'I am excited now' ("Psychology,"

p. 191). The latter, like all hypotheses and singular statements of science, is subject to revision, since no statement of the system language can be "strictly speaking 'verified'" ("Die physikalische Sprache," p. 440; see also "Psychology," p. 191). The former, however, "being an epistemological point of departure, cannot be rejected" ("Psychology," p. 191). The elements of the Protocol are "the sentences that need no justification but serve as foundation for all of the remaining sentences of science" ("Die physikalische Sprache," p. 438).

It would be less than a year before Carnap would give up this way of distinguishing between system language and protocol language. In 1932 his system of beliefs on this topic was already unstable. At the same time that he was drawing a sharp distinction between the two languages on the basis of their revisability or lack of it, he was also arguing for the physicalist doctrine that every meaningful sentence can be translated into the language of physics. (What the "language of physics" is remains, of course, forever undefined in view of the uncomfortable fact that physicists will talk as they please in centuries to come.) Yet the language of physics, whatever else it might be, is a system language, and all sentences of a system language are, according to Carnap, revisable. Thus, protocols cannot, strictly speaking, be verified, for otherwise there would be a sentence in the system language, the translation of a protocol, that would, strictly speaking, be verified. Carnap could not hold for long that (a) protocols are unrevisable, (b) all sentences of the physicalist language are revisable, and (c) protocols can be translated into the physicalist language. Under the pressure of Neurath's and Popper's arguments (a) was soon to be dropped.

The shift to the material mode rendered the standard empiricist problems even more puzzling and difficult (perhaps impossible) to solve. Since the time of the *Aufbau* Carnap had been explaining that there is nothing to meaning beyond extension and psychological representations. In 1931 he had extended this list to include relations between sentences. The "formal mode" version of verificationism was that a sentence was meaningful when there were protocols that confirmed it and others that refuted it. This raised the problem of what confirmation and refutation could be when interpreted as relations between sentences – as opposed to what sentences in a language say – and the even more serious problem of the meaning of protocols. Verificationism in its formal mode could obviously not apply to them. Their meaning and their truth should then emerge from experience. But how? And whence do these protocols acquire the character of epistemic unmoved movers? Again, surely from their link with experience. But what, exactly, was that link?

Now that the discussion had been transported to the formal mode, the question was, What epistemic relation between ink and experience could possibly constitute the foundation of knowledge? Or what relation between structural features of the distribution of sound waves and reality could possibly be the basis of all certainty? How could one even make sense of the idea of a sentence being compared with experience? One sentence might be compared with another or with a physical object with respect to size, color, and so on; one sentence might be longer or darker than another. These are physical relations, and therefore positivists had nothing against them. But to say that the sentence 'John is blond' could be compared with the fact that John's hair is dark, or with an experience of the color of John's hair, seemed absurd. The positivists greatly disliked Russellian talk about facts as entities subsisting "out there"; but even if they had granted their existence, they would have thought a comparison between them and the sentence would hardly have shed any light on meaning and truth. Many people had often pointed out that it is what sentences *say* that agrees or conflicts with facts or experience. But as we saw in Schlick's early doctrine, it hadn't been so easy to explain what that kind of link was supposed to be.

One very popular theory claimed that the link was causal. In England, Russell and Ogden had put forth views of this type. In *The Analysis of Mind* (1921) Russell had argued that all verification is reducible to an operation that is, in a sense, the converse of memory: "Instead of having first sensations and then images accompanied by belief, we have first images accompanied by belief and then sensations" (p. 269). What is verified is always an expectation, and to verify it is to have a certain type of sensation: "When an image accompanied by an expectation-belief is thus succeeded by a sensation which is the 'meaning' of the image, we say that the expectation-belief has been verified" (p. 269). Russell then raised the question of how expectation should relate to the expected occurrence in order for verification to obtain and concluded that the most promising approach was "to take a more external and causal view of the relation of expectation to expected occurrence" (p. 270):

We have first an expectation, then a sensation with the feeling of expectedness related to memory of the expectation. This whole experience, when it occurs, may be defined as verification, and as constituting the truth of the expectation. . . . The whole process may be illustrated by looking up a familiar quotation, finding it in the expected words, and in the expected part of the book. (p. 270)

Carnap would try to articulate Russell's causal model, although, of course, as a mere proposal not intended to conflict with anyone else's views on this matter ("Erwiderung," p. 182). In Carnap's version, the idea was to think of the scientist's utterance of a protocol sentence as essentially indistinguishable from an ammeter displaying a scale reading. The noises the scientist makes while stating a so-called opinion are to be taken as a bare physical fact on a par with all other extralinguistic physical facts. One may, of course, say that protocol sentences mean something, in the same sense in which one says that the fact that the ammeter needle is on the number 4 "means" that electric current is going through the wire. In both cases, the significance of the given event lies entirely in the causal network to which it belongs. What matters about such protocol noises is not their Fregean sense but the fact that humans emit them regularly under given circumstances.[1] Just as smoke is a more reliable indicator of fire than lunacy is of genius, the utterance of 'red here now' is a more reliable indicator of the presence of red than the utterance of Schrödinger's equation is of anything at all.

It is this conclusion that was not easy to defend without circularity. On Carnap's version of experience, observation sentences were lifeless entities with no preferences or rejections of their own. He would conclude, at least for a while, that it is *we* who must give them life by acts of convention. In years to come, other philosophers would embrace the circularity and naturalize epistemology; still others would conclude that the matter is best ignored, dropping altogether the question of how experience is linked to reality.

Wittgenstein, as we know, had a perfectly definite answer concerning the link between "elementary propositions" and experience. He had argued that the link is not external, as in a mere causal relation between stimulus and response, but internal to the proposition. "For me, there are only two things involved in the fact that a thought is true, i.e. the thought and the fact; whereas for Russell, there are three, i.e. thought, fact and a third event which, if it occurs, is just recognition" (*Philosophical Remarks*, p. 63). His point was that to understand a genuine proposition is (in part) to grasp a certain procedure that has as its outcome an item of human experience; and what the sentence *says* is that that procedure will have a certain outcome. "To understand the sense of a proposition (*Satz*) is to know how one is to decide whether it is true or false" (*Philosophische Bemerkungen,* p. 77). Against Schlick's doctrine in "The Nature of Truth in Modern Logic," that verification is only a *criterion* of truth, Wittgenstein claimed: "How we verify a proposition is what it says. . . . The verification is not *one* sign (*Anzeichen*) of truth, but is *the* sense of the proposition" (*Philosophische Bemerkungen,* p. 200). Wittgenstein's proposition is, in effect, an expectation of a certain event together with a procedure that will generate either that event or another one that will fully refute that expectation. In this sense we may endorse a realist picture according to which we compare propositions with reality or with experience; and there is no mystery in this comparison, since what we contrast are two elements in the same space (like the meterstick and what it measures): the expected event and the outcome of the process. To compare the claim that the clock will strike in five minutes with reality is simply to compare the expectation that I will hear a certain type of sound under given circumstances with the actual sound I hear once I bring about those circumstances. The mystery of the comparison between a claim and experience is solved by placing experience within the claim.

From this perspective, we do not have Schlick's judgment *J"* and then the fact it describes together with an additional correlation. This would be to assume that "the relation of proposition to fact is an external relation; this is not correct. It is an internal relation" (Wittgenstein, *Lectures, 1930–32,* p. 9; see also *Philosophical Remarks,* p. 63). All we have is the proposition, whose very sense is a procedure that places us in a perceptual space with a certain expectation as to what will happen in it. What we contrast is not *J'* and *J"* but the expectation associated with *J'* and an actual occurrence. (The problem with this view is, as we saw, how to avoid the solipsism to which it seems to lead.)

In "The Turning Point in Philosophy" (1930) Schlick endorsed Wittgenstein's doctrine of the proposition. He argued that the statement of a problem, for example, must be associated with a characterization, however implicit, of the road leading to its solution:

For it turns out that the indication of this road is basically equivalent to stating its meaning; the traversing of the road in practice can of course be prevented by factual circumstances, such as defective human capacities. The act of verification, in which the road to solution finally terminates, is always of the same kind: it is the occurrence of a particular state-of-affairs, ascertained by observation and immediate experience. It is thus, in fact, that the truth (or falsity) of every statement is established, both in science and everyday life. There is no other way, therefore, of testing and confirming truths, save by observation and experimental science. (*Philosophical Papers,* vol. 2, p. 157)

But Schlick added an un-Wittgensteinian twist to the theory by attributing to factual propositions a feature that Wittgenstein thought only a priori statements could display.

In the preceding chapter we saw that the essential function of science in Schlick's view was to make predictions that are tested by experience. One such prediction would be "If, at such and such a time, you look through a telescope focussed in such and such a manner, you will see a speck of light (a star) coinciding with a black line (cross-wires)." "Let us assume," he said, "that on following these instructions the event prophesied actually occurs; this means, of course, that we make an ascertainment (*Konstatierung*) for which we are prepared; we pass an observational judgement that we *expected*" ("On the Foundations of Knowledge" [1934], *Philosophical Papers,* vol. 2, p. 382). Schlick's "ascertainments" resemble those life events that one encounters at the end of the verification process of a Wittgensteinian proposition. But Schlick treated them as if they were propositions in their own right. Moreover, in order to support their unshakable certainty, he claimed that disagreements as to their truth value are inconceivable.

In true Wittgensteinian style, Schlick went on to explain the character of his basic propositions in terms of what it is to understand them. Their nature is best grasped, Schlick thought, in relation to analytic propositions. Analytic statements are such that anyone who understands them must be fully aware of their truth value; for to understand "means in fact nothing else but to be clear about the rules for employment of the words involved; but it is precisely such rules which make the proposition analytic" ("On the Foundations of Knowledge," *Philosophical Papers,* vol. 2, p. 384). Carnap would have granted these points but not the additional, tacit, constructivist assumption that led Schlick to conclude that "in an analytic judgement, to understand its meaning and to discern its *a priori* validity, are *one and the same process*" (p. 385).[2]

Schlick's position on this matter is not coherent. On the one hand, he said that only in the process of verifying the ascertainment can we understand it; on the other, he assumed that those who do not verify it can understand it. For instance, he offered examples of ascertainments in situations where it is clearly implied that Schlick's readers as well as others can understand what they cannot verify. Here is a case in point:

Suppose a physicist wants me to check some project. He gets me to look through a telescope in his laboratory and asks: "What is there now in the visual field?" I answer (truthfully, let us assume): "There are two yellow lines there." ("Introduction and on 'Affirmations' from *Sur le Fondement de la Connaissance*" [1935], *Philosophical Papers,* vol. 2, p. 409)

If this is, as Schlick claimed, an ascertainment, then by his own standards only he could understand it.[3]

It would be implausible to assume that the fallibilists had a clear picture of Wittgenstein's account of the link between statements and experience and that they rejected it in full awareness of what they were doing. Most likely, they had only a vague idea of what the theory was, since Wittgenstein's syncopated explanations of it were not easy to understand, and those whom Wittgenstein had managed to convince (Schlick and Waismann) became thoroughly inarticulate when the time came to offer reasons for their position. But it would be equally erroneous to depict the positivists in the way favored by Wittgenstein's friends, as a group of silly fumblers, blind to the depths of insight available only a few blocks away from their meeting place. If they did not understand Wittgenstein's view, they certainly had the right question in mind when they examined it: What would be an example of the sort of proposition Wittgenstein was talking about? A transcendental argument had led him to "deduce" in the *Tractatus* that there must be objects. Now, a decade later, he had begun to worry about the fact that he knew no examples of objects; by the early 1930s he had decided that there are no objects in the intended sense. But now he was about to go through the same process all over again: If there is to be meaning in the strict sense of the word, there have to be decidable propositions that tie up to experience in the indicated fashion (the new form of his transcendental reasoning); but again, he could offer no examples of such propositions.

Enter Neurath

Until about 1930 most of the members of the Vienna circle seem to have taken for granted that observational statements were known with certainty and there was really no significant problem associated with them. Even Reichenbach, who from the very beginning had placed probability at the heart of his considerations, was talking about "facts of zero level" or "immediate perceptual experience," noting that "the facts of zero level are completely certain precisely because they are merely reports of sensations" ("Ziele und Wege der physikalischen Erkenntnis," p. 15). But early in the 1930s (if not before) Neurath started pressuring Carnap and others on this very point.

In response to Carnap's "Die physikalische Sprache als Universalsprache der Wissenschaft," Neurath asserted that protocol sentences cannot be statements that do not need justification. "Even a protocol sentence can suffer the destiny of being overthrown. There is no '*Noli me tangere*' for any sentence, as Carnap asserted for the case of protocols" ("Protokollsätze," p. 209). The main argument he offered for this conclusion was that an ambidextrous scientist might write a protocol sentence with one hand and its denial with the other. Neurath concluded that one of those protocol sentences would have to go and that therefore even protocols can be abandoned. Neurath was probably the first to draw the conclusion that would soon be common opinion in the analytic tradition: Cartesian certainty is entirely beyond our reach. If even protocols are revisable, then absolutely everything we believe is subject to revision and all of our beliefs are fallible.

Neurath's doctrine of fallibilism was only one part of his more general rebellion against traditional views on science. In order to appreciate his influence on other members of the Vienna circle, we should look at several of the other theses that characterized his position. First, there is the thesis that science is the measure of all things, the final word on everything factual, and the main guide to epistemology. Of course, many others before Neurath had taken science to be the paradigm of knowledge and rational activity. This was an idea that Schlick, Reichenbach, and others had been promoting for more than a decade. But Schlick and the others also thought they had to give a reason for this belief in the epistemic supremacy of science; they thought that science was so good because there were certain standards of rationality and empirical adequacy that science met more fully than did anything else. Neurath may be the first to have come up with the remarkable view that science is, indeed, superior to all other intellectual activities, but that there is no way we could possibly offer a defensible argument for that claim. Schlick and others agreed that the scientific enterprise itself cannot be expected to define the standards on which one might ground a justification of science, for the simple reason that anything that characterizes an activity cannot be part of what that activity brings into existence. One must have some prior idea of rational pursuit and then present arguments to show that science conforms to them. But, Neurath answered, if science embodies the totality of methods of rational pursuit of knowledge, then to take a stand outside of science is to take an unreasonable stand. It *can* be done, but why would anyone want to?

From the standpoint of its justification, then, science is no better or worse off than, say, the Christian Scientist's or the shaman's attitude toward reality. Others would soon draw from Neurath's premises the inevitable relativistic conclusion that science is just one more way of looking at things. Neurath chose not to do so. Thus, he was the first positivist to articulate a doctrine of what we might call dogmatic relativism: Even though there are no standards extrinsic to the actual practice of science that can stand in judgment of it (relativism), science is (dogmatically) asserted to be overwhelmingly superior to any other system of beliefs (like metaphysics or religion) and indeed can stand in judgment of them. By Neurath's own standards, his decision to adopt the doctrine of dogmatic relativism cannot be distinguished from a religious leap of faith. Alternatives to science are not given the slightest consideration, even though (or perhaps because) Neurath's argument left no way of reasonably displaying their inadequacy.

Neurath's idea that there is no standard over and above science was intended to include the idea that we do not compare scientific claims with experience or with reality. To compare claims with experience or anything else but other claims would be to try to get outside the domain of our convictions in order to compare them with the world. But we cannot jump out of our convictions any more than we can jump out of our shadow. "Thus *statements are always compared with statements,* certainly not with some 'reality', nor with 'things', as the Vienna Circle also thought until now" ("Physicalism" [1931], *Philosophical Papers,* p. 53). Statements are to be accepted or rejected not on the basis of their correspondence with the world or our experience of the world, but on the basis of comparisons with other statements:

> *Assertions are to be compared with assertions,* not with "experiences" or with a world, or with anything else. All of these senseless *duplications* belong in a more or less refined metaphysics and are therefore unacceptable. Each new assertion will be contrasted with the totality of those available assertions that have already been brought into harmony with each other. *An assertion is called "correct" when it can be incorporated* into this totality. What cannot be incorporated will be rejected as incorrect. Instead of rejecting the new assertion one can also change the total system of available assertions so that the new one may be incorporated into it; in general, however, this decision is taken with hesitation. ("Soziologie im Physikalismus," p. 403)

Nor does 'truth', if one is going to use that term at all, have anything to do with any kind of correspondence to facts or the world:

> If a statement is made, it is to be confronted with the totality of existing statements. If it agrees with them, it is joined to them; if it does not agree, it is called 'untrue' and rejected; or the existing complex of statements of science is modified so that the new statement can be incorporated; the latter decision is mostly taken with hesitation. *There can be no other concept of 'truth' for science.* ("Physicalism," *Philosophical Papers,* p. 53)

Popper, like Neurath, had come to see that all sentences are revisable under conceivable circumstances (Carnap, "Intellectual Autobiography," p. 32). But he did not agree with all of the other theses that Neurath advocated. His most telling criticism of Neurath's doctrine was that it

> must be completed through the declaration of a process that limits the arbitrariness of the "eliminations"; by not taking this into account Neurath unwittingly throws empiricism overboard. Empirical statements are no longer distinguished in relation to arbitrary systems of sentences; *every* system becomes defensible if one can simply delete protocol sentences that are inconvenient. In this way not only can one rescue any system, in the manner of conventionalism; but given an adequate supply of protocol sentences, one will be able even to confirm it, by the testimony of witnesses who have testified, or protocolled, what they have seen and heard. (*Logik der Forschung,* pp. 54–5)

This criticism is devastating, but it affects Popper's own proposal no less than Neurath's. For Popper's own positive account was as follows: "From a logical standpoint the testing of a theory goes back to its basic sentences, and these are acknowledged by convention. Thus it is *conventions* that decide the destiny of theories" (*Logik der Forschung,* p. 64). Consequently, the difference between Popper's standpoint and that of a conventionalist like Neurath is that "we see the characteristic feature of the empirical method in that what we determine by convention are not the general sentences but the particular ones, the basic sentences" (*Logik der Forschung,* p. 64). The main difference with positivism is that "the decisions about the basic sentences are not 'justified' by our experiences but, logically speaking, are *arbitrary conventions* (psychologically speaking, purposeful responses)" (*Logik der Forschung,* p. 65). Popper's ambiguity is once again exemplified in his decision to accept the distinction between basic statements and theoretical statements and yet reject the reason that made it reasonable: He insisted on the distinction but insisted also that basic statements are as theoretical as any others. As to what reasons there are for regarding one set of basic sentences as more truthful than any other, Popper failed to be more communicative than Neurath. As we shall see, foundationalists would soon be pressing this point on the proponents of the new doctrine of protocols.

Schlick was quite willing to endorse the view that all statements within the language of science are hypotheses and therefore revisable (Schlick, "Uber das Fundament der Erkenntnis," pp. 293–4). He remained a foundationalist nonetheless. Schlick could not understand how a distinction could be drawn between genuine knowledge and pseudoscience without relying on the existence of singular statements (protocols or, as Schlick called them, *"Konstantierungen"*) that are absolutely certain and provide the foundation of all empirical knowledge. Given the unrevisable character of these basis elements, he simply regarded them as statements of a language disjoint from that of science.

Carnap took Neurath more seriously, however. In "Uber Protokollsätze" he came to acknowledge that besides his old conception of the protocol language there is another view (attributed to Neurath and Popper), according to which the protocols are elements of the system language. The choice between these two language forms is, like so many things since 1932, a matter of convention. Moreover, even within the second language form the choice of a specific syntactic form for protocols, as between Neurath's, Popper's, or some other proposal, is, once more, a matter of convention. This seemingly harmless change of mind was to have major implications.

Empiricism at sea

Experience, objectively construed, is a process that involves a large element of human activity and convention, but it also involves something else. We may or may not have the concepts required to formulate electromagnetic conjectures; we may choose to design an experimental set-up or not; we may choose to open our eyes in front of the voltmeter or not. But if we do all of these things, we are no longer free to choose to see the needle pointing at the number 4. In experience, as in the Wittgensteinian proposition, there is a constructive process in which the human will is in command and, at its end point, there is an encounter with a circumstance entirely beyond our will. In this resistance to or independence from our will, Dilthey had identified the very essence of our conception of an external world.[4] It is this final stage that reveals, through its independence from us, the presence of a second party in the epistemic process, the "external" world. Only the most extreme and less coherent forms of idealism will seriously put forth a theory of experience that does not allow for this extraconventional element. Neurath's theory was precisely of this sort.

Around 1935 there was a running joke to the effect that a fallibilist would have a hard time at a restaurant, since he would be unable to check whether what the waiter brought him corresponded to the menu item he had ordered (see, e.g., Rougier, "Allocution finale," pp. 88–9). The origin of the joke was a remark that Russell had made in summing up his argument against Neurath's position. Russell had pointed out that when he went into a restaurant and ordered chicken, the aim was not to make his words "fit into a system with other words, but to bring about the presence of food" (*An Inquiry into Meaning and Truth*, p. 141). In his reply Neurath objected to the expression 'The bringing of rabbit instead of a chicken does not satisfy the desire expressed by Russell's order': "I propose only that we should transform the expression into: 'the word-thinking of Russell, "A chicken will appear"' (in connection with his order) seems to be contradictory to his word-thinking: 'no chicken appeared'" ("Universal Jargon and Terminology" [1941], *Philosophical Papers*, p. 227). Of course, Russell may word-think (whatever that may be) "no chicken appeared" because the pope told him to think so, or because he looked at the tray and saw the rabbit. According to Neurath, this difference is epistemologically insignificant. Hahn once asked Neurath why, in his view, physicists should do experiments. No answer was recorded in the protocols of that session of the Vienna circle, but if he were to remain consistent, Neurath could only have answered that there was no reason whatever. That empiricism and rationalism should have come to this is, perhaps, the greatest irony of these Viennese developments.

The blunt candor with which Neurath stated his position makes its refutation unnecessary. Yet one must cope with the astonishing fact that these ideas greatly influenced Carnap, and that after clearly displaying their obvious untenability, Popper went on to put forth a position essentially indistinguishable from Neurath's. There must have been a force within the positivist tradition leading strongly in the direction of idealism.

The root of the difficulty is that a theory of empirical knowledge requires a theory of its link with experience (what was sometimes called a theory of experience). Decades of only partially successful efforts had shown how hard the problem was. Neurath's characteristic solution was to deny the existence of the problem: Since those who try to explain the link between knowledge and experience often say obscure or confused things, we should not talk about the topic. We should instead talk about the link between sentences. As Popper and later Russell put it, the least one can say about Neurath's position is that it signifies an abandonment of empiricism. But even the most diehard idealist had preserved a link of sorts to reality by assigning to statements of experience a privileged role. Neurath denied not only the dogmatic correspondence picture of things, but also the fact that experience is a form of access to reality preferable to all others. This is the heart of the protocol-sentence debate. Neurath's position was the glorification of syntactic ascent: We can talk only about talk. In the process, any link between knowledge and experience had been severed.

On this issue, as with almost everything else, Carnap's attitude was a delicate mixture of indecision, reluctance to become entangled in philosophical speculation, and obscure insight that there was a truth higher than all those under consideration. Semantic conventionalism was the philosophical instrument of Carnap's hesitation; and he appealed to it frequently in his less thoughtful utterances about the matter of protocols. Carnap repeated often enough that Schlick, Neurath, and their followers shouldn't get so angry at one another because it was all a matter of convention. And he did a little more; he tried to figure out how to solve the problem of protocols. His attitude toward them, both before and after the acknowledgment of Tarski's discovery, shows the lingering force of idealist thought patterns in Carnap's repressed philosophy.

Carnap's first serious attempt to face the issue was in reply to a challenge issued by Zilsel in "Bemerkungen zur Wissenshaftslogik." The main question Zilsel posed was accurately synthesized by Carnap as follows:

Logically speaking, each conceivable class of protocol sentences is as justified as every other. For each class of protocol sentences one can construct a scientific system that is, first of all, consistent and that is also sufficiently confirmed by the corresponding protocol sentences. *How are we to distinguish our science, the "real" or "true" science,* which we decidedly prefer to all fantasy science and to the other conceivable systems? ("Erwiderung," p. 179)

Carnap's answer was that

we shall designate as "real protocol sentences" those statements or written assertions (as physical-historical configurations) that stem from certain people, especially from the scientists of our cultural circle. . . . It would be conceivable that each person could make his protocol sentences agree with those of others only with great difficulty or not at all . . . luckily, in science we are in fact in a position to bind together our protocols with those of a hundred other people in a common elaboration. ("Erwiderung," p. 180)

In principle, of course, our luck need not hold. Carnap went on to say that even in cases of disagreement, however, experience is not the arbiter:

If someone now appears who, on the basis of his protocols, builds a science that is not consistent with the one constructed by our hundred people, then we vote him down; we say of him (depending on the circumstances) that he is colorblind, or a poor observer, or a dreamer, or a liar, or a madman. If we found that against our one hundred there is another one hundred with a common science that cannot be reconciled with ours, then we couldn't vote them down. In case further research would not lead to agreement we should simply accept the fact that different groups possess unalterably diverse scientific systems. Luckily, this is not the case. (p. 180)

Shortly thereafter, Hempel, who had recently joined the fallibilist ranks, drew the obvious conclusions: Truth is coherence and (echoing Neurath)

statements are never compared with a "reality," with "facts." None of those who support a cleavage between statements and reality is able to give a precise account of how a comparison between statements and facts may possibly be accomplished. . . . Therefore that cleavage is nothing but the result of a redoubling metaphysics. ("On the Logical Positivists' Theory of Truth," pp. 50–1)

Schlick's response to Hempel displays clearly how strongly foundationalists felt about the issue under debate:

I have been accused of maintaining that statements can be compared with facts. I plead guilty. I have maintained this. But I protest against my punishment: I refuse to sit in the seat of the metaphysicians. I have often compared propositions to facts; so I had no reason to say that it couldn't be done. I found, for instance, in my Baedeker the statement: "This cathedral has two spires," I was able to compare it with 'reality' by looking at the cathedral, and this comparison convinced me that Baedeker's assertion was true. Surely you cannot tell me that such a process is impossible and that there is a detestable metaphysics involved in it. ("Facts and Propositions" [1935], *Philosophical Papers,* vol. 2, p. 400)

Neurath, like all idealists, was appalled by the idea that one could adopt a position outside our opinions from which to judge their adequacy to their topic; he was equally appalled by the possibility of taking a stand outside science in order to judge the validity of its assertions. This is the point of his most celebrated metaphor: "We are like sailors who must rebuild their ship on the open sea, never able to dismantle it in drydock and to reconstruct it there out of the best materials" ("Protocol Sentences" [1932–3], in Ayer, *Logical Positivism,* p. 201). Neurath replied to Schlick:

When I say I 'compare' what is printed in a guidebook about a church with the church itself, this would be expressed according to our proposals: "The guidebook contains the statement 'this church has two steeples'" and "I formulate the statement 'this church has two steeples'." The two 'inserted' statements coincide; to put it less carefully: the guidebook is confirmed by experience. ("Physicalism and the Investigation of Knowledge" [1936], *Philosophical Papers*, p. 163)

Usually we distinguish between talk about things that are not sentences and talk about things that are sentences. When we say that the Baedeker contains a report that St. John's Cathedral has two spires, we are talking about a sentence; when we say that St. John's Cathedral has two spires, we are talking about certain things that are not sentences. Schlick's simple point was that we often decide (and science often *should* decide) the truth value of certain sentences by looking at the things they are about and seeing whether these things have the properties attributed by those sentences. Neurath's denial of this point must be frankly recognized for what it is, the offspring of confusion. Neurath thought that granting this simple point he was committed to the idea that we can get out of the domain of thinking in order to compare it with that of reality. Of course, when we look at St. John's Cathedral, we think, 'That has two spires', the same thought conveyed by the statement in the book. But the *origin* of the former statement (pace Popper) makes an essential difference, which is lost in Neurath's, Carnap's, and Popper's accounts. Syntactic ascent was a dreadful idea in connection with epistemology, because one lost the independence of experience. Why should I compare the two sentences 'The Baedeker says "*xxx*"' and 'I say "*xxx*"' rather than 'The Baedeker says "*xxx*"' and 'I say "not-*xxx*"'? If one acknowledges the role of experience, there is no doubt what the answer is: It's not up to me! For all the creativity, inspiration, and convention that goes into the act of experience, there is still a little something imposed upon me. But that little something, reality, had completely vanished when Carnap and Neurath made their syntactic ascent. The tragic result of their climb was the conventionalism of the empirical basis.

Truth reconsidered

Lukasiewicz once noted that Polish philosophers were "too sober" to agree with the Viennese doctrines ("Logistic and Philosophy" [1936], p. 233), and a few years later Russell would synthesize their viewpoint on protocol truth by noting that according to it "empirical truth can be determined by the police" (*An Inquiry into Meaning and Truth*, p. 140). It was easy to make fun of the fallibilists, but it was not so easy to determine what was wrong with their reasoning.

They had begun with the seemingly harmless and widely accepted thesis of metalogic. Protocols became the honest version of facts or states of affairs; meaning and truth for *other* statements were defined through verificationism or the correspondence theory. But, as we saw, this raised the major question of how the meaning and truth of protocols were to be characterized. The question of the meaning of protocols was treated by the new positivists as a syntactic issue. This was the source of their concern about the form of protocol sentences. To solve the problem of the meaningfulness of protocols was to identify a form such that every sentence of that form was a (meaningful) protocol. The odd thing about Carnap's solution was that almost any form would do, for the matter was conventional (see "Uber Protokollsätze"). The question of protocol truth, however, was more elusive.

In the early stages of this development, in which protocols were re-garded as mere reformulations of talk in the material mode, there was still a rigid link between states of affairs and protocols that accounted for the inevitable truth of those protocols that we honestly accept. This connection was not mere truth but certainty: Protocols were the ambas-sadors of states of affairs in the linguistic world of knowledge, not merely because they depict states of affairs as they are but because we *know* that they do. The reason for their select status among sentences is that our knowledge of protocols is as good as knowledge ever gets. Most of those who were amused by the fallibilists' bind had been willing to follow them up to this point. What they failed to see is that, from *that* point on, the argument for coherentism was fairly tight.

The new positivists' case against certainty was, we now think, conclu-sive. As the belief in certainty became weaker, however, the only gener-ally acknowledged link between protocols and facts became looser. Truth and meaning remained, as always, a sort of match with protocols, but now protocols had no particular connection with reality. And when the form of protocols became a matter of convention, truth became a match between sentences and other sentences of conventionally speci-fiable form or, equivalently, a certain sort of match between the class of all accepted sentences. As to which sentences to choose for the initial matching Protocol, no sensible rule could be given other than: Listen to what the scientists tell you. Science is fine as it is. As Neurath put it, there are no philosophical problems *"in which scientific knowledge itself becomes a problem"* ("Radikaler Physikalismus und 'Wirkliche Welt,'" p. 347). In the end, Carnap's formal mode and the demise of certainty had transmuted the correspondence theory into the coherence theory and had thereby led positivism from its early prescriptivism to a radically descriptive stand.

The common assumption of both the fallibilists and the foundational-ists, like Schlick, who opposed them was that knowledge can be said to represent reality only if there are propositions that are known with certainty and that establish a link between knowledge and reality. By 1935, however, some fallibilists had come to question this common assumption. Their faith had been shaken by Tarski's work on the nature of truth. It is symptomatic that while foundationalists such as Russell and Schlick greeted Tarski's theory with a merely polite interest for its technical achievement, many fallibilists quickly hailed it as a liberating breakthrough.

In his "Intellectual Autobiography" Carnap recalled the meeting with Tarski when he first heard of the possibility of defining truth:

I assumed that he had in mind a syntactical definition of logical truth or provability. I was surprised when he said that he meant truth in the customary sense, including contingent factual truth. Since I was thinking only in terms of a syntactical metalanguage, I wondered how it was possible to state the truth-condition for a simple sentence like "this table is black." Tarski replied: "This is simple: the sentence 'this table is black' is true if and only if this table is black." (p. 60)[5]

When Carnap met Tarski again in Vienna in the spring of 1935, he urged him to deliver a paper on truth at the Paris International Conference taking place in September. Tarski "thought that most philosophers . . . would be not only indifferent, but hostile" ("Intellectual Autobiography," p. 61). As far as some positivists were concerned, he was right. Neurath, Arne Ness, and later Kaufmann and Reichenbach initially argued that Tarski's semantics involved an intolerable metaphysics. Carnap saw clearly that it did not, and in his own contribution to the Paris conference he finally put the necessary emphasis on the distinction Kantians and positivists had refused to take seriously: truth and confirmation.

A number of philosophers who, before Tarski, were immersed in the Kantian–positivist confusion concerning truth and who started using the notion of truth after they read Tarski, initiated the story that *only* after Tarski's work did it become possible to talk responsibly about truth. However understandable from a psychological standpoint, this account is untenable. The mathematical and formal value of Tarski's work is beyond dispute. The concept of truth had not previously been the target of real problems, however, but only of monumental confusions specific to the Kantian–positivist traditions, confusions that had not affected the semantic tradition. Tarski's work allowed positivists to join those who had kept their heads when Kantians and positivists seemed to have lost theirs. But to see it as a monumental step forward for philosophy is no more than a parochial appreciation of things.

Carnap's endorsement of Tarski's doctrine would eventually lead him to his famous exercises in semantics. But its most immediate philosophical payoff was little more than the recognition of the old Fregean distinction between the content of a statement and its assertion. Carnap's "Truth and Confirmation" (1936) is the first carefully worked out presentation by a positivist addressed to fellow positivists in which a clear distinction is made between *saying* something and *claiming that it is true* – which is not, of course, the distinction between truth and confirmation. At this point the positivist tradition began to converge with the better side of the semantic tradition. Carnap had reached the point where Bolzano had begun.

That the intended distinction was content versus assertion rather than truth versus confirmation emerges from Carnap's essentially unaltered stand concerning realism. In the draft of the paper read at the conference, after the resounding endorsement of Tarski's views, Carnap added, "The construction of so-called reality depends however, as we know, on the structure of the language being used at the time; it is in each case different, for example, in primitive thought, in classical physics, and in quantum physics." (The original text of this draft appears to be lost. The quotation is taken from Schlick's letter to Carnap of 14 November 1935, RC 102-70-11, ASP.)[6] Schlick did not attend the conference, but when he saw Carnap's draft, he wrote:

It is typical that you talk here of "construction" whereas I would say "description." I would propose that we talk of the construction of reality, say, in the building of a house or the construction of a canal, but that we call the construction of a science or of a world view "description." In any case it seems to me obvious that the two are completely different things. No one will convince me that it is inappropriate and dangerous to say that primitive and modern physicists have different world views but live in the very same reality. . . . If one takes your words literally, one would assert that reality is created through language and that therefore the primitive physicist and the quantum physicist live in different realities. One can, after all, say that; but I would have expected to find that type of claim in Keyserling or Simmel (who without doubt must be regarded as a relativistic metaphysician) rather than in Carnap! (Schlick's letter to Carnap of 14 November 1935, RC 102-70-11, ASP)[7]

In response to this, Carnap acknowledged that the sentence was too brief and misleading (Letter to Schlick of 4 December 1935, RC 102-70-10, ASP) and replaced it by a longer passage in which he discussed the expression "comparing a statement with the facts." The sentence was misleading, he now said, because talk about "the facts" or "reality"

can easily lure us to an absolutistic conception according to which it would be possible to ask about an absolute "reality" whose nature is established in and of itself, quite independently of the language chosen for its description. The answer to a question about 'reality' does not depend exclusively upon this 'reality', however, or 'the facts', but also upon the structure of and the concepts available in the language chosen for the description. In translating from one language to another the factual content of a factual sentence will not always be preserved unchanged, as when the structures of both languages differ in essential respects. For example, many sentences of the language of modern physics can indeed be completely translated into the language of classical physics, but other sentences cannot be translated at all, or only deficiently. This is the case when in the sentences in question use is made of concepts (such as 'wave function' and 'quantization') that do not appear and – this is the essential point – cannot be added to the language of classical physics because they presuppose a different language form. . . . (It is not only that sentences accepted at an earlier stage are later rejected, but that, for some sentences – independently of whether they are held true or false – it is not at all possible to construct a corresponding sentence in the new language.) ("Wahrheit und Bewährung," p. 22; see also Carnap's "Von der Erkenntnistheorie zur Wissenschaftslogik," p. 39)

In sending the corrected version to Schlick, Carnap noted that "there remains . . . a difference of opinion" between them,

for I do not believe in translatability without loss of content, and therefore I think that the content of a world description is influenced to a certain degree by the choice of a language form. But that certainly does not mean that reality is created through language. (Letter to Schlick of 4 December 1935, RC 102-70-10, ASP)[8]

Schlick had said in his "Are Natural Laws Conventions?" (*Philosophical Papers,* vol. 2) that experience "can never compel" the abandonment of a convention. This was his main reason for drawing a sharp line between statement of fact and statement of convention. The implication of his reasoning is that experience *can* compel the abandonment of a statement of fact. This had been assumed by Popper in order to formulate his position. Most people, including Popper, soon came to see the untenability of this position; most people, excluding Popper, realized they had to revise their views as a consequence of that observation. The sharp distinction could hold only if one had something else to appeal to. The obvious candidate was the facts: A factual claim is one to which the facts can say no, whether we know it or not; a conventional claim is something different. This had sounded like awful metaphysics to the positivists. Now Tarski's theory of truth allowed for some measure of ease in talking this way.[9]

From this point on, coherentist pronouncements among positivists become increasingly rare, and the distinction between truth and certainty inspired Carnap and others to develop semantic and inductive logic as separate branches of philosophy. Another outcome was a moderation of the radical descriptivism of Carnap's "Erwiderung auf die vorstehenden Aufsätze von E. Zilsel und K. Duncker." Except for a few diehards (Neurath, Popper), the problem of the grounds of our belief that knowledge corresponds to reality disappeared among fallibilists as a genuine problem of epistemology.

Notes

Chapter 1

1. See C. Knüfer, *Grundzüge der Geschichte des Begriffs 'Vorstellung' von Wolff bis Kant.* Kant's views on representation differed from those of his predecessors in some significant respects. For example, by the time of his *Dissertation* of 1770 he had drawn a sharp distinction between two faculties of representation – sensibility and understanding – and he would soon draw an equally sharp division between the representations they generate. Moreover, he would assume, for reasons never disclosed, that singular representations are (among human beings) the privilege of sensibility, while general representations emerge only from the understanding. Wolff had classified representations as "either of singular or individual things, or of universal" (*Logic*, p. lxxi); and since he, like Lambert and Meier, identified representation and concept, he thereby acknowledged individual concepts. (On the identification of representation and concept see G. F. Meier, *Auszug aus der Vernunftlehre*, sec. 249; C. Wolff, *Vernänftige Gedanken von den Kräften den menschlichen Verstandes*, sec. 4; J. R. Lambert, *Neues Organon*, sec. 6.) Kant emphatically rejected this identification: "A singular concept is not a concept at all" ("Conceptus singularis ist gar kein Conceptus," *Philosophische Enzyklopädie*, p. 18). Having consigned all individual representations to the domain of sensibility and all general representations to the understanding, he called the former 'intuitions' and reserved the word 'concept' for the latter. Thus, Kant concluded that the idea of an individual concept is a *contradiction in adjecto*. L. W. Beck has argued that the introduction of the two sorts of representations and of the corresponding representational powers is the most prominent and original feature of the strategy that led Kant to the formulation of his critical philosophy (Beck, "Kant's Strategy").

2. Other passages worth looking at are Kant, *Logik Blomberg*, p. 41; *Logik Philippi*, p. 410; and *Vorlesungen über die Metaphysik*, pp. 135–7. In the last we find, for example, "If God were to bring light directly into our soul, so that we could be conscious of all of our representations, then we would see all bodies in the world clearly and distinctly, just as if we had them before our eyes" (p. 136).

3. In the case of nongiven, constructed concepts, analysis is a triviality, for in that case *we* have decided what the constituents of the concept are to begin with. For *given* concepts, however, far from being a triviality, analysis constitutes the very essence of genuine philosophical activity.

4. See, e.g., Waismann, *Wiener Logik*, p. 841: "In the end, one always comes to the part concepts, which are simple, and they can only be clear to us." See also Kant, *Logik Philippi*, p. 342.

5. Leibniz had also noted a difficulty in this area: "It appears not to be within human power to analyze concepts sufficiently to be able to arrive at primitive concepts, or at others that are composed of them. But the analysis of truths is more within human power" (*Opuscules et fragments inédits de Leibniz*, p. 514). The "problem of indefinables," as Russell came to call it, will figure prominently in later chapters.

6. The qualification 'thought in' is essential for Kant since, like Leibniz, Kripke, and Putnam, he thought that the constituency of given concepts depends not on what we know but on what the facts of the matter are. Leibniz, for example, had written that "the word 'gold' does not signify only what the person who pronounces it knows of it – for example, something yellow, very heavy – but also what he does not know and what another may know, i.e., a body endowed with an internal constitution from which proceeds color and weight and from which spring still other properties that he admits to be known by experts" (*Nouveaux essais*, bk. 3, chap. II, sec. 24; see also bk. 4, chap. 6, secs. 8–11). Kant echoed this opinion in the *Critique*, A727–8/B755–6. These uncharacteristic passages do not reflect, in my opinion, a mind-boggling anticipation of the causal theory of natural kinds but yet another consequence of the confusion between concept and object, a confusion whose presence elsewhere in the writings of these philosophers can be established without the shadow of a doubt. In any case, if the constituents of a concept A may be disclosed as a result of empirical research, then we cannot define analyticity without an appeal to what "is thought" in the concept, for 'A is B' might be a posteriori even though B is contained in the concept A. In order for 'A is B' to be analytic it does not suffice that B is part of A; we must also be aware (even though preferably obscurely) that B is part of A.

7. The only "reason" I have been able to find for this claim in Kant's writings occurs in "Lose Blätter zu den Fortschritten der Metaphysik," *Kants gesammelte Schriften*, vol. 23, p. 340. Kant's point is, of course, an utter triviality if he means by 'analytic' 'nonampliative'; but then he still owes us an argument for the claim that some necessary judgments are, in that sense, not analytic.

8. Kant's principle may be regarded as a response to Lambert's problem when he admitted that the "*fons possibilitatis duos ideas combinandi* has not been fully discovered" (*Uber die Methode die Metaphysik, Theologie und Moral richtiger zu beweisen*, p. 9; cited in Beck, *Early German Philosophy*, p. 407). There may also be a link with Leibniz. In a draft of the reply to Eberhard, Kant conjectured that Leibniz's principle of sufficient reason was an effort to formulate the principle of synthetic judgments ("Vorarbeiten zur Schrift gegen Eberhard," *Kants gesammelte Schriften*, vol. 20, p. 376).

9. In the case of transcendental knowledge, which is not, properly speaking, expressed in synthetic judgments but in synthetic *Grundsätze*, the synthesis of the corresponding concepts is grounded by the possibility of experience

(*Critique*, A783/B811). The link with intuition comes from the fact that "intuitions in general . . . constitute the field, the whole object, of possible experience" (*Critique*, A95).

10. Moore noted in *Principia Ethica* that since *good* is indefinable (unanalyzable), everything we say about it must be synthetic, and Russell had expressed the same opinion regarding indefinable ideas in general in his *Critical Exposition of the Philosophy of Leibniz* (sec. 11). It is not surprising that they found hosts of synthetic a priori statements in mathematics, logic, ethics, and several other places.

11. Alternatively, one could accept the principle of synthetic judgments as a trivial consequence of the *second,* nonnominal definition of analyticity; but then, in the appropriate (second) sense of 'synthetic', Kant has given us absolutely no reason to believe that there are synthetic a priori judgments.

12. In Kant's day it was common to draw the distinction and uncommon to observe it. Wolff, for example, wrote in his *Psychologia Empirica,* 2d ed. (1738): "If some object is represented in the mind, one must distinguish the mental act by which this representation occurs" (sec. 48). But Knüfer notes that Wolff himself failed to take the distinction at all seriously (*Grundzüge der Geschichte des Begriffs 'Vorstellung' von Wolff bis Kant,* p. 15). Though not the first to draw this distinction, Bolzano would be the first postmodern philosopher to realize clearly the devastating consequences of failing to observe it (see Chapter 2, this volume).

13. Kant did not call (**) analytic, but rather "tautological" (*Logik,* sec. 37, p. 111) and "explicitly identical"; it is "void of consequences," unlike "implicitly identical" judgments such as (*). Sometimes Kant excluded tautological judgments from the category of analytic judgments (*Preisschrift über die Fortschritte der Metaphysik,* p. 322).

14. Leibniz had recognized that "we know that identical propositions are necessary propositions without any understanding or analysis of their terms, for I know that A is A, whatever may be understood by A" (*Philosophical Papers and Letters,* p. 187). Presumably he would have said the same thing about 'All As and Bs are A'.

Chapter 2

1. For details on the nature of Lagrange's proposal see *Théorie des fonctions analytiques.* For Cauchy's refutation of it see Grabiner, *The Origins of Cauchy's Rigorous Calculus,* p. 36.

2. For contemporary appraisals of Bolzano's contributions to these fields consult, e.g., P. Dugac, "Des fonctions comme expressions analytiques aux fonctions représentables analytiquement"; D. M. Johnson, "Prelude to Dimension Theory: The Geometrical Investigations of Bernard Bolzano"; B. van Rootselaar, "Bolzano's Theory of Real Numbers"; and Detlef Laugwitz, "Bemerkungen zu Bolzanos Grossenlehre." The last compares Bolzano's work on actual infinitesimals with Laugwitz's own development of Robinson's nonstandard analysis.

3. Pierre Dugac, one of the leading historians of early-nineteenth-century math-

ematics, has judged that "among early 19th century mathematicians, Bolzano was probably the one who posed the deepest questions on the foundations of analysis" ("Fondements de l'analyse," p. 339). Elsewhere, referring specifically to Bolzano's "Rein analytischer Beweis des Lehrsatzes," Dugac said that Bolzano's proof of the intermediate-value theorem shows that he was the first to have the immense merit of understanding the logical sequence of theorems that leads to the intended result, including the theorem about the upper bound of a set of numbers, the "Cauchy" criterion – which Bolzano states in his memoir anticipating Cauchy; Bolzano's proof of the sufficiency of his condition – an incomplete proof, to be sure – adumbrates, if only vaguely, the need to "construct" the set of real numbers ("Des fonctions comme expressions analytiques aux fonctions représentables analytiquement," p. 16).

4. With the possible exception of Cauchy, all the others in this list were directly inspired by Bolzano's work. Grattan-Guinness has (implausibly) argued that Cauchy stole Bolzano's ideas in his "Bolzano, Cauchy and the 'New Analysis' of the Early Nineteenth Century." But also see Freudenthal's reply in "Did Cauchy Plagiarize Bolzano?" and J. Grabiner's analysis in *The Origins of Cauchy's Rigorous Calculus,* esp. chap. 3.

5. Upon occasion Bolzano seemed to be inspired by a perverseness of purpose: He was the first to discover a continuous function that is nowhere differentiable. (Weierstrass was the first to *publish* an example of this sort.)

6. Clearly, also, Bolzano is here skirting the toughest problem in his tradition: the sense in which the topic of semantics has any substance. We shall soon see this problem grow (Chapters 4, 5, and 6) and lead eventually to the peculiar Viennese attitude toward ontology.

7. The same confusion inspired a famous argument in Kant's *Critique* to the effect that space cannot be a concept because space is infinitely divisible and "no concept as such can be thought as containing an infinite number of representations within itself" (B40). Bolzano identified this clear instance of the fallacy when he noted that Kant was assuming that "since space itself consists of infinitely many parts, therefore the concept of space must also consist of infinitely many parts" (*Theory of Science,* p. 84). A much more important example is the failure to distinguish between the constitution of representations and that of the objects they represent. The astonishing resilience of this confusion will be one of the dominant themes of Part II.

8. Let us note in passing that Klein's proof of the independence of the parallel postulate in 1871 is best understood in light of Bolzano's new standpoint. Let P be the parallel postulate and E the conjunction of the remaining Euclidean axioms; then what Klein showed is that $E \Rightarrow P$ is not necessary, in Bolzano's sense. But he certainly did not show that (in Leibniz's sense) there is a conceivable world in which $E \Rightarrow P$ is false. As we shall see, Frege – and many others – could make no sense of Klein's claim, and he argued that one *could not* prove the independence of the parallel postulate. He was probably thinking in terms of the Leibnizian approach, having failed to grasp the force of Bolzano's insight.

9. Our *grammatical admissibility* interprets Bolzano's *Gegenständlichkeit.* A

proposition whose subject term is 'the man x' will remain *gegenständlich* while we substitute names of men for 'x', but it will lose its *Gegenständlichkeit* if we write, e.g., 'the man 7'. The requirement appears to be inspired by some of the same considerations that later led Russell to his theory of types and Wittgenstein to his doctrine of the form of objects.

10. Bolzano's *analytic* is not closed with respect to his *logical consequence*: 'This triangle has angles adding up to 180 degrees' is analytic – since grammatical admissibility (*Gegenständlichkeit*) demands that 'this' always stand for the representation of a triangle, but 'All triangles have angles adding up to 180 degrees' is not analytic (see *Theory of Science*, pp. 195–202; see also sec. 59). One century after Bolzano defined '*allgemeingültig*', however, Gödel proved a theorem to the effect that all "generally valid" formulas of a first-order language are provable in an appropriate axiomatic system, such as the one designed by Frege. Gödel did not explain what he meant by '*allgemeingültig*' (Tarski did, a few years later, as we shall see); but he could have used Bolzano's characterization relativized to the logical notions of his first-order language.

11. Bolzano made the same point in "Allgemeine Mathesis" (1810), *Gesamtausgabe*, ser. 2A, vol, 5, p. 31.

12. Kant's principle of synthetic judgments was also challenged in *Grossenlehre*, p. 86. In the same treatise, Bolzano offered as an explanation for Kant's appeal to intuition in mathematics the same considerations that Russell would offer early in our century; he suggested, in effect, that the incompleteness of logical theory led Kant to think one had to appeal to an extraconceptual source (p. 88).

13. For a revealing indication of how far Bolzano's standpoint has now become common ground, see Bochenski's interpretation of the same Aristotelian passage in his classic *Formale Logik*, p. 54. Bochenski comments that "the thought expressed is quite clear: Aristotle . . . draws a sharp distinction between the validity of the inference and the truth of the premises. These texts contain the historically first formulation of the idea of a *formal* logic, universally valid and independent of content (*Stoff*)." But the notion of form is not even suggested in these passages, whether in Bolzano's sense (the one Bochenski seems to have in mind) or in any other.

14. Bolzano, of course, *applied* the incomplete-symbol strategy to his rigorization of the calculus; but he does not seem to have recognized the role that this idea could play in philosophical semantics.

15. This implausible claim should not be confused with the absurd opinion that the numbers 35 and 53 – the *objects* of those representations – have the same constituents.

Chapter 3

1. The roots of this analysis of modality can be detected in Kant's pre-critical writings. In the *Beweisgrund* of 1763, for example, he said that "possibility is abolished not only if internal contradiction is encountered, as in logical impossibility, but also when no matter or datum for thought exists" (p. 69).

2. The answer is, of course, anybody as clever as Gauss.

3. Upon occasion Kant got so carried away that he said that "concepts are altogether impossible ... if no object is given for them" (*Critique*, A139/B178). He didn't mean it; in his *Nachträge*, he corrected this statement, replacing "become impossible" with "are, for us, without meaning" (p. 28). Kant's position was that the consistency of a concept can be established independently of its "objectivity" or "objective validity." The concept of a regular decahedron, for example, is perfectly consistent but lacks objective validity ("Uber Kästners Abhandlungen" [1790], *Kants Gesammelte Schriften*, vol. 20, pp. 414–15), since no object can be presented in intuition that conforms to it (there is no "construction of the concept," p. 416). Frege had somewhat stricter demands; he seems to have thought that the only way to prove the consistency of a concept was by identifying an instance. If so, we could not be certain of the consistency of the concept of a regular decahedron or, for that matter, of that of a satellite of the moon.

4. The only way to have an intuition of a line is to draw it in thought (*Critique*, A162–3/B203); moreover, drawing in thought involves the representation of a process in time – hence of a psychological process (see *Critique*, A102).

5. Kemp Smith thinks that in these passages Kant should have referred to the schemata of concepts rather than to images (*A Commentary to Kant's 'Critique of Pure Reason'*, pp. 337–8). But since the schema of a concept represents a method that associates with each instance of the concept an image of it, the problem discussed below arises also in the case of the schema. In any case, in A239f/B298f Kant explained that pure intuition gives only the forms of objects and that even pure concepts are without meaning if we do not construct objects for them in empirical intuition: "The mathematician meets this demand by the construction of a figure, which, although produced *a priori*, is an appearance present to the senses. In the same science the concept of magnitude seeks its support and sensible meaning in number, and this in turn in the fingers, in the beads of the abacus, or in strokes and points which can be placed before the eyes" (*Critique*, A240/B299).

6. In *De mundi sensibilis atque intelligibilis forma et principiis* (1770), p. 403, Kant had written that geometry thinks of its objects not by means of universal concepts but "by subjecting it to the eyes by means of a singular intuition as happens with things sensitive." Also, "the mathematics of space (geometry) is based upon this successive synthesis of the productive imagination in the generation of figures" (*Critique*, A163/B204).

7. Bolzano envisaged this first possibility when he wondered in *Beyträge zu einer begründeteren Darstellung der Mathematik*, "How do we proceed from the intuition of a single object to the feeling that what we observed is also valid for all others? Through what is unique and individual or through what is general in this object? Obviously only through the latter, that is, by means of the concept and not by means of the intuition" (pp. 243–4).

8. Mill allowed for one exception: "That the same thing should at once be and not be – that identically the same statement should be both true and false – is not only inconceivable to us, but we cannot imagine that it could be made conceivable. We cannot attach sufficient meaning to the proposition, to be

able to represent to ourselves the supposition of a different experience on this matter. We cannot therefore even entertain the question, whether the incompatibility is in the original structure of our minds, or is only put there by our experience" (*Hamilton's Philosophy,* p. 70). By implication he is saying that we *can* attach sufficient meaning to the remaining strictly inconceivable propositions to describe the circumstances in which we would regard them as conceivable and even true.

9. For details of Mill's attempts to explain the a priori from the "Law of Inseparable Association" see, e.g., *Hamilton's Philosophy,* chap. 14.

10. It wasn't successful. See Hilbert, *Grundlagen der Geometrie,* app. 5.

11. This third point involves the observation that the geometry does not determine the metric, something that even Reichenbach did not fully appreciate but that does find detailed recognition in Grünbaum's writings (e.g., *Philosophical Problems of Space and Time,* chap. 3, sec. B).

12. Helmholtz's original goal in "On the Facts Underlying Geometry" was to show that given the three-dimensionality and the infinity of space, free mobility entailed that space must be Euclidean. Free mobility was shown to entail constant curvature, and the assumption of infinity ruled out spherical spaces (curvature > 0). Then, in 1869, Beltrami brought to Helmholtz's attention his own "An Attempt to Interpret Non-Euclidean Geometry," in which, as we saw, he studied spaces of constant *negative* curvature that satisfy both free mobility and the postulate of infinity. Helmholtz's "On the Origins and Significance of the Axioms of Geometry" is essentially a philosophical meditation on Beltrami's discovery.

It is worth noting that the search for an "interesting" set of conditions sufficient for Riemann's metrical form soon came to be known as "der Raumproblem." What should count as an interesting set of conditions was never very well defined, but it was generally assumed that they had to be somehow known with greater certainty than the Riemannian form they were intended to justify. Lie soon showed that Helmholtz had not quite solved the problem or that, if he had, he had grossly misdescribed the premises of his proof; for the axiom of free mobility that might be thought to be grounded on experience is one that refers to finite motions, whereas Helmholtz's reasoning involves an appeal to a version of the principle that applies to infinitesimal motions. Like many other people at the time, Helmholtz seems to have thought of infinitesimal motions as finite but very tiny motions. Thus, he concluded that one could infer from his finite version of free mobility to the infinitesimal version (what is true of all finite motions must also be true of the tiny ones). Lie, in contrast, was sensitive to the idea (stemming from Bolzano's work) that infinitesimal "motions" were no motions and infinitesimal "distances" were no distances, and that talk concerning infinitesimals was to be construed as, in effect, involving what Russell came to call incomplete symbols. Helmholtz's totally fallacious reasoning can be seen as a paradigm case of Whitehead's "fallacy of misplaced concreteness," and Lie's point as a striking and enlightening application of the doctrine of incomplete symbols. For an illuminating account of the relevant facts see Torretti's *Philosophy of Geometry from Riemann to Poincaré,* chap. 3, Pt. 1.

13. The fact that is, in effect, observed by the members of both universes, and that was perhaps intended by Helmholtz to count as the factual ground of geometry, is what Grünbaum has called "Riemann's concordance assumption," the claim that solid objects that coincide at one time and place will coincide at other times and places, independently of how they have been transported. All Riemannian spaces – including those of variable curvature – satisfy this condition (geometrically reinterpreted as the path independence of congruence judgments). This new fact can hardly be regarded as a new candidate for the empirical foundation of geometry, however, since Weyl's infinitesimal geometry, for example, allows for spaces that violate Riemann's concordance assumption. For references see my "Elective Affinities: Weyl and Reichenbach."

14. In "Uber die thatsächlichen Grundlagen der Geometrie" (1868), Helmholtz had made the very same statement, adding, "This investigation is quite independent of the further question of the origin of our knowledge of the statements of factual content" (p. 610). This topic was the central subject of "On the Origin and Significance of the Axioms of Geometry."

15. Riehl did not do any better. In *Der philosophische Kriticismus* he explained that in analytic judgments "we analyze the content of the given concept and we thereby illuminate or clarify our understanding of it. If, on the other hand, different concepts are put in a judgment complex, the ensuing unity of representation is synthetic; it widens our knowledge of the subject concept. The synthetic judgment enriches our knowledge. The staying at a point in the given concept in one case, the going beyond it to another concept, in the second case, signifies the difference between analytic and synthetic" (vol. 1, pp. 318–19). Without further ado, he concluded, "Judgments whose connecting ground is a concept are analytic judgments; judgments whose ground of unity is intuition are synthetic. Analytic judgments are purely conceptual judgments; synthetic judgments are intuition judgments" (p. 320).

16. See also Riehl's *Führende Denker und Forscher,* chap. 9, esp. pp. 228–9.

Chapter 4

1. See also Kant, *Critique,* A715–18/B743–6. It is interesting that Bolzano referred to this very claim in *WL,* vol. 4, p. 291, observing that mathematics now uses the method that Kant attributed to philosophy, since it entirely avoids intuition.

2. See Russell's letter of 15 January 1904 to Meinong, in which he identified his conception of logic with Meinong's *Gegenstandstheorie.*

3. This often ignored distinction will play a decisive role in the characterization of two types of realism (attributed to Helmholtz and Planck, respectively) in Chapter 9. Note, for example, that in *Begriffsschrift* Frege illustrated what he meant by the "conceptual content" as what is common to 'The Greeks defeated the Persians at Plataea' and 'The Persians were defeated by the Greeks at Plataea' (van Heijenoort, *From Frege to Gödel,* p. 12). The effort to preserve something more than logical form is transparent.

4. The goal, he had written, is precisely to define the concept of number (*The Foundations of Arithmetic*, p. 5). This must be done, he argued, without appeal to the psychological conditions that preceded the formation of this concept. No description of mental processes "can ever take the place of a genuine definition of the concept" (p. 34).

5. Here is a sample of Bolzano's troublesome account of the nature of intuition: "As soon as we direct our attention upon the change that is caused in our mind by an external body, e.g., a rose that is brought before our senses, the *next* and *immediate* result of this attention is that the *representation* of this change arises in us. Now, this representation has an *object*, namely, the change that takes place in our mind at that very moment, and nothing else" (*WL*, vol. 1, p. 326; see also *Grossenlehre*, sec. 6).

6. The objective representation of an individual is apparently the individual itself. In this period, Frege did not see any difference between the objective representation of a place and the place itself (*The Foundations of Arithmetic*, p. 37). This is a feature characteristic of semantic monism (see the section on semantic dualism).

7. See also "Ueber den Zweck der Begriffsschrift," *Begriffsschrift*, p. 101, and *Nachlass*, p. 273.

8. In his early writings (*Begriffsschrift* and elsewhere) Frege talked as if the concept were not there until we "create" it by carving it out in one way or another. But, of course, it is hard to see how we could find a concept in a cpj if it had not been there to begin with.

9. Frege's remarks are obviously valid only when referred to symbols (as the parenthetical remarks indicate); but they are claimed to apply to their semantic correlates. Once again, Frege's primarily semantic thought pattern seems to be dominated by syntactic factors. (Carnap could have pointed to these developments as proof of the misleading character of the material mode of speech; see Chapter 17.)

10. See Chapter 6 for Russell's first theory of denoting. The novelty of Frege's approach may be underscored by noticing that twenty years later, in *Principles*, Russell would argue that the propositions *if x is a man, then x is mortal, for every x* and *all men are mortal* are equivalent but not identical. The former is said to be really a conjunction of infinitely many propositions – presumably its instances – whereas the latter is a simple proposition whose subject term is whatever 'all men' denotes.

11. Frege's characterization of the meaning of molecular expressions (in *Begriffsschrift* and elsewhere) is the only reason I know of to ascribe to him the view that meaning (i.e., sense) consists of truth conditions. The reason is, in fact, not very good, since obviously this construction process applies only to molecular expressions and it is intended to give, in effect, the meanings of the logical connectives. It is not clear that Frege recognized the uniqueness assumption involved in saying that $p \lor q$ is *the* cpj that is true precisely when p is true or q is true; but this assumption does have a ring of truth-conditional semantics. There is, however, no reason to think that Frege held a similar view for the crucial case of atomic sentences. Nothing in Frege's writings on

geometry, for example, suggests that he would have given a truth-conditional account of the way in which atomic expressions in geometry mean what they mean.

12. More than three decades later he would reiterate the point: "An object can be determined in different ways, and every one of these ways of determining it (*Bestimmungsweisen*) can give rise to a special name; and these different names then have different senses" (Letter to Jourdain [1914], *Philosophical and Mathematical Correspondence,* p. 80).

13. Translators do not agree on how to render *'Bedeutung'* into English, although most of them agree that 'meaning' and 'significance' are bad translations (favorites are 'reference', 'denotation', 'designation', *'nominatum'*). It so happens that 'meaning' and 'significance' are what *'Bedeutung'* means in German. Moreover, it seems reasonable to assume that the best translation of a given term as used by a given philosopher into language *L* is the one he or she would have chosen if in full command of *L.* How would Frege have translated *'Bedeutung'* into English? We do not know for sure, but he once told Peano that he would translate *'Bedeutung'* into Italian as *'significazione'* (see Letter to Peano [undated], *Wiss. Briefwechsel,* p. 196); and in reply to inquiries from Jourdain, he used the word 'signify' as a name of the relation between sentence and truth value. It is hard to believe that had Frege written in English, he would have chosen anything but 'meaning' or 'significance' as equivalent to his *'Bedeutung'.* If Russell had written in German, *his* 'meaning' would have become *'Bedeutung',* and no doubt subtle hermeneuticians would have rendered it back into English as 'reference', *'nominatum',* or worse.

Chapter 5

1. See, e.g., Meinong's "The Theory of Objects" (1904), p. 76; Russell's "Meinong's Theory of Complexes and Assumptions," *Essays in Analysis,* p. 21, and "On Denoting," *Essays in Analysis,* p. 110.

2. Psychology, he argued, is the theoretical science closest to logic. See letter to Husserl of January 1905 in appendix to *Wahrheit und Evidenz,* where Brentano said, for example, "What is the general law of contradiction if not the statement: whoever both acknowledges and rejects (explicitly or implicitly) the same thing, or, in other words, whoever contradicts himself, thinks absurdly?" (p. 156). See also Brentano's *Die Lehre vom richtigen Urteil,* containing lectures on logic and theory of knowledge given between 1874 and 1895, in which Brentano argued that psychology is the ground of logic.

3. Brentano wrote to Kraus in 1909, "I never drew on Bolzano in the slightest" (*Psychology,* p. 383). In his letter to Husserl of January 1905 ("You praise Bolzano as your teacher and guide," he complained), Brentano called Bolzano's domain of thought things "absurd" (*Wahrheit und Evidenz,* p. 157).

4. Brentano's own position on this matter remains a subject of speculation. His emphasis on the immanent and in-existent character of his "objects" suggests that he denied them an independent life. In response to the rising tide of Platonism within his school, he once wrote, "When I talked of an 'immanent

object', I introduced the expression 'immanent' in order to avoid a misunderstanding, for some call object what is outside the mind. As opposed to this, I talked of an object that pertains to representation, whether or not there is anything outside the mind corresponding to it. It has *never been my view that the immanent object is identical with the 'represented object'*. The representation does not have as object the 'represented thing' but 'the thing'; thus, e.g., the representation of a horse does not have the 'represented horse' but 'horse' as its (immanent) object, and thus the only one properly to be called object. But this object has no being" (*Wahrheit und Evidenz*, pp. 87–8). (There seems to be here an implicit reference to Twardowski; see below.) Yet in 1909 he wrote to Kraus, explicitly acknowledging that his original intention coincided with that of the Meinongians (in *Psychology*, p. 383). Whatever the historical truth, the fact is that the elder Brentano thought the turn to semantic ontology elicited by his earlier studies indefensible.

5. Husserl was second only to Frege in his understanding of this situation. For example, he commented on Twardowski's (later Meinong's and Russell's) reasons for accepting nonexistent objects as follows: "The contradictory properties [of the subject expression] do not apply to the represented object, for what does not exist cannot have properties; they are merely represented as applying to an object" ("Intentional Gegenstände" [1894], *Aufsätze und Rezensionen (1890–1910)*, p. 308).

6. See, e.g., Moore's review of Brentano, *The Origin of the Knowledge of Right and Wrong*, and Russell's several papers on Meinong and his school in *Essays in Analysis*.

7. By the time of *Analysis of Mind*, Russell had rejoined the idealists in denying this distinction and denouncing Brentano for having drawn it.

8. Some Frege scholars prefer to include as part of the *meaning* of unsaturatedness the fact that concepts cannot occupy subject positions. I prefer to look upon this thesis as an alleged consequence of unsaturatedness. There are, of course, two distinguishable issues involved: (a) whether the concept is an entity that, unlike objects, can unify other entities (objects *or* concepts) into new (propositional) complexes and (b) whether entities of that peculiar sort can occupy subject positions. Frege and Russell agreed on what I am calling unsaturatedness but disagreed on the latter issue.

9. The mind dependence in question is one that has nothing whatever to do with the temporal location of mind relative to physical objects. Kant would have had no difficulty in accepting the theory of evolution and granting that there were physical objects *before* there were any minds. The temporal reference implicit in this claim places us already within the domain of the constituted world of experience, and Kant's philosophy has no implications concerning the order of mind and matter within it. If, however, we want to refer to an order outside that constituted realm, the word 'before' has lost all sense.

10. The first suggestion of this view occurs in the famous letter to Frege of 1902 (van Heijenoort, *From Frege to Gödel*, pp. 124–5), in which he reported on the paradox. The view is further developed in "On Some Difficulties in the Theory of Transfinite Numbers and Order Types," *Essays in Analysis*, esp.

pp. 137–8 and 163–4. In "On the Substitutional Theory of Classes and Relations," *Essays in Analysis,* we are warned against "false abstractions" (p. 165), which are to be avoided through an appropriate holistic semantic analysis.

Chapter 6

1. These fragments encapsulate and link the two central ideas concerning representation that seem to underlie Wittgenstein's constructivism. On the one hand, there is the well-known concern with isomorphism in representation, as prominent in the *Tractatus* as in Wittgenstein's doctrines of the late 1920s; on the other, there is the seemingly unrelated concern with the notion of "searching" or "looking for," which is invisible in the *Tractatus* but prominent around 1930. The link between these notions emerges from Leibniz's text: In order for a representation truly to represent an object it must consist either in the actual giving of the object (intuition) or else in a method that leads us to the object – in other words, we must be able to look for what we are concerned with; otherwise, we cannot be said to have a semantic link with the object in question. Moreover, the kind of looking cannot be one that leads us to the object, as it were, accidentally.

2. See A. Marty, "Uber das Verhältnis von Grammatik und Logik" (1893), and also *Gesammelte Schriften,* vol. 2, pt. 1, p. 219. Twardowski's confused arguments on this matter are in *On the Content and Object of Presentations,* chap. 14.

3. Leibniz called a mode of thinking "*blind* or *symbolical*" when we are not thinking of all the ingredients of the appropriate notion and operate instead with words or symbols (as in algebra, arithmetic, and "in fact universally"). When we think all the ingredient notions, "I call the cognition *intuitive.*" Leibniz added, "Of the primary elements of our notions, there is given no other knowledge than the intuitive" ("Meditationes de cogitatione, veritate et ideis" [1684], quoted by Mill in *Hamilton's Philosophy,* pp. 319–20).

4. We have seen that Frege toyed with this idea in his letter to Marty (?) quoted on p. 70. The idea then vanished from Frege's philosophy. In a letter to Russell of 1902, Frege explained that one must not confuse these conjunctive complexes – which he apparently regarded as legitimate – with classes (*Wiss. Briefwechsel,* pp. 222–4).

5. Russell's views on quantification in *Principles* consist of two parts: his theory of denoting and the notion of formal implication, borrowed from Peano. The latter notion is only loosely related to Frege's idea of quantification and is drastically inferior to it. Russell's snide remark about Frege's account of quantification in his otherwise admiring appendix on Frege's writings is a clear indication of how poorly he understood Frege's great discovery.

6. See my "Russell as a Platonic Dialogue" for further discussion of this point.

7. Adding to the confusion, in his review article, "Meinong's Theory of Complexes and Assumptions," *Essays in Analysis,* there appears to be a recurrence of the Brentanophile stage. The confusion becomes monumental when in "On Denoting" Russell manages to present himself as entirely oblivious to

the points he had made in chapter 5 of *Principles*. In later years Russell insisted that until he discovered the theory of "On Denoting," he saw no way of rejecting Meinong's reasoning that if the golden mountain did not have some sort of being one should conclude that 'the golden mountain has no being' is meaningless (see, e.g., *My Philosophical Development*, p. 84). He certainly had thought this before he discovered his first theory of denoting. He couldn't possibly have thought it afterward.

8. This was far from being Frege's own account of definite descriptions. For Frege the particle 'the' did not merely introduce a number statement but, beyond this, had a "reductive" effect, bringing the types of the entities under consideration to the lower, objectual level – as Russell might have put it.

   Our version of definite descriptions allows for a simple explanation of the distinction between primary and secondary occurrences. The distinction applies to those cases in which the sentence under consideration can be interpreted in two ways, either as 'The *F* is *G*' or as '*H*(the *F* is *G*)'. Thus, one can say that the difference concerns the decision of how much of the sentence under consideration must be included as part of the predicate concept *G*. For example, 'Scott is not the author of *Waverley*' could be interpreted either taking *G* to be '*x* is not identical with Scott' or taking it to be '*x* is identical with Scott', in which case *H* would be 'It is not the case that *p*'. In the first case we would be saying that there is exactly one author of *Waverly* and that he is identical with Scott; in the second, that the following is not true: that there is exactly one author of *Waverley* and that he is not identical with Scott. The truth conditions of these claims are different, since the latter (but not the former) would be true if there were more than one author of *Waverley*.

9. Russell, of course, had a second "objection," contained in "On Denoting." He argued that "the relation of the meaning to the denotation involves certain rather curious difficulties which seem in themselves sufficient to prove that the theory which leads to such difficulties must be wrong" (*Essays in Analysis*, p. 111). These curious difficulties emerged from an effort Russell made in mid-1905 to work out the details of his theory of denotation. After a number of unsuccessful tries (contained in "On Fundamentals," written in 1905, 230.030710, Russell Archives), Russell came to the conclusion that we cannot talk either *about*, or *by means of*, his denoting complexes. The argument for this conclusion in "On Denoting" is entirely grounded on Russell's celebrated inability to keep the use–mention distinction straight. Through reasoning that defies reconstruction, Russell came to conclude that it is impossible to talk of denoting complexes, that there really are not any, and that consequently "the whole distinction of meaning and denotation has been wrongly conceived" (*Essays in Analysis*, p. 113).

10. Church once noted that *Principia Mathematica*, no less than Milton's *Paradise Lost*, is part of the English language.

11. This describes Russell's treatment of definite descriptions in the terminology that he preferred to use. But one might rephrase his point in terminology that became current after Wittgenstein, saying that Russell's strategy associates with every sentence in which an incomplete expression occurs a statement

of its truth conditions – formulated without appealing to the expression in question and in a more perspicuous language.

12. See Urmson, *Philosophical Analysis,* p. 29, and Pears, *Bertrand Russell and the British Tradition in Philosophy,* pp. 107–11.

13. The very same argument occurs in Whitehead and Russell, *Principia,* p. 70.

Chapter 7

1. The extra machinery has to do with his theory of cardinality, which Russell had complemented – along lines similar to Frege's and consistent with Cantor's intentions – plus the theorem that the power set of a set cannot have a cardinality smaller than that of the given set.

2. The claim occurs in his letter to Frege of 24 June 1902 (Frege, *Wiss. Briefwechsel,* p. 216). One possible line of reasoning would be as follows: To everything in the universe there corresponds its singleton, so there are no more things than classes; and there surely can be no more classes than things, since each class is a thing in the universe. By the Cantor–Bernstein theorem, it "follows" that the two classes are equinumerous.

3. The paradox remained unrecognized for several months, perhaps longer. Russell first communicated it to Frege in a letter dated 16 June 1902 (van Heijenoort, *From Frege to Gödel,* pp. 124–5). The account given in the text is a slightly Lakatosian (i.e., erroneous) reconstruction of the events leading to the paradox. The unvarnished truth is told in my "The Humble Origins of Russell's Paradox."

4. See, e.g., the letter to Frege of 29 September 1902 (Frege, *Wiss. Briefwechsel,* pp. 230–1); Russell, *Principles,* sec. 500, p. 527; Russell, "On Some Difficulties in the Theory of Transfinite Numbers and Order Types," *Essays in Analysis,* p. 142.

5. In July 1902 Russell wrote to Frege: "Each day I understand even less the real meaning of 'Umfang eines Begriffes' [Frege's term for 'class']" (Frege, *Wiss. Briefwechsel,* p. 221); and in August he insisted, "but I am still completely lacking in the direct intuition [*Anschauung*], the direct insight [*Einsicht*], of what you call Werthverlauf," i.e., of Frege's extensions of concepts and relations (p. 226).

6. In the mid-1920s Ramsey reinterpreted the doctrine of *Principia Mathematica* in an extensional framework, abandoning the primacy of intension. Russell's reaction is worth noting. Ramsey had, in effect, taken "correlations" to be collections of ordered pairs. Russell wrote: "Now such a collection exists if somebody collects it, or if something either empirical or logical brings it about. But, if not, in what sense is there such a collection? I am not sure whether this question means anything, but if it does it seems as if the answer must be unfavorable to Ramsey" (Review of Ramsey's *The Foundations of Mathematics and Other Logical Essays* [1932], p. 85). In a 1931 review ("Review of *Foundations of Mathematics* by F. P. Ramsey," p. 478), Russell said that Ramsey had tried to preserve the formulas of *Principia Mathematica* (except for the reducibility axiom) while changing the intended meanings. Russell's "middle course" on the issue of intensionalism is

illustrated in his correspondence with Jourdain. At one point (in 1905) Jourdain wondered why intensions were necessary for classes, noting that mathematicians behave like gods in their abstract domain. Russell replied that "even a Creator has to be able to make up his mind what he is creating" (Grattan-Guinness, *Dear Russell – Dear Jourdain,* p. 54). But a few sentences later the other side of his personality reasserted itself: "I do not hold that definition by extension is *logically* limited to finite classes, but it is humanly, because we are not immortal" (p. 55).

7. He even went on to challenge (in what would now be called a "Wittgensteinian" mood) Cantor's proof that there are more classes of finite numbers than there are finite numbers. According to Russell, his argument showed only that "no one denumerable set of formulae will cover all classes of finite numbers; but the class shown to be left over in each case is defined by a formula in the process of showing that it is left over. Thus this process gives no ground for thinking that there are classes of finite numbers which are not definable by a formula" ("On Some Difficulties in the Theory of Transfinite Numbers and Order Types," *Essays in Analysis,* p. 163).

8. Russell's account of this discovery is in a letter to Jourdain of 15 March 1906 (Grattan-Guinness, *Dear Russell – Dear Jourdain,* p. 80).

9. A final new axiom, the notorious axiom of reducibility, was also required in the system of *Principia,* although it is not, of course, required in the simplified (extensional) version of the theory of types due to Ramsey (see note 6, this chapter). This axiom elicited some remarkably eloquent complaints. Here is a fine example: "Especially with regard to the second point [Russell's axiom of reducibility], mathematics manifests its full participation in the servile revolt of the positive sciences against philosophy, the revolt of the anti-spiritual mind, with its democratic leveling process, against the spiritual mind and its hierarchic structure, which changed the question: 'What is your intrinsic nature and what does this nature bring forth?' into the other: 'What can you be used for? What profit do you yield when you are made to play your part in the process of production standardized by such and such axioms?' Brouwer's intuitionist mathematics represents the restoration of mind to its old and sacred rights" (H. Weyl, "Consistency in Mathematics" [1929], p. 150).

10. See also "The Regressive Method of Discovering the Premises of Mathematics" (1907), *Essays in Analysis,* pp. 273–4, 282.

11. Ramsey attributed to Russell the view that a logical truth is a true statement that contains only logical primitives (*The Foundations of Mathematics and Other Logical Essays,* p. 4). In his review Russell did not challenge this historical point.

12. "Now," he added in his review, "following Wittgenstein's definition of logic, I agree that they are tautologous generalizations" (p. 477). But a few years later, in *Principles,* he candidly conceded that "it is by no means easy to get an exact definition of this characteristic [i.e., being tautological or analytic]" (p. ix). And then he added that logical propositions are those that are true "in virtue of their form" (p. xii); that "if an adequate definition of logic is to be found," we must explain the meaning of "true in virtue of its form"; and,

finally, that "I am unable to give any clear account of what is meant by saying that a proposition is 'true in virtue of its form'" (p. xii). In short, Russell still did not know what logic was.

13. Russell had written in a reply to Bradley: "I do not myself admit necessity and possibility as fundamental notions: it appears to me that fundamentally truths are merely true in fact" ("Some Explanations in Reply to Mr. Bradley," p. 374).

14. The "cannot" is a revealing slip; Russell had no noncircular explanation of what it could possibly mean.

15. "[No] one definite entity, of any sort or kind, is ever a constituent of any truly logical proposition" (Russell, *Theory of Knowledge*, pp. 97–8).

16. "Acquaintance with the fact is only possible when there is such a fact" (Russell, *Theory of Knowledge*, p. 130).

17. Russell explained a few years later that Wittgenstein's criticism had led him to contemplate suicide. He is said to have considered dropping deep philosophy; but he kept writing rather profusely on things such as the so-called problem of the external world.

18. Elsewhere Russell explicitly invoked that notion in his doctrine of geometry. For example, he wrote that "it is, undoubtedly, by analysis of perceived objects that we obtain acquaintance with what is *meant* by a straight line in actual space" ("Non-Euclidean Geometry," p. 593).

19. I have attempted an examination of the relevant geometric facts in my "From Geometry to Tolerance."

20. For example, Frege thought that "deducing something by logical inferences from Hilbert's pseudoaxioms is about as possible as cultivating a garden plot by means of mental arithmetic" (*On the Foundations of Geometry and Formal Theories of Arithmetic*, p. 105).

21. Notice, in passing, the revealing inference from "intuition-free" to "purely logical, like arithmetic." As Bolzano had noted, there is a gap between those two.

22. Like Frege, Russell started by rejecting this viewpoint; but, unlike Frege, Russell was far too sensitive to scientific trends to let the opinions of the experts go unheeded for long. As the first of a very long series of epicyclic revisions of his theories, Russell endorsed, circa 1900, the idea that geometry asserts only the implications from its axioms to its theorems; and by 1902 he had generalized this doctrine to the totality of mathematics: "Pure Mathematics is the class of all propositions of the form 'p implies q', where p and q are propositions containing one or more variables, the same in the two propositions, and neither p nor q contains any constants except logical constants" (*Principles*, p. 3). On this topic see my "Russell and Kant." On its sources in geometry see Russell's *Principles*, pp. 7–8, 372–3, 429, 430, 441–2.

23. Propositionalism also prevented Frege from understanding what Hilbert regarded as the most important results of nineteenth-century geometry: the independence proofs. Such proofs presupposed that logic is fully applicable to systems of only partially interpreted sentences. They regarded specific, fixed "interpretations" as something with which logicians need not concern themselves. All talk about models and interpretations in the now standard

sense would have been anathema to Frege, since it presupposes that a language can be developed and that logic can be applied to it without assuming that the nonlogical signs have any specific meanings. The best Frege could make of the formalists' "interpretations" was in terms of the exemplification relation. For example, Frege thought that

(1) If 2 is greater than 0, then 2 is less than 1, was an "interpretation" in the formalists' sense of the improper sentence:

(2) If x is greater than 0, then x is less than 1.

(See "Uber die Grundlagen der Geometrie," *Kleine Schriften,* pp. 301–2.) On this approach, the interpretation of hyperbolic geometry that proves the independence of the parallel postulate, for example, is understood as follows. Instead of (2), the implication to be "interpreted" has, as antecedent, the conjunction of Hilbert's axioms minus the parallel postulate and, as consequent, the denial of that postulate. Call this implication (3). Then Klein's "interpretation" is a true proposition (call it (4)) that stands to (3) precisely as (2) stands to (1). Frege granted that (1) does prove the independence of something, although not of the proposition *2 is less than 1* from *2 is greater than 0* (since we do not know what *that* would mean), or of the improper sentence 'x is less than 1' from 'x is greater than 0'. What is proved is the independence of the concept *being less than 1* from the concept *being greater than 0*. In cases like the inference from (3) to (4), Frege admitted, it is harder to describe the entities whose independence is being proved. They are the "meanings of the parts" of the antecedent and consequent of (3). In the simpler cases we have concepts, but "we lack a short designation for the meaning of such parts" in the general case (*The Foundations of Arithmetic,* p. 316).

In *Grundlagen,* before he developed his official semantics, Frege went along with general opinion uncritically acknowledging that geometers (presumably, Klein) had established the independence of some postulates (see p. 21). But he soon noticed the inconsistency between that standpoint and propositionalism, and decided that proofs such as Klein's or Hilbert's do nothing whatever to establish what they are designed to establish – the independence of certain geometric propositions. One could be confused into thinking that they do only if, like Hilbert, one failed to distinguish true axioms from sentences with only partial meaning. Moreover, as far as Frege could tell, there is *no* way to prove its independence from the remaining Euclidean axioms. Since the axiom is true, there is no question of finding a domain in which the other axioms are true and *it* "becomes" false (whatever that might mean). So according to Frege, the matter of independence was still an open question; perhaps the parallel postulate could be proved after all. See Hilbert's letter to Frege of 29 December 1899 in Frege, *Wiss. Briefwechsel,* pp. 65, 68.

Chapter 8

1. In the *Notebooks* he said that the concept *this* is "identical with the concept of *object*" (16 June 1915 (4), p. 61); thus, objects appear to be what we refer

to. For further evidence of semantic monism in Wittgenstein, see his treatment of identity in 4.241–3, entirely hostile to Frege's distinction between *Sinn* and *Bedeutung.* Recall that identity was the factor that triggered Frege's speculations on his distinction. In 6.232 Wittgenstein claimed that the distinction is unnecessary to solve Frege's problems. Just as Russell had placed Mont Blanc in the propositions about it, Wittgenstein was puzzled by the fact that a watch must be in propositions about *it* and that, consequently, changes in the watch would seem to entail changes in what we are saying about it. See, e.g., entries 16 June 1915 (8), p. 61; 18 June 1915 (9), pp. 64–5; and 22 June 1915 (5), p. 70.

A rather striking illustration of Wittgenstein's inability to see beyond the monistic framework comes in a Cambridge lecture given in 1934–5 in which he says that "the sentence 'I see a man' is not explained by '(Ex) I see $x \cdot x$ is a man'. For the latter leaves the use of x unexplained. It might be an explanation of saying 'I see a man' if this were said of a dark patch in fog, or of a human-looking figure which behaved like a man, or of a roll of carpet with a man in it" (*Lectures, 1932–5,* p. 125).

2. See also: "The phrase 'that so and so' has no complete meaning by itself, which would enable it to denote a definite object as (e.g.) the word 'Socrates' does. We feel that the phrase 'that so and so' is essentially incomplete, and only acquires full significance when words are added so as to express a judgment, e.g. 'I believe that so and so', 'I deny that so and so'" (Russell, "On the Nature of Truth and Falsehood" [1910], p. 151).

3. He let it drop until chapter 3 of part 2, in which he finally acknowledged that his effort to define 'proposition' had failed: "This instance suggests, what is also suggested by many other considerations, that our definition of a proposition is inadequate . . . when we say that *'aRb'* has 'meaning', it seems impossible to maintain that we *mean* that somebody understands it. If it has meaning, it *can* be understood; but it still has meaning if it happens that no one understands it. Thus it would seem that we must find some non-psychological meaning for the word 'proposition'" (*Theory of Knowledge,* p. 134). But the manuscript ends without even a hint of what this theory might be. One is reminded, once again, of Whitehead's remark, that Russell was an entire Platonic dialogue in himself. The manuscript of *Theory of Knowledge* would be easier to understand if different paragraphs were attributed to different persons.

4. "My fundamental thought is that the 'logical constants' do not represent (*vertreten*)" (*Tractatus,* 4.0312).

5. Wittgenstein added that the subject–predicate form is not the only one suggested by ordinary language, but as Frege's work shows (*sic*), it can be forced upon a great deal of discourse – such as mathematical discourse. "Only we must be clear about the fact that now we are not dealing with objects and concepts as the result of an analysis, but with molds into which we have squeezed the statement. . . . But squeezing something into a mold is the opposite of analysis" (*Philosophische Bemerkungen,* p. 137). At about the same time, Wittgenstein wrote in his typescript for vols. 1–4 (p. 17): "The subject–predicate form is not itself another logical form and it is the medium

of expression of innumerable fundamentally different logical forms. . . . 'The plate is round', 'the man is large', 'the patch is red' have nothing in common concerning their form" (Die Subjekt-Prädikatform ist an sich noch keine logische Form und sie ist Ausdrucksmittel unzähliger grundverschiedener logischer Formen. . . . "Der Teller is rund", "der Mann ist gross", "der Fleck ist rot" haben in ihrer Form nichts gemeinsames; Wittgenstein Papers, 208).

6. Reflecting on his earlier views, Wittgenstein wrote around 1930: "Here 'object' means 'reference of a not further definable word'" (*Philosophische Grammatik*, p. 208). And here is an example of what Wittgenstein had to say on indefinables in 1913: "Indefinables are of two sorts: names and forms. . . . A proposition must be understood when *all* its indefinables are understood. The indefinables in *'aRb'* are introduced as follows: (1) *'a'* is indefinable, (2) *'b'* is indefinable, (3) whatever *'x'* and *'y'* may mean, *'xRy'* says something indefinable about their meaning" (*Notebooks*, p. 98). (*'R'* stands not for a relation but for a form. The same is probably true in the celebrated *Tractatus*, 3.1432, which is why that statement does not support a nominalist interpretation.)

7. Explaining the *Tractatus* to Desmond Lee, Wittgenstein once said that "objects etc. is here used for such things as a colour, a point in visual space etc. . . . 'Objects' also include relations; a proposition is not two things connected by a relation. 'Thing' and 'relation' are on the same level. The objects hang as it were in a chain" (*Lectures, 1930–32,* p. 120).

8. Shortly after his visit to Wittgenstein, Ramsey wrote that "according to Wittgenstein, with whom I agree . . . we are not acquainted with any genuine objects or atomic propositions, but merely infer them as presupposed by other propositions" ("Universals" [1925], *Foundations*, p. 28). In 1932 Wittgenstein is reported to have said to his Cambridge students: "Russell and I both expected to find the first elements, or 'individuals', and thus the possible atomic propositions, by logical analysis. . . . And we were at fault for giving no examples of atomic propositions or of individuals. We both in different ways pushed the question of examples aside. We should not have said 'We can't give them because analysis has not gone far enough, but we'll get there in time'" (*Lectures, 1932–35,* p. 11; see also p. 109; compare with *Notebooks,* 16 June 1915 (6), p. 61). Actually, in pre-Tractarian writings Wittgenstein had made a few tries at identifying objects, including as possible candidates a point in the visual field, a patch in the visual field, the visual picture of a star, the material points of physics, and the primary colors (see *Notebooks,* pp. 45, 64, 69; Waismann, *Vienna Circle,* p. 43). In the *Blue Book* he gave redness, roundness, and sweetness as examples of "elements" or "individuals" (p. 31). In *Philosophische Bemerkungen* he explained, "What I once called 'objects', simples, were simply what I could refer to (*bezeichnen*) without running the risk of their possible nonexistence; i.e. that for which there is neither existence nor nonexistence" (p. 72), and he gave as examples "three knocks" (as in 'three knocks on the door') and "6 feet" (as in '6 feet high'). The *Notebooks* had explained that "relations and properties, etc. are *objects* too" (16 June 1915 (5), p. 61).

9. Es ist klar, dass es keine Relation des "Sich Befindens" gibt, die zwischen einer

Farbe und einem Ort bestünde, in dem sie "sich befindet". Es gibt kein Zwischenglied zwischen Farbe und Raum. Farbe und Raum sättigen einander. Und die Art, wie sie einander durchdringen, macht das Gesichtsfeld.

10. Quine has wondered why Russell thought that the doctrine of incomplete symbols could help solve his problems with the paradox. In Russell the theory of types is offered as a solution to the intensional paradoxes, not to the problem of the class of classes not belonging to themselves. The solution to the intensional paradoxes solves the problem with Russell's class and with many other paradoxical classes. But Russell had come to distrust the existence (subsistence, etc.) of *all* classes (not so for intensions, of course), and therefore wanted to get rid of commitments to them before he tried to solve the remaining, intensional paradoxes. The latter seemed to call for a far more discriminating surgery.

11. Apparently, Wittgenstein used a notation that associates with each adicity a corresponding copula. Thus, 'ϵ_1' seems to stand for the property copula, 'ϵ_2' for the dyadic-relation copula, and so on.

12. As I read this text, Wittgenstein was using quantifiers in connection with form much as Russell had in his *Theory of Knowledge.* Thus, Wittgenstein's '$(Ex,y)\epsilon_1(x,y)$' would stand for (the form of?) the property copula (something like 'x is attributed to y', perhaps), and 'Something is human' would stand for a single unsaturated entity, suspiciously like Frege's concept x *is human.* For clear indications of this use of quantification see, e.g., Wittgenstein's *Notebooks,* last entry for 15 October 1914, pp. 13, 104. By 1 November 1914 Wittgenstein no longer thought that $(Ex)\phi x$ was the form of ϕa (p. 22). Here he said for the first time that the form of a statement must already be given in the form of its constituents (p. 23).

13. Wittgenstein once wrote: "I could imagine an organ whose stops were to be operated by keys distributed among the keys of the manual that looked exactly like them. There might then arise a philosophical problem: 'How are silent notes possible?' And the problem would be solved by someone having the idea of replacing the stop keys by stops which had no similarity with the note keys" (*Philosophische Grammatik,* pp. 193–4).

14. In the *Tractatus* he had written, "When two expressions can be substituted for one another, that characterizes their logical form" (6.23(2); see also *Philosophical Remarks,* pp. 118–19).

15. Upon occasion Wittgenstein said that this or that is a form (e.g., that space, time, and being a color are forms of objects; see *Tractatus,* 2.0251). What he meant, apparently, was that it is not a constituent of a "propositional complex" (to use a non-Wittgensteinian phrase), but a feature of the sorts of arrangements in logical space of which the constituents we will actually encounter are capable. The central idea was that some words in ordinary language do not really stand for any thing, but only for possibilities of some of the things for which other words do stand. What is so misleading about ordinary language is that it treats (syntactically) in the very same manner what stands for objects and what stands for forms of objects, what we can speak about and what can only be shown. See the following section.

16. Wittgenstein did not assign a major role to the notion of a complex in the

Tractatus. This was probably the result of a conscious effort not to associate his views with those of Russell, Meinong, and the other philosophers who had placed it at the center of their semantics. But clearly Wittgenstein had that concept firmly in mind. This is revealed by several entries in his *Notebooks* (some quoted earlier) and by later remarks, such as this one from a later manuscript, quoted by André Maury in "The Concepts of *Sinn* and *Gegenstand* in Wittgenstein's *Tractatus*": "I said once (in the *Tractatus*) that the 'elementary statement' is a concatenation of names. For objects correspond to the names and to the statement corresponds a complex of objects. When the statement 'the jar is to the right of the glass' is true, what corresponds to it is the complex consisting of the jar, the glass and the relation Right–Left (or however one wishes to designate it)" (pp. 112–13).

17. The Sv is a combination of objects (*Tractatus,* 2.01) and is constituted by that configuration of objects (2.0272). Two quotations from Maury's "The Concepts of *Sinn* and *Gegenstand* in Wittgenstein's *Tractatus*" suggest a very intimate link between the concept *configuration of objects* and the concept *complex.* In a remark from the late 1930s Wittgenstein exclaimed, "The ungrammatic use of the words 'object' and 'complex'!!" In a text from 1944, in a very similar context we find, "The ungrammatic use of the words 'object + configuration'!" (p. 113).

18. Further evidence derives from the *Prototractatus,* 4.01221 and 4.10224, which makes a certain claim about *Sinn* that is then corrected to apply to the (possibly more general) notions of *Sachlage* and possible *Sachlage.* Presenting (*darstellen*) is intimately related to showing, but it demands bipolarity: We cannot present logical forms (4.12). We cannot present the *Sinnlos* but only *Sinn.*

19. The sentence expresses the thought (*Gedanke; Tractatus,* 3.12), but it presents (*darstellt*) its sense (2.221, 2.202, 4.031).

20. In his 1913 "Notes on Logic" Wittgenstein had stated, "Logical inferences can, it is true, be made in accordance with Frege's or Russell's laws of deduction, but this cannot justify the inference; and therefore they are not primitive propositions of logic" (*Notebooks,* p. 100).

21. Quine would appeal to this traditional understanding of things many years later in his first critique of conventionalism. His charge was that the conventionalist really means to say that logic is derivable from conventions *plus logic;* his basic reason is, in effect, that given that one has defined A as B, one still needs logic (the principle of identity and the law of substitution of identicals) in order to prove that A is B. This presupposes an anticonventionalist construal of logic (though, to be sure, the standard construal) and therefore begs the relevant question.

22. Trying to draw a clear-cut division between his own view of the matter and that of his predecessors, Wittgenstein wrote in 1914 that "logical propositions are neither true nor false" (*Notebooks,* p. 108) and that a logical "proof" of a logical proposition does not prove that it is true, "but proves *that* it is a logical proposition" (p. 108). "Therefore, if we say that one *logical* proposition *follows* logically from another, this means something quite different from saying that a *real* proposition follows logically from *another.* . . .

Logical propositions *are forms of proof:* they shew that one or more propositions *follow* from one (or more). Logical propositions *shew* something,
because the language in which they are expressed can *say* everything that
can be *said*" (p. 108).

Chapter 9

1. Schlick had read Russell's review of Meinong's *Uber Annahmen,* but evidently had not grasped the significance of that notion, which first had been
   detected quite clearly in Frege's writings. We can formulate the point simply
   by noting that in the assertions 'If *p,* then *q*' and '*p*', *p* appears unasserted in
   one case and asserted in another; yet if modus ponens is to be valid, they
   must express the very same thing. So what is expressed or said by a statement, its content, what is relevant not only to logical inference but to argument in general, must be quite independent of assertion or judgment, of
   epistemic grounds, of propositional attitudes toward contents. Consider, for
   example, reductio ad absurdum arguments.
2. The idea that once I have a concept, I still have to do something more, to
   coordinate it with objects, in order for it to have an extension, would reap-
   pear in Reichenbach's notion of a coordinative definition.
3. On the exhaustive character of these two forms of definition, see "Experience, Cognition and Metaphysics" (1926), *Philosophical Papers,* vol. 2, p.
   101.
4. Schlick was clearly unaware of the nature or magnitude of the problem he
   had just touched upon and of how poorly one can understand what science
   has done with the concept of silver in terms of standard ideas of explicit
   definition.
5. The problem of false judgment has received a remarkable twist: "A *false*
   judgement must obviously be one whereby the designation of facts would
   come to have two or several meanings" (Schlick, "The Nature of Truth in
   Modern Logic," p. 97). Suppose, for example, we say, 'This tree is red' in front
   of a green tree. If I accept the judgment in question as a name of the corresponding state of affairs, "I would never know . . . what the proposition: 'The
   tree is red' actually means; . . . For . . . I would not know whether it is really
   talking about a red tree or a green one. . . . A negative judgement . . . is
   therefore nothing else but a sign for the fact that the corresponding positive
   judgment would yield several possibilities of coordination, and is thus unus-
   able" (p. 97).
6. For details see, e.g., Gerold Prauss, *Kant und das Problem der Dinge an sich;*
   and Werkmeister, "The Complementarity of Phenomena and Things in Themselves," esp. p. 303.
7. Kant's own reluctance to choose between these two interpretations is illustrated by his conflicting remarks on the topic in letters written within a
   period of ten days. On 7 August 1783, he wrote to Garve that "all objects that
   are given to us can be interpreted in two ways: on the one hand, as appearances; on the other hand, as things in themselves" (Kant, *Philosophical
   Correspondence, 1759–99,* p. 103). On 16 August, he wrote to Mendelssohn

that "there are other objects in addition to the objects of possible experience – indeed, they are necessarily presupposed, though it is impossible for us to know the slightest thing about them" (*Philosophical Correspondence, 1759–99*, p. 107). More often than not, Kant preferred to sit on the fence: "We can never know [things-in-themselves] except in the way in which they affect us" (*Grundlegung zur Metaphysik der Sitten*, p. 4).

8. For a recent example of this position, see G. Maxwell's "Scientific Methodology and the Causal Theory of Perception." Maxwell argued, in Quine's presence, that no one had ever seen Quine – or any other physical object, for that matter.

9. If the parties in this debate had distinguished between meaning, justification, and topic, Mach might have granted to Planck that experience is not the topic of science and Planck might have granted to Mach that experience plays a greater role than he thought in assigning meaning and in justifying science.

10. Schlick was, in effect, joining an affirmative action movement on behalf of the given that had considerable currency at the time. Whitehead gave eloquent formulation to its central idea as follows: "What is given in perception is the green grass. This is an object which we know as an ingredient in nature. The theory of psychic additions [i.e., the "one-world materialist" view] would treat the greenness as a psychic addition furnished by the perceiving mind, and would leave to nature merely the molecules and the radiant energy which influence the mind towards that perception" (*The Concept of Nature*, pp. 29–30). For us, "the red glow of the sunset should be as much a part of nature as are the molecules and electric waves by which men of science would explain the phenomenon" (p. 29). Whitehead's point is an echo of Schlick's.

11. A decade later, Carnap would face Schlick's difficulty in his familiar Genesis style, by merely creating one more universe between the private auto-psychological domain and the qualityless world of physics. This is what he called in the *Aufbau* the "physical world," a version of Kant's world of outer sense and of Sellars's "manifest image." Whether Schlick failed to see the alternative or thought instead that he had quite a handful of universes already, the fact is that he refused to acknowledge a halfway world between the topic of phenomenological psychology and that of physics. In *Einstein's Theory of Relativity*, Cassirer dismissed Schlick's identification of the Kantian doctrine of the ideality of space as a gross misunderstanding (pp. 451–2). In "Critical or Empiricist Interpretation of Modern Physics," Schlick replied that he "was well aware that Kant defines 'intuition' in a quite different way. . . . Kant certainly wanted to purge [intuition] of everything psychological – but I shall never be able to persuade myself that he succeeded" (*Philosophical Papers*, vol. 1, p. 331). In correspondence, Cassirer had raised the same objection, and Schlick had replied as follows: "That my concept of thing-in-itself coincides with Kant's concept of the empirical object is largely correct, but in my opinion they do not coincide exactly, and indeed the reason for that is simple, because the concepts of appearance and empirical object in Kant's system do not seem to me to be constituted in a way that is

free of contradiction." (Dass mein Begriff des Dinges an sich mit dem Kantischen des empirischen Gegenstandes zusammenfällt, trifft im grossen Ganzen zu, aber meines Erachtens doch nicht genau, und zwar einfach deshalb, weil mir der Begriff der Erscheinung und des empirischer Gegenstandes in Kants System überhaupt nicht widerspruchsfrei konstituiert zu sein scheint; Letter of 30 March 1927, VCA).

It is worth adding that in 1920 Reichenbach had already written to Schlick saying, "There [i.e., in *AE*] you define the 'thing in itself' the way the Kantians usually define the object of appearance" (Sie [definieren] dort das 'Ding an sich' . . ., wie die Kantianer sonst den Gegenstand der Erscheinung definieren. Letter of 29 November 1920, VCA). See also Reichenbach's review, "Moritz Schlick, *Allgemeine Erkenntnislehre.*"

12. Since Schlick thought that intuition was the only human mode of access to quality or content, and since he did not recognize semantic content as an alternative to psychological content, it is easy to see why Schlick was so pleased with Carnap's structuralist version of knowledge in the *Aufbau.*

13. In conformity with this firmly held view, Schlick said that the psychological concept *red* designates the experience of perceiving red (*GTK,* p. 312). Hence, expressions like 'perceiving red' are highly misleading in that they suggest that red is not the experience itself but the (intentional) target of a relation involved in the experience. After explaining for years what was wrong with Schlick's way of thinking about representation, Russell embraced, in *The Analysis of Mind,* a position very similar to Schlick's.

14. Schlick did not see where his requirement that "I need a series of premises about the nature of the processes through which these sensations are aroused" could lead. Fifty years later Paul Feyerabend in *Against Method* would carry this reasoning to its tragic logical conclusion when he argued that those Aristotelians who refused to accept Galileo's telescopic observations had (Feyerabendian) methodology on their side. The reason is that Galileo did not have a decent theory of optics capable of grounding the appropriate inferences concerning the moon, etc. By Feyerabend's logic, Tycho Brahe should have taken off his glasses each time he made an astronomical observation in order to increase its reliability.

Chapter 10

1. Heute morgen habe ich Ihre Abhandlung ueber Cassirer mit wahrer Begeisterung gelesen. So scharfsinnig und wahr habe ich schon lange nichts gelesen.

2. Reichenbach's arguments in support of this (and related implications) are highly unclear and seem to be based on a number of unstated assumptions that Kant would readily reject. The arguments are also marred by technical confusions. For example, he talks of "non-Euclidean coördinates" and of the "metric of these coördinates" (*RAK,* p. 24), and he claims that "the requirement of general relativity leads to non-Euclidean coördinates" (p. 24).

3. In a review article on the philosophies of relativity, Reichenbach describes this book as the "masterful presentation of a historian to whom systematic analysis gave breadth of vision, and whose superior competence lacks any

dogmatism. His every sentence evinces a command of critical analysis that is bent not on a *preservation of Kant's doctrines,* but on a *continuation* of Kant's *methods*" ("The Present State of the Discussion on Relativity," pp. 25–6).

4. Ten years later Neurath would cut the very thin string tying Reichenbach's ship to reality (see Chapter 18).

5. As a proper Kantian, Reichenbach believed that all empirical observation is "theory laden" (although he also seems to have believed the opposite, since perception is the criterion for the uniqueness of coordination). That is why he did not say we compare a prediction with an observation but rather we compare one computation emerging from theory with another emerging from data. In Cassirer's words: "Abstract theory never stands on one side, while on the other side stands the material of observation as it is in itself and without any conceptual interpretation. Rather this material, if we are to ascribe to it any definite character at all, must always bear the marks of some sort of conceptual shaping. We can never oppose to the concepts, which are to be tested, the empirical data as naked *'facta';* but ultimately it is always a certain logical system of connection of the empirical, which is measured by a similar system and thus judged" (*Substance and Function,* p. 107). In 1925 Reichenbach wrote: "There are no facts, proclaims the idealist. . . . In a certain sense, this is true. Every experiment performed by a natural scientist presupposes a theory, in order that it may be utilized as a fact at all" ("Metaphysics and Natural Science" [1925], *Selected Writings, 1909–1953,* vol. 1, p. 289).

6. This is an allusion to Einstein's early and repeated statement to the effect that the content of his theory in the end reduces to statements about coincidence events, events in which two world lines coincide. This is one of many manifestations of Einstein's early operationist reductionism that, much to his later regret, inspired both quantum physicists and positivists to adopt an antirealist stance.

7. Weyl's approach to the traditional "problem of space" (*das Raumproblem*) was designed to answer this very question by identifyng a priori conditions that entailed the Riemannian expression for *ds.* See, e.g., his Spanish lectures, *Mathematische Analyse des Raumproblems,* and also *Philosophy of Mathematics and Natural Science,* pt. 2, chap. 1. Weyl eventually abandoned the project. For further references and an analysis of Weyl's attempts, see my "Elective Affinities: Reichenbach and Weyl."

8. Er erklärte sie und rechtfertigte ihre Geltung, indem er die allgemeinsten Gesetze der Natur zugleich als die Prinzipien der Natur*erkenntnis* enthüllte (als Prinzipien der Möglichkeit der Erfahrung). Mit anderen Worten (denn für ihn war dies dasselbe): er identifizierte die evidenten allgemeinen Sätze der Naturwissenschaft mit den Prinzipien, die den Erfahrungsgegenstand konstituieren. Gerade hierin, d.h. in der Vereinigung der beiden von Ihnen sehr richtig unterschiedenen Begriffe des Apriori, scheint mir ein so wesentlicher Gedanke des Kritizismus zu liegen, dass man nicht daran rütteln kann, ohne sich weit ausserhalb der Kantischen Philosophie zu stellen.

9. . . . die extremste Sensualismus, von dessen Unhaltbarkeit ich natürlich eben-

so wie Sie überzeugt bin. Mir ist die Voraussetzung gegenstandskonstituierender Prinzipien so selbstverständlich, dass ich, zumal in der "Allg. Erkenntnisl." nicht nachdrücklich genug darauf hinwies.

10. Es bestehen ja aber ausserdem noch die beiden Möglichkeiten, dass jene Prinzipien Hypothesen oder dass sie Konventionen sind. Nach meiner Meinung trifft gerade dies zu, und ist der Kernpunkt meines Briefes, dass ich nicht herauszufinden vermag, worin sich Ihre Sätze a priori von den Konventionen eigentlich unterscheiden. . . . Die entscheidenden Stellen, an denen Sie den Charakter Ihrer apriorischen Zuordnungsprinzipien beschreiben, erscheinen mir geradezu als wohlgelangene Definitionen des Konventionsbegriffs (pp. 2–3).

11. Sie fragen mich, warum ich meine Prinzipien a priori nicht *Konventionen* nenne. Ich glaube, über diese Frage werden wir uns sehr leicht einigen. Obgleich mehrere Systeme von Prinzipien möglich sind, ist doch immer nur eine *Gruppe* von Prinzipien-Systemen [*sic*] möglich, und in dieser Einschränkung liegt eben doch ein Erkenntnisgehalt. Jedes mögliche System besagt in seiner Möglichkeit eine *Eigenschaft* der Wirklichkeit. Ich vermisse bei Poincaré eine Betonung, dass die Willkürlichkeit der Prinzipien eingeschränkt ist, sowie man Prinzipien kombiniert. Darum kann ich den Namen "Kovention" nicht annehmen. Auch sind wir nie sicher, dass [wir] nicht zwei Prinzipien, die wir heute nebeneinander als konstitutive Prinzipien bestehen lassen und die also beide nach Poincaré *Conventionen* [*sic*] sind, morgen wegen neuer Erfahrungen trennen müssen, sodass zwischen beiden Konventionen die Alternative als synthetische Erkenntnis auftritt.

12. Ich glaube, dass nur die undefinierte Seite, durch Vermittlung der Wahrnehmung, die begriffliche Seite bestimmt, nicht aber umgekehrt. Jene Lehre scheint mir darauf zurückzuführen zu sein, dass man so leicht den *Begriff* der Wirklichkeit mit der Wirklichkeit selbst verwechselt . . . ein Schein, dem die Marburger Neukantianer zum Opfer gefallen sind. Die Festlegung der Länge eines Stabes (S. 38) scheint mir z.B. nicht zur Definition des wirklichen Stabes zu gehören – das Wirkliche ist immer jenseits aller Definition – sondern sie ist Bestimmung eines Merkmals unseres *Begriffes* von dem Stabe.

Chapter 11

1. . . . nur deuchte mir, dass dieser Wissenschaft [i.e., die Physik] noch eine andere vorhergehen sollte, in der erst dargethan und erklärt würde, dass wir, und unter welchen Umständen wir berechtigt wären, so manche *Erfahrungsurtheile* zu fällen. Denn dass die meisten Urtheile, die wir Erfahrungen nennen, von uns nicht unmittelbar erkannt, sondern erst aus gewissen andern gefolgert würden, das hatte ich schon als ein Knabe gefühlt, und mich nicht selten in dem Nachdenken darüber, aus was für Vordersätzen wir dergleichen Folgerungen eigentlich ableiten mögen, verloren. Lächeln Sie immerhin über die Nutzlosigkeit solch einer Untersuchung; ich gestehe doch, dass ich noch heut zu Tage glaube, es sollte eine solche Wissenschaft

geben, nur das ich nicht mehr meine, sie müsste von Jedem, der Physik studieren will, voraus betrieben werden.

2. Die ex[akten] Wiss[enschaften] arbeiten häufig mit Begriffen (die zuweilen gerade ihre Hauptbegriffe sind), von denen sie nicht exakt sagen können, was sie bedeuten; und andrerseits: die traditionellen Methoden der Philosophie können hier wenig helfen.

3. Since both the Kantian and positivist traditions had taken experience to be the touchstone of sense, it was natural to take experience as the target of this reductionist project.

4. Carnap used the term 'quasi-X' to signify the very best he could do to produce what other people call an X.

5. At this point there emerges a radical divergence with Russell concerning the problem of indefinables. Carnap said: "It has sometimes been thought that a physical magnitude (e.g., time) has a sense in and of itself, quite independently of how it is to be measured; the question of how it is to be measured is then a further question. On the contrary, one must emphasize strongly that the sense of each physical magnitude consists in this, that certain physical objects are associated with determined numbers. So long as one has not determined how this association is to proceed, the very magnitude is not determined, and assertions about it are senseless" (*Physikalische Begriffsbildung,* p. 21).

6. See "Über die Abhängigkeit der Eigenschaften des Raumes von denen der Zeit," p. 337, for Carnap's use of 'about'. In the *Aufbau,* sec. 32, Carnap considered the case in which, instead of an assertion about *a,* we have a context with zero or more free variables, and here the condition of adequacy for the "translation" is that the extensions of *definiendum* and *definiens* coincide.

7. In the *Aufbau,* Carnap did not seriously address the issue of exactly what is to count as a legitimate "translation" rule. The little he did say appears to entail that for the case of sentences, all that need be preserved is truth value (see, e.g., sec. 86). This is obviously absurd. Soon after the publication of the *Aufbau,* Carnap recognized that identity of extension could not possibly be a sufficient condition of adequacy. See Kaila's reference in his "Logistic Neo-positivism," pp. 7–8, to a private communication from Carnap on that issue.

8. See also the reference in sec. 7 of *Abriss der Logistik.* Apparently Carnap had not read "On Denoting."

9. The expression to which the translation rule applies need, of course, have no variables. What will have a quantified variable is the statement of the rule, since it must refer to a class of sentences indicating, for each member of the class, how the translation is to be performed. But as we shall see in Chapter 16, Carnap was not on friendly terms with the object language–metalanguage distinction during these years.

Chapter 12

1. . . . scheint es mir zweifelhaft, ob man so wie sie es tun, von der Beziehung der Gegenstände auf etwas Wirkliches abstrahieren darf. . . . Gewiss können Sie das Realitätsaxiom ein metaphysiches nennen; aber ohne dieses Axiom wäre

Ihr Konstitutionssystem nur ein Schachspiel, und die ganze Wissenschaft auch. . . . Ich glaube . . . dass Ihre Neutralität ein schöner Traum ist.

2. In 1927 M. Scheler published a monograph entitled "Idealism and Realism," in which he argued that those two doctrines share a false presupposition: "the assumption that we cannot separate what we call the existence or reality of any object (whether of the internal world, the external world, another self, a living being, an inanimate thing, etc.) and what we call its nature (its contingent nature as well as its essence, *essentia*) when we are dealing with the question of what is, or what can or cannot be, immanent to knowledge" (p. 289). Scheler argued that once the two issues are detached, one can see the truth (and the falsehood) in both metaphysical standpoints: Idealists are right in claiming that essence is immanent to consciousness; realists are right in denying immanence to existence. Husserl explained in the preface to the English edition of *Ideas* that "the real world indeed exists, but in respect of essence [it] is relative to transcendental subjectivity" (p. 21). Carnap's holism (as discussed later) may be regarded as an intelligible version of the claim that essence is immanent.

3. Carnap discussed the bad interpretation of problems of reality in pt. 5, chap. D of the *Aufbau* and in pt. 2, chap. B of *Pseudoproblems.* The best statement of his position occurs in the story of the geographic expedition in sec. 10 of *Pseudoproblems.* The *worst* statement occurs on the preceding page of *Pseudoproblems* and in sec. 176 of the *Aufbau.*

4. One can find an effort of this sort in Mill's *Logic,* bk. 1, chap. 3, sec. 2. On Dummett's interpretation, Frege's holistic aphorism addresses this very point.

5. Alles, von dem man überhaupt sprechen kann, muss sich auf von mir Erlebtes zurückführen lassen. Alle Erkenntnis, die ich haben kann, bezieht sich entweder auf meine eigenen Gefühle, Vorstellungen, Gedanken usw. oder sie ist aus meinen Wahrnehmungen zu erschliessen. Jede sinnvolle Aussage über noch so entlegene Gegenstände oder über noch so komplizierte wissenschaftliche Begriffe muss sich *übersetzen* lassen in eine Aussage, die von meinen eigenen Erlebnisinhalten, und zwar meist von meinen Wahrnehmungen spricht.

6. This passage is missing in the English translation. See Carnap, *LSW,* p. 49.

7. Elsewhere Carnap said that "all real objects . . . are quasi objects" (*LSW,* sec. 52, p. 72).

8. Thus, Carnap's attitude seems to reflect an overwhelming reluctance to accept the notion of reference. Around 1935 Tarski would explain to Carnap that he could accept that notion without altering any of his basic philosophical principles. Around 1930 Wittgenstein displayed a similar concern about reference (for an interesting example, see *Lectures, 1930–1932,* pp. 45–6). Echoes of this Carnapian attitude are clearly audible in the neutral language of *Meaning and Necessity.*

9. In "Dreidimensionalität des Raumes und Kausalität," after complaining, in effect, that neo-Kantians had not been sufficiently phenomenalistic, Carnap added that "their true achievement, namely, the proof of the object-creating function of thought, remains correct" (p. 108). A few years later Carnap was

no longer so sure whether we construct objects or concepts, and the confusion was reflected in his failure to draw a sharp distinction between those two notions in the *Aufbau* (see, e.g., secs. 5, 27, 158).

10. The quotations are from lectures that Carnap delivered in 1934 at the University of London.

11. In 1925 Carnap had written to Reichenbach that his preferred title was "Prolegomena zu einer Konstitutionstheorie der Wirklichkeit" ("Prolegomena to a Theory of Constitution and Reality"; Letter of 10 March 1925, RC 102-64-11, ASP). Carnap remained unhappy about this title right up until publication time. In December 1927 he sent to Schlick a "Frage äuer die Wahl des Buchtitels" in which he wondered whether "Der logische Aufbau der Welt" was such a good idea after all. After noting that in his view a constitution system with a physical basis was just as feasible as the one presented in the *Aufbau* and that the former was best for science (*Realwissenschaft*) whereas the latter was best suited for epistemology (*Erkenntnistheorie*), he added: "Which of the two systems deserves more the name the 'constitution of reality'? The first constitutes the world of knowledge (or consciousness); perhaps one can also say: reality (as known reality; one cannot even talk about any other). The second system, however, can perhaps make stronger claim to the name: it constitutes reality as the totality of everything that happens in space and time; and isn't it above all this viewpoint that we have in mind in science with the word 'reality'?" (Welches der beiden Systeme verdient mehr den Namen eines 'Aufbaues der Wirklichkeit'? Das erste baut die Erkenntnis- (oder Bewusstseins-) Welt auf; vielleicht kann man auch sagen: die Wirklichkeit (als erkannte Wirklichkeit; von einer andern kann ja nicht die Rede sein). Das zweite System kann aber vielleicht stärkeren Anspruch auf den Namen geltend machen: es baut die Wirklichkeit auf als das gesetzmässige Gesamtgeschehen in Raum und Zeit; und ist es nicht vor allem dieser Gesichtspunkt, den wir in der Realwiss. bei dem Wort 'Wirklichkeit' vor Augen haben?)

He then added that at a later time he would like to develop the second, physicalist system of constitution. (This is the idea that Neurath thought Carnap had stolen from him in the early 1930s.) He continued: "I might *choose the book title now already taking into consideration this later plan.* Perhaps now 'Logic of Knowledge'; the later one: 'Logic of Reality'? Add to it the earlier subtitle? Or: 'the Logical Structure of Knowledge', later: 'The Logical Structure of the World'?"(Ich möchte den *Buchtitel nun schon mit Rücksicht auf diesen späteren Plan wählen.* Vielleicht jetzt 'Erkenntnislogik'; das Spätere: 'Wirklichkeitslogik'? Dazu der frühere Untertitel? Oder: 'Der logische Aufbau der Erkenntnis', später: 'Der log. Aufbau der Welt'?) (VCA).

12. In hindsight one can see, for example, some of Cassirer's work as struggling toward a formulation of this point. Characteristically, the closest he came to it was in statements reminiscent of Frege's holistic maxim. Thus, in *The Philosophy of Symbolic Forms,* Cassirer opposed what he called the copy theory of knowledge, the idea that truth comes before what he called objects (pp. 105–14). This formulation may perhaps be interpreted as a foreboding

of the transvaluation of idealism that was about to take place in the hands of the new positivism.

13. *The Logical Syntax of Language* deals with another question, for a large portion of that book tries to make sense of theses like 'Natural numbers are really classes' and 'Natural numbers are really certain types of constructions'. The solution in this case relates not to conceptual holism but to what Carnap called the "thesis of metalogic." The matter is discussed later.

14. Die *Frage* nach dem *Wesen der Gegenstandsarten* ist falsch gestellt; was gemeint ist, ist zu beantworten durch Angabe der *Zusammenhänge der Begriffe.* Zusammenhänge der Begriffe bedeutet: *Zusammenhang der Sätze,* in denen sie vorkommen.

15. One must bear in mind that Frege had burdened that word with a fatal ambiguity.

16. Therefore, Carnap's "naturalism" leaves room for a specifically philosophical activity. Science is in charge of deciding what there is, and philosophy is in charge of explaining what it is that science has decided. It might seem that Quine thinks there is no such role for philosophy. But what science is it that decides who is right in the conflict over ontology between Carnap and Quine, and to what science do their writings on this matter belong?

17. The inexperienced homophonist will think that at this point it is necessary to take a stand and say that reference is a pseudorelation (*Abriss der Logistik,* p. 21). But Tarski would soon explain to Carnap that the homophonist can relax and join the realist even on that portion of the homophonist's language. (What Carnap said in the *Abriss* is that *Bedeutung* is a pseudorelation.) Given the ambiguity with which Frege had burdened that word, the statement may be read as an allusion to holism. It may be worth remembering, also, that in 1913 Wittgenstein wrote to Russell that the word *'Bedeutung'* is an incomplete sign (Letter to Russell of November 1913, *Letters,* p. 35).

Chapter 13

1. Ich bin mit *sehr, sehr* vielen Formulierungen des Buches [i.e., der "Abhandlung"] heute nicht einverstanden . . . alles (oder doch das meiste) was "Elementarsätze" & "Gegenstände" betrifft hat sich nun als fehlerhaft erwiesen & musste gänzlich neugearbeitet werden.

2. The book would surely have passed unnoticed (and maybe unpublished) had it not been for Russell's introduction. As is well known, Wittgenstein requested to his publisher that the introduction be deleted. On 6 May 1920 he wrote to Russell: "Your Introduction is not going to be printed. . . . You see, when I actually saw the German translation of the Introduction, I couldn't bring myself to let it be printed with my work. All the refinement of your English style was, obviously, lost in the translation and what remained was superficiality and misunderstanding" (*Letters,* p. 88).

3. The only reliable source for what went on in these meetings is the record kept by Waismann during the years 1929–32. We do not know how often the group met in 1927 and 1928. (Carnap's notes record five meetings in 1927 – on Ramsey, Esperanto, the occult, religion, and ethics; RC 102-78-07, ASP.)

They met at least four times in 1929, nine in 1930, four in 1931, and one in 1932. The sessions were discontinued when Wittgenstein decided that Carnap was stealing his ideas (even though Carnap had been excluded from the group of allowed visitors in January 1929).

4. Unaccountably, a number of Wittgenstein's British friends have assumed that whenever the logical positivists attributed an opinion to Wittgenstein, this was usually based on a misunderstanding of the *Tractatus*. Quite apart from the fact that no one can seriously claim to understand clearly what the *Tractatus* says about anything, there is the further relevant fact that the positivists had been talking to Wittgenstein for years since 1927 and might therefore be assumed to have been reporting on the views he was holding at *that* time rather than a decade earlier.

5. Here are some of the issues on which Wittgenstein was changing his mind:

(1) The theory of *Bedeutung:* The old concept of *Bedeutung* had been inspired "in a primitive philosophy of language" based on a misunderstanding of the function of naming – as in semantic monism (see, e.g., *Philosophical Grammar,* p. 56, and the beginning of *Philosophical Investigations*). "But the meaning of a word does not consist in something's corresponding to it, except in a case like that of a name" (*Philosophical Grammar,* p. 311). Now the *Bedeutung* of a word was not an object but a place, its place in grammar. Talk of *Gegenstände* became apologetic and eventually vanished, to be replaced by talk of grammatical rules and the way they constitute meanings.

(2) The theory of analysis: "I too thought that logical analysis had to bring to light what was hidden (as chemical and physical analysis does)" (*Philosophical Grammar,* p. 210; see also *Lectures, 1932–35,* p. 11); "I used to believe that philosophy had to give a definitive dissection of propositions so as to set out clearly all their connections and remove all possibilities of misunderstanding. I spoke as if there was a calculus in which such a dissection would be possible. I vaguely had in mind something like the definition that Russell had given for the definite article, and I used to think that in a similar way one would be able to use visual impressions etc. to define the concept say of a sphere" (*Philosophical Grammar,* p. 211). Now he thought that the search for the (hidden) atomic propositions whose logical product constitutes some given claim was a misguided project (*Philosophical Grammar,* pt. 1, app. 4, p. 210–12; *Lectures, 1932–35,* p. 11; Waismann, *Vienna Circle,* p. 182).

(3) The theory of infinity: In the *Tractatus* he had assumed that infinity was a number (*Lectures, 1930–32,* p. 119); hence, the constructivist analysis of infinity and the associated doctrine of hypotheses were at least partly new.

(4) The picture theory: There is a steady decline in the role played by the idea that propositions are pictures.

(5) The correspondence theory of meaning: It was abandoned. "In the *Tractatus.* . . . I said something like: it [i.e., pictorial character] is an agreement of form. But that is an error" (*Philosophical Grammar,* p. 212).

6. For example, after saying that a search presupposes that I know what I am looking for without what I am looking for having to exist, he added: "Earlier I

would have put this by saying that searching presupposes the elements of the complex, but not *the* combination that I was looking for. And that isn't a bad image: for, in the case of language, that would be expressed by saying that the sense of a proposition only presupposes the grammatically correct use of certain words" (*Philosophical Remarks*, p. 67).

7. "The word 'proposition', if it is to have any meaning at all here, is equivalent to a calculus . . . in which $p \lor -p$ is a tautology (in which the 'law of excluded middle' holds). When it is supposed not to hold, we have altered the concept of proposition" (*Philosophical Grammar*, p. 368). Thus, what Dummett now regards as a condition for realism in a field is what Wittgenstein regarded as a condition for there to be a proposition concerning that field.

8. Before 1930, possibly even at the time of the *Tractatus*, Wittgenstein thought that the primary language was "necessary" (*Philosophical Remarks*, p. 51) and, no doubt, superior to ordinary language. By the late 1920s he had changed his mind, but he still thought that the translation of ordinary language into phenomenal language, even though not "more correct," would serve at least "to show clearly what was logically essential in the representation" (*Philosophical Remarks*, p. 88).

9. Wittgenstein thought, for example, that there are certain things he called "visual tables" that do not consist of electrons. The tables that do contain electrons are, if anything at all, things that would have no being in the absence of minds or language. Also "objective," "physical" space is "only a construction with visual space as its basis" (*Philosophical Remarks*, p. 100).

10. Schlick seems to have been greatly impressed by Dilthey's position on this matter. See *GTK*, sec. 23.

11. The old method looked for constituents, as in chemical analysis (*Philosophical Grammar*, p. 210; *Lectures, 1932–35*, p. 11); the new method identifies languages that express the same facts in a less misleading way.

12. In his notes of conversations with Wittgenstein, Waismann described this language incorrectly (*Vienna Circle*, p. 49). Of course, we do not know whether Wittgenstein explained himself improperly or whether Waismann's notes were inaccurate.

13. In *Philosophical Remarks*, p. 85, Wittgenstein wrote, "We are tempted to say: only the experience of the present moment has reality." He (barely) resisted the temptation to say it, not because it isn't true, but because it is one of those profound meaningless truths that can only be shown.

14. "'Space' in this sense meant everything of which you must be certain in order to be able to ask a question" (*Lectures, 1930–32*, p. 17). Since the time of the *Tractatus*, Wittgenstein had been assuming that, for example, whenever something appears to be the case in a certain "space," there is another space where it really is the case. Thus, if we are drunk or dizzy, physical objects will *appear* to change their physical location; ipso facto, that determines that there is a space, *visual space*, where "they" do change their location even though they remain unmoved in physical space. See *Lectures, 1930–32*, p. 70; also *Philosophical Remarks*, p. 72: "The visual table is not composed of electrons."

15. Waismann's notes have Wittgenstein saying, "If I can never verify completely

the sense of the statement, then I couldn't have said anything with it. In that case the statement says nothing at all" (*Wiener Kreis,* p. 47).

16. "The point of talking about sense-data and immediate experience is that we are after a non-hypothetical representation. If a hypothesis cannot be verified conclusively, it can simply not be verified, and there will be for it neither truth nor falsehood" (Wittgenstein, *Philosophische Bemerkungen,* p. 283; see also p. 285).

17. "The definition of a concept indicates the method of *verification,* the definition of a number-word (a form) shows the way to a *construction*" (Waismann, *Wiener Kreis,* p. 226).

18. . . . der eigentliche mathematische Satz ein Beweis einen soganante mathematischen Satzes ist.

19. More generally, "When I hear a statement of, e.g., number theory, but do not know its proof then I do not even understand the statement. . . . When I learn the proof I learn something *completely new,* not just the way to an already familiar goal" (*Philosophische Bemerkungen,* p. 183). "The mathematical statement – in contrast to a proper statement – is *essentially* the last term of a proof that shows it to be correct or incorrect" (*Philosophische Bemerkungen,* p. 192). See also *Philosophical Grammar,* p. 370: "The verbal expression of the allegedly proved proposition is in most cases misleading, because it conceals the real purport of the proof . . . the proof is part of the grammar of the proposition!"

20. "The difficult mathematical problems are those for whose solution we don't yet possess a *written* system. The mathematician who is looking for a solution then has a system in some sort of psychic symbolism, in images, 'in his head', and endeavours to get it down on paper" (*Philosophical Remarks,* p. 176).

21. Completely misunderstanding the point of Russell's doctrine of knowledge by description, Wittgenstein went on to add: "Indeed Russell has really already shown by his theory of descriptions, that you can't get a knowledge of things by sneaking up on them from behind and it can only *look* as if we knew more about things than they have shown us openly and honestly. But he has obscured everything again by using the phrase 'indirect knowledge' " (*Philosophical Remarks,* pp. 200–1). Russell's ambiguities on the issue have been discussed in Chapter 6, but there can be little doubt that his reference to "indirect knowledge," i.e., to knowledge by description, was not the obscuring of anything, but the natural consequence and indeed the whole point of Russell's work.

22. It should be clear that this complaint is a very close relative of the one issued by Carnap against those who *ask* questions such as whether there are classes (regardless of how they answer them).

Chapter 14

1. Wittgenstein expressed his recognition of this point by accusing Carnap of stealing his ideas. The charge was first made in a letter to Schlick of 5 January 1932 (VCA), in which Wittgenstein explained that Carnap's "Die phys-

ikalische Sprache" (1932) presented his own ideas without attribution. The charge was absurd, but it displays the recognition of what many of Wittgenstein's students have failed to notice: That both in problems and in solutions, the leading "subtle positivist" and the leading "philistine positivist" were not that far from each other. (We borrow this terminology from Pears's *Ludwig Wittgenstein,* pp. 184–6.)

A few months earlier another Viennese philosopher, Otto Neurath, had sent Carnap fiery telegrams explaining that Carnap's "Die physikalische Sprache" contained *his* ideas (RC 029-12-65 and RC 029-12-68, ASP). Since Neurath's complaint reached Carnap before publication, Carnap added a long footnote in which he grossly exaggerated the value of Neurath's ideas and their significance. No doubt he would have done the same had Wittgenstein's charges reached him on time. Shortly thereafter, the Viennese mathematician Karl Menger raised the question of why Carnap did not acknowledge that the principle of tolerance was *his* own idea (an issue Menger has recently made public; actually Menger's "tolerance" was a combination of Russell's if–thenism and a proto-Popperian fallibilism with no deep connection with Carnap's idea). Only a few months earlier, Carnap had endured some painful correspondence with Schlick, who insisted that Carnap acknowledge that Wittgenstein was the *true owner* of the principle of tolerance. The moderation, balance, and delicacy with which Carnap responded to these ludicrous charges and inquiries are quite astonishing. As Schlick once wrote to Waismann (in connection with Wittgenstein's charge), "It is lucky that Carnap is such a calm man!" (Ein Glueck, dass Carnap ein so ruhiger Mensch ist! Letter of 24 August 1932, VCA).

2. See also "Some sentences are propositions, and other sentences look like propositions and are not"; the latter are "rules of grammar" in disguise (*Lectures, 1932–35,* p. 65).

3. Here is Kant's statement: "If intuition must conform to the constitution of the objects, I do not see how we could know anything of the latter *a priori;* but if the object (as object of the senses) must conform to the constitution of our faculty of intuition, I have no difficulty in conceiving such a possibility" (*Critique,* Bxvii).

4. The parenthetical "or none" is, perhaps, the key difference with Carnap; see Chapter 19. See also D. Lee's notes for 1931 (Wittgenstein, *Lectures, 1930–32*), p. 58. Ambrose's notes for 1932–33 have the following remark: "The objection that the rules [of grammar] are not arbitrary comes from the feeling that they are responsible to the meaning. But how is the meaning of 'negation' defined, if not by the rules? $-p = p$ does not follow from the meaning of 'not' but constitutes it" (Wittgenstein, *Lectures, 1932–35,* p. 4). See also lectures 6 and 7 in Ambrose's notes for 1934–5, e.g.: "Can I deduce the rules [concerning what the king is in chess] once I get hold of the idea in the chess player's mind? No. The rules are not something contained in the idea and got by analyzing it. They constitute it. . . . It seems at first sight that the rules for the use of a symbol are deducible from the idea connected with it. . . . The idea and the rules stand in the relation of a symbol and the rules for its use. So far as the idea is a static mechanism, what follows from it is hypothetical, and so far as it is not, what follows is *a priori.* We can say *a priori* only what we

ourselves have laid down" (p. 85). To be sure, our account of Wittgenstein's views on the a priori ignores many of the hesitations, ambiguities, and inconsistencies in his treatment of the issue. For example, for a while Wittgenstein seems to have regarded the a priori as applying to the domain of "phenomenology" (the various phenomenal spaces); see *Lectures, 1930–32,* pp. 76–7. Here, the a priori seems to be something quite different from the constitutive: It is what we "see" to be true without any need to verify. For example, when you are presented with three objects, "you do not have to *count* the objects – you see them as three. And there is no further verification possible as this is a proposition about your sense-data" (*Lectures, 1930–32,* p. 77). This kind of "a priori" should not be confused with the topic of this chapter; it is the direct ancestor of Schlick's *"Konstatierungen."*

5. Spricht die Geometrie von Würfeln? Sagt sie, dass die Würfelform gewisse Eigenschaften habe? . . . So spricht die Geometrie nicht vom Würfel, sondern konstituiert die Bedeutung des Wortes " Würfel" u.s.w. Die Geometrie sagt nun z.B., die Kanten eines Würfels sind gleich lang, und nichts liegt näher als die Verwechslung der Grammatik dieses Satzes mit der des Satzes "die Seiten des Holzwürfels sind gleich lang." Und doch ist das eine eine willkürliche grammatische Regel, das andere ein Erfahrungssatz.

   Ambrose's notes for 1933–4 contain the statement: "Geometry is not a physics of *geometrical* straight lines and cubes. It constitutes the meaning of the words 'line' and 'cube'"; and also, "if we alter the geometry we alter the meaning of the words used, for the geometry constitutes the meaning" (Wittgenstein, *Lectures, 1932–35,* p. 51).

6. Moore's notes contain the following remark attributed to Wittgenstein: "The meaning of a word is no longer for us an object corresponding to it" ("Wittgenstein's Lectures in 1930–33," p. 255). Notice the "no longer for us."

Chapter 15

1. Ich sehe hauptsächlich drei Phasen: 1. 1925–30, im Mittelpunkt: Wittgensteins Tractatus, nebenbei: mein Aufbau Auffassung, die alles sehr vereinfacht; Gefahr des Dogmatismus. Ablehnung der Metaphysik durch ein zu stark vereinfachten Schema. Alle Schwierigkeiten scheinen gelöst. Der Drache ist getötet. Jetzt braucht nur noch ein wenig durch Erläuterungen geklärt zu werden. 2. Die neue Phase kommt aus zwei Neuerwerbungen: 2a. (Hauptsächlich seit 1929?) Physikalismus, Einheitswissenschaft; Brücken zwischen den Fächern; die Aufmerksamkeit geht nicht nur auf Physik, sondern weiter auf Psychologie und Soziologie. 2b. Syntax hauptsächlich seit 1931 (mein erster Entwurf: Jan 1930 [*sic*]; starker Einfluss durch Tarskis Vorträge in Wien, Februar 1930, missachtet von Schlick und Waismann). Allmählich wird uns immer klarer: alle unsere Probleme sind syntaktische Probleme. Dient zur Bekräftigung der These der Einheitswissenschaft. Nicht: alles ist gelöst, sondern eine Menge neuer Aufgaben, die in Angriff zu nehmen sind.

2. Meine "Syntax" hat historisch zwei Wurzeln: 1. Wittgenstein, 2. Metamathematik (Tarski, Gödel).

3. We should emphasize that the sources on which we have based our account

of Wittgensteinian grammar derive largely from texts that either did not exist
or Carnap could not have seen before 1931.

4. Its basic results are summarized in Carnap's "Bericht über Untersuchungen
   zur allgemeinen Axiomatik."

5. The notion of *inhaltlich* was used by Hilbert and others as roughly equivalent to 'meaningful', as opposed to 'purely formal'. Usually, *inhalt* was associated with intuition – in the standard Kantian fashion.

6. . . . sonst würden sie uns nicht in den Stand setzen, zu handeln; und De-
   duzieren ist Handeln, denn es bedeutet: aus vorgegebenen Zeichenzusam-
   menstellungen nach festen Regeln andere Zusammenstellungen bilden.

7. . . . das System der logischen Sätze, dessen Voranstellung wir für jede Axiomatik gefordert haben, nicht selbst ein AS in dem hier gemeinten Sinne sein
   kann.

8. Carnap ignored the distinction between the name of a PM formula containing
   'R' as its only nonlogical sign and that formula itself. Under appropriate
   assumptions there will be for every formula of that sort a sign 'g' in PM such
   that 'g(R)' is provably equivalent (though, of course, not identical) to the
   given formula ('g(R)' is what Carnap would later call an "abbreviation" of the
   original expression). The failure to recognize this distinction may explain
   why Carnap thought that the inference from a formula containing 'R' (i.e.,
   from $f(R)$ to 'Eϕ(ϕ(R))') is trivial. We shall make no effort to disambiguate
   Carnap's claims since his treatment of these matters collapses once the use–
   mention distinction is observed.

9. Carnap's early constructivist bias is extensively documented in his Nachlass.
   The constructivist language I of *The Logical Syntax of Language* was the
   only legitimate language in the early stages of that book. Carnap's correspondence with Kaufmann (whose *Das Unendliche in der Mathematik und seine
   Ausschaltung* offers a constructivist analysis of infinity) contains further
   evidence of Carnap's belief that discourse about infinity must be seen as an
   abbreviated manner of discourse about the finite (Letter of 3 February 1928,
   RC 028-25-13, ASP) and that the domain of the nondenumerable is to be
   rejected (Letter of 7 April 1929, RC 028-25-05, ASP).

10. . . . "erfüllt", wenn es ein Modell hat: (E)f; somit "k-erfüllt", wenn ein Modell
    angegeben werden kann; *"leer",* wenn es kein Modell hat: (E)f.

11. Besitzt [es] eine kontradiktorische Folgerung, so heisst es *"widerspruchsvoll"*
    . . .: (Eh) [$f \Rightarrow$ (h & $\bar{h}$)]; somit "k-widerspruchsvoll", wenn eine derartige
    Aussagefunktion angegeben werden kann. . . . Wenn ein AS fR eine kontra-
    diktorische Folgerung, so heisst es *"widerspruchsfrei"*:$\overline{(Eh)}$ [$f \Rightarrow$ (h & $\bar{h}$)].

12. In "On the Limitations of the Means of Expression of Deductive Theories"
    (1935, *LSM*), Tarski proved that every categoric axiom system is nonramifia-
    ble. In note 1 of that paper (p. 384) he stated that the theorem was announced
    in 1927 and that the result "is mentioned in Fraenkel, A. [*Einleitung*], p. 352,
    note 3." Lest the reader conclude that Carnap was merely reproducing results
    that he knew were available, we quote here the relevant part of Fraenkel's
    footnote, which refers to current mathematical studies on completeness: "See,
    for example, Dubislav . . . Carnap . . . (as well as deeper but unpublished
    works by these authors and A. Tarski) . . ." (Vgl. etwa DUBISLAV . . . CARNAP

... (sowie tiefergehende noch unveröffentlichte Arbeiten dieses Autors und A. TARSKIS) . . .). Carnap's "unpublished work" is likely to be the "Untersuchungen," of which Fraenkel had seen a draft.

13. ... ein Verfahren angegeben werden kann, durch das in jedem Falle die Folgerung nachweisbar ist.

14. Das AS fR sei leer: $\overline{(E)}f$ (1)

   ($\sim$) L26: $f \to f$ (2)

   Tautologisch gilt (L19): $f \to f$ (3)

   Aus (2) und (3), nach L21: $f \to (f \& \overline{f})$ (4)

   ($\to$) $(Eh)\,[f \to (h \& \overline{h})]$ (5)

15. gR sei k-leer; das bedeutet, dass im Beweise von Satz 2 (1) beweisbar ist. Daraus ist dann, wie oben gezeigt, (4) beweisbar; . . .

16. See Menger's account of Tarski's visits to his seminar in his "Memories of Moritz Schlick."

17. Carnap had taken three courses with Frege in 1910–14. He obviously recognized them as significant – they are the only lecture notes from that period preserved in Carnap's Nachlass. But he chose to take Russell, rather than Frege, as his first model in the field of logic.

18. The interpretation of Frege put forth by Dummett conflates these two elements. Dummett regards it as obvious and not worth discussing that the step from Frege's semantics to current post-Tarskian semantics was a very modest one (see, e.g., *Frege: Philosophy of Language,* pp. 81–2). But if Dummett is right, it would be hard to understand why Frege reacted against Hilbert the way he did. In fact, the step in question demanded a major change in our understanding of logic. To a large extent, Carnap's ontogeny recapitulates the phylogeny of logic.

19. *Decision-definiteness* is defined by the condition that one can prove in PM either

$$(x)(y) \ldots (F(x, y, \ldots) \Rightarrow (S(x, y, \ldots))$$

or

$$(x)(y) \ldots (F(x, y, \ldots) \Rightarrow -S(x, y, \ldots))$$

for each $S(x, y, \ldots)$. Tarski's and Carnap's explications certainly differed in content. For example, whereas for Carnap all three of Fraenkel's notions of completeness collapse into one, for Tarski they do not (see, e.g., theorem 10 in "Limitations of the Means of Expression of Deductive Theories," *LSM,* p. 391).

20. In all of Tarski's writings before "Limitations of the Means of Expression of Deductive Theories," his explication of 'consequence' was syntactical and, indeed, proof-theoretic. (It was a d-concept rather than a c-concept in Carnap's sense.) In chapter 3 of *LSM,* for example, he said that the consequence of a set of sentences is "obtained by means of certain operations called *rules of inference*" (p. 30); in chapter 4, that in the propositional calculus, "The consequences of a set of sentences are formed with the help of two operations, that of *substitution* and *detachment*" (p. 40; see also chap. 5, p. 63). In chapter 3 'consequence' is taken as a primitive term to be characterized by

axioms that count, in effect, as conditions to be satisfied by admissible rules of inference. One of these axioms asserts that any consequence of a set X of sentences must be a consequence of a finite subset of X. Since the language under consideration is arbitrary, and not first order, this condition is most likely suggested by the intuition that rules of inference may have only finitely many premises and may be used only finitely many times (a condition that, as we shall see, Carnap's syntactic but not proof-theoretic analysis of consequence in *The Logical Syntax of Language* would reject). Moreover, in Tarski's early papers there was no clear distinction between truth and proof; in chapter 3 (published in 1930) the consequences of the empty class were called the *"system of all logically true sentences"* (p. 33), and in chapter 5 (also from 1930) the same set was called the *"system of all logically provable or logically valid sentences"* (p. 71). One might add that even in "The Concept of Truth in Formalized Languages," the notion of consequence remained syntactical, even though Gödel's "Uber unentscheidbare Sätze" had already suggested that the syntactic analysis of consequence "has been effected without remainder" (p. 252; see also parenthetical remark on p. 257).

Chapter 16

1. It is possible to reconstruct part of the story of Carnap's writing of *LSL* from his correspondence with Schlick. On 7 December 1931 Carnap wrote that the text of his "Metalogik" (as he then called it) was almost ready, consisting of 160 typed pages (RC 029-29-15, ASP); on 15 March 1932 he referred to a second part, not yet written (RC 029-29-14, ASP); on 30 June 1932 he reported that part II was ready except for a final chapter (RC 029-29-11, ASP; also Gödel's, comments in his letter of 11 September 1932, note 2, this chapter, refer to part II, which must therefore have included the treatment of language II); on 28 November 1932 Carnap sent to Schlick the concluding, philosophical chapter of "Semantik" (as he now called it, following a suggestion of Gödel and Behmann; RC 029-29-02, ASP); on 19 June 1933 he reported having devoted the preceding months to a revision of the book and to the writing of a new chapter (presumably, part IV) on syntax for arbitrary languages (RC 029-29-27, ASP). The manuscript of *LSL* was sent to Springer on 14 December 1933 (Letter of 21 December 1933, RC 029-29-25, ASP). It may be worth noting that on 10 November, 1934 Nagel wrote from Poland reporting that Adjukiewicz had received a copy of Carnap's book and added, "He also asked me to express his regret at being unable to send you the German translation of Dr. Tarski's book" (RC 029-05-21, ASP), referring, presumably, to Tarski's *Introduction to Logic and to the Methodology of Deductive Sciences,* which first appeared, in Polish, in 1936.
2. We refer, of course, to published statements. A letter from Gödel to Carnap of 11 September 1932 (RC 102-43-05, ASP) indicates that (as one might expect) Gödel had also seen and probably solved the problem. In this letter Gödel announced that in the sequel to "Uber unentscheidbare Sätze" he would include a characterization of truth.

3. Tarski had claimed that since the rule requires infinitely many premises, "it cannot easily be brought into harmony with the current view of the deductive method, and finally that the possibility of its practical application in the construction of deductive systems seems to be problematical in the highest degree" ("Some Observations on the Concepts of w-Consistency and w-Completeness," *LSM,* p. 295). In contrast, Carnap thought that there was "nothing to prevent the practical application of such a rule" (*LSL,* p. 173). It would be impossible to prove infinitely many theorems in the object language one by one; but a metatheorem might prove them all at once.

4. The key reason for Tarski's negative conclusion was his commitment to the theory of semantic categories. The link will be explained later.

   In his 1935 contribution to the Paris conference, Tarski withdrew these negative conclusions and offered a definition of consequence (see *LSM,* chap. 16). After stating that "the first attempt to formulate a precise definition of the proper concept of consequence was that of R. Carnap" (p. 413), he added in a footnote (concerning his "Some Observations on the Concepts of w-Consistency and w-Completeness"): "My position at that time is explained by the fact that, when I was writing the article mentioned, I wished to avoid any means of construction which went beyond the theory of logical types in any of its classical forms." He then went on to indicate that "in his extremely interesting book," Carnap had properly emphasized the need to distinguish derivability from consequence (p. 413).

5. Nehmen wir z.B. die Formel $(F)F(0) \lor \overline{F(0)}$; um festzustellen ob sie analyt. ist, muss man dies für alle Formeln der Gestalt $P(0) \lor \overline{P(0)}$ tun. Zu diesem Zweck muss man jedes konstante Prädikat P durch sein Definiens ersetzen; in diesem können aber wieder gebundenes Prädikat-Variable vorkommen u.s.w., so dass man auf einen regressus in inf. kommt. Am deutlichsten wird dies dadurch, dass u.U. *dieselbe* Formel immer wiederkehren kann. Setzt man z.B. in der Formel $(F)F(0) \lor 0 = 0$ für das konst Präd $(f)F(x)$ ein und bringt auf die Normalform, so erhält man wieder die ursprüngliche Formel. Dieser Fehler lässt sich m.E. nur dadurch vermeiden, dass man als Laufbereich der Funktionsvariablen nicht die Präd. einer bestimmten Sprache, sondern alle Mengen u. Relationen überhaupt ansieht. Dies involviert nicht etwa einen platonistischen Standpunkt, denn ich behaupte, dass sich diese Df. für "analyt" innerhalb einer bestimmten Sprache, in der man die Begriffe "Menge" u. "Rel" schon hat, durchführen lässt.

6. In *LSL* Carnap gave a different reason for abandoning the substitutional interpretation: "It may happen that, though all these sentences [the '$M(Pi)$'s] are true, '$M(F)$' is nevertheless false – in so far as M does not hold for a certain property for which no predicate can be defined in II . . . we will follow Gödel's suggestions and define 'analytic' in such a way that '$M(F)$' is only called analytic if M holds for every numerical property irrespective of the limited domain of definitions which are possible in II" (pp. 106–7). In "On Definable Sets of Real Numbers" (chap. 6, *LSM*) Tarski had discussed the problem of definability, noticing that in view of the enumerability of the propositional functions in any given language, there had to be nondenumerably many classes of reals that are not definable in any given system.

7. There is no indication in the correspondence with Gödel or in the notes Carnap took of conversations with him that the idea of evaluation was suggested by Gödel – or by anyone else. This, together with the fact that Carnap was extremely careful, indeed generous, in attributing ideas and suggestions to others, makes it likely that the idea is entirely his own.

8. It should be emphasized that the reason we are justified in making this statement is not *primarily* that it is true but that we can *prove* it in the language on which we are standing as we make our syntactic considerations. Carnap had explained: "The method of derivation [as opposed to the method of consequence] always remains the fundamental method; every demonstration of the applicability of any term is ultimately based upon a derivation. Even the demonstration of the existence of a consequence-relation . . . can only be achieved by means of a derivation (a proof) in the syntax-language" (*LSL*, p. 39).

9. The exclusion of semantic primitives establishes that if the OL is a system of physical theory, all one needs to define truth for it is the primitives of physics and those of syntax. This was intended to make the notion of truth acceptable to physicalists.

10. It is worth emphasizing that Tarski's convention (T) demands the provability (in ML) of $\phi(X) = p$, not its truth. Tarski would likely have agreed with Carnap's remarks in *LSL* concerning deducibility and consequence (see the first section of this chapter). Hence Tarski's decision to endow ML with an axiomatization M.

11. *We* may see Tarski's languages as the conjunction of a formal language plus an interpretation and then abstract the notion of "truth in an interpretation" from what he was doing. In Part I we endeavored to detach this Hilbertian picture of things from the Fregean picture; for the latter there was a certain perversity in the decision to detach the interpretation from the rest of the language. Tarski's presentation was entirely Fregean in spirit. The point is that there is a third, "formalist" alternative between the two that Tarski considered: (a) languages endowed with a fixed, unique interpretation and (b) "sciences to the signs and expressions of which no material sense is attached," for which "the problem here discussed has no relevance" (*LSM*, p. 166).

12. That Tarski's focus was on axiomatized OLs and, indeed, on mathematical theories is emphasized by the fact that when Tarski discussed the possibility of offering a "structural definition" of truth, i.e., one in terms of a metalinguistic axiomatic system, he failed to include among objections the otherwise obvious and devastating one that the procedure could not possibly work for contingent sentences (see pp. 163–4). Even so, Tarski was far more keenly aware than Carnap of the fact that the definition of truth "alone gives no general criterion for the truth of a sentence" and that in this respect it "does not differ at all from the greater part of the definitions which occur in the deductive sciences" (p. 197). As we shall see, Carnap had explained essentially the same point to Schlick, but he lost his grasp of it again by the time he raised the question of whether one can hope to define truth in syntax.

13. Kleene may have been the first to see that one could simplify Carnap's

definition by reformulating it in a way that paralleled the definition of a well-formed formula; see his review of *LSL,* esp. p. 83, and also his "On the Term 'Analytic' in Logical Syntax," preprint, 1939 (available from the author). In his review of the latter work Carnap wrote: "When Tarski constructed his method for defining the semantical concept of truth, it became clear that an analogous method could be used in syntax for the definition of 'analytic' (or 'provable') in systems with indefinite rules. It seems that the simplified definition proposed by Kleene is this analogue" (p. 158).

14. As we saw in Chapter 8, the notion of semantic category is similar to Wittgenstein's idea of *form;* it is even closer to Carnap's concept of *genus (Gattung;* see *LSL* sec. 46). Carnap did not endorse the theory of semantic categories and so was in a position to offer in *LSL* a definition of truth for the infinitary language II. He apparently learned the use of transfinite levels from Hilbert and Gödel (*LSL,* p. 189).

15. Having abandoned the idea of defining truth explicitly for infinitary languages, Tarski explored the possibility of introducing the concept of truth in the appropriate metalanguages by appealing to the axiomatic method, introducing 'truth' as an undefined metalinguistic primitive and adding a number of axioms (including, perhaps, all instances of convention (T)) to specify its meaning. Even though this axiomatic account is hardly philosophically illuminating, Tarski noted that in a certain sense the resulting theory would be categoric. If the axiom of infinite induction were added, making the metalinguistic theory w-complete, then any two interpretations of *Tr* would be coextensional.

16. We know that Tarski had read carefully and corrected a number of errors in Carnap's *LSL* before its publication in English in 1937. (Carnap thanked Tarski in 1935 for some of the corrections – see, e.g., *LSL,* p. 88.) It would be interesting to know if Carnap's more "tolerant" attitude on this semantic matter had any influence on Tarski's change of mind.

17. The failure to allow for a concept of truth prevented Carnap from offering a coherent version of Lesniewski's argument. Presumably, what we wanted to state in his condition (a), for example, is that the sentence '*Tr*(*N*) iff *S*' is true in OL; but the closest he would want to get to that statement would be to say that the sentence in question is determined by given rules. As stated, Carnap's reasoning does not observe the use–mention distinction.

18. Carnap occasionally suggested otherwise (e.g., "Intellectual Autobiography," p. 60), but this is only a manifestation of his extreme reluctance (so uncommon among his Viennese contemporaries) to present his earlier work in a favorable light.

Chapter 17

1. Picture the cat as forever yearning for a cup of tea.
2. These are restrictions to mathematics of the three standard issues of epistemology discussed in Chapter 11, this volume.
3. Not, of course, the particular sentence but all "translations" of it as well, in a sense of translation that does not presuppose the picture of meaning being

challenged. Perhaps the best way to articulate the intended sense of translation is via Sellars's dot quotation. For example, .point. is the class of all expressions that play the same linguistic role as 'point' does in the geometry to which it belongs.

4. If the analogy with geometry gave some plausibility to Carnap's deontologizing conjecture, his specific arguments against the ontological implications of logic did the exact opposite. Carnap's arguments on that matter were, without exception, flawed; and the rather striking superficiality of some of them is proof of how reluctant he was to give any serious thought to the matter that most foundationalists before and after him regarded as absolutely essential. As to Carnap's specific arguments, we prefer to pass over in silence this embarrassing corner of his early philosophy.

5. Concerning logical symbols, for example, he said that "the meaning of these symbols . . . arises out of the rules of transformation" (*LSL*, p. 18).

6. These two doctrines of the factuality of meaning seem to be independent. One can claim that for every language and every syntactically correct but seemingly meaningless claim in it, there is a context in which the claim is meaningful. (A typical example of this position is the poem concluding with Chomsky's famous line: "Colorless green ideas sleep furiously.") Yet one could consistently insist that there can be language only under context-independent conditions.

7. Popper has repeatedly complained against those who call him a positivist, but perhaps one should not argue about words.

8. In accord with the conventionalist fashion, Popper argued that whether scientific laws are strictly universal or equivalent to finite conjunctions of singular statements is not a question of fact but "can be settled only by an agreement or a convention" (*The Logic of Scientific Discovery*, sec. 13, p. 63). But his instincts were better than his philosophy, and thus he rightly rejected Reichenbach's view – rather than describe it as a different convention.

9. Putnam has reported that in connection with similar questions concerning whether there is a fact of the matter, Quine's answer is that "there is not fact of the matter to the question whether there is a fact of the matter." The answer to that is, "Is *that* a fact?" One is committed either to the factuality of conventions at some level or else to what one might call w-conventionalism. The former doctrine faces exactly the same difficulties as the first-level conventionalism it is designed to challenge; the latter leaves *every* answer in that denumerable chain without a support in fact, and thereby with no reason to hold it.

10. This is the paper that elicited Wittgenstein's charge of plagiarism. From his correspondence with Schlick, it appears that Wittgenstein worried about Carnap's priority of publication. If so, the ideas he was worrying about must not have been present in the *Tractatus*. Which of the ideas contained in "Die physikalische Sprache als Universalsprache der Wissenschaft" (1932) were not already in the *Tractatus* and were developed by Wittgenstein since then?

11. Roughly speaking, F is a "universal word" if 'Fa' is analytic for all a's of the

appropriate type (*LSL*, pp. 292–3). It is not clear what notion of analytic Carnap had in mind, since he said that 'object' is a universal word and there is nothing in his own definition of analyticity that entails that consequence.

12. Among instances of the "worse" category we may include this: Carnap showed that for certain language forms, the traditional formulation of traditional philosophical questions (as stated, e.g., in *LSL*, pp. 322–3) is in some sense equivalent to a syntactic formulation. In view of the fact that the equivalence relation is symmetric, it would appear that one needs some additional reason to conclude that the "real" meaning of all those traditional questions is the one displayed in their syntactic formulation. Yet without further ado, Carnap assumed that the alleged discourse about objects is merely alleged. Carnap was well aware of the fact (*LSL*, p. 236) that if truth were definable in his syntax languages, then *every* sentence would really be about language, for we could always translate every "material" statement ('Snow is white') into a "formal" counterpart ('Snow is white' is true). Since, as Tarski showed, truth *is* definable in what Carnap called a syntax language, the whole argument is reduced to absurdity.

Chapter 18

1. The matter of ontology and the associated issue of realism were not much discussed in Vienna in the early 1930s. Carnap had given his final word on the matter in the *Aufbau*. Wittgenstein was still within the solipsist's fly bottle, in which Schlick had recently joined him. Neurath condemned every form of realism (and everything else he disliked) as nonsensical metaphysics. Even Popper argued in *Grundprobleme* that neither realism nor idealism "can be grounded and must therefore be rejected as unscientific (dogmatic-metaphysical)" doctrines (p. 74). After defining idealism as the claim that the world exists only as my representation, and realism as the claim that things exist independently of my representation, Popper concluded, "The opposition: idealism–realism can be considered an example of an undecidable antinomy" (p. 73). He added that Kant "no doubt correctly" held that "whenever we have an undecidable antinomy, neither of the assertions can be grounded and therefore both are to be rejected as unscientific (dogmatic-metaphysical)" (p. 74). A simple syllogistic inference leads to the conclusion quoted above. Among philosophers of science only Reichenbach and – in an odd sort of way – Schlick thought that there was more truth than confusion in realism and more confusion than truth in its alternatives.

2. Perhaps the most impressive testimony of Carnap's peculiar sense of what it is reasonable to do to science is his translation (at the end of *LSL*) of the first few paragraphs of Einstein's 1905 relativity paper from the dangerous material mode in which Einstein wrote it into the proper syntacticist formal mode.

3. The essential unity of their standpoints should not be obscured by the fact that each of them regarded the other's work as worthless. Neurath also regarded Popper's work as worthless (and vice versa). All three regarded

Wittgenstein's work as worthless. Wittgenstein's opinions about *their* work (and Carnap's) are better passed over in silence. Carnap thought that all of them had a point.

4. The surviving parts of the manuscript of *Two Problems* were published by Popper in 1979. The published text includes a number of clarifying remarks added in 1978. We shall usually omit them in quotations from the 1932 text.

5. In *The Logic of Scientific Discovery* Popper did say that "after all, 'the whole of science' might err" (p. 29). But he said this in a polemical context, in the process of trying to refute Reichenbach's transcendental maxim, the principle of utilizability.

6. Very little has survived from part 2 of Popper's manuscript. It is not clear to what extent part 2 (on the problem of demarcation) had been completed.

7. In the English version of *The Logic of Scientific Discovery, Geltung* is translated as "how to establish the truth" (p. 28), although, when it proves convenient, *Geltung* is elsewhere translated as "truth" (e.g., in *Geltungswert*) or as "justification" or "validity" (p. 31). It should also be noted that this English translation contains several "clarifications" not explicitly indicated as such. For example, where the German text says "man könnte sie etwa als Lehre von der *deduktiven Methodik der Nachprüfung* kennzeichnen" (p. 4), the English has "It might be described as the theory of *the deductive method of testing,* or as the view that a hypothesis can only be empirically *tested* – and only *after* it has been advanced" (p. 30).

8. In 1951 Wittgenstein was still writing that Goethe's theory of color "is not a theory that has proved to be unsatisfactory, but it is, strictly speaking, not a theory at all. Nothing can be predicted with it" (*Remarks on Colour,* p. 11).

9. At about the same time he was writing in his notebooks: "When I say that a hypothesis is not conclusively verifiable, that does not mean that there is a verification of it that we may approach ever more nearly, without ever reaching it. That is nonsense – of a kind into which we frequently lapse. No, an hypothesis simply has a different formal relation to reality from that of verification. (Hence, of course, the words 'true' and 'false' are inapplicable here, or else they have a different meaning.)" (*Philosophical Remarks,* p. 285).

10. If there were such propositions it would, indeed, be reasonable to detach their semantics from that of hypotheses. Whether there *are* such propositions was the subject of the major confrontation among positivists in the early 1930s, which is the topic of our concluding chapter.

11. Weyl had written in 1929: "I cannot conceive of a grosser misunderstanding than that of making the legitimacy of this procedure [complete induction] which refers to the *possible* depend, as Russell does, on the actual existence of infinitely many objects in the real world. I believe that here we strike the root of the mathematical method in general: the *a priori* construction of the *possible* in opposition to the *a posteriori* description of what is actually given" ("Consistency in Mathematics," pp. 153–4).

12. Hilbert's new version of formalism illustrates the extraordinary revival of intuition as the source of the mathematical a priori in the 1920s. In "On the Infinite" he explained that Frege and Dedekind tried "to provide a foundation

for arithmetic which was independent of both intuition and experience" (p. 139). "In contrast to the earlier efforts of Frege and Dedekind," he added, "we are convinced that certain intuitive concepts and insights are necessary conditions of scientific knowledge, that logic alone is not sufficient. Operating with the infinite can be made certain only by the finitary" (p. 151).

13. Apparently the point made an impact on Ramsey, since in "Law and Causality" (1929) he wrote that a "belief of the primary sort," i.e., a Wittgensteinian proposition, "is a map of a neighbouring space by which we steer. It remains such a map however much we complicate it or fill in details. But if we professedly extend it to infinity, it is no longer a map; we cannot take it in or steer by it. Our journey is over before we need its remoter parts" (*Foundations,* p. 134).

14. This doctrine of hypotheses as instructions should not be confused with the type of conventionalism for physics that Poincaré had promoted in France and Eddington in England. Conventions can never conflict with facts; nomic instructions can and often do. The essential feature of these nomic instructions is, to repeat, their capacity to generate predictions that may be and often are falsified. Under such circumstances the law must be abandoned. Wittgenstein and Schlick would not say that under such circumstances the law has been "refuted," because they thought that the sense of truth and falsehood that applies to basic statements cannot apply to universally quantified ones. See the section on the new Carnap, this volume, for further evidence of the conflict between this standpoint and conventionalism. The conflation of Schlick's and Wittgenstein's views with nomic conventionalism is promoted by the tendency to confuse Wittgenstein's "instructions" with what he called "rules" (of grammar), which are, indeed, definitions and conventions. For the distinction between rules and instructions see, e.g., Wittgenstein's *Lectures, 1932–35,* p. 153.

15. As a solution, this would rank with the idea that the nature of logic is clarified by the doctrine that logic says nothing. Since 'chinchulin' also says nothing and yet no one is striving to incorporate it into the system of *Principia,* an account of the nature of logic must consist of something more than that celebrated slogan. As we saw in Chapter 8, Wittgenstein's doctrine of logic was not simply that it says nothing, but that it shows something.

16. For example, if $W(Fx) = p$, $W(Gy) = q$, and $W(Fx$ probabilistically implies $Gy) = u$, then $W(Fx \lor Gy) = p + q - (p \cdot u)$.

17. In a footnote to p. 47 added in 1978, Popper said that the concessions to Hume offered in these remarks were merely provisional and that they were challenged in the second, lost part of the book. If so, the second part of the book undermined the reasoning in the first, since clearly the latter would imply that Kant's "solution" was no solution at all.

18. The 1979 text adds a footnote: "I should have written 'can be established as true or false.'"

19. The 1979 text says "[demonstrably] true. . . ."

20. The 1979 version reads: "but [we should] not [ascribe to it] a positive one."

21. In his "Intellectual Autobiography" Popper proudly records his first performance at a meeting of the Aristotelian Society (in 1936). Russell had given a

paper on the limits of empiricism. Popper was, as usual, reluctant to make his presence felt; but Ayer insisted that he speak up and so he said that "the whole trouble was due to the mistaken assumption that *scientific knowledge* was a species of *knowledge* – knowledge in the ordinary sense in which if I know that it is raining it must be *true* that it is raining, so that knowledge implies truth. But, I said, what we call 'scientific knowledge' was hypothetical, and often not true, let alone certainly or probably true (in the sense of the calculus of probability). Again the audience took this for a joke, or a paradox, and they laughed and clapped" (Schilpp, *The Philosophy of Karl Popper,* p. 87). They would have laughed even louder had they known that Popper thought science "is knowledge writ large."

22. Strictly speaking, as we know, it did not extend to *anybody's* position, not even to Wittgenstein's or the early Carnap's, as *they* intended their theories to be taken. What Carnap tolerated, here and elsewhere, were only the views of those who were tolerant – and there did not seem to be too many of those, even in Vienna. The various targets of Carnap's tolerance were not other people's opinions but the reformulation of those positions as proposals.

23. The implicit distinction is between statements that seem to say something about reality but do not and those that seem to and do. The negation of Schlick's distinction and of *his* type of conventionalism may be based either on the old propositionalist line that every apparent knowledge claim does say something about reality or on the modern pragmatist claim that *no* single claim says anything at all about reality.

24. Schlick detected the very same confusion behind Carnap's and Neurath's position concerning protocols ("Introduction and on 'Affirmations' from *Sur le Fondement de la Connaissance,*" *Philosophical Papers,* vol. 2, p. 407).

25. In a letter to Carnap dated 14 November 1935, Schlick wrote, "I always believe that the main difference between us derives from your mathematical temperament and my physical one" (Ich glaube immer, dass der Hauptunterschied zwischen uns in Deinem mathematischen und meinem physikalischen Temperament begründet ist) (RC 102-70-11, ASP).

26. The extraordinary amount of space devoted to the matter of the embeddability of syntax in the object language was motivated not only by early Wittgensteinian concerns about a unique language but also by the desire to solve this conflict between the pragmatist and the syntacticist side of his approach. At first Carnap seems to have thought that Gödel's methods allowed for a complete translation of syntax; but he soon found out that they did not, and he explained the point quite clearly in several places in *LSL.* Yet at *other* places – when he wore his Neurathian personality – he talked as if this fact could be overlooked. For example, he claimed that "we regard syntax not as a special domain outside that of the rest of science but as a subdomain of science as a whole, which forms a single system . . . having a single language S_1," (*LSL,* p. 286). On its most natural reading, this conflicts with the detailed proof that the central syntactic notion of 'analytic in L' cannot be defined in L for the languages discussed by Carnap (sec. 36).

27. Here is a relevant passage from Carnap's "Intellectual Autobiography": "At that time [1940–1, at Harvard] I gave a talk on the relation of mathematics to empirical science in a large discussion group of faculty members interested in the foundations of science. My main thesis was that mathematics has no factual content and, therefore, is not in need of empirical confirmation. . . . I thought that this was an old story and at any rate a purely academic question. But to my great surprise, the audience responded with vehement emotions. Even before I had finished my lecture, excited objections were raised. Afterwards we had a long and heated discussion in which several people often talked at the same time. Richard von Mises stated bluntly that the sentence '2 + 2 = 4' (if taken, not as a theorem in an uninterpreted axiom system, but in its customary interpretation) was just as much of an empirical nature as the sentence 'Solid bodies expand when heated'. I thought: are we now back with John Stuart Mill?" (pp. 64–5).

Chapter 19

1. Several decades later Feyerabend endorsed this doctrine under the name of the "pragmatic theory of observation." Quine's theory of protocols avoids Chomsky's objections in that it does not make the rather implausible assumption that all persons will say 'red here now' every time they see anything red; his view is that under those circumstances, if prompted by an appropriate question, there will be assent to the protocol.
2. We discussed Carnap's refutation of this point in *LSL* in Chapter 17. Schlick remained unimpressed, appealing to Wittgenstein's doctrine that we understand a mathematical proposition only after we have proved it (Letter to Carnap of 14 November 1935, RC 102-70-11, ASP).
3. Schlick added an un-Wittgensteinian link between verification and a sense of personal fulfillment: "The joy in knowledge is joy in verification, the exaltation of having guessed correctly. . . . The question concealed behind the problem of the absolutely certain foundation of knowledge is, so to speak, that of the legitimacy of the satisfaction which verification fills us with" (*Philosophical Papers*, vol. 2, p. 383). Schlick, no doubt, had in mind the average physicist making an average laboratory prediction. But some may also predict death from cancer or nuclear holocaust.
4. As we know, Schlick endorsed the idea; Carnap claimed that it entails the subjectivity of butter (since butter bends to our will).
5. This description of the episode illustrates the mine field of misleading information the historian of positivism must go through. The reference to "logical truth or provability" might lead one to think that at the time of *LSL* Carnap had no conception of logical truth other than theoremhood. The diagnosis of Carnap's surprise ("since I was thinking only in terms of syntactical metalanguages") has got to be wrong since, as we know, *LSL* allows for syntactic metalanguages that include translations of their object languages. It was argued in Chapter 17 that a better diagnosis of Carnap's difficulty involves his verificationist leanings.

6. Die Gestaltung der sog. "Wirklichkeit" hängt aber, wie wir wissen, von der Struktur der jeweils verwendeten Sprache ab; sie ist z.B. jeweils eine andere im primitiven Denken, in der klassischen Physik, in der Quantenphysik.

7. Es ist typisch, dass Du hier von "Gestaltung" sprichst, wo ich "Beschreibung" sagen würde. Ich würde nämlich vorschlagen, von "Gestaltung" der Wirklichkeit etwa beim Bau eines Hauses, beim Anlegen eines Kanals zu reden; den Aufbau einer Wissenschaft, eines Weltbildes aber "Beschreibung" zu nennen. Auf jeden Fall scheint mir auf der Hand zu liegen, dass beides etwas total Verschiedenes ist. Niemand wird mich überzeugen, dass es unzweckmässig und gefährlich wäre, zu sagen, dass der Primitive und der moderne Physiker verschiedene Weltbilder haben, aber in einer und derselben Wirklichkeit leben. . . . Nimmt man Deine Aeusserung wörtlich, so würde sie behaupten, dass die Wirklichkeit durch die Sprache geschaffen werde und dass daher der Primitive und der Quantenphysiker in verschiedenen Wirklichkeiten leben. Man kann das schliesslich sagen, aber ich würde einen solchen Satz doch eher bei Keyserling oder Simmel (den man wohl einen relativistischen Metaphysiker nennen muss) erwarten als bei Carnap!

8. . . . bleibt . . . eine Meinungsdifferenz, weil ich nicht an die restlose Uebersetzbarkeit glaube und daher meine, dass auch der Inhalt der Weltbeschreibung in einem gewissen Grade durch die Wahl der Sprachform mitbeeinflusst wird. Dass heisst aber gewiss nicht, dass die Wirklichkeit durch die Sprache geschaffen werde.

9. See my "Carnap's *Sprachanschauung* circa 1932," pp. 222–4, for the argument that Carnap's views did not change essentially with his acceptance of Tarski's theory.

References

Abbreviations or shortened forms of titles used in the text are indicated in brackets at the beginning of an entry.

Unpublished sources

Foreign-language quotations from unpublished sources are translated by the author; the original quotations are provided in the notes.

[ASP] Archives of Scientific Philosophy in the Twentieth Century, Department of Special Collections, University of Pittsburgh Libraries. Citations specify the file number of the item quoted or referred to. The file numbers of items in the Rudolf Carnap Collection of the ASP are preceded by "RC"; those of items in the Frank P. Ramsey collection are preceded by "FR"; and those of items in the Hans Reichenbach Collection are preceded by "HR."

[Russell Archives] Bertrand Russell Archives, McMaster University. Citations of items other than letters specify the file number of the item quoted or referred to.

[VCA] Vienna Circle Archive, University of Amsterdam.

[Wittgenstein Papers] *The Wittgenstein Papers,* microfilm edition, G. H. Wright, ed. (Cornell University Library); catalogue in *Philosophical Review 78* (Oct. 1969):483–503. Citations specify the catalogue number of the item quoted or referred to.

Published sources

If a citation is made to a published English translation of a quotation, the translation in the text is that found in this English translation; if the citation is to a non-English version, the translation is the author's.

Allison, H. E., ed. and trans. *The Kant–Eberhard Controversy.* Johns Hopkins University Press, Baltimore, Md., 1973.

Aristotle. *Prior Analytics.* In *The Complete Works of Aristotle,* J. Barnes, ed., vol. 1. Princeton University Press, Princeton, N.J., 1984.

Arnauld, A., and Nicole, P. *La logique ou l'art de penser.* Flammarion, Paris, 1970.

Ayer, A. J. *Logical Postivism.* Free Press, New York, 1959.

424 References

Beck, L. W. *Early German Philosophy.* Harvard University Press, Cambridge, Mass., 1969.

"Kant's Strategy." *Journal for the History of Ideas 28* (1967):224–36.

Becker, O. [*Mathematische Existenz*] *Mathematische Existenz, Untersuchungen zur Logik und Ontologie mathematischer Phänomene.* Niemeyer, Halle, 1927.

Beltrami, E. [*Opere matematiche*] *Opere matematiche di Eugenio Beltrami,* vol. 1. Publicate per cura della Facoltia di scienze della R. Universita di Roma. University Hoepli, Milan, 1902.

Bennett, J. "Substance, Reality, and Primary Qualities." *American Philosophical Quarterly 2* (1965):1–17.

Berkeley, G. *The Analyst.* In *The Works of George Berkeley,* A. Luce, ed., vol. 4. Nelson, London, 1951.

Berthelot, M. *La chimie au Moyen Age,* vol. 3. Zeller, Osnabrück & Philo Press, Amsterdam, 1967.

Bochenski, I. M. *Formale Logik.* Alber, Freiburg, 1956.

Bolzano, B. *Beyträge zu einer begründeteren Darstellung der Mathematik.* In *Early Mathematical Works (1781–1848).*

Early Mathematical Works (1781–1848), L. Novy, ed. Institute of Czechoslovak and General History CSAS, Prague, 1981.

[*Grossenlehre*] *Einleitung zur Grössenlehre und erste Begriffe der allgemeinen Grossenlehre,* J. Berg, ed. In Bolzano, *Gesamtausgabe,* ser. 2A, vol. 7.

Gesamtausgabe, E. Winter, ed., vols. 1–15. Frommann, Stuttgart-Bad Cannstatt, 1969–87.

Lebensbeschreibung. Seidelsche, Sulzbach, 1836.

Paradoxes of the Infinite, D. A. Steele, trans. Routledge & Kegan Paul, London, 1950.

"Rein analytischer Beweis des Lehrsatzes." In Bolzano, *Early Mathematical Works (1781–1848).*

Theory of Science, R. George, ed. and trans. University of California Press, Berkeley and Los Angeles, 1972.

"Uber der Begriff des Schönen." *Untersuchungen zur Grundlegung der Aesthetik.* Athenaeum Verlag, Frankfurt, 1972.

[*WL*] *Wissenschaftslehre,* Wolfgang Schultz, ed. Meiner, Leipzig, 1929.

Borges, J. L. *Obras completas,* vol. 1. Emece Editore, Buenos Aires, 1974.

Bradley, F. H. *Appearance and Reality.* Clarendon Press, Oxford, 1959.

"Reply to Mr. Russell's Explanations." *Mind 20* (1911):74–6.

Brentano, F. *Die Lehre vom richtigen Urteil,* F. Mayer-Hillebrand, ed. Francke Verlag, Bern, 1956.

[*Psychologie*] *Psychologie vom empirischen Stundpunkte.* Duncker & Humblot, Leipzig, 1874. [Translated as *Psychology from an Empirical Standpoint.*]

[*Psychology*] *Psychology from an Empirical Standpoint,* O. Kraus, ed.; A. C. Rancurello, D. B. Terrell, and L. L. McAlister, trans. Routledge & Kegan Paul, London, 1973.

Wahrheit und Evidenz, O. Kraus, ed. Meiner, Leipzig, 1930.

Brouwer, L. E. J. "On the Foundations of Mathematics." In *Philosophy and Foun-*

dations of Mathematics, A. Heyting, ed., vol. 1 of Brouwer, *Collected Works.*
  North Holland, Amsterdam, 1975.

Carnap, R. *Abriss der Logistik,* vol. 2 of *Schriften zur wissenschaftlichen Welt-
  auffassung,* P. Frank and M. Schlick, eds. Springer, Vienna, 1929.

"Bericht über Untersuchungen zur allgemeinen Axiomatik." *Erkenntnis 1*
  (1930):303–7.

"Diskussion über Wahrscheinlichkeit." *Erkenntnis 1* (1930):260–85; Carnap's
  remarks are on pp. 268–9, 282–3.

"Dreidimensionalität des Raumes und Kausalität." *Annalen der Philosophie
  und philosophischen Kritik 4* (1924):105–30.

["Erwiderung"] "Erwiderung auf die vorstehenden Aufsätze von E. Zilsel und K.
  Duncker." *Erkenntnis 3* (1932–3):177–88.

"Intellectual Autobiography." In Schilpp, *The Philosophy of Rudolf Carnap.*

[*LSW*] *The Logical Structure of the World.* In Carnap, *The Logical Structure of
  the World and Pseudoproblems in Philosophy.*

The Logical Structure of the World and Pseudoproblems in Philosophy, R. A.
  George, trans. University of California Press, Berkeley and Los Angeles, 1969.

[*LSL*] *The Logical Syntax of Language.* Routledge & Kegan Paul, London, 1937.

[*Aufbau*] *Der logische Aufbau der Welt.* Weltkreis-Verlag, Berlin, 1928. [Trans-
  lated as *The Logical Structure of the World.*]

Meaning and Necessity. University of Chicago Press, Chicago, 1967.

Philosophy and Logical Syntax. Kegan Paul, Trench, Trubner, London, 1935.

Physikalische Begriffsbildung. Wissenschaftliche Buchgesellschaft, Darmstadt,
  1966. [Unchanged reproduction of the first, 1926 edition.]

["Die physikalische Sprache"] "Die physikalische Sprache als Universalsprache
  der Wissenschaft." *Erkenntnis 2* (1932):432–65. [Translated as *The Unity of
  Science,* M. Black, trans. Kegan Paul, Trench, Trubner, London, 1934.]

[*Pseudoproblems*] *Pseudoproblems in Philosophy.* In Carnap, *The Logical
  Structure of the World and Pseudoproblems in Philosophy.*

["Psychology"] "Psychology in Physical Language." In Ayer, *Logical Positivism.*

Review of S. C. Kleene, "On the Term 'Analytic' in Logical Syntax." *Journal of
  Symbolic Logic 5* (1940):157–8.

"Uber die Abhängigkeit der Eigenschaften des Raumes von denen der Zeit."
  Kant-Studien 30 (1925):331–45.

"Uber Protokollsätze." *Erkenntnis 3* (1932–3):215–28. [Translated as "On
  Protocol Sentences," R. Creath and R. Nollan, trans., *Nous 21* (1987):457–
  70.]

["Uberwindung der Metaphysik"] "Uberwindung der Metaphysik durch logi-
  sche Analyse der Sprache." *Erkenntnis 2* (1932):219–41. [Translated as
  "The Elimination of Metaphysics Through Logical Analysis of Language." In
  Ayer, *Logical Positivism.*]

"Von der Erkenntnistheorie zur Wissenschaftslogik." *Actes du Congreàs international de philosophie scientifique, Sorbonne, Paris, 1935 388* (1936):
  36–41 [Hermann, Paris].

"Wahrheit und Bewährung." *Actes du Congreàs international de philosophie
  scientifique, Sorbonne, Paris, 1935 391* (1936):18–23 [Hermann, Paris;

English translation is part of "Truth and Confirmation," in *Readings in Philosophical Analysis,* H. Feigl and W. Sellars, eds. (Appleton-Century-Crofts, New York, 1949)].

Carroll, L. *Symbolic Logic,* W. W. Bartley, ed. Potter, New York, 1977.

Cassirer, E. [*Einstein's Theory of Relativity*] *Einstein's Theory of Relativity Considered from the Epistemological Standpoint.* In Cassirer, *Substance and Function and Einstein's Theory of Relativity.*

The Philosophy of Symbolic Forms, vol. 1: *Language,* R. Manheim, trans. Yale University Press, New Haven, Conn., 1953.

Substance and Function. In Cassirer, *Substance and Function and Einstein's Theory of Relativity.*

Substance and Function and Einstein's Theory of Relativity, W. C. Swabey and M. C. Swabey, trans. Open Court, Chicago, 1923.

[*Einstein'schen Relativitätstheorie*] *Zur Einstein'schen Relativitätstheorie, Erkenntnistheoretische Betrachtungen.* Cassirer Verlag, Berlin, 1921. [Translated as *Einstein's Theory of Relativity.*]

Clarke, S. *The Leibniz–Clarke Correspondence,* H. G. Alexander, ed. Manchester University Press, Manchester, 1956.

Coffa, J. A. "Carnap's *Sprachanschauung* circa 1932." In *PSA 1976,* F. Suppe and P. Asquith, eds. (1977):205–41.

"Elective Affinities: Weyl and Reichenbach." In *Hans Reichenbach, Logical Empiricist,* W. Salmon, ed. Reidel, Dordrecht, 1979.

"From Geometry to Tolerance: Sources of Linguistic Conventionalism in 19th Century Geometry." *From Quarks to Quasars,* R. Colodny, ed., University of Pittsburgh Series in the Philosophy of Science, vol. 5. University of Pittsburgh Press, Pittsburgh, 1986.

"The Humble Origins of Russell's Paradox." *Russell 33–4* (1979):31–8.

"Russell and Kant." *Synthese 45* (1980):43–70.

"Russell as a Platonic Dialogue." *Synthese 45* (1980):43–70.

Cohen, H. *Kants Theorie der Erfahrung.* Dümmlers, Berlin, 1885.

Couturat, L. "Essai sur les fondements de la géométrie par Bertrand Russell." *Revue de Métaphysique et de Morale 6* (1898):354–80.

Dostoevsky, F. *The Idiot,* C. Garnett, trans. Macmillan, New York, 1948.

Dugac, P. "Des fonctions comme expressions analytiques aux fonctions représentables analytiquement." In *Mathematical Perspectives,* J. W. Dauben, ed. Academic Press, New York, 1981.

"Fondements de l'analyse." In *Abrégé d'histoire des mathématiques, 1700–1900,* J. Dieudonneé, ed., vol. 1. Mermann, Paris, 1978.

Duhem, P. *The Evolution of Mechanics,* M. Cole, trans. Sijthoff & Noordhoff, The Netherlands, 1980.

Dummett, M. *Frege: Philosophy of Language.* Harper & Row, New York, 1973.

Truth and Other Enigmas. Harvard University Press, Cambridge, Mass., 1978.

Eddington, A. *The Nature of the Physical World.* University of Michigan Press, Ann Arbor, 1958.

Feyerabend, P. *Against Method.* Redwood Burn Limited Trowbridge & Esher, London, 1980.

Fraenkel, A. [*Einleitung*] *Einleitung in die Mengenlehre.* Springer, Berlin, 1928.

Frege, G. *The Basic Laws of Arithmetic,* M. Furth, ed. and trans. University of California Press, Berkeley, and Los Angeles, 1964.

[*Begriffsschrift*] *Begriffsschrift und andere Aufsätze,* Ignacio Angelelli, ed. Olms, Hildesheim, 1964. [Translated in van Heijenoort, *From Frege to Gödel.*]

["Booles rechende Logik"] "Booles rechende Logik und Begriffsschrift" (1880–1). In *Nachlass.*

[*Collected Papers*] *Collected Papers on Mathematics, Logic, and Philosophy,* B. McGuinness, ed.; M. Black, V. H. Dudman, P. Geach, H. Kaal, E-H. W. Kluge, B. McGuinness, and R. M. Stoothoff, trans. Blackwell Publisher, Oxford, 1984.

The Foundations of Arithmetic, J. L. Austin, trans. Harper & Bros., New York, 1953.

[*Grundgesetze*] *Grundgesetze der Arithmetik,* vol. 1. Olms, Hildesheim, 1962. [Translated as *The Basic Laws of Arithmetic.*]

[*Grundlagen*] *Die Grundlagen der Arithmetik.* Olms, Hildesheim, 1961. [Translated as *The Foundations of Arithmetic.*]

Kleine Schriften, Ignacio Angelelli, ed. Olms, Hildescheim, 1967.

[*Nachlass*] *Nachgelassene Schriften,* H. Hermes, F. Kambartel, and F. Kaulbach, eds., vol. 1 of *Nachgelassene Schriften und wissenschaftlicher Briefwechsel.*

Nachgelassene Schriften und wissenschaftlicher Briefwechsel, vols. 1 and 2. Meiner Verlag, Hamburg, vol. 1 in 1969, vol. 2 in 1976.

On the Foundations of Geometry and Formal Theories of Arithmetic, E-H. W. Kluge, trans. Yale University Press, New Haven, Conn., 1971.

Philosophical and Mathematical Correspondence, G. Gabriel, H. Hermes, F. Kambartel, C. Thiel, and A. Veraart, eds.; M. Kaal, trans. University of Chicago Press, Chicago, 1980.

[*Translations*] *Translations from the Philosophical Writings of Gottlob Frege,* P. Geach and M. Black, eds. Basil, Blackwell & Mott, Oxford, 1960.

"Uber Sinn und Bedeutung." In Frege, *Funktion, Begriff, Bedeutung: Fünf logische Studien,* Günther Patzig, ed. Vandenhoeck & Ruprecht, Göttingen, 1969.

[*Wiss. Briefwechsel*] *Wissenschaftlicher Briefwechsel,* G. Gabriel, H. Hermes, F. Kambartel, C. Thiel, and A. Veraart, eds., vol. 2 of Frege, *Nachgelassene Schriften und wissenschaftlicher Briefwechsel.*

Freudenthal, H. "Did Cauchy Plagiarize Bolzano?" *Archive for History of the Exact Sciences* 7 (1970–1):375–92.

Gödel, K. ["Uber unentscheidbare Sätze"] "Uber formal unentscheidbare Sätze der *Principia mathematica* und verwandter Systeme I." *Monatshefte für Mathematik und Physik 38* (1931):173–98. [Translated as "Some Metamathematical Results on Completeness and Consistency." In van Heijenoort, *From Frege to Gödel.*]

Grabiner, J. *The Origins of Cauchy's Rigorous Calculus.* M.I.T. Press, Cambridge, Mass., 1981.

Grattan-Guinness, I. "Bolzano, Cauchy and the 'New Analysis' of the Early Nineteenth Century." *Archive for History of the Exact Sciences* 6 (1969–70):372–400.

Dear Russell – Dear Jourdain. Duckworth, London, 1977.

Grünbaum, A. *Philosophical Problems of Space and Time.* University of Minnesota Press, Minneapolis, 1968, 1st. ed.: Reidel, Dordrecht, 1973, 2d ed.

Helmholtz, H. von. [*Einleitung*] *Einleitung zu den Vorlesungen über theoretische Physik,* vol. 1, pt. 1, of *Vorlesungen über theoretische Physik,* A. König and C. Runge, eds. Barth, Leipzig, 1903.

Epistemological Writings, M. F. Lowe, trans., Boston Studies in the Philosophy of Science, vol. 37, R. S. Cohen and M. W. Wartofsky, eds. Reidel, Dordrecht, 1977.

Schriften zur Erkenntnistheorie, P. Hertz and M. Schlick, eds. Springer, Berlin, 1921. [Translated as *Epistemological Writings.*]

"Die Thatsachen in der Wahrnehmung." In Helmholtz, *Vorträge und Reden,* Fünfte Auflage. Vieweg, Braunschweig, 1903.

"Uber das Sehen des Menschen." In Helmholtz, *Philosophische Vorträge und Aufsätze,* H. Hörz and S. Wollgast, eds. Akademie, Berlin, 1971.

"Uber die thatsächlichen Grundlagen der Geometrie." In Helmholtz, *Wissenschaftliche Abhandlungen,* vol. 2. Barth, Leipzig, 1883.

Hempel, C. "On the Logical Positivists' Theory of Truth." *Analysis 2* (1934–5):49–59.

Hilbert, D. *Gesammelte Abhandlungen,* vol. 3. Springer, Berlin, 1935.

Grundlagen der Geometrie. Teubner, Leipzig, 1930.

"On the Infinite." In *Philosophy of Mathematics,* P. Benacerraf and H. Putnam, eds. Prentice-Hall, Englewood Cliffs, N.J., 1964.

Höfler, A. *Logik.* In Höfler, *Philosophische Propädeutik,* pt. 1. Tempsky, Vienna, 1890.

Hume, D. [*Enquiry*] *An Enquiry Concerning Human Understanding,* E. Steinberg, ed. Hackett, Indianapolis, Ind., 1977.

A Treatise of Human Nature, L. A. Selby-Bigge, ed. Clarendon Press, Oxford, 1888.

Husserl, E. *Aufsätze und Rezensionen (1890-1910),* B. Rang, ed. In *Husserliana,* vol. 22. Nijhoff, The Hague, 1979.

Ideas, W. R. Boyce Gibson, trans. Allen & Unwin, London, 1969.

Introduction to the Logical Investigations, P. J. Bossert and C. H. Peters, trans. Nijhoff, The Hague, 1975.

Logical Investigations, J. N. Findlay, trans., vols. 1 and 2. Routledge & Kegan Paul, London; Humanities Press, New York, 1970.

Logische Untersuchungen, vols. 1 and 2. Niemeyer, Tübingen, 1968. [Translated as *Logical Investigations.*]

Philosophie der Arithmetik, L. Eley, ed. In *Husserliana,* vol. 12. Nijhoff, The Hague, 1970.

[*Begriff der Zahl*] *Uber den Begriff der Zahl,* Habilitationsschrift, 1887. In *Philosophie der Arithmetik,* International Congress for the Unity of Science, ed. *Actes du Congreàs international de philosophie scientifique, Sorbonne, Paris, 1935,* vols. 1–8. Hermann, Paris, 1936.

Joachim, H. *The Nature of Truth.* Clarendon Press, Oxford, 1906.

Johnson, D. M. "Prelude to Dimension Theory: The Geometrical Investigations of Bernard Bolzano." *Archive for History of the Exact Sciences 17* (1977): 261–5.

Kaila, E. "Logistic Neopositivism." In Kaila, *Reality and Experience,* R. S. Cohen, ed. Reidel, Dordrecht, 1979.

Kant, I. *Anthropologie.* In *Kants gesammelte Schriften,* vol. 7.

[*Critique*] *Critique of Pure Reason,* N. Kemp Smith, trans. St. Martin's Press, New York, 1965.

De mundi sensibilis atque intelligibilis forma et principiis. In Kant, *Werke in Zehn Bänden,* W. Weischaedel, ed., vol. 5. Wissenschaftliche Buchsgesellschaft, Darmstadt, 1975.

[*Beweisgrund*] *Der einzig mögliche Beweisgrund zu einer Demonstration des Daseins Gottes* [The one possible basis for a demonstration of the existence of God], G. Treash, trans. Abaris Books, New York, 1979.

Grundlegung zur Metaphysik der Sitten. In *Kants gesammelte Schriften,* vol. 4.

Kants gesammelte Schriften, vols. 1–29, Königlich Preussischen Akademie der Wissenschaftlicher und Deutsche Akademie der Wissenschaften zu Berlin, eds. De Gruyter & Reimer, Berlin, 1910–83.

[*Kritik*] *Kritik der reinen Vernunft,* Raymund Schmidt, ed. Meiner Verlag, Hamburg, 1956. [Translated as *Critique.*]

Logic, R. Hartman and W. Schwarz, trans. Bobbs-Merrill, Indianapolis, Ind., 1974.

Logik. In *Kants gesammelte Schriften,* vol. 9. [Translated as *Logic.*[

Logik Blomberg. In *Kants gesammelte Schriften,* vol. 24, pt. 1.

Logik Busolt. In *Kants gesammelte Schriften,* vol. 24, pt. 2.

Logik Philippi. In *Kants gesammelte Schriften,* vol. 24, pt. 1.

Logik Pölitz. In *Kants gesammelte Schriften,* vol. 24, pt. 2.

[*Nachträge*] *Nachträge zu Kants kritik der reinen Vernunft,* B. Erdmann, ed. Lipsius & Tischer, Kiel, 1881.

Philosophical Correspondence, 1759–99, A. Zweig, ed. and trans. University of Chicago Press, Chicago, 1967.

Philosophische Enzyklopädie. In *Kants gesammelte Schriften,* vol. 29.

Preisschrift über die Fortschritte der Metaphysik (1804). In *Kants gesammelte Schriften,* vol. 20.

Prolegomena to Any Future Metaphysics, L. W. Beck, ed. Bobbs-Merrill, Indianapolis, Ind., 1950.

Reflexionen zur Logik. In *Kants gesammelte Schriften,* vol. 16.

Uber die Methode die Metaphysik, Theologie und Moral richtiger zu beweisen. In *Kant Studien,* Ergänzungshefte, K. Bopp, ed., no. 42. Reuther & Reichard, Berlin, 1918.

[*Untersuchung über natürlichen Theologie*] *Untersuchung über die Deutlichkeit der Grundsätze der natürlichen Theologie und der Moral.* In *Kants gesammelte Schriften,* vol. 2.

Vorlesungen über die Metaphysik. Wissenschaftliche Buchgesellschaft, Darmstadt, 1964.

Wiener Logik. In *Kants gesammelte Schriften,* vol. 24.

Kaufmann, F. *Das Unendliche in der Mathematik und seine Ausschaltung.* Deuticke, Leipzig, 1930.

Kemp Smith, N. *A Commentary to Kant's "Critique of Pure Reason."* Humanities Press, Atlantic Highlands, N.J., 1984.

Kleene, S. C. Review of Rudolf Carnap, *The Logical Syntax of Language. Journal of Symbolic Logic 4* (1939): 82–7.

Kline, M. *Mathematical Thought from Ancient to Modern Times.* Oxford University Press, New York, 1972.

Knüfer, C. *Grundzäge der Geschichte des Begriffs 'Vorstellung' von Wolff bis Kant.* Olms, Hildesheim, 1975.

Königsberger, L. *Hermann von Helmholtz,* vol. 1. Vieweg, Braunschweig, 1902.

Lagrange, J. L. *Théorie des fonctions analytiques.* In *Oeuvres de Lagrange,* M. J.-A. Serret, ed., vol. 9. Gauthier-Villars, Paris, 1881.

Lambert, H. M. *Neues Organon.* Wendler, Leipzig, 1764.

Laugwitz, Detlef. "Bemerkungen zu Bolzanos Grossenlehre." *Archive for History of the Exact Sciences 2* (1962–5):398–409.

Leibniz, G. W. *Logical Papers,* G. H. R. Parkinson, ed. and trans. Clarendon Press, Oxford, 1966.

  [*Nouveaux essais*] *Noveaux essais sur l'entendement humain.* Garnier-Flammarion, Paris, 1966.

  Opuscules et fragments inédits de Leibniz, L. Couturat, ed. Olms, Hildesheim, 1961.

  Philosophical Papers and Letters, L. E. Loemker, trans. and ed. Reidel, Dordrecht, 1956.

Lukasiewicz, J. "Logistic and Philosophy." In Lukasiewicz, *Selected Works,* L. Borkowski, ed. North-Holland, Amsterdam, 1970.

Marty, A. *Gesammelte Schriften,* J. Eisenmeir, A. Kastil, and O. Kraus, eds., vol. 2. Niemeyer, Halle, 1918.

  "Uber das Verhältnis von Grammatik und Logik." In Marty, *Symbolae Pragenses,* Deutsche Gesellschaft für Alterthumskunde in Prag, ed. Tempsky, Vienna, 1893.

Maury, A. *The Concepts of* Sinn *and* Gegenstand *in Wittgenstein's* Tractatus, *Acta Philosophica Fennica 29,* no. 4 (1977).

Maxwell, G. "Scientific Methodology and the Causal Theory of Perception." In *New Readings in Philosophical Analysis,* H. Feigl, W. Sellars, and K. Lehrer, eds. Appeteon-Century-Crofts, New York, 1972.

Meier, G. F. *Auszug aus der Venunftlehre.* Gebauer, Halle, 1752.

Meinong, A. *Gesamtausgabe,* R. Haller, R. Kindinger, and R. Chisholm, eds., vol. 2. Akademische Druck- & Verlagsanstalt, Graz, 1971.

  "The Theory of Objects." In *Realism and the Background of Phenomenology,* R. M. Chisholm, ed. Free Press, Glencoe, Ill., 1960.

  Uber Annahmen. Barth, Leipzig, 1928.

Menger, K. "Introduction." In H. Hahn, *Empiricism, Logic, and Mathematics,* B. McGuinness, ed. Reidel, Dordrecht, 1980.

  "Memories of Moritz Schlick." In E. Gadol, *Rationality and Science.* Springer, Vienna, 1982.

Mill, J. S. [*Hamilton's Philosophy*] *An Examination of Sir W. Hamilton's Philosophy,* J. M. Robson, ed., vol. 9 of *Collected Works of John Stuart Mill.* University of Toronto Press, Toronto; Routledge & Kegan Paul, London, 1979.

References   431

[*Logic*] *A System of Logic.* Longman's, Green, London, 1965.
Moore, G. E. *Principia Ethica.* Cambridge University Press, 1980.
"The Refutation of Idealism." In Moore, *Philosophical Studies.* Littlefield, Adams, Paterson, N.J., 1959.
Review of Brentano, *The Origin of the Knowledge of Right and Wrong. International Journal of Ethics 14* (1903):115–23.
"Truth and Falsity." In *Dictionary of Philosophy and Psychology,* J. M. Baldwin, ed., vol. 2. Smith, Gloucester, Mass., 1960.
"Wittgenstein's Lectures in 1930–33." In Moore, *Philosophical Papers.* Collier, New York, 1962.
Neurath, O. [*Philosophical Papers*] *Philosophical Papers, 1913–1946,* R. S. Cohen and M. Neurath, eds. Reidel, Dordrecht, 1983.
"Protokollsätze." *Erkenntnis 3* (1932–3):204–14. [Translated as "Protocol Sentences." In Neurath, *Philosophical Papers,* and Ayer, *Logical Positivism.*]
"Radikaler Physikalismus und 'Wirkliche Welt.'" *Erkenntnis 4* (1934):346–62.
"Soziologie im Physikalismus." *Erkenntnis 2* (1932):393–31. [Translated as "Sociology in the Framework of Physicalism." In Neurath, *Philosophical Papers.*]
Newton, I. [*Principia*] *Newton's Mathematical Principles of Natural Philosophy and His System of the World,* A. Motte, trans., rev. by F. Cajori. University of California Press, Berkeley and Los Angeles, 1962.
Pasch, M. *Vorlesungen über Neuere Geometrie.* Teubner, Leibzig, 1882.
Peano, G. [*Formulaire*] *Formulaire de mathématiques,* vols. 1–4. Bocca, Turin; Carre & Naud, Paris, 1895–1903.
Opere scelte, vol. 1. Edizioni Cremonese, Roma, 1957.
Pears, D. F. *Bertrand Russell and the British Tradition in Philosophy.* Random House, New York, 1967.
Ludwig Wittgenstein. Viking Press, New York, 1970.
Planck, M. "Positivismus und reale Aussenwelt." *Forschung und Fortschritte 6* (1930):448–68. [Translated as chaps. 1 and 2 of Planck, *The New Science,* J. Murphy, trans. Meridian Books, New York, 1959.]
"The Unity of the Physical World-Picture." In *Physical Reality,* S. Toulmin, ed. Harper & Row, New York, 1970.
Poincaré, H. "Analyse de ses travaux scientifiques." *Acta Mathematica 38* (1921):126–31.
"Des fondements de la géométrie." *Revue de Métaphysique et de Morale 7* (1899):251–79.
"Sur les principes de la géométrie." *Revue de Métaphysique et de Morale 8* (1900):72–86.
Popper, K. *Conjectures and Refutations: The Growth of Scientific Knowledge.* Harper & Row, New York, 1963.
[*Grundprobleme*] *Die beiden Grundprobleme der Erkenntnistheorie,* T. E. Hansen, ed. Mohr, Tübingen, 1979.
The Logic of Scientific Discovery. Hutchinson, London, 1968.
Logik der Forschung. Springer, Vienna, 1934.
Prauss, G. *Kant und das Problem der Dinge an sich.* Bouvier Verlag, Bonn, 1974.

432 References

Ramsey, F. P. *Foundations: Essays in Philosophy, Logic, Mathematics and Economics,* D. H. Mellor, ed. Routledge & Kegan Paul, London, 1978.

The Foundations of Mathematics and Other Logical Essays, R. B. Braithwaite, ed. Routledge & Kegan Paul, London, 1931.

Reichenbach, H. "Bemerkung." *Erkenntnis 3* (1932–3):427–8.

"Diskussion über Wahrscheinlichkeit." *Erkenntnis 1* (1930):260–85; Reichenbach's remarks are on pp. 263–4, 269–70, 274–7, 282, 284.

[*E & P*] *Experience and Prediction.* University of Chicago Press, Chicago, 1938.

"Moritz Schlick, *Allgemeine Erkenntnislehre.*" *Zeitschrift für angewandte Psychologie 16* (1920):341–3.

"On Probability and Induction." *Philosophy of Science 5* (1938):21–45.

The Philosophy of Space and Time, M. Reichenbach and J. Freund, trans. Dover, New York, 1958.

"Der physikalische Wahrheitsbegriff." *Erkenntnis 2* (1931):156–71.

"The Present State of the Discussion on Relativity." In Reichenbach, *Modern Philosophy of Science,* M. Reichenbach, ed. and trans. Routledge & Kegan Paul, London, 1959.

Relativitätstheorie und Erkenntnis Apriori. In *Die philosophische Bedeutung der Relativitätstheoreie,* vol. 3 of *Gesammalte Werke in 9 Bände,* A. Kamlah and M. Reichenbach, eds. Vieweg, Braunschweig, 1979. [Translated as *The Theory of Relativity and a Priori Knowledge.*]

"Rudolf Carnap, *Der logische Aufbau der Welt.*" *Kant Studien 38* (1933):199–201.

Selected Writings, 1909–1953, M. Reichenbach and R. S. Cohen, eds., vols. 1 and 2. Reidel, Dordrecht, 1978.

The Theory of Probability, E. H. Hutten and M. Reichenbach, trans. University of California Press, Berkeley and Los Angeles, 1949.

[*RAK*] *The Theory of Relativity and a Priori Knowledge,* M. Reichenbach, ed. and trans. University of California Press, Berkeley and Los Angeles, 1965.

"The Verifiability Theory of Meaning." *Proceedings of the American Academy of Arts and Sciences 80* (1951):46–86.

"Ziele und Wege der physikalischen Erkenntnis." *Allgemeine Grundlagen der Physik,* M. Thirring, ed., vol. 4 of *Handbuch der Physik,* H. Geiger and K. Scheel, eds. Springer, Berlin, 1929, pp. 1–80. [Translated as "The Aims and Methods of Physical Knowledge." In *Selected Works,* vol. 2.]

Riehl, A. *Führende Denker und Forscher.* Quelle & Meyer, Leipzig, 1922.

[*Phil. Krit.*] *Der philosophische Kriticismus und seine Bedeutung für die positive Wissenschaft,* vols. 1 and 2. Engelmann, Leipzig, 1879.

Rootselaar, B. van, "Bolzano's Theory of Real Numbers." *Archive for History of the Exact Sciences 2* (1962–5):168–80.

Rougier, L. "Allocation finale." *Actes du Congrès international de philosophie scientifique, Sorbonne, Paris 1935, 8* (1936):88–91 [Hermann, Paris].

Russell, B. *The Analysis of Matter.* Dover, New York, 1954.

The Analysis of Mind. Allen & Unwin, London, 1961.

"The Basis of Realism." *Journal of Philosophy 8* (1911):158–61.

A Critical Exposition of the Philosophy of Leibniz. Cambridge University Press, 1900.

An Essay on the Foundations of Geometry. Dover, New York, 1956.

Essays in Analysis, D. Lackey, ed. Braziller, New York, 1973.

"Geometry, Non-Euclidean." *Encyclopedia Britannica,* 10th ed., vol. 4. 1902.

An Inquiry into Meaning and Truth. Penguin, Harmondsworth, 1962.

Letter to Meinong, 15 December 1904. *Russell 9* (1973):15–16.

"Logical Atomism." In Ayer, *Logical Positivism.*

My Philosophical Development. Allen & Unwin, London, 1959.

Mysticism and Logic. Barnes & Noble, New York, 1971.

"The Nature of Truth." *Mind 15* (1906):528–33.

"Non-Euclidean Geometry." *Athenaeum 4018* (1904):592–3.

"On the Nature of Acquaintance." In Russell, *Logic and Knowledge,* R. C. Marsh, ed. Allen & Unwin, London; Macmillan, New York, 1968.

"On the Nature of Truth." *Proceedings of the Aristotelian Society* 7 (1906–7):28–49.

"On the Nature of Truth and Falsehood." In Russell, *Philosophical Essays.* Simon & Schuster, New York, 1966.

Our Knowledge of the External World. Allen & Unwin, London, 1972.

Portraits from Memory. Allen & Unwin, London, 1956.

[*Principia*], see Whitehead and Russell.

[*Principles*] *The Principles of Mathematics,* 2d ed. Allen & Unwin, London, 1956.

The Problems of Philosophy. Oxford University Press, 1976.

"Review of *Foundations of Mathematics* by F. P. Ramsey." *Mind 46* (1931):476–82.

Review of Ramsey's *The Foundations of Mathematics and Other Logical Essays. Philosophy* 7 (1932):84–8.

Russell's Logical Atomism, D. Pears, ed. Fontana/Collins, London, 1972.

"Some Explanations in Reply to Mr. Bradley." *Mind 19* (1910):373–8.

"Sur les axiomes de la géometrie." *Revue de Metaphysique et de Morale* 7 (1899):684–707.

Theory of Knowledge: The 1913 Manuscript, E. R. Eames and K. Blackwell, eds., vol. 7 of *The Collected Papers of Bertrand Russell.* Allen & Unwin, London, 1983.

Scheler, M. "Idealism and Realism." In Scheler, *Selected Philosophical Essays,* D. R. Lachterman, trans. Northwestern University Press, Evanston, Ill., 1973.

Schilpp, P. A., ed. *The Philosophy of Karl Popper.* Open Court, La Salle, Ill., 1974.

The Philosophy of Rudolf Carnap. Open Court, La Salle, Ill., 1963.

Schlick, M. [*AE*] *Allgemeine Erkenntnislehre,* 2d. ed. Springer, Berlin, 1925.

[*GTK*] *General Theory of Knowledge,* A. E. Blumberg, trans. Springer Verlag, New York, 1974.

"The Nature of Truth in Modern Logic." In Schlick, *Philosophical Papers,* vol. 1.

Philosophical Papers, H. L. Mulder and B. F. B. van de Velde-Schlick, eds.; P. Heath, trans., vols. 1 and 2. Reidel, Dordrecht, 1979.

Problems of Ethics, D. Rynin, trans. Dover, New York, 1962.

"Uber das Fundament der Erkenntnis." In Schlick, *Gesammelte Aufssätze, 1926–1936.* Gerold, Vienna, 1938.

"Das Wesen der Wahrheit nach der modernen Logik." *Vierteljahrsshrift für wissenschaftliche Philosophie und Soziologie 34* (1910):386–477. [Translated as "The Nature of Truth in Modern Logic."]

"What Is Knowing?" In Schlick, *Philosophical Papers*, vol. 1.

Tarski, A. "The Concept of Truth in Formalized Languages." In Tarski, *LSM*.

Introduction to Logic and to the Methodology of Deductive Sciences, O. Helmer, trans. Oxford University Press, New York, 1965.

[*LSM*] *Logic, Semantics, Metamathematics*, J. H. Woodger, trans. Clarendon Press, Oxford, 1956.

Torretti, R. *Philosophy of Geometry from Riemann to Poincaré*. Reidel, Dordrecht, 1978.

Twardowski, K. *On the Content and Object of Presentations*, R. Grossman, trans. Nijhoff, The Hague, 1977.

Urmson, J. O. *Philosophical Analysis*. Clarendon Press, Oxford, 1960.

van Heijenoort, J., ed. *From Frege to Gödel: A Source Book in Mathematical Logic*. Harvard University Press, Cambridge, Mass., 1967.

Waismann, F. "Hypotheses." In Waismann, *Philosophical Papers*, B. McGuinness, ed. Reidel, Dordrecht, 1977.

[*Vienna Circle*] *Wittgenstein and the Vienna Circle*, B. McGuinness, ed.; J. Schulte and B. McGuinness, trans. Harper & Row, New York, 1979.

[*Wiener Kreis*] *Wittgenstein und der Wiener Kreis*, B. F. McGuinness, ed. Blackwell Publisher, Oxford, 1967. [Translated as *Wittgenstein and the Vienna Circle.*]

Werkmeister, W. H. "The Complementarity of Phenomena and Things in Themselves." *Synthese 47* (1981):301–11.

Weyl, H. "Consistency in Mathematics." In Weyl, *Gesammelte Abhandlungen*, K. Chandrasekharan, ed., vol. 3. Springer, Berlin, 1968.

Mathematische Analyse des Raumproblems. Springer, Berlin, 1923.

Philosophy of Mathematics and Natural Science, O. Helmer, trans. Princeton University Press, Princeton, N.J., 1949.

Whewell, W. *History of Scientific Ideas*. Parker, London, 1858.

Whitehead, A. N. *The Concept of Nature*. Cambridge University Press, 1920.

Whitehead, A. N., and Russell, B. [*Principia*] *Principia Mathematica to *56*. Cambridge University Press, 1962.

Wittgenstein, L. *Blue Book*. In Wittgenstein, *The Blue and Brown Books*. Harper & Row, New York, 1965.

[*Lectures, 1930–32*] *Wittgenstein's Lectures, Cambridge, 1930–1932*, D. Lee, ed. Rowman & Littlefield, Totowa, N.J., 1980.

[*Lectures, 1932–35*] *Wittgenstein's Lectures, Cambridge, 1932–35*, A. Ambrose, ed. Rowman & Littlefield, Totowa, N.J., 1979.

Letters to C. K. Ogden, G. H. von Wright, ed. Blackwell Publisher, Oxford; Routledge & Kegan Paul, London, 1973.

[*Letters*] *Letters to Russell, Keynes and Moore*, G. H. von Wright, ed. Cornell University Press, Ithaca, N.Y., 1974.

[*Notebooks*] *Notebooks, 1914–1916*, G. H. von Wright and G. E. M. Anscombe, eds. Harper & Row, New York, 1961.

Philosophical Grammar, R. Rhees, ed. University of California Press, Berkeley and Los Angeles, 1974.

Philosophical Investigations, G. E. M. Anscombe, trans. Macmillan, New York, 1958.

Philosophical Remarks, R. Rhees, ed.; R. Hargreaves and R. White, trans. University of Chicago Press, Chicago, 1975.

Philosophische Bemerkungen, R. Rhees, ed. In *Schriften von Ludwig Wittgenstein,* vol. 2. Suhrkamp Verlag, Frankfurt am Main, 1964. [Translated as *Philosophical Remarks.*]

Philosophische Grammatik, R. Rhees, ed. Barnes & Noble, New York, 1969. [Translated as *Philosophical Grammar.*]

Prototractatus, B. F. McGuinness, T. Nyberg, and G. H. von Wright, eds. Cornell University Press, Ithaca, N.Y., 1971.

Remarks on Colour, G. E. M. Anscombe, ed. University of California Press, Berkeley and Los Angeles, 1977.

Remarks on the Foundations of Mathematics, G. H. von Wright, R. Rhees, and G. E. M. Anscombe, eds., G. E. M. Anscombe, trans. Blackwell Publisher, Oxford, 1967.

[*Tractatus*] *Tractatus Logico-Philosophicus.* Routledge & Kegan Paul, London, 1949.

Wolff, C. *Logic,* W. Clarke and R. Collins, trans. Hawes, London, 1770.

Psychologia Empirica. In Wolff, *Gesammelte Werke,* J. Ecole, ed., pt. 2 Abt., vol. 5. Olms, Hildesheim, 1968.

Vernünftige Gedanken von den Kräften des menschlichen Verstandes, 4th ed. Halle im Magdeburgischen, 1725.

Zilsel, E. "Bemerkungen zur Wissenshaftslogik." *Erkenntnis 3* (1932–33):143–61.

Index

analyticity, 33–5, 38–9, 57, 58–9, 123, 252, 379, 382; *see also* Bolzano, B.; Carnap, R.; Kant, I.; Schlick, M.

Aristotle, 33, 38–9, 69, 85, 100, 114, 125, 379

arithmetic, 9, 18, 22, 26, 28, 29, 35, 41, 42–3, 45, 47–8, 56, 72, 74, 76, 101, 193; *see also* Frege, G.; Gödel, D.; Kant, I.; logicism

arithmetization of the calculus, *see* rigorization of the calculus

Arnauld, A., 9, 15

Austrian realism, 83, 87–8, 93, 212; *see also* Russell, B.

Avenarius, R., 183–4, 185, 189, 207

axiom of choice, 114, 117–21, 308, 309, 322

axiom of infinity, 120–1

axiom of free mobility, 54–5, 133–4, 381

axiom system (AS), 46–7, 61, 117, 197, 274–5, 309–10; *see also* Carnap, R.

Becker, O., 253

Bedeutung, 79, 220, 384; *see also* Frege, G.; Wittgenstein, L.

Beltrami, E., 381; *see also* pseudospherical model

Beltrami–Klein model, *see* pseudospherical model

Bennett, J., 180

Berkeley, G., 24–5, 41, 94, 228

Bochenski, I. M., 379

Bolzano, B., 2, 8, 21, 22–3, 26–7, 39–40, 67, 69, 85, 89, 99, 109–10, 120, 145, 172, 257, 373, 377–8, 379, 383, 384
 analyticity, 33–5, 37–9, 378, 379
 classes, 103
 conceptual ground of the a priori, 36–7, 39, 140, 198, 380
 form, 37–9, 379
 grammatic admissibility, 34, 378–9
 intermediate-value theorem, 27–8, 378
 intuition and the synthetic a priori, 28–

9, 39, 43, 45, 74, 75, 140, 379, 381, 382, 390
 isomorphism in representation, 31–2, 40, 64, 100, 378
 propositions, 32, 34
 representation vs. object, 30–2, 67, 79, 84, 87, 105–6, 225, 238, 339
 rigorization of the calculus, 26, 27, 210, 211
 subjective vs. objective representations, 29–30, 32, 35, 40, 66–7, 225

Boole, G., 65, 69

Borel, E., 117

Borges, J. L., 8, 10, 178–9

Bradley, F. H., 94–6, 103–4, 112

Brentano, F., 84, 85–8, 100–2, 107, 145, 146, 171, 199, 212, 384–5

Brouwer, L. E. J., 117, 252–3, 255, 307, 389

calculus, 22, 23–6; *see also* Bolzano, B.; rigorization of the calculus

Cantor, G., 28, 74, 102, 114, 115, 117, 119, 211, 271, 300, 311, 389
 power set theorem, 115–16, 388

Carnap, R., 1, 8, 76, 128, 159, 189, 206, 207–8, 213, 214, 285, 312, 346, 372, 373–4, 383, 401, 404–5, 411, 412, 417–18, 420, 422
 analyticity, 287–8, 290–3, 294, 298, 299, 300, 301–2, 303, 304, 313, 322, 331, 332, 351, 352, 362, 413, 414–15, 416–17, 420, 421
 a priori, 2–3, 139, 259–60, 263, 266, 267, 268, 271, 309, 322, 324, 353
 Aufbau, 149, 189, 208, 214–18, 221, 223, 224–5, 279, 328, 331, 348, 358, 397, 398, 401, 403, 417
 axiom systems (AS), 275–8, 279, 280, 282
 conceptual holism, 218, 221–2, 224, 230, 231–3, 402